THE LAND IN BETWEEN

Edmundston, seen from across the river in 1890. CDEM PC2-16

THE LAND IN BETWEEN

The Upper St. John Valley

from

Prehistory to World War One

Béatrice Craig & Maxime Dagenais

with the collaboration of

Lisa Ornstein & Guy Dubay

Tilbury House, Publishers, Gardiner, Maine
The Maine Acadian Heritage Council, Madawaska, Maine
Acadia National Park and The Saint Croix Island International Historic Site
Bar Harbor, Maine

Tilbury House, Publishers
103 Brunswick Avenue • Gardiner, Maine 04345
800–582–1899 • www.tilburyhouse.com

Maine Acadian Heritage Council
PO Box 88 • Madawaska, ME 04856
207–728–6826

Acadia National Park & The Saint Croix Island International Historic Site
PO Box 177 • Bar Habor, Maine 04609
Acadia: www.nps.gov/acad • 207-288–3338
Saint Croix Island: www.nps/gov/sacr • 207-454-3871

First paperback edition: July 2009
10 9 8 7 6 5 4 3 2 1

Library of Congress Cataloging-in-Publication Data
Craig, Béatrice.
  The land in between : the upper St. John Valley, prehistory to World War I / Beatrice Craig, Maxime Dagenais with the collaboration of Lisa Ornstein, Guy Dubay. -- 1st pbk. ed.
      p. cm.
  Includes bibliographical references and index.
  ISBN 978-0-88448-319-9 (pbk. : alk. paper)
  1. Saint John River Valley (Me. and N.B.)--History. 2. Borderlands--United States. 3. Borderlands--Canada.
I. Dagenais, Maxime, 1979- II. Title.
  F1044.S2C73 2009
  971.5'5--dc22
                          2009011388

Cover designed by Geraldine Millham, Westport, Massachusetts
Editing assistance by Virginia Reams and Sujata Guptan, NPS, Bar Harbor, ME
Production managed by Tilbury House, Publishers
Printed and bound by Versa Press, East Peoria, Illinois

...une vallée est toujours le berceau de quelque chose. Témoin la vallée du Nil, la vallée du Tigre et de l'Euphrate.

—Antoine Maillet et Rita Scalabrini,
L'Acadie pour quasiment rien

CONTENTS

PREFACE

The Land in Between is the first volume of a new history of Madawaska. The second volume, *The Land Divided,* will cover the period from World War I to the present. We had three goals when writing *The Land in Between:* to provide individuals interested in the upper St. John Valley with a survey of its history; to put in the hands of professionals (teachers, librarians, archivists, museum personnel) a reference book that would facilitate their work; and finally, to incite others to continue investigating and writing the history of this region.

The organization of the volume reflects those three goals. The narrative chapters are followed by suggestions for further readings which identify material written for non-specialists. The sources sections list the printed material we have used to write the chapters (the full citations are found in the bibliography). For the sake of brevity, we have not listed archival material, but most can be identified reasonably easily from the references included in the printed sources. The chapters are followed by appen-dices regrouping technical, genealogical or statistical material, as well as documents in the original English or translated from the French.

This volume would not have been possible without the material and moral support provided by the Acadia National Park & Saint Croix Island International Historic Site and the Maine Acadian Heritage Council, whom we want to thank most heartily. We have also benefited from the able assistance of numerous archivists: William Davis at the US National Archives, who explained to us where to find US government documents in Ottawa; Robbie Gilmore at the Provincial Archives of New Brunswick; Garry Shutlak at the Provincial Archives of Nova Scotia; and the personnel of the Archives de la Côte-du-Sud and of the Maine State Archives. We also owe some special thanks to the various people at the Library and Archives of Canada, especially Isabelle Charron, from the Archives Conservation Center (Cartographic Division), who went a-sleuthing after the elusive Bainbrigge notebook.

LISTS OF FIGURES, TABLES, MAPS, ILLUSTRATIONS, AND ABBREVIATIONS

List of Figures

List of Tables

List of Maps

List of Illustrations

List of Sidebars

List of Abbreviations

AA   Acadian Archives/ Archives acadiennes (Fort Kent, ME)

AAQ   Archives de l'archevêché de Québec.

CDEM   Centre d'études Madawaskayennes (Edmundston, NB)

CIHM   Canadian Institute for Historical Micro-Reproductions.

LAC   Library and Archives of Canada (Ottawa, ON)—formerly known as National Archives of Canada (NAC) and National Library of Canada (NLC); other previous names: Public Archives of Canada (PAC) and Dominion Archives of Canada.

NSARM   Nova Scotia Archives and Record Management (formerly known as Provincial Archives of Nova Scotia or PANS).

PANB   Provincial Archives of New Brunswick (Fredericton, NB).

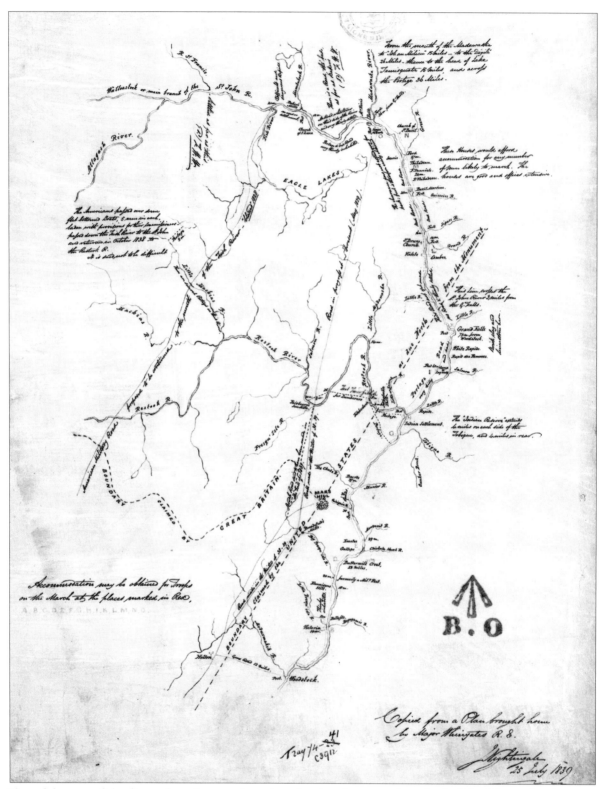

Plan of the area of the disputed northeastern boundary showing the route along the St. John River taken by troops, as well as the military road made by the Americans to the Fish River and other roads under LAC NMC-6839

INTRODUCTION

This book takes its inspiration from Father Thomas Albert's *Histoire du Madawaska*, a historical survey of the upper St. John Valley published in 1920. Father Albert, a parish priest, used research notes that Madawaskayan Prudent Mercure compiled while employed at the Dominion Archives of Canada (now Library and Archives of Canada), supplemented with material provided by fellow antiquarians like the Reverend W. O. Raymond and by senator Patrick Thériault of Maine, regional genealogists, and oral tradition.

Histoire du Madawaska was a remarkable achievement for its time and has done long service as a reference for anyone interested in the history of the area. Not surprisingly, however, the book shows its age in a variety of ways. In the first place, a lot of time has elapsed since the book was published. Over the past eighty-nine years, many historical documents and primary source materials inaccessible to Father Albert have surfaced, shedding new light on the past. In addition, recent developments in technology during this same period have produced new means to make these old sources "talk." For example, thanks to computers, it is now possible to thoroughly process data in historical documents such as parish registers, land records, and census surveys. Finally, the field of historical scholarship has itself evolved, producing a discipline with well-developed methods for gaining an in-depth understanding of the past.

Father Albert's priorities and goals for writing *Histoire du Madawaska* were very different from those of modern-day historians. He was in fact not a historian, but a doctor of theology and of canon law. Both these disciplines are deductive: they reach their conclusions by determining, through rigorously logical methods, the consequences of an agreed-upon

starting point, which for Catholic theologians of the period were the indisputable Truths of the Catholic Church. Clerical scholars of Albert's generation acquired their deductive skills through the study of philosophy, the capstone of Catholic classical college studies. Nineteenth-century Canadian clerics, as well as graduates of classical colleges, frequently viewed history as a branch of philosophy, whose purposes were to uncover the role of the Holy Providence in human affairs and God's ultimate plan for mankind. Like many of his fellow theologians, Father Albert's priorities in writing *Histoire* were pastoral and didactic, rather than scholarly.

Father Albert's means for writing his book were also markedly different from those of a contemporary historian. In the first place, his full-time responsibilities as a parish priest in Shippagan left little leisure time or financial means to travel in search of missing documents. In addition, he had no access whatsoever to modern-day research conveniences, such as interlibrary loan and the Internet. He therefore had to make do with the knowledge he had acquired during his studies, documentation he had been given, and information other scholars were willing to share with him. In addition to limiting his access to documentation, this situation also prevented Father Albert from double-checking his sources for accuracy, as a result of which his Histoire contains a number of factual errors. For instance, he dates the abolition of the oaths that prevented Catholics from being elected to the Provincial Legislature to 1837, but the oaths had been abrogated in 1830.[1]

Father Albert was also hindered in his efforts by the fact that archives in his day were few and far between. The Dominion Archives in Ottawa were a relatively new establishment, created in 1872, and were still a division of the federal Ministry of Agriculture at the time Albert was writing. The Provincial Archives of New Brunswick only came into existence in 1967.

Over the past seventy-five years, archives on both sides of the Canadian border have collected, transcribed, organized, and inventoried material that was scattered and often not easily accessible to the general public. Twentieth-century technological innovations, such as microfilms and, more recently, digitization, have increased access to material for researchers who cannot travel. Archives have also produced finding aids to their collections, which facilitate the location of specific documents and the search for information. Most recently, searchable on-line archival databases have proliferated, allowing researchers like us to track down plenty of needles that were formerly lost in the haystacks. For instance, all pre-1800 Québec notarial records (including civil contracts of all kinds, prenuptial agreements, and post-mortem settlements of estates) have been indexed in a searchable database called Parchemin.

When Parchemin first became available at the National Library of Canada, we decided to test it by looking for records involving Acadians who had escaped deportation in 1755 and found refuge in Québec's lower St. Lawrence region. Entering "Thibodeau" in the search box made records about Jean-Baptiste Thibodeau and Jean-Baptiste Cormier, whom we recognized as two of the Madawaska territory's earliest settlers, appear on the screen. The database revealed that in January 1768, J-Bte. Thibodeau and J-Bte. Cormier sold a sawmill that they co-owned in Montmagny (a town east of Quebec City on the south shore of the St. Lawrence River). *Notaire* Collin had written the contract. Since Collin's papers were available on microfilm, we were able to track down the sale contract and learned that Thibodeau and Cormier had purchased the mill in February 1765. The implications of this information made our head spin. Weren't Cormier and Thibodeau refugees? How on earth were they able to *buy* a sawmill less than ten years after escaping from Beaubassin, presumably with no more than the shirts on their back? Their extraordinarily speedy economic recovery and entrepreneurial success simply did not mesh with conventional thinking about the lives of Acadian refugees. Time to investigate!

What happened to us at the National Library is typical of the historian's work. Like archaeologists and astronomers, historians regularly stumble across new information that forces them to reconsider what they know and to revise their interpretations accordingly. Rewriting history, a legitimate and ongoing process among professional historians, is certainly not about "tampering" with the past. The past is what happened and is unalterable. History, on the other hand, is a form of interpretive narrative about the past. In writing their narratives, historians obey specific rules, the most fundamental of which are that history must be based on verifiable evidence, and that this evidence either must have been produced at the time of the events described or, if produced later, must have been written by individuals who participated in or witnessed those events. (Historians call this type of evidence *primary source*.) Oral and material history similarly have their own rules and methods. History, therefore, is dependent upon the availability of these sources, and the discovery of new sources can require the rewriting of history, in the same way as the discovery of a previously unknown site can lead to the rewriting of archaeology.

What historians write about is also dependent upon the kinds of questions they ask themselves, and people from different time periods and different backgrounds are interested in different questions. Father Albert was both a theologian and a man of his time, and his *Histoire du Madawaska* reflects these interests and perspectives. An early twentieth-century French-Catholic priest, he was, like many of his colleagues, a firm believer in *La Survivance*, a then-popular French Canadian clerico-nationalist ideology that urged French North Americans to conserve their language, religion, and traditions, and to mistrust changes, urban life, and modernity in general. Like many proponents of *La Survivance*, Father Albert also believed that Holy Providence had bestowed a mission on the French of North America to catholicize the continent. Father Albert's vision of this providential mission clearly shaped his interpretation of the past throughout *Histoire du Madawaska*; in fact, his very last words, "Geista Dei per Franco" (Deeds of God through the Franks), quote the title of medieval Benedictine theologian Guilbert de Nogent's narrative of the First Crusade. The *Survivance* ideology, however, went out of fashion in the 1960s.

An up-to-date history of the Madawaska territory is therefore in order, covering events to the present using the full range of documentation now available, new methodologies where appropriate, and an organizational framework relevant to the contemporary world. We have chosen to use the concepts of "borderland" and "bordered lands" as our organizing principles. The borderland approach was actually developed in the 1920s and is currently enjoying a comeback among U.S. historians. It is an approach well-suited for an exploration of this particular part of the world, and a timely one as well.

"The Valley" (to use the local term for the upper St. John Valley) is an unusual place in a number of respects, two of which are particularly pertinent to the "borderland" concept. First, this is a region where Acadian and French Canadian settlers met and blended. Second, despite the Valley being split between different powers early in the nineteenth century, its residents have done a remarkable job of behaving as if this division did not exist. As a consequence, they have developed a sense of being a people "in between" and of being different. In these post-9/11, post-Patriot Act days, when going "across" (to use the local term for crossing the St. John River along the international boundary) to gas up the car, pick up groceries, or visit *mémère* now requires a passport and the potential involvement of the secretary of state, understanding how past people negotiated their position "in between" throughout history is—perhaps more than ever—relevant and useful.

Borderland historians document the transforma-tion of "frontiers" into "borderlands" and of "borderlands" into "bordered lands." Frontiers are regions where boundaries are undefined or ill-defined. The various groups who inhabit them are free to interact as they see fit. This interaction may be violent or peaceful. Borderlands are areas contested by rival powers. Imperial and international conflicts may intrude into local people's lives, but they still manage to preserve a large degree of autonomy, and informal relations still predominate. As the borders become clearly defined and enforced, borderlands become bordered lands. Local interactions are increasingly restricted, channelled from above, and subordinated to the policies and priorities of the distant governing powers.

According to these definitions, the area that now encompasses northwestern New Brunswick, northeastern Maine, and eastern Québec was a frontier area until the first Treaty of Paris in 1763. Before the arrival of Europeans, Natives traveled back and forth between the Gulf of Maine and St. Lawrence River. They entered into various forms of exchange of raw material, tools, technological knowledge, and other cultural products that have left behind no archaeological remains. As Europeans settlers arrived, all three regions were claimed by both the French and English, who used them, but did not control them. The Natives continued using the region as they saw fit, trying to play off French against English to protect their homelands and way of life. The American Revolution prolonged this frontier era because the region was part of the territory contested between Loyalists and Revolutionaries. After 1783, it was clear that boundaries existed between the United States and British North America (as present-day Canada was called before 1867) and between Québec and New Brunswick, even if the exact locations of some of these boundaries were contested. The upper part of the St. John River was at the heart of one of these disputed territories, but this did not stop Acadians and French Canadians, New Englanders, and Provincials from seeking their livelihoods along its banks—often in flagrant disregard of anyone's claim to sovereignty. The Valley had become a borderland.

The Valley remained a borderland even after the Webster–Ashburton Treaty conclusively established an international boundary in 1842, splitting the Madawaska territory and its people. There are three main reasons for the Valley's enduring borderland status. First, its inhabitants had not been asked their opinion about the matter and were therefore disinclined to inconvenience themselves to fit into diplomats' notions of territoriality. Second, Maine, New Brunswick, Britain, and the United States did not want to disturb the trans-border economy that had emerged in the Valley and benefited all of these governments. Third, natural means of communication and transportation firmly linked the upper St. John Valley to the port of Saint John, New Brunswick. Communications with the rest of Maine were impractical, when they existed at all. Economically speaking, northern Aroostook County was really part of New Brunswick, not the United States, until the construction of the Bangor and Aroostook Railway in the 1890s. As railroads brought new means of communication with the outside and a new economy based on lumber and agricultural exports, American and Canadian tariff and immigration policies drove a wedge between the two halves of the Valley. In this same period, however, cultural bonds between the two were being strengthened by the ideology of *La Survivance* and possibly of the Acadian Renaissance movement. Thus, on the eve of World War I, the Valley was "in between"—neither a true borderland nor a pair of fully fledged bordered lands—and its people faced many choices and challenges in finding an identity that was operational in the contemporary world.

Historians use frameworks to organize and order the study of the past. Different frameworks bring different issues to the forefront and push others into the background. The framework we have chosen highlights the commonalities between the residents of both sides of the St. John River, the emergence of their sense of distinctiveness, and their interactions with the world around them. We also deliberately emphasize successes (of which there were many) rather than victimization (upon which Acadians in the past tended not to dwell). While we hope that *The Land in Between* contributes significantly to an understanding of and appreciation for the history and the people of the upper St. John Valley, we know full well that ours is not a "complete" history. Indeed, we hope that our readers understand that in history—by which we mean the written narrative—there is really no such thing as the "final word." As we hope will be amply obvious in the chapters that follow, history is subject to constant revisions, because new questions bring different issues into the spotlight, and because new documents and new methods cast new light on old questions. Like archaeologists, historians are too dependent on the "luck of the find" to claim to have a final answer to anything.

In his introduction, Father Albert very deliberately presented *Histoire du Madawaska* not as a definitive work, but rather as the first step in establishing a historical narrative for the region, one that he hoped future historians would revise and expand. *The Land in Between,* which will be published in two volumes, belatedly answers Father Albert's call, and, like him, we hope it will stimulate further scholarship on this remarkable part of the world. Like Albert, we say to our readers: "Pick up the mantle."

ENDNOTE
1. PANB, RS24, Legislative Assembly: sessional records, S:38, B53, Bill for the relief of His Majesty's Roman Catholic Subjects in New Brunswick, passed 17-2-1830: 78. Microfilm, reel F17401.

1

THE PHYSICAL ENVIRONMENT

The Madawaska territory is part of two important geographic entities: the St. John River basin and the Maritime Peninsula. The St. John River basin is the largest in the Northeast and occupies almost half of the Maritime Peninsula (see Map 1-1). The Maritime Peninsula extends from the Kennebec River through southeastern Québec, Maine, and New Brunswick all the way to Nova Scotia and Cape Breton Island. In geological terms, the peninsula is of recent origins: it is a mere 13,000 years old. For about 10,000 years before that time, it was covered by glaciers. The Madawaska territory shares the same overall characteristics as the peninsula: a not-too-generous soil, initially forested and teeming with wild animals, well irrigated by a dense network of rivers, and subjected to a rigorous continental climate. Those characteristics determined how Native people and Europeans could make their living in the region; they also contributed to shaping political events from the seventeenth to the nineteenth centuries.

I.   WHAT IS "MADAWASKA"?

What is the historical region known as Madawaska? Present-day maps of northern Maine and north-western New Brunswick show a Madawaska County (N.B.), Madawaska River (N.B.), Little Madawasaka River (Maine), Madawaska Lake (Maine), and town of Madawaska (Maine). At one point there was even a "Madawaska *seigneury*" in Québec, surrounding Lake Témiscouata (see Map 1-2). However, one will *not* find a region called "Madawaska" (for example, "Madawaska Settlement" or "Madawaska Territory") on the map. Where do these terms come from, and what do they mean?

In the early nineteenth century, the New Brunswick government defined the "Madawaska territory" as the "unorganized portion of the civil parish of Kent" (see Map 8-2, page 105). Devoid of precise boundaries, the Madawaska territory was the land occupied by French settlers on the upper St. John River and grew as their settlement spread. Half a century into its existence, the territory was split between three political entities: Maine, New Brunswick, and Québec. The Madawaska territory is therefore neither a political or administrative unit, nor a geographic region. Instead, it is a socio-cultural entity whose distinctive identity was forged by its inhabitants, something that regional historian Prudent Mercure noted at the turn of the last century:

> The territory known as Madawaska includes all the settlements on both banks of the St. John River. From the Grand Falls to the Seven Islands a distance of 140 miles.... By the treaty of 1842, all the settlements on the north bank...remained

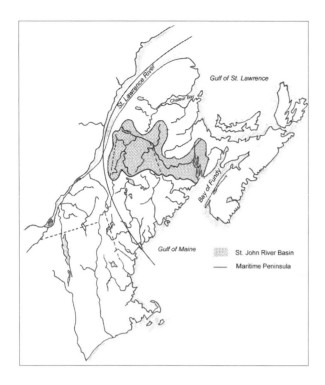

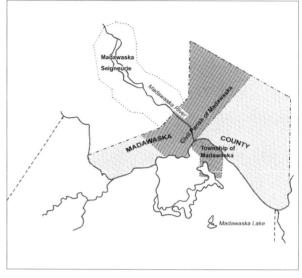

Map 1-1 (left): Maritime Peninsula
Map by B. and S. Craig
Map 1-2 (above): Madawaska Place Names
Map by B. and S. Craig

to the English government and all the establishments on the south bank became a part of the United States.... The people are of the same origin having the same customs, language, habits, and religion and the same family names; indeed it is one people but divided only as to government.[1]

We use Mercure's definition here; for the purposes of our study, Madawaska includes all lands in the upper St. John Valley in present-day Maine and New Brunswick, as well as Témiscouata and the territory at the southern edge of Kamouraska, Bellechasse, and L'Islet counties in Québec. After 1785 however, we will mainly focus on the current county of Madawaska in New Brunswick and the northern tier of townships in Aroostook County in northern Maine.

II.   QUATERNARY GEOLOGY AND GEOGRAPHY

A. Deglaciation and the "Great Lakes" Age

The Maritime Peninsula was largely covered with ice until about 13,000 years ago (or BP, before the present)[2] (see Map 1-3). The massive Laurentian ice sheet covered most of Canada from Alberta eastward and pushed down into northern New England and the Great Lakes region. Around 13,000 BP, a deepening bay called the Goldthwait Sea appeared where the St. Lawrence estuary is now located. It gradually extended westward and caused the formation of the Champlain Sea between present-day Ottawa and Quebec City. The Goldthwait Sea separated the part of the Laurentian ice sheet located over the Maritime Peninsula from the rest and made it melt faster than the remainder. The northern edge of this

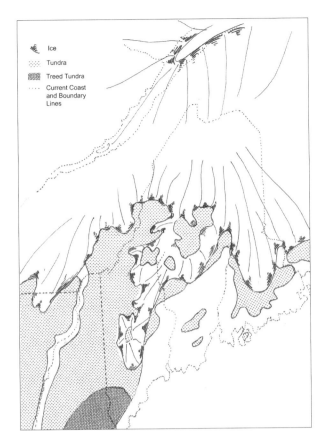

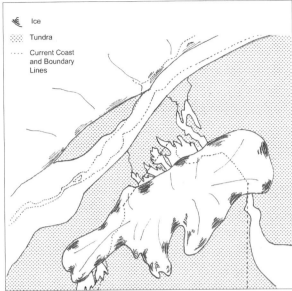

Map 1-3 (left): Maine around 13,000 BP
Map by B. and S. Craig
Map 1-4 (above): Northern Maine around 12,000 BP
Map by B. and S. Craig

Map 1-5 (below): Northern Maine around 11,000 BP
Map by B. and S. Craig

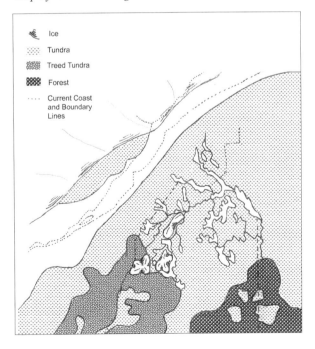

smaller icecap ran roughly parallel to the Notre Dame Mountains, between the current St. Lawrence and St. John Rivers. Melting waters accumulated between the remaining ice and the Notre Dame Mountains and formed several interconnected glacial lakes that drained into Goldthwait Sea (see Map 1-4). The western part of the basin deglaciated first, and when the early (or paleo-) St. John River was formed, it flowed northwards into current Lake Témiscouata. Water from the lakes on the current St. Francis River flowed through the Cabano River into Lake Témiscouata, which drained north through either the Aberish or Des Aigles Rivers. An ice plug west of Edmundston held another lake in the Frenchville area called Lake Ennemond. Glazier and Beau Lakes and Lake Pohenegamook along the St. Francis River, as well as Baker Lake, are remnants of those glacial lakes.

By 11,000 BP, only residual ice could be found

in the region (see Map 1-5). Two very large lake systems emerged in northern Maine between 12,000 and 11,000 BP. One was glacial Lake Madawaska. The waters of this 130-km body of water stretching from Grand Falls to the head of Témiscouata Lake were held by a drift dam at Grand Falls (a drift dam is made of debris and rocks left behind by retreating ice). Glacial Lake Madawaska initially drained north, as the Grand Falls dam was then at a higher altitude than the Aberish and Des Aigles outlets. The other major lake system was glacial Lake Guerette, which drained north into the St. John River through the Fish River and south through the Aroostook River. Two additional, but smaller, lake systems were located on the Allagash and in the Big Black-Shield Branch Valley.

B. Emergence of the Modern River System

Those extensive lakes lasted until about 10,000–9,500 BP, after which they drained relatively quickly (over a 200-year period). Témiscouata, Touladi, Squatec, and des Aigles Lakes are remnants of those glacial lake systems. By then, the waters were flowing to the south and east, a reversal of the earlier direction. Water flow reversal and draining of the lakes were the consequences of complex geological events accompanying deglaciation. Waters initially flowed northward because the weight of the Laurentian ice mass was pushing the surface of the earth down, whereas the recently freed land to the south rose (a process called isostatic rebound). After 10,500 BP, the Laurentian ice sheet receded. The north shore of the St. Lawrence River rose, tilting the land back towards the south. The climate changed at the same time. Winters had been dry until then; now, snowfalls were abundant. This led to heavy spring meltdown, and the flood water began to spill over the Grand Falls drift dam. At flood time, the St. John River was laden with sediments that fell to the bottom of the lake or were deposited on the flood plain. Glacial Lake Madawaska drained when isostatic rebound continued raising the land to the north and erosion cut a channel through the Grand Falls dam. River channels remained unstable until about 7,700 BP, and the St. John kept shifting over the old lake bed. Floods were much more important then than they are now: a terrace at Siegas on the left bank of the St. John River below the Madawaska River, formed by sediments deposited by floods, is six meters higher than the highest recorded flood in historic time. Interestingly, the contours of glacial Lake Madawaska and Lake Ennemond correspond, by and large, to the area settled by 1870. People opened farms first on the very, very old lake bottoms. Geological events that occurred nine millennia ago shaped people's decisions as to the best place to settle in the nineteenth century.

III.   PALEO-ENVIRONMENTS

The recently deglaciated upper St. John River basin was quite cold and dry; precipitation (rain and snow) was not abundant. As the Laurentian sheet receded, the climate became warmer and moister, until about 4,000 BP when the temperature cooled down again. The deglaciated regions were colonized by vegetation that constantly changed as the climate warmed up, and new species moved into the region. Animal species accompanied the vegetation, followed by their predators—including humans. (See Table 1-1,

Environmental and Cultural Chronology.)

A. The Pleistocene Era—to 10,000 BP

Around 11,500 BP the deglaciated land masses began to be colonized by lichen and mosses (including the attractively named "grey reindeer moss"), grasses, sedges, small shrubs like alders, and finally willows. This vegetal environment is called a tundra. It lasted until about 10,000 BP. In other parts of

Table 1-1: Environmental and Cultural Chronology

AD/BC	BP	ERA	Cultural tradition	Geologic events in the upper St. John River basin	Vegetation in upper St. John River basin	Human occupation in upper St. John River basin
1950 AD		Holocene	Present			
1500 AD			Historic period			Campsites mouth Madawaska and St. Francis Rivers (mostly Maliseets)
1000 AD	1,000		Late ceramic			Dickey-Lincoln sites: Témiscouta (Davidson) site
0	2,000		Middle ceramic			
400 BC	2,400					
1000 BC	3,000		Early ceramic	Stabilized physical environment	Mixed forest	
	4,000		Late Archaic			
4000 BC	5,000		Late Archaic			
	6,000		Middle Archaic			
6000 BC	7,000		Middle Archaic	River chanel shifting	Closed forest	Unspecified
	8,000		Early Archaic			
8000 BC	9,000		Early Archaic / Late Paleo-Indian	Draining of lakes and water flow reversal	Parkland (treed tundra)	Dégelis sites (Archaic); Squatec sites (Paleo-Indians); Témiscouata and Shield Lake sites (Paleo-Indian)
	9,500					
	10,000		Early Paleo-Indian	Glacial lakes formation	Herb-, then shrub-tundra	Unknown
10000 BC	11,000	Pleistocene			Glacial desert	None
12000 BC	12,000		None	Deglaciation	None	None

North America, Pleistocene tundras supported large grazing animals such as mammoths, North American camels and horses, musk oxen, bison, and tundra caribou. The paucity of animal remains makes it difficult to know exactly which of those large mammals roamed the Maritime Peninsula. Occasional remains of prehistoric horses, musk oxen, mammoths, and possibly bison have been found in Maine, in addition to caribou. It is impossible to say how common those animals were in the peninsula and, except for caribou, whether they were hunted by humans.

B. The Holocene Era
(10,000 BP to the Present)

Between 10,500 and 9,500 BP, the temperature rose and precipitation increased, but the climate was probably still cooler and dryer than now. The glacial lakes drained fairly rapidly, and freshly uncovered lake bottoms were heavily colonized by new vegetal species, such as spruce, poplar, birch, fir, and pine. Those types of trees also grew in scattered thickets through the shrub tundra, which gradually gave way to a parkland environment: the poplar woodland.

North American fauna also underwent some dramatic changes around 10,000 BP. Most of the large species became extinct. Only seven species weighing more than 20 kg (45 lb) survived in the northern Appalachian region: moose, white-tailed deer, elk, cougar, timber wolf, black bear, and bison. Tundra caribou migrated north, to be replaced by forest caribou.

The forest gradually thickened and closed, and by 9,500 BP, northern Maine and adjacent New Brunswick were covered by white pines, oaks, yellow birch, and hemlock. New animal species moved in, including beavers, small mammals, fish, and fowl. Those animals still inhabit the region today. The vegetation cover continued to evolve, and between 7,500 and 4,900 BP, conifer and hardwood dominated. Around 4,000 BP, the temperature cooled again, and winter precipitation increased noticeably, causing spring floods. The tree mix also changed, and spruce, fir, and larches became more common while hemlock declined. By 4,000 BP, the type of vegetation that characterizes the Maritime Peninsula at the present was in place.

IV.   CONTEMPORARY CLIMATIC CONDITIONS

Overall, the upper Valley has experienced the same type of continental climate over the past 200 years as in the past 4,000. The summers are short, hot, and relatively dry; the winters are long, cold, and characterized by heavy snowfalls. This can cause significant spring flooding. The summer months (June, July, and August) can get extremely warm. By mid-September, the temperature of the region becomes noticeably colder. The first snowfall is usually in early to mid-November, and by the middle of the month, the rivers and lakes start to freeze. The coldest part of the year begins on the first of January and can last up to March 20. The mercury often goes down to 20°F below zero, but in some cases can even go down to 30°F or even 35°F below. Snow cover is

on average three feet deep. By mid-April, the snow starts to melt, and the rivers, streams, and lakes start to break up. By May, the mornings and days are warmer, and farmers can start planting. The growing season averaged 120 days in the nineteenth century, with killing frosts occurring until the third week in May and starting again in the third week of September. Low-lying pieces of land along the river have been more susceptible to late and early frost than back hills. At the present, frosts hard enough to kill tomato plants can happen in the Valley in late August

The climate has also changed over time. Some of the changes were induced by human activities. Nineteenth-century New Brunswick settlers believed that clearing the land of its dense and wild forests influenced summer and winter temperatures: winter was deemed to be much longer in regions where the forest had not been cleared. The tree cover retarded the melting of snow and the start of the growing season. The climate also varied over time independently of human activities. Peter Fisher, the first historian of New Brunswick, provides us with a description of climatic conditions until the late 1830s. The 1800s began with a period of mild winters and cool summers, interrupted by the famous "year without a summer" (1816). The weather then gradually improved until 1822, when bumper crops were harvested through the province. Drought struck in 1825, so severely that the entire Miramichi Valley went up in flames, destroying thousands of acres of timber. The reverse problem occurred in the early 1830s: the summers were cold and wet, even frosty. Two unusually cold winters (1835 and 1836) were followed by an excessively dry summer (1836) that almost destroyed the pastures.

Records of killing frosts for Maine show that the length of the growing season fluctuated widely. Between 1829 and 1845, the only pre-1900 period for which data are available, the growing season in northern Maine ranged between 75 and 200 days. The growing seasons were unusually long in the early 1830s, dropped precipitously to 80–85 days in the middle of the decade, increased to an average of 140 days at the end of the 1830s, and dropped again below 100 days for the rest of the period for which data exist. We have not found other detailed descriptions of the climate for the later period, but this example is sufficient to demonstrate that farmers were very vulnerable to its vagaries. Dry or wet summers reduced yields; late spring frosts prevented timely sowing; and early fall ones could destroy crops before they had been harvested.

V.   CONTEMPORARY SOIL AND SUITABILITY FOR AGRICULTURE

Most of the soil of the St. John Valley is good by Maritime/New England standards. Part of the upper and middle St. John and Aroostook river valleys flow through a large stretch of Caribou loam, a light, well-drained soil extremely suitable for potatoes. In the eastern half of the Madawaska territory, a gravelly loam prevails. The soil of the hills that frame the valley is often stony. When not sloping excessively, it is suitable for pastures. Most of the hills have never been cleared for farming, and most of what has been cleared has since been abandoned and is reverting to forest.

The attractiveness of the St. John River (all the way to the Bay of Fundy) resides in the intervales that line its banks. The intervales are made of fine material deposited by the river. In their natural state, they were covered with hardwoods that, contrary to evergreen, produce humus. And some intervales were flooded every spring, which contributed to their fertility. In some parts of the valley, including the eastern half of the Madawaska territory, the intervales extend up to three miles away from the river.

Nineteenth-century government officials, geologists, and agronomists described the valley's agricultural potential in glowing terms. In an 1832 report, land commissioner Thomas Baillie claimed:

> These interval lands...could scarcely fail to attract attention for their evident fertility, and for the very remarkable luxuriance of their vegetation...and enormous growth...[which indicates] great fertility of the soil supporting them.[3]

Although reports such as these should be taken with a grain of salt (most were written to attract new settlers), they were not completely fanciful. Madawaska was a good agricultural region.

The upper St. John basin belongs to the Great Lakes/St. Lawrence ecological belt, which is a mixed forest where maple trees and yellow birch are very common alongside hemlocks, white pine, fir, and spruce. Locally, different species may dominate. This vegetal cover was in place about 4,000 BP. The forest is quite different from the one in the rest of Maine. It is an extension of the Canadian Shield rather than of the New England Seaboard or the Appalachian Plateau.

Certain species of hardwood and softwood have proved to be particularly useful for local use or export. Maple, a hardwood, is abundant throughout the region and is a valuable indigenous tree. The wood can be used to make furniture, and, of course, the live trees produce a sweet sap that can be turned into syrup and sugar. The tree can grow to a great size: 2 feet in diameter and 60 feet high. It normally grows on land suitable for farming. The beech is another common species of hardwood, but signals poor agricultural soil. Its wood was commonly used in the building of sleds and farm tools. White ash is common in the area and signals good soil. It may reach a height of 60 feet and diameter of 2 feet. The wood is flexible and was often used in making oars, staves, and various agricultural tools.

Softwoods include fir, cedar, spruce, and pine. Fir, an evergreen wood, is especially durable even when wet and was often used in the manufacturing of tubs, buckets, and barrels. It was also often planted around houses to act as shelter and insulation from the cold winds of winter. Cedar, another softwood common in the region, is usually found in low, swampy lands. The tree does not grow very big, but was used commonly for fencing and shingles. Since it resists rotting, it was ideal for making shingles. Finally, black spruce is found in a variety of soils. It grows to a height of 40 to 50 feet. It is now one of the region's most important species of wood, as it ranks second to pine in the production of deals (very thick planks) and boards.

The most important species of wood, however, has been white pine. It is this species that fed the timber and then lumber industries for most of the nineteenth century. White pine is the largest and straightest tree of the North American forest, often reaching 160 feet in height and a 4-foot diameter. Some have even reached the height of 200 feet with a diameter of 5 feet. Not only do pines grow very straight and tall, but they have no branches on the lowest part of their trunk. This means that there are no knots in the lumber made from this section of the tree. It is also a very stable wood that does not greatly expand and contract in response to humidity levels, and it is easy to work. New England and Canadian settlers used pine for furniture, which they painted. The British authorities believed those very tall and very straight trees made perfect masts for their ships. Consequently, they reserved the best pines for the use of the Royal Navy. Those trees were identified by a special mark (the King's Broad Arrow), and local people were forbidden to cut them, even if the trees were on their land. Other wood products initially cost too much to ship to Britain and could not compete with wood from Scandinavia and Russia.

Pine and spruce also make good construction lumber, and rapid deforestation in the northeastern United States, coupled with rapid urbanization, created a strong demand in the United States for Canadian construction lumber from the middle of the nineteenth century onwards. Later in the century, ways of turning wood into paper were discovered, and the forests of Maine and New Brunswick became sources of raw material for pulp and paper manufacturing.

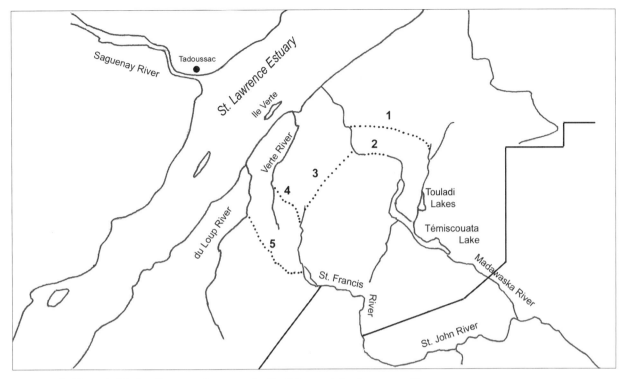

Map 1-6: Historic Native Portages between the St. John and St. Lawrence Rivers:
 1. Touladi Lake and Des Aigles River
 2. Aberish and Trois Pistoles Rivers
 3. Trois Pistoles to St. Francis River (Rivière St Francois)
 4. Rivière Verte to St. Francis River
 5. Du Loup to St. Francis River through Lac Pohenegamook
 Map courtesy A. Burke

VII.   HYDROGRAPHY

The river system of the Maritime Peninsula allowed communications between all its parts (see Map 1-1). The major river in the region is the St. John. The Madawaska region lay astride its upper valley.

  The St. John River (*Woolastuk,* or "beautiful river" in Maliseet) is the second longest river flowing into the North Atlantic (about 673 km or 418 miles long). French explorer Samuel Champlain named it after Saint John the Baptist, because he discovered it on that saint's feast day on June 24, 1604. It was also called River Saint John's or River Saint John in the seventeenth and eighteenth centuries. Its source is located in northwestern Maine, near the sources of

the Etchemin and Chaudière Rvers, which flow into the St. Lawrence south of Quebec City. The river flows north through Maine, then eastwards to Grand Falls or Grand Sault (originally known as "the Great Falls of the River Saint John's"). At this place, about 200 miles from its mouth, the river falls 58 feet into a pool below. These falls offer quite a spectacular sight and attracted tourists as early as the nineteenth century. Below the falls, the river veers south and continues its course through New Brunswick and finally ends into the Bay of Fundy. The river is now the boundary between Maine and New Brunswick from the St. Francis River to a few miles above Grand

Falls. The St. John River drains an area of 54,600 square kilometers (21,330 square miles), which is larger than Switzerland. Fifty-one percent of the drainage area of the basin is situated in the Province of New Brunswick. The remaining areas are located in the state of Maine (36 percent) and the Province of Québec (13 percent) (see Map 1-1).

Both its length and number of tributaries made the St. John River the main artery in the Maritime Peninsula until the building of the railroads, connecting the St. Lawrence River with the Gulf of St. Lawrence, Bay of Fundy, and Gulf of Maine through several alternate routes. The St. Francis and Lake Témiscouata/Madawaska Rivers, which flow into the St. John from the north, have been used as travel routes between the St. John and St. Lawrence for time immemorial (see Map 1-6). The Grand River joins the St. John a short distance above Grand Falls; its head is close to the head of the Restigouche, which flows in Chaleur Bay. The two rivers were therefore an important communication artery in prehistoric times. Further down, several rivers flowing into the left bank of the St. John offer ways to reach the headwaters of the Miramichi, Richibucto, and Cocagne Rivers, which flow into the Northumberland Strait opposite Prince Edward Island. Lastly, the Kennebecassis, which enters the St. John River a short distance above St. John, allowed inland connection with the Petitcodiac River and Shepody Bay at the head of the Bay of Fundy. On the left bank, several rivers made communications possible with the St. Croix and Magadavic, and from there to the Bay of Fundy and Gulf of Maine.

The region's Natives made use of this network to reach hunting grounds and trade with each other. Europeans who came to the region soon learned about them and used those communication routes for their own purposes. The first Europeans to have used the portages between the upper St. John and the St. Lawrence appear to have been three Catholic missionaries on their way from Acadia to Québec in 1624. The Madawaska region, with its three major portages towards the St. Lawrence, a connection to the Restigouche, and another to the Kennebec and Penobscot, was this system's major hub. As we shall see in the subsequent chapters, the region's river system was as important as soil, climate, and vegetation to the life of the region's Natives and white inhabitants.

ENDNOTES
1. Mercure, *Papiers de Prudent L. Mercure*, 33.
2. To avoid having to renumber their chronological sequences every ten years or so, scientists have agreed that "the present" used as reference would be the year 1950.
3. Baillie, *Account of the Province of New Brunswick*, 18.

FURTHER READINGS
Acadian Culture in Maine. http://acim.umfk.maine.edu, section 3, "Maine Acadians and the Land."
Laing, David. "Out of Chaos." In *The County: Land of Promise*, ed. A. Mcgrath. 1989: 9–17.
Dubay, Guy. *Chez Nous: The St. John Valley.* 1983: 1–14.
Connell, Allison. "Governed by Nature: Bioregions in the St John River Watershed." *Echoes, Northern Maine Journal* 51 (January-March 2001): 32–34 and 47.
Folster, David. " 'I Am a St. John River Person': Creating a Mystique." *Echoes, Northern Maine Journal* 35 (January-March 1997): 2 and 48–52.
Tyrrell, Merle E. "The Year with No Summer: Snow and Ice in June." *Echoes, Northern Maine Journal* 36 (April-June 1997): 2 and 18–20.
Olmstead, Kathryn. "Celebrating the River: Bells in 60 churches rang at noon and the people of the St. John River were united." *Echoes, Northern Maine Journal* 27 (January-March 1995): 31–33 and 47.
Flagg, Gale L. "Pearls along the River: Scattered among the common flora along the St. John River are dozens of Maine's rarest plants." *Echoes, Northern Maine Journal* 27 (January-March 1995): 34–35 and 38.
Judd, Richard W. *Aroostook: A Century of Logging in Northern Maine.* 1988.
Wynn, Graeme. *Timber Colony: A Historical Geography of Early Nineteenth-Century New Brunswick.* 1981.
Harris, R. Cole and Geoffrey J. Matthews. *Historical Atlas of Canada,* vol. 1. 1987: plates 1, 17 and 20.

SOURCES
This chapter covers a long time span and relies on a long list of sources. Borns (1986), Newman (1986), Hughes, Borns *et. al.* (1986), Lowell (1986), and Davis and Jacobson (1985) cover the deglaciation process. The emerging

landscapes were studied by Davis and Jacobson (1985). For southern Québec, see Parent (1985) and Richard (1985). Kite (1983), and Kite and Stickenrath (1988 and 1989) have studied the early geology of the upper St. John River. Madawaska geology has been studied by Rampton (1988). Bonnichsen *et. al.* (1986) have looked at the changing environment and its suitability for human occupation. Nicholas, alone or with Kite and Bonnichsen (1981 and 1988), provides information on the early archeology of the Upper St. John Valley. Eighteenth- and nineteenth-century observations of the physical environment are found in P. Campbell (1792), Fisher (1838), Gesner (1847), Lugrin (1884), and Monro (1855). Nineteenth-century climate has been studied by Baron and Smith (1996). Contemporary assessments of Madawaska soil quality can in found in Arno (Maine Madawaska) and Langmaid *et. al.* (New Brunswick Madawaska) (1964 and 1980).

Part One

FROM NATIVE FRONTIER TO IMPERIAL BORDERLAND

Human occupation began along the upper St. John River a very long time before the arrival of the first white settlers—more than 11,000 year ago, to be precise. At the dawn of human occupation, the upper St. John River basin appears to have been a fairly self-contained environment, and its inhabitants were members of the human vanguard into the Maritime Peninsula. Soon, however, the region emerged as a zone of contact between the St. Lawrence Valley and Maritime Peninsula, and thus as a Native frontier. When the Europeans (Portuguese, Basques, and French) first appeared on the shores of the St. Lawrence and later along the Gulf of Maine and Bay of Fundy in the 1500s and early 1600s, their activities meshed with those of the Natives; they fished, and they traded European-made goods for fur. Europeans used the river in the same way as the Natives, as a means of communication between the St. Lawrence and the Bay of Fundy. The upper St. John River continued to be at the heart of a frontier area. Before long, however, the French and English began claiming land as dependent territories, or colonies; European rulers sought to create New World colonies as a means of expanding both their economic resources and imperial prestige. The French opened fur-trading and fishing stations on the St. Lawrence starting in 1599, and the St. Lawrence Valley became the colony of Canada. The first French settlement in the Maritime Peninsula was established on St. Croix Island in 1604; a vaguely defined territory stretching from Cape Breton Island to Maine and from the Bay of Fundy to the Chaleur Bay became the colony of

Acadia. Canada, Acadia, and later Louisiana constituted New France. The English established settlements in Massachusetts Bay (1620 and 1629), and their population spread outward from there. France and England tried to prevent each other's colonies from growing and captured them from each other when they could. The Natives did not accept the invasion passively; they fought to preserve control over their land and its resources and to protect their way of life. The strategically located St. John River Valley became a borderland between the French and English colonies, between the Natives and European newcomers, and later between the British and the American Revolutionaries. Throughout the period, it was a critical component in the French—and later British—communication system.

Who were those first humans who lived in the upper St. John River basin and used its resources? How did they interact with each other? What were their ways of life? How were they affected by the arrival of the Europeans? What use did the Europeans make of the river and its upper reaches? How did eighteenth-century conflicts shape the life of the Natives and European inhabitants of the St. John Valley? And finally, why did Natives and later French settlers leave the lower St. John to resettle in the Madawaska territory? The chapters in this first section will take us through a chronology of events to answer those questions.

Timeline Part One: From the Sixteenth to the Eighteenth Century

Dates	International Events	North American Events	Events in the Maritime Peninsula	St. John River Valley
1534			Jacques Cartier (F) explores the Chaleur Bay	
1535		Cartier sails up the St. Lawrence		
1570s			First European explorers along the Maine coast	
1535–80		Iroquoians vacate the St. Lawrence below Montreal		
1580			John Walker (E) explores the mouth of the Penobscot and steals 400 hides from the local Native village.	
1581		Normandy merchants organize a company to trade in fur along the St. Lawrence		
1600		Founding of Tadoussac (F)		
1603				Samuel de Champlain encounters Maliseets near Tadoussac
1604			French winter over on St. Croix Island	
1605			St. Croix colony transferred to Port Royal (Nova Scotia)	
1606			English colony attempted at Popham (Maine)	
1607		Founding of Jamestown (Virginia)		
1608		Founding of Quebec City by Champlain (F)		
1613			Samuel Argall (E) destroys French posts at Port Royal and Mount Desert Island	
1617–19			The "Great Dying": first recorded epidemic of European disease among the Natives	
1620		Plymouth Colony founded (E)		
1621			King of England grants Nova Scotia to the Scottish Earl of Sterling	
1624		The Dutch start a colony on Manhattan (New Amsterdam)		
1629		English take Quebec City.		
1629		Founding of Massachusetts Bay Colony (E)		
1632	**Treaty of Saint-Germain en Laye**		**France regains Acadia**	Charles de La Tour starts a Fort and trading post at mouth of St. John River
1633			France claims the Kennebec as the boundary between the French and English possessions	
1635			Founding of Pentagouet at the mouth of the Penobscot River by Charles Menou d'Aulnay	
1634			Smallpox epidemics	
1635–55			"Beaver Wars" among Amerindians	
1640–70			Iroquois attack Natives on Maritime Peninsula	
1654			English capture Port Royal, Fort La Tour and Pentagouet	
1667	**Treaty of Breda**	Dutch cede New Amsterdam to England	**France regains Acadia**	
1670			Saint-Castin arrives at Pentagouet	
1671			Founding of Beaubassin	
1675–78			**King Philip's War**	
1676–78			Jesuit Mission at Rivière du Loup	
1674			English capture Port Royal; destroy Pentagouet, Machias, Jemseg	
1678			Part of Kennebec Abenakis move east of Penobscot river	
1680			**France regains Acadia**	

Dates	International Events	North American Events	Events in the Maritime Peninsula	St. John River Valley
1680		Founding of Abenakis mission on the St. Lawrence , at Saint-François (Onandaka)	Acadians move to the Des Mines basin (Grand Pré)	
1680s			Jesuits establish Missions at Norridgewock and Pentagouet	
1684				Grants to the D'Amours brothers of four seigneuries on the St. John
1686				Grant of the Madawaska seigneury to Aubert de la Chesnay
1685				Probable beginnings of Maliseet village of Meductic.
1688				Mgr. de Saint-Vallier travels to Acadia through the St. John River and leaves account of journey
1689				Probable founding of Catholic Mission at Meductic
1688–99	War of the League of Augsburg		**King William's War**	
1689			English capture Port Royal	
1692				Lamothe Cadillac travels the St. John River to Témiscouata Lake and leaves account of journey
1692				Governor De Villebon establishe capital of Acadia at Nashwaak (Fort St. Joseph)
1694–96			Epidemics	
1696			English establish Fort Pemaquid	English fail to capture Nashwaak
1696				John Gyles accompanies Maliseets hunting party to upper St. John River and leaves account of the journey
1697	Treaty of Ryswick		**France regains Acadia**	
1698			Foundation of Shepody (Hopewell N.B.) and Petitcodiac (Hillsborough N.B.) settlements by Acadians.	
1702–13	War of Spanish Succession		**Queen Ann's War**	
1704		Founding of second Abenakis mission on the St. Lawrence, at Bécancourt (Wolinak)	Pentagouet taken; Passamaquoddy destroyed.	
1710			Port Royal taken by the British	
1713	Treaty of Utrecht	**France cedes Acadia "within its ancient limits" to the British**	Port Royal renamed Annapolis Royal	
1710s				Beginnings of Native village at Aukpac or Aukpaque
1720			Beginning of construction of Louisbourg	
1721-27			Dummer's War (Natives and British)	
1724			Destruction of Norridgewock	
1725			Articles of Boston—end of Dummer's war.	
1727			Dummers' Treaty	
1741-48	War of Austrian Succession			
1744-48			**King George's War**	
1744			French and Amerindian troops from Canada attack Annapolis Royal, but fail to take it	Captain Pote captured at Annapolis Royal and brought to Quebec City; leaves account of journey up the St. John River.
1745			Massachusetts declares war on the Abenakis; fall of Louisbourg	Catholic Mission transferred from Meductic to Aukpac

Dates	International Events	North American Events	Events in the Maritime Peninsula	St. John River Valley
1746				Opening of the Grand Portage Route
1748	**Treaty of Aix La Chapelle**		Louisbourg returned to the French in exchange of Madras (India)	
1749			Foundation of Halifax in N.S. Erection of Fort Halifax in Winslow (Me.)	
1750			French build Fort Beauséjour and Gaspareau. Relocation of Acadians on St. John Island and north of Messagoueche River; destruction of village of Beaubassin by the French	
1754			**French and Indian Wars begin**	
1755			Destruction of Fort Beauséjour and Gaspareau by the British.	Some Acadians take refuge at Jemseg and Sainte-Anne des Pays-Bas
			Deportation of Acadians	
1756	**Seven-Year War begins in Europe**			
1758			Fall of Louisbourg	Destruction of Jemseg
1759			Fall of Quebec	Destruction of Sainte-Anne
1760			Fall of Montreal - surrender of the French on the lower St. John—Battle of the Restigouche	
1762				Founding of Maugerville
1763			**Treaty of Paris**	
1763				Simonds, Hazen and White at Portland Point (Saint John)
1765		Peace of Boston ratified by St. John River Natives.		
1764				St. John River Company established; grants issued the following year
1767-68				First group of Acadians returning the St. Lawrence settle on proprietors' land on lower St. John
1768			First post-deportation grants to Acadians in New Brunswick	
ca. 1768				French village at Hammond River
1774		**Americans declare their independence**		
1776			Jonathan Eddy's attack against Fort Cumberland (formerly Ft. Beauséjour) fails	
1777				John Allan expedition against lower St. John; constructions of Fort Howe at mouth of the river
1779			British destroy American fleet at the mouth of the Penobscot	
1782			Catholics allowed to own land under normal conditions in Nova Scotia	
1783	**Treaty of Paris**	American independence recognized by Britain	Arrival of Loyalists	Arrival of Loyalists in the fall Rebuilding of the Grand Portage Route
1784			**New Brunswick becomes a separate province**	

2

A NATIVE FRONTIER: THE PREHISTORIC
UPPER ST. JOHN VALLEY[1]

The term "prehistory" refers not to a period of the human past when nothing significant happened, but rather to a period in that past that has left behind no written documents. In North America, prehistory ends with European colonization. Because our understanding of what occurred in human society before the adoption of writing derives largely from archaeological evidence, knowledge of the prehistoric past depends largely on the existence—and discovery—of archaeological sites. Archaeological sites in the North American northeast offer relatively little information because the region's acidic soil digests organic material over time, leaving almost nothing for scholars to work with besides stone artifacts and pottery fragments. Anthropologists therefore use those objects, as well as the way of life they reflect (hunter-gatherer versus farmer, for instance) to distinguish between different successive or overlapping cultural traditions (see Table 1-1 in previous chapter).

While no archaeological sites have been discovered along the St, John River between Edmundston and Tobique, numerous sites have been investigated along the uppermost St, John/Allagash and Black rivers, around Munsungun and Chase Lakes, and farther north around Lake Témiscouata. At present, archaeologists rely on evidence from those sites to understand the prehistory of the upper St, John River basin.

I. PALEO-INDIANS

A. Early Paleo-Indians

The earliest North American people are called Paleo-Indians. Paleo-Indians were also the earliest habitants of the Maritime Peninsula. Paleo-anthropologists distinguish between early and late Paleo-Indians based on the highly distinctive shape of their projectile points. Early Paleo-Indian sites have been found in the Maritime Peninsula in Maine and Nova Scotia, as well as in southern Québec (Megantic), Massachusetts, New Hampshire, and Vermont (see Map 2-1). They all date from about 10,500 BP. Their inhabitants most likely moved from the southwest following herds of the large grazing animals they hunted. Living in a frigid, almost treeless environment, Maritime Peninsula Paleo-Indians had to know how to build snug, windproof, and watertight shelters, and how to make tailored garments from animal hides (possibly resembling traditional clothing worn until recently by High Arctic Inuit). For their encampments, early Paleo-Indians favored stretches of well-drained, sandy soil distant from lakes and rivers. Munsungun appears to have attracted Paleo-Indians because the area was rich in chert, a hard stone used for tool making. Paleo-Indians were highly skilled tool makers, with fine-tuned

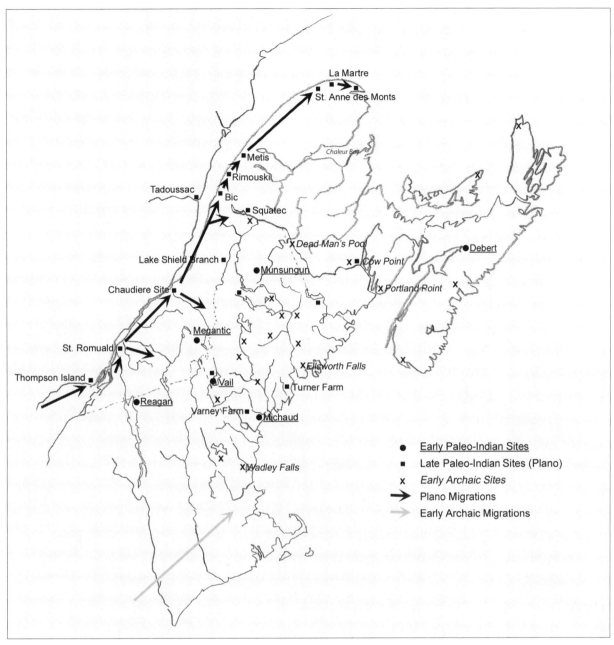

Map 2-1: Early Native Sites and Plano Migration
Map by B. and S. Craig

knowledge of the properties of the materials available to them. The stone objects they produced are beautifully crafted and strikingly elegant. We do not know whether Maritime Peninsula Paleo-Indians ever hunted woolly mammoth or prehistoric bison. There is some evidence they hunted tundra caribou, and the variety of tools found suggests they hunted other animals as well. They probably also ate fish, berries, and nuts in season.

Because tundra caribou are very mobile herd animals, their hunters likely gathered at one place in fairly large numbers to take part in communal hunts, but they did not necessarily stay together year round. Neighborhood groups exchanged information while remaining culturally distinct. For instance, while the fluted projectile point was a universally used form, Munsungun and Vail fluted points were made using different techniques. What happened to Paleo-Indians when the temperature warmed up, flora changed, and animals upon which they relied for subsistence either migrated north or became extinct is as yet unknown. They may have followed their prey north or stayed where they were and adapted to the new circumstances.

B. Late Paleo-Indian and Archaic Cultures

Two major cultural traditions coexisted in Maine and southern Québec between 10,000 and 8,000 BP: late Paleo-Indians or "Plano people," and Early Archaic. (For anthropologists and archaeologists, "Archaic" means less old than "Paleo.") Plano people were hunters, fishermen, trappers, and gatherers. They lived in a tundra forest or open forest environment, hunting large, solitary animals (moose, elk, deer, and bear) as well as smaller prey.

A significant number of Plano sites have been found on the south shore of the St. Lawrence, especially along the Gaspé Peninsula. They are located on beaches at the mouth of rivers leading to the interior. The Plano people may have fished as well as hunted sea mammals like seals, walruses, or beluga whales; they were also likely hunting land game, trapping, and gathering. The Plano people appear to have migrated from present-day Manitoba, following an eastward route along the Great Lakes and the St. Lawrence. Plano sites have been found near Témiscouata Lake in Squatec. Archaeologists do not know whether Témiscouata was reached from the north or south. Some think the Plano migrated south following north/south valleys. Other anthropologists believe some Plano people followed a route

through the Chaudière Valley, northern Maine, and Lake Témiscouata to reach the St. Lawrence again (see Map 2-1).

Early sites in the upper St, John River basin are rare outside the Témiscouata area. One possible reason is that Paleo-Indians found the environment inhospitable. Anthropologist George Nicholas thinks otherwise. He believes the glacial lake basins were a mosaic of micro-environments: shallow ponds, wetlands, and small streams, all supporting different flora and fauna and providing mobile populations with a great variety of resources. The upper St, John was then a "landscape of opportunities."[2] However, by the middle Holocene, the environment had become more uniform, and humans preferred other regions where resources were more abundant, such as major river valleys and the coasts, and the upper St. John was used less frequently, primarily for travel. However, the scarcity of early sites is not necessarily evidence of a lack of occupation, or even use, but may be due to a lack of discoveries.

The earliest evidence of human occupation in the upper St. John River basin is a late Paleo-Indian/ Early Archaic site on a terrace that overlooks glacial Lake Shields Branch. It dates from the early Holocene. The site is very large and was probably a base camp from which small groups detached themselves for hunting and foraging expeditions. Some of the artifacts found on the site were made of stones from the interior of Maine and from the mouth of the St. John River, which suggests extensive trade and river travel.

A few Plano sites have been found in southwestern Maine (Varney Farm in Turner) but not in New Brunswick. Most prehistoric Maine sites from this period belong to the Early Archaic tradition. Did the two groups meet and mix? We do not know. The occupation of the territory between the St. Lawrence and northern Maine appears to have been a complex process, involving contacts between people of different origins.

Recent excavations (2000–02) conducted at Squatec by archaeologists Dumais and Rousseau in the Témiscouata district brought this complexity to light. The site dates from 9,000 to 8,400 BP. Most artifacts are made from chert from Touladi in the Témiscouata district, but some objects are made from Munsungun chert. Most artifacts belong unmistakably to the Plano tradition but display marked differences from the Plano artifacts found in Maine and in the Lower St. Lawrence and Gaspé areas. Some objects, however, were made using a technology belonging to an earlier tradition. The Squatec people were a chronological as well as geographical "border people." Their artifacts suggest they had limited contact with other groups along the St. Lawrence but more extensive contact with people from northern Maine.

This position as a "people in between" was to characterize all later prehistoric occupants of the Témiscouata region. Local remains from the Archaic culture are scarce. Most were found at Dégelis or along the Madawaska River. Those artifacts bear witness to contacts with north and south; the influence of the south is, however, more pronounced. The arti-

Illus. 2-1 at bottom: Stone tools found on Lake Touladi site CkEe2-22 and the source of raw material used (Maine, N.B., N.S.).
Courtesy A. Burke

Illus. 2-2 below: Biface (stone tool) made of Ramah quartzite from Labrador, 1,350 km away (850 miles), found on site CjEd-5 on Madawaska River.
Courtesy A. Burke

Illus. 2-3: Biface of Ramah quartzite found in Saint-Honoré, Témiscouata. The material is translucent.
Courtesy A. Burke

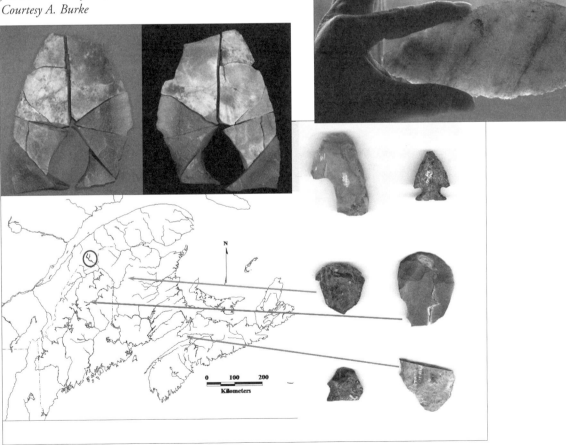

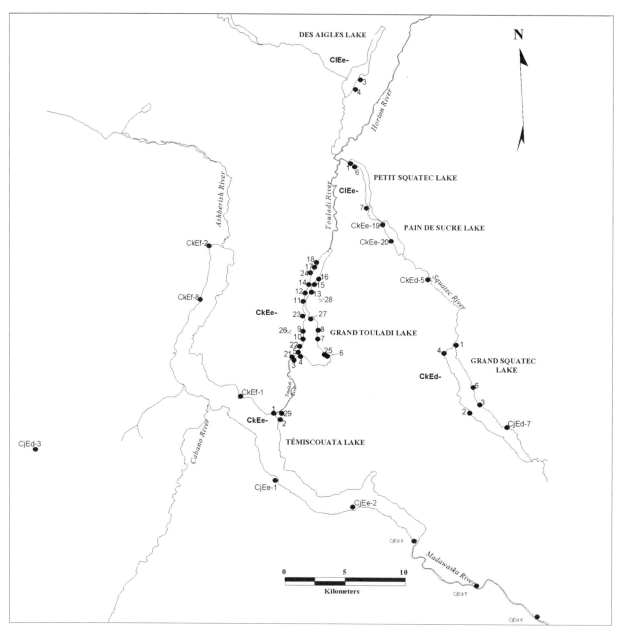

Map 2-2: Archaeological sites around Témiscouata Lake
Courtesy A. Burke

facts do not look like the stone ones found in the St. Lawrence Valley, resembling instead the kind found in New England sites. Dumais and Rousseau, who investigated the Dégelis and Madawaska River sites, concluded they had been occupied by human groups moving from the south and reaching the upper limits of their familiar ecosystem. As those groups occu-pied sites along a major communication route, they had contacts with people from the north as well: their artifacts are made of Touladi chert as well as material from the St. Lawrence Valley and New England. Touladi chert was not exported north, but objects made with it have been found on the lower and middle St. John River. The Dégelis, Madawaska, and Squatec sites, therefore, were part of a larger space where various cultural groups either coexisted or met: Plano culture on the south shore and Gaspé Peninsula; Gulf of Maine Archaic (a culture relying on marine resources) on the north shore of the St. Lawrence; Early Archaic in the Maine interior. Dumais and Rousseau concluded that:

> It is probably at that time that geographic space gradually acquired a political dimension and that its occupants for the first time had to internalize the concept of "frontier"; the notion of a periphery which, although fluid and unfixed, would have curtailed their mobility. On this count, it seems increasingly plausible that at the time, the St. Lawrence south shore and the interior of Maine would have constituted a checkerboard.[3]

The upper St. John Valley had become a frontier.

Sidebar 2-1: Glooscap and the Giant Beaver: Algonquian Memories of Prehistoric Landscapes?

Glooscap (Gluskap) is a character found in various northeastern Algonkian folktales (Montagnais, Penobscot, Passamaquoddy, Mi'kmaq, and Maliseet), but most of his adventures occurred along the St. John. Memories of a very distant past—when the Pleistocene megafauna roamed across a Maritime Peninsula studded with meltwater lakes—seem embedded in those tales. They describe a universe originally inhabited by giant animals. Glooscap brought them down to size by petting them. A beaver escaped, however, and built a dam at the mouth of the St. John so high that all the land behind it flooded. Glooscap smashed the dam with his axe, creating the Reversing Falls (at the entrance of present-day Saint John, N.B.). But when he tried to pet the beaver, the animal escaped upriver. Glooscap chased him in vain, and the rocks (and even snowshoes) he threw at the elusive beast created various islands and rocks in the river. In one version, the beaver escaped to the St. Lawrence, which it dammed, creating the Great Lakes; in another, the Annapolis Valley in Nova Scotia is the remnant of a giant beaver pond drained by Glooscap. The Grand Falls is yet another breached giant beaver dam, which used to hold another great lake.

During the Pleistocene era, the Maritime Peninsula was covered with ice-dam lakes. The lakes drained over a relatively short time after the arrival of the first humans in the region. A species of beaver (*Castoroides Ohioensis*) the size of a black bear lived in most of North America until about 6,000 BP (although no fossil has yet been found in the Maritime Peninsula). Did Paleo-Indians who moved to the peninsula believe the giant lakes they encountered had been created by now-invisible giant beavers? Were the Glooscap tales ways to account for the dramatic changes that occurred in their environment after their arrival? Are the tales "fossil memories" of the prehistoric age, faint echoes of the voices of people who lived here ten thousand years ago?

Sources: Beck (1972), Jack (1895), and Leavitt (1995). See also: http://website.nbmmnb.ca/Koluskap/English/Stories/StoryList.php

---

II.   THE WOODLAND OR CERAMIC PERIOD

A. Locations

The later prehistoric cultures are called "Woodland" or "Ceramic." Their main distinctive trait is their use of baked clay pots. Woodland people were usually horticulturalists: they cultivated small fields with hoes. As very few Maritime Peninsula inhabitants were horticulturalists, anthropologists use the label "Ceramic" to refer to those among them who used pottery. Archaeologists draw distinctions between the various groups according to differences in pottery techniques and types of decoration. The Ceramic period has left more sites and sites richer in artifacts than previous cultures, suggesting higher population density and more complex use of resources. Archaeologists have, for instance, identified forty-five sites around Lake Témiscouata, and most date from this period (see Map 2-2). Some Témiscouata sites, like the Davidson one at the mouth of the Touladi River, have been occupied repeatedly since the early Ceramic period. The sites contain stone artifacts, pieces of pottery, and occasional bones. The projectile points are of a style unknown along the St. Lawrence but widespread in the Maritimes among

Illus 2-4: St. Lawrence Iroquoian and Middle Woodland pottery fragments originating from the St. Lawrence Valley and found on Lake Témiscouata.
Courtesy A. Burke

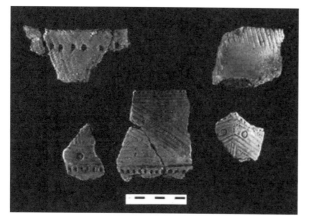

late prehistoric Mi'kmaq and Maliseets. Stone artifacts are made mostly of Touladi chert, with pieces made of material from Tobique, Munsungun, the Bay of Fundy, Labrador, and New York/Ontario. Only five sites contained pottery. The ones found at Davidson were made of clay found near present-day Quebec City and used the same decorative style as St. Lawrence potteries. At another site (Pelletier site), the technique used (tempering the clay with crushed shell) was typical of Maritime pottery made between 1,000 and 1,500 AD but unknown along the St. Lawrence. The occupants of the Témiscouata sites were therefore familiar with pottery-making techniques and decorative styles from those two regions—or were able to acquire pottery from them. Except for the Davidson site, none of the sites bore the imprint of even semi-permanent occupation until the Ceramic period. The Témiscouata was a hunting-fishing-trapping-gathering territory, travel corridor, source of raw material (Touladi chert), and later, towards the end of the Ceramic period, a place to live.

The sites on the uppermost St. John River and the Black and Allagash Rivers were also travel sites (see Map 2-3). Nothing older than 3,000 BP has been found there yet. The artifacts resemble those found on the middle Saint John River, but also on the Penobscot and Kennebec. The sites' locations also indicate that they were not primarily bases from which the Natives gathered food, but rather where they stopped while traveling. The number of sites attests to the intensity of travel through those rivers. David Sanger concluded from his excavation of the Dickey-Lincoln area that "in the northeast, there are areas serving vital functions that are not immediately involved in the food quest."[4]

George Nicholas surmises that those routes served for regular travels between the Maine coast, Maine interior, and St. Lawrence. Prehistoric people traveled from place to place to reach other food

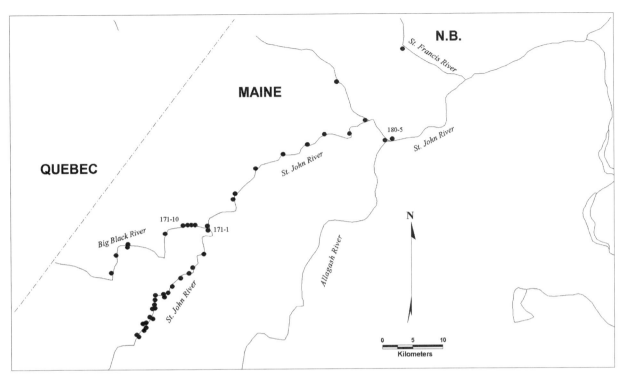

Map 2-3: *Archaeological sites on Uppermost St. John.* Courtesy A. Burke

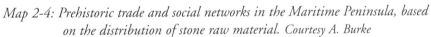

Map 2-4: *Prehistoric trade and social networks in the Maritime Peninsula, based on the distribution of stone raw material.* Courtesy A. Burke

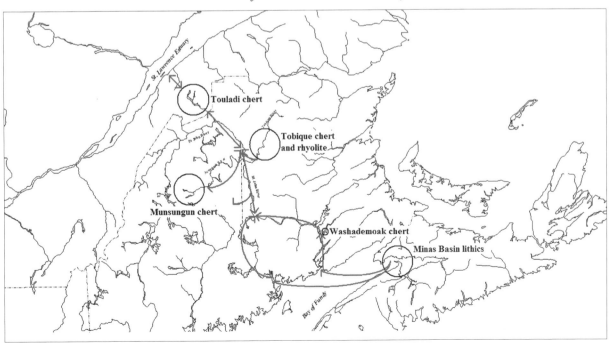

resource areas, but also for exchanges, as evidenced by the mixed origins of the material used in the Témiscouata region (see Map 2-4).

B. Sixteenth-Century Native Groups

Late sixteenth- and early seventeenth-century explorers left accounts of the people they encountered, and this allows us to gain a better picture of the ethnic divisions among the people who occupied the Maritime Peninsula. In 1535, Jacques Cartier had encountered Montagnais on the north shore of the St. Lawrence estuary and Iroquoian horticultural villages between Quebec City (Stadaconna) and Montreal (Hochelaga). The Iroquoians' presence extended farther down the estuary, but the groups downriver did not cultivate fields. Instead, they hunted, fished, and caught sea mammals, especially beluga whales. They are known to have occupied sites at Tadoussac, Ile Verte, and Trois Pistoles. The Iroquoians belonged to a different linguistic family than their neighbors, who were all Algonquian-speaking. They clashed with other natives whom they called "Toudamans" and who were Mi'kmacs or Maliseets, or both. In the first few years of the seventeenth century, Champlain encountered "Souriquois" east of the St. John River (called "Tarrentines" by the English); "Etchemins" (Maliseet, Passamaquoddy, and Penobscot) between the St. John and Kennebec Rivers; and "Almouchiquois," who were horticulturalists farther west and all the way to Massachusetts Bay. Another group, the Abenakis, lived seven days travel south of Quebec City, on the Kennebec River. They too were horticulturalists (see Map 3-1 in the next chapter).

C. Ways of Life

Early Paleo-Indians and their successors differed in at least one fundamental way. The first chose flat, sandy locations distant from water for their encampments; the later groups, on the other hand, systematically chose sites close to water, usually at the junction of two rivers or at the head of rapids. Rivers played a different role in their lives and in their search for food than they had for their predecessors. Archaic people are probably the ones who began to make dugout canoes by hollowing out the trunks of very large trees (before them, trees were not large enough for that purpose). Ceramic people made birchbark canoes, which not only were easier to maneuver, but also could be carried over portages (see Map 2-5). The use of wood as a raw material was reflected in Archaic and Ceramic people's tools: they continued making chipped stone tools like the Paleo-Indians, but they also made polished stone tools, especially axes and gouges suitable for working wood. Otherwise, their toolkit was the one of nomadic hunters and gatherers. They hunted large game, trapped small animals, fished (with nets or weirs), and gathered berries, nuts, and roots. They made use of wood and bark containers for storage and cooking. Cooking was by means of dropping very hot stones in a bark container filled with water and the item to be cooked. The introduction of ceramics simplified cooking. The pots usually had a pointy bottom and could be stuck into the ground or among the fire's embers. Clay pots, however, are heavy and break easily, which suggests that those who used them had a less nomadic way of life; some groups adopted pottery for a while and then abandoned it because it was too cumbersome for their lifestyle.

Evidence from the Davidson and other large sites and historical evidence from the time of contact suggest that bands made of several extended families each claimed a particular territory. Native people recognized kinship on the mother's and father's side, which facilitated the movement of people between groups and bands. Archaeologists used to believe the Ceramic people spent summers on the coast and wintered in the interior. They thought the patterns early European explorers had observed applied to earlier people as well. They now believe that patterns of occupation were the opposite in the pre-contact period, and that not all Natives alternated between the coast and interior. Passamaquoddy Bay Natives lived off shellfish in winter and moved to the islands

Map 2-5: Section of a map of New France entitled "Carte pour servir à l'éclaircissement du papier terrier de la Nouvelle France, [J. B. L. Franquelin, 1678]." Although the map is not very accurate, the author is aware of the existence of rivers and portages forming communication routes between the St. Lawrence and the St. John. Note the illustration showing Native people carrying their canoe over a portage.
LAC, NMC-17393

to catch cod in summer. On the Miramichi, Natives used semi-permanent base camps where they stored food and from which they launched hunting, fishing, and gathering expeditions. We know that the Natives traded with their neighbors, because archaeologists keep finding non-local material, including very distant material, in the various sites.

For the time being, our most-detailed description of the life of St. John River interior groups is the one left by John Gyles, who was captured by the Maliseets as a small boy in 1689. He lived with them for nine years. The Maliseets had at that time a base camp at Meductic (see Map 3-1). Their village contained long houses, wigwams (birchbark, portable, covered structures), hearths, tanning pits and frames, and smokehouses (to preserve food). The Meductic Natives cultivated corn, but it seems horticulture had recently been introduced among them by Abenakis refugees. The summers were occupied with river fishing, hunting, and gathering edible plants, in addition to tending the cornfields. Smaller groups could detach themselves from the gathering for brief forays into the nearby forest. Meat and fish were smoked, and hide was prepared. In the fall, the gathered crowd began to disperse in smaller groups. October and November were the best time for the bear hunt, as the animals had considerably fattened to sustain themselves during the long period of hibernation. Before the first snowfall, canoes were put in storage, and snowshoes were made. Winter was the time of maximum dispersion. Gyles was included in a small party that went north to hunt and camped at Madawaska (see Appendix C). Very small groups hunted moose and caribou and trapped smaller animals, for this was the time of year when animal fur was the thickest. When spring came, the canoes were retrieved and repaired (a well-made canoe could last ten years); new ones were made if needed, as well as birchbark containers and shelters. Fishing resumed until it was time for the annual summer gathering. Groups of eighty to a hundred individuals could then gather in semi-permanent sites. Larger gatherings (200–300 persons) appear to have taken place only where certain resources were particularly abundant (sturgeon and salmon on the lower St. John, for instance). The junctions of rivers and entrances of key portages were the favored places for summer gatherings. In Gyles' days, the Meductic Natives did not travel south to fish on the coast, despite the relatively short distance, but this may have been a recent development like horticulture.

Conclusion

In the Prehistoric period, the rivers penetrating deep into the interior of the Maritime Peninsula (the St. John, Penobscot, Kennebec, and their tributaries) played an important role in the life of the Natives. They made contacts between the groups living along the Gulf of Maine/Bay of Fundy and those living on the lower St. Lawrence possible. The Madawaska-Témiscouata-Aberish-des Aigles sector emerged as an important crossroads between the east-west route (the St. Lawrence) and a north-south one (the St. John-Témiscouata-Saguenay). In the sixteenth century, the St. Francis-Rivière du Loup also played an important communication role. Archaeological finds make it clear that the Natives took full advantage of those opportunities to trade with each other. Other forms of interactions may have occurred, but as they left no archaeological traces, we do not know about them. With the exception of the late Pleistocene era, however, humans appear to have shown limited interest in living that far into the interior. Locations distant from the coast were used as resting places while traveling or during hunting expeditions, or as sources of material to make tools and weapons; they were used much less frequently as sites of semi-permanent camps. This had not been the case in the earliest period of human occupation when very different environmental conditions both on the coast and the interior had made the interior, including the upper St. John River basin, a desirable place to live.

ENDNOTES

1. In Canada, "Indian" and most of the phrases including this term are no longer used, unless they are historical ones like "Indian Treaties" or "Indian Act." The first inhabitants of the Americas are referred to as "Natives" (always with an upper case), "Amerindians," or "First Nations." The phrases "American Indians" or "Native Americans" are unheard of. As the descendents of most of the people we are discussing in this chapter and the following are Canadians, we will use the Canadian terminology to describe Native peoples.

2. Nicholas, "Archeology of the upper St. John River," 139.

3. Dumais et Rousseau, "De limon et de sable...," 72.

4. Sanger, "Archaeological Survey...," 23.

FURTHER READINGS

Leavitt, Robert M. *Maliseet and Micmac: First Nations of the Maritimes.* 1995.

Bourque, Bruce J. *Twelve Thousand Years: American Indians in Maine.* 2001.

Tuck, James A. *Maritime Provinces Prehistory.* 1984. (beginning to date).

Buckner, Phillip A. and John G. Reid. *The Atlantic Region to Confederation: A History.* 1994: ch. 1.

Judd, Richard W., *et. al. Maine: The Pine Tree State from Prehistory to the Present.* 1995: ch. 1.

Bear Nicholas, Andrea and Harald Prins. "The Spirit of the Land, the Native People of Aroostook." In *The County: Land of Promise,* ed. A. Mcgrath. 1989: 19–37.

The material about the Prehistory of eastern Québec is in French (see Sources below).

Harris, R. Cole and Geoffrey J. Matthews. *Historical Atlas of Canada,* vol. 1. 1987: plates 2 to 9 and 14.

SOURCES

To find information about Native occupation and use of the upper St. John River basin, consult the work of Maine, New Brunswick, and Québec archaeologists. In addition to Bourque and Tuck listed above, *Recherches amérindiennes au Québec* (1978), Chapdelaine (1985, 1995, 1996, and 2004), Deal and Blair (1991), Doyle (1985), and Robinson, Petersen, and Robinson (1992) provide good overviews of each region. Burke, Chalifoux, Dumais, and Rousseau have conducted extensive and recent archaeological searches in the Témiscouata-Madawaska region; Burke's doctoral thesis (2000—available on microfiches from the National Library of Canada), and his 2006 article are particularly useful. Bonnischen is the authority on the Munsungun region. Nicholas, Kites, and Bonnischen (1981) and Sanger (1978) offer the most readable material on the archaeology of the uppermost St. John. For southern Québec, see also Tremblay (1998), Martijn (1990), and Plourde (1999). Some useful information can be gleaned from Ganong (1899).

3

FROM NATIVE FRONTIER TO IMPERIAL BORDERLAND: THE ST. JOHN RIVER IN THE SIXTEENTH AND SEVENTEENTH CENTURIES

The first contacts between Europeans and Natives occurred in the sixteenth century and preceded the production of detailed written documents by at least a century. In 1497, John Cabot made landfall on the island of Newfoundland, which he claimed for England. By 1505, the Portuguese, French, English, and Basques were launching fishing and whaling expeditions off the island and in the Gulf of St. Lawrence. In their spare time, they traded with the Natives. Unbeknownst to the Natives, the newcomers would profoundly transform their lives. The contacts that were initially beneficial soon turned detrimental. Nonetheless, until the beginning of the eighteenth century, the Natives managed to preserve their autonomy, although their numbers were considerably reduced by disease and warfare.

No direct information about the upper St. John River or Madawaska-Témiscouata is available until the last quarter of the seventeenth century, and what exists is very limited. We can nonetheless make educated guesses about the nature of human activities in the area. The river systems of the Maritime Peninsula were critical to Natives and Europeans alike for trade, conquest, and defense. The upper St. John remained an important bridge between north and south for Natives and, increasingly, for the French who were starting trading stations and settlements on the Bay of Fundy and along the St. Lawrence. In addition, the St. John Valley slowly turned into a borderland between the Natives and English, and between the French and English empires, as both powers intensified their presence in the Maritime Peninsula and New England.

I.   THE SIXTEENTH CENTURY

After Cabot's landfall, European fishermen and whalers made extensive contacts with the Natives along the coast of the Gulf of St. Lawrence. In 1534, French explorer Jacques Cartier sailed up Chaleur Bay (see Map 3-1). There he encountered Natives who spoke broken Portuguese, evidence of sustained contacts with visiting fishermen. Initially, trade along the St. Lawrence was limited to the river's estuary. The Natives remained hostile to fur traders sailing farther upriver, and, until 1580, the Europeans believed sailing beyond Tadoussac was unsafe. The

Stadaconians vacated the St. Lawrence Valley around that time, for reasons that are not entirely clear. Some scholars believe they were driven away by the Mohawks who wanted to trade directly with the Europeans; others argue that adverse climatic conditions destroyed agriculture at the very limit of its ecological niche. Some of the Stadaconians may have sought refuge among the Abenakis, traveling south through the Chaudière River. Most moved west and joined the Hurons.

Beginning in 1581, French merchants from

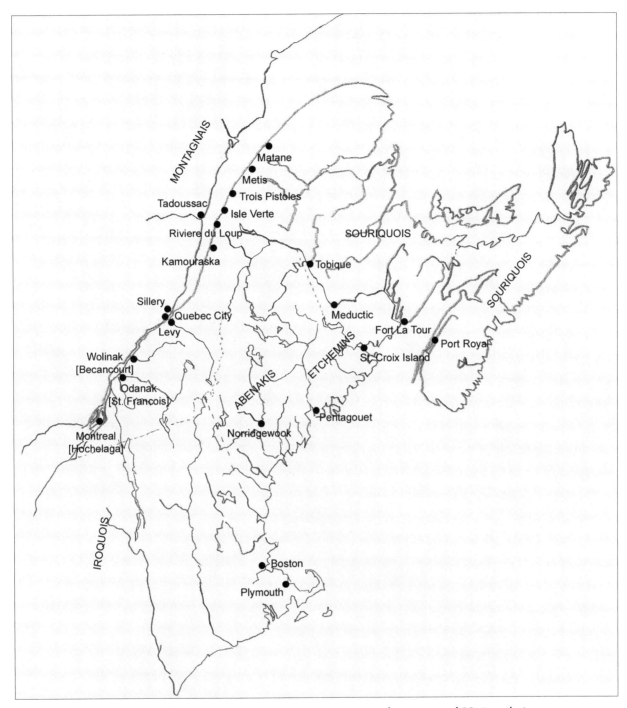

Map 3-1:. Sixteenth- and seventeenth-century European trading posts and Native ethnic groups
Map by B. and S. Craig

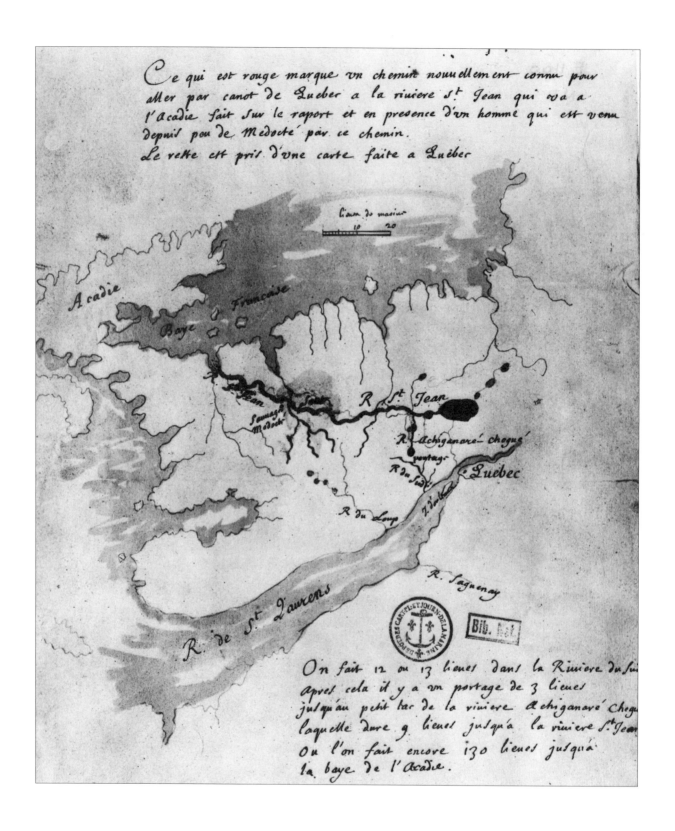

Ce qui est rouge marque un chemin nouuellement connu pour aller par canot de Queber a la riuiere s.t Jean qui va a l'Acadie fait sur le raport et en presence d'vn homme qui est venu depuis peu de Medocté par ce chemin.

Le reste est pris d'vne carte faite a Queber

(map labels)

Acadie

Baye Francoise

R. S.t Jean

R. Achiganaré choqué

portage

R. du Sud

R. Vaulbec

Quebec

R. du Loup

R. Saguenay

R. de St Laurens

On fait 12 ou 13 lieues dans la Riuiere du Sud Apres cela il y a vn portage de 3 lieues jusqu'au petit lac de la riuiere Achiganaré Choqué laquelle dure g lieues jusqu'à la riuiere S.t Jean Ou l'on fait encore 130 lieues jusqu'à la baye de l'Acadie.

Map 3-2: Map of a new portage route to travel from Québec to Acadia entitled "Plan du chemin por aller de Québec en Accadie. 13 noe 1685," by Jacques-René de Brisay, marquis de Denonville, 1685. LAC, NMC-25106. The map is upside down—that is, the north is at the bottom, and the south at the top. The texts (in French) read: At the top: "What is in red indicates a route recently learned about to go by canoe from Quebec to the River Saint John which goes to Acadia and traced according to the report of a man recently arrived from Medocté this way. The rest is taken from a map made in Quebec." At the bottom: "One travels 12 or 13 leagues on the Rivière du Sud, after that there is a three-league portage to the small lake on the Achiganavé-Chégis River, which river flows for 9 leagues till the River Saint John over which one travels 130 leagues to reach the Bay of Acadia."

Normandy began organizing fur-trading expeditions up the St. Lawrence. They traded principally at Matane, Ile Verte, Tadoussac, and Quebec City. In addition, they sent small trading vessels as far as Trois Rivières (at the mouth of the St. Maurice River) and perhaps even to Montreal. By the end of the 1500s, Natives from the coast of Nova Scotia to Labrador were used to the Europeans' seasonal visits. Their contacts ranged from friendly and mutually profitable to hostile and murderous; on the whole, they were friendly. The relationships between European fishermen and Montagnais on the north shore of the St. Lawrence were good enough for the Europeans to store their coastal boats with the Natives when they returned to Europe at the end of the fishing season.

Tadoussac was the most important trading location because it was located at a crossroads between an east-west communication route (the St. Lawrence) and a north-south one (the Saguenay and Témiscouata-Madawaska-St. John route). After the Stadaconians' departure from the St. Lawrence estuary, Montagnais and other Algonkians from the north shore and Mi'kmaq and Maliseets from the Maritime Peninsula moved into the vacated territory. This put the Mi'kmaq and Maliseets in a good position to act as middlemen between Europeans on the St. Lawrence estuary and western Maine and Massachusetts Natives, from whom they obtained not only fur, but also agricultural products. In 1603, French explorer Samuel de Champlain encountered a group of Etchemins in the St. Lawrence estuary on their way to Tadoussac to trade. When Europeans began to explore the coast of Maine and the Bay of Fundy at the turn of the seventeenth century, they were

struck by the extent of Native-European exchange already taking place. Mi'kmaq and Etchemins wore European-made clothing and sailed "shallops," substantial boats copied from the ones the European fishermen left behind when they returned home. Messamouet, chief at La Have in Nova Scotia, had even gone to France and been a guest of the mayor of Bayonne, in the French Basque country, in 1580. The Mi'kmaq, who were superb seamen, probably made contacts with the Europeans along the coast of Gaspé and brought their goods back by boat. The Etchemins, who lived between the Kennebec and St. John, were more likely to have traveled first through the St. John and Témiscouata or St. Francis route, and subsequently through the Kennebec-Chaudière route to meet the European traders—routes that they described in detail to Champlain. The only Europeans known to have traveled through the former route prior to the mid-1600s were three French missionaries going from Acadia to Québec in 1624, and they left no firsthand account of the river. As the Europeans became familiar with the geography of the region, they discovered new routes between Acadia and Québec (see Maps 3-2 and 3-3)

Natives saw the fishermen and whalers as additional people with whom they could trade. Europeans wanted fur, especially beaver fur, as beaver hats had come into fashion in Europe and remained so until the early nineteenth century. Metal objects and textiles were the trade items favored by the Natives, who had developed neither metal-producing technology nor looms for textiles. Trade goods included copper pots and kettles (the most-prized objects), metal tools and weapons (like swords), and woolen

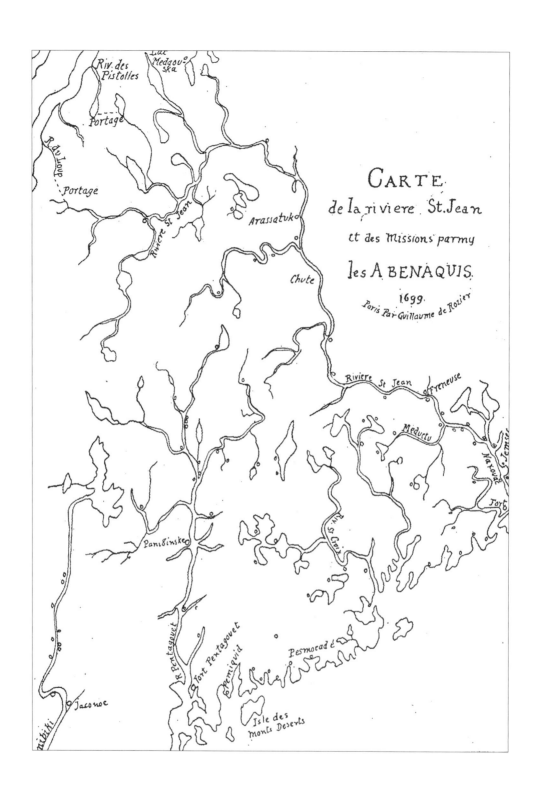

Map 3-3: Native camp sites along the St. John, St. Croix and Penobscot Rivers in 1699. W. Ganong reproduced this French map by Guillaume de Rozier, whose original seems lost, in his "Additions and Corrections to the Monograph on Cartography," Proceedings and Transactions of the Royal Society of Canada, *1906, 60. The map was visibly drawn from the point of view of a canoeist. De Rozier used the term "Abenakis" as a generic term for christianized Maritime Natives. The European posts and sedentary missions are identified by name. Ganong believed the dots represented campsites. The only campsites on the upper St. John are at Grand Falls and at the mouth of the St. Francis; another can be seen on Touladi Lake. There is none mentioned at the mouth of the Madawaska River.*

blankets and glass beads. By the end of the sixteenth century, the range of goods had broadened to include a greater variety of textile products, clothing, and guns and ammunition, as well as sailor's provisions—dried peas and beans, biscuits, and prunes. The Europeans also started providing the Natives with alcohol. As the latter were unfamiliar with intoxicating substances, binge drinking and drunkenness became a serious problem, deplored by Native chiefs and European officials alike. With this exception, trade was not detrimental to the Natives: they traded on their own terms and gained access to a wider variety of goods. This started to change in the seventeenth century, when the newcomers began to colonize the Maritime Peninsula and neighboring regions. With colonization came warfare, alien conceptions of sovereignty and landownership that marginalized the Natives, and disease.

II. THE LONG SEVENTEENTH CENTURY (1600–1713): WARFARE AND ITS CONSEQUENCES

Europeans began exploring the coasts of Maine and the Maritime Peninsula at the end of the sixteenth century and soon established permanent settlements along the St. Lawrence, in Nova Scotia, and along the Gulf of Maine. The French opened a trading post at Tadoussac in 1599; Pierre Dugua, Sieur de Mons, tried to do the same on St. Croix Island in 1604. After a disastrous winter that left most of his men dead, he relocated to Port Royal (present-day Annapolis, Nova Scotia). In the 1630s, two French adventurers who subsequently became governors of Acadia, Charles de La Tour and Charles D'Aulnay, set up forts at the mouths of the St. John (Fort La Tour) and the Penobscot (Pentagouet). After the failed Popham Colony (1606), the English established a settlement in Plymouth, Massachusetts, in 1620, followed by coastal fur-trading and fishing stations, the Massachusetts Bay colony in 1629, and a string of small farming settlements that gradually crept up the coast of Maine. The European presence rapidly led to almost constant conflicts—first among the Natives, then between the Natives and Europeans, and finally among the European themselves—and to Native migrations within the Maritime Peninsula.

A. Conflicts

1. Conflicts Among Natives
In the first half of the seventeenth century, Maritime Peninsula and lower St. Lawrence Valley Natives fought with each other. The Mi'kmaq strove to prevent groups farther west from trading directly with the Europeans who were beginning to ply the waters of the Gulf of Maine, by attacking their villages and stealing their furs. Soon, fur-bearing animals became scarce along the coast, forcing the Natives to push farther and farther inland. To the north, Souriquois, Etchemins, and Montagnais were fighting over the control of the south shore of the St. Lawrence in the 1630s. The Montagnais were even hunting and trapping on the upper St. John, in Etchemin territory.

The missionary Father Le Jeune, who wintered with Montagnais in 1634, spent some time with them around Lake Témiscouata. And as we have seen above, the Iroquois may have chased the Stadaconians away from the St. Lawrence in order to trade directly with the Europeans. Collectively, these inter-tribal conflicts are known as "the Beaver Wars."

Conflicts among the Natives, however, were not purely the result of trade with the Europeans. The Iroquois (Five Nations Confederacy) were trying to surround their territory with a ring of allied or tributary tribes and were willing to engage in ferocious warfare to achieve their goals. The Mohawks, in particular, inspired tremendous fear among the Maritime Peninsula Natives. Among their targets, their attacks generated stories like the one of the Iroquois

---

Sidebar 3-1: Malobiana's Many Faces

The Mohawks were the implacable enemies of the Maritime Peninsula Natives, who greatly feared them. Thomas Albert's readers are familiar with the story of Malobiana (also known as Malabeam), the young Maliseet maiden who sacrificed her life to save her people by luring a party of Mohawks warriors to their death over the Grand Falls. Malobiana was also the heroine of an 1873 poem by New Brunswick antiquarian James Hannay. Canadian poets Charles G. D. Roberts (1887) and Archibald Lampman (unfinished, published posthumously in 1900) also used the story for their poems. New Brunswick antiquarian W. O. Raymond told the story in prose in his *River St. John*. In this account, the unnamed Native woman did not plunge to her death over the falls with the Mohawks; she escaped, but lost her sanity as a consequence of her ordeal. The Natives, however, told a much less dramatic version of the story. Here is the tale as written down by M. F. Foster in 1873:

> It is a tradition of the Micmacs that in a remote age two families of their tribe were on the upper St. John hunting, and were surprised by a war-party of the strange and dreaded Northern Indians. The latter were descending the river to attack the lower Micmac villages, and forced the captured women to pilot them down. A few miles above the falls, they asked the unwilling guides if the stream was all smooth below, and on receiving an affirmative answer, lashed the canoes together into a raft, and went to sleep, exhausted with their march. When near the Grand Falls the women quietly dropped overboard and swam ashore, while the hostile warriors, wrapped in slumber, were swept down into the rapids, only to awaken when escape was impossible. Their bodies were stripped by the Micmacs on the river below, and the brave women were ever afterward held in high honor by the tribe.

> Under the pen of non-Native authors, the story celebrating bravery, cunning, and success became a typical Victorian tale of sacrifice to the community. The Euro-American rendition of the story, in the words of literary scholar D. M. R. Bentley, was also "consonant with the prevailing view that female heroism consisted primarily of suffering and the wide-spread belief….that Canada's Native people were the doomed relics of a race characterized by both savagery and nobility." Malobiana and the Mohawks exemplified those two characteristics.

Sources: Bentley (2005). Bentley reproduces the text quoted above; a slightly longer, buy equally factual version of the story can be found in Rand (1894).

lured to their death over the Grand Falls (see Sidebar 3-1). The conflict with the Iroquois intensified in the 1640s, when the Mohawks launched raids as far east as the Kennebec. In 1661, a Mohawk delegation demanded that the Kennebec Abenakis submit to them and become one of their client nations, a demand the Abenakis rejected. The Montagnais, Etchemins, and Mi'kmaq then created a defense league against the Iroquois. The Iroquois threat diminished only after the French brought to North America veterans of the war against the Turks in Eastern Europe, the Carignan-Salières Regiment (1666). The Iroquois made their peace with the French (and their allies) in 1701.

2. Conflicts Between the Natives and Europeans

Inter-tribal wars were aggravated by the conflicts between the Natives and Europeans. The Natives, as a rule, enjoyed good relations with the French. The French were not very numerous and were more interested in trade and fishing than agriculture. They occupied either territory deserted by the Natives (the St. Lawrence Valley) or unoccupied by them (the Nova Scotia marshland). The English, on the other hand, were more numerous and their population was expanding rapidly. Moreover, since they were primarily farmers, the New England colonists competed with the Native horticulturalists for the same tracts of land. In 1674, a Massachusetts chief known as "Philip" decided to fight back. He had the support of all the southern New England tribes, as well as the Abenakis and Penobscot Etchemins. King Philip's War lasted until 1678. It was a disaster for the Natives, who were either killed or forced out of New England, except in Maine, where they drove the English out for a while. The Kennebec River became a no-man's land between the French and English, and the local Abenakis fled east or north. Subsequent conflicts between the Europeans and Natives were the result of Europeans wars.

3. Conflicts Among the Europeans

When their mother countries were at war, so were

North American colonies. Sparsely populated Acadia was very vulnerable to English attacks, and even relatively well-populated Quebec City was temporarily overtaken by the English in 1629. Port Royal was destroyed for the first time in 1613, and the English subsequently controlled Acadia between 1627 and 1632, 1654 and 1667, and finally 1674 and 1680. Port Royal was captured again in 1689, to be returned to France in 1697. Until the eighteenth century, Acadia, or parts of it, was always returned to France at the end of the hostilities in exchange for some English possession seized by the French. However, when war broke out again in 1702, Port Royal was captured again, and this time, Britain kept Acadia for good.

During all those conflicts, the Maritime Peninsula Natives normally sided with the French, whom they thought less dangerous, but their assistance could never be taken for granted. The Natives did not see themselves as subjects of the French king, whatever the latter claimed, but as independent nations free to conclude alliances and fight when they saw fit. They pursued their own goals: they wanted their sovereignty recognized and their way of life preserved. Unfortunately for them, the French were no more ready to recognize Native sovereignty over their territory than the English were. As far as both groups were concerned, the Natives were not "civilized" and thus could not be sovereign (see Sidebar 3-2).

B. Population Movements and Declining Numbers

Trade and warfare led to Native migrations. In western Maine, fear of the Mohawks led some of the Abenakis to submit to the English for protection. Others simply moved out of the way temporarily or permanently. Because of their location on the Kennebec-Chaudière route, the Abenakis had made contact early with the French at Quebec City and had endeavored to redirect the St. Lawrence fur trade toward their territory. They traveled north to acquire

Sidebar 3-2: Sovereignty and Land Ownership in European and Native Culture

When John Cabot made landfall in Newfoundland in 1497, he took possession of the land in the name of the King of England. Jacques Cartier did the same in the name of the French king on the St. Lawrence in 1535, despite the very visible presence of a Native village nearby. What made the Europeans believe they could claim for themselves land that belonged to others?

The answer was religion. When the Spaniards stumbled upon the Americas in their search for a route to India, they encountered populations who were not Christians. The pope decreed that land not belonging to Christian princes was free for the taking. In return, Christian princes were expected to convert the Natives to Catholicism, thus saving them from damnation. Protestants princes embraced this principle as eagerly as Catholics ones. Kings, however, also had non-religious reasons to want colonies: colonies could be rich in precious metals, stimulated trade, and were a source of prestige.

Native people through the Americas, therefore, could not be sovereign, because they were pagans. Sovereignty and land ownership, however, are two different things. Colonial powers did not think Natives were sovereigns, but sought to define the extent of the latter's property rights in the land they used. The legal consensus among Europeans (codified in the seventeenth century by the famous legal theoretician Grotius), was that occupation of a given territory conferred ownership. However, whereas Grotius equated occupation with cultivation of an unspecified nature, those who applied the law equated it with European-style farming. Hunters and gatherers, therefore, were not considered landowners. It was almost impossible for Europeans to think of hunting grounds, seasonal camp sites, and the travel routes linking them as "property." Native horticulturalists had a hard time convincing the Europeans that their property should not be limited to their fields. Different groups of Europeans, however, were more or less restrictive in their understanding of Native ownership. The Quakers (in Pennsylvania) and the Dutch (in Manhattan) bought the land from the Natives. The New Englanders initially scoffed at the idea, but subsequently adopted it. The French never had to address the issue, since they occupied land the Natives were not using.

Purchasing land from the Natives did not solve the ownership problem. Natives and Europeans understood "ownership" in radically different and incompatible ways. Western legal systems understood ownership as an absolute, exclusive, and transferable right, restricted only by a king's or lord's rights of eminent domain. Nobody could use a piece of property without the consent of the owner. The Natives understood "property" as a right to use the resources of the land for one's own needs or for the needs of the group, and no more. Land rights were not individual rights, and rights of usage were not exclusive, either. When Natives "sold their land" to white settlers or officials, they merely sold a non-exclusive right for use. They often continued to use the land in question to hunt, trap, fish, grow crops, or live. Europeans viewed this as trespassing. Natives also believed that they could legitimately allow more than one European to use the land in question and therefore "sold" the same piece of land to several people. Europeans viewed this practice as dishonest. But as far as the Natives were concerned, the Europeans' attitude toward land and property made no sense and was merely a device to evict them from their ancestral land under false pretences. Land ownership was a source of multiple and mutual misunderstandings between Europeans and Natives fur, and the St. Lawrence Natives (Huron) traveled south to their settlements. The Abenakis benefited from the fact that English trade goods were cheaper and of better quality than the French ones. The Abenakis were also the first Natives in the Maritime Peninsula to embrace Christianity (Catholicism). This led to the French authorities using the term "Abenakis" as a generic for Maritime Peninsula Christian Natives. During and after King Philip's War, about 1,500 Abenakis took refuge along the St. Lawrence, where the authorities settled them at Bécancourt (Wôlinak) and Saint François (Onandaka) (see Map 3-1). In 1688, Mgr. de Saint-Vallier, bishop of Québec, traveled to Acadia; at Madawaska, he encountered some Christian Natives from Sillery (the first Christian Native reservation set up by the French—the Sillery Natives were Algonkians) as well as some converted Mi'kmaq. In 1692, the adventurer and future founder of Detroit, La Mothe-Cadillac, described Madawaska as a place where the Abenakis (Canibas) were taking refuge when conditions in their territory were dangerous (see Appendix C). The upper St. John, nonetheless, was still considered part of Etchemin territory, which, according to Governor Villebon in 1698, extended all the way to Rivière du Loup.

After King Philip's War, other Abenakis retreated east, where they mingled with the Etchemins. On the Penobscot, the mix was mostly Abenakis, but on the St. Croix and St. John Rivers, the Abenakis assimilated to the Etchemins. For their part, some of the Etchemin moved north across the St. Lawrence and joined the Montagnais alongside the Saguenay River. Around that time, the French began to use Native terms to refer to them. The Souriquois were now referred to as Mi'kmaq, the Kennebec-Penobscot tribes as Canibas, and the tribes on the St. Croix and St. John as Maliseets. According to the Jesuit missionaries, there were four "Abenakis" villages regrouping about 350 warriors and their families in the Maritime Peninsula by 1709: Norridgewock, Pentagouet, Passamaquoddy, and Meductic, the last two inhabited by Abenakis and Maliseets (see Map 3-3). The mission-aries never mentioned a village at Madawaska. The Natives divided hunting grounds among themselves, each corresponding to a separate river.

At the same time, epidemics were sharply reducing the number of Natives. The Europeans brought not only trade goods to North America, but also germs. The Natives had no immunity to European diseases and died in large numbers from them (a phenomenon known as "virgin-soil epidemic"). Missionary Father Briard in 1612 reported that diseases had ravaged the Mi'kmaq before the Europeans even settled in the Maritime Peninsula, and that the Natives blamed contacts with fishermen for the epidemics. In 1617, the first epidemics swept through the Etchemins and traveled as far as Massachusetts, wiping out the Native population of the villages in which the Pilgrim Fathers settled. The Puritans viewed this as a sign that God himself wanted them to have the land. Smallpox broke out at Plymouth in 1634 and swept through the surrounding Native communities. Europeans often survived the disease, but not the Natives, who almost always died from it. Additional epidemics further reduced those numbers. By 1696, the Native population in Acadia was estimated at 1,119, with only 294 Natives in the entire St. John Valley (see Table 3-1).

All through the period, the French population was very small and lacked women. The men consequently took Native wives, marrying them in the Church or in accordance with Native customs. Charles de la Tour's first wife was a Native woman, and the baron de Saint-Castin married the daughter of a Penobscot chief. Interracial marriages were initially encouraged by the French authorities, who thought it a good way to "civilize" the Natives. In Europe, women had to obey their husbands; therefore the authorities thought French men would control their Native wives and oblige them to adopt French mores. Instead, however, many of the men "went Native"—that is, adopted their wives' way of life. In the eighteenth century, the English would view this mingling of blood as a reason to consider the Acadians as dangerous and unreliable.

Table 3-1: Losses Due to Epidemics Among Maritime Peninsula Native Populations

	Pre-epidemic Population (1600–1610)	Post-epidemic Population (circa 1650)	Mortality Rate
Maliseet-Passamaquody	7,600	2,500	67%
Eastern Abenakis	13,800	3,000	78%
Western Abenakis	12,000	250	98%

Source: Snow (1988): 24.

III.   TRADE AND SETTLEMENTS

A. Trade Along the St. John River

Because the St. John River connected the St. Lawrence with Acadia, it was used to circumvent trading regulations in Canada. The French trading post at Tadoussac (see Map 3-1) held a monopoly on the shipping of fur to France, which entitled its holder to levy heavy taxes on the exports. In 1694, the inhabitants of the south shore of the St. Lawrence petitioned the French government to be exempted from the Tadoussac monopoly, arguing that Natives had never resided in the area, and that those with whom they traded came from the St. John River, Pentagouet, and Boston. They won. In 1685, they were granted the right to trade with the Natives who visited them, but not to go and trade in Native territory. However, in 1690, the young New England captive John Gyles was part of a Maliseet winter hunting expedition on the upper St. John that stopped at Madawaska on their way home, where an old man had a trading post. The old man may have been an independent or an agent of Charles Aubert de La Chesnay.

La Chesnay, a merchant trader and member of the Executive Council of New France (*Conseil souverain*), acquired a large number of seigneuries along the St. Lawrence south shore (Percé in Gaspé in 1672, Rivière du Loup in 1673, Kamouraska, Saint Jean Port Joli, and finally le Bic). He also obtained a grant of the land surrounding Lake Témiscouata in the name of two of his young children as the Madawaska seigneury (1683) (see Map 3-4). A seigneury was a manorial estate. The holder, or seigneur, had to pledge allegiance to the king, bring in settlers and develop the infrastructure (e.g., mills, wharves). The settlers, or *censitaires*, received perpetual leases at fixed rents but had to cultivate the land and use the holder's mill and other facilities. La Chesnay was interested in the fisheries, agriculture, and lumbering, but above all he was interested in the fur trade. Denis Riverin, the holder of the Tadoussac lease, accused him of diverting the fur trade from Tadoussac to Rivière du Loup, launching fur-trapping expeditions on the north shore, and shipping the fur south through the St. John River and Port Royal, where he had a trading post. Riverin wanted the French authorities to levy a tax on the fur exported through Acadia, but they refused, fearing this would incite traders to take their goods to Boston instead. La Chesnay died in 1702, leaving an estate burdened with debts. This led to the selling of the Rivière du Loup and Madawaska seigneuries to

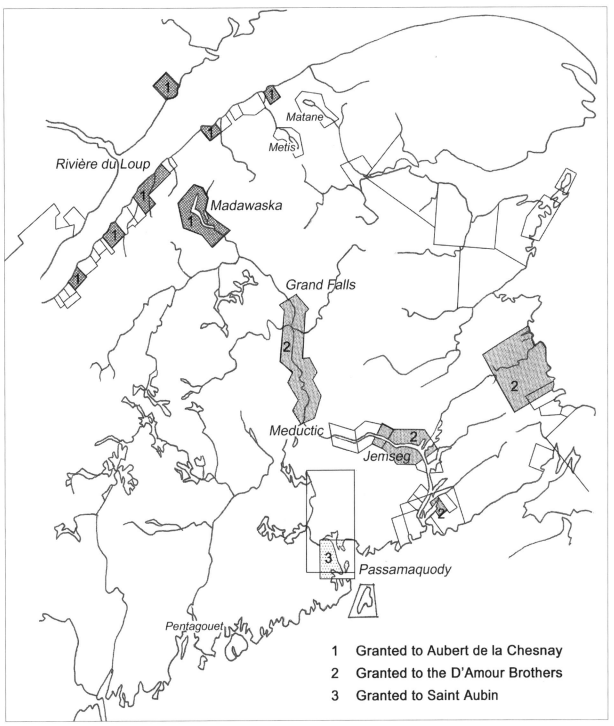

Map 3-4: Lower St. Lawrence and St. John River seigneuries at the end of the seventeenth century.
W. F. Ganong, "A Monograph of Historic Sites in the Province of New Brunswick," Proceedings and Transactions
of the Royal Society of Canada, 1899, 275 and R. Cole Harris and Geoffrey J. Mathew. Historical Atlas of
Canada, vol. 1, 1987, plate 51

Legend in map:

1 Granted to Aubert de la Chesnay
2 Granted to the D'Amour Brothers
3 Granted to Saint Aubin

Place names in map: Matane, Metis, Rivière du Loup, Madawaska, Grand Falls, Meductic, Jemseg, Passamaquody, Pentagouet

Joseph Blondeau dit Lafranchise. Blondeau made no more efforts at developing the Madawaska seigneury than his predecessor. In 1723, there were six acres of land cleared on the Madawaska seigneury, and no resident. For Blondeau as for La Chesnay, the Madawaska seigneury was useful primarily as a base from which to conduct fur trade between the two rivers. The same was true of the men who received seigneuries farther down river.

B. The *"Seigneuries Sauvages"* (see Map 3-4)

Other Canadian merchant traders were aware of the resources in fish, timber, and fur held by New Brunswick. They secured seigniorial grants along the coast, along the St. John, and around Chignecto isthmus. Mathieu d'Amours (another member of the Executive Council) and his four sons were granted Matane, Metis, and very large tracts along the St. John. One of the seigneuries, Clignancourt (granted to Mathieu's son René), extended from Grand Falls to Meductic. In return for the grants, the d'Amours were required to entice the Natives to settle on their land (they convinced some), bring white settlers (they mostly failed), develop the tract (they tried), and support the Church (we don't know if they did). The d'Amours brothers made farms and built a store and sawmill, but they attracted few settlers. In fact, in 1714, there were fewer than fifty Euro-Americans on the St. John River. The limited development of the d'Amours's seigneuries earned them the nickname *seigneuries sauvages* (Native seigneuries, but in French *sauvage* also means "in a natural state"). The brothers' main activity was the fur trade. There were other *seigneuries sauvages* at the mouths of the St. Croix and Penobscot. Although their holders traded in fur and married in the local Native communities, those grants had been made for strategic reasons. The St. Croix seigneury was given to Jean Serreau de Saint-Aubin, whose sons married Native women and were assimilated by the Natives (later we will meet a possible descendent of Saint-Aubin). Further west at Pentagouet, the baron de Saint-Castin, a lieutenant in the French military, also traded with the Natives and married the daughter of a Penobscot chief. Their son inherited the seigneury and the title, and became an Abenakis chief as well as a French baron. Those seigneurs also failed to develop their seigneuries.

C. The Extension of French Settlements

After Acadia was returned to France in 1667, Acadians from peninsular Nova Scotia began to move to the head of the Bay of Fundy and into present-day New Brunswick. The Beaubassin settlement began in the 1670s. It was an agricultural and fur-trading establishment, which traded mostly with New England rather than France. By the 1680s, there was a gristmill and sawmill there as well. Settlements began in the Minas Basin at about the same time. The Shepody settlement was started in 1698, when Pierre Thibodeau, a miller from the Port Royal area, scouted the river. He wintered over for the first time in 1699–1700. He built a sawmill on the river with machinery acquired from Boston and traded in fur as well. In 1702, there were close to fifty people on the Shepody and Petitcodiac Rivers. Shepody and Beaubassin were typical of the peculiar relationship between Acadia and New England: when not at war, they traded with each other. Those settlements are important for us, because some of the Acadian founders of the Madawaska settlements (such as the Cyr, Cormier, Thibodeau, and Thériault) came from this area.

D. Native Villages on the St. John River

Most St. John River Natives settled at Meductic, where they built a village and grew crops in summer. In winter, they hunted in the interior. The village was mentioned for the first time in a document by Mgr. de Saint-Vallier, bishop of Québec, in 1688 (see Appendix C). Its creation probably followed the retreat of some of the Abenakis to the St. John River, and the latter probably introduced horticulture in the region. The bishop believed this would be a good place for a mission and appointed Father Simon-Gérard de La Place at about that time to minister to the Natives. Subsequently, there would always be a missionary priest at Meductic, until the mission was moved to Aukpac in the second half of the eighteenth century. There was a permanent Mi'kmaq village at Nashwaak, about which we know very little. The Maliseets appear to have concentrated their forces on the lower reaches of the river. From there, they tried to defend their traditional territory between the St. John and Penobscot Rivers from English encroachments. There is no evidence there was a permanent or even semi-permanent Native settlement at Madawaska at that time, despite the Natives hunting there.

IV.   KING WILLIAM'S WAR, 1689–99

During the War of the League of Augsburg (King William's War, 1688–99), the English conquered Port Royal again (1690) and the St. John remained the only part of Acadia in French hands. Joseph Robineau de Villebon, the governor of Acadia, withdrew from Port Royal to the mouth of the St. John, first at Jemseg and then at Nashwaak, where he built a fort next to the Native village. Villebon was desperately short of soldiers and needed all the Native assistance he could muster. The St. John-Témiscouata route became crucial for communicating with Québec, securing supplies and ammunitions for the Natives, and for moving troops. French and Native soldiers used the river to come down from Québec under the command of Pierre Le Moyne d'Iberville and then sailed to attack English coastal positions. Reinforced by Maliseet warriors, they took Fort Pemaquid in 1696. The same year, the English attacked the fort at Nashwaak, but failed to take it. At Pentagouet, the baron de Saint-Castin organized the successful resistance of the Franco-Native forces against the English. In 1697, the Treaty of Ryswick returned Acadia to France, and three years later, the new governor, Jacques-François Monbetan de Brouillan, moved back to Port Royal.

Conclusion

The St. John River had been a major Native communication route between the Bay of Fundy and the St. Lawrence. By the end of the seventeenth century, intertribal wars and conflicts with the English had made it a place of refuge for the Abenakis. During King William's War, it even became the last bastion of French Acadia—a place to hold, and from which to launch raids on the English, with the assistance of Native warriors.

We know very little about human activities along the upper St. John during the seventeenth century. The river was an important Native communication route and the boundary between Maliseet and Mi'kmaq territories. The Maliseets traveled upriver to hunt, trap, and trade with the St. Lawrence French. The Maliseets were known to hunt and trade in the Madawaska area in 1696. The Gaspé Mi'kmaq also probably hunted there, as well as the Abenakis who had taken refuge in Québec. It also seems that at the end of the seventeenth century, the Penobscot Natives (Canibas) were using Madawaska as a refuge. Some of the Natives preferred to trade their fur with the French on the south shore of the St. Lawrence rather than take them down the St. John River. Canadian merchant traders intent on exploiting the natural resources of the area and the Gaspé Peninsula also noticed the fur trading potential of the area between the two rivers and obtained suitably located seigneuries to pursue the trade more effectively. Their presence simultaneously asserted French sovereignty over the region and made the consolidation of Franco-Native alliances easier.

FURTHER READINGS

Bear Nicholas, Andrea and Harald Prins. "The Spirit of the Land, the Native People of Aroostook." In *The County: Land of Promise,* ed. A. Mcgrath. 1989, provides a Native perspective on the events described in this chapter.

More conventional accounts in:

Buckner, Phillip A. and John G. Reid. *The Atlantic Region to Confederation: A History.* 1994: ch. 2–5.

Judd, Richard W. *et. al. Maine: The Pine Tree State.* 1995: ch. 2–5.

Raymond, W. O. *The River St. John.* 1943.

Fortin, Jean-Charles *et. al. Histoire du Bas Saint-Laurent.* 1993: ch. 2.

SOURCES

For Maine Natives, see Bruce Bourque (1989 and 2001) as well as Bourque and Holmes (1985). The Maliseets are discussed by Prins (1986, 1992), Johnson (1994 and 1998), and Tremblay (1998). Dickason (1986) and Reid (1981) provide useful information on Native-European interactions. For the impact of European diseases on native populations, see Snow and Lamphear (1988). The Native concept of land tenure is further explained in Ray (1973). Bourque Campbell (1994 and 1995) discusses the "seigneuries sauvages" and their holders. The *Dictionary of Canadian Biography* (accessible on-line on the National Library of Canada website), includes notices on the following: La place, Simon-Gérard; Aubery, Jacques; Loyard, Jean-Baptiste; Danielou, Jean-Pierre; Gyles, John; D'Amours de Clignancourt, René; D'Amours de Freneuse, Mathieu; D'Amours de Chauffours, Louis; d'Amours de Chauffours, Mathieu; Aubert de la Chesnay, Charles; Aubert de la Chesnay, Louis; Abbadie de Saint-Castin, Jean Vincent; Abbadie de Saint-Castin, Bernard-Anselme; Abbadie de Saint-Castin, Joseph; Serreau de Saint-Aubin, Jean; Aprendestiguy, Martin; Robineau de Villebon, Joseph. Stanwood (2004) incorporates recent archaeological discoveries at Pentagouet to provide an updated analysis of Saint-Castin's activities. Ganong (1899, 1904, and 1906) is still useful.

4

FROM BORDERLAND TO FRONTIER AND BACK, 1713–76

Between 1713 and 1763, the St. John River and its European and Native inhabitants were at the heart of a territorial conflict between the French and British. After 1763, the region became a commercial frontier between New England and the province of Québec, before again becoming contested terrain, this time between the British and Americans during the Revolutionary War.

War had resumed between France and England in 1702. The French lost, and in 1713 ceded Acadia to Britain[1] in the Treaty of Utrecht. They kept Cape Breton Island (Ile Royale) and Prince Edward Island (Ile Saint-Jean). This treaty worsened the situation of the Natives between the Kennebec and St. John Rivers. They struggled for the next half-century to preserve their sovereignty and way of life. For their part, the French quickly claimed that the territory between the Penobscot River and Chignecto Isthmus was not part of Acadia, and therefore was still French. This turned the St. John River into a key communication route between the different French possessions in the Maritime Peninsula and Québec. War resumed in 1744, and with the exception of a truce between 1748 and 1754, lasted until 1763. The war concluded with the first Treaty of Paris in 1763. France surrendered all her colonial possessions in North America, Africa, and India to Britain, and kept only some fishing stations in the Gulf of St. Lawrence, two sugar islands in the West Indies, and some trading posts in West Africa and India.

After 1763, all of North America east of the Appalachians was British, but not for long. The British colonists resisted attempts at regulating their economic activities and taxing them, as well as at preventing them from settling west of the Alleghenies. They revolted. Nova Scotia did not. The St. John Valley became again a frontier between two warring parties—and a key communication route for the British. The Revolutionaries won. In the second Treaty of Paris (1783), Britain recognized the independence of thirteen of its American colonies, triggering the exodus of a large number of refugees, the Loyalists, to its remaining North American possessions.

Those events had a dramatic impact on the peninsula's Natives and on the Acadians. The Natives lost their sovereignty and control over their territory. Between 1755 and 1763, the British removed all the Acadians they could capture from the region. A fair number, however, managed to remain in the area. Others escaped to Canada and came back after the end of hostilities. After peace was concluded, Natives, Acadians, New Englanders, and members of the British elite scrambled for control of the resources of the St. John River. The Acadians cooperated economically and then militarily with the British. The future founders of the Madawaska settlement belonged to this last group.

ECONOMIC FRONTIER AND POLITICAL BORDERLAND 1713–63

A. The Natives

The Maritime Peninsula Natives were astonished—and angry—when they learned the French king had ceded Acadia to Britain. How could he give away something that was not his to begin with—namely, their land? Disagreement between the Natives and British over sovereignty and the right to use the land led to Dummer's War (1722–27), the defeat of the Natives and their signing the Peace of Boston in 1725, and Dummer's Treaty in 1727. In them, the Natives recognized the sovereignty of the British king over their land and agreed to let Euro-Americans settle among them. The British promised not to interfere with their religion and let them fish and hunt as they had in the past. The treaties were based on mutual misunderstanding (and were probably mistranslated to boot). The British understood treaties as final agreements backed by signed papers. The Natives viewed them as alliances to be renewed at intervals through rituals and exchanges of gifts. The British considered gifts to be bribes; lack of gifts led the Natives to conclude the alliance had lapsed, especially as too many English people were not respecting the terms of the treaties in the first place. The French, on the other hand, were solicitous: they provided the Natives with resident missionaries and made sure they were given gifts on behalf of their king. So the Natives, still thinking they were sovereign people, allied themselves with the French, who, like them, wanted to drive the British out of Acadia. Mi'kmaq, Maliseets, and Passamaqoddy used the conflict between the two imperial powers to attempt to preserve control over their ancestral land and preserve their traditional way of life. In the end, they partially succeeded. As historian Oliva Dickason has noted, those nations are the only ones in the peninsula who are still living on the land of their ancestors.

B. Contested Ownership

The French immediately denied that the area between the Penobscot and the Chignecto Isthmus was part of the Acadia they had surrendered. Although the British disagreed, in practice they treated the Missiguash (or Messagoueche) River as the boundary between peninsular Nova Scotia and the French possessions. Beaubassin was therefore British, but Shepody, Memramcook, and the Petitcodiac were French, and their settlers were expected to fight the British in case of war. The French also tried to entice the peninsular Acadians and the Mi'kmaq to move to Ile Royale, where they began to build a fortress (Louisbourg) in 1720, or to Ile Saint Jean. Neither group was willing to do so: Ile Royale lacked game and was unfertile, and Ile Saint Jean would have to be cleared of its forest. The British were not eager to see the Acadians move and strengthen the French side, and consequently did not take any measure to incite them to leave.

The French needed their Native allies to keep New Brunswick; the French also needed to keep the St. John River under their control. Consequently, they supported a succession of missionaries at Meductec and in 1716 built a stone church there. About 300–400 Natives habitually resided at the village at that time. In the late 1710s, the Natives built another village a few miles below Meductic, at Aukpac. Meductic declined rapidly afterwards. By 1731, it comprised only 20 families (about 100 people). Father Germain, the missionary, moved the mission to Aukpac in 1745. The Natives also began to winter over at Beaubassin, where they could get supplies from the French. The St. John was well traveled, not only by Native hunting parties and government couriers, but also by ordinary Acadians. The young adults of Beaubassin and Shepody, for instance, traveled up the Petitcodiac and St. John River to go to Quebec City and receive the Sacrament of Confirmation by the bishop of Québec.

C. The Last Wars, 1744–63

When war resumed in 1744, the governor of New France, La Jonquière, had a road cut between Lake Témiscouata and Rivière du Loup to facilitate communications between Canada and the French possessions in the Maritimes. Supply depots were created near the Grand Falls and along Lake Témiscouata. The Natives kept their own supplies at this lake. Some Maliseets and Mi'kmaq used the St. John River to take refuge along the St. Lawrence at Levy, Saint-Michel, Pointe à la Caille, and Kamouraska during this war. Six hundred French soldiers and Native warriors came down from Québec via the St. John in 1745 to attack Annapolis Royal, which they did not take. The New Englanders retaliated by attacking and capturing Louisbourg. At the other end of the world, the French captured Madras, a British possession in India. At the Treaty of Aix la Chapelle (1748), Madras was swapped for Louisburg, to the fury of New Englanders.

In 1749, tensions intensified when the British founded Halifax, against the violent opposition of the Mi'kmaq who viewed this as a trespass on their territory and therefore harassed settlers. The French built two forts north of the Missiguash River, at Beauséjour and Gaspereau, and the British built Fort Lawrence at Beaubassin. The new commander of the French force on the St. John, Boishebert, built a fort near the mouth of the St. John River. This consolidated French control over the river and allowed them to supply the Natives with weapons and provisions from Québec without danger of being attacked by the British. Social and economic intercourse between Canada and the remainder of French Acadia continued. Canadian merchants like J-Bte. Grandmaison did business at Beaubassin in the early 1750s (see Sidebar 4.1). In the same period, the French were putting pressure on the Acadians from the Windsor and Chignecto area to move to Ile Saint Jean or north of the Missiguash River. In 1750, some 2,000 Acadians from the head of the Bay of Fundy moved to Ile Saint-Jean, from which many moved to Québec later

in the conflict. Worse off were the Beaubassin settlers. In 1750, the missionary Le Loutre and his Native warriors forced the villagers (about 1,000 people) to move to the other side of the Missiguash, and torched the village and church. The refugees had great difficulties eking out a living in the new settlement, which was overcrowded. The French were also dispatching agents in the area to keep the Natives on their side. Numbers should have favored the French. At the beginning of 1755, the bulk of the population east of the St. Croix River was French—about 8,200 in peninsular Nova Scotia, 4,300 in what later became New Brunswick, and 6,000 in Prince Edward Island and Cape Breton. On the other hand, there were less than 3,000 British settlers in Nova Scotia.

The French efforts at keeping control over the area were nonetheless in vain. In the summer of 1755, the British captured Fort Beauséjour and Gaspereau. Shortly afterwards, they began removing all the Acadians they could round up from the territories they controlled. About 6,000 Acadians were taken from Nova Scotia to British colonies farther south, and when some were refused entry by the local colonial authorities, they were taken to England. Many Acadians, however, were able to escape before being captured. They traveled through well-known routes towards the New Brunswick coast and Chaleur Bay or toward the St. John River, where they took refuge between Jemseg and Sainte-Anne. In 1758, Louisbourg fell for the second time; Prince Edward Island was also taken; and the residents of the two islands escaped to Québec or were sent to France.

In the wake of Louisburg's capture, Colonel Robert Monkton sailed up the St. John to eliminate the remaining French strongholds. He managed to destroy the French positions as far as present-day Maugerville. The Acadians escaped farther north; some stayed at Sainte-Anne, assuming winter would prevent the British from reaching them. Others continued toward the St. Lawrence. In February, Monkton put his men on snowshoes and destroyed

Grandmaison, a carpenter from Quebec City, moved to Beaubassin after the death of his first wife in 1749. In 1752, he married Marguerite Thibodeau, daughter of Jean-Baptiste and Marguerite Leblanc, and granddaughter of the founder of Shepody. In 1754, he sold his property for a large profit to the commander of Fort Beauséjour, who paid him (illegally) with goods from the military store. He then moved to Kamouraska, where in 1757 he was buying property and being referred to as a "merchant trader" (*négociant*). He was also the administrator of the Kamouraska seigneury owned by Jean-Baptiste d'Amours and commander of the French forces on the St. John River. (D'Amours was the son of one of the lower St. John seigneurs seen in Chapter 3.)

Some Acadians refugees joined Jean-Baptiste Grandmaison after 1755—and in 1761 Marguerite Grandmaison-Thibodeau was godmother to her niece Marguerite Cyr, daughter of Joseph and Marguerite Blanche Thibodeau, the future Tante Blanche (see Side bar 6.1). Joining Grandmaison was a wise move, since he had widespread business contacts and could help the refugees. Some French, Acadians, and Natives kept fighting in northeastern New Brunswick after the fall of Montreal in 1760. The British destroyed the French vessels in the Battle of Restigouche, and Murray, military governor of Québec, send an emissary to the Restigouche Acadians to convince them to lay down their arms; he even promised them land in what is now eastern Ontario. This emissary was Jean-Baptiste Grandmaison, who was wounded in the process and subsequently received a pension from the government.

About 1768, Grandmaison settled at Cacouna and became a militia captain. He engaged in a variety of economic activities, operated a mill at Rivière Ouelle, and owned a boat. His business partners included Malcolm Fraser, by then seigneur of Rivière du Loup. Unfortunately, Grandmaison went bankrupt, and his creditors even garnished his pension. His daughter, Marguerite, and her second husband Antoine Gagné, were among the first Madawaska settlers.

Source: Hudon (1998)

Sainte-Anne. This time, the Acadians were less lucky; some were caught and killed. Some Acadians and Natives regrouped around Oromocto and used this as a base to harass the British. Boishebert by that time had been sent to the coast near Shediac. In the fall, the French learned that Québec had fallen; the next spring, Montreal had to capitulate because the British supply ships reached the St. Lawrence before the French ones. Natives and Acadians had to make their peace with the British, and the 200 St. John River Acadians who surrendered at that time were held at the fort at the mouth of the river. The prisoners included J-Bte. Cyr and his family, whose nine sons were among the first white Madawaska settlers. The Natives made their peace in 1760 (and again in 1766), and the French, as we have seen, abandoned their North American colonies to the British in 1763. At the time of the treaty, the Acadians were widely dispersed, but the largest groups were to be found in France and in Québec (see Table 4-1).

In 1763, Acadians refugees in Québec could be found in places where the Natives had taken refuge during the previous war, where they knew people, such as Grandmaison, or where they could use their fishing, lumbering, or fur-trading skills. Some married into the Canadian population. The future founders of the Madawaska settlement were all part of that group, with the exception of the Mazzerolle family, which was deported to Massachusetts. For instance, Jean Baptiste Thibodeau was godparent to some of Grandmaison's children or witness to the marriage of some others. J-Bte. Cyr, Jr., married a Canadian woman at Kamouraska in 1767. His brother Jacques was a pilot at Saint-Thomas de la Pointe à la Caille between 1765 and 1768. J-Bte. Thibodeau and his cousin J-Bte. Cormier acquired a sawmill at Pointe à la Caille in 1765 and sold it in January 1768.[2]

The Acadian refugees were used to fishing and trading as well as farming and fitted very well in the local economy. The lower St. Lawrence was no economic backwater, despite being thinly populated. People spilling from older parishes took land to farm. But many engaged in other activities as well—the fur trade; exploitation of maritime resources (cod fishing in the gulf, eel fishing along the coast, and porpoise hunting); manufacturing of timber and lumber and shipbuilding; coopering; salt-making; tar manufacturing; and shipping. Fish and fur were stepping stones to general trade, manufacturing, and ship-

Table 4-1: Geographic Distribution of Acadian Population in 1763	
	Number of People
New England	1,700
Middle Colonies	1,460
Southern Colonies	500
Louisiana (Spanish colony)	300
Nova Scotia	1,250
St. John River	100
Chaleur Bay	700
Prince Edward Island	300
Quebec	2,000
England	850
France	3,500
Total	12,660

Source: Harris and Matthews (1987): vol. I, plate 30

ping, and success in those ventures could in turn lead to appointments as seigneurs' agents or commissions in the militia. Kamouraska traders' activities also extended east to Gaspé and south towards the St. John.

III.   THE ST. JOHN RIVER VALLEY FRONTIER, 1763–85

After the first Treaty of Paris, peace was quickly reestablished in Nova Scotia, allowing economic activities to resume. George III, who became king in 1760, took a personal interest in British and American affairs, contrary to his predecessor. He was very keen to display his royal benevolence and extend it to the Acadians and Natives. Nova Scotia Indian Agent Michael Francklin convinced the St. John Valley Natives to sign a treaty in 1766 recognizing their subjection to the British king. The Acadians similarly accepted the fact they were now British subjects. Some of those Acadians had never left Nova Scotia or New Brunswick; others were former St. Lawrence refugees moving into the now-pacified St. John Valley, where economic activities were starting again (see Map 4-1). Several groups of people were keenly interested in the lower St. John. Québec merchants, New England settlers, and land speculators and their

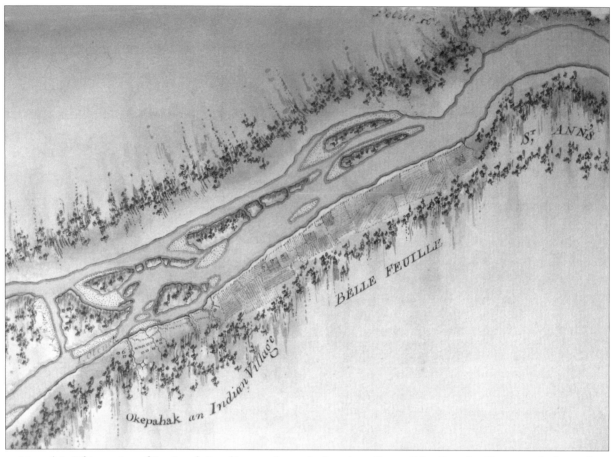

Map 4-1: This section of Lt. Joseph Peach's map shows the location of one of the French villages on the lower St. John. A few buildings surrounded by garden, and fairly extensive fields, are clearly visible. The Native village is immediately to the left. It is not known whether this site was already re-occupied, or whether the fields, gardens, and buildings were remnants from a pre-war settlement. LAC: Lt. Joseph Peach of the 4th Regt, A plan of the River of St. John's, from Fort Frederick in the Bay of Fundy, to the River of Medouesqua, 1762, NMC-14312

agents hoped to make money through the sale and lease of real estate. Merchants and developers like Beamsley Glazier and New England merchants Simonds, Hazen, and White hoped to make their fortune through trade in addition to real estate. The Acadians could help them further their plans in addition to pursuing their own interests.

A. The Fur Trade

Commercial ties between the lower St. Lawrence and the St. John River resumed at the end of the war.

Lower St. Lawrence merchants and their Quebec City patrons actively sought to channel the St. John River fur trade toward their stores and warehouses. Hunting and trapping was normally done by the Natives, who exchanged fur for European goods with merchant firms' agents (known as *coureurs des bois*). In 1765, at the Natives' request, British officials forbade white people from trapping and hunting on the St. John. Trading with the Natives was limited to those who had a government-issued license. Some Acadian families were particularly fit for the St. John River fur trade, since they were originally from the area. Such was the case of the Robichauds, who had lived on the lower St. John for most of the eighteenth century and had Native blood (they were descendents of Saint-Castin). In 1768, a Québec merchant trader engaged Pierre Robichaud to trade with the St. John River Natives; Robichaud's son Regis succeeded him in 1774, assisted by his nephews Michel and Anselme after 1780. By 1788, Michel and Anselme were in business on their own, supplied by the House of Fraser and Young from Quebec City. Later, the Robichauds suffered serious competition from other merchants, particularly the Scot Alexander McLennan who settled at Kamouraska in 1778 and soon married the stepdaughter of the new (and also Scottish) seigneur de la Pocatière. Around 1779, McLennan took a partner, Pierre Duperré, who did the trading with the Natives. The partnership lasted till 1786. By then, McLennan had purchased a seigneury in Gaspé to engage in fisheries, and Duperré was living at Madawaska and competing directly with the Robichauds in the St. John River fur trade.[3]

The fur trade was bringing Canadians and Acadians to the St. John River, but the Church, Nova Scotia authorities, and Natives were unhappy with the situation. The authorities feared the traders were filling the heads of the Natives with all sorts of nonsense about the French regaining control of the region. The local authorities, local priest, and Catholic hierarchy complained the traders plied the Natives with liquor.

The Natives had their own grievances. In July 1768, the governor and Council of Nova Scotia received a visit from two chiefs from St. Ann's Point, Pierre Tomma or Thomas and Ambroise Saint-Aubin (a probable descendent of the Saint-Aubin of St. Croix, met in the previous chapter). Among their complaints were that rum and liquor were too easily available; François Belisle Robichaud (Pierre Robichaud's other son) had taken the ornaments of their church with him to Canada during the war and his widow was refusing to return them; and some Acadians were hunting on their ground on the St. John River and taking all the beavers. They singled

out two families belonging to Paul Barnaby and Paul Laurence who had made themselves at home in their village and who, they said, "we shall be glad were removed." The Executive Council promised to act on all those grievances, and soon a letter was sent to the governor in Québec asking him to prevent Canadians and Acadians from coming down the St. John and trapping the area out of its beavers—and to intervene with Mrs. Robichaud. A week later, a letter was also sent to John Anderson, one of the justices of the peace at Maugerville (opposite St. Ann's Point), enjoining him to enforce existing liquor license laws and to remove the Acadians who were settled on the king's land and among the Indians. A month later the provincial secretary asked the local justices of the peace to give the Acadians notice that they had to move to some other part of the province, where they would get a grant upon applying for one. Six families chosen by the priest would be allowed to stay. The Acadians did not all obey, and in March, the provincial secretary threatened to bring the force of the law upon those who remained on the king's land without permission.

Through the 1760s, 1770s, and 1780s, Québec trading houses extended their tentacles down the St. John River, hiring Canadians and Acadians with pre-existing links with the area to trade with the Natives, to the dismay of Nova Scotian authorities and Native chiefs alike. Québec trading houses, however, were not the only ones to see opportunities on the St. John River. Tentacles were also reaching up from the south, and their senders also relied on the services, skills, and connections of Acadians.

B. The New England Connection

In 1763, Massachusetts merchants Simonds, Hazen, and White opened a trading post at Portland Point, at the mouth of the St. John River, which soon grew into a small colony of about 150 persons. Later the partners opened another trading post at Oromocto, near Maugerville. They traded in fur, feathers, and fish; burned lime; and made barrel staves. Lower St.

John Natives and settlers were drawn into the activities of Simonds, Hazen, and White as suppliers of trade goods and foodstuff, as laborers, and as customers. The merchants provided them with imported textiles, metal and metal-ware, and West Indian goods. In their 1764–66 St. John River account book, "Amiable and Peter Dowsett," Victor Richard, and Charles Levron are provided with supplies and tools to fish cod in the Bay of Fundy. "John" Martin was listed in the 1778–1779 account book. He bought shots, shoes, fabric, thread and buttons, cups and saucers, and rum, and was given some cash. He paid in labor. "Peter" Cormier is listed in the account book for 1779, buying bread, flour, beef, potatoes, and rum. Since he was buying agricultural products, he was obviously not farming. Five Acadians appear in a seventy-eight-page account book covering the years 1775–79: John and Francis Robichaud (Jean and François), Augustin White (Leblanc), Oliver Thebedo junior (Olivier Thibodeau), and Francis Violet (François Violette). They bought cooking utensils, window sashes and glass panes, blankets, tobacco, rum, powder and shots, and farm implements. Robichaud purchased a coffee pot, pewter dish, and some red camlet (an expensive fabric). They paid for their purchases with cash, labor, or farm products.[4]

In 1779, the merchants secured a contract with the British navy; they hired the settlers to cut timber and masts and purchased bread grain from them. Joseph Thériault, an Acadian and brother-in-law to the J-Bte. Thibodeau we met earlier, led a masting crew on the Kennebecassis River. A few Acadian families lived there with him: François Violette, Charles Levron, Olivier Thibodeau, Alexis Comeau, and Jean and François Robichaud, as well as the Canadian Joseph Boucher. (Later, Violette, Thibodeau, and Thériault moved to Madawaska.)

The Acadians possessed other skills that were in demand in the region. Simonds, Hazen, and White had hired Acadians to dike a marsh that was part of their holding at the mouth of the river. The Sunbury County land record book shows that there were at least three boat builders in Maugerville between 1776 and 1784. The Acadians knew how to build boats and therefore could have found work with them. And then there was Joseph Doucet, who made a coat for the Reverend David Burpee in December 1777—Doucet who, according to Hannay, was one of the Maugerville settlers, and who, according to the Studholme Report, had been a resident above St. Ann's since 1763. He, too, appears in Simonds, Hazen, and White's 1764–65 account book, and is specifically identified as a "Frenchman." One of his payments was in beaver. We should not, therefore, assume that the Acadians were merely self-sufficient farmers because they had land and stock. Farming may have been a secondary activity for them, as well as for their Anglo-Protestant neighbors.

The French settlers did not have titles to the land they occupied. In August 1767, the governor of Nova Scotia presented the provincial Executive Council a petition from eleven Acadians asking for land on the lower St. John. The council determined that the land where they had settled was already granted, but gave them permission to stay, nonetheless. The petitioners are unfortunately not named in the minutes, but the Studholme Report, a 1783 document, identifies Daniel Godin, Paul Cire, Pierre Cire, Jean-Baptiste Cormier, François Cormier, Jacques Cormier, Amant Cormier, Pierre Tibeaudo, and Paul Potier as having lived in the area since 1767, and they are most likely part of that group.[5] They had all spent the war years on the St. Lawrence, except possibly Godin. Almost all were originally from the Beaubassin-Mines area and related to each other. The expulsion order of 1768 mentioned above, directed at those who were settled without permission on the king's land, clearly did not apply to this group, which was settled on *granted* land with the council's permission. Those Acadians may have been willing to stay on land they could never expect to own because the location offered them desirable economic opportunities.

C. British Favorites: The St. John River Society

The Acadians had not been able to get a grant on the lower St. John because they were Catholics, but also because they had arrived too late. The lower St. John was also coveted by would-be farmers from New England and people dreaming of owning large estates cultivated by tenants. In 1762, a group of Massachusetts families, encouraged by a land speculator with grandiose plans, Alexander McNutt, had started a settlement across St. Ann's Point. Unfortunately, the governor of Nova Scotia, as instructed by London, had reserved the land on the lower St. John for veterans of the last war, and in July 1763, the white settlers on the lower St. John were consequently informed they had to move. Among those were the New Englanders of McNutt's settlement, as well as a handful of unnamed Acadians. The Nova Scotia provincial agent in London, Joshua Mauger, lobbied on behalf of the New Englanders, who received a grant for a 12-square-mile township, which they named Maugerville, in December of the same year.

The Acadians were not included. Their status in postwar Nova Scotia was still uncertain, largely on account of their religion, which at the time mattered to authorities much more than language or ancestry. In Britain, Catholics were still subjected to discriminatory laws (called Penal Laws). They could not vote, be elected, attend universities, enter the professions, or receive commissions in the military, and could hold land only directly from the king (they were not allowed to buy land or receive any as gifts; they could not inherit from Protestants, either). A 1758 Nova Scotia law similarly restricted Catholic landownership in the province. Nova Scotia did not allow Catholics to hold land on the same terms as Protestants until 1783, five years after Britain had passed a law to the same effect.

Although soldiers and subaltern officers were entitled to grants on the lower St. John, they rarely received any from the government. Instead, in 1765, Halifax issued twenty grants totaling 750,000 acres on the lower St. John (see Map 4-2); Alexander McNutt and twenty-two others received a grant for 10,000 acres above and below the Keswick River, known as McNutt's or Frankfort. The St. John River Society received five grants. It was a partnership of sixty-eight very well-heeled individuals, started by British officers in Montreal. Those were soon joined by partners from Massachusetts, New York, and even Ireland, and by Sir Frederick Haldimand. Their local agent was Colonel Beamsley Glazier,[6] whose nephew John we shall meet in subsequent chapters.

The grants were conditional: the proprietors had to pay a small annual fee to the Crown called a "Quit Rent," clear a given number of acres every year, and bring a specified number of Protestant settlers within four years. Between 1764 and 1767, Glazier endeavored to make this happen on behalf of the proprietors, most of whom were merely speculators with no intention of ever living on the St. John. Glazier believed the region had immense economic potential, with natural resources in abundance. Farming was good, and one could engage in the cod fisheries from the mouth of the river. Cattle and lumber could be shipped to Massachusetts, and potash exported to Britain. In December of 1764, he laid out his plans in detail in a letter to the proprietors. Convincing people to settle in the wilderness was always difficult. Glazier recommended a policy followed by most colonization agents in North America: give away land to the first comers. Those first settlers cleared farms, cut roads, built bridges and wharves, erected mills, set up smithies, and opened taverns and general stores, which made the place attractive and raised the value of the land. Proprietors subsequently sold the land to the later comers. Those who did not have the necessary capital leased it until they had saved enough money to buy. Glazier also intended to scatter his first settlers, convinced that they would later want additional acreage. He would then lease it to them.

> ...the New England people must have some lands given them outright at first, after that they will take up others and pay Rent, the only way will be to Intermix them among our lands; by their improvement our lands is improved.[7]

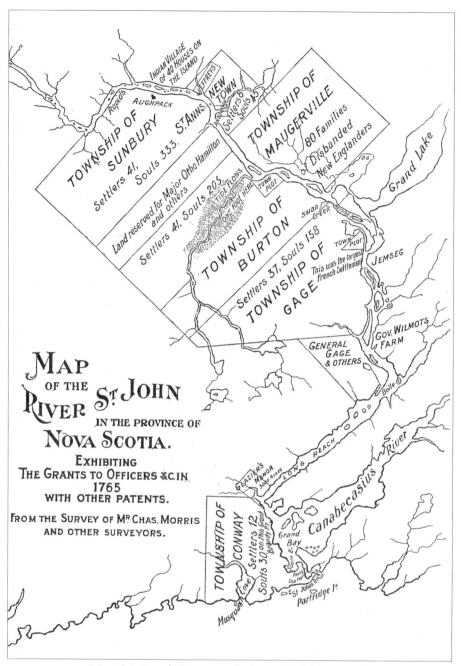

Map 4-2: Land Grants on the Lower St John in 1767
From W. O. Raymond, "Papers relating to Townships of the River St. John,"
New Brunswick Historical Society Collections, 1905, 305

Proprietors made their profit from the late comers who preferred moving into an established community to carving one in the wilderness.

Glazier also told the proprietors that "Any French who has taken the oath of allegiance may become your settler." [8] He was mistaken—when the grant was issued a few months later, it specified that the settlers had to be Protestants. Catholic settlers would not count towards meeting the grant's requirements. Not all the proprietors seem to have been aware of this—or cared: Jean Martin came in 1768 by liberty from one of the proprietors, John Collins of Canada, and was still there in 1783 (Collins was deputy-surveyor of the province). The Acadians' Catholicism did not make them entirely useless: they could help develop the infrastructure that would make the land valuable and attractive to other settlers. Glazier believed there was great potential for trade in lumber between the area and Massachusetts. This could be what attracted J-Bte. Thibodeau and Cormier and incited them to sell their Montmagny mill; they may have hoped to go into lumbering in an area that had far more trees than Saint-Thomas de Montmagny. Otherwise, their behavior makes little sense.

Glazier did not rely entirely on the settlers to develop the region's infrastructure. He set up a store from which the pioneers could draw provisions; brought cattle, including a bull; tried to settle craftsmen; and supervised the building of a dam and sawmill on the Nashwaak. By 1767, however, he was disgusted by the inaction of most of the proprietors, who were not even paying their subscription to the St. John River Society and were leaving him short of capital. He went back to his regiment in the summer. Very few of the proprietors made any effort to fulfill the terms of their grants, and none succeeded. One of those who tried was the Irishman Richard Shorne, who moved to St. Ann's Point in 1767 and also acted as an attorney for another proprietor, the Reverend Curryl Smith, from Ireland. Smith did not succeed, either. Another was James Simonds, the merchant established at the mouth of the river. He would have succeeded, had American privateers not destroyed his settlement during the Revolution.

Those huge grants later complicated the process of resettling the Loyalists (and settling the Acadians). Although almost empty, the land could not be granted, because it was no longer in the possession of the Crown. The land first had to be forfeited on account of non-compliance with the terms of the grant. The process, called escheating, was cumbersome and slow. The first governor of New Brunswick, Carleton, bypassed this process by requiring the re-registration of all Nova Scotia grants. Absent proprietors, as he expected, did not re-register and lost their property, and the rights of only a handful of people, like Simonds, Hazen, White, or Shorne had to be examined.

IV.   THE REVOLUTIONARY PERIOD

During the American Revolution, the lower St. John was in turmoil. Most Maugerville settlers were pro-Americans. The Acadians sided with the British. They pointedly refused to join Jonathan Eddy and his band of American rebels when they launched an ill-fated attack on Fort Cumberland (the old Fort Beausejour) in 1776, despite their being headquartered nearby. In fact, lower St. John Acadians actively supported the British cause, serving as couriers, scouts, and pilots. Future Madawaska settlers like the Mercure brothers (Michel and Louis), the Martin brothers (Jean, François, and Simon), Joseph Thériault, and François Violet, as well as Louis Godin and Augustin LeBlanc, were among the couriers. Louis and Michel Mercure carried the mail between Halifax and Quebec City, and Thériault, Violet, Godin, and Leblanc carried it within New Brunswick.

The Natives, for their part, split. Some, under

Illus. 4-1: A View of the Great Falls on the Height of Lands on the River St. John's, taken by Henry Holland, Lieut. 70th Regt., 1782. *The Great Falls of the River Saint John attracted sightseers as early as 1782. Note the British military men at the bottom left corner. One is sketching the falls; others are picnicking.* LAC, C-149840

Peter Tomma, remained loyal to Britain. Others, following Saint-Aubin, sided with the Americans and moved to Machias (Maine) with Eddy after the failure of the attack on Fort Cumberland. Most Natives played one against the other—this, after all, was not their quarrel, and they sought to exploit the situation to their advantage. Michael Francklin gathered representatives of the region's tribes at Fort Howe at the mouth of the river in 1778. He obtained a promise they would not take arms against the British, but could not get them to agree to fight against the Americans.

At the very end of the Revolution, some Acadians got secure tenure for their holdings from the proprietors. In 1783, Oliver Thibodeau had a 999-year lease from Richard Shorne at St. Ann's Point, and François Cormier similarly received a title from one of the grantees. By 1782 and early 1783, the proprietors who were still active were very worried and were even giving away land to people on the condition *they* bring settlers. But these men were the exceptions—most of the proprietors had long lost interest in their grant. Nonetheless, most of the Acadians were squatters and were not the only ones. By the 1780s, the children of the Maugerville settlers had come of age, and some were establishing new farms on land that did not belong to them.

Conclusion

In the eighteenth century, the St. John Valley was not an empty space at the rear of European colonies (Québec, Acadia, and New England). Instead, it was first a key constituent of the French colonial communication system, providing land links between the various French possessions and blocking British expansion. After 1763, it was more than the thinly populated northern fringe of Nova Scotia or an isolated extension of Massachusetts, with minimal contacts with either. Instead it became a meeting place and the contested frontier between two commercial networks, one centered on Massachusetts and the other on Quebec City. It was also the object of undisguised land lust from well-heeled British speculators and would-be estate owners. All of them could and did use Acadians and French Canadians to try to achieve their goals—and the Acadians and French Canadians collaborated because it fit their own goals as well.

ENDNOTES
1. After James I (of England, also James VI of Scotland) came to the throne and until 1706, England and Wales, on the one hand, and Scotland on the other, were two independent kingdoms, with their own parliaments, but sharing the same sovereign. The two kingdoms were united in 1706, the Scottish Parliament abolished, and the new entity referred to as "Britain." Since 1706, "England" has referred only to a part of the United Kingdom.
2. AQQ, Greffes de Notaires, Greffes de Me. N.C. Lévesque of Québec, 10-3-1765 and 17-1-1768. Thibodeau could sign his name, too.
3. McLennan also went bankrupt in late 1788 and disappears from the records after 1790.
4. NSARM, Simonds, Hazen and White papers, #12 Account book St John River 1764–1766, Microfilm

12710; NBM, Hugh T. Hazen Collection, Hazen and White account book, 1775–79, Microfilm F82.
5. They were joined the following year by Jean, Simon, Francis and Amant Martin; Oliver, Jean Baptiste, Jacques, Joseph and Francis Cire; Joseph Thériault; Louis Lejeune; Joseph Roy; and François Maurin. In 1769, it was the turn of Joseph and Paul Mazerolle; Jean Baptiste and Joseph Daigle; Joseph and Jean Hebert; Bernard Labrie; Baptiste Niemo; Pierre Pinette; and Michael Mercure to settle above St. Ann's Point. The Cormiers (Francis, Joseph, and Pierre Jr. and Sr.) rounded up the group of early comers in 1770. The bulk of those people were also Beaubassin Acadians who had spent the war years on the St. Lawrence's south shore. A French translation of the Studholme Report can be found in Albert (1920 and 1982), and a transcription of the original English in the collections of the N.B Historical Society and on-line.
6. Glasier (Glasior, Glazier), Beamsley (Belnsley, Bensley) Perkins, 1714-84. Army officer, land agent, and officeholder. See full biography at http://www.biographi.ca/EN/
7. Letter from Glazier to Capt Falconer and Committee of the St. John River Society in Montréal, December 14, 1764; Cited by Raymond in "Papers relating to the townships of the St. John...," 311.
8. Ibid., 313.

FURTHER READINGS

Bear Nicholas, Andrea and Harald Prins. "The Spirit of the Land, the Native People of Aroostook." In *The County: Land of Promise*, ed. A. Mcgrath, 1989, provides a Native perspective on the events described in this chapter.

More conventional accounts in: *Acadian Culture in Maine*, http://acim.umfk.maine.edu , section 2, "Roots of Maine Acadian Culture."

Daigle, Jean, "L'Acadie de 1604 à 1763, synthèse historique." In *L'Acadie des Maritimes, études thématiques des débuts à nos jours*, Jean Daigle, (dir.), 1993: 1-44.

Buckner, Phillip A. and John G. Reid. *The Atlantic Region to Confederation: A History*. 1994: ch. 6, 7, 8.

Judd, Richard W. *et. al. Maine: the Pine Tree State*. 1995: ch. 6–7

Raymond, W. O. *The River St. John*, Sackville. N.B. Tribune Press, 1943.

Griffiths, Naomi E. S. *The Context of Acadian history, 1686-1784*. 1992.

Bourque, Bruce J. *Twelve Thousand Years: American Indians in Maine*. 2001: ch. VII.

Dubay, Guy. *Light on the Past*: 30–36 for reproduction of documents about Acadian commercial activities.

Harris, R. Cole and Geoffrey J. Matthews. *Historical Atlas of Canada,* vol. 1. 1987: plate 47.

SOURCES
Raymond's work remains an excellent secondary source for the history of the St. John Valley in the eighteenth century (1894–98, 1899–1905, 1921, 1943); this can be supplemented by Hannay (1894–95) and Ganong (1899, 1904, and 1906). Hudon's work on lower St. Lawrence merchants (1995, 1996, 1998, and 1999) and Johnson and Martijn (1994) are good sources for the fur trade in that period. The role of Maine-New Brunswick Natives in eighteenth-century conflicts is covered by Ghere (1993). Johnson's "Louis Thomas Saint-Aubin et sa famille" (1998) focuses on the fate of one Native-French family. For anti-Catholic legislation, see Bastarache *et. al.* (1993). Short, factual accounts of the Acadian Deportations of 1755–63 can be found in every Canadian history textbook. Online, a reliable one can be found at http://fortress.uccb.ns.ca/search/AcadiaPaperE.html. A good, visual overview of the Acadian deportations and returns is found in the *Historical Atlas of Canada,* vol. I, table 30. Dickinson (1994) discusses the fate of the Acadians in the St. Lawrence Valley.

5

FROM NATIVE HUNTING GROUND TO FRENCH VILLAGE: MADAWASKA, 1776–1790

In 1782, Pierre Lizotte, then a boy of fourteen years of age, strayed from his home in Canada, and found his way to the Indian settlement at the mouth of the Madawaska River, where he continued during the following winter. On his return to his friends, his representations were such as induced his half brother Pierre Duperré to accompany him to the same place for the purpose of trade with the Indians. The year following they commenced their business on the south side of the St John, from two to three miles below the mouth of the Madawaska River. They were the first persons who commenced their residence at Madawaska.[1]

The village where Lizotte spent the winter was a new one. Maliseets and Abenakis had used the site for a very long time as a camp site when hunting, as a resting place while traveling, and as a refuge. The first indication of a Native village at the mouth of the Madawaska River is found on a 1778 British map (see Map 5-1).[2] A marginal note on the map informs us that the Natives had not cleared any land and were exclusively living from hunting and fishing, which suggests a very recent settlement. The village may have expanded rapidly—otherwise, Pierre Duperré, one of Rivière Ouelle fur traders, would have known it was large enough to warrant a permanent trading post without his younger brother telling him. Within ten years, the Natives were joined by Acadians and French Canadians. By 1790, the French village numbered close to two hundred people, and kept growing. The Native village, however, rapidly dwindled to

a handful while the Valley's French settlement continued growing.

The two villages were a consequence of the American Revolution. The traditional explanation is that the French village had been founded by Acadians from the Fredericton area driven from their farms by Loyalists with the aid of the New Brunswick government. The refugees chose to relocate on the upper St. John Valley to put as much distance as possible between themselves and their persecutors.[3] According to local historian Abbé Albert, the Natives would then have generously given their land to the French, in whom they recognized a superior "civilized" race, and then vanished into the wilderness.

There are problems, and even factual errors and omissions, with these explanations. Why the Natives established a village at the mouth of the Madawaska River is not explained. The reason given why the village melted away in the early years of the nineteenth century is unconvincing. First, it is extremely doubtful the Native chief ever uttered the words Father Albert puts in his mouth—the Native chief may not even have spoken French.[4] Second, given that the St. John River was the I-95 highway, or the Trans-Canada, of its era, and that intense fur-trading activities were taking place along its banks, its upper part made an improbable choice for a hiding place. Third, documentary evidence shows that the arrival of the Loyalists in 1783 had an adverse effect on French and English settlers alike. The French settlers received grants for their lower St. John holdings from the New Brunswick government. They sold their property or

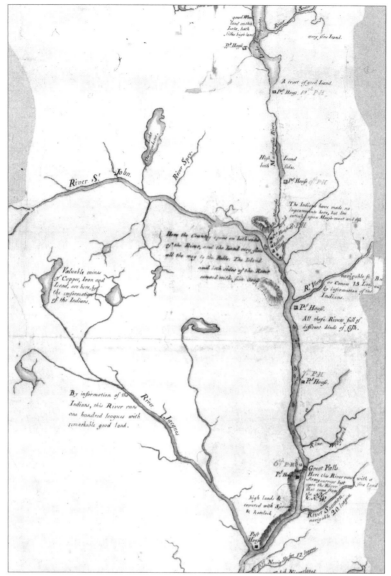

Map 5-1: Upper St. John and Madawaska River in 1778. Native village at Madawaska in 1778, from a map entitled "St. John River from its mouth to its source." LAC, NMC-10867

their claims and moved to Madawaska with the blessings of two provincial governments. Fourth, this story discounts the important role played by French Canadians in the founding of the Madawaska settlement.

The Native and French villages were both consequences of the American Revolution. The Natives were most likely driven by a desire for safety, and the destruction of their economic base probably accounts

for the village's disappearance. The French village was partly a creation of the British authorities, who wanted to protect the St. John-Grand Portage route after the end of the Revolution. Economic and cultural factors, rather than ethnic cleansing, provide better explanations as to why some of the lower St. John French took advantage of the authorities' plight—and they can also account for the arrival of French Canadians.

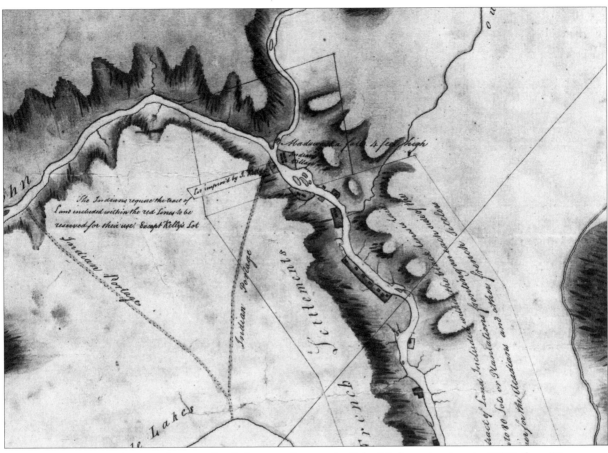

Map 5-2: Native village and Native land claim at the mouth of the Madawaska river in 1787, from "A survey from the Great Falls of the River St. John to the head of Lake Tamasquata with part of the portage leading from that lake to the River St. Lawrence. Taken in July and August 1787 by George Sproule Esqr. Surveyor General of New Brunswick by order of His Excellency Lieut. Governor Carleton. [Plus a survey of the continuation of the aforementioned portage to the St. Lawrence by Mr. Collins Deputy Surveyor of the Province of Quebec.] A note on the map reads: "The Indians request the tract of land included within the red lines to be reserved for their uses, except Kelly's lot." LAC, NMC 18184

I.   THE NATIVE VILLAGE

The reasons for the existence of a Native village at Madawaska are unknown. Anthropologist Vincent Erickson suggests that the Natives at Madawaska relocated from the lower St. John after the arrival of the Loyalists in 1783 undermined their economy. As a member of New Brunswick Executive Council Edward Winslow said, "They were, of course, compelled to leave the banks of the rivers [particularly the St. John] and hunt on other grounds." [5]

Pierre Lizotte, however, reported what seems to have been an established village in 1782. It may have resulted from Natives fleeing the conflicts between British and American forces along the Maine coast (much as the Abenakis had used Madawaska as a wartime refuge in the seventeenth century), augmented by the arrival of refugees from the newly independent American colonies. The trial of Charles Nichau Noïte for a murder committed at Madawaska (see Appendix D) provides indirect evidence to this effect. Noïte was a Penobscot whose family had been killed by the English. Machias, at the mouth of the Penobscot River, had been the site of intense activities during the revolutionary period. The marriages, baptisms, and burials of Natives recorded in the Valley parish register before 1800 also support this interpretation: most Natives are identified as Maliseets, Mi'kmaq, or Abenakis. By 1787, the village numbered about sixty families who hunted along the St. John River and its tributaries. They kept their Grand Annual Council at Madawaska and were served by a Catholic priest of their own choosing from Canada.

Once a large number of Natives settled year round at Madawaska, traders soon arrived. Some were familiar names from Canada: Duperré and Lizotte were early residents. Jean-Baptiste Crock traded on behalf of Québec merchant Pierre Duchauguet, who had obtained a license to send one canoe to the St. John River in March 1783. In 1784, James Kelly had a trading post above the Madawaska village and a lot reserved to him in 1787 (see Sidebar 5-1 and Map 5-2). Complaints about merchants (including the Robichauds and Natives from the Abenakis village of Saint-François) selling liquor to Natives show that others were present as well; and Louis Mercure made similar complaints about American merchants from the Kennebec River in 1789.

The village was unlikely to be viable in the long run. Even in the best of times, the region was probably not capable of supporting a population of several hundred, and the fur trade was accelerating the depletion of local game and fur-bearing animals. Natives from as far away as Lorette (near Quebec City) were hunting in the area as well. The arrival of the French settlers sealed the fate of the Native village by further increasing the size of the local hunting population. Some evidence also suggests that the loss of traditional hunting land was compounded by the actions of a government indifferent to Native property rights. For instance, a 1792 Native petition for land at the mouth of the Madawaska River was turned down. Depredations from the neighbors' animals were an additional problem that limited the Natives' ability to farm. In 1800, Duperré filed a petition claiming the Natives had freely sold him a piece of their land, because it "is of no benefit to their persons by reason that it is not in their power to secure the same from the destroying of the grain every year by the inhabitants' cattle."[6] (The Executive Council of the province did not give him the grant.)

Although the village was still significant in 1793, Mgr. Plessis, Bishop of Québec, found only two wigwams when he visited the area in 1812. Most Maliseets had moved, some to Tobique, which was founded in 1801 and became their major settlement in New Brunswick, and others to Ile Verte, where they had had a camp since the mid 1750s. (In the 1820s, they were granted a reserve called Viger at that location.[7])

II.   POST-REVOLUTIONARY ADJUSTMENTS

At the end of the Revolution, the British found themselves in possession of a much-reduced North American empire whose communication system had to be reorganized. They also had to settle in their remaining colonies a fairly large number of Loyalists, whose arrival over a very short period challenged the local authorities. In southern New Brunswick, the Loyalists' arrival turned a sparsely populated but ethnically diverse region of farmers, fur traders, and lumbermen into an overwhelmingly Anglo-Protestant region engaging in a more traditional agrarian economy. This seriously disturbed the life of the Acadians, who decided to try to start again elsewhere.

A. Protecting the St. John–Grand Portage Route

After the United States gained its independence in 1783, the St. John–Grand Portage route became a critical component of the eastern British communications system, and Governor-General Haldimand had upgraded it.[8] The following winter, Royal couriers began using it on a scheduled basis. The St. John–Grand Portage route was unsettled for most of its length and dangerously close to American territory, making it, and the men using it, vulnerable to attacks.

Haldimand's solution to this problem was to create new white settlements along the St. John River. In November 1783, Louis Mercure, one of the Royal couriers, made him an attractive proposition: Some lower St. John Acadians wanted to move to Québec for the sake of their religion. Haldimand decided to grant them land above the Great Falls, which at the time was considered part of the province of Québec, and he promptly communicated the scheme to the governor of Nova Scotia, John Parr.

Mercure was the son of a petty nobleman and had served as captain in the Ile Saint-Jean (Prince Edward Island's) garrison. During the Revolutionary War, he was a lieutenant in a volunteer regiment raised in New Brunswick in 1780, the King's Rangers, whose primary functions were scouting and intelligence. In 1780, Mercure moved to the lower St. John (where his brother Michel had lived since 1769) and built a mill on his lot. He served as a Royal courier between Castine, Halifax, and Québec, and was therefore well placed to be aware of the problems with the Grand Portage route.[9] He was also likely to

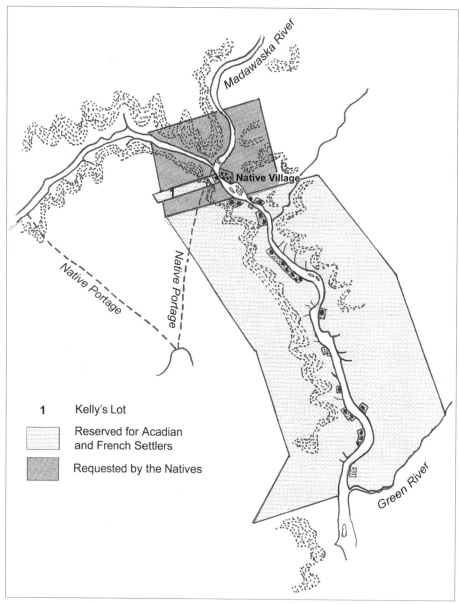

Map 5-3: Madawaska settlement in 1787, showing land reserved for French settlers, and land requested by the Natives. Adapted from Sproule 1787 by B. and S. Craig

know a large number of colonial troops were going to be disbanded on the lower St. John, since petitions for land began arriving in Halifax as early as 1782. His knowledge and government connections allowed him to act as an intermediary between the British authorities and potential upper Valley settlers.

Soon after, Haldimand left for England on leave

and did not come back. In 1786, he was replaced as governor in chief of British North America by Guy Carleton, Lord Dorchester. Dorchester shared Haldimand's views concerning the necessity of settling the St. John River. So did his younger brother, Thomas Carleton, who was appointed lieutenant governor of the newly established province of New

Brunswick in 1784.[10] In January 1785, the New Brunswick governor and council promised 200 acres to anyone who would settle at Madawaska and in August of the same year, reserved the land between the Madawaska and Green River for the French; the land was surveyed in 1787 (see Map 5-3). The security of the St. John–Grand Portage route was further reinforced by the establishment of two small garrisons at the mouth of the Presqu'Isle River (now known as the Prestile Stream) and at the Grand Falls in 1790. The portage, however, was allowed to fall into disrepair, and it is not until after the War of 1812 that the British authorities settled former soldiers at intervals along it. The men lasted as long as the authorities provided them with supplies—then they left. The best known of the Grand Portage settlers was not, however, a former soldier but a retired courier named Philip Long. Long settled above Lake Témiscouata and was paid two shillings a day under the condition of providing room and board for couriers and other worthy travelers. (Two shillings, or forty cents, was slightly less than the daily wages of a farm laborer. See the note on money in Appendix B.)

B. The Impact of the Loyalists' Arrival

1. The French Want to Leave

In early 1783, the Acadians of the lower St. John had few reasons to want to leave. The provincial Catholic Relief Act was to remove the main obstacle to their getting land. Economic opportunities were plentiful: they had land on which to grow their food and raise their stock; they engaged in the fur trade, in the fisheries, in lumbering; they worked for wages for merchants; and some were craftsmen like the Doucet encountered in the previous chapter. Their economic prosperity, however, depended on having access to a range of resources: land, fish, trees, and fur-bearing animals. Their difficulties in securing a resident priest likely troubled them more; most of the heads of families were getting on in years, and the afterlife was much closer than it was when they had left the lower St. Lawrence River. This apparently incited

some to support Mercure's plan to relocate to Madawaska in the fall of 1783. Mercure himself had no intention to move upriver at that time. Within a couple of months, he received a grant for an island opposite one of the French villages, and his land at the mouth of the Madamkeswick had been surveyed so that a grant could be issued. A year later (1784), however, a disenchanted Mercure petitioned both the Québec surveyor general and the governor of the newly created province of New Brunswick for land at Madawaska.

The letter was co-signed by twenty-four other people: twenty residents of the lower St. John, as well as Duperré, Pierre Lizotte and his brother Jean Lizotte, and Augustin Dubé, a French Canadian who had also worked for McLennan. The Canadians probably signed Mercure's petition when the latter was stopped at their place of residence en route for Quebec City. Mercure's was not the only petition for land at Madawaska: in 1784, the Cyrs, Daigles, Ayottes, and Sansfaçon also sent a petition to the governor general, and the Daigles appear to have taken a petition to the governor of New Brunswick the following year. In September 1784, Mercure, by then colonization agent for the newly named Madawaska territory, sold his grant on the lower St. John for £150 ($600) to Fredericton merchant William Garden and moved north. Within ten years, almost all the French settlers above St. Ann's Point and on the Kennebecassis River had left either for the upper St. John Valley, Memramcook area, or Chaleur Bay and Caraquet. What had happened?

2. Troubled Waters

Mercure and his neighbors were tired of the chaos prevailing on the lower St. John. In the spring of 1783, there were only 18,000 white people in Nova Scotia, 1,400 of them on the lower St. John. In the last three months of the year, some 30,000 American Loyalists were literally dumped on the shores of Nova Scotia, 12,000 of them at the mouth of the St. John River. Little was ready to accommodate them. The short-staffed Nova Scotia government was overwhelmed by the tasks at hand. To give an example, the provincial surveyor general swore in twenty deputies without any assurance London would pay their salary, and then, because he had no budget, had to pay for their surveying instruments out of his own pocket. (He was refunded more than £2,000 in 1784—the equivalent of 8,000 days of work at common laborer's wages.) The situation was even worse on the St. John, because distances to the seat of government compounded the problems. The trip was difficult, especially when the weather was bad. It took a week to go from the mouth of the river to Halifax, but only thirty hours to sail from Saint John to Boston.

Many lower St. John Loyalists were disbanded volunteer regiments, whose officers often had connections in London. They conducted their own surveys and some of the block grants they laid out included already-settled land. Sharks soon began to prey in the troubled waters, as a descendant of the Maugerville settlers explained later in the century:

> All the loyalists were not honest and gentlemen-like, be it known to you, and had more knowledge and were abler dealers than some of the old inhabitants, for some of them visited Halifax and examined the records of the land office, and whenever they found grants not taken out, or where settlers had gone without proper authorities, they applied for those lands, got grants and dispossessed many of the early settlers.[11]

The "old inhabitants" and "early settlers" referred to in this document were *not* the Acadians, but the Anglo-Protestant Maugerville settlers. In their desire to lay claim to territory on the lower St. John, speculators disregarded religious affiliation or ethnicity.

3. Securing Titles to the Land

Neither the "old inhabitants" nor the Loyalists were satisfied with the way the provincial government in Halifax was dealing with the crisis. Reading the minutes of the Executive Council for 1783–84 is like reading a long jeremiad: complaints, complaints, and more complaints, from all quarters. Nova Scotia

Governor Parr soon joined the chorus, complaining to his superiors in London about the ungratefulness of all those demanding people whom nothing could satisfy. The Loyalists pressed for secession from Nova Scotia. In 1784, New Brunswick was formed into a province, with Sir Thomas Carleton as governor. Carleton and his Executive Council spent most of their first year of existence allocating land to all those who were eligible. These included both "old inhabitants" and Acadians. The Natives, however, were not included in the distribution.

The Acadians of the lower St. John do not appear to have been treated worse than the "old inhabitants" or even the Loyalists, who experienced their own share of difficulties. The Acadians sent relatively few petitions to the New Brunswick government for compensation, and this is not because they were meek or subservient: at the time, the Acadians had the deserved reputation of being quite insistent and forthright in pressing their causes with the government. And in the long run, they usually got what they wanted.

But grants do not seem to have solved the Acadians' problems. Within a few months (and in some cases, within a few weeks) of receiving a title to their lands, almost all the Acadians sold their property and left. For instance, ten of the eighteen Acadians included in the grant to Augustin "White" [Leblanc] in January 1786 sold their holdings within six months. In January 1785, the governor and council decreed that not only the Acadians leaving the lower St. John could sell their improvements, but that whoever claimed the land afterwards would have to show proof of purchase in order to receive the grant. Consequently, some of the French did not even wait for a title before selling. The prices received by the Acadians fell within the range of the ones obtained by the old inhabitants who were also selling land to the newcomers.

A combination of factors spurred the lower St. John French to leave. To begin with, many felt that the government was too slow in responding to their petitions for grants to their land. In August 1784,

The Land in Between

Augustin Leblanc and two dozen others petitioned Parr to ask that land that had been surveyed and allotted to them by the previous governor be officially granted. Nothing was done, because by that time Parr no longer had jurisdiction over New Brunswick. In November 1784, Augustin Leblanc presented his petition to Carleton. The survey was conducted before the year was over, but the titles were not delivered. In March of the following year, Leblanc petitioned again, asking for an assurance in writing that each applicant would get the 200 acres surveyed for him. He was told the grants would be issued "in due time." They were not issued till January 31, 1786. These delays made some of the Acadians nervous, and they indicated they would be satisfied with a grant elsewhere, if it would speed up the procedure. Imperfect surveys were also a common problem: the surveyors were not drawing the lines where the occupants believed they should be, and then one had to go through the tiresome petition process to get redress, which was also slow. Jean, Simon, and Joseph Martin of Lower French Village complained about the survey in 1787, but got their title only in 1799.

4. Economic, Family, and Religious Concerns

A secure title issued in a timely fashion was only a partial solution to the many dilemmas facing the French of the lower St. John as a result of the Loyalists' arrival. After enjoying almost twenty years of relatively undisturbed frontier existence—except for American attacks during the Revolution—they suddenly found themselves hemmed in on all sides by a people who neither spoke their language nor shared their religion. Settlement put an end to the fur trade, as well as to lumbering activities, because all the nearby trees were on private land. They could still farm, but how could they possibly settle their children, now that the available local land had become such a scarce commodity? How could they preserve their religion? These two last concerns were uppermost in the petition for land at Madawaska presented by Olivier Thibodeau, Joseph Thériault, and

François Violette in 1789. They stated that they were:

> ...encumbered with large families whose settlement in life they look forward with much anxiety [and it was] their earnest wish to see them settled around them on land of their own, which they cannot expect in the part of the country where they now reside. That your petitioners are informed that Government offers encouragement in lands to such persons as shall settle high up the River Saint John, which your petitioners are desirous of doing, not only in order to obtain such lands for their families, but that they may have the assistance of a Priest in the performance of the rites and ceremonies of their religion and in the superintendence of their children's education.[12]

Thibodeau, Thériault, and Violette had between them twenty-three sons, eight of whom were over the age of sixteen. They were neither landless, nor squatters: they had been included in a 1787 grant. Thériault may even have been a miller. In August 1785, he had petitioned the governor and council for the right to start a gristmill on a nearby stream, and his petition had the support of a dozen of his Loyalist neighbors. Having a mill would have made him one of the leading men in the parish.

However, whatever their relative security as land owners, the arrival of literally thousands of new immigrants on the lower St. John meant that the old mixed economy based on fur, trees, and farms was no longer feasible, and there was no land left for their children. The other reason the three men put forward echoed the one given by Mercure in 1783: they wanted to be near a priest. The prospect of their community ever becoming large enough to support a resident priest had been destroyed by the arrival of the Loyalists.

Religious and economic factors offer compelling reasons as to why the Acadians streamed out of the lower St. John in the 1780s. Their response was also typical of the era. Selling one's property in a densely settled part of the country in order to relocate on the frontier—where land was cheap and plentiful and where one could therefore provide sons with their own farms—was a common practice among French- and English-speaking people alike in North America until the nineteenth century. The behavior of the lower St John Valley French was therefore not extraordinary. Some left for Madawaska, others for the New Brunswick coast, instead.

Not everyone was happy with Madawaska: the Mazzerolles, Jean Tardif, Alexandre Bourguoin, and some of the Martins went back and received grants at Kingsclear before the century was over. The Mercures similarly did not linger on. In July 1792, Louis Mercure sold his lot to Michel Martin. In 1793, he applied for, and received, a 500-acre grant in Tring Township (St. Joseph de Beauce) on the Chaudière River, as a "reduced lieutenant" in the "late corps of Loyalists commanded by Col. Rogers."[13] At the time, a cattle trail went from the Kennebec River to Quebec City through this valley, and the government was also planning to open post relays along it. But Louis seems to have soon given up the idea of opening an inn or becoming a post master in Beauce. In 1809, he and his son Louis Michel, "of River de Chute, Yeomen," sold Joseph Young of Woodstock a lot with a sawmill at River de Chute (N.B.) for £50; it seems Mercure had been on the land since 1790.[14] As for his brother Michel, he had obtained a grant for 200 acres at Salmon River (another good mill site), six miles below the Grand Falls, in May 1792, which he sold to John King of Saint John in 1808.[15] The Mercures had apparently hoped to benefit from a trade in lumber that did not materialize—like Olivier Thibodeau and Joseph Thériault at Kennebecassis.

III. FAMILY REUNION: CANADIANS MEET ACADIANS ON THE UPPER ST. JOHN

The Acadians (and Canadians) moving north to Madawaska were promptly joined by Canadians moving south. The Canadians' migration was only a matter of time. Duperré and Lizotte were at the vanguard of waves of French Canadian migration to the Valley from Québec's lower St. Lawrence Valley (now referred to as the Côte-du-Sud) which lasted until the twentieth century. Most of the French-speaking people who moved to the upper St. John Valley came from the parishes which dot the Côte-du-Sud between l'Islet and Kamouraska, where many Acadians had taken refuge after 1755.

This migration was of a type repeated over and over throughout North America from the beginnings of European settlement to the late nineteenth century: old settlements filled up until land became scarce and the scarcity forced the upcoming generation to move and seek land elsewhere. Those economically motivated migrations usually occurred "under family auspices" and took the form of chain migrations: a small group left first, found a place to its liking, and sent the message back home. They were then joined by family members, neighbors, and co-parishioners, who in turn sent the message back to where they came from, and as the place filled up, the process started again. By the 1780s this process affected the entire Côte-du-Sud. Migration from the Côte-du-Sud toward the St. John Valley began shortly after Duperré and Lizotte opened their trading post in 1783. It was greatly facilitated by the recent improvements on the Grand Portage road that made it useable by carts in the summer.

Migrations from the south and from the north were under family auspices, too. Not all lower St. John Acadians relocated to Madawaska—a large number chose the New Brunswick coast, instead. Regis S. Brun discovered that those who moved to the Memramcook region were descendent of Acadians who had lived near Beaubassin before the deportation. Those who moved to Madawaska were either Canadians or married to Canadians or were likely to have a Canadian brother- or sister-in-law (see appendix F for a list of charter families, with their relationships to each other). No Acadian with a

Illus. 5-1: A sketch of Philip Long's farm by Lower Canada surveyor Joseph Bouchette, around 1815. Madawaska farms probably looked the same. LAC, E-001201329

Canadian connection migrated east. The timing of the first migrations was, however, less a matter of improved roads than of opportunity: British authorities were granting free land to people willing to set-tle there. The fact that moving to the upper St. John Valley offered the chance to reunite with family and acquaintances moving there from southern New Brunswick added to the attractiveness of the place.

V. BEHIND THE TALE OF EXPULSION

The Acadian migration to Madawaska left a lasting legacy of bitterness. In 1790, Surveyor Park Holland, who happened to visit the new Madawaska settle-ment, mentioned that the settlers had moved there "in anger." Why were the Acadians angry? A June 1785 letter from Charles Blanchard and Joseph Thériault, two of the Acadians included in Hammond's[16] grant on the Kennebecassis, to G. D Lud-low, member of Council and chief justice for New Brunswick gives us some clues.[17] The letter (in English) concluded:

When M. Francklin divided the tract among us and administered the oath again to us, we had no doubt of holding this land and enjoying the priv-ileges of English subjects, equally with others that settled in the country. As we have faithfully adhered to our oath when some on the river have not and have been ready to assist when called upon; in our old age [unreadable word] with helpless women and children to be set adrift seems to us unjust, inhumane and contrary to the generosity we might expect from Britain.[18]

What had triggered the letter was, on the one hand, the imperfect survey that had deprived them of some intervale land, and on the other, the demand that they pay rent, which they deemed "exorbitant," on that land. Now that the tract was filling up, Hammond was presenting the bill to his "tenants." Petition and letter produced the desired results: Hammond's grant was escheated (forfeited by the court); the Acadians got freeholds; and Thériault got additional acreage.

The letter is interesting on several counts. First, Blanchard and Thériault did not contest the proprietor's right to charge rent, only the amount, which they deemed disproportionate to the income the property could generate. They were the victims not only of a bad survey, but also of rack-renting, and wanted redress. Second, they displayed a very keen sense of the reciprocity of obligations between subjects and their sovereign or his representatives. The two men were angry because they believed they had fulfilled their part of the bargain and were not getting their dues in return. However, the bargain was not what they thought it was. Francklin's affidavit was explicitly neither a grant nor even a location ticket, but a license of occupation; it gave the Acadians the right to use the land until its owner (Crown or proprietor) decided what to do with it. The Acadians were so sure it was as good as a grant that they annexed it to one of their petitions.

The letter also shows that the two men accepted current notions of the proper structure of society. They talked about the *privileges* of English *subject*s (not the Rights of Men) and of the *generosity* they expected from Britain (not of justice), and referred to Ludlow as "*gracious*" and expressed their *gratitude* for his "graciousness." And they were trying to secure the help of an extremely powerful individual who could intervene in their favor. They accepted without question the hierarchical nature of eighteenth-century society. The "lower orders" (as working class people were called at the time) were supposed to defer to and obey the "better sort" (those with pedigrees and privilege). In return, the "better sort" took paternal care of the "lower orders." As a result, eighteenth-century society functioned as a vertical network of upper-class patrons and lower-class clients. The "lower orders" went along with this system—but they expected favors to flow in return for their deference. When the favors went undelivered, they were known to protest, petition, or riot.

The French settlers in the lower St. John shared this vision of society and felt cheated when their "betters" did not fulfill their part of the bargain. Blanchard and Thériault were a case in point. They won their case and may have stopped being angry. Their friends and relatives upriver, on the other hand, may have felt that they, too, had fulfilled their part of a bargain, but that their "betters" were not delivering. Not all felt their problem had been solved satisfactorily.

The Acadians probably expected better-than-average treatment from the British authorities at the end of the American Revolution because of their wartime loyalty and services to the Crown. They were getting it from Parr, but did not receive it from Carleton. After restrictions on Catholic landownership were removed, Parr began issuing grants and survey warrants to the French. Mercure was one of the first to be served, on account of his connections. In October 1783, John Parr informed Haldimand that:

> I have made Mercure very happy by giving him the island he so much wished for; it gives me pleasure to have in my power to assist men of merit and those who behaved well during the late Rebellion, but particularly those recommended by your Excellency.[19]

Some land was also laid out for him and the Martins at the mouth of the Madamkeswick River, but New Brunswick was separated from Nova Scotia before Parr could sign the grant.

When the Loyalists suddenly poured into the region, the Acadians' military service no longer made them special, and they did not receive preferential treatment. The thousands of Loyalists who flooded in to the region in 1783 represented a far larger constituency. The creation of the province of New Brunswick and the installation of a new set of governmental administrators effectively removed any advantage the Acadians and their patrons might have had with the Nova Scotia administration. Hazen seem to have been able to quickly rebuild his network, by linking with the extremely well-connected mayor of Saint John, G. G. Ludlow. It is most likely through Hazen that Blanchard and Thériault got in contact with Ludlow's brother. But when Mercure petitioned the new governor asking that the land set aside for him by Nova Scotia be granted to him, his petition joined the many that were addressed to the governor, instead of being fast-tracked on account of his services and connections.

Suddenly being treated like a common farmer must have been particularly galling to someone as well pedigreed as Louis Mercure. The Martins eventually got the grant. There is no evidence Mercure got his. We can imagine him sharing his dismay—or his anger—with his son, and the story being passed down from one generation to the next, losing some of its details at each passing to become a stark story of dispossession by vindictive anti-Acadian Anglos. Louis Mercure's descendent, Prudent Mercure, did find examples of Acadians dealing with bad neighbors, bad surveys, and long waits for their titles, but never wondered whether the "old inhabitants" and the Loyalists had been treated differently. He assumed the Acadians had been singled out for ill treatment.

Conclusion

The history of the founding of the Madawaska French settlement is a tale of multiple players and multiple interests, playing out against the setting of a huge postwar population displacement and consequent bureaucratic disarray. For the Natives, it meant another relocation to Tobique and Viger. On the French side, it includes both lower St. Lawrence fur traders seeking their fortune on the upper St. John and French Canadians seeking remedy for over-crowding in their parishes caused by rapid population growth, as well as Acadian settlers from the lower St. John facing overcrowding and disruption caused by the massive influx of Loyalists. On the English side, it includes governmental officials seeking to shore up the main communication artery between Halifax and Québec while floundering in the logistical nightmare of trying to minister, with completely inadequate staffing, to the needs of a new province and some twelve thousand displaced Loyalists. To their credit, the Acadians were not mere passive victims, meekly accepting the fate dealt to them by Providence. They petitioned for their rights, sought redress, and, given their limited options, were rather successful. Ultimately, their move to the Valley gained them property rights in one of the best farming districts of the region, as well as access to timber resources. The Acadians and French Canadians who remained or came back to the Fredericton area, on the other hand, got land but were assimilated within three generations.

ENDNOTES
1. Deane and Kavanagh, "Report," 480.
2. LAC, Map collections, HI/210/St. John River [1778], microfiche 10867.
3. For instance: Albert, *Histoire du Madawaska,* 76, and Bernard, *Histoire de la survivance Acadienne,* 187–88.
4. When he met the French-speaking governor Haldimand in 1784, he needed an interpreter. So did the Native witnesses at Noïte's trial (see Appendix D).
5. Raymond, *Winslow papers,* 510.
6. PANB, RS108, Land grant and application book, York County petitions, application from Pierre Duperré July 18, 1800, microfilm reel F1041.
7. The story of the Viger reservation is told in details in Fortin, *Histoire du Bas Saint Laurent.*
8. Haldimand, Sir Frederick (baptized François-Louis-Frédéric), army officer and colonial administrator; b. 1718 in Switzerland, son of François-Louis Haldimand, receiver for the town; d. there unmarried 1791. See full biography in the *Dictionary of Canadian Biography* at http://www.biographi.ca/EN/
9. See Louis Mercure's biography in the *Dictionary of Canadian Biography.*
10. Carleton, Guy, 1st Baron Dorchester, army officer and colonial administrator; b. 1724 in Ireland, d. 1808 in Eng-

land; third son of Christopher Carleton and Catherine Ball; m. 1772 Lady Maria Howard, third daughter of the 2nd Earl of Effingham. Carleton, Thomas, army officer and colonial administrator; b. *c.* 1735 in Ireland, d. 1817 in England; youngest son of Christopher Carleton and Catherine Ball; m. 1783 Hannah Foy, *née* Van Horn. See the biography of the Carleton brothers in the *Dictionary of Canadian Biography*; Thomas Carleton biography also provides a good survey of early New Brunswick History.

11. Hannay, "The Maugerville Settlement," 84.

12. PANB, RS108, Land petitions and application book, King's county petitions, petition dated 21/12/1789, microfilm reel F1036; (cited and copied in M. Pelletier, *Van Buren: A History*).

13. LAC, RG1 L3, Lower Canada Land Papers, 1793, Vol. 1: 272, microfilm reel C-2493; 1793, vol. 12: 3839, microfilm reel C-2496; 1795, Vol. 12: 4282 microfilm reel C-2496.

14. PANB, RS108, Land petition and application book, York county petitions, microfilm reel F1452

15. LAC, RG1 L3, Lower Canada Land paper, Exploration of Roads, Craig Road, Road to New Brunswick, 1810–1819, vol. 27, microfilm reel 2504

16. Hammond or Hamond, Sir Andrew Snape, naval officer and colonial administrator (1738-1828); see full biography in *Dictionary of Canadian Biography*.

17. Ludlow, George Duncan, b. 1734 in Long Island, NY; m. 1758 Frances Duncan; d. 1808 in Fredericton, N.B. In 1783, Ludlow and his brother Gabriel George had joined other well-heeled New Yorkers in London, where they had lobbied for the creation of New Brunswick into a separate province. G. D. Ludlow was appointed chief justice of the colony and came back to North America with the newly appointed governor, Sir Thomas Carleton. His brother was appointed the first mayor of Saint John, and was the second most important person in the colony. When Carleton left the colony in 1803, he became administrator, commander-in-chief, and president of the Council, for five years. See biography at *Dictionary of Canadian Biography*. PANB, RS108, Land petitions book, King's County petitions, Letter from Charles Blanchard and Joseph Thériault to the Hon. G. D. Ludlow 29-6-1785, microfilm reel F1024.

19. Raymond, *Winslow Papers*, 162; for the grant, see NSARM, Crown land grants, old book 15:58

FURTHER READINGS

Acadian Culture in Maine, http://acim.umfk.maine.edu, section 2, "Roots of Maine Acadian Culture."

Thériault, Léon. "L'Acadie de 1763 à 1990, synthèse historique." In *L'Acadie des Maritimes, études thématiques*

des débuts à nos jours, Jean Daigle (dir.). 1993: 45–92.

Buckner, Phillip A. and John G. Reid. *The Atlantic Region to Confederation: A History.* 1994: ch. 8–9

Judd, Richard W. *et. al. Maine: The Pine Tree State from Prehistory to the Present.* 1995: ch.7

Bourque, Bruce J. *Twelve Thousand Years: American Indians in Maine.* 2001: ch. VIII.

Fortin, Jean-Charles *et. al. Histoire du Bas-Saint-Laurent.* 1993.

Laberge, Alain *et. al. Histoire de la Côte du Sud.* 1993.

Bear Nicholas, Andrea and Harald Prins. "The Spirit of the Land, the Native People of Aroostook." In *The County: Land of Promise*, ed. A. Mcgrath. 1989, provides a Native perspective on the events described in this chapter.

Dubay, Guy. *Chez Nous: The St. John Valley.* 1983, gives the perspective of a local historian.

Also see Dubay, Guy. *Light on the Past.* 1995, for reproduction of documents.

SOURCES

Raymond (1899–05, 1904–05, 1907, 1943, and 1972) is a good secondary source for the events leading to the founding of the Madawaska settlement. He can be supplemented with Hannay (1893–94 and 1909) and Ganong (1899, 1901, 1904, and 1906) as usual. The story of the Grand Portage has been told by Marie-Victorin (1918), Raymond (1921), and more recently, W. E. Campbell (2005). For the Maliseets, see Johnson and Martijn (1994), Tehatarongnatase (2000), and S. Tremblay (1998). The relocation of some of the Maliseets in Québec is covered in Chapter 6 of Fortin (1993). Paradis (1989) and Andrew (in the *Dictionary of Canadian Biography*) have both produced a short biography of Mercure. Migrations out of the lower St. John are discussed by Craig (1983, 1984, and 1986) and Brun (1969). Dionne (1989) has inventoried the Acadian land grants in New Brunswick (however, the information on the Kennebecassis is erroneous). Petitions for land and land grants can be found in two on-line databases on the web site of the Provincial Archives of New Brunswick. Any investigation of land holdings must also use the land registry books, as land grant registration was not complete.

Part Two

A DISPUTED TERRITORY, 1785–1851

This period in the history of Madawaska is framed by three events: the founding of a French settlement on the upper St. John on the one hand, and the signing of the Webster-Ashburton treaty in 1842, which put an end to the boundary dispute between Britain and the United States, followed by the resolution of the Interprovincial boundary dispute in 1851, on the other. The settlers had hardly begun clearing their farms in the 1780s when jurisdiction over their territory was contested, first by Québec and New Brunswick, and then by Britain and the United States. The dispute was initially of little concern to the settlers, since they were too busy recreating a community and developing their economy to worry about diplomatic disagreements. The beginnings of the lumber industry, however, brought the dispute to a head, with Britain and the United States defending their claims militarily.

In this section, we are going to examine what happened to the Madawaska settlers between 1785 and 1851. First, what kind of economy did they build once relocated on the upper St. John? What accounted for the continuing immigration from Lower Canada to the Valley? What was life like in the Valley in the first half if the nineteenth century? How did New Brunswick exercise jurisdiction over the Valley, and what were the consequences for the settlers? And finally, what triggered the resolution of the two boundary disputes, after they had been allowed to simmer for about half a century?

Timeline Part Two: 1763–1851

Dates	Diplomatic Events	Political Events	Bundary Issues	Administrative Events
1763		Royal proclamation—fixes southern boundary of province of Quebec		
1783	**Treaty of Paris**	Treaty of Paris defines northeastern boundary of the United States.		
1785				New Brunswick promises grants to Madawaska settlers
1787				Quebec Executive Council authorizes grants at Madawaska
1787			Surveyor general of Quéebec (Holland) and of New Brunswick (Sproule) disagree on location of border between the two provinces.	First location tickets at Madawaska issued by New Brunswick
1789		The Robichauds sue Duperré and Dubé in Quebec		Mercure, Duperré, and Costin petition for local elections
1790			Mazzerolle grant issued by N.B.	Quebec commissions two militia captains at Madawaska

Dates	Diplomatic Events	Political Events	BundaryIssues	Administrative Events
1791			N.B. appoints a justice of the peace at Madawaska	
1791		Constitutional Act creates provinces of Upper and Lower Canada . Disabilities against Catholics removed in both provinces.		
1792			Quebec and New Brunswick refer the boundary dispute to Great Britain	**Foundation of parish of St. Basile**
1793				First milita company at Madawaska under N.B. authority (Independent Cie.)
1795		Madawaska French try to participate in N.B. elections		
1798	St Croix River identified; eastern line of the state drawn		St Croix River identified; eastern line of the state drawn	
1803		Madawaska French try to participate in N.B. elections		
1810		**N.B. Catholics get the right to vote**		
1812	War of 1812 between the U.S. and Britain			
1814	Treaty of Ghent, ends the War of 1812			
1818			First Americans on the upper St. John	
1824			N.B. issue first timber licenses at Madawaska	Creation of the 4th Battalion York Militia (first regular militia battalion at Madawaska)
1824	Britain issues moratorium on timber licenses at Madawaska			
1825			Maine and Massachusetts land agents Coffin and Irish visit Madawaska territory Rebuilding of Grand Portage route by Lower Canada	
1827			Arrest of John Baker	
1830		**Catholic Relief Act in N.B.;** first Catholic justice of the peace at Madawaska (Francis Rice)	Britain divides territory north of the St. John along the Madawaska River; Western section attributed to Lower Canada and the rest to New Brunswick	
1831	King of Netherlands arbitration in boundary dispute		Deane and Kavanagh visit the disputed territory	
1833		Establishment of Carleton County		
1837		First Madawaska candidate at elections (L. Coombs)		
1838				Creation of parish of St. Bruno
1839	"Aroostook War." Governor of Maine sends the militia to northern Aroostook; booms erected across the rivers and forts erected on both sides of the St. John			
1842	**Webster–Ashburton Treaty (Also called "Treaty of Washington")**			Creation of parish of Ste. Luce.
1846		N.B. attempt at incorporating civil parishes in the former disputed territory disallowed on account of interprovincial boundary dispute.		
1851		Resolution of Interprovincial boundary dispute.		

6

ECONOMY AND POPULATION, 1785–1845

Once arrived at Madawaska, the new settlers had to build an economic base as quickly as possible. Their economy was always commercial. It initially rested on agriculture and the fur trade. After the first lumber camps opened in the upper St. John River basin, lumbering replaced the fur trade as the second mainstay of the local economy.

Agriculture was the most reliable economic activity, and everybody had a farm. The soil was fertile, and, by the late 1700s, some farmers were growing significant surpluses. After the War of 1812, the Madawaska settlement began to ship large quantities of wheat beyond its boundaries, and it continued to do so until environmental problems made growing wheat unreliable. It then had to find substitute commercial crops. In the meantime, the wheat trade stimulated the building of gristmills and drove up the price of farmland.

The nature of the local economy shaped local society, as well. Economic opportunities attracted people; economic crises drove them out. Different types of activities also attracted newcomers, and lumbering allowed many people without any prior connection to the Valley to successfully resettle there, leading to the creation of a stratified society by the middle of the century.

I.   THE FUR TRADE

Since 1765, hunting and trapping above the Grand Falls was reserved for the Natives. Trade with the Natives should have been under license issued by the governor-general, but it appears that this regulation was poorly enforced. As a result, unlicensed traders plied their goods along the St. John. Business was initially quite profitable. In 1788, traders Duperré and McLennan sued a former clerk, claiming his accounts were short, and proffered books for the October 1784–July 1786 period as proof. The traders had sent $163 worth of goods (or, in colonial currency, £40 16s 4³/₄d) to Madawaska and collected $1,148 worth of merchandise in return (£286 11s 7d). Trade dwindled very rapidly as fur-bearing animals became increasingly rare. In 1809, the priest claimed that hunting was no longer worth the effort. However, while hunting could no longer be relied upon as a main source of income, it could provide supplementary income. Well into the 1830s, priests were complaining that some of their parishioners were paying their tithes, not in farm products as they were supposed to, but in fur at their own valuation.

A. The Eighteenth Century

Settlers began clearing land for farms as soon as they arrived. By 1799, some of those farms were capable of feeding not only their own residents, but also people in additional households. They may also have had surpluses left to sell outside the St. John Valley. We know how much Madawaska farmers grew in the last year of the eighteenth century. They petitioned the bishop for a resident priest, claiming they could support one, and, to prove their point, they reported the amount they had tithed in the past year and the amount they would tithe in the next. Farmers were supposed to tithe one-twenty-sixth of their field crops, therefore a simple calculation tells us how much they grew. Historian Betty Hobbs Pruitt estimated that eighteenth-century Massachusetts farms

producing at least forty-three bushels of grain could cover all their needs and be left with significant surpluses to sell. She considers those farms "commercial." Farms producing between thirty-four and forty-three bushels covered their needs and were "subsistence" farms. Those below 34 bushels had to supplement farm production with wage work or craft work. The fifty-six Madawaska farms which paid tithes in 1799 were collectively able to reach the forty-three-bushel benchmark (see Table 6-1, and Table 1 in Appendix H). However, there were seventy-two households at Madawaska that year; the other farms probably were not developed enough to grow crops. The fifty-six tithe payers could have fed everyone, and still have had ten bushels to spare (see Table 6-2, and Table 2 in Appendix H). Despite occasional setbacks, such as a crop-destroying insect

Table 6-1: Production per Farm (in bushels) for Selected Crops and Years*

	Number of Farms	Wheat	Buckwheat	Oats	Potatoes
1799	56	53	1	11	70
1830s	159	111	3	74	356
1833	159	37	3	29	229
1842**	61	46	7	81	227

Table 6-2: Production per Household (in bushels) for Selected Crops and Years*

	Number of Households	Wheat	Buckwheat	Oats	Potatoes
1799	72	42	1	9	56
1807	100	44	no data	11	78
1830s	403	45	1	20	143
1833	403	15	1	11	90
1842**	250	11	2	20	55

* For more detailed tables, see Tables1 and 2, Appendix H.
** Parish of St. Luce, only   Sources: See list of censuses, p. 409.

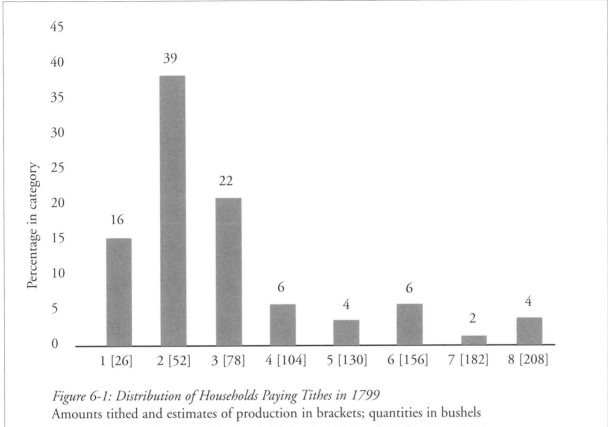

Figure 6-1: Distribution of Households Paying Tithes in 1799
Amounts tithed and estimates of production in brackets; quantities in bushels
Sources: AAQ, Lettres de prêtes missionaries du Madawaska à l'évêque de Québec, 3 mars 1799

infestation in 1792, Madawaska agriculture had started off on the right foot. Not everyone, however, was equally productive. Pioneer farming tends to conjure images of equality among all farmers. This was not the case. There were, for a start, the sixteen households that had not tithed. The estimated production of the others ranged from 26 to 208 bushels. Simon Hébert produced 208 bushels of grain and soon built a gristmill at Madawaska. Production therefore varied considerably from farm to farm (see Figure 6-1).

B. The Early 1830s

After the War of 1812, observers noted that the upper St. John Valley had become one of the region's main wheat producers. Peter Fisher, the first historian of New Brunswick, and Joseph Bouchette, surveyor general of Lower Canada (see appendix A for geographic terminology), noted in 1824 and 1825 that Madawaska was shipping grain and flour to Fredericton.[1] On the other hand, in an 1827 letter to the governor of Maine, two American Madawaska settlers, John Baker and James Bacon, mentioned that:

> Great crops have been raised in Madawaska for several years past—latterly sufficient for their own consumption and the support of emigrants thither, besides exporting four or five thousand bushels to Canada.[2]

The trade was made possible by the rebuilding of the Grand Portage route from 1821 to 1823. According to Alexander Fraser, owner of the Madawaska seigneury, "330 loaded horses, chiefly wheat from Madawaska have traveled this way since the 8th of

Illus. 6-1: One of the resting place on the Grand Portage route between Rivière du Loup and Lake Temiscouata was Camp Saint François, *north of the lake at the point where the Grand Portage crossed the St. Francis River. Note the wide bridge, the several houses, and the traveler on a cart. LAC, Millicent Mary Chaplin Fonds, watercolor, July 1842, C-000919*

January, with at least twice the number of people." [3]

For his part, Alexander Wolff, the Lower Canadian road commissioner responsible for repairing the Grand Portage, reported in 1829 that:

> There is a man known as Captain Hebert, principal merchant at Madawaska, who brings to Canada through this road between 20 and 30 carts, which return loaded with merchandise from Canada to Madawaska every year.[4]

Tables 6-1 and 6-2 show that, at that time, Madawaska farms were still producing much more than required for mere subsistence. That is, established farms could feed the entire population and have crops left over. Thanks to a document produced in the winter of 1833, we know exactly how much

Madawaska farmers had been growing in the early 1830s, as well as how many horses, cattle, sheep, and pigs they owned, and the size of their families. The document allows precise calculations of the size of the wheat surplus in the previous years: 6,000 bushels. Madawaska settlers could have indeed sold 4,000 to 5,000 bushels in Lower Canada, and have 1,000 to 2,000 bushels left to grind into flour and ship downriver. As in 1799, not all farms were equally productive. Out of 401 farms listed in the report, only 156 reported a crop in the previous years (the others had a few animals or, at the very least, a cow), and the size of their surplus varied greatly. In large part, this was because most farms had been started recently. The report produced by Maine land

Illus. 6-2: Philip John Bainbrigge, Crossing Lake Etchemin on the ice, December 12, 1836. *Crossing Temiscouata Lake in winter would not have been different. LAC, C-11904*

agents John J. Deane and Edward Kavanagh in 1831 indicates how long people had been on their claim and the extent of their improvements. As Figure 6-2 shows, clearing was proceeding at a rapid pace, but this meant that a lot of farms were not yet fully productive.

C. Income

If our average early 1830s farmer was able to sell all his field crop surpluses, he could have earned between $120 and $160 from the sale. Placed in the context of local land prices and wage levels, this was good. Between 1830 and 1834, a 200-acre farm on granted land sold for an average of $552 (£138). Land without a grant fetched about half that price (about $280 or £70). In 1843, the priest was leasing out a well-located farm belonging to the Church for $60 a year. In other words, a farmer renting a holding and producing average surpluses could save

enough to buy an established farm within five years. This was more profitable than wage work. In the 1840s, male laborers earned about 2 shillings a day (40 cents); they got 25 shillings a month or $5 (with room and board) when hired by the month. Males hired for the year received about £15 or $60. (We could not find earlier data on wages.) The farmers' potential earnings were, therefore, significant when we compare them either to laborers' earnings or the price of land. Madawaska in the 1830s was prosperous, and this prosperity was linked with participation in the wheat trade after the War of 1812. One of the consequences of the increasing commercialization of agriculture was an increase in the price of land. Prices reported in the Registry of Deeds climbed steadily after the war; in particular, they jumped immediately after the Grand Portage Road was rebuilt (see Figure 6-3).

Selling crops was not the pioneers' only source of

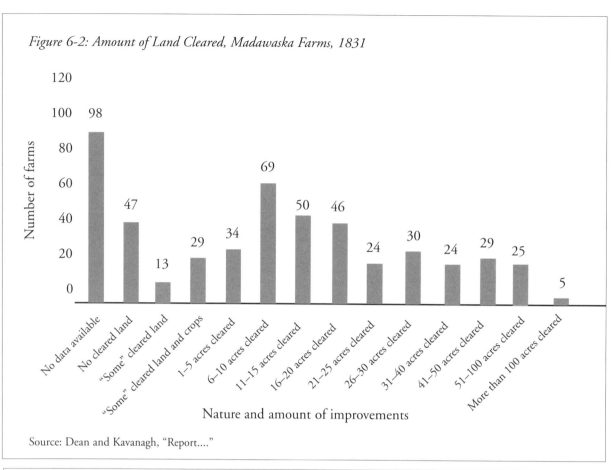

Figure 6-2: Amount of Land Cleared, Madawaska Farms, 1831

Source: Dean and Kavanagh, "Report...."

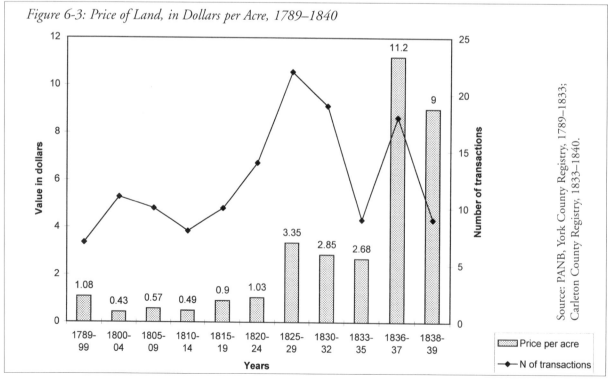

Figure 6-3: Price of Land, in Dollars per Acre, 1789–1840

Source: PANB, York County Registry, 1789–1833; Carleton County Registry, 1833–1840.

Illus. 6-3: Picture taken at the turn of the last century of Georges Bernier's boat (a similar boat can be seen in Illustration 4 in Chapter 9). This type of boat was ubiquitous on the St. John River until the end of the nineteenth century, as the following description shows: "Formerly the larger portion of the supplies for the lumber camps and also for the stores along the river was boated up the river from Fredericton. The boats used were large, flat-bottomed scows with a cabin built upon the after end in which the boatman ate and slept and upon the top of which the helmsman stood and steered the boat by means of a huge rudder. Some of these boats are capable of carrying 200 barrels of pork and are drawn up the river by horses."
Wiggin, History of Aroostook, *194. Picture from Chad Pelletier's collection.*

income. Between 1818 and 1831, the New Brunswick government was paying bonuses to those who grew bread grains on land cleared in the past two years. The sums were significant: the province was paying a shilling (20 cents) per bushel of wheat. After 1825, settlers had a third source of income: timber. Bona fide settlers were allowed to cut the timber on their holdings if it had been granted to them, or if they had been issued a location ticket (a permission to settle pending the issuance of a grant). They took advantage of this. They also cut trees on public land and passed the logs off as their own. New farmers could therefore earn money selling the trees they were removing from their claim, sow grain among the stumps, harvest the crop, eat it, and still get money for it.

Some of the men collected very large bonuses.

They were clearly combining logging with growing grain on the land they had just cleared. They probably hired men to assist them in cutting, unless they had several grown sons. Otherwise, there is no way to account for the staggering quantities of grain they were producing. The Daigle brothers, Hilarion and Dominique (sons of Joseph), collected the bonus seven and eight times, respectively. Together, they received slightly over £100 ($400) from the government. They became substantial landowners. In 1831, Hilarion claimed three farm lots, two of which he had acquired in 1826 and 1827; he had ninety acres cleared. Dominique also claimed three lots, but cleared only thirty acres. David Cyr (Simon Hébert's adopted son) collected the bonus four times for a total of £ 32 4s 11d ($129), the last time for 559 bushels in 1831. He was an innkeeper who claimed three lots in 1831 and had a large stable of draft animals, which would have been useful in the woods. There was also a school operating on his property. Simonet Hébert, son of Simon, large landowner, large stock owner, and parish officer, collected £24 8s ($96) over four years. Michel Martin received the bonus only twice, but, as he reported 443 bushels of grain in 1827, he received a total of £28 3s 10d ($112) from the government. In 1831, he claimed four lots and cleared 176 acres. In 1833, he was, with the Hébert brothers, one of the three largest stock owners in the settlement.

D. Pluriactivities

The opportunities offered by the trade in bread grain encouraged some to build gristmills. One of the highest tithe payers in 1799 was Simon Hébert, who built such a mill in 1807. Profitable mills also changed hands. Pierre Duperré acquired Louis Mercure's former mill site at the end of the eighteenth century, and sold it in 1808 with a grist and sawmill, for the then-astronomical sum of £610 9s 0d ($2,440) to Peter Fraser and John Robinson. Robinson was perhaps the best-heeled Loyalist in New Brunswick; his father, Beverley, son of another John, administrator of Virginia, had been a childhood friend of George Washington. Our Robinson was a merchant, member of the provincial legislature, later provincial treasurer, mayor of Saint John, member of the executive council, and president of the Bank of New Brunswick.[5] The mill then passed into Louis Bellefleur's hand. Bellefleur was a merchant from Berthier who had engaged in the wheat trade in Lower Canada before moving to Madawaska around 1807. According to Deane and Kavanagh, he paid Peter Fraser $1,000 for the mill, and invested a further $2,000 in it. In 1831, Bellefleur claimed a grist and sawmill and three houses, as well as two other farm lots in the settlement. He may have bought the mill on credit and not discharged the mortgage. In 1836, Peter Fraser was dead. The executor of his will, Beverley Robinson (John's son), sold "a lot lately in possession of Louis Bellefleur" at Madawaska, 300 acres in size, with a grist and sawmill to François Thibodeau (Firmin's son). In 1845, the Americans issued a grant for the lot, less the mill site, to the heirs of P. Fraser and J. Robinson.[6] Thibodeau registered his deed to the property very shortly thereafter. The grain trade may then have attracted outside entrepreneurs, encouraged people to clear land quickly, and also driven up farm prices.

E. Crisis

Soon, however, the pendulum swung in the opposite direction. Wheat production declined precipitously from 1833 onwards. By 1850, very little was grown. Oats production, on the other hand, increased significantly, and buckwheat stopped being a marginal crop (see Tables 6-1 and 6-2, and Appendix H). The immediate cause of the decline was a catastrophic crop failure in 1833. Recovery was difficult because a parasite, the wheat midge, was sweeping across New England and making its way toward Lower Canada. It reached the Valley in the mid 1830s. To compound these difficulties, the wheat crop was also attacked by rust (a fungal disease). Wheat had become an uncertain crop.

Bad crops were not new. Crops had failed in 1787, 1797, 1814, 1816, 1817, and 1828. They had also possibly failed in 1832. They failed dramatically in 1833, 1836, and 1842 on account of the weather. Previously, production had always bounced back, but this time wheat growing did not. The growing season shortened in the 1830s as winters grew longer, and the midge refused to go away. But there was also a new phenomenon: western competition. By the mid 1830s, western New York and Pennsylvania, the Great Lakes states, and Upper Canada were producing large quantities of wheat and at lower cost than the eastern seaboard. The Erie Canal, which opened in 1825, and the building of canals around the rapids of the St. Lawrence and Niagara Falls in the 1830s and 1840s made it possible to ship this cheap western wheat eastward. By the time the midge was ravaging eastern wheat fields, western flour was available, and farmers from New England to Lower Canada switched crops and started eating bread made from store-bought flour. Madawaska was no different: inexpensive imported flour appeared in the region in the 1830s. Crown Land Commissioner Baillie priced the flour at 40 shillings ($8) a barrel (196 pounds) in his 1832 *Account of the Province of New Brunswick*. Barreled flour at 30 shillings ($6) appeared in the accounts of one of the Madawaska priests from 1835 to 1837. This was a considerable drop in price, and by that time Madawaska farmers had largely decided wheat was no longer worth their time. The bigger farmers continued growing an acre or two of wheat, but the others simply gave it up.

By the 1830s, a double economy was in place at Madawaska. On one side were well-established farmers engaged in truly commercial agriculture. They fed their families and neighbors from their farms and shipped surpluses outside the Valley. They also engaged in additional activities, such as large-scale land clearing, which allowed them to sell timber and collect provincial bonuses, and milling, if they had the available resources. On the other side were pioneers who had to find outside sources of income until their farms could support them. In earlier years, they probably participated in the fur trade. Later, they could exchange labor for food with their neighbors. After 1825, they could also work for wages in the upper St. John River lumber camps. Then, they could use the money to buy what they needed. This double economy depended on links with two provinces: workers transported grains over the Grand Portage to Lower Canadian markets, and floated wood to Fredericton and Saint John. Local people were very aware of the advantages of living on the boundary between two provinces. In an 1823 report, Alexander Wolff noted that, despite the poor state of the road, Madawaska storekeepers preferred to get their supplies from Quebec City rather than Fredericton. They noted that they could not travel to and from Fredericton in less than nine days, "whereas in the same time or a little less, they can travel to Québec, and back again, with the advantage of getting their goods at a much lower rate."[7]

III.   MIGRATIONS

The Madawaska population increased rapidly between 1785 and 1850 (see Table 6-3), thanks to a high birth rate, low infant mortality, and continuous immigration. Except for isolated exceptions, Acadian migrations to Madawaska stopped with the arrival of the last lower St. John French settlers around 1789. Migrations from Lower Canada continued unabated, and, after 1820, a few New Englanders and Catholic Irish also began to trickle in. After 1800, the New Brunswick government could no longer issue grants because of the boundary dispute, but its surveyors laid out lots and issued location tickets until 1825 to those who asked for one. Immigration was initially limited to a couple of families per year but gained momentum after 1825, when lumber camps opened in the region. The peaks and troughs in Figure 6-4 reflect the health of the local economy.

Family ties continued to play an important role in migrations until 1825. Newcomers who had a relative in Madawaska before they arrived almost always settled there permanently, but only one family in three without such a relative stayed. The chil-

Table 6-3: Non-Native Population, 1790–1840*

			Year		
1790	1799	1808	1820	1830	1840
			Population		
174	418	456	1,171	2,476	3,460

* A more detailed table can be found in Appendix E.
Sources: See list of censuses, pp. 408–09.

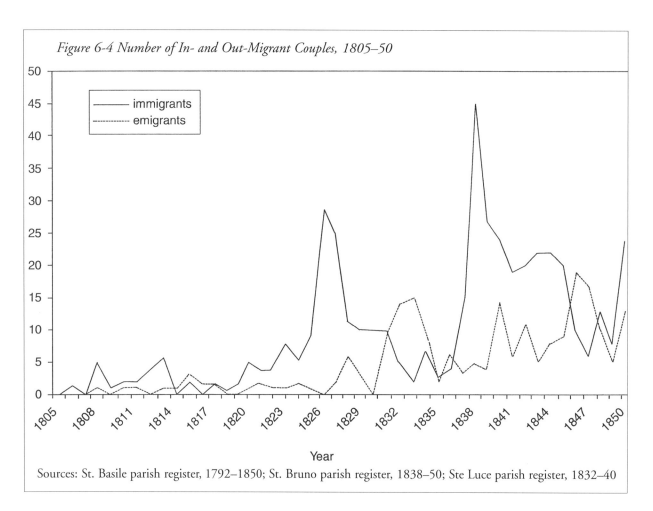

Figure 6-4 Number of In- and Out-Migrant Couples, 1805–50

Sources: St. Basile parish register, 1792–1850; St. Bruno parish register, 1838–50; Ste Luce parish register, 1832–40

dren of those who remained married the children of charter families (that is, families established in the Valley before 1800), and the settlement continued to be made up of interrelated families. Family ties also continued to influence one's choice of location after 1820. Pioneering was, in large part, a cooperative venture, and settlers tried to stay as close to immediate relatives as possible. But relatives continued to offer some security even after the pioneer stage was over. For example, in the event of sickness or acci-

dents, such as when the cow died or the house burned down, one usually could not count on anybody's help but the neighbors'. That help was likely to be more forthcoming if the neighbors were also relatives (see Sidebar 6-1). At that time, the Church offered little assistance to people in trouble. Indeed, in the first half of the century, it provided no services to Madawaskayans, with the exception of occasional schooling. Family networks were the only available safety net.

IV. SOCIAL STRATIFICATION

Things changed in the second quarter of the century: two large waves of immigrants arrived from the St. Lawrence, and the Valley lost many people in the 1830s. The Canadian migrants differed from their

predecessors in more ways than just numbers. By 1830, half of those newcomers had no relatives living in Madawaska; by 1840, three-quarters of the immigrants were in this situation. However, this lack of

Sidebar 6-1: Tante Blanche

Kin and neighbors were very important for survival during the pioneering days. They offered the first line of defense in the case of mishap. When cooperation among siblings and neighbors was inadequate, the larger network of kin could be called upon. The story of "Tante Blanche" is a case in point. In 1797, the crops froze, and a starving Madawaska settlement petitioned Fredericton for relief. In the meantime, Madawaska women faced the difficult task of feeding their families with insufficient resources. Marguerite Blanche Thibodeau, wife of Joseph Cyr from Grande Rivière, earned a place in local folklore for her efforts. Her story has been passed down from generation to generation, and, to this day, several versions of her story still circulate in the Valley. The one written down by Abbé Albert in 1920 is among the better known. Behind the inevitable embellishments, one can discern the outlines of a plausible episode.

According to Albert, when the settlement ran out of food, the men left to go hunting. Going from door to door, Marguerite Blanche supervised the sharing of available food and kept the community's morale up until the hunters came back. One can, of course, wonder how she managed to redistribute food in a community that had "eaten its last peck of boiled wheat and killed its last cow." The story, however, is plausible if it were Grand Rivière Village that had run out of food. The men could have gone hunting. Marguerite Blanche, at the time the second oldest woman at Madawaska, could have trekked the forty miles separating Grande Rivière from St. Basile. She had numerous nephews and nieces of her own in the upper St. John Valley, and her husband's eight brothers were also established at Madawaska. Almost every door she could have knocked on would have been that of a niece or nephew. These family members would probably have been willing to spare some food for their relatives in the Grand Rivière, enabling the starving lot to survive until the men's return. At her death, Marguerite Blanche was buried in the parish church, an honor normally reserved for males. The fact that the earliest and most famous local hero is actually a heroine—and an old woman to boot—reinforces the notion that women were agents in their own right in late eighteenth-century Acadian society.

Source: Albert (1920): 123–24.

family connections no longer posed an obstacle to permanent relocation to Madawaska: two-thirds of those families stayed (a third more than in the 1800 to 1825 period). Lack of previous family connections, however, remained an obstacle to integration into the existing community; migrants without relatives were the early equivalent of the people from the wrong side of the tracks. Charter family members did not marry newcomers or their children, for instance. Nor could newcomers make purchases on credit at the general store like their more established neighbors. And priests tended to view them as undesirable rowdies trying to escape the social constraints of better-established parishes. By 1850, the division was even noticeable to outsiders. British agronomist J. F. W. Johnston remarked:

> The Acadian French, who are settled in numbers in the upper part of this valley, are described as fine industrious men; but the Lower Canadians who came across from the shores of the St. Lawrence, are represented by the English settlers as a "miserable set." This probably arises from the fact that, as the Irish do with us, the poor Lower Canadians come into and through the country as beggars in great numbers.[8]

By mid-century, Madawaska society had stratified: the top layer was deemed "Acadian" and the bottom layer "Canadian." It is true that Acadian families were, on average, better off than the newly arrived Canadians: they had more land, better land, more productive farms, and often controlled the mill sites. But Johnston's "Acadians" included people like the Lizottes and Fourniers The label "Acadian" was applied indiscriminately to charter families and wealthier community members, instead of being limited to people who could trace at least part of their ancestry back to pre-1755 Acadia.

The opening of the lumber camps in the Valley during the winter of 1824–25 triggered changes in both the volume and composition of the migratory groups. Migrants from Canada were looking for land to farm, but land must be cleared before it can be farmed. Before 1825, newcomers depended on established settlers to survive during this stage. Established settlers naturally gave preference to their cousins. After 1825, newcomers could work in the shanties during the winter and use the money earned to buy necessities from their neighbors or merchants. They could also sell the trees on their claim as timber. Not having a local cousin was no longer a great handicap. Newcomers, however, remained vulnerable to economic problems; if the crops failed or the timber did not sell, they were the first to feel the pinch. The two immigration peaks in Fgure 6-4 correspond to good years in the forest industry; the out-migration surge in the mid-1830s, however, corresponds to a severe crop failure. Another group of people had also begun to move in the Valley in the 1820s. They were not Canadians, but New Englanders from the Kennebec Valley. They sought trees, not land, and they settled in relative isolation to the west of the French settlement. We will meet them again in Chapter 8.

V.   LEAVING THE VALLEY

Out-migration also began in earnest during the 1830s. The Old Town/Orono/Milford/Bradley area on the Penobscot River was one of the migrants' destinations after the opening of the road between Houlton and the St. John River in 1838. A few French were already there in 1835 before the road was even completed. They included Alexandre and Charlotte Ouellette, a couple from Saint-André de Kamouraska who had moved to Madawaska around 1826. Zebulon, a.k.a Eusèbe Sirois Duplessis, a member of one of Madawaska's charter families, married Alexandre and Charlotte's daughter at Old Town. Joseph Ouellette (unrelated to Alexandre), also a member of one of the charter families, married Zebulon's cousin. Alexandre and his family stayed on the Penobscot for about fifteen years and then disappeared. Zebulon and his wife came back to Madawaska and then moved back to Old Town in 1849. Joseph stayed in Old Town. Other St. John Valley men and occasionally their families moved farther away, to the Great Lakes region and even Wisconsin. Many relocated in communities very similar to what the St. John Valley had been a generation or two previously: heavily forested frontiers with plenty of land available for farmers.[9]

Conclusion

Pioneer settlements usually conjure images of self-sufficiency and subsistence agriculture. The pioneers allegedly lived off the land and engaged in limited exchanges only when absolutely necessary. For example, they sold small surpluses to acquire necessary goods they could not produce themselves, such as salt or metal. Visitors to the Madawaska territory between 1820 and the mid-1830s, on the other hand, describe the region as a breadbasket, whose farmers were able to sell bread grains and flour in large quantities to southern New Brunswick via the St. John River and to Québec via the Madawaska and St. Lawrence Rivers. American officials such as Deane and Kavanagh usually minimized trade relations between the Valley and the rest of British North America; howevcr, it was in the interest of their cause to do so.

Images of commercial farmers were not a figment of people's imaginations. The region's farmers were already enterprising and outreaching in this early period. This trade lasted for a generation until a combination of bad weather, insect infestation, and outside competition made commercial wheat growing unprofitable. Meanwhile, the Valley's overall prosperous economy, abundant land, and wage-earning opportunities in the lumber camps attracted many newcomers. They significantly contributed to population growth after 1820 and permanently changed the character of the settlement. Over the next twenty years, the Madawaska settlement changed from a large, close-knit family clan strung along the river into a society stratified by lines of ancestry and segmented by ethnicity. Charter families (the descendants of the eighteenth-century settlers) also rapidly emerged as economic and social leaders.

ENDNOTES

1. Bouchette visited the settlement for the first time in 1807, but his comments at the time were particularly laconic: "Les chaumières sont pour la plupart proprement baties et les champs et les jardins biens cultivés." [Most cabins are well built and the fields and gardens well tended.] Bouchette, *Description topographique de la province du Bas Canada,* 561.
2. John Baker and James Bacon (for the American Citizens of Madawaska Committee) to Enoch Lincoln, governor of the State of Maine, January 9, 1827, in Sprague, "Documentary History of the Northeastern Boundary," 351.
3. Journal of the House of Assembly of Lower Canada (9 Geo IV, 1829, Appendix P), Alexander Fraser to J. A. Wolff, Esq., letter dated February 19, 1827, Early Canadiana Online, http://www.canadiana.org.
4. Journal of the House of Assembly of Lower Canada, 1829, Appendix P, A. Wolff's report, August 10, 1826.
5. Robinson, John, businessman, office holder, and politician; b. 1762 near New York City, third son of Beverley Robinson and Susanna Philipse, and grandson of John Robinson, former president of the Council and administrator of Virginia; m. 1787 Elizabeth Ludlow, second daughter of George Duncan Ludlow, chief justice of New

Brunswick (see Chapter 5, note 17); d. 1828 in Saint John, N.B. See full biography in the *Dictionary of Canadian Biography* at http://www.biographi.ca/EN/. Later in his career, Fraser became vice president of the Bank of New Brunswick.
6. PANB, Carleton County Registry Office, 1845.
7. A. Wolff's report, August 10, 1826.
8. Johnston, J. F. W., *Notes on North America,* 70.
9. Bourbonnais County in Illinois was a common destination for Madawaskayans who left the territory. The county boasted an identifiable population of French Canadians between the two World Wars.

FURTHER READINGS

Craig, Béatrice. *Backwood Consumers and Homespun Capitalists: The Emergence of a Market Culture in Eastern Canada in the Nineteenth Century.* 2009.
Dubay, Guy. *Light on the Past.* 1995: 18–29 for reproduction of documents.
Acadian Culture in Maine. http://acim.umfk.maine.edu. Section 2, "Roots of Maine Acadian Culture."

SOURCES

This chapter draws on Craig's previous work, and sources can be found in the bibliographies or footnotes. Besides the volume listed above, also see Craig (1983, 1986a, 1986b, 1993a, 1993b, and 1995). For out-migrations, see Craig (1984) and Sorg (1984). Contemporary descriptions of the Valley can be found in Bouchette (1815 and 1831, vol. II), Fisher (1825 and 1838), Deane and Kavanagh (1831), Ward (1841), Gesner (1847), and Johnston (1850 and 1851). For background, see Judd *et. al.* (1995), Chapters 10 and 11, but note that the section on the St. John Valley is dated. For New Brunswick, see Buckner and Reid (1994), Chapters 1 and 2, as well as Acheson (1993). To understand the society from which the Madawaska migrants came, see Laberge, *et. al.* (1993), especially Chapters 2, 3 and 5, and Fortin et. *al.* (1993), Chapters 3 to 5. For Bourbonnais, see Langellier (1999). Blais (2005), and Dickinson (1994 and 1998), which discuss Acadian resettlement in Chaleur Bay and Québec's Richelieu Valley and provide interesting comparative material.

7

WAYS OF LIFE

What was life like at Madawaska during the late eighteenth and early nineteenth centuries? Because of its location along a major communication route, its proximity to a natural wonder—the Grand Falls—and the dispute over the boundary, many people traveled through the region. Some even stayed a while, taking time to investigate life in the territory. These individuals often left detailed accounts of their observations. The settlement also shared some general characteristics with Maine and New Brunswick pioneer communities, which contextualize these visitor reports. These various sources provide us with a picture of the settlement at variance with some well-entrenched, but inaccurate, images of the St. John Valley and "traditional" French Canadian society. They also contradict many stereotyped images of pioneer communities.

I. AN AGRICULTURAL SETTLEMENT

Farming was critical to survival in the area. One could purchase tea, sugar, spices, and even staples, such as flour or fish from the stores, but that was about it. Moreover, one also needed to have something to exchange for store items. Therefore everyone farmed. At mid-century, even merchants and professionals had a farm for safety. We have few descriptions of early Madawaska farming, but what exists suggests it was similar to pioneer farming elsewhere in the province.

A. Pioneer Farming

Before being able to farm, a settler usually had to make a farm. The first thing an aspiring New Brunswick farmer did when taking possession of his lot was to cut some trees to erect a shelter. The first house was normally made with round, 15- to 20-foot logs and chinked with moss or clay. The roof was covered with boards, and then with birch or spruce bark held in place with poles and ties. A wood-framed chimney matted with clay allowed a source of heat. The typical New Brunswick pioneer log house had one window and one door (with a window sash). There was a root cellar under the floorboards and a loft above the first floor. Later, the farmer usually built a frame house and converted the log building into a barn or storage shed.

Once a shelter had been built, the pioneer felled more trees, which he either burned or used for fencing (there is no reference to the practice of tree girdling in New Brunswick or Madawaska). The stumps could not be removed until they had rotted. The result, as described by Thomas Baillie is as follows: "After ten years, he has a new log or frame house with stone chimney, a frame barn, 25 or 30 acres cleared admitting in many places the plough, a horse, two oxen, a pair of steers, two cows, a calf,

Illus. 7-1: A romantic representation of pioneers clearing up land in the forest. The picture emphasizes the size of the trees, which are made to dwarf the humans. PANB, David Janigan Collection, MC2946

eight to ten sheep, and half a dozen of hogs."[1] However, Baillie was trying to attract immigrants to New Brunswick, and his calendar seems to have been optimistic: this result was more likely to take fifteen year to achieve. The amount of stock was particularly generous for a farm still encumbered by stumps.

Until the stumps were removed, farmers could not plow their fields. They broadcasted their seeds over the surface and covered them using a triangular horse-drawn harrow or a hoe. The New Brunswick and Nova Scotia Land Company, a colonization company that owned land in the mid-St. John Valley, claimed that, through this method, one could get three good successive upland crops without using any manure. The company's promotional literature also claimed that intervale land (or flat land along the

river) never required fertilizer. Wheat, oats, and potatoes, which were planted in hills (small mounds of soil) and cultivated with a hoe, constituted the first three crops. After that, the field was left as grass until the stumps could be removed. The company recommended mixing grass seeds with grain crops, so some hay could be raised after the harvest. Indian corn, pumpkins, cucumbers, peas, and beans were also hilled like potatoes, whereas other grains, turnips, hemp, flax, and grass seeds were broadcasted and harrowed over. Pioneers also had gardens where they grew salad greens, various types of kale, and asparagus. Peas, a common crop in French settlements, were grown in the fields, but frost-susceptible beans were planted in gardens.

Mid-nineteenth-century New Brunswick farm-

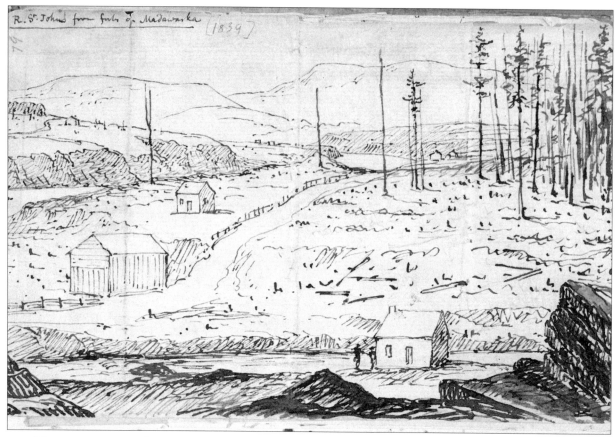

Illus 7-2: A more realistic view of a clearing at the mouth of the Madawaska River in the late 1830s. The building in the foreground belonged to Simon Hebert. It then served as an inn. The one on the other side of the river was Native captain Periz's, and the one in the background belonged to Francis Rice (see Map 7-1). Philip John Bainbrigge, "River St. Johns from Forks of Madawaska, 1839," LAC C-049610

ers apparently practiced the same kind of agriculture as seventeenth- and early eighteenth-century New Englanders: they cultivated the same piece of land for six or seven years and then turned it into pasture for the same length of time. Farmers knew about fertilizers and used manure on their potatoes; they also began to use mineral fertilizers, such as plaster of Paris, lime, and alluvial deposits, in the 1830s. There is no way to know how widespread the practice was, though, especially since farmers apparently relied on cultivating new land to maintain production levels. In 1856, New Brunswick agronomist James Robb described the process in these terms:

> Thus a virgin soil can cheaply produce at any time, and when it has been once exhausted by

cropping, the field may be laid down to pasture until fertility is restored, with another piece of the forest brought in to undergo the same treatment. This may not be the best method, but at all events, it is a natural one for poor men to follow inasmuch as it involves the least outlay of skill, labour or capital.[2]

Making a farm thus took at least ten years, during which the farmers' options were limited. He had to earn money, support his family, and buy stock and equipment, but could not expand production to meet his needs. For all practical purposes, he could only plant the fields cleared during the previous two years; the others remained covered by grass until the stumps could be removed.

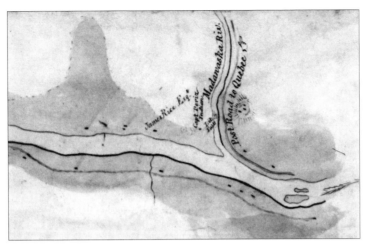

Map 7-1: Section of a map of the Saint John River by New Brunswick surveyor John Wilkinson in 1840, showing the Petit Sault in 1840. It identifies the houses of James Rice, Esq. (a British honorific title suitable for a member of Parliament), and of Native Captain Periz(?). The buildings can be seen on Illustration 7-2. The dots on top of the hill are the fort and ancillary buildings. LAC, NMC-14310-2

B. Madawaska Agriculture

Madawaska farmers likely practiced the same type of husbandry as their colleagues in other parts of New Brunswick, as well as, across the northeast frontier. Contemporary visitors' accounts comment do not suggest otherwise. Park Holland visited the settlement in 1790 while doing a survey. He noted that the settlers:

> ...have a Church and priest, cattle, horses, sheep, and hogs, raise wheat, oats, barley, and peas, and flax, and tobacco, which, though of a poor quality answer for smoking, make their own cloth, etc.... Their houses are built of logs, and those we entered were neat and in order. They make their meat into soup to which they add onion and garlic, which grow wild upon the banks of the river.[3]

The following year, another visitor, Patrick Campbell, found a thriving agricultural settlement at Madawaska. Farmers raised "the strongest crops imaginable of wheat, barley, oats, and vegetables of most kinds (except Indian corn) in great plenty." The settlers had gardens in which they grew onions, turnips, cabbages and "other garden stuffs," and yields were extremely high.[4]

The 1831 observations of American land agents Deane and Kavanagh suggest that there had been few changes since the days of Park Holland. The crops were largely the same, except for the addition of potatoes. The stock consisted of "small-boned cattle, Canadian horses, large-bodied, coarse woollen sheep, and swine."[5] The inhabitants purchased their cattle in Lower Canada. The most common type of cow in the province was a small, thrifty animal, which was, nonetheless, a good milk cow—a good choice for people with limited resources. The Canadian horse that the Valley settlers raised enjoyed such a good reputation that Lower Canadians bred it for export to the United States.

These visitor descriptions corroborate the conclusions one can draw from early statistics. Until the 1830s, settlers practiced a mixed kind of agriculture and grew as wide a variety of crops as local conditions would allow. St. John Valley agriculture was unexceptional in terms of types of crops and stock and flock varieties. The crops grown in Madawaska could be found everywhere else in eastern Canada and the northeastern United States. The stock was similar to

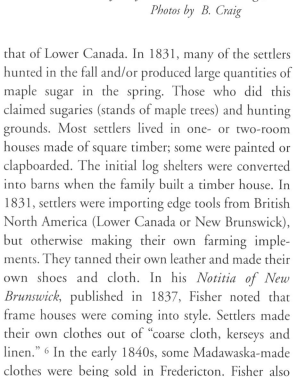

Illus. 7-3: The Roy house at the Acadian village in Van Buren is the oldest surviving house in the Valley. It dates from 1790. Note the slightly curved roof edge projecting away from the walls of the house. This roof line is similar to the one of the house on the cover, and reflects Québec influence.

Illus. 7-4: A St. John Valley cupboard from the first half of the nineteenth century. Roy House, Acadian village, Van Buren, Maine.

Photos by B. Craig

that of Lower Canada. In 1831, many of the settlers hunted in the fall and/or produced large quantities of maple sugar in the spring. Those who did this claimed sugaries (stands of maple trees) and hunting grounds. Most settlers lived in one- or two-room houses made of square timber; some were painted or clapboarded. The initial log shelters were converted into barns when the family built a timber house. In 1831, settlers were importing edge tools from British North America (Lower Canada or New Brunswick), but otherwise making their own farming implements. They tanned their own leather and made their own shoes and cloth. In his *Notitia of New Brunswick*, published in 1837, Fisher noted that frame houses were coming into style. Settlers made their own clothes out of "coarse cloth, kerseys and linen." [6] In the early 1840s, some Madawaska-made clothes were being sold in Fredericton. Fisher also claims that the settlers procured their salt and manufactured goods from Fredericton and Canada.

Visitor descriptions of the St. John Valley from the late 1830s to the early 1850s point to a shift in crops by the early to mid-nineteenth century. In his autobiography, Lieutenant Colonel Baird reminisces about a visit to the Madawaska settlement in 1838, describing loaves resembling "huge knots sliced from a tree, and the bread dark but sweet." [7] This obviously was not wheat bread. In 1851, British agronomist J. F. W. Johnston mentions the extensive cultivation of buckwheat in New Brunswick "since the wheat has become so precarious a crop." He deplored the cultivation of this plant; it was too easy to grow and, therefore, encouraged laziness among the farmers. It also forced women to cook every day when their time would have been better spent doing something else. [8] Visitors also identified the lumber camps as a market and source of employment for local people. Edmund Ward stated in 1841 that the Valley boasted several substantial farmers who raised large quantities of oats and grains "with which they supply the lumbering parties in their immediate vicinity."[9] Therefore, until the 1830s, visitors found a prosperous agricultural community. After the War of 1812, they described it as engaging in subsistence *and* market farming. Stocks seem to have remained the same throughout this period, but crop choices evolved. Wheat appears to have become a commercial crop after the War of 1812 and to have been abandoned by the late 1830s. At that time farmers switched to buckwheat and lumber camp supplies, such as oats.

II.   WHAT DID THEY EAT?

When elderly people decided to retire, they often exchanged all or part of their property for support until their death. Their exchange contracts, or deeds of maintenance, provide useful information about settlers' diets because they list in great detail everything the retirees expected to receive: food items, clothing, small cash allowances, a furnished room, and cordwood, as well as services, such as the use of a cart and horses, and funeral and memorial masses

(see more information about deeds of maintenance in Chapter 16 and examples in Appendix J). The goods were to be delivered once a year; the food items, therefore, were all nonperishable, but one can assume that fresh food was also available in season, even if was not listed. A typical retiree's food allowance can be found in Table 7-1.

Some women wanted a cow, to be fed and stabled by the person who took over their farm; they

Table 7-1: Typical Retirees' Weekly Food Allowance in the First Half of the Nineteenth Century

Food Product	Amounts
Potatoes	7 pounds
Bread*	9 pounds
Mess pork (salt pork)**	2 pounds
Beef or mutton	1 pound
Dried peas	1¼ pounds
Rice or barley (for soup)	1½ ounces
Sugar	½ pound
Butter	½ pound
Tea***	½ ounce (equivalent of about 6 tea bags)
Lard	2 ounces
Salt	½ bushel (yearly)
Pepper	Small amount
Milk, eggs, poultry, vegetables	Varied by season
Onions, cabbages and salted greens	Varied (typically stored for winter use)

* When retirees ceased to ask for "wheat made into flour," they asked instead for store-bought flour *(farine de quart or farine du magasin)*. Buckwheat was rarely mentioned in the first half of the century.
** One retiree, Leon Bellefleur, specified it must be without bones.
*** Tea consumption increased after mid century.
Sources: PANB, York County registry, 1789-1833; Carleton County registry, 1833–51; Victoria County registry, 1851–73; Fort Kent, ME, Northern Aroostook Registry of the Deeds, 1845–75.

Illus. 7-5: James Bucknall Bucknall Estcourt, "Two women and a child, Madawaska, September 1844." This sketch is one of only two pictures showing early nineteenth-century Madawaska costume; the women are wearing tops with the mutton sleeves in fashion at the time, neckerchiefs tucked into the front of their short gowns, plain petticoats, wrap-around aprons, and moccasins. The headgear does not look at all like the one contemporary Acadian women in the Maritimes were wearing. Estcourt was one of the surveyors who drew the boundary line between the United States and British North America on the ground.

Illus. 7-6: James Bucknall Bucknall Estcourt. "Two women holding two children by the hand, Madawaska." In this other sketch, the woman on the right seems to be the same as the one on the left of the previous one. Her companion is also wearing a mutton-sleeve top, and a broad-rimmed hat similar to the one worn by the woman in Illus. 9-4. LAC, C-135256 and LAC, C-135255

also asked for plowed and manured garden patches that were large enough to plant a few bushels of potatoes. While these deeds never mention any fruits or vegetables, such as apples, corn, and beans, they do occasionally include requests for chocolate or spices. Some retirees also asked for wines (especially port) or spirits (rum or brandy). The quantities were not very large (a gallon of wine a year was common). Beer and whiskey were never mentioned. And tobacco was listed with food: men requested smoking tobacco and pipes, women occasionally requested snuff.

Such food allowances provided a diet that was both qualitatively and quantitatively adequate. But it

was also bland and monotonous and would nowadays be considered too heavy in fat and salt. It also shows that some exotic items—such as rice, spices, tea, and chocolate—had made their way in the Valley diet, and that coffee and beans were not yet items of consumption. Settlers in the Valley were also clearly not prohibitionist, but they were not great drinkers either. The notebook of carpenter Joseph Audibert suggests that the consumption of alcohol was linked to the celebration of Christmas or the New Year, since he bought his liquor in December. Since wine was believed to have medicinal value, port may also have been reserved for that purpose.

Illus 7-7: We do not have any representation of Madawaska male costume. However, it seems very likely that Madawaska men wore typical French Canadian capots and soft red woollen hats, like these hunters. Hunting was a common winter activity. In this watercolor, Millicent Davis Chaplin depicted a moose hunt. LAC, C-000895

III.   CLOTHING

The only pictures we have of Madawaska female costume are rough sketchs from the 1840s; they show women wearing fashionable mutton-sleeve tops with small neckerchiefs tucked in the opening, straight skirts covered with a wraparound apron, moccasins, and conical headdresses, rather than caps. We can also form a reasonably precise picture of the composition of Madawaska wardrobes from local deeds of maintenance. In the first quarter of the century, women received every year a suit of homespun clothes ("homespun" was the name given to a type of hand-woven fabric), an under-petticoat (back then a petticoat was a skirt; the undergarment was called an under-petticoat), a calico suit, a calico *mantelet* (a type of loose blouse), a muslin cap, one to two aprons, two to three linen and flannel shirts, stockings, mittens, shoes, and cotton handkerchiefs They

might receive fabric instead of ready-made clothing.[10] Other items sometimes mentioned included silk handkerchiefs, silk bonnets, cotton stockings, umbrellas, and shawls.

Naturally, a woman's wardrobe consisted of more than the items she received every year, and worn-out clothes were recycled. New suits were likely used as Sunday best clothes, and the previous year's Sunday best clothes became the current year's daily outfit. Last year's weekday suit could be used for doing dirty work. New homespun aprons were requested so rarely it seems likely that women converted old gowns and petticoats into aprons. Cotton aprons were easier to wash, but homespun ones, which were thicker and partly made of wool, provided greater flame resistance and would have been more appropriate for doing the laundry and soap-making. Children's clothes could be made from the good parts of adults' used garments. Old woolen garments could also be cut into strips and used as weft for bed rugs (a heavy type of bead covering) or, when beyond recycling, they could be thrown into the wool churn, a tool that shredded used woolen material so that it could be re-spun and woven into blankets and other items. Women darned mittens and re-footed socks before finally tossing them into the wool churn. The best parts of used cotton garments could be turned into aprons, caps, kerchiefs, towels, baby shirts, and weft for bed rugs; the worst ones became rags.

A typical 1830s supply of men's clothing included a homespun suit, two flannel and two linen shirts, an extra pair of homespun trousers, possibly under-trousers or drawers made of wool, socks, mittens, hats, and shoes. Cotton and silk handkerchiefs, broadcloth waistcoats (or the material to make them), beaver hats, and overcoats were delivered every two to four years. Upon retirement, men usually received a great coat, which was to last them the rest of their lives.

Firmin Thibodeau, who retired in 1831, had much more sartorial tastes. He wanted, in addition to the usual annual allotment, a complete suit of "super fine cloth," half a dozen homespun and as many fine shirts, five pairs of moccasins, shoes and

boots, a beaver hat, a silk one, and two cambric and two cotton handkerchiefs., His wife did not request anything unusual, except black worsted stockings and six shirts instead of the customary three. But she wanted her clothes to be made of the best material. If the Thibodeaux were typical of other settlers, well-to-do men were much fancier dressers than their wives. And, as early as the late 1820s, prominent men frequently wore fine garments, beaver hats, and silk handkerchiefs as neckties.

Cotton had appeared in women's wardrobes as early at the turn of the century, but only for small items: handkerchiefs, muslin caps, and calico nightcaps. One exception was Frosine Martin, who requested a calico gown or petticoat and short gown as early as 1805. She, however, requested one that would last "forever." This was not an article for daily wear. By the 1820s, cotton suits and mantelets were becoming normal components of a woman's wardrobe, along with cotton aprons. By the 1850s, cotton shirts for both men and women replaced linen ones. Silk appeared in the 1820s but was only used for bonnets and handkerchiefs or neckerchiefs. It took one to one-and-a-half yards of silk to make a bonnet, suggesting quite a bit of ruffles and flounces! (A muslin cap required only one yard.)

IV.   FAMILIES AND HOUSEHOLDS

"This man's wife has had twenty children," noted James Maclauchlan in the margin of his 1833 report on the Madawaska settlement. The man he was referring to was Lawrence Terrio. Numerous visitors to Madawaska commented on the large size of the families; all those who mentioned family size also commented on their encounters with one or more families with twenty children. This, of course, fits the traditional view of French Canadian families as extremely large. A lot of people also continue to believe that girls during this period married at age fifteen or sixteen and boys at eighteen; that the couple would then have twenty children (one every year);

and that the man and wife were dead before their forty-fifth birthdays, the women presumably from childbirth. There is, of course, a slight problem with dying young in childbirth and simultaneously producing twenty children. Demographers have shown that this was far from an accurate picture of past families. This finding holds true for Madawaska families, as well.

For example, Laurent Thériault married Reine Cyr in 1808. They indeed had twenty children, but since eight of them died before their first birthday, they did not have a twenty-children-strong family. They were also very unusual: only three couples mar-

Table 7-2: Average age at First Marriage, Madawaska Marriages, 1792–1842

	Born in Madawaska	Born Outside Madawaska
Men	25	31
Women	21	26

Sources: St. Basile parish register, 1792–1842; St. Bruno parish register, 1838–42.

ried before 1840 had twenty children. So what did the "typical" Madawaska family look like?

Men and women did not marry in their teens, and the children of immigrants married significantly later than the others (see Table 7-2). On the other hand, very few people never married. Marriage was common, in part, because it was an economic necessity. Marriage was a means of making a living for both men and women because a family farm could not function smoothly without a male and female at the helm. Priests put forward this economic function of marriage when they asked the bishop for permission to marry cousins (marriages between first and second cousins were prohibited by the Church unless there were some extremely compelling reasons to allow them; marriages between third cousins also required special permission, but they were more readily granted).

The following statements written by the Madawaska priests illustrate this point:

1821: "A widower for a year and a half, he wants to marry his first cousin. He has several young children and needs somebody to keep his house. The girl is hardly twenty, but cannot expect any inheritance, and her suitor is a well-off party."

1822: "He is in a position to support his uncle [the bride's father] better than any of his children."

1826: "The girl does not have a mother and is forced to hire herself as a servant."[11]

The list goes on. Newly married couples were getting established: they were creating a new economic unit, and this unit was expected to become quickly self-supporting. In a way, young people in Madawaska married for the same reason young people these days take jobs: to be able to support themselves and become independent from their parents.

Despite those practical considerations, marriage was not purely mercenary. The priest's letters sometimes allude to an emotional dimension, as well. A young man told he would never be allowed to marry his first cousin kept coming back in tears, for instance. She was clearly the love of his life, and that was that. (A new bishop eventually approved the union.)

Because marriage was an economic necessity, one would expect widows and widowers to remarry at the first opportunity. But this is not what happened. Older widows and widowers were more likely to remain unmarried. Younger men were far more likely to remarry than younger women (see Table 7-3). Children were the determining factor. Men with young children were desperate for a wife, since they had no clue how to care for infants. But men were not very willing to marry a woman with her own little ones whom they would have to support. Men also remarried faster than women (see Table 7-4). The "marriage market" clearly discriminated against widows with children.

Even though families were not as large as initially assumed, married couples did have lots of children—an average of 10.3 per completed family. (A completed family is one where neither the husband not the wife died before the wife's forty-fifth birthday.) Families usually had thirteen or fourteen children.

Table 7-3: Rates of Remarriage, 1792 -1842

	Women		Men	
	Number	Percentage	Number	Percentage
Total number of widows and widowers	68		138	
Remarried	42	49 %	95	69 %
Did not remarry	44	51 %	43	31 %
Older than 45 when widowed and not remarrying	24	55 %	25	58 %

Sources: St. Basile parish register, 1792-1842; St. Bruno parish register, 1838–42.

Table 7-4: Distribution of Widowed People Who Remarried, by Length of Widowhood

	Men	Women
Less than a year	44%	29%
1 year	26%	34%
2 years	7%	19%
3 or more years	22%	19%

Sources: St. Basile parish register, 1792–1842; St. Bruno parish register, 1838–42.

Babies, however, did not appear every year like clockwork. The first one usually came along ten to thirteen months after the marriage. After that, babies were born, on average, every year and a half; that interval lengthened as the woman got older. The last ones were usually three years apart. Very few women had children past age forty-three. Madawaska enjoyed an unusually low infant mortality rate. (Infant mortality refers to children who die before they reach their first birthday.[12]). Families with thirteen to fourteen children rarely had that many children living at home at the same time. By the time the youngest came along, the oldest were gone.

Despite the burden such large families must have been, Madawaska parents did not put their children into service as New Englanders had done in the colonial period. According to the 1850 and 1851 censuses, 85 percent of children ages fifteen years and older still lived at home with their parents. Children not living with their parents or a close relative, such as an older brother, are listed as orphans, lodgers, or servants. Children under age ten are usually listed as orphans, ten- to fifteen-year-olds are listed mostly as servants, and children over age fifteen are almost always listed as servants. Ten then appears to have been the age at which children were expected to "pull their weight."

Servants in Madawaska were substitutes for the children one did not have, and were usually adolescent. In 1851, the median age was eighteen for female servants and twenty for male servants. This means that half the female servants were under age nineteen and half the males were under age twenty-one. Few families with servants had more than one, and three out of four families with servants did not have children older than fifteen. However, the heads of these households were usually old enough to be their servants' parents. Two out of three servants were also males. Apparently, Madawaska families believed it was the man of the house who needed help, not the mother with her brood. Alternately, women may have relied on informal help networks and "borrowed" girls for a day or two.

V.   THE WORLD OF THOMAS MARTIN AND MARIE-LUCE CYR

Statistics, however, tell us little about the nature and quality of family life. To understand that, one needs qualitative sources, such as letters, diaries, memoirs, and autobiographies. Unfortunately, these kinds of sources are almost nonexistent in the Valley, with one exception: five letters sent to carpenter Joseph Audibert between 1852 and 1854 (see Appendix N). Three were sent to Audibert at Fort Kent by his sisters and brother-in-law from Quebec City and two—one from his father-in-law Chrysostome "Thomas" Martin, and another from his mother-in-law, Marie-Luce Cyr—were sent to Portland, where he, his wife and a sister-in-law spent the summer of 1852. His reasons for being in Portland are not known.[13]

Thomas and Marie-Luce's letters are particularly interesting. Because neither of them could write, they dictated their letters to their neighbor, school teacher Jacques Hamel. Unaware of letter-writing conventions, they said what they felt and narrated events occurring around them in the same way they would have verbally updated someone coming back after an absence. The letters are thus detailed and spontaneous.

The tone of each letter is affectionate, but not overly sentimental. The letters also seem to suggest that the writer and recipient were comfortable sharing their feelings with each other. Marie Luce made critical but good-natured observations on her little society. The atmosphere suffusing the letters is surprisingly genteel. Jane Austen and her characters would have felt at home in the Valley.

Thomas, on the other hand, wears his heart on his sleeve. He starts his letter with these words:

I received your affectionate letter dated from the 11 current, which caused us as you can expect the greatest pleasure in learning that you were all in perfect health. I told myself the Lord deign answer our prayers. I bless him and would bless him even more if he deigned make our wishes come true and bring you back among us.

Thomas clearly misses his children a lot and does not hesitate to say so, but avoids falling into typical Victorian mawkishness. He sounds more like an eighteenth-century "Man of Feelings": emotions are natural; emotionalism is silly. Conversely, his wife seems more inclined to convey her feelings through actions rather than words. Joseph Audibert's sisters articulate their feelings in the same manner as Thomas. They also believed that it is natural for morally deserving people (like their brother) to acquire a good station in life.

Thomas and Marie-Luce missed their adult children who had left Madawaska. Children's deaths however did not elicit very emotional responses from their family. The death of a grandchild shortly after birth is merely mentioned. The young mother's reaction seems to have been one of anger rather than sorrow: she would have two the next year. It is as if she were saying: "And there, Death! *That* will show you!" A four-year-old drowning in the river is "bad news," but not of the kind one wants to linger on. None of this, of course, means that people did not care about their children. Rather, they were used to children dying and, since there was little one could do about it, they would shed their tears and move on. Their attitude was similar, it seems, to the way we handle the death of elderly people today. But as the children got older, they were less likely to die, and families became increasingly attached to them. It was the departure of the twenty-something one had expected to have for neighbors until one died that was a cause for grief.

The family clearly provided a mutual help network. Audibert's absence from Fort Kent was possible because his father-in-law was taking care of his affairs. Thomas for example, had someone shear his daughter's sheep. He wanted to know whether she wanted the wool processed, or sent to her in Portland as is. Thomas also cut his son-in-law's hay. In return, he asked Joseph to inquire about a logging permit for him while he was downstate. Thomas Martin also made use of his son-in-law's Quebec City connection to get mercantile information, namely the price of flour. Audibert used the same Quebec City relatives to acquire a lathe, which his brother-in-law shipped to him; José Nadeau, another of Thomas Martin's son-in-law, used the same channel to obtain trade goods from the same place.

In addition to mutual help networks, the families also served as information conduits. Martin and Audibert acquired information, official documents, and goods through personal contacts. Friends and acquaintances further extended and reinforced those networks. Audibert's sisters got news from their brother, not only through letters, but also through people traveling between Quebec City and the Valley. Audibert's wife Marguerite would have got her fleece through a Mr. Jackson who traveled back and forth between the Valley and Portland. And neither literacy nor even the sending of letters was required to exchange information.

Madawaskayans were also quite mobile. The three Audibert sisters paid a visit to their brother in 1854. They were, however, of modest means, since their husbands were blue collar workers (a carpenter, a shoemaker, and a day laborer.) Vacations were not for the middle or upper class only. Audibert went to Portland with his family for a stay that was clearly not meant to be permanent since he kept his meadow and flock back in the Valley. Jacques Hamel, the school teacher, went back and forth between Quebec City (where he worked as a ship carpenter) and

Madawaska (where he taught school). Hamel's father-in-law, courier Philip Long, had lived on Témiscouata Lake.[14] When he died, his daughter Suzanne went to Quebec City, her mother's hometown, where she met and married Hamel. And as the letters indicate, the Great Lakes states exercised an irresistible attraction for many.

The letters also provide us with a glimpse of leisure activities during that time in the Valley. For example, summer was clearly wedding season, and weddings presented the perfect opportunity for dancing. Everybody joined in. These dances, however, were very different from contemporary, and even late nineteenth- and early twentieth-century dances. One did not dance in pairs. Marie-Luce Cyr's description suggests figure dances or even some form of pantomime. Dancing was a very energetic activity—it splintered the floorboards. Marie-Luce commented that "you would have thought that any moment they were going to fall into pieces, but they came out of there in one piece as they got into and I can assure you that they had more luck than the floorboards because splinters were flying all over the place." Thomas threw himself wholeheartedly into the activity, under the amused gaze of his wife.

The letters reveal a world of close-knit, affectionate families, relying on each other to carry out the ordinary business of life, but they also suggest Madawaskayans were a bit old-fashioned when it came to leisure.

Conclusions

Paul-Louis Martin, in a review of Jane Cook's book on the material culture of the St. John Valley in the nineteenth century, dismissed the Madawaska area as a minuscule settlement, almost completely cut off from the rest of the world.[15] The statement is inaccurate but excusable. The image of pioneer communities as small and isolated is an enduring one—and the location of the Madawaska settlement, which lay miles from other inhabited areas, adds to the stereotype.

However, one should not confuse distance and rudimentary means of communication with isolation. We saw in the previous chapter that the Valley's remoteness did not prevent trade. Nor was trade a one-way street. The Valley sold grain and timber to outsiders—and used the proceeds to acquire what were then called "new groceries" (tea, spices, sugar, chocolate, and tobacco), as well as products such as rice and cotton from southern states. The retirees' allowances show that by the 1830s exotic goods were commonly consumed in the Valley. One should not, therefore, assume that just because a community had the means to be self sufficient, it ignored or avoided trading opportunities.

The Martin, Audibert, and Hamel families also show that, in the early nineteenth century, ordinary people had developed very effective communication mechanisms. They used these mechanisms not only to get news about each other, but also to gain information about trade, get their paperwork done, and obtain "mail order" goods unavailable locally. Even outside fashion influenced the way people dressed. The Valley's openness to the outside world—a theme that emerged in the previous chapter—is thus corroborated by those few letters.

Madawaska's links with the outside world depended, in large part, on personal, and often family, networks. Internally, Madawaska economy and society were also structured through family networks. Marriage was consequently a momentous event in a young person's life. Not only was it the union of two people who were attracted to each other (there are no indications whatsoever that parents controlled their children's marriages), but it was also the founding of a new productive and reproductive unit, which integrated and extended existing networks.

ENDNOTES
1. Baillie, *Account of the Province of New Brunswick*, 17.
2. Robb, *Agricultural Progress*, 15.
3. Bangor Historical Society, Bangor, ME. Transcript of: Park Holland, "Life and Diary," unpublished manuscript, 1790, n.p.
4. Campbell, *Travels in the Interior*, 97.

5. Deane and Kavanagh, "Report," 455–56.
6. Fisher, *Notitia of New Brunswick*, 98.
7. Baird, *Seventy Years of New Brunswick Life*, 90. Johnston also described the local bread as a dark one made from a mixture of buckwheat, barley, and rye. A bread made of one part each wheat, rye, buckwheat, and barley is indeed dark and sweet—and surprisingly very palatable. Johnston, *Report on Agricultural Capabilities*, 69.
8. Johnston, *Report on Agricultural Capabilities*, 68 and 79.
9. Ward, *Account of the St. John*, 86.
10. A suit required seven to eight yards of material; a short gown or blouse took two to three yards; and an apron or a cap took one yard.
11. AAQ, Lettres des prêtres missionnaires du Madawaska à l'Évêque de Québec, 1792–1850.
12. When Marcella Sorg and B. Craig calculated Madawaska's infant mortality rate in 1983, it was the lowest known infant mortality rate in seventeenth- to nineteenth-century North America: Sorg and Craig. "Patterns of Infant Mortality in the Upper St. John Valley."
13. A copy of the Audibert papers is available at the Acadian Archives at the University of Maine at Fort Kent.
14. Philip signed his name "Long" with an "o"; his descendants spell it with either an "o" or an "a."
15. "Un îlot relativement clos, presque un isolat social": Martin, review of Cook, 610.

FURTHER READING
The texts listed in the previous chapter are also appropriate for this one.
Dubay, Guy. *Chez Nous: The St John Valley*. 1983: 87–103.
Acadian Culture in Maine, http://acim.umfk.maine. edu. Section 3, "Maine Acadians and the Land."

SOURCES
See Craig's report entitled "Madawaska families and households, 1785–1850" at the Acadian Archives, as well as Craig and Sorg on infant mortality (1983). For descriptions of Madawaska and New Brunswick farming and pioneer life see Baird (1890), Baillie (1832), Campbell (1792), Deane and Kavanagh, "Report" (1831), "Wilderness Journey" (1980), Fisher (1839), Gesner (1847), Johnston (1850 and 1851), Holland (1780), McGregor (1828 and 1832), New Brunswick and Nova Scotia Land Company (1843), Robb (1856), Ward (1841), and Joseph Treat's journal in Pawling (2007). The *Lettres des prêtres missionnaires du Madawaska à l'évêque de Québec, 1792–1850*, located at the Archives de l'Archevêché de Québec, have been microfilmed and are available through interlibrary loan.

8

HOW MADAWASKA BECAME PART OF NEW BRUNSWICK

In 1783, Charles Nichau Noite (see Chapter 4 and Appendix D) was tried in Quebec City for a murder committed in the Valley, because the Québec authorities considered Madawaska as part of their province. New Brunswick soon challenged this belief, and the matter was referred to Great Britain in 1792. By that time, the disagreement between Britain and the United States about the exact location of the international boundary had surfaced, and the matter of the interprovincial boundary was left in abeyance. In the following years, New Brunswick exercised jurisdiction over the Madawaska territory. It promptly integrated the Madawaska settlers into its own political system, administrative and legal structure, and defense organization. Canada however did not relinquish her claims to the area, and reasserted them after the international boundary was established in 1842. The Catholic Church, for its part, continued to treat the Madawaska territory as a *de facto* part of Québec.

I. HOW NEW BRUNSWICK ACQUIRED A PANHANDLE

A. Bad Maps Make Fuzzy Boundaries

Britain acquired Canada in 1763 through the Treaty of Paris, and the king immediately issued a proclamation (the Proclamation of 1763), which, among other articles, defined the southern boundary of the province, now renamed the province of Québec:

> Along the Highlands which divide the river that empty themselves into the ... river St. Lawrence from those which fall into the sea, and also along the North Coast of the bay of Chaleurs....

This boundary was reaffirmed by the Québec Act of 1774, and the northern boundary of Nova Scotia (which New Brunswick inherited in 1784) was always described as identical to the southern boundary of Québec.

The Treaty of 1783, which recognized the independence of the thirteen American colonies, defined the northern boundary of Massachusetts (in the District of Maine) as identical to the southern boundary of Québec. The boundary between Massachusetts and Nova Scotia followed the St. Croix River to its source, and then proceeded due north until it crossed the Highlands described above. The treaty negotiators had relied on Mitchell's map of 1755, but the map contained many errors, and gave wrong names to some of the rivers. In reality, no river was called St. Croix. Difficulties arose immediately: which of three local rivers approximately fitting the description of the "St. Croix" was the true one, as none bore that particular name. The Americans, of course, argued that St. Croix referred to the easternmost river, but the British claimed it was the westernmost ones (see Map 9-1). A British-American commission chose the river now renamed St. Croix in 1798 and drew the due north line, which cut across the St. John River a few miles west of Grand Falls.

B. New Brunswick Reaches North

The "Highlands" turned out to be equally problematic. No unbroken height of land divides the St. Lawrence River watershed from the rivers flowing into the Atlantic Ocean. In addition, a boundary line following this watershed line would have placed Témiscouata Lake outside the limits of Québec. However, in the seventeenth century, Québec had granted the lake and the land surrounding it as a seigneury. The land on the southern tip of the lake was, thus, historically part of Québec.

Controversy broke out when New Brunswick issued the first location tickets at Madawaska in 1787. The surveyor generals of the two provinces, who were supposed to draw the line, disagreed on its location. Samuel Holland, the Canadian surveyor, proposed a line from the Restigouche to the Grand Falls, which New Brunswick surveyor George Sproule immediately rejected as contrary to common sense. By that time, Governor-in-Chief Lord Dorchester had grasped the implications of the drawing of that line: the farther to the north the interprovincial boundary line was drawn, the farther to the north the international boundary would be.

The committee appointed by Dorchester to consider the matter, noted that the old seigneury was located south of the watershed line, but also took into account the new settlement:

> Beside, the Accadians [*sic*] already settled above the great falls of the St. John River, and such people as may chuse hereafter to settle there would be greatly incommodated [*sic*] if these parts should be included in the province of New Brunswick. Their commercials dealings will be with this country for they must from their situation be supplied with European and West Indian commodities from Quebec.[1]

Sproule, on the other hand, claimed that the Acadians wanted to remain part of New Brunswick. And in a 1790 letter to British Secretary of State Grenville. New Brunswick Lieutenant-Governor Carleton referred to a petition presented by the Madawaska Acadians stating they wished to remain under New Brunswick jurisdiction.

C. Double Jurisdiction

For a brief period both provinces exercised jurisdiction over the Madawaska territory. In July 1787, the Québec Executive Council was still authorizing its surveyor general to provide grants to would-be Madawaska settlers, especially Acadians. Dorchester commissioned Acadian brothers François and Jacques Cyr as captain and lieutenant of the militia in September 1790, and it appears that Madawaska debtors were sued in Quebec City. Québec authorities included the Madawaska territory in their 1790 census as well. After appointing the Cyr brothers, Dorchester informed his younger brother Carleton that the best way to avoid problems stemming from the uncertain jurisdiction over the area was for the governors of each province to commission the same men as militia officers. Carleton promised to do just that, but there is no evidence that he commissioned the Cyr brothers in the New Brunswick militia. Furthermore, Carleton informed his brother Dorchester that militia officers were not allowed to exercise civil jurisdiction in New Brunswick since they were in Québec. Therefore, he suggested appointing justices of the peace, and proposed the names of Pierre Duperré and Louis Mercure. Dorchester must have reminded his brother that justices of the peace had to be Protestant and, therefore, Duperré and Mercure did not qualify. Militia officers were allowed to exercise civil powers in Québec precisely to go around that requirement. The double jurisdiction was therefore tricky to administer. Carleton appointed Thomas Costin, a Protestant residing in Madawaska, justice of the peace for the territory in March 1791. The New Brunswick government also promised Madawaska land to settlers in 1785, issued location tickets in 1787, and granted land in 1790 and 1794.

D. Conflicts

This situation could not last very long. Matters came to a head in 1789, following a turf war between men trading with Natives. That May, Duperré, Augustin Dubé, also a trader, and some of their men intercepted a few canoes belonging to the Robichaud brothers and seized their goods, alleging the Robichauds' license to trade with Natives was invalid. Then in July, Mercure, Duperré, and Costin asked the New Brunswick authorities to appoint a judge and a militia captain at Madawaska (see Sidebar 8-1). In August, Robichaud sued Duperré and Dubé for loss of trade in the Québec Court of Common Pleas. Duperré and Dubé argued the court had no jurisdiction over the area as it was part of New Brunswick. The judge, however, rejected their claim and found them guilty in September 1790; an arbitrator estimated damages in January 1791. That summer, justice of the peace Costin informed officials in Fredericton that he had fined the Robichauds £5 for causing a disturbance and selling liquor to the Native. In November 1791, the *Quebec Gazette* published a notice that the sheriff was going to sell Duperré's Madawaska property, but it is not clear whether this action was carried out.

The following year, the Robichaud brothers won another suit in recovery of debt before the Court of Common Pleas, this time against Duperré's neighbor, François Albert. François and Jacques Cyr were charged with seizing and auctioning some of Albert's goods. Costin arrested Jacques Cyr and jailed him at the Grand Falls barracks. Cyr had to compensate Albert to secure his release but was subsequently refunded by the Québec government. Québec then called on the mother country to settle the dispute. But by that time, the disagreement between the United States and Britain over the boundary was beginning to surface. Dorchester appealed to his brother's patriotism and Carleton let the matter rest. In 1798, the St. Croix question was settled, but this decision placed the entire Madawaska district west of the boundary. The only way for Britain to hold onto the Madawaska region was to claim a line south of the Grand Falls, which she did.

E. Britain Steps In

Although New Brunswick stopped pressing its boundary claim, it did not stop exercising *de facto* jurisdiction over Madawaska. Britain confirmed this situation in 1830. The Colonial Office's identical instructions to the governors of both provinces delineated the territory over which they had jurisdiction. The old Madawaska seigneury and the land west of the Madawaska River went to Canada, and the remainder to New Brunswick.

II. CIVIL GOVERNMENT IN NEW BRUNSWICK UNTIL 1845

In many ways being a resident of Québec—or Lower Canada as it was called after 1791—rather than New Brunswick did not make much difference. Both provinces were meant to be oligarchic societies governed by close-knit gentries, parliaments on a tight leash, and an established, or state, church. The latter was, of course, the Protestant Church of England, although the Catholic Church had a semi-official status in Lower Canada. By 1783, British people on both sides of the Atlantic had concluded that Britain had lost the thirteen American colonies due to too much democracy in their government. The errors of the past had to be avoided in the remaining colonies, and, when the United States descended into anarchy, as surely it would, British North America would stand as a beacon of peace, order, and good government. In one respect, however, being a resident of Lower Canada, as opposed to New Brunswick, did matter: New Brunswick Catholics were subjected to discriminatory laws much longer than Lower Canadians, and this hindered their ability to take part in the governing process.

A. Governors and Councils

Throughout British North America, provincial constitutions strengthened the powers of the London-appointed governors, kept elected assemblies under control by limiting their power and the right to vote, and restricted input in local government.[2] Local government as we know it was nonexistent. At the head of the system were the provincial lieutenant governors.[3] These London appointees were normally career officers from the mother country. They held this office "at the pleasure of the Crown" and could, therefore, be replaced at any time. ("The Crown" was the term used to refer to the government; in this case, it meant the one in London.) These lieutenant governors were accountable to London, not to the provincial assembly. A council of their choosing assisted them in their executive functions. The legislative branch of the government included a legislative council, also appointed by the lieutenant governor, and an elected assembly. Since the population of New Brunswick was small, the same men sat on both councils. In 1834 London ordered the two councils to be made of (mostly) different men.

B. Local Government

1. Counties, Parishes, and Quarter Sessions

The governor and Council, as the executive branch was then known, appointed people equivalent to modern-day civil servants, such as customs officers and postmasters. Sheriffs, responsible for county law and order, were similarly Crown appointees. Patronage, in the form of government appointments, was a way to reward supporters. The governor and Council also appointed the men in charge of local government. The province was divided into counties, further divided into civil parishes. The counties were the units of local government. The Madawaska territory initially consisted of "unassigned" land in York County. This area became part of the newly established Parish of Kent in 1821. It became a civil parish in 1833 when the northern part of York County

became Carleton County. The new Parish of Madawaska included all territories in Carleton County north of the Parish of Perth (see Maps 8-1 and 8-2).

Until 1877, local government in New Brunswick used the English system of "sessions and grand juries." (England had established the same system in Colonial Virginia.) The governor and Council appointed parish magistrates, or justices of the peace, to govern the counties. The justices of the peace for each county met a few times a year in sessions to handle judiciary matters as well as appoint and supervise the work of county and parish officials. Their powers were extensive: they managed statute labor (compulsory work repairing local roads and bridges); regulated ferries, booms, timber driving, and local markets; ordered the collection of taxes for common jails, workhouses, almshouses, and parish police; issued regulations to prevent vices, such as the profanation of the Sabbath, abating public nuisances, and preventing animals from running at large; licensed inns and taverns; enforced provincial laws regarding public health, Crown land (public land), navigation, highways, and the militia; and appointed parish officers in charge of day-to-day operations. These parish officers included an overseer of the poor, market clerk (if there was a market), constables, parish assessors, parish clerk, fence viewers (the men who made sure no one encroached on their neighbor's property by moving their fence), pound keepers, hog reeves (who dealt with runaway pigs), and sundry others deemed necessary.

2. The Grand Juries

The democratic elements in this system should have been provided by the provincial assembly and grand juries. The grand juries' influence however, was limited both by the way their members were chosen and the restrictions placed on their power. In New Brunswick, only jurors owning real estate worth at least £10 ($40) or a personal estate worth at least £100 could be appointed. They played a judicial role by deciding whether or not there was sufficient evi-

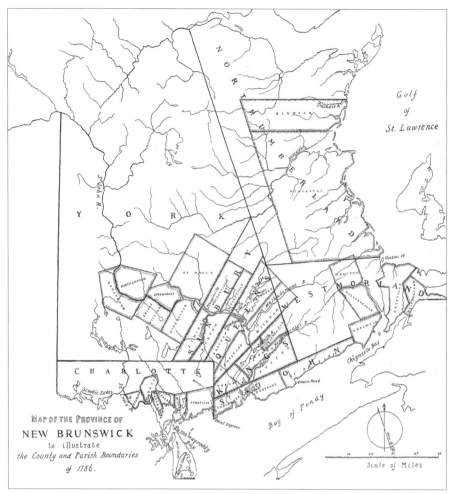

Map 8-1: New Brunswick County and civil parish boundaries in 1786; W. F. Ganong,
"Monograph of the Evolution of the Boundaries of the Province of New Brunswick,"
Proceedings and Transactions of the Royal Society of Canada, 1901, 418.

dence to put accused people on trial. Their governmental role, on the other hand, was purely advisory. (They proposed names for parish officers, for instance.)

On paper, it may appear as if the governor and Council controlled both the sessions and grand juries. In practice, however, governors did not wield that much power, especially in rural areas, because the number of people suitable for a given position was usually very small. Governors tried to appoint men who had some wealth (which gave them limited immunity from community pressure), some educa-

tion (since records had to be kept), and preferably the respect of their communities. Nominations, therefore, inevitably went to a community's leading men—and, despite the formal authority the governors exercised over them—competent appointees exercised considerable managerial freedom over their counties. The lack of local democracy does not seem to have bothered people too much: the most common complaints were not that the system was undemocratic, but that the justices of the peace were incompetent or abused their powers.

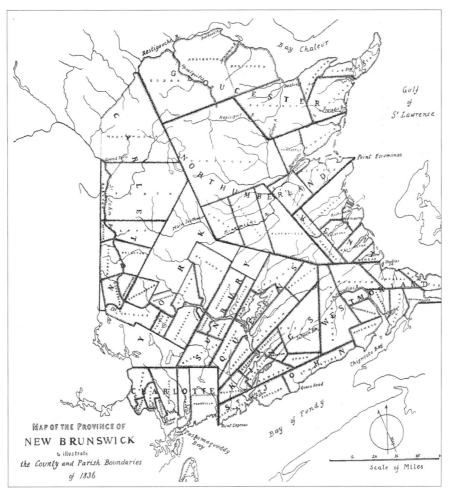

Map 8-2: *New Brunswick County and parish boundaries in 1836; W. F. Ganong,*
"Monograph of the Evolution of the Boundaries of the Province of New Brunswick,"
Proceedings and Transactions of the Royal Society of Canada,1901, 424.

3. Local Government at Madawaska

Few records about Madawaska local government exist for the years between 1785 and 1845. We have seen that Thomas Costin, a Protestant married to a Catholic woman, was appointed justice of the peace in 1791. He was relieved of his function in 1796, but no one replaced him for years. James MacLauchlan, warden of the disputed territory after 1825, was also a justice of the peace and thus could serve the Madawaska population. The next local person to become a justice of the peace was Irish schoolmaster Francis Rice. He was appointed in 1830 after dis-

criminatory laws against Catholics were finally abolished. Leonard Reed Coombs, a Protestant, was the next appointee in 1833. C. A. Hammond joined their ranks in 1842. The government still preferred Protestants, as well as people who spoke English and had some education.

The identity of parish officers remains even more elusive. An undated document written by Costin (who left the territory by 1799) lists Simon Hébert and Pierre Lizotte as surveyors, Bénoni Thériault and François Thibodeau as constables, and François Martin as road commissioner. Existing county records

Francis Rice tried to convince Dr. Landry, the military surgeon at Fort Ingal, to settle at Madawaska. In a letter to his fiancée, Landry described Rice in those terms:

> *You have often heard me mention Mr. Rice and surely, you want to know something about him. He is a militia captain and magistrate at Madawaska. He has been busy supervising the construction of a new road to that place, This is why he is staying here. He is Irish and well educated, and owns his fortune to his talents. He left his father's house when he was a young man to come to Canada with an uncle, and fate wanted that they be shipwrecked on the Isle Rouge opposite Ilse Verte. He lost everything, and for a few years had to rely on the help of charitable people for his support. He started in the world, far from his family, with nothing, and at present can be proud of himself. He has the trust of the governor of the province, to the point of being able to advise him. He is 39; his countenance is open and honest and he is generous and sensible.*

Source: Dr. Jean Landry to Caroline Lelièvre, August 19, 1839.

cover the years 1821 to 1823 and 1832 to 1833. Parish officers, such as highway surveyors, fence viewers, and clerks, were almost all drawn from charter families (families established at Madawaska before 1800). For example, Pierre Duperré and Michel Mercure served as highway commissioners and overseers of the poor during the 1820s; similarly David Cyr and Anselme Albert were pound keepers. Léon and Antoine Bellefleur, who could read and write, were parish clerks from 1821 to 1823. There was not an English name in sight during those two years. Two English names, however, appeared between 1832 and 1833: Leonard Coombs and Michael Tighe (an Irish-Catholic man married to a woman from a charter family) were parish clerks; Coombs was also a highway commissioner. Even before Madawaska became a separate parish, it was administered by its residents and, although the record keeping positions went to English-speakers during the early 1830s, other positions remained in French hands.

Distances, however, discouraged Madawaska residents from using most government services. One had to go to Fredericton, or later Woodstock, to go to court, probate wills, administer estates, or register deeds. Consequently, French names are very few and far between in those records. According to Maine land agents Deane and Kavanagh, people used local arbitrators instead of going to court.

This scattered evidence suggests that Madawaska settlers, like residents of other parishes, took part in local government. But one can see that their religion was a serious obstacle until 1830 and worked to their disadvantage even afterwards; illiteracy and lack of

English also limited the offices they could fill. The need to travel long distances further discouraged them from using government services.

C. The House of Assembly

1. A Not-So-Deferential Body

Local government was, in reality, assumed by the House of Assembly, which made local laws and retain power over the purse. The New Brunswick House of Assembly's journal is cluttered with pieces of legislation and appropriations that look more like local housekeeping issues than matters of concern to a *provincial* assembly.

The House of Assembly was the only elected governing body. This soon turned it into a forum where one expressed dissatisfaction or voiced complaints. This occurred despite the fact its members were not democratically chosen. The first two houses, elected in 1785 and 1791, had both cooperated with and deferred to the wishes of the lieutenant governor. But when the economy took a turn for the worse in the late 1780s, the lieutenant governor was held responsible. An opposition made up of all those who felt excluded from Carleton's Loyalist New Brunswick appeared in the assembly during the early 1790s. Among its members were Stair Agnew, a large Fredericton landowner who rejoined the rank of the governor's supporters after 1800, and the far more radical James Glennie, who denounced the government's incompetence and wastefulness.[4] One example of this incompetence and wastefulness was the expenditures on garrisons at Presqu' Isle and Grand Falls to protect settlements that everyone but the lieutenant governor, knew were on American soil. The House of Assembly's ability to impose its view was, however, limited by the fact all colonial laws had to be approved by the province's Legislative Council, the lieutenant governor, and London officials. The lieutenant governors could also dissolve a contrary assembly, which is exactly what Carleton did in 1795, when the House of Assembly vetoed a defense appropriation.

2. Voting Rights

The right to vote for the House of Assembly, or franchise, was not universal. It was limited to freeholders (people who owned a piece of land) worth £25 ($100) or more. Candidates had to own a freehold worth at least £200. Restricting the franchise to property owners was the norm, not the exception, during the late eighteenth and early nineteenth centuries; this was a way to limit formal political participation to the "middling sort" and their better. Property qualifications were even the norm in the United States until the 1820s. Because the vote was not secret (voters informed the sheriff of their choice), landlords and employers could easily blackmail poor people. The vote was, therefore, restricted to people who were economically independent. But it was not hard for muscled or armed supporters of a given candidate to intimidate property owners as well. Elections were often rowdy, if not downright violent, affairs. Voting irregularities were also quite common as the sheriff, who supervised the elections, sometimes allowed ineligible people to vote or, prevented eligible people from voting.

3. Catholics' Political Rights

Political rights were not immediately extended to Catholics. In Britain, Catholics had very few rights, and public opinion was not in favor of extending them. Nova Scotia had followed the English lead: members of the assembly and of councils had to take the state oaths: they swore allegiance to the king and his Protestant heirs (Oath of Allegiance), denied the temporal authority of the pope, although not the spiritual one (Oath of Supremacy), and rejected the Stuarts' claims to the throne (Oath of Abjuration). They also had to subscribe to the Declaration against Transubstantiation (denying a fundamental Catholic belief).[5] Voters had to take the oaths and make the declaration when asked by the sheriff. The decision was entirely up to him. Catholicism could, therefore, disqualify voters.

Some Catholics voted in the pre-1795 New Brunswick elections, but the assembly invalidated the results, declaring the Catholic votes as contrary to the laws of England. By then, however, the disfranchisement of Catholics was no longer the norm in the rest of British North America. Nova Scotia had given Catholics the right to vote in 1789 and Upper and Lower Canada followed suit in 1791. New Brunswick's first electoral laws in 1795 required voters to take the state oaths but not the declaration. Whereas the Oaths of Allegiance and Abjuration posed no problems for Catholic voters, many found the Oath of Supremacy hard to swallow. In 1795, legislators were still in no hurry to enfranchise Catholics. By the early 1800s, however, the wind had turned. Peter Fraser, a reformer elected in 1810, introduced a bill that would enfranchise Catholics.[6] The new law called for a religiously neutral oath of allegiance in place of the state oaths. Catholics, however, could not be elected to public office, since members of the assembly still had to take the state oaths and make the declaration. In 1829, Britain passed the Catholic Emancipation Act, and New Brunswick followed suit in 1830. Madawaska settlers, however, remained at a disadvantage. The British government had stopped issuing land grants in the territory due to the boundary dispute. Only the holders of one of the seventy-four eighteenth-century grants were eligible to vote. As far as we know, these individuals took part in elections. Elections, however, occurred at the county level. York County, to which Madawaska belonged until 1833, was entitled to four members, who usually came from the southern part of the county. Carleton County was entitled to two members, who were almost always from the Woodstock area. The first Madawaska resident to run was Leonard Coombs in 1837, but he lost.

D. Participation of Madawaskayans in Provincial Politics

1. The 1789 Petition

Some Madawaska residents were demanding greater political rights as early as 1789. When Louis Mer-

cure, Pierre Duperré, and Thomas Costin asked for a justice of the peace and a militia captain, they did not ask Carleton to nominate them, but to call a meeting to elect them (see Sidebar 8-1). This was a peculiar, seemingly "American" request. Mercure and his group were trying to introduce bad New England practices into the king's domain. Had Carleton acquiesced, he would have erected a little Madawaska Republic on the upper St. John. Of course he knew better and did no such thing.

2. The 1795 Elections

The issue of political rights re-emerged after the elections of 1795 (the election that followed the lieutenant governor's dissolution of the assembly after it vetoed his requested military appropriation bill). In the fall of 1795, Duperré led a group of Acadians to the voting station at the Grand Falls garrison; they were told, however, that they could not vote in the provincial elections unless they took oaths contrary to their religion (see Sidebar 8-2).

Duperré's simple rendition of this story, however, is deceiving. If we look past the obvious fact that Catholics were told they could not vote, what do we see? At the Grand Falls garrison, these voters met Stair Agnew, a candidate, warning them that they would be "lost" if they took the Oaths. But Agnew was a Protestant who likely believed Catholics were "lost" anyway.[7] Moreover, what was Agnew, a resident of Fredericton, doing at Grand Falls? Especially since he claimed he was not seeking the support of the Acadians, the only non-Native people living above Woodstock? The 1795 election was an acrimonious one, which pitted the lieutenant governor and his Loyalist council against members of the assembly who were questioning his decisions and policies. Because Agnew was a member of that opposition, his presence at that polling station suddenly takes a much broader dimension. The politicians were playing games, and the Acadians had innocently, or perhaps not so innocently, begun to take part in them.

The sheriff, a government appointee, had set up a polling station in a region over which Carleton was

To the Honourable Thomas Carleton, Esqur., Lieutenant Governor and Commander in Chief of the Province of New Brunswick & & &.

Your Petitioners humbly Showeth that

The Inhabitants of this New Established Place, and Whereas it is the Desire of the Government of this Province, that this place should be settled and Regulated, And Whereas there is great Prospect of its being well Inhabited in a short Time, they humbly Requests of Your Excellency and the Honourable Council, to grant them their Request.

Two Members of the Peace, One for a judge, and the other for Captain of Militia, being well wishers to Render themselves Under the Discipline, Rules and regulations of this Province, and where as they take the Liberty of Proving our Necessity to your Honour, and the Danger of being in such a Distant Place. If your Honour dos not Take them in Consideration Then his merchants from the River Cenibeck comes trading in this Place with Merchandize and strong liquor and not Only that but gives bad advice t the Savages and Number of others who comes and gos Which we cant give Your Honour any Account of; Therefore humbly Prays That it would please Your Honour to accord to your Worthy Petitioners there demand with a Power to Examining all such strugglers and Merchants who may sell and retail liquors in this Place, or who ever thay may be found on this River without Having permission from their superiors. And has we are will wishes not Live like the Wild Nations but like Christians and submit to their lawful superiors and to defend the Law - - -

They humbly Pray of your Excellency if your Honour should accord to His Majesty's faithful Subjects their Demand, to give an Order in Writing that they may Make a general Assembly in this place and to go by Votes, which will be the most capable of undertaking the said Commissions for that purpose - - -

And thus in Duty bound prays

Your Honours,

> *Most Obedient and Most*
> *Humble Servants*
> *Louis Mercure*
> *Pierre Duperre*
> *Th Costin*

At Madawaska
July the 16th 1789

Note: The petition's handwriting looks like Duperré's. The spelling is exactly as we left it. This was obviously not written by an English-speaking person.

Source: PANB, RS-330, J-1789/1, petition of Louis Mercure.

Sidebar 8-2: Madawaska Settlers Prevented from Voting in 1796

A petition of Pierre Duperré on behalf of himself and nineteen other French Acadians, complaining that they were prevented from giving their votes at the late election in the county of York by improper representations being made to them respecting the oaths requires by law to be taken.

The petition of Pierre Duperré, most humbly showeth

That your petitioner together with 19 other French Acadians, freeholders and inhabitants of the county of York, and good faithful and loyal subjects of our gracious sovereign King George the third, appeared at the poll held at the Grand Falls for the election of members to serve for the said county in the present general assembly on the fifteenth day of September last- that your petitioner together with the said nineteen others aforementioned then and there tendered their votes at the said poll and were thereupon told by Stair Agnew esq. one of the candidates at the said election, that they, your petitioner and the said other French Acadians abovementioned, would be required to take an oath which if they should take it they would abjure their religion and be forever lost. That the said Stair Agnew esq. further at the same time informed them that he did not want their votes, but that he came to inform them of the consequences of their taking the said oath and to save them from being forever lost, that your petitioner on behalf of himself and the said others above-mentioned requested to have the said oath read and explained to them by the sheriff holding the said poll, but that the said oath was not read or offered to be read, and was not explained to your petitioner and the said others in any other manner than as abovementioned by the said Stair Agnew esq. and that your petitioner and the said others abovementioned did not themselves consent or offer to take the said oath.

That your petitioner has since seen the oaths required to be taken by law, particularly the oaths of allegiance, supremacy and abjuration translated into the French language, and now understanding the meaning thereof, is ready and willing to take the same and that he would have taken the same at the said poll, if the meaning of the same had been then explained to him; and your petitioner verily believes and has good cause to believe, that the said other French Acadians abovementioned would in like manner have taken the same had the meaning thereof been explained to them and that they are now ready and willing to take the same.

Your petitioner therefore for himself and on behalf of the said Acadians above mentioned most humbly prays to be heard by counsel at the Bar of this Honourable House to substantiate the foregoing fact, and that the votes of your petitioner and the said nineteen others may be allowed to them and be considered as good and valid for the candidates for whom they severally declared their intention to vote at the said poll, the names of which candidates appear subjoined by the said sheriff to the poll book of the said election.

And in duty bound shall ever pray

P Duperré

Note: Duperré is the only individual who signed this document (and he did it with a huge flourish!).
Source: PANB, RS24, S10, Legislative Assembly, Sessional papers, 1796, P5, February 18, 1796: 469, microfilm, reel F14923.

very eager to assert the province's jurisdiction against Canadian claims and American pretenses (the due-north line between New Brunswick and Maine was not agreed upon until 1798). Unfortunately, the only freeholders around were Catholic. There was a way around the problem: it was up to the sheriff to administer the oaths, which was normally done before the freeholder cast his vote. But the Acadians voted (orally), and *then* were told that they would have to take oaths tantamount to renouncing their religion. The informant, however, was not the sheriff, but Agnew.

Had the Acadians cast their vote for the government candidates? Would Agnew, despite his denials, have been happy to let their votes stand if they had voted for him? Had he shown up in this remote corner of York County because he suspected the Acadian delegation would support the government? One would need the poll books (where the votes were recorded) to answer these questions, but the books have not survived. Religion certainly does not look like the real issue. And what about Duperré himself? Did he take a group of Acadians to the poll to reaffirm that the Madawaska territory belonged to New Brunswick and not Lower Canada, and thus ensure that no Québec court or Québec-appointed militia officer could fine him or seize his property? And what should we make of the fact that Duperré alone signed his "petition," and it does not contain even the names of the nineteen other Acadians? Was this a case of patron and clients, where the clients voted as their patron wanted them to because this was the way things were done in the eighteenth century?

3. Peter Fraser Secures the Franchise for Catholics

The story does not end there. As mentioned, Peter Fraser spearheaded the drive to enfranchise the Catholics after his election in 1809. The move may not have been entirely altruistic. In 1794, Duperré, who was still trading in fur but obviously had burned his bridges in Lower Canada, started doing business with one of the main fur traders on the lower St. John—a man called Peter Fraser! Fraser ran for elec-

tion in 1802 as an opposition candidate but lost. The House of Assembly received two petitions from Madawaskayans, who complained that they had not been able to vote because the poll had been set up too far (at Woodstock) and had closed early. The wording of each petition was identical, they were witnessed by Duperré, and they were each signed by exactly twenty people—the number of men in a militia company. This suggests that Duperré had a hand in this. According to D. M. Young, "In 1802 French-speaking Madawaska settlers had protested when they were denied the opportunity to vote, and their petitions had been looked upon as being in support of Fraser and McLeod."[8] After the Catholics were enfranchised, the Madawaska settlers apparently voted for Fraser, who was not defeated until 1827—the first election following Duperré's death in 1825. Was Duperré the one who steadfastly delivered his clients' votes to his patron?

Besides throwing light on eighteenth-century electioneering, the Grand Falls incident shows that Madawaska settlers were both political pawns and political agents. The patron/client culture of the times canalized their agency. But, given the times, this was nothing unusual. Later, Mgr. Langevin, the St. Basile priest, played the same advocacy role for his community, as well as that of patron for his parishioners. He was in good terms with the successive governors, whom he advised regarding the best course of action toward the Valley. For example, Langevin interceded when the governor refused to allow settlers to cut wood on their claims, and he obtained governmental relief when the crops failed (see Appendix O). Madawaska settlers were as much part of the political system as their social standing, education, and, until 1830, religion, allowed. In this respect, they were no different from other residents of the province.

A. The New Brunswick Militia

The relationship between Fraser, Duperré, and the Madawaska settlers was not exclusively political. The men also met on the training field, since they were all part of the provincial militia. The House of Assembly set up the provincial militia through several successive acts, beginning in 1787. The purpose of the militia was to provide the province's first line of defense and provide a pool of trained men from which to recruit provincial regiments during times of conflict. All able-bodied male residents of the province between the ages of sixteen and sixty had to enlist in the militia. They served under the commanding officer of the area where they resided. There was only one unit per county, and men residing in outlying areas were allowed to join independent companies. Such a company, commanded by a captain and two subalterns, existed at Madawaska in 1793.[9] Although the assembly created the militia, the lieutenant governor as commander in chief chose the officers. (Individuals could apply for a commission but without guarantee they would receive one). He selected men who were prominent and influential in their community; often those men held civil appointments or served as members of the assembly. Since appointments reflected a person's social standing, they were sought after. The lieutenant governor also appointed lower-ranking officers, but these appointments were based on senior officers' recommendations. In some American colonies, troop members elected militia officers. Neither the assembly nor Carleton ever entertained the idea. In fact, Carleton made it very clear this method of selection was unacceptable when a rumor circulated that such a democratic selection had occurred at Madawaska in 1793.

B. Madawaska Militia Regiments and Officers

Until 1794, the militia existed mostly on paper: people had other things to do. Later, in the nineteenth century, conflicts between the House of Assembly and the lieutenant governor further compromised the militia's standing. The assembly refused to appropriate money for the militia's equipment or inspections to retaliate against actions by the lieutenant governor it did not like. The militia was taken seriously only when a threat loomed. This occurred periodically, such as during the early 1790s when the province feared a French invasion, during the 1807 Embargo, the War of 1812, the boundary dispute beginning in the late 1820s, and, finally, during the Fenian scare of the late 1860s.[10] During the boundary dispute, militiamen were even issued uniforms. In 1824, New Brunswick organized the 4th Battalion York County Militia. Captain Duperré was transferred there from 1st York. Peter Fraser was commissioned commanding officer with the rank of major. The twenty other officers were all Madawaska residents, and only Francis Rice, Michael Tighe, and Michael Farrel were not French. (They had, however, married local Frenchwomen.) Maine saw the organization of this battalion as an infringement of her sovereignty. New Brunswick, of course, saw it as a way to protect its territory from a possible American invasion. The 4th York later became the 3rd Carleton (after the creation of a new county). Fraser was its first lieutenant colonel, followed by Coombs in 1846. The 3rd Carleton disappeared after 1849, when it merged with two other Carleton battalions after the formation of Victoria County. The new battalion became the 1st Victoria Battalion.

Forty-two of the ninety-one men who ever held commissions in the 3rd Carleton were French. Non-Valley residents constituted a small fraction (about a quarter) of the officers and do not appear until the mid 1840s. The successive lieutenant governors had no difficulties commissioning French men; Acadians, on the other hand, were never commissioned to the highest ranks. Lieutenant colonels and even majors had to be able to read the drill manual, so illiteracy and lack of English posed as much of an obstacle to becoming an officer as they did to becoming a justice of the peace. Religious prejudices may also have influenced choices. The only French major before 1845 was Antoine Bellefleur, who was promoted in 1837, but he was an anomaly as he was literate and came from a military family. Madawaska Acadians nonetheless fared better than their cousins in other parts of the province, whose names rarely appear on historic records of militia officers during that time. This was true in counties such as Kent and Restigouche that boasted large Acadian populations. The three Carleton battalions saw active duty during the boundary dispute, garrisoning forts, manning observation posts, guarding ammunition depots, and through their presence, asserting New Brunswick jurisdiction over the St. John River.

C. The Post-1842 Militia—A Social Institution

Interest in the militia remained strong in the immediate aftermath of the signing of the Webster–Ashburton Treaty. By 1850, however, the perceived need for a militia—and the assembly's willingness to appropriate money for it—had disappeared. The militia existed again only on paper. Officers resorted to providing a keg of beer or spirits to entice enlisted men to attend the yearly training session, which became more festive than militaristic. Finding suitable officers also became more difficult. In the late eighteenth century, officers had always been men with military experience; by the 1820s, officers were drawn from Loyalist and Acadian families. By the 1840s, however, immigrants and their sons began to be commissioned; ancestry was no longer a deter-

mining factor, and officers were drawn from the ranks of the "middling sort," that is from the ranks of storekeepers, farmers, merchants, and artisans. People still applied to become officers in the militia because their fathers and grandfather had been officers, but also because of their family's position in the community, because they believed it would help them in their business, or simply because the annual training session was a way to break the monotony of rural life. This new type of officer was likely to neglect his duties or simply resign when it became too inconvenient. One of the consequences of this democratization of the officers' corps, however, was the social integration of immigrants and people from different social strata into the community. Madawaska followed this trend. Only after 1848 was the 3rd Carleton's officers corps not comprised entirely of Loyalists, such as Coombs, or men who were either members of charter families or who had married into such a family, such as Rice. The 1848 regiment included two recently arrived French Canadians and some Irish Catholics, such as John Costigan. A militia commission could also be a stepping stone to a government position. For example, Fraser served as judge of the Inferior Court of Common Pleas for York County. Rice, who was an adjutant (a staff officer in charge of record keeping, correspondence and drilling) in the 3rd Carleton, succeeded Coombs as lieutenant colonel of the 1st Victoria in 1864. He was also the first Madawaska resident to be elected to the assembly (1850) and to be appointed to the Legislative Council (1855).

IV. A QUEBEC INSTITUTION: THE CATHOLIC CHURCH

The early Madawaska settlers (Natives included) were all Catholic. The settlement was erected into a parish (St. Basile) by the bishop of Québec in 1792. In 1829, the Maritime Provinces were turned into a separate diocese with a see at Charlottetown. Large-scale Irish immigration in New Brunswick led to the

formation of the bishopric of Fredericton in 1842 (the see was subsequently moved to Saint John). The Maritime bishops were English-speaking Irishmen and, by tacit agreement, the bishop of Québec continued appointing priests from Québec to Madawaska. In 1838, the New Brunswick government decided to pay a priest to minister to the St. John River Natives. The priest chose to stay in the Valley and have his church, which was dedicated to Saint Bruno, erected there. Ste. Luce, initially a relief chapel for St. Basile, became a parish in its own right in 1842.

Although very devout, the Madawaska French were also unruly. The priests complained they dragged their feet to pay the tithes or to make necessary church or rectory repairs. The people wanted their priests to say mass, teach catechism, and administer the sacraments, but otherwise stay out of their business. The priests, however, had other ideas and wanted to reform their parishioners to fit their image of the perfect flock. Behavior at mass appears to have been a problem, with the men coming and going during service to refresh themselves at the nearest tavern. In 1820, an exasperated priest decided to have the church doors locked after the beginning of mass to end the nonsense. Duperré arrested him on the spot for sequestration and did not release him until he had paid a hefty fine. If we are to believe the priests' letters to the bishops, Madawaskayans simply ignored orders and prohibitions that did not suit them. This did not prevent priests from thinking they were the natural leaders of their community and act accordingly, as Mgr. Langevin's letters show.

Besides mass, catechism, and sacraments, the Church provided no services to the population at that time. Whatever else was provided, such as limited schooling, was always at the priest's initiative. Female religious orders, which typically provided educational and medical services, did not arrive at Madawaska until the 1850s.

Conclusion

Britain and New Brunswick were both keen to exercise their jurisdiction over the Madawaska territory. There were practical reasons for this. Eighteenth- and early nineteenth-century authorities viewed groups living beyond the reach of established jurisdictions with great suspicion, In their eyes, those people were trying to hide. Madawaska residents likely did not want to be left entirely to their own devices either, but, by and large, they managed on their own. They appear to have used the services of the sheriff and of the courts when it was worth their time, and petitioned for relief when crops failed. Researchers have not yet investigated Madawaskayan—or even Acadian—use of the provincial justice system.

As far as the British authorities were concerned, there were also political reasons to exercise power over the region. By introducing political and military institutions to the area, New Brunswick asserted provincial jurisdiction and British sovereignty over a waterway critical to its communication system. In the process, the New Brunswick political elite were forced to face an uncomfortable issue: full civil rights for Catholics. They could not, however, quite bring themselves to extend those rights. Consequently, Madawaska settlers became as much (or as little) a part of the provincial political system as their social standing, education, and, until 1830, religion would allow. In this respect they were no different from farmers from other counties. They were also eventually integrated into the province's defense system. When this finally occurred, they fared better than Acadians in the rest of New Brunswick, and dominated their battalion's officer corps.

People on the ground could play the game to their advantage as well. Lower Canadian Pierre Duperré did not hesitate to proclaim Madawaska a New Brunswick territory when it suited him. He did this despite the fact that part of the population was Canadian and despite the fact that Catholics enjoyed greater civil rights in Lower Canada. He won because the governors of the two provinces did not want to cause trouble and because the Madawaska settlers preferred being New Brunswickers. This state of affairs may have lasted well into the nineteenth century had it not been for lumberers reaching the upper St. John Valley in the 1820s, which brought the boundary dispute to a head.

ENDNOTES

1. LAC, MG11, Great Britain, Colonial Office Records, "Report of the Committee of Council appointed to consider the boundary between the province of Québec and New Brunswick and the means of encouraging the communication and settle the land in that vicinity," "Q" series, vol. 60. 18 October 1787, 157, microfilm, reel C 11907. See also summary in Brymer, *Report on Canadian Archives for the Year 1891* (1892), State Papers, Lower Canada, Q series, vol. 60.

2. Provincial constitutions differed greatly from the American Constitution: they were not written documents detailing the province's rules but an aggregate of instructions to lieutenant governors, imperial and colonial statutes, and local practices.

3. The position of governor-in-chief was created in 1786. It was held by the governor of Québec, and later by the governor of Lower Canada. The governor-in-chief was the supreme military commander of British North America. The governors of the other provinces were called lieutenant governors

4. Glenie, James, army officer, military engineer, businessman, office holder, and politician (1750–1817); see full biography in the *Dictionary of Canadian Biography* at http://www.biographi.ca/EN/

5. People who took the three oaths and made the declaration were said to "take the Test." New Brunswick voters, therefore, did not "take the Test," but members of the assembly did.

6. Faser, Peter, merchant, magistrate, politician, and militia officer (1765–1840); see full biography in the *Dictionary of Canadian Biography*.

7. Agnew, Stair, landowner, politician, justice of the peace, and judge (1757–1821). See full biography in the *Dictionary of Canadian Biography*.

8. Quoted in entry for Stair Agnew, *Dictionary of Canadian Biography*.

9. Previously, the governor of Canada had commissioned Jacques and François Cyr as officers, but after New Brunswick assumed jurisdiction over the territory, militia commissions were issued solely by this province's lieutenant governor. Duperré was captain of the New Brunswick Militia Company; his subalterns appear to have been Firmin Thibodeau and François Albert.

10. The Fenians were a movement started in the 1850s by Irish Americans to secure Irish independence from Britain. Since they were not able to attack Britain, the Fenians tried to invade British North America instead, launching a raid against New Brunswick in April 1866 and two against Niagara and southern Québec in June of the same year.

FURTHER READINGS

Buckner Phillip A. and John G. Reid. *The Atlantic Region to Confederation: A History.* 1994: ch.12–14.

SOURCES

MacNutt (1963) and Buckner and Reid (1994) are good sources for those wishing to understand the broad lines of the New Brunswick political system and its evolution. To read about the position of Catholics in Maritime society in general, and of voting rights in particular, see Murphy (1984) and J. Garner (1953). Facey-Crowther is the leading researcher for the New Brunswick militia. See also Muir's short article (1964). Lists of parish officers, justices of the peace, and militia officers can be found in *The New Brunswick Almanac and Register* or *The Merchants' and Farmers' Almanac* for the appropriate year; those have been reproduced by CIHM. Elections results (including the number of votes cast) have been published in *Elections in New Brunswick, 1784–1984.* The conflict between Duperré and the Robichaud brothers can be pieced together through court transcripts transcribed by Chipman (1838) and discussed by Raymond (1907); Massé (1999) has also written an article in French on the topic. Biographies of Carleton, Agnew, Glennie, and Peter Fraser can be found in the *Dictionary of Canadian Biography*.

9

HOW PART OF MADAWASKA BECAME AMERICAN (AND THE REST REMAINED PART OF NEW BRUNSWICK)

In February 1819, our old acquaintance Pierre Duperré put pen to paper to inform the New Brunswick Attorney General Thomas Wetmore of a troublesome development:

> ...Captain Nathan Baker came to Madawaska twelve months ago. At that time he wished to introduce the laws of the States; brought a magistrate along with him from the States to form a corporation, and desired my concurrence.... Some of the inhabitants forbade him to cut wood upon their lots; he said it did not belong to them, but to the States.... He appears to be a man who takes much upon himself.[1]

In the 1790s, Duperré had tried to use the interprovincial boundary dispute to serve his economic interests. But some Americans were now playing the same game—or he imagined they were going to play it. The creation of a settlement at Madawaska had been a political and even diplomatic move. So had the settlers' participation in New Brunswick political and military life. These activities represented methods of asserting British sovereignty over the Valley. The Americans who came to the upper St. John Valley clearly understood this. What was at stake this time was timber. The boundary dispute between Britain and the United States had become economic.

I.   A CONFLICT OVER TIMBER

The upper St. John Valley's white pine forests began to attract attention in 1816 and 1817, when a handful of men from southern Maine made their way north to exploit this resource. These men included the Bakers, from Moscow in the upper Kennebec Valley, and John Harford and his son, also named John. In 1818, the men's families joined them. John Baker, who was single at the time, continued on to the Miramichi and Chaleur Bay, where he worked in lumber camps. His brother Nathan Baker settled at the mouth of the Meruimticook River (later renamed Baker Brook) and quickly cleared land and built both a house and a saw and gristmill. By the winter of 1818–19, Nathan had entered into an arrangement with Samuel Nevers, a Saint John merchant of pre-Loyalist stock. Nevers had a provincial

timber license; after 1820, both Nathan and John worked for him as timber cruisers (a timber cruiser was a man who crisscrossed the forest to locate merchantable timber). Soon thereafter Nathan died, and John took over the farm and mill and married his sister-in-law, Sophia Rice. Thus, Americans were actively participating in the lumber industry on the upper St. John River, but their involvement hinged on cooperation with a provincial merchant. The activity ignored boundaries. Whoever had jurisdiction over the territory had rights to its timber, and, therefore, lumbermen had a stake in resolving the dispute. Jurisdiction over the disputed territory was no longer merely a matter of debate for surveyors and diplomats. The arrival of the forest industry in the St. John basin brought the boundary dispute to a head, thereby forcing its resolution and, subsequently, the resolution of the interprovincial boundary dispute. But it also created an international economy in the Valley, an economy the terms of the 1842 treaty were careful not to disrupt.

A. The Beginnings of the Timber Trade in the Maritimes

The birth of the colonial timber trade resulted from Europe's Napoleonic Wars. Since the seventeenth century, Britain, which could not meet its own timber requirements, had been importing timber and lumber from the Baltic region in northeastern Europe. Although its North American colonies were heavily forested, they were too distant to be competitive on the British market. As a result, North Americans only exported masts and spars to Britain. In 1806, Napoleon, who controlled most of continental Europe, cut off British imports and exports. Deprived of its supply of timber, Britain turned toward British North America for supplies. Colonial merchants responded enthusiastically but also lobbied for a preferential tariff that would offset transatlantic shipping costs once the war was over. They succeeded. In 1810, British officials taxed foreign timber entering their ports at 65 shillings per load ($13), and colonial timber at 5 shillings ($1). Between 1821 and 1842, the colonial preference was barely reduced; duties during that period were fixed at 55 shillings per load ($11) and 10 shillings per load ($2) respectively. Colonial timber thus enjoyed a protected market in Britain.[2]

Exports of ton timber from New Brunswick reached an all-time high in 1825 and represented two-thirds of the value of all exports out of the province. The production of ton timber declined shortly thereafter, but the decline was eventually balanced by an increase in the production of lumber, such as deals, boards, and planks, cut from both pine trees too small for timber, and from spruce. As lumbermen culled the best pine stands, however, the main centers of timber and lumber production shifted. The Tobique and the Miramichi were the most intensely exploited areas between 1820 and 1825. Government officials issued the first timber license specifically for the upper St. John during the 1823–24 season. The expanding timber trade also attracted Lower Canadian merchants and entrepreneurs. The British Admiralty allowed a few men to cut on Crown land located behind Kamouraska and Saint-André. Lower Canadian officials began auctioning timber licenses for this area in 1826. Lumbering also took place on the seigneurial land which was surrounding Lake Temiscouata, and which had been purchased by lumbering interests.

B. A Territory in Dispute

1. Strategic Importance of the Territory

Both the St. John and Aroostook Rivers flowed through the disputed territory (see Map 9-1). The emerging timber industry brought the boundary conflict to the forefront. The dispute stemmed from the same faulty map that triggered the interprovincial boundary dispute. A joint commission had easily settled the north-south boundary between Maine and New Brunswick in 1798. However, neither the 1798 commissioners, nor a subsequent group surveying the area between 1816 and 1821, could agree on the location of the remaining boundary line. Britain, for her part, was determined to maintain control of the St. John–Témiscouata route. It not only provided a critical mail route, but it was also needed to transport troops traveling across British North America during the winter. Some regiments used that route during the War of 1812 and again during the rebellion of 1837 in Upper and Lower Canada. Nonetheless, neither country was willing to go to war over the issue; they probably would have reached a compromise had they had been free to do so. But in 1820, Maine, until then part of Massachusetts, became a state. Its political leaders adopted an intransigent attitude and refused to let the U.S. federal government relinquish any part of the disputed territory.

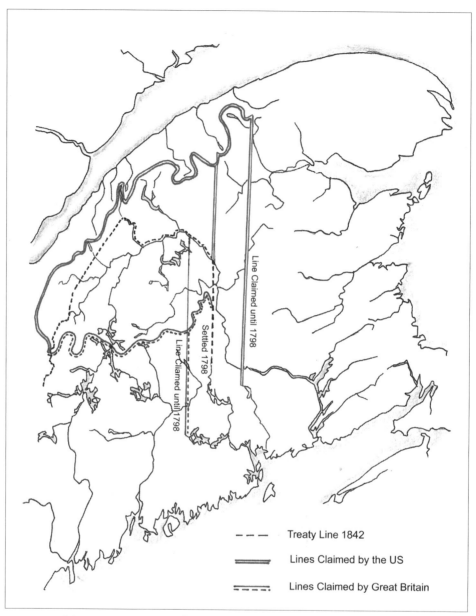

Map 9-1: *International Boundary Dispute. Map by B. and S. Craig*

2. Opportunities for Illegal Logging

Lumbering in the disputed territory exacerbated the dispute. Pines were a valuable resource. Governments earned revenue from these trees by granting timber licenses or selling forested land; New Brunswick, in addition, taxed timber export. Maine, Massachusetts (which still owned half of Maine's public land under the terms of the 1820 separation), and New

Brunswick were all unwilling to forego this income. None of the parties involved were willing to watch as rogue lumber parties stripped the region of its marketable timber while London and Washington tried to solve the boundary issue.

As a result of Maine's objections, New Brunswick suspended the issuance of timber licenses in the disputed territory. New Brunswick officials appointed James A. MacLauchlan, a veteran of the War of 1812, as warden of the same territory. MacLauchlan received the same instructions as the Maine state land agents: illegally cut timber was to be seized and sold, and the money was to be put into a trust fund. But lumbermen fought back. They went to court and often won, since the jury was often comprised of men linked to the timber trade. One way for the New Brunswick authorities to save face was to allow contraband timber through but fine it. MacLauchlan, who understood the reality of the situation, reminded trespassers they were breaking the law but did not try very hard to put a stop to their activities—unless they were American. American authorities, for their part, remained more lenient toward their own. Local people, on the other hand, did not discriminate against people of any nationality. "Provincials" could supply Yankee teams and vice versa, and they banded together to thwart officials from both countries.

As the boundary dispute worsened, New Brunswick authorities intensified the battle to stop illegal logging. Trespassers, though, were full of tricks. Not all cutting in the disputed territory was illegal, a situation they used to their fullest advantage. Owners of granted land could cut whatever they wanted on their property without government permission: this included the owners of the seventy-four lots Fredericton had granted at Madawaska during the eighteenth century. The owners of the Madawaska seigneury, which surrounded Témiscouata Lake, also fell into this category. By 1838, one-third of the seigneury belonged to the Témiscouata Pine Land Company, an American company headquartered in Portland, Maine. Lumbermen could take trees cut around the lake out of the seigneury only via the Madawaska and St. John Rivers. New Brunswick authorities also allowed holders of location tickets to cut and sell up to a hundred tons on their land. Trespassers, therefore, had no difficulty disguising illegally cut timber. They could also claim they had purchased the timber from settlers. For their part, the settlers also passed

timber cut on public land as their own.

To complicate matters, Lower Canadian authorities, who controlled the northernmost part of the disputed territory, issued licenses to lumbermen cutting along the Touladi River and Squatec Lake, east of Lake Témiscouata. This wood was also floated down the Madawaska to the St. John River. Sir John Caldwell, a lawyer and businessman actively involved in Lower Canada's timber trade, had built a sawmill in Grand Falls on land leased to him for twenty-one years (see Map 9-2).[3] The authorities allowed him to cut large quantities of timber behind the Kamouraska, St. André, and Rivière-du-Loup seigneuries to feed his mill. By 1839, he was also purchasing timber from the settlers.

New Brunswick's increasing efforts to ascertain the exact origin of all timber rafts floating down the river created bureaucratic tangles as redoubtable as log jams on the river. One good example of this is the wrangling between Charles Beckwith and his partners and the Crown Land Office. Beckwith appears numerous times in Crown land agent Baillie's correspondence because of his extensive lumbering activities in the St. John River basin. Baillie apparently suspected him of sailing too close to the wind. In June 1836, Baillie wrote to Beckwith to inform him that timber belonging to him and to his partners, Madawaska residents Francis Rice and Leonard Coombs, had been seized. Baillie wanted to know where it had been cut. Beckwith immediately replied, noting that he and his partners had cut 1,375 sticks (a stick was a tree shorn of its branches), and all but 155 of those sticks had been cut on the land of settlers holding location tickets, and with their permission; some had been purchased from holders of granted land. He added he had cut some of the timber in the Témiscouata seigneury. Unconvinced, Baillie checked Beckwith's story with a seigneurial agent two days later. The following year, Beckwith's agent (and brother) at Saint John tried to prevent further difficulties by writing Baillie in April before rafting his wood down the river. He wanted to know if the timber could be inspected before it went downriver. We do not have Baillie's answer. In October, however, Baillie informed the lieutenant governor that Beckwith, Coombs, and Rice had cut timber without a license above the Grand Falls. He advised against treating them differently from other trespassers and suggested letting them get away with paying an 8-shilling-per-ton fine ($1.60).

In 1838, Beckwith apparently decided to limit his operations to the seigneury and, in April, received permission to cut from the Témiscouata Pine Land Company. An incriminating report from MacLauchlan aroused Baillie's suspicion and in July, he asked his deputy to investigate the origin of Beckwith's timber. In August, a visibly irritated Beckwith and his new partner, John Glazier, wrote to Baillie to explain the timber's origins, noting that the 5,821 tons in question had been cut on the seigneury. Beckwith and Glazier concluded by stating: "Although we meet you in this...straightforward manner, we cannot but feel ourselves aggrieved by the manner in which we have been dealt with."[4]

The Beckwith saga took an ironic turn in 1839; Baillie appointed a man by the name of M. Berton as Saint John's seizing officer, only to discover shortly thereafter that Berton was Beckwith's brother-in-law, Berton had also been one of the first persons to receive a license to log along the upper St. John. We do not know whether or not Baillie's suspicions concerning Beckwith's activities were justified. If they were, it means that Beckwith managed to escape legitimate penalties and that corruption had spread through the official ranks; Beckwith's two partners, Rice and Coombs, were justices of the peace and militia officers at Madawaska. However, if Beckwith was an honest lumberman, Baillie's actions made it very difficult for him to carry out his business and were tantamount to harassment. But distinguishing legal from illegal activities and repressing the latter while allowing the former to continue was almost impossible.

3. Local Lumbermen and Outside Entrepreneurs

Information about lumbering along the upper St. John River before the treaty is very limited and unsystematic for obvious reasons. The activity was however unmistakably international in nature and the local population was heavily involved. Americans opened the first lumber camps but, as we have noted, they were working for a Saint John merchant. Those receiving licenses to cut along the upper St. John from 1823 to 1825 included local men and men from southern New Brunswick. They also included the provincial firm of Peters and Wilmot, who intended to mill their logs locally. In September 1823, they applied for a license of occupation, which they did not receive, at the Grand Falls to build a sawmill and cut a canal. The following year, they purchased some land from two local Frenchmen; unfortunately, the precise location of this land is unclear. In September 1825, they had purchased half a local sawmill belonging to Samuel Nevers and petitioned for a license to cut logs to feed it. At about the same time, they hired two Americans, Daniel Savage and James Walker, to build a double sawmill for them on the Fish River. They operated it for a year, went bankrupt in 1828, and handed over the mill to the two Americans in lieu of payment. By 1845, Fredericton merchant Frederic Hathaway had come into possession of the mill. Peters and Wilmot had obviously intended to establish themselves as one of the main businesses along the upper St. John, but the collapse of the timber trade in 1825 eventually destroyed their enterprise.

Three of the eight persons licensed to cut timber during the 1823–24 and 1824–25 seasons were local Frenchmen: Alexandre Bourguoin, Firmin Thibodeau, and Louis Bellefleur. Both Thibodeau and Bellefleur owned sawmills at Madawaska. The French, as locatees and grantees, could also legally cut trees on their land. This, coupled with the fact that public land abutted their lots, made it easy for

Map 9-2: The Grand Falls site in 1839, showing Sir John Caldwell's mill and house, and the military buildings. LAC, Bainbrigge, Philip John, Roads along the Frontier, 1839, 101. G1139.21.P2B34, 1840.

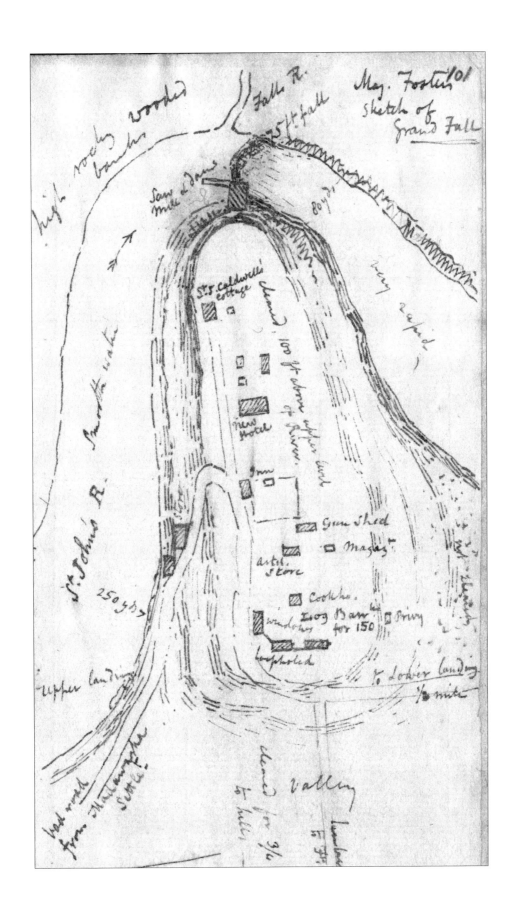

Maj. Foster's
sketch of
Grand Fall

121

them to cut illegally. Local Frenchmen led—and perhaps even outfitted—several of the 1838 logging parties identified by land agent George Buckmore. A Frenchman by the name of Dubé logged 400 tons at the Grande Rivière. Joseph Michaud, a local militia captain, identified by W. O. Raymond[5] as an important local lumberman, cut 3,000 tons on the St. Francis River.

Names of men from neighboring regions are sporadically mentioned in various sources during this time. For example, Buckmore mentioned in 1839 that Woodstock merchants supplied some of the trespassing crews. Beckwith and his business partner Coombs, as well as John Glazier, were provincial men who moved upriver to log. Sir John Caldwell, leaseholder for the Grand Falls site, was from Lower Canada. British American entrepreneurs were, there-fore, interested in upper St. John Valley lumber, but strove to give the impression they were operating within the law. The same was probably true of New Englanders. For example, the Portland-based Temiscouata Pine Tree Company had purchased part of the old Madawaska seigneury surrounding Témiscouata Lake. American lumbering interests were, therefore, as aware of the St. John River basin's economic possibilities as their provincial counterparts. But these merchants preferred to stay clear of the area until government authorities resolved the boundary dispute. Running afoul of the law was not in their long-term business interest. Their involvement was not even necessary because the local population was actively engaged in lumbering and could supply them with logs.

II.   RESOLUTION OF THE DISPUTE

By the 1837–38 season, trespassers were entering the St. John and Aroostook Valleys on a massive scale. Wooded areas behind the Grande Rivière and Rivière Verte settlements and along both sides of the Madawaska, St. Francis, and Fish Rivers teemed with crews. In December 1838, Buckmore estimated that fifty to seventy-five men, along with ten teams of horses and sixteen yokes of oxen, were busy preparing for the season along the banks of the St. John and its northern tributaries. He believed they could cut 75,000 tons of timber worth $100,000, with a third of the total volume coming from the Fish River.

Maine was largely responsible for the ongoing boundary dispute. Its politicians had turned the boundary into an electoral issue: Whigs and Democrats, who were vying for the control of the state government, outdid each other in jingoism. London and Washington officials had been ready for a compromise for a good while. In 1830 they had asked the king of the Netherlands to act as an arbiter in the dispute. In 1831, the king determined that a boundary could never be drawn according to the stipulations of the Treaty of Paris and proposed halving the disputed territory along the St. John. London officials, who cared only about keeping the communication line intact between Halifax and Québec, would have accepted the proposal. Convinced that the land north of the river was very poor and reluctant to fight over a few thousand acres of pine, spruce, and tamarack, Washington officials would also have accepted the proposal. But Mainers rejected the king's compromise. And to assert their claim, they incorporated the territory into a township in March 1831.

The boundary dispute almost turned into an armed conflict in 1839. Governor John Fairfield, who was elected in 1838, decided Maine should take the matter into its own hands. Alarmed by Buckmore's report, he sent another land agent, Rufus McIntyre, and a posse to stop the trespassing. McIntyre was promptly captured by lumbermen and handed over to provincial authorities. Sir John Harvey, lieutenant governor of New Brunswick, accused the American posse of invading provincial territory and placed some British regulars along the St. John (see Map 9-3); Fairfield sent the state militia. Secre-

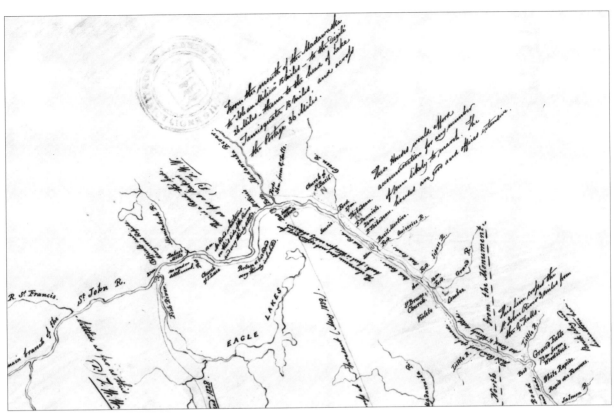

Map 9-3: Plan of the area north of the disputed north eastern boundary showing the route along the St. John River taken by troops as well as the military road made by the Americans to the Fish River and other road under construction, by Frederick Wm. Nightingale Whinyates, Royal Engineer. The map lists the houses where men on the march could rest. LAC NMC-6839

tary of State John Forsyth and Prime Minister Henry Fox of Britain proposed an agreement whereby New Brunswick would continue keeping some British regulars and the provincial militia along the St. John, Maine would withdraw its militia but keep an armed posse on the Aroostook. Britain would control the Madawaska territory, and the United States, the Aroostook Valley. Washington sent General Winfield Scott, a confirmed troubleshooter, to Maine to convince Fairfield to endorse the Fox-Forsyth agreement. Scott also happened to be a long time friend of Harvey, which helped smooth the process. The Ameri-

cans built a blockhouse and boom across the Fish River at Soldier Pond and then another boom and a blockhouse (which is still standing) at the mouth of the river (see Map 9-4 and illustrations). They also built a blockhouse and boom at Fort Fairfield. The booms were to prevent trespassers from floating illegally cut lumber in the St. John. They also finished the "Fish River Road" between Masardis and the newly named Fort Kent. Federal troops moved to Fort Kent and Fort Fairfield in 1841. Similarly the British improved roads on their side, built two blockhouses at the head of Témiscouata Lake and at Little

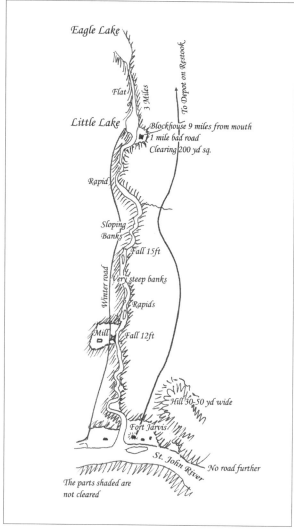

Falls (currently Edmundston), and erected several military stations between the Aroostook River and Grand Falls, as well as one at Dégelis (see Maps 9-5 and 9-6 and illustrations). The provincials built a boom on the St. John below the mouth of the Aroostook and refused to let any timber from the disputed territory through.

By 1840, the provincial and state officials' combined efforts had put an end to illegal logging in the territory—but had also severely impaired legal logging. Two years later, Washington and London finally settled the dispute, by designating the St. Francis and St. John rivers as boundaries. Maine kept the Aroostook Valley. Free navigation rights along the

Map 9-4a: Fish River in 1838. Map by B. and S. Craig from a sketch in Lieut. Bainbrigge's report to the Lieut.-Governor of New Brunswick, November 18, 1839, LAC, RG7-G:7, vol. XX-1839, microfilm, C-47.

Illus. 9-1 (top, right): The American Fort at Fort Kent (originally Fort Jarvis); under construction; sketch in Lieut. Bainbrigge's report to the Lieut.-Governor of New Brunswick, November 18, 1839. LAC, RG7-G:7, vol. XX-1839, microfilm, C-47 (also see Map 9-4).

Illus. 9-2 (center, right): The Americans also built a boom across the river at Soldier Pond (then called Little Lake), and a small fort; Bainbrigge's report, November 18, 1839.

Map 9-4b (below): Plan of the Fort Jarvis (Fort Kent) site. Map by B. and S. Craig from a sketch from Lieut. Bainbrigge. LAC, Bainbrigge, Philip John, Roads along the Frontier, 1839, 81. G1139.21.P2B34,1840.

Map 9-5 (bottom, right): The Petit Sault in 1839, showing the site where the block house was built. LAC, C-017787

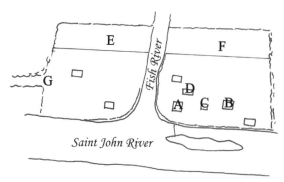

A - *Block House*
B - *Block House*
C - *Stable for 25 horses, bullet proof 20ft logs*
D - *Cook House*
E - *Abattis*
F - *Abattis*
G - *Opening of road to settlement*

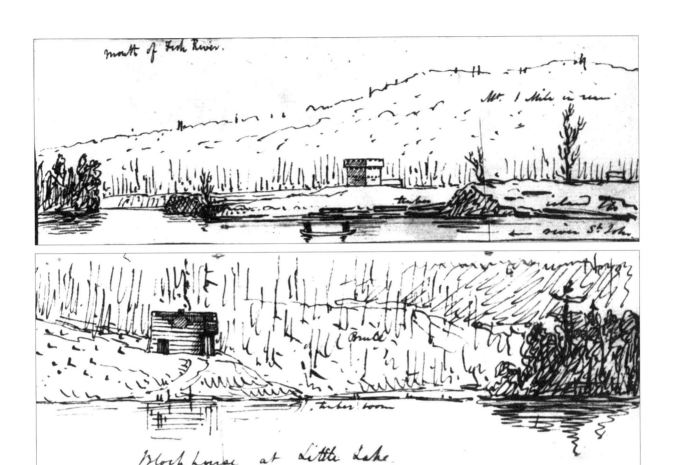

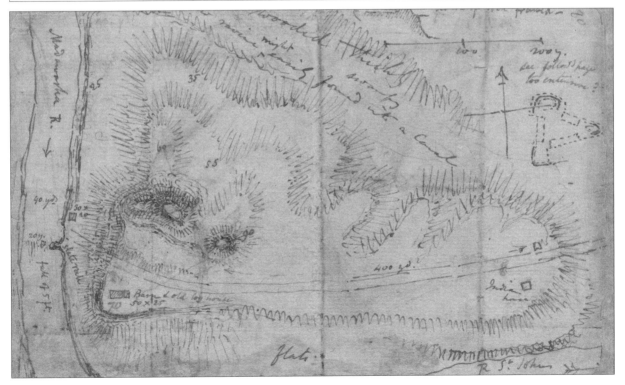

How Part of Madawaska Became American

Illus. 9-3: The British built a block house at the Petit Sault (also see Map 9-5). LAC, C-40144

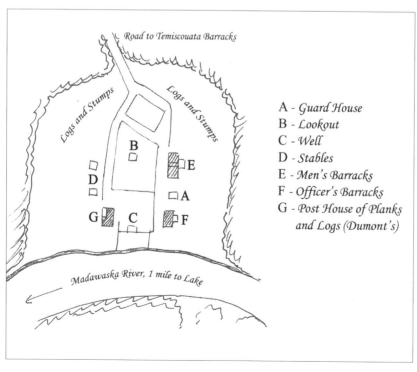

Road to Temiscouata Barracks

Logs and Stumps

Logs and Stumps

B

D

G   C   A

F

E

Madawaska River, 1 mile to Lake

Map 9-6: Plan of the Dégeli barracks in 1839. Map by B. and S. Craig from a sketch from Lieut. Bainbrigge, LAC, C-049662.

A - *Guard House*
B - *Lookout*
C - *Well*
D - *Stables*
E - *Men's Barracks*
F - *Officer's Barracks*
G - *Post House of Planks and Logs (Dumont's)*

The Land in Between

Illus. 9-4: By the 1840s, the British had some soldiers stationed at the Dégelis, at the junction between Lake Témiscouata and the Madawaska River; the individual in the central yard between the buildings is wearing a red coat; Goods were carried in small boats in summer (also see Map 6-6).
View of the Madawaska River, c. 1840, (attributed to) Arianne Saunders Shore (Canadian, 1790–1868), oil on panel, 18.4 x 23.2 cm, gift of Lord Beaverbrook, Beaverbrook Art Gallery, Fredericton, NB, Canada.

St. John for both forest and unprocessed agricultural products were guaranteed. This clause satisfied the the lumbermen; without it the lumber industry could not have expanded in the American St. John River basin. New Brunswick could have charged lumbermen whatever it wanted for the right to float wood below the Grand Falls, or even prohibit American timber rafts altogether. Britain retained the Témiscouata route, and bona fide settlers (those with at least six years' residence) were to receive titles to the land they occupied. A concerted newspaper campaign, a bit of blackmail from Washington, and pressure from the various lumber interests convinced Maine politicians to acquiesce. John Baker found himself in an uncomfortable situation: his extensive holdings were all on the British side of the river. Webster and Ashburton reached a "gentleman's agreement" to handle this situation (see Sidebar 9-1).

Illus 9-5: The British also built a larger fort on the shores of Temiscouata Lake.
Philip John Bainbrigge, Fort Ingall. 1839, LAC, C-17787

Sidebar 9-1: A Special Agreement Between Daniel Webster and Lord Ashburton
Concerning John Baker

MacLauchlan to Reade, Esq., private secretary to the lieutenant governor
Madawaska
November 11th, 1842
Sir,
I have the honor to acquaint you for the information of his Excellency the Lieutenant Governor, that Mr. John Baker, an American citizen residing at the entrance of the Meruimticook River, North side of the Saint John and 6 miles below the American armed fort at the Fish River called upon me today having received a letter which I have read from W. Kent the late governor of the State of Maine, acquainting him that as the boundary Commissioners from the State of Massachusetts and Maine were fully aware of the unpleasant situation Mr. Baker must be placed in on the settlement of the north eastern boundary, by having his property brought within the British Territory; had in consequence entered into an understanding with Lord Ashburton, through Webster the Secretary of State, that in the event of Mr. Baker not wishing to remain under the British government upon the ratification of the treaty, he should then be allowed to privilege of having his property valued by and paid for by that government.

I am therefore requested by Mr. Baker to state to his Excellency that, as he does not feel disposed after all that has transpired in this section of the Province, to remain under the British Government, begs that his Excellency will be pleased on the ratification of the Treaty to direct the property to be appraised agreeable to the understanding of both governments.

Reade responded that MacLauchlan should not do the appraising himself and recommended referring the matter to a man by the name of Mr. Baby. As we know, Baker continued living at Meruimticook until his death.

Soource: LAC, MG9A2, Lieutenant Governor of New Brunswick Fonds, Vol. 6, 1831-1842, p. 2.

YANKEES, FRENCH, AND THE BOUNDARY DISPUTE

A. The Americans

How did this drawn-out boundary conflict affect the local population? Outwardly, the small group of Americans who arrived in the first quarter of the century reacted very differently from the French. They loudly supported Maine's position, whereas the French kept a low profile. Nonetheless, underlying their differences, one can detect similar concerns and goals. The French, like the Americans, wanted above all to secure the means to be economically independent and, if possible, reap extra profits from the timber trade.

The Americans raised a commotion vastly disproportionate to their numbers. Between 1816 and the late 1820s, a dozen or so New Englanders, some with their families, settled between the Meruimticook and St. Francis Rivers. Most Americans, like John Baker, were originally from southern Maine, but some came from farther afield, such as Charles McPherson from Rhode Island and Jesse Wheelock from Northborough, Massachusetts. Some moved directly to the upper St. John Valley. Others followed a more circuitous route. Baker first went to Chaleur Bay, while Wheelock initially settled in Saint John, New Brunswick, and owned a share in a vessel. There, Wheelock may have met Barnabas Hunnewell, another Kennebec man, who spent the early 1820s in the port city before moving to the upper St. John Valley. McPherson came to the St. John Valley via the Restigouche. These men were unexceptional in many respects. Their brief biographies, as told by Edward Wiggin in his *History of Aroostook,* resemble those of early settlers in most Aroostook County communities included in this volume: they came from southern Maine, Massachusetts, New Hampshire, and New Brunswick. They may have come directly from their place of origin to northern Maine or they may have wandered around prior to their arrival in the area, but they always lived in regions involved in the timber trade. They settled in areas with few or no permanent residents, built mills, brought shingle and clapboard machines, and opened stores and taverns, forming the nucleus of new settlements. They usually combined farming with their other activities. They may have gone into partnership with others, and their partners may have been provincial men. Most of these men came after the resolution of the boundary dispute; the Meruimticook New Englanders were only noteworthy because of the precocity of their endeavors.

John Baker quickly emerged as their leader. On July 4, 1827, he organized an Independence Day celebration, erected a liberty pole, and hoisted an American flag. The New Englanders attended the celebration, but the French stayed away. Baker used the opportunity to proclaim the independence of the "Madawaska Republic" and called on both the French and American populations to ratify its compact. That compact stated, in part, that as soon as it was feasible, the "Republic" would request to join the United States. The French again demurred. During the summer, Baker prevented a local constable from serving a warrant against a debtor and tried to intercept the royal mail when he chanced to meet the courier on the Madawaska River. The courier was not intimidated, and the mail went through.

His Majesty's Government was not amused; in September, a provincial posse arrested Baker, took him to Fredericton, and charged him with inciting sedition, obstructing the mail, trespassing on Crown land, and logging without a permit. Unable to post bail, Baker spent eight months in jail awaiting trial. When the court met, Baker denied it had jurisdiction over him. He was an American citizen who had been arrested on American soil for actions that had occurred in an American territory.

The prosecution promptly retaliated, bringing forth evidence that Baker had tacitly acknowledged provincial jurisdiction in the past. A provincial surveyor had laid out his land; he had asked provincial magistrates for help in recovering his debts; he had paid the alien tax; and he had accepted the provincial bounty for grain grown on new land. How could he then pretend the Madawaska territory was not British? He was sentenced to two months in jail and a £5 fine ($20), a rather lenient sentence considering the charges against him.

The incident did not quiet Baker. In August 1831, he called a town meeting to organize a municipal government in the newly incorporated Madawaska Township and to select a representative to the state legislature. This time, the posse that tried to arrest him was led by no less than New Brunswick's lieutenant governor and by the attorney general. Baker, now a bit wiser from past experience, escaped before their arrival. He reappeared in 1840, when he called another town meeting, had himself elected moderator, and organized local presidential elections. As the trial testimonies demonstrated, Baker's ardent American patriotism was relatively new. Previously, both Baker and his brother Nathan had treated the upper St. John as British. In 1820, Nathan applied to Fredericton for a grant on the land where he had built a house and mill. He applied, not in his own name, but in the name of his two-year-old son, who had been born in British North America. Because Nathan was an alien, he was not eligible for a grant. His request was turned down. In 1824, John, who took over his brother's family and property when Nathan died, had Samuel Nevers apply for a grant for the same piece of property. According to local historian R. Paradis, the scheme almost worked. Some time later, we find John Baker in Fredericton trying to become a naturalized British subject. While on the way to the provincial capital, he met two American land agents, George Coffin and James Irish, who gave him a grant. It is only after that incident that Baker became a stalwart American, protecting the territory of the republic against foreign trespasses and planting American institutions in the wilderness. His fellow citizens at the Meruimticook followed suit.

B. The French

The French were much quieter than their American neighbors. They were not invisible, though. Maine (and Massachusetts) representatives became aware of their existence very early. Twice state officials sent their land agents to the upper valley to ascertain their claims—and their allegiance. Agents Coffin and Irish, who visited the settlement in 1825 immediately after their chance encounter with Baker in Fredericton, lacked the time to do more than post promises of land on the church door and at Thibodeau's inn, where they had stayed. Coffin and Irish liked Firmin Thibodeau very much. He refused any payment from the two men. He also gave them the impression he was pro-American. "Mr. Thibodeau is very friendly to the Americans," they reported, "and desirous of having an organized government at Madawaska and to be represented in the General Court, to have parish officers and officers of their own choice in the militia. He observed he was now a captain of the militia, commissioned from the government of New Brunswick, but he would never call his men out under that commission."[6] However, the minute the Americans left, Thibodeau handed the proclamation they had left behind to his commanding officer, Peter Fraser. In that proclamation, the state land agents promised a hundred acres to anybody who applied to the Houlton state land agent; the grants were free except for the surveying costs. Thibodeau was clearly playing both ends against the middle.

Maine land agents John J. Deane and Edward Kavanagh spent several weeks at Madawaska in the summer of 1831. Kavanagh, a Catholic who had attended a Jesuit college in Montréal, could speak French. The two men entered the Valley through the Allagash, thus escaping MacLauchlan's notice for quite a while. Deane and Kavanagh visited the settlers along both sides of the St. John until they reached the Fish River, then they continued on the south bank until they reached the boundary line. They proceeded to cross the river and were ready to continue their investigation on the north bank when MacLauchlan appeared and let them know he considered them trespassers. (The king of Netherlands' decision, which awarded the river's north bank to the British, had just been made public.) He allowed the two men to continue their journey, but not to question settlers.

Deane and Kavanagh had until then gathered very specific information, in part, by interviewing prominent settlers. With few exceptions, the French had received them very well and willingly answered their questions. Their information, when compared to other sources, is remarkably accurate. After they were intercepted by MacLauchlan, the two Americans had to rely almost entirely on direct observation or indirect testimonies from the few who were still willing to speak to them. Most settlers became uncommunicative. The two men left the St. John Valley convinced the French were pro-American, but did not dare to make their feelings public for fear of British reprisal, the same conclusion Coffin and Irish had reached six years previously. They claimed that a significant number of French people had told them in confidence that they wished to be American.

New Brunswick officials, who had exercised jurisdiction over the settlement since the eighteenth century, never doubted the loyalty of the French settlers. They took this loyalty so much for granted that they rarely broached the issue, although they occasionally complained that the Americans were attempting to "bribe" the French away from them.

Concrete evidence available at the time seemingly supported this belief: in the 1820s and 1830s, the French took part in the provincial militia, voted (when they owned granted land) served as parish officers, appeared before the grand jury, collected grain bonuses on their new land, registered deeds at Fredericton, and petitioned the lieutenant governor for assistance when their crops failed. Very few took part in Baker's meetings. Those who did participate but subsequently ran into trouble claimed the innocence of their intentions.

It was in the French settlers' best interest not to take sides publicly and to let both the Americans and the British believe what they wanted. The boundary dispute was, after all, a *querelle d'anglais* (a quarrel among Englishmen). The French settlers' primary concern was to keep their land. They probably welcomed Deane and Kavanagh because the Maine land agents had indicated their intention to issue land grants to the settlers. There was no way of predicting which side would win, so the French sought to keep their options open. The Americans were in an altogether different position: as aliens, they were ineligible for land grants from New Brunswick. American settlers also failed in their attempts to secure grants through their minor children or through friends. They believed their only hope to own land was through an American victory, hence their vigorous support of the American cause. In short, both French and American settlers pursued the strategy best suited to their economic needs.

IV.   HOW NEW BRUNSWICK KEPT ITS PANHANDLE

The settlement of the international boundary dispute resurrected the interprovincial one. New Brunswick claimed the land that it had administered for half a century and that it had been ready to defend during the Aroostook War. New Brunswick officials also pointedly remarked that their Canadian counterparts had not lifted a little finger to protect the territory against the Americans.[7] Canadian officials replied that New Brunswick's land claim upheld the American interpretation of the 1783 treaty. If Britain now adopted that claim, it would tell the world it had lied during the recent negotiations. To complicate matters, the Webster–Ashburton Treaty of 1842 assigned Britain a strip of territory north of the St. John, south of the watershed line, and west of the due north line; which province had jurisdiction over this area was far from clear (see Map 9-1).

As with the international boundary dispute,

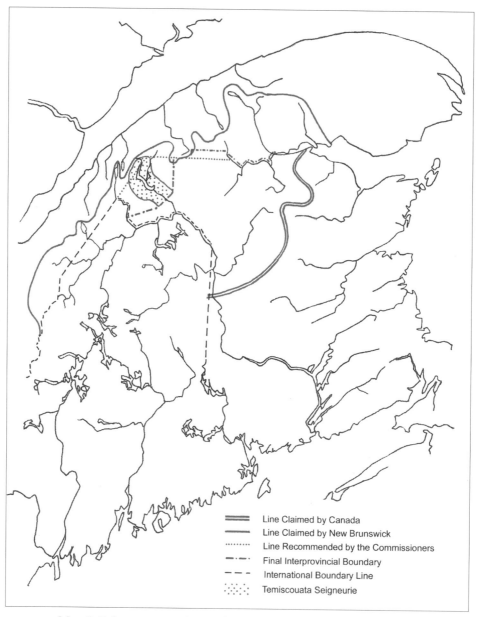

Map 9-7: Interprovincial Boundary Dispute. Map by B. and S. Craig.

lumbermen brought the matter to a head. They wanted to log in that strip of land, as well as along the St. Francis River. But who would issue licenses and collect stumpage fees? The two provinces unofficially respected each other's permits by placing the money collected from stumpage fees in a disputed territory fund. That money was to be distributed after the settlement of the boundary. This, however, provided only a short-term solution. Officials from the two provinces appointed commissions, which produced reports, proposals, and counterproposals. By 1846, it had become obvious that their positions were irreconcilable, and the home government in London had to step in. It appointed its own commission, which presented its report in 1848. The commissioners gave the old seigneury to New

The Land in Between

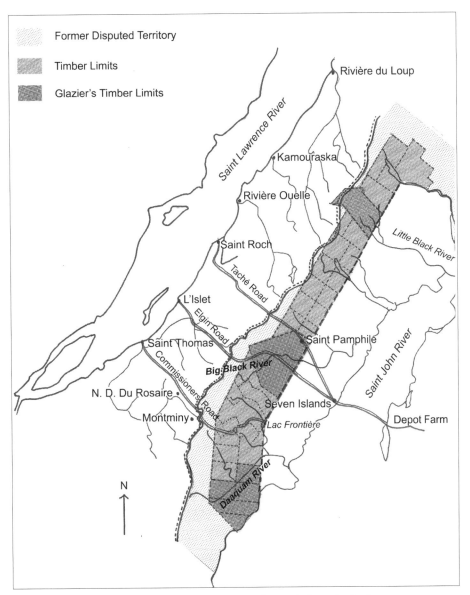

Map 9-8: Uppermost St. John and Côte-du-Sud.
Adapted from Laberge et. al., Histoire de la Côte du Sud, *180, 182 & 187, by B. and S. Craig.*

Sidebar 9-2: From Disputed Territory to Lower Canadian Townships
(See Map 9-8)

Part of the former disputed territory now lies along the Québec-Maine border at the rear of Bellechasse, Montmagny, and L'Islet Counties in the Côte-du-Sud region. The ink was barely dry on the Webster–Ashburton Treaty when roads leading from the St. Lawrence to the new border and beyond were opened. The first road was the "Route des Commissaires" (the Commissioners' Road), used by bound ary surveyors. This road linked Saint-Thomas de Montmagny with Lac Frontière, then known as Lac des Anglais. This led to the settlement and creation of Montminy Township in 1857. The Elgin Road, connecting Saint-Jean-Port-Joli with the boundary line and Seven Islands on the uppermost portion of the Saint John, opened in 1856, but plans for its construction date as far back as 1827. By 1865, there were already 130 families living along this road, specifically at Saint-Damase, Sainte-Perpétue, and Saint-Pamphile. The Taché Road opened shortly after that; it started at Saint-Roch and, like the Elgin Road, terminated at Seven Islands. The Canadian government issued timber licenses for most lots in the once-disputed territory as soon as the interprovincial boundary was established. In 1853, the main licensees included the Glaziers, William Price, John Jenkins, and George Young. Some lumbermen brought their families, and, by 1870, thirteen out of the eighteen townships eventually erected in the former disputed territory had come into existence.

Sources: Laberge *et. al,* (1993): 186–87; Mercier (1981); Rouillard (1901); St. Pierre, "Les chemins de colonization,"http://www.encyclobec.ca

Brunswick and the strip of land between the watershed and the St. John River to Canada. New Brunswick officials were willing to accept the proposal, but Canadian officials rejected it (see Map 9-7). The ball was back in London's court. Governor General Earl Grey, who still wanted the provinces to reach a mutual understanding, tried another approach. Each province was to appoint an arbitrator; the arbitrators would then select a third one; and then the three men would draw the boundary line. If the arbitrators could not agree, London officials would decide the matter. They could not agree because Canada's arbitrator vetoed his colleagues' proposal. When the British government intervened, it adopted the proposal of the 1848 commission, keeping the old Madawaska seigneury within Canada. In August 1851, the British Parliament passed an act establishing the boundary between Canada and New Brunswick. Provincial surveyors drew the line in 1853, thus putting an end to the seventy-year dispute. Although a section of the disputed territory was now formally a part of Lower Canada, its connections with Maine and New Brunswick were not broken; roads led from the St. Lawrence to the uppermost portion of St. John, and New Brunswick lumbermen continued to exploit its resources (see Sidebar 9-2).

Conclusion

Between 1783 and 1842 the geopolitical status of the Madawaska territory was in dispute, but this did not prevent people from exploiting the Valley's natural resources. During that period, lumbering along the upper St. John River was widespread, illegal, and transnational. French Canadian immigrants worked in the shanties in the winter and laid claims to farm lots in the summer. Lumbermen could be local men as well as outsiders. and were of various nationalities. Their suppliers were local or provincial, but their financial underwriters could be located as far as Quebec City, Fredericton, Boston, or Glasgow.

This industry negated boundary lines separating Lower Canada, New Brunswick, and Maine, which greatly angered Mainers. It also turned the Valley into a true borderland. In the end, the treaty left the forest industry undisturbed. Britain kept its communication route; New Brunswick kept most of the territory awarded to Britain; and Madawaska residents received titles to their land—and in the case of those on the southern bank, unexpected citizenship. While Maine got an established boundary, it was not the one it wanted. For the next fifty years, Mainers also wondered if the river's southern bank belonged to them on more than a nominal level.

ENDNOTES

1. U.S. Congress. Senate, *Message from the President of the United States*, 20th Cong., 1st session, 1828, 30.

2. A "ton" of timber was equal to 40 cubic feet, a "load was equal to 50 cubic feet.

3. Caldwell died in Boston in 1842 while visiting Daniel Webster, the key negotiator of the Webster–Ashburton Treaty.

4. PANB, RS663/E/2/a, Timber Correspondence, Beckwith and Glazier to Baillie, 6/8/June 8, 1838.

5. Raymond, "Introduction" to Deane and Kavanagh's report.

6. Maine State Archives, Land Office Records, *Journal of Massachusetts Land Agent George W. Coffin on his journey up the St. John River,* Sept. and Oct. 1825.

7. During 1837 and 1838, Lower Canada had to quell a rebellion within its boundaries, leaving minimal time and resources to intervene in the conflict.

FURTHER READINGS

Dubay, Guy, *Chez Nous: The St. John Valley.* 1983: 25–34.

Judd, Richard W., *et. al. Maine: the Pine Tree State.* 1995: ch. 15.

Acadian Culture in Maine, http://acim.umfk.maine.edu, section 2, "Roots of Maine Acadian Culture."

Green, Jere W. "Aroostook Becomes a County." In *The County: Land of Promise,* ed. A. McGrath, 1989: 63–73.

Jones, Howard. *To the Webster–Ashburton Treaty: A Study in Anglo-American Relations, 1783–1843.* 1977.

Scott, Geraldine T. *Ties of Common Blood: A History of Maine's Northeast Boundary Dispute with Great Britain, 1783–1842.* 1992.

SOURCES

The boundary dispute, not surprisingly, has generated a large amount of writing. We are partial to Howard Jones's account, although it focuses mostly on the diplomatic aspects of the dispute. Carroll's account is the most recent (2001). G. T. Scott (1992) provides a less academic account of the dispute, but pays greater attention to what occurred on the ground. Melvin's account (1975) is easily available in Aroostook County libraries; Burrage (1919) is still worth consulting despite its age. Also of interest is Paradis on John Baker (1972), Lowenthal on the role of the press (1951), McDonald on the Fort Kent blockhouse (1990), Scott on fortifications (1990), Hale on the Northeastern Boundary Commission (1957), and Wagner on General Winfield Scott (1995). Gary Campbell is currently writing a doctoral thesis at the University of New Brunswick on Baker and MacLauchlan. One can easily access many primary sources, such as Sprague's *Documentary History of the North Eastern Boundary Controversy* (1910), Chipman's *Remarks upon the Disputed Points of Boundary* (1838), or the *Documentary History of the North-Eastern Boundary Controversy* in the Maine state papers (1828–29); to those, one can add documents from the twentieth Congress of the United States (1828). Information about lumbering can be found in Judd (1989), Wood (1935), and Wynn (1981), as well as at the Provincial Archives of New Brunswick under the heading "Department of Natural Resources and Crown Land." Documents describing the settlement during the last years of the dispute include the last pages of Joel Wellington's field notes while surveying the Fish River Road (1828) and Coffin and Irish's diary (1825). Both of those documents are available at the Maine State Archives. Deane and Kavanagh's report (published in 1907) and their diary (published in 1980) also describe this population. Ganong (1901) covers both the international and interprovincial boundary disputes.

Part Three

STILL A BORDERLAND, 1845–79

By 1850, the Madawaska territory was divided among three independent political entities: the state of Maine, the British colony of New Brunswick, and the British colony of Canada. What would happen to its inhabitants? Would they be able to preserve the integrity of their community, or would they start dividing along British and American lines? The Americans assumed the Madawaska settlers would willingly assimilate. The British assumed they would continue as they had always been, as French-speaking Catholics.

The settling of the boundaries allowed the various governments to exercise jurisdiction over their respective share of the territory, set up land-granting procedures, extend citizenship rights to some of the residents, and create institutions—such as post offices and schools—which brought these settlements firmly under the control of either the United States or New Brunswick. Those institutions, however, did not succeed in pulling apart the two halves of the community. The institutions remained fairly weak, and people soon used them in ways that perpetuated the bond between them, Nor could political and administrative forces counter the impact of continued immigration from French Canada, which kept the Valley French-speaking and Catholic. Institutional forces were also much weaker than economic ones. The local economy remained a regional one so firmly tied to Saint John that some questioned whether northern Aroostook County was truly American.

Throughout this period, the Madawaska settlement was vulnerable to the vagaries of the timber trade. We chose 1873 as the terminal date for this period because a severe crisis in the forest industry led to its lasting reorganization. Five years later, the railroad also reached the Valley, creating different economic opportunities. First, we will look at the forces that should have divided the settlement between 1842 and 1873, such as land grant policies, politics, and institutions. Second, we will look at the ties between the two halves of the Valley, such as the forest industry, agriculture, business, and the emergence of a consumer society. Third, we will look at the ways generations succeeded each other on the land.

	Maine	New Brunswick
1827		Britain introduces a new system for alienating Crown land in her colonies: the land must be purchased
1833	Maine levies a tax on banks to support public schools	New Brunswick Common School Act provides public funding for one school per civil parish
1837		The Legislative Assembly of New Brunswick gains control over Crown land in the province
1841	Construction of the Telos Cut	
1842	**Webster–Ashburton Treaty**	
1842	Upper St. John Valley becomes part of the diocese of Fredericton	
1842		First post office in St. John Valley (at Madawaska, N. B.)
1843	First U.S. Post Office in St. John Valley (in Fort Kent)	New Brunswick introduces a new licensing system for logging on Crown land
1844	Maine and Massachusetts survey the south bank of the river and issue deeds to settlers	
1847		New Brunswick Parish School Act creates a provincial board of education and sets up a normal school in Fredericton
1847	John Glazier blows up the Chamberlain dam; did it again the following year.	
1848		New Brunswick surveys the north bank of the river and issue deeds to settlers
1848		Ministerial responsibility introduced in New Brunswick (Responsible Government)
1848	Timber markets in Britain collapsed; depression in timber-producing regions	
1849		New Brunswick passes a Land Labor Act: settlers can pay for their land in road duty
1851		First telegraph in St. John Valley (Halifax to Quebec City line through Edmundston)
1853	**Canada–New Brunswick boundary established**	
1854	**Maine buys back Massachusetts' share of Maine public land** **Creation of the "Know Nothing" party (American Party) in Maine**	**First Acadian elected to New Brunswick House of Assembly (Amand Landry from Westmorland)**
1854	Creation of the Diocese of Portland	
1854	Maine Common School Law creates school districts run by elected committees	
1854	**Reciprocity treaty between the United States and British North America signed.**	
1855		Secret ballot introduced in New Brunswick elections; only British subjects can vote in New Brunswick elections
1858		The St. Basile Academy opens
1861	State of Maine takes over the schools in the St. John Valley	John Costigan (Grand Falls) elected to New Brunswick House of Assembly
1861	Beginning of the American Civil War	
1864		Beginning of negotiations for Confederation
1866	End of the American Civil War	
1866	**Reciprocity treaty between the United States and British North America repealed.**	
1866	**Pike Act (re-entry of forest products into the U.S.)**	
1867		**Creation of the Dominion of Canada (Confederation) on July 1**
1867		Founding of the *Moniteur Acadien,* the first French-speaking newspaper in the Maritimes
1868	Maine sells remaining public land in Aroostook to the E&NA railroad for $1	
1868	Frenchville's Father Sweron opens a high school in his parish	
1870	American Madawaska becomes part of the diocese of Portland.	
1870	Common School Act reorganize school system in the state. St. John Valley schools regain their autonomy	
1872		Free Grant Act passed in New Brunswick: bona fide farmers can get free land.
1872		New Brunswick grants remaining public land in Victoria-Madawaska to railroad
1873	Economic crisis ("Panic of 1873")	
1875	Saint John firm of Jewett and Pitcher fails, leading to business failures in the St. John Valley	

10

TERRITORY AND POPULATION

The most immediate impact of the 1842 treaty was the formalization of land ownership: titles were given to those with six years of residence and procedures were established for others to acquire public or Crown land. Land alienation policies were not identical on both sides of the river. Moreover, disagreements between Maine and Massachusetts over which policy to pursue, coupled with the unsettled interprovincial boundary, delayed the issuance of land grants. Access policies, availability of land, and the American Civil War affected both the growth rate and the geographic location of new settlements. The Valley's population, nonetheless, continued to grow, and the settled area expanded (see Map 10-1). Some hardy pioneers even established their homes at the mouth of the Allagash River (see Sidebar 10-1 and Map 10-2).

I. LAND GRANTS UNDER THE TREATY

Article V of the Webster–Ashburton Treaty stated that the United States would recognize British grants in the Valley; it also stated that those who had been genuine settlers at Madawaska for six years at the time of the treaty would receive a title to their claim. Maine and Massachusetts, who jointly owned the land south of the river, and New Brunswick sent surveyors to the Valley in 1843 and 1844, respectively, to lay out settlers' lots. Maine and Massachusetts issued grants for 293 river lots and 24 rear lots, as well as some of the islands, in 1845. These various grants totaled 52,300 acres. The surveyors also laid out the lots of 147 people who had begun settling them before the treaty but had not accumulated the required six years of residence. Surveyors issued grants to these individuals, who occupied 14,900 acres, in 1854 after Maine bought Massachusetts's share of the public land. New Brunswick, however, did not re-issue eighteenth-century grants like Maine and Massachusetts; instead, it gave titles to 450 additional claimants in 1848. The New Brunswick grants totaled 77,000 acres. Provincial surveyors also laid out insufficiently improved lots, so that their holders could purchase them without additional expenses. However, this sale of land was put on hold because Lower Canada was claiming part of British Madawaska. The surveyors further reserved several tracts of land for government purposes, and laid out "town plats" opposite the mouth of the Fish River and at the mouth of the St. Francis. This meant the land would be sold out as town—and not farm—lots. A town had already been laid out at the Petit Sault, and in due time it became the town and then city of Edmundston. Another one was laid out at Grand Falls (briefly called Colebrooke). The small Native reservation in St. Basile remained in place.

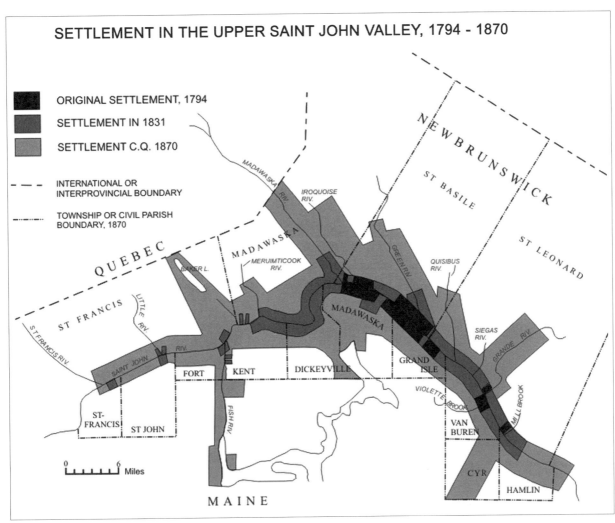

SETTLEMENT IN THE UPPER SAINT JOHN VALLEY, 1794 - 1870

Map 10-1: Population Expansion 1790-1870
Design by B. Craig; cartography by Sam Herald

II. LAND POLICIES AFTER THE TREATY

A. Maine

When Maine separated from Massachusetts and became a state in 1820, Massachusetts had retained ownership of half the public land in its former northern district. Public land was held jointly by the two states, and land titles issued pursuant to the treaty were granted in the names of both states. But the two states could not agree on a common policy concerning the rest of the public land. Massachusetts wanted to use it for revenue, while Maine believed it should be sold as quickly as possible. The issue was resolved when Maine finally purchased Massachusetts' share in 1854.

Maine then rapidly disposed of her public land in the former disputed territory, since her policy had always been to put public land into private hands as quickly as possible. It classified public land as either "settling land" or "timberland." The rapid liquidation policy applied mostly to timberland, which was difficult to police and Maine did not want to pay for the cost of building roads and bridges through it. To prevent lumbermen from purchasing the best timberland, leaving the rest in the hands of the state, Maine auctioned off timberland in quarter, half, and whole townships. Lumbermen usually had to pool their resources to purchase this much land, which they then held "in common"; This means that they did not divide the land among themselves, but shared profits in proportion to their investments. Shares of townships could be sold as well. Local historian Guy Dubay found a rather extreme case in the 1860s, when E. G. Dunn of Ashland and E. S. Coe of Bangor granted cutting rights on two townships to A. S. Flint. Dunn owned $3/8$ of $31/52$ of $1/8$ of one township and $31/52$ of half of another; Coe owned $21/52$ of $1/8$ of one and $21/52$ of half the other. Shares of timberland circulated very rapidly among lumbermen who bought and sold in rapid succession, driven either by cash flow problems or speculation. By mid-century lumbermen owned the bulk of the land that had not been allocated to settlers north of the tenth line of townships. This meant that timber holdings were quickly concentrated in a few hands. For example, David Pingree of Salem, Massachusetts, owned 38 of the 138 townships north of the tenth line in 1853.

Since 1838, Maine land reserved for settlers had

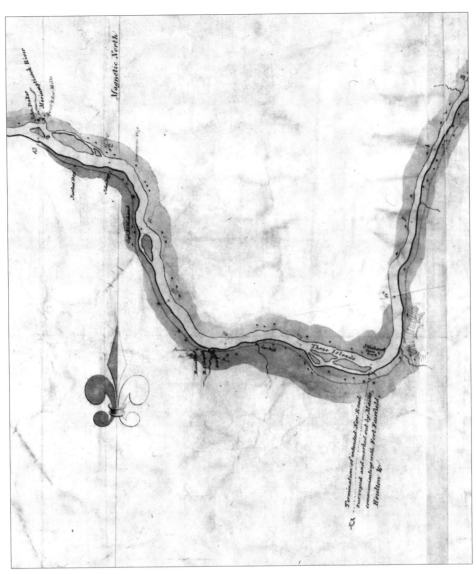

Map 10-2: Sainte Luce in 1840; Section of 1840 map of the Saint John River by New Brunswick surveyor John Wilkinson showing John Baker's grist and sawmill at the mouth of the Meruimticook river, then from left to right, "Justus Deg" (? Daigle), "John Deg" (Jean Baptiste Daigle), Captain Romain Michaud, the burial ground and Sainte Luce's church (on the left of the brook), a gristmill on the right of the same brook, a sawmill at the mouth of the next brook, the termination of an intended route to Fort Fairfield, and J. Michaud's tavern and ferry across the river. Each dot is a house, and the shaded areas represent improved land. The area south of the river is now Frenchville. LAC, NMC- 14310-2

Illus. 10-1: The two houses in this image show clearly how housing evolved as farms got more established. The picture shows a typical clearing, with a house under construction, and a shanty in the yard. The shanty was a small log structure which sheltered people until they built a house; it was subsequently used for animals. Note that the roof is different from the one of the Roy house (Illus. 7-3). The legend says "Petit Sault in 1815," which is impossible because photography did not exist in 1815. CDEM, PC1-16

been sold for 50 cents an acre. One-fourth of the price was to be paid in cash over a four-year period, and the rest in "settling duties," or work on roads and bridges. This policy made land accessible to men of limited means. But in 1868, Maine sold one million acres of timberland in the St. John and Penobscot River basins for one dollar to the European and North American Railroad; some of that land was located immediately behind the treaty lots. There were already some settlers clearing farms on that land, but the state overlooked their presence and made no provisions for them. This led to a "squatter" problem that took twenty years to resolve (see Chapter 17). In 1873, 393 families were settled on propri-

etors' land behind the treaty lots. Eighty-four of the lots thus occupied had been taken in the 1840s, 227 in the 1850s, and 117 in the 1860s.

B. New Brunswick

New Brunswick policies concerning the disposal of Crown land were initially less generous. In 1827, London stopped granting free Crown land in British North America. After 1827, Crown land was disposed of in one of two ways. Would-be settlers could petition for 200-acre lots. The Crown Land Office set the price, which buyers had to pay for in four equal installments. New Brunswick also sold large

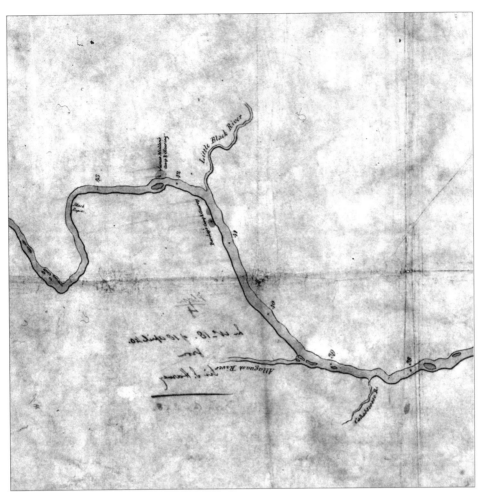

Map 10-3: Allagash section of map of Saint John River by New Brunswick surveyor John Wilkinson in 1840. It shows Barclay's camp and clearing almost opposite the mouth of the Little Black River and James Mullen's camp and clearing immediately to the left of this river. The strange characters are the date, which was written on the back of the map, and bled through. LAC, NMC-14310-1

tracts (two to ten square miles) at public auctions, but forbade removal of timber until the land was fully paid. Lumbermen, however, preferred logging under a provincial license and usually did not buy timberland. Between 1848 and 1856, settlement lots at Madawaska sold for three shillings an acre (60 cents). A would-be farmer purchasing a hundred acres of public land on the British side of the Valley was charged £15, Halifax currency ($60), which had to be paid entirely in cash in four yearly installments.

If he purchased the same amount of land from the State of Maine, he owed $50, $12.50 to be paid in four cash installments and the rest in road labor.

In 1849, the assembly, which had gained control over Crown land in 1837, passed a Labor Act allowing settlers to pay for their land with labor on local public roads. After 1872, groups of settlers could obtain a block grant under the Free Grant Act. Unfortunately, in 1872, New Brunswick granted the Quebec and New Brunswick Railway 100,000 acres

Illus. 10-2: An "American" and a "Canadian" house stand side by side on the bank of the river. The "Canadian houses" were built parallel to the river, and the "American ones" perpendicular to it. CDEM, PB1-12

of land per mile of road constructed, with most of this land in Victoria County. At the beginning of the twentieth century, New Brunswick bought some of the land back to make it available for settlement. Both Maine and New Brunswick thus subsidized the construction of railways on their territories through the giving of massive tracts of land (one million acres in Maine and more than two million in New Brunswick), but both also had to buy back some of that land.

III. POPULATION GROWTH

Both halves of the Valley continued growing after the treaty, and they grew even faster than the counties of which they were part. In 1840, the southern bank of the Valley comprised one-fifth of Aroostook County's entire population; in 1870, it comprised a quarter of the county's population. Nonetheless, overall population growth had slowed on both sides of the river by the mid-nineteenth century, dropping from 8.5 percent per year between 1835 and 1850 to slightly more than 5 percent between 1850 and 1870 (see Table 10-1 and Appendix E). Difficulties between proprietors and settlers and the American

Illus. 10-3: By 1848, many houses built at Madawaska were similar to the O'Neill house in this picture: a one-story building with roof projecting over a gallery, and side utility building. CDEM, PA1-15

Table 10-1: Population Growth on the North and South Banks: 1840–71

| | South Bank (US) | | North Bank (NB) | |
	Population	Annual Increase	Population	Annual Increase
1840	1,876			
1850-51	2,917	5.5 %	1,584	10.6 %
1860-61	5,234	7.9 %	3,434	3.2 %
1870-71	7,443	2.9 %	7,324	6.1 %

Source: See list of censuses pp. 408–09.

Civil War probably explain why population growth dropped significantly on the American side of the river between 1860 and 1870.

The Valley was following regional trends: by the 1860s, overseas migration into New Brunswick had slowed considerably, and foreign migration into Maine was largely comprised of British North Americans. Out-migration from Maine and New Brunswick was also increasing. Mainers were migrating to the Great Lakes region, especially to Bourbonnais, some twenty miles southwest of Chicago. New Brunswickers either flocked to Boston or migrated to Maine, Michigan, Wisconsin, and Minnesota. Those states still had decent farmland available. Logging was also an important activity in all of the Great Lakes states, and former residents of both Maine and New Brunswick could take advantage of the skills they had gained in the woods back home.

But as these early Valley residents were moving out, French Canadians were moving in. New Brunswick historians believe that only the continuous growth of the Acadian districts of Madawaska, Northumberland, and Restigouche (due, in part, to a higher than average birth rate and, in the northern counties, continued French Canadian immigration) prevented the province from experiencing a net population loss. The situation was not as dire in Maine, but Madawaska clearly contributed more than its share to the growth of Aroostook County. The occasional information one can glean from Madawaska sources about the destination of out-migrants suggests an intriguing hypothesis: charter families probably went to the Great Lakes states or Boston, while French Canadians, who only stopped at Madawaska for a few years before continuing on, went to New England's mill towns. People born and bred at Madawaska would then have followed the New Brunswick immigration pattern described above, and French Canadians passing through, the French Canadian pattern.

IV.   ORIGINS OF THE POPULATION

One consequence of lower immigration rates to the Valley after 1850 was a reduction in the percentage of people born and married outside its boundaries. In 1831, for example, 49 percent of the male heads of household and 30 percent of the female ones listed in Deane and Kavanagh's report were born in Lower Canada. Between 1870 and 1871, though, only 38 percent of the male heads of household listed in the census and 19 percent of the females were born in that province.

The censuses do not tell us where couples married, but they do indicate their children's place of birth. Few couples seem to have immigrated into the area between their marriage and the birth of their first child. The proportion of couples with Canadian-born children should, therefore, be a reasonable estimate of the proportion of couples who had married in Canada. It dropped from 26 percent in 1831 to 7 percent in 1870–71 (see Table 10-2). This means that the proportion of Canadian-born adults had declined only modestly, but the proportion of couples who had immigrated to the Valley after marriage had shrunk significantly. As the century progressed, more and more Canadian-born immigrants had spent a large part of their life at Madawaska.

Surprisingly, the proportion of people on both the New Brunswick and Maine sides of the Valley who declared their birthplace as the other side of the Valley was extremely small. This may have been the consequence of the way the census was taken. We can imagine the scene:

Census taker: And what would your name be, sir?

Farmer: Jean-Baptiste Cyr, à Joseph à François.

Census taker: And how old were you on your last birthday sir?

Farmer: Forty-one.

Census taker: And where were you born sir?

Farmer: Well, here, lived here all my life.

The census taker would then jot on his form,

Table 10-2: Distribution of St. John Valley Couples According to Birthplace

	1831	1850–51	1870–71
Number of couples	404	958	2,062
Percentage of husbands born in Canada	49%	45%	38%
Percentage of wives born in Canada	30%	42%	19%
Percentage of families with Canadian-born children	26%	12%	6%

Sources: Deane and Kavanagh, "Report": Langlois (1971); for censuses, see pp. 408–09.

"Birthplace: Maine." The head of one of the households counted in Maine in 1850 had even moved to New Brunswick in time to be enumerated by the province the following one. In the American census, he is listed as native of Maine, and in the provincial one as native of the province.

This vagueness regarding birthplace tells us something: for many Valley people, the Valley remained a single geographic entity. This, however, is not good news for the historian—we cannot use those censuses to determine the extent of migration from one bank of the river to the other.

V. OCCUPATIONAL STRUCTURE

In 1851, more than 80 percent of the male heads of household on the New Brunswick side of the Valley were farmers. One out of ten farmers was listed as a "tenant," which corresponds with what historians have found in other parts of the northeast. Renting a farm was a common but short phase in one's life cycle; it was a time to save money to buy land and, equally important, to build up one's stock. Non-farmers included rural craftsmen, such as blacksmiths, wheelwrights, saddlers, tinsmiths, and shoemakers. Others were in the service industry, such as innkeepers (New Brunswick only), boatmen, millers, merchants, and traders. There were eighteen lumbermen, fifteen carpenters, and one tailor in St. Basile.

The 1850 American census is, on the other hand, of limited use. An inordinate number of heads of household are listed as "laborers," despite having been granted land five years previously. Very few people were neither farmers nor laborers. Yet, it is hard

to believe that there were no blacksmiths or millers in Van Buren, for instance. The only explanation for these anomalies is that the census marshal listed as "farmers" only those who clearly could make a living from their holding (which relegated new farmers to the ranks of laborers). Village artisans and millers were listed as "farmers," not as artisans or millers, because they also owned a farm. This way of listing occupation reveals what was in the census taker's mind: economic self-sufficiency required an operational farm; any additional source of income was a bonus.

Between 1870 and 1871, the occupational structure on the American side of the Valley had changed: 70 percent of the male heads of household were listed as farmers and 22 percent as laborers. Other individuals fell into a range of manufacturing and service occupations. Laborers were concentrated in Fort Kent, Saint John, and St. Francis. Those laborers may have been new farmers; more likely, they were men who derived most of their income from wage work in the woods or in the mills, as suggested by their proximity to lumber production centers. On the New Brunswick side, the proportion of farmers among male household heads had dropped and 16 percent of the heads of household in Madawaska Parish were listed as neither farmers nor laborers. The range of occupations was wider in Madawaska/Edmundston: heads of household included five inn- or hotel-keepers, one boarding-house keeper (Vital Hébert's widow), three merchants, three storekeepers, two physicians (Florent Fournier and François Bernier—see Sidebar 24-1), six schoolteachers, one tailor, one saddle maker, and one baker. Hébert's widow also had a photographer, a storekeeper/member of the Church of England (Hilaire Pelletier), and the storekeeper's clerk (Michael Tighe) lodging at her residence. A surveyor was staying at Prudent Babin's hotel; Babin was also the census taker. William Hartt, son of merchant John Hartt, Esq., was a telegraph operator at St. Basile. More significant was the presence of twenty-three merchants, storekeepers, and traders in the entire Valley—or one store for approximately one hundred households. The 1870 and 1871 censuses show that the Valley was moving away from being an agricultural–lumbering settlement. Its economy was beginning to diversify, and this diversification resulted in the emergence of proto-urban centers.

Conclusion

After the signing of the 1842 treaty, land in the Valley ceased to be a natural resource available to all who claimed it. State and provincial governments reasserted their rights over it and used it to further their own aims. Massachusetts and the British authorities believed public land should be used to produce revenues for the state. Maine and New Brunswick legislators thought otherwise. They wanted to use this land to entice people to settle in the state or province and prevent population decline. Their views prevailed, and after mid-century farm-land was available almost free of charge to those interested. Unfortunately for would-be farmers, both the state and the province also decided to use public land to subsidize railway building, with rather mediocre results.

Populationist land policies were unsuccessful. They could not prevent the large-scale westward migration that slowed population growth in both Maine and New Brunswick and even caused the population to decline in some districts. Nonetheless, the population in the northern parts of Maine and New Brunswick grew, thanks in large part to Canadian immigration. It is not clear if cheap land contributed to this growth. Regional rates of population growth do not reflect changes in land-granting policies. On the other hand, growth rates were adversely affected by political problems, such as the inter-provincial boundary dispute and the American Civil War.

Migrants were looking for land. They and their children contributed to the rapid growth in the number of farms between 1850 and 1870. However, by 1870, the Valley's occupational structure was beginning to show signs of the changes yet to come. Wage earners headed more and more households, especially in the part of the settlement closer to the lumber camps. Villages like Fort Kent and, more particularly, Edmundston were attracting a population with a wider range of occupations. This included those in service occupations such as lawyers, physicians, and photographers. However, by 1870, the Valley was more homogeneous in terms of the origins of its population, whose numbers now included more people born and raised in the Valley. It had, however, ceased to be an undifferentiated mass of farmers sprinkled with a few rural craftsmen. Its economic and social structure was on the brink of change.

The Land in Between

FURTHER READINGS

Dubay, Guy. "The Garden of Maine." In *The County: Land of Promise,* ed. A. Macgrath. 1989: 153–60.

Dubay, Guy. "The Land in Common and Undivided: the Lumber World of Western Aroostook." In *The County: Land of Promise,* ed. A. Macgrath. 1989: 145–52.

Dubay, Guy. *Light on the Past: Documentation on our Acadian Heritage.* 1995. (This contains transcriptions of early censuses and copies of early maps.)

SOURCES

Population figures can be calculated from the schedules of the various American, New Brunswick, and, after 1867, Canadian censuses (see list pp. 408–09). For Maine land policies, see D. C. Smith (1969) and for New Brunswick, see Ganong (1904). For Acadian and French Canadian immigration to New England, see Brookes (1976), Vicero (1968), and Leblanc (1988). The story of lumbermen holding timberland in common is found in Dubay's "The Land in Common..." on page 146.

11

POLITICS AND RELIGION, 1845–67

The 1842 treaty split the Valley between two entities whose political systems and philosophies were very different. On one side was a fairly democratic republic that allowed extensive grassroots input into the political process. On the other side was a colony whose mother country controlled the decision-making process and circumscribed popular participation.

Maine life was highly politicized and shaped by both national and state issues. In the 1840s and 1850s, those issues so severely disrupted traditional alignments that they led to the emergence of new parties, one of which (the Republicans) still exists today. In New Brunswick, there were no parties—and no group of politicians officially called itself a party before 1925. Through most of the nineteenth century, New Brunswickers subscribed to the "compact" view of government—governments were ad-hoc coalitions of politicians that could fall apart for

any number of reasons. Personalities, not party affiliation or ideologies, were what mattered. When Madawaskayans on the south bank of the river became American citizens, they did not instantly adopt American political culture (about which they knew almost nothing). The little evidence about Valley political life that has survived suggests that Valley people continued to adhere to their political traditions and practice "compact" politics.

At first glance, one would think that the treaty did not affect religion, as churches remained independent from governments. Church officials, however, were getting involved in politics, and parishioners on the American side of the river complained that the cross-border parishes had become unmanageable; they asked to be incorporated into an American diocese—a decision likely influenced by local politics.

I. NEW BRUNSWICK: FROM COLONIAL TO RESPONSIBLE GOVERNMENT AND CONFEDERATION

A. Evolution of the System

As we saw in Chapter 8, in the early 1840s the provincial political system was deliberately undemocratic, although it did not entirely shut common people out of the decision-making process. In that decade and the next, the provincial political system underwent profound changes. In the 1840s, reformers managed to put "casual revenues" (which

included income from timber licenses) under the control of the assembly rather than the governor's. This gave the House of Assembly power over the purse. Next, in 1848, London accepted the extension to the colonies of the principle of responsible government, in which the Executive Council had to secure the confidence of the assembly or resign. If the House of Assembly did not like what the Executive Council was doing, it could pass a motion of non-confidence and dissolve the government. Then, the lieutenant governor could either appoint a government that had the confidence of the majority of the assembly members or call an election. This meant that the parliamentary system was established in New Brunswick at about the same time it was established in the other British North American colonies.

The electoral system also democratized slightly, which made it possible for craftsmen and professionals who owned little real estate to vote. Universal male suffrage, however, did not occur until 1889. (Women had to wait until after World War I and Natives until 1960.)[1] The electoral law passed in 1855 introduced the secret (or "Australian") ballot and restricted the right to vote to British subjects. (All people born in British North America were British subjects, as were all people born in the British Isles.)

Despite the fact that politicians had lined up under the Reform and Tory banners during the struggle for responsible government, these could not be considered parties in the traditional sense, since the alignments did not last. Subsequently, some politicians were known as "conservative" or "liberal" (with the latter in favor of further democratization of government, moral reform, such as Prohibition, and secularization of public life), but liberals and conservatives did not form lasting alliances among themselves and were known to strike deals with politicians of the opposite tendency to gain power. Governments were comprised of allied politicians who got together to run the province, who knew how to make the system work, and who carefully distributed patronage appointments and public work expenditures among themselves and their constituents. Furthermore, until 1855 individual members could introduce money bills in the assembly, which they could then use to finance local projects, such as byroads and bridges. "Earmarks," in other words, have venerable antecedents. "Opposition" parties regrouped individuals whose goals and ambitions had been thwarted by the current government, and politicians moved freely from opposition to govern-

ment. At election time, family ties and personal connections figured prominently in the nomination process. Candidates identified themselves as "friends of the government" or "friends of the opposition" and ran on personal planks. There were no party platforms. Each candidate issued his own election card in which he informed electors of his position on the issues affecting them, stated the reasons why they should vote for him, and pledged to attend to local needs and concerns. To further convince the limited number of voters that they were their friends, candidates treated them to food and drinks and even paid them to vote. In return, people voted for candidates who they thought could defend their interests or to whom they felt bound by personal ties. Until the adoption of the secret ballot, physical intimidation at the polls also influenced electoral results. Political life was, therefore, parochial, personal, and dominated by cliques or compacts; elections were, at best, boisterous events reminiscent of a militia muster and, at worst, violent, mob-controlled affairs.

One consequence of parochial politics noted by historian Robert Garland was that "compact coalitions built upon a co-existence of diversities that confined polarization to just below the surface."[2] Much later, Catholic/Protestant and French/English antagonisms would come out into the open, but before 1866 whatever the Protestants thought of the Catholics and the English of the French (and vice versa) had a muted impact on politics. Assembly members were elected by county-wide, multi-member constituencies; this usually made minimizing ethnic or religious divisions desirable.

B. The Contested 1854 Elections

The personal and local nature of elections and the marginal impact of religious affiliation and language on those elections became very visible during the contested 1854 Victoria election. (Madawaska was then part of Victoria; see Table 11-1.) In that election, shared economic interests determined a candidate's supporters. Victoria was entitled to two seats in

Table 11-1: British Administration of Madawaska

1821	Madawaska territory formally integrated into the new civil parish of Kent
1833	Carleton County established (shire town: Woodstock)
1833	Madawaska territory turned into a civil parish
1844	Victoria County established; creation vetoed due to the interprovincial boundary dispute.
1851	Victoria County re-created (shire town: Grand Falls)
1851	Civil parishes of St. Francis, Madawaska, St. Basile, and St. Leonard established

the House of Assembly, and the two candidates with the highest number of votes across the county would get elected.

Francis Rice (from Madawaska) and James Tibbits (from Andover) received the highest number of votes cast. The results were close: 422 for Tibbits and 420 for Rice. Charles Watters from Andover lost with 392 votes. At the opening of the session, the House of Assembly was presented with three separate petitions. Tibbits, who instigated one of them, claimed Rice had been illegally elected (through violence, influence peddling, and corruption). Mgr. Langevin, the St. Basile priest, said irregularities had taken place at the Andover poll where supposedly ineligible voters had cast votes for Tibbits. Langevin claimed Watters should have been elected. Watters, a Catholic, was a personal friend of Langevin. Leonard Coombs, Firmin Thibodeau, and Léon Bellefleur, for their part, denounced the violence perpetrated by Watters' supporters at the St. Francis, Madawaska, St. Basile, and St. Leonard polls. They said Tibbits's supporters had been driven away at St. Francis, noting that the troublemakers had come from Maine. Eighty-seven individuals, none bearing a French name, signed Tibbits's petition. Coombs's petition was backed by 308 people, many of whom were local businessmen. This included merchants, such as J. Emmerson, P. C. Amiraux, and J. Hodgson; lumbermen, such as four members from the Glazier family and three members from the Beardsley family; millers or future millers, such as Joseph Cyr and P. O. Byram; innkeeper Augustin Perron; and others, such as Simonet Hébert

and his sons, Vital and Beloni, Squire Firmin Thibodeau, Francis Thibodeau, and several Bellefleurs. Langevin's petition had the greater number of supporters (342) but included only three leading men: Dr. Florent Fournier, Joseph Hébert, and Régis Thériault. The other names all appear to have been those of farmers.[3]

Madawaska businessmen, regardless of the nature and scope of their business, or their ethnicity and religion, rallied together to support the election of one of their own: lumberman James Tibbits. A large number of farmers led by one of the priests, however, opposed him. No Madawaskayan, on the other hand, appeared ready to challenge the election of a local candidate: Francis Rice. Politics created divisions between businessmen and farmers, and local men and outsiders; it also split extended families. However, national origin, language, and religion do not seem to have played much of a role in those divisions. Watters did gain a seat at the partial election of 1855, held when Rice had to resign because of his appointment to the Legislative Council.[4] In that race, Watters defeated "John" Cyr, 411 to 381.

C. John Costigan and Confederation

John Costigan was elected to the New Brunswick Assembly in 1861. He died while still a federal senator in 1916. (See his biography in Sidebar 26-1.) His political career was, therefore, a very long one. Costigan's father, also named John, was a native of Ireland who immigrated to Lower Canada in 1830. He worked as an agent for Sir John Caldwell, subsequently moving to Grand Falls where Sir John had a sawmill. He eventually became a postmaster at Grand Falls. After finishing his education at the college in Sainte-Anne-de-la-Pocatière, the younger Costigan became registrar of the deeds for Victoria County in 1857 and then a judge in the Inferior Court of Common Pleas. He also married in 1857. In 1861, he ran for the assembly and was elected on a "conservative" ticket. (This meant he did not align himself with the reformers or "Smashers," led by Samuel Leonard Tilley. That group advocated prohibition, assembly control of all public expenses, a non-sectarian public school system, and "honest government.") Prohibition was the biggest political issue in New Brunswick in the 1850s. In 1853, the assembly passed a prohibition law modeled on the "Maine Law"; however, it proved unenforceable and was abrogated the next year, only to be reinstated by the new government in 1855. This time it was enforced much to the outrage of most of the population. The government fell as a consequence. Tilley (who was provincial secretary at the time) was not re-elected, and the new government again repealed prohibition. Reformers were, however, back in power in 1858, and stayed in power for the next ten years. They were not particularly inclined to recognize linguistic or religious rights: instead, they promoted an English, secular, and dry society. The conservatives were usually not prohibitionists and believed religion had a role to play in public affairs. It was that latter conviction that led to occasional Protestant-Catholic alliances.

Costigan's election in 1861 was part of a changing of the guard that had begun in the mid-1850s, in which men from the lower ranks of society were replacing politicians from old, mostly Loyalist families. Amand Landry, for example, was the first Acadian to gain an assembly seat when he was elected in Westmorland in 1854. Another Westmorland politician, Albert Smith, had recognized the electoral weight of the Acadians and was actively courting their vote. Rice was similarly elected in 1854, and

became the first Madawaskayan to be elected to the House of Assembly. The new men soon faced an issue that polarized political life in the Maritimes: Confederation.

As mentioned earlier, the various British North American colonies were autonomous units—independent from each other but subject to imperial control (see Appendix A). By the 1860s, Britain was finding its colonies expensive and wanted them to join together to ensure their own defense. Railroad interests also wanted the provinces to join together to enhance their ability to raise capital on financial markets. Manufacturers in central Canada wanted the provinces to join together to expand their market, especially since the United States was raising tariffs, making it increasingly difficult to export manufactured goods there. At the same time, Upper and Lower Canada wanted a divorce, because their "united" province had become hopelessly impossible to govern—the French and English simply could not agree with each other on anything. Their premier, John A. Macdonald, had come to the conclusion that diluting "the Canadas" into a larger union would solve the problem. In 1864, the men who were later called the "Fathers of Confederation" devised a plan for a confederation of the British North American provinces at conferences in Charlottetown (P.E.I.), Quebec City, and London.

Upper and Lower Canada were both in favor of Confederation. The Catholic hierarchy in Lower Canada was particularly favorable. Maritimers, however, were divided. The Tilley government supported the move. The Irish Catholic New Brunswickers opposed it, since they were afraid of being swallowed by a sea of Protestants. The Maritime Catholic hierarchy was similarly divided. Bishop Sweeny of Saint John was quietly opposed; Bishop Rogers of Chatham more openly in favor; and Archbishop Connelly of Halifax was very openly in favor. The Acadians were generally opposed: they did not want to become a French minority in an English state. However, the conservative Israel Landry, founder of the *Moniteur Acadien,* was in favor. Most opponents, regardless of their religion and language, were also very much aware of the fact that Lower and Upper Canada were more populous and economically developed; they feared those central Canadians would control the government and run it for their own interests. To make matters worse, the province of Canada was in debt, which the new entity, if formed, would assume; in short, Maritimers would end up paying for central Canada's internal improvements. Westmorland politician Albert Smith consequently called the Confederation scheme "a plan born of the oily brain of Canadian [that is, Ontario and Québec] politicians."5

In 1865, Tilley called an election that turned into a referendum for or against Confederation. The anti-Confederation forces led by Albert Smith won. Those forces were particularly strong in the northern (Acadian) counties; Victoria, for example, returned an anti-Confederation slate. Costigan joined the new government led by Smith. The new government, however, was made up of people united solely by their opposition to Confederation, and it soon fell. At the 1866 elections, the pro-Confederation forces won. They had received some unexpected help: American members of the Fenian Brotherhood, an Irish organization fighting for home rule (internal autonomy) in Ireland, had decided to attack the nearest British possessions, thereby launching raids in Upper Canada and southern New Brunswick. The Americans did little to stop them, and British North Americans concluded that the United States was ready to attack and annex them into the Union. Confederation suddenly seemed like a good move. Canada also filled the electoral coffers of pro-Confederation candidates in the province.

Westmorland, Kent, and Gloucester Counties returned Confederation opponents to the assembly thanks to Acadian support. This led some pro-Confederation newspapers, especially the virulently anti-Catholic *Saint John Daily Telegraph,* to denounce the ignorant and illiterate French, or the "half savage from Tracadie," for their choice. In Victoria, pro-Confederation candidates James Beveridge and Vital Hébert led the polls. Costigan, assumed to be pro-Fenian because he was Irish, came in third and was, therefore, not elected.6 The following year, despite his initial opposition to Confederation, Costigan ran for a seat in the federal parliament as a conservative and won.

II.   MAINE POLITICS FROM THE REFORM ERA TO THE CIVIL WAR

Maine politics during this time were quite different from New Brunswick politics. Its political horizon stretched farther than her boundaries, since she was part of a federal state. Local government was in the hands of locally elected people, and the state legislature did not have to worry about every byroad in the state (see Appendix G, "Maine Local Government"). Maine also had clearly identifiable political parties. Extreme verbal violence, however, characterized the campaigns, as each party was convinced it was the only true repository of American values. When Maine became a state, the Democratic Republicans dominated the state political scene just as they dominated the federal one. The party, however, grouped people with sharply differing views regarding the proper role of government. One faction wanted state and federal governments to actively support commerce and manufacturing. It advocated tariffs against the import of manufactured goods to protect American industries, subsidies for internal improvements, and the creation of a national bank. The other faction was highly suspicious of policies linking governments to manufacturing and commercial interests, believed banks were parasitical institutions, and favored decentralization coupled with greater state rights.

After Andrew Jackson was elected president in 1828, the two factions hardened into two separate parties: the National Republicans (soon renamed the Whigs) and the (Jacksonian) Democrats. Jackson also introduced the "spoils system" in which active supporters of the winning party filled public offices. This practice enhanced neither the reputation of public officials nor that of politicians. Farmers and craftspeople tended to be Democrats and business people Whigs.

From 1820 to the recession of 1837, Democrats in favor of limited government dominated Maine political life. Many, however, blamed the 1830s recession on Jackson's economic policies. The ensuing Whig ascendancy was short-lived, and the Democrats were back in power until 1842 when reformer Republicans captured the state; they remained in power until 1854. The years 1842 to 1856, however, were politically confusing because reform movements and the issue of slavery splintered existing parties and led to the temporary or permanent regrouping of dissidents into other political parties.

The 1820s, 1830s, and 1840s were the "age of reform" in the northeastern states. Reformers were usually members of an evangelical church; they believed human beings were perfectible and therefore had a duty to improve themselves. They also believed that Christians had a God-given duty to facilitate the process through both moral persuasion and legislation. The reform movements that had the greatest impact on Maine in the 1840s, when the southern part of the Valley became American, were Nativism, Prohibition, and opposition to slavery. The Nativists were intensely anti-immigration and anti-Catholic. The slavery issue destroyed the Whig Party, almost destroyed the Democrats, and led to the creation of the Republican Party, which became the dominant party in Maine in 1856 and remained so until the early 1900s. In Maine, the Prohibition issue also significantly contributed to party fragmentation and realignment.

Initially, the Valley was part of Maine's political mainstream: it voted Democrat like the majority of the state's electors. However, it did not switch affiliations in the 1850s like the rest of the state. The Valley was also wet, French-speaking, and Catholic, which made it an inevitable target of Nativists and Prohibitionists, and consequently, of many Whigs and Republicans.

A. The Reform Impulse in Maine

In the early 1840s, the issues that dominated Maine political life were linked to the reform impulse. Nativism was on the rise, and the first Prohibition law passed in 1837. Nativism complicated the integration of Valley people into Maine politics. Their refusal to endorse the Prohibition movement put them at odds with an extremely vocal and efficient pressure group.

Nativism was a backlash against Irish Catholic immigration. Many perceived Irish Catholics as clannish, intemperate, prone to brawling, and subservient to their priests. They were also prompt to become citizens and get involved in politics (and normally threw their support behind the Jacksonian Democrats). Many native-born Americans, therefore, viewed them as not only objectionable but also as threats to American principles and institutions. Those with strong anti-immigrant feelings gathered in the American Party, more commonly known as the "Know Nothing Party." Know Nothingism attracted many people from the disintegrating Whig Party in the late 1840s, and the Maine Know Nothing Party was founded in 1854. Nativism led to some nasty incidents: anti-Catholic riots in Portland, the burning of Catholic churches in Bangor and Bath, and the tarring and feathering of Father John Bapst in Ellsworth. Maine Nativists, however, condemned mob actions; they believed that the proper solution was to make the acquisition of American citizenship more difficult.

Nativism was undistinguishable from anti-Catholicism. In 1843, when Maine legislators appointed Governor John Fairfield to the U.S. Senate (at the time, legislators, not electors, chose senators), the president of the Maine State Senate took his place, as provided for in the Constitution. He was the Québec-educated, Catholic Democrat Edward Kavanagh. Kavanagh should have been automatically chosen as his party's gubernatorial candidate in the next election. Instead, the Democrats chose the Protestant Hugh Anderson. They denied that religion influenced their decision, but few were convinced. Although Kavanagh was not on the ballot, 3,000 people voted for him in protest. Religion—or rather Catholicism—remained the issue that would not go away.

In Maine, Know Nothingists were also ardent Prohibitionists. Prohibition was particularly strong in the state, whose legislature passed Maine's first prohibition law in 1837. That resolution, however, lacked teeth. Portland Mayor Neal Dow (a Whig) secured the passage of a stronger law (the "Maine Law") in 1851. Maine was the first state in the Union to become dry and, with a short interlude, remained so until 1933. Prohibition had more support among Whigs than Democrats, and Prohibitionists usually supported other reform movements, particularly the anti-slavery movement. French Canadians and Acadians were strongly opposed to the Maine Law even though they often joined temperance societies organized by their priests. They believed in drinking in moderation, not abstinence, and volunteerism, not coercion. This put Madawaskayans at odds with a powerful political force in the state. It didn't help that this force was also anti-Catholic.

B. Opposition to Slavery and the Birth of the Republican Party

When the southern part of the Valley became American, Mainers had just replaced a Whig governor with a Democratic one. Succeeding governors were all Democrats until 1854, when the Prohibitionist Lot M. Morril was elected. In the 1850s, the Democratic Party lost favor because it had become associated with the wrong side of the slavery issue.[7] Mainers, like almost all New Englanders, condemned slavery as immoral. However, they disagreed about what should be done about it. As in the rest of the United States, opponents to slavery were divided. The more radical group, the Abolitionists, advocated

abolishing slavery across the Union. Another group, the Free Soilers, wanted to allow slavery to continue where it already existed but prevent its extension; they believed that slavery would die out on its own in due time.[8]

Neither option was palatable to slaveholding states. They feared that if the free states became the majority in the Union, they would abolish slavery sooner or later. They, therefore, aligned themselves with the Democratic Party because it had always supported state rights. The Democrats themselves were divided. In Maine, they split between two factions in 1849, the Woolheads, who were militantly opposed to its extension (as well as drinking), and the Wildcats, who were more open to compromise. The 1854 Wildcat gubernatorial candidate was Shepard Cary, who condemned both abolitionism and Prohibition. Opponents to slavery were more likely to gravitate toward the more interventionist-minded Whig Party, and after the Whig party began to disintegrate, toward the short-lived Liberty and Free Soil parties that emerged in the 1840s and 1850s.[9] Anti-slavery Democrats also bolted from their party in increasing numbers to join anti-slavery parties. The remaining Democrats were, therefore, looking more and more like accomplices of the hated southern "Slavocrats." In 1861, many Democrats opposed going to war to keep the southern states in the Union, leading to a new split between "peace" and "war" Democrats. Democrats usually opposed the Maine Law as well.

This led to the founding of the Republican Party in 1854. It was a gathering of anti-slavery Democrats, leftover Whigs, Know Nothingists, Free Soilers, Prohibitionists, and other reformers. The Republicans fielded their first gubernatorial candidate in 1856, won the elections, and kept winning them until long after the Civil War had ended. Being a Democrat in Maine in the late 1850s and 1860s amounted to quite a bit more than supporting a minority party. It made the person morally suspect, if not downright "un-American," in the eyes of Republicans.

Table 11-2: Gubernatorial Election Results in the Valley, 1844-66

	Percent Whig or Republican	Percent Democrat	Party Winning the Election
1844	14.2	85.8	D
1845	0	100	D
1847	2.6	97.4	D
1848	5.2	94.8	D
1849	7.3	92.7	D
1850	41	59	D
1852	--	--	W
1853	59.3	37.5	W
1854	45	5	Other
1855	24.1	75.9	D
1856	21	79	R
1857	40.9	59.1	R
1858	14.8	85.2	R
1859	20.2	79.8	R
1860	40.6	59.4	R
1861	--	--	R
1862	52.6	9.9a	R
1863	19	81	R
1864	12.2	87.8	R
1865	45.6	54.4	R
1866	18.5	81.5	R

a. Plus 37.5 percent for the "War Democrat" candidate
Information missing for 1852 and 1861.
Sources: *Belfast Republican; Kennebec Journal.*

C. Voting Patterns in the Valley

Valley electors had supported Democratic gubernatorial candidates in the 1840s and early 1850s. This had made them part of the electoral mainstream. However, when the state turned Republican, they did not follow suit and continued voting Democrat, even during the Civil War (with the exception of 1853 and 1863). The Republican vote in the Valley oscillated between 12 percent in 1864 and 59 percent in 1853 (see Table 11-2). Madawaskayans were,

nonetheless, not wedded to the Democratic Party. In 1849, 1850, and 1854, their state representatives were Whigs. The Valley similarly sent two delegates, François Thibodeau and Firmin Cyr, to the county Republican convention in 1858. Presidential elections attracted few voters in the Valley, except in 1852. The Whig candidate was a familiar figure: General Winfred Scott, a prominent figure during the Aroostook War. Scott lost the election, but 204 of the 324 Madawaska voters supported him.

This did not prevent the Whig/Republicans

from violently denouncing the French for their Democratic leanings and claiming that their bad political choices were somehow a consequence of their lack of English. They also accused Madawaskayans of the same sins as many immigrants: they allegedly sold their votes for personal favor, money, and booze. Partisan prejudices coupled with anti-immigrant and anti-Catholic hostilities led many Whigs and later Republicans to depict the Valley French as a menace to American political values anytime local electoral results worked against their favor. (But as Sidebar 11-1 shows, Democrats

---

Sidebar 11-1: Finger Pointing

Democrats
Extract from a letter to the editor printed in the *Republican Journal*, (Belfast, Maine), from a writer in Saint John, dated September 20, 1844. (The *Republican Journal* was Democrat; it was founded in the days when the Democratic Party was still known as the Democratic Republicans). The author is an unhappy Democrat.

About one week before the elections, several federal emissaries [the administration is Whig] came upon this river from the Aroostook and Houlton, and in addition to these, the feds had the influence of their British allies on the other side of the river. As soon as certain one of these emissaries came upon the river, he hired as many as he thought necessary to accompany him up and down the river. He engaged a dinner for their party at Madawaska and prepared a hundred at the house where the meeting was held, and his party did the same at Hancock Plantation and Van Buren Plantation. It was publicly stated that all persons voting the Whig ticket should have dinner gratis, and very many stated to me that they were offered pay for they day's work, and as much rum as they could drink for the day, if they would vote the Whig ticket from the foregoing, you can form some idea of what the Democrats had to contend with, among a population wholly unacquainted with our laws, and rules regulating elections.

Whigs/ Republicans
This statement by James Pike, responsible for investigating accusations of electoral frauds in the Valley in 1858, shows that Democrats indulged in the same behavior.

In 1844, all these plantations [Hancock, Madawaska, and Van Buren] voted for members of Congress in the Eastern district; but the votes were all rejected by the Governor and Council [Democrats] for alleged informalities and illegalities, the principal informality being, most probably, that the votes were given for the wrong candidate....

It was the custom for the candidates for office in New Brunswick, or their friends, to provide gratuitous entertainment on the day of elections to their supporters. And in this way, frequently large sums of money were expended. And when by the treaty of 1842 the French settlement on the South and West side of the Saint John River fell within the jurisdiction of Maine, the same course of treatment was expected from the candidates for offices in Maine, as had been practices in New Brunswick. Unscrupulous and scheming politicians were not slow in finding this out and profiting by the occasion.

Source: Maine Public Documents. *Report of the Joint Committee Appointed to Investigate Frauds....* (1858): 2–3.

were no better than Republicans.)

We do not know whether Madawaskayans continued to prefer Democrats because they were traditionally the party of farmers or because they were the party in power when they became Americans. One may also surmise that the presence of Nativists and Prohibitionists among the Republicans alienated many, although not all Madawaska residents felt that way. Madawaskayans were, however, aware that their origins made them suspect. When asked where he was born during the 1858 investigation into electoral fraud, François Thibodeau answered, "I was born here and I have always lived here." He did not clarify what he meant by "here"—and based on the location of his father's homestead, he was probably born on the New Brunswick side of the river.

D. The Continuation of Compact Politics

The political system in Maine was more egalitarian than in New Brunswick, and the party system more fully developed. The Valley residents, however, continued to engage in compact politics as they had when they were part of New Brunswick—and to endorse the same political class. The Reverend Henri Dionne's letter to John Hubbard, Maine former Democratic governor, reflects the same kind of relationship Langevin had established with the governor of New Brunswick, as well as the need to solve the same kinds of problems (see Appendix O). Dionne and Hubbard corresponded in French, as had Langevin and the lieutenant governor of New Brunswick. Hubbard had secured money for Madawaska roads in the past and Dionne visibly expected money for the schools he sponsored and wanted Hubbard to keep an eye on this. Finally, Dionne asked Hubbard to clarify settlers' rights to timber.

Both the top-down New Brunswick system and the bottom-up United States one identified the same individuals as the natural local leaders. New Brunswick appointed justices of the peace and militia officers who were closely related to those elected

in the United. In a few cases, the same person simultaneously filled the various functions on both sides of the border. François Thibodeau, who had been a militia lieutenant since 1840 and became a New Brunswick justice of the peace in early 1849, was elected to the Maine House of Representatives in the fall of 1849. He remained a member until 1852, when he was succeeded by his brother-in-law Paul Cyr. Joseph Nadeau, an innkeeper at Fish River, eventually replaced Cyr and stayed in that position until 1857 when one of François Thibodeau's nephews, Firmin Thibodeau, had his turn. Cyr replaced the younger Thibodeau again from 1859 to 1861.

François Thibodeau was one of the community's leading men. His wife had financed the building of a shrine over an allegedly miraculous spring in Grand Isle on the American bank. François was important enough for the bishops of Boston to stay at his place when they conducted pastoral visits in the American Madawaska. Two of his daughters were among the dozen or so pupils boarding at the St. Basile Convent School in 1871, and one of them later joined a convent in Saint John. And as we saw, in 1858, Thibodeau took part in the county Republican convention, whose participants elected former storekeeper Abraham Dufour (also Thibodeau's cousin) as vice president of the county party organization. Thibodeau and a few others were shifting from compact to partisan politics. Nonetheless, French-speaking politicians in American Madawaska remained closely related to each other and closely related to New Brunswick justices of the peace and militia officers. François' brother, Vital, for instance was commissioned as a militia captain in 1842 and as a justice of the peace in 1847.

E. A Case of Electoral Fraud: The Elections of 1858

From the time the Valley first held elections, losing parties questioned the validity of the results. In 1858, the accusations grew more serious and led to a formal inquiry led by Senator James Pike of Calais, Maine. And, indeed, there were reasons to be suspicious. In Hancock Plantation where, in the past, 150 to 175 voters had cast a ballot, 360 votes had been registered. Pike's report describes an appalling situation throughout the Valley: federal officials, who due to the spoils system, were all Democrats appointed by a Democratic administration, supervised the elections, and interfered with voters. They had openly bought votes and circulated lists of eligible voters after the fact. In Madawaska and Van Buren, the plantation clerk and assessors were almost all illiterate in English, if not illiterate in general. In Hancock, these individuals were Americans but also appallingly incompetent (see Sidebar 11-2). And that was not the worst of it: in addition to all the irregularities and illegalities that had occurred in the two other plantations, a Hancock Democratic candidate for the state senate, William Dickey, was the one holding the ballot box; the poll opened before the plantation clerk

---

Sidebar 11-2: Hubbub

As evidenced by the following statements to James Pike during the 1858 investigation into allegations of fraud, extreme confusion—and voting irregularities—were rife in the St. John Valley in the mid-1850s.

Statement by Firmin Cyr (à Paul), clerk of Van Buren Plantation:
There was no old list [of voters] and I made up the one which was posted, by request of the assessors, from my own knowledge. I could find no old list but the one of 1850. I know most of the voters in this plantation. We counted the checks on our list, and compared them with the ballots, and found them to agree. I made up the list sent to the Secretary of State from my checks. We admit all to vote who swear they were born on the disputed territory. Those who come from Canada and were on the other side of the line at the time of the treaty we do not admit (p. 21).

From the statement of William H. Cunliffe, clerk of Hancock Plantation:
I am clerk of Hancock Plantation. I do not know who are the voters in this plantation and who are not. I do not know anything about the rules for receiving votes. There are no regularity about them. I do not know whether any names are ever handed to our assessors or not, to be put on our voting list. At the last election, everything was in a hubbub (p. 30).

From the statement of Martin Savage, assessor of Hancock Plantation:
There are about 25 voters above the Hancock Plantation line on the St. John River. There is a settlement at the mouth of the Allagash and Little Black rivers, and along on the river. We received all the voters from that quarter who come. The townships above us never send us any list of name to put on our voting list. There is no established rule about voting as far as I can find or get hold of. The people who come from Canada, I think, have to be here 10 or 12 years to entitle them to vote; American born have to be here three months; but there is no fixed rule (p. 32).

Source: Maine Public Documents. *Report of the Joint Committee Appointed to Investigate Frauds....*_(1858).

arrived; and, to top it off, Dickey's supporters had treated voters to a liberal quantity of alcohol.

Pike, a Republican reporting to a Prohibitionist governor, referred his report of the incident to a select joint committee headed by Elijah Hamlin, a former Whig gubernatorial candidate. Some of the accusations levied at the French were the kind of stock accusations Nativists routinely levied against immigrants and Catholics. Parties not in control of the White House also routinely accused the federal government of using federal officials to produce the desired electoral results. In this particular case, however, the complaints appear to have reflected more than crude stereotypes. For a start, Pike, although clearly partisan, was not prejudiced. He was very much aware of the fact that the problems in the Valley could feed negative stereotypes about its people, and he went to great length to counter them. He also tried to understand why the problems had occurred in the first place—and, in doing so, he has provided modern historians with glimpses into how Valley people were adapting to the American political system. Pike concluded that the allegations about voting irregularities, corruption, and fraud were true, but also determined that the French clerks and assessors had been conscientious election supervisors. The same could not be said of the Americans in Hancock, where the worst abuses had taken place.

> In justice to this people, it should be borne in mind that the plantation, in which the frauds were committed at the last election, is the one which is not officered by the French. In Hancock, the three assessors and the clerk are native born or regularly naturalized citizens. The French voters were not parties to it farther than to have allowed themselves to be made, in part, blind instruments of its perpetration, and in this, only to a limited extent.[10]

The voters, acquainted only with New Brunswick-style elections were, he believed, "made the prey of designing reckless men, mainly the agents of the federal government."

Pike concluded that it was urgent to provide the Valley with a decent education system where the children would be taught in French, reasoning that one cannot teach children in a language they do not know and expect good results. The committee reviewing the matter blamed the Democrats for their role in the incident. They also proposed that plantations not be larger than townships, and that a former law allowing residents of unincorporated townships to vote more or less where they chose would be repealed. The goal was to make it possible for the clerk and assessors to know whether the people trying to vote were indeed eligible.

Beneath the surface of Pike's report, one detects a New Brunswick compact political culture. Everybody agreed people had been paid to vote. Joseph Nadeau of Fort Kent even described this payment as fair compensation for people's time, noting, "Voters get paid for their day's work." And indeed there was a going rate, which appears to have ranged from 50 cents (an average laborers' daily wages) and $1.50 (the cost of hiring a man and his team for a day). In New Brunswick, most electoral contests revolved around who would be most capable of getting money to fix potholes or other such weighty issues, and not every adult male was even granted the privilege of taking part in the process. One can easily understand why voters, many of whom lived quite a distance from the polling station, would not interrupt their work to go and vote unless they were given some additional incentive. They probably did not see why the situation should be different in Maine. Some of the candidates for the state legislature also adopted a New Brunswick campaign style. A candidate named Bradbury was rumored to have promised Valley people that he would get the state to buy three tiers of township for them if elected. (We will see in Chapter 17 that access to settling land had become a problem in the county.) In other words, he was not campaigning on national issues, such as slavery, or even state ones, such as Prohibition, but was presenting himself as a man who could directly benefit his supporters. Compact politics could also explain why Madawaskayans were uninterested in presidential elections. According to statistics published in Maine newspapers, the only time Valley residents actively participated in such an election was when General Scott ran. And they supported him despite his being a Whig.

III.   ECCLESIASTICAL ISSUES

Religion was a political issue in Maine and New Brunswick, and many Protestants viewed Catholics as politically suspect. Religious men also got involved in politics. Evangelical Protestant ministers supported, and sometimes initiated, reform movements. Catholic, Anglican, and Episcopalian bishops tended to be conservative and support the political status quo. As we have seen above and in Chapter 8, parish priests acted as representatives of their flock and tried to defend their interests through direct appeal to political leaders. This was still a world of strong executives and patron/client relationships—a remnant of eighteenth-century politics.

After 1842, Valley parishes continued to encompass both sides of the river. Priests, therefore, found themselves playing a political role on both sides as well. In December 1857, Watters, recently re-elected to the New Brunswick Assembly informed Father Henri Dionne of Ste. Luce that he would endeavor to do his best to "serve those purposes, which yourself and our late dear friend Mgr. Langevin and the other clergymen desires in the country, and I will continue to do so." He added, "I did not consult the wishes or advise with Emmerson or any other of the enemies of the French people, and I regret that M. McGuirk [the new St.Basile priest] should prefer their advice and counsel to yours."[11] Not surprisingly, Dionne and McGuirk were soon at loggerheads, the former accusing the latter of consorting with women. McGuirk, for his part, accused Dionne and Rice of opposing government grants to the St. Basile Convent (a girls' school). Dionne also had a stormy relationship with New Brunswick Justice of the Peace Prudent Gagnon, whom he accused of behavior so scandalous than even the Protestants were shocked. What exactly Gagnon did remains unclear—Dionne's correspondence is richer in invectives and denunciations than facts. What the correspondence makes clear, however, is that politics and, by extension, political attacks were personal matters. It also shows that priests did not stay above the political fray.

The new boundary, on the other hand, could be a convenient way of escaping a priest deemed meddlesome or imperious. As early as 1843, St. Basile's American parishioners asked to be placed under the jurisdiction of an American bishop. They argued that problems associated with the exchange of currency, the difficulty of crossing the St. John in the winter, and the fact that the St. Basile priest failed to provide them with vital records such as death, birth, and marriage certificates made the transfer a logical choice. What they did not mention is that they were also fighting with their priest, Mgr. Langevin. Six years later, they petitioned the bishop for Langevin's recall. The situation worsened under Langevin's successor, Hugh McGuirk. (McGuirk seemed a troubled man and showed signs of mental illness after his transfer to Saint-Louis-de-Kent.)

American Madawaska was not integrated into an American diocese until 1870, a long delay considering parishioners' years of petitioning and the Church's policy to make diocesan boundaries coincide with national ones. In 1842, such a transfer would have been extremely unpractical, as Maine was part of the Diocese of Boston, and communications with the rest of the state were primitive. The Valley, therefore, remained part of the Diocese of Fredericton established in 1842 as a result of large-scale Irish immigration into the province. As there were very few French-speaking priests in the diocese, Fredericton's bishop, Mgr. Dollard, let the bishop of Québec continue appointing priests to the settlement. It was not until the 1850s that these various bishops began discussing how to handle Valley parishes. Maine was then part of the Diocese of Portland, created in 1854, also in response to Irish immigration.

In November and December 1859, Mgr. Connelly, archbishop of Halifax; Mgr. Sweeney, bishop of Saint John; and Mgr. Bacon, bishop of Portland, agreed that dividing the Madawaska Catholics was not a good idea. The people did not want the division, said Connelly, adding that keeping the former settlement ecclesiastically united would preserve its French character and diminish the risk of conversions. Connelly also argued that the Portland bishopric was too new and inexperienced to address Valley residents' needs. For instance, very few priests in the Diocese of Portland could speak French. Mgr. Rogers, bishop of the newly created (1860) Diocese of Chatham to which the Valley belonged, had no preference for who had jurisdiction over the area, but also felt it should not be divided. At the beginning of 1860, Bacon reversed his position and asked for the Valley parishes to be included in his diocese. Nothing happened to the diocesan boundaries, which were fixed by Rome. New parishes, on the other hand, were created in the Valley through the division of older ones, and those were always wholly in Maine or wholly in New Brunswick. Cross-river parishes thus gradually shrunk in size.

American Madawaskayans who were still part of the Parish of St. Basile, began to chafe at being part of a "foreign" bishopric. In 1864, 1,017 heads of families led by Louis Cormier, the register of the deeds and secretary of the Catholic Association of Aroostook, petitioned Rome for detachment from Chatham and inclusion in the Diocese of Portland. They used the same arguments as their fathers had a generation earlier, namely blaming the river as the main problem: in the winter, blocks of ice made it impossible to cross, which often made residents miss mass. Across the river in St. Basile, Sylvain Daigle and Luc Albert circulated an opposing petition, but it gathered only 137 signatures. Interestingly, Mgr. Bacon no longer wanted the settlement, claiming

that, as a result of the tensions between the United States and Britain, it would be foolish to divide the territory right then. The issue was finally resolved on August 7, 1870, after Bishops Rogers of Chatham, Sweeny of Saint John (where the Fredericton Diocese had been transferred), and Bacon of Portland went to Rome to settle the matter. The pope granted American Madawaska to the Diocese of Portland.

Conclusion

Political life at Madawaska after 1842 remained the same as before: parochial, personal, and led by the same group of men. Political leaders continued to be drawn from closely related charter families. Priests stepped into the political arena and relied on their personal relationship with governors to secure funding or promote policies that helped their flock. In New Brunswick, where the franchise was still restricted, most issues were local and the political horizon limited to the province, compact politics could still work.

Antebellum Maine was different. The most-heated political debates of the period were not local but statewide or national ones, namely Nativism and Prohibition, which alienated Valley French. (Historically, North American French have always opposed Prohibition.) Political principles and ideologies played a growing role in Maine's political life, and party life hardened. Mainers saw New Brunswick style back pocket politics—which was characterized by a mix of paternalism and street violence—as not only dysfunctional and illegitimate but potentially a threat to "Americanism." The Valley's continued preference for the Democratic Party further marginalized the region.

The Valley also fit uncomfortably within the structure of the Catholic Church. It was French-speaking, while the majority of Catholics outside Québec were Irish or Scottish, with an overwhelmingly Irish hierarchy. The bishops found ways to service the Valley with French-speaking priests, but it took them thirty years from the passage of the treaty to come to the logical conclusion to include the southern bank of the river in an American diocese.

ENDNOTES

1. The electoral law was even "corrected" in 1848 to specify that voters had to be male property owners, because in some counties widows with property had presumed to cast ballots, a behavior which, of course, could not be allowed to continue!

2. Garland, *Promises, Promises...*, 19.

3. PANB, Journal of the House of Assembly, Contested elections, 106, and supporting petitions, 1854–55.

4. Watters was also a friend of the Ste. Luce priest, Rev. Dionne. He did not get along with Langevin's successor, Hugh McGuirk, and got embroiled in local squabbles between priests and parishioners. Archives de la Côte-du-Sud et du Collège de Sainte-Anne, Fonds Collège de Sainte-Anne, Fond Abbé Henri Dionne, F100/34/LXIII, LXXIV, LXXXI, LXXXIV, LXXXVII, and XXXVIII and 35/XVIII, LXXVIII.

5. *Morning Telegraph,* January 23, 1865, cited in Wallace. "Albert Smith...," 289.

6. According to Albert, the county court in Grand Falls had to decide the winner of the election in St. Basile and Andover because there had been procedural errors. Anglo-Protestants from the Tobique area surrounded the courthouse, but were soon confronted by Madawaskayans and Irish Catholics. To prevent a riot, Costigan withdrew his candidacy, and Hébert and Beveridge were elected. However, the electoral records show Hébert ahead of Costigan, and Albert wrongly claims Costigan supported Confederation.

7. Slavery had been formally abolished in the British North American provinces by the early 1830s. However, slavery had ceased to exist well before that time, as British North American courts had refused to support it or force escaped slaves to return to their masters from the late eighteenth century onwards.

8. Free Soilers did not want slavery to be extended to the current states of California, Nevada, Arizona, and New Mexico, which were conquered in 1848, as well as Texas, a Mexican province that gained independence in 1836 and later joined the United States. Anti-slavery groups blamed southern slave holders for the war with Mexico.

9. There was a Liberty Party in Maine in 1841, and a Free Soil Party, comprised of Whigs and anti-slavery Democrats, in 1848.

10. Maine Public Documents, *Report of the Commission appointed to investigate alleged elections frauds...*, 19.

11. Archives de la Côte-du-Sud et du Collège de Sainte-Anne, Fonds Collège de Sainte-Anne, Fond Abbé Henri Dionne, F100/34/LXXIV.

FURTHER READING
Dubay, Guy. *Chez Nous: The St. John Valley.* 1983: 71–86.

SOURCES

For the evolution of the colonial political system, see Mac-Nutt (1963), Buckner and Reid (1994), ch. 14 and 15. Thériault (1993), Doucet (1993), and Landry and Lang (2001) provide overviews of Acadian involvement in politics.

See (1993 and 2004) has examined mid-century anti-Catholic riots in New Brunswick. The development of New Brunswick local government is described in Whalen (1964). Pre-Confederation electoral results can be found in *Elections in New Brunswick 1784–1984* (1984) and G. Boucher (1973). Garland (1979) provides an analysis of the results. For more information on Confederation, see Belliveau (1977) and G. Sirois (1973). The *Canadian Biographical Dictionary* (available online through the National Archives of Canada website) includes entries on the major provincial political figures.

For Maine, older histories such as Coe (1928) and Hebert (1952) remain valuable. Electoral results for the Valley need to be culled from contemporary newspapers. Information about the 1858 election fraud accusations are found in the 1858 *Report of the Commission Appointed to Investigate Election Frauds* at the Maine State Archives. Maine's system of local government is described in Kingsbury (1872) and Stetson (1898).

Albert (1920) remains the best source on the Valley's ecclesiastical history. Stevenson and Mount (1992) have written a short history of how the parishes split; their research is based mostly on documents kept in the Vatican Archives. For a broad overview of religious life, see Thériault (1993).

12

EDUCATION AND POSTAL SERVICES

Political institutions were not the only ones affected by the resolution of the boundary dispute. Communications and educational institutions were also transformed. The postal and educational systems were reorganized on the New Brunswick side of the river. On the American side, they had to be created, and education was the main tool used by the Maine government to try to integrate and assimilate Valley residents. Different—or divided—institutions pushed people apart, but the way people used those institutions tended to minimize those centrifugal forces.

I.   POSTAL SERVICES AND TELEGRAPH

The modern postal system emerged in most western countries by the nineteenth century, when postal services became available at low cost to everyone. New Brunswick integrated the former disputed territory into its existing postal system in the same manner as it had integrated it into its other institutions. The United States postal service took longer to reach the area, partly because of a lack of roads.

A. New Brunswick

1. Early Postal System

Colonial authorities had encouraged the settlement of the upper St. John Valley in order to protect a major mail route. In the eighteenth century, the British government had also established a series of post houses between Fredericton and Rivière du Loup to accommodate mail carriers and travelers, although the latter were of secondary importance. Most of those houses were not manned. The post houses were not post offices in the modern sense of the term, since the mail system was not a public service. It existed to carry government dispatches. Post houses were places where Royal Mail carriers could rest in relative safety. (See Map 5-1, p. 58.)

2. Development of a Public Mail Service

The very first public post office in New Brunswick opened in Saint John in 1784. By 1823, there were nine public post offices in the province. By 1830, people in Saint John could post letters for Fredericton and Canada every Friday; mail from Canada and Fredericton arrived every Thursday. The New Brunswick mail was part of the Colonial Postal System until 1843, when the province acquired its own postmaster general. The following year, there were twenty-three post offices throughout the province. New Brunswick acquired complete control over its postal service in 1851, the year the postage stamp was introduced. (Before the introduction of stamps, the person receiving the letter paid the postage, which was proportional to the distance the letter traveled). Throughout the years, the postal service expanded to eventually include a total of one hundred offices. In 1867, the newly created Dominion of Canada took over the control of postal services, and by 1870, there were 438 offices, serving every part of the province.

3. Madawaska Post Offices

Historian Georges Sirois dates the first post office at Madawaska to 1837, but none is listed in the various almanacs for New Brunswick before 1842. John Costigan was appointed deputy *Canadian* postmaster at Grand Falls in May 1837; his commission remained valid until 1843. The elder Costigan was the father of politician John Costigan whom we met in the previous chapter. In 1840, P. C. Amiraux replaced C. L. Beckwith as postmaster at Madawaska (Petit Sault, later Edmundston); John T. Hodgson succeeded him in 1847. In 1850, the post office was located on the premises of Hodgson's brother-in-law, John Emmerson. In 1851, three new offices opened at St. Leonard, Baker Brook (run by John Baker), and St. François. (And in 1853, a woman named Mary Ann Kelly operated the St. Basile post office.) The volume of mail increased considerably after 1841, when a regular steamship line began running between Halifax and London, making transatlantic mail communications much speedier. In winter, mail could not travel to Québec and Montreal by boat and had to be carried over land through the St. John River route.

Madawaska residents could thus send mail to Saint John and Canada and destinations in between early on. In 1845, the province appropriated £20 a year for a weekly courier service between Madawaska and St. Francis. The very first *New Brunswick* postal route out of the Valley began in 1850, from Edmundston to Grand Falls and Woodstock. One could send a letter every Tuesday, Thursday, and Saturday mornings from Edmundston; it would usually arrive at Grand Falls the same day by 3:00 P.M. and at Woodstock by the following morning. After 1870, mail traveled six times a week over this route. In 1864, a second route opened, linking Edmundston to Rivière-du-Loup three times a week. Finally, in 1878, a one-mile route opened, connecting Edmundston to Madawaska, Maine. The Edmund-

ston post office played a significant role in the lives of both Madawaska and New Brunswick residents. On March 3, 1843, a man named John Smith Gray of Lincoln (in New Brunswick) sent John and Stephen Glazier a letter, care of John Emmerson at Little Falls, Madawaska. The letter, mailed from Fredericton, was stamped first in Woodstock on March 4, and then at the Madawaska (Maine) post office on March 6. Since there were no official mail routes between the two sides of the river at this time, local people must have made their own arrangements to forward mail. Louis Cormier, the northern registrar of deeds, provides another example. Cormier, who lived in Grand Isle, sent a letter in April 1850 to Hiram Hunt of Fort Kent. Cormier mailed the letter from Little Falls.

4. Postal Services

There were no official post office buildings at this time, and the postmasters' houses often doubled as a post house. The Edmundston post office, for instance, followed John H. Hodgson from the Emmerson store to a location on Church Street back to the Emmerson store in 1870. The postmaster's duties included keeping a diary of his activities, providing a list of offices where people could send letters, and prioritizing the mail: letters that had a stamp already on them or had been paid for in cash got first priority. They could also register letters containing money upon payment of a fee. Finally, in 1863, postmasters were given the right to issue money orders for up to $100. Postal routes were auctioned to the lowest bidder (the person who agreed to handle mail for the lowest annual fee). Each contract was good for a maximum of four years, but many were renewed. William Hartt, an innkeeper at Grand Falls, and John Curran, a farmer at Grand Falls, held contracts for the route between Edmundston and Grand Falls until 1876; William Newcomb, an innkeeper at Andover, and Charles Gaudry, a merchant in Rivière-du-Loup, carried the mail from Edmundston to Rivière-du-Loup between 1864 and 1875.

B. Maine: The Establishment of Post Offices in Aroostook and Madawaska

Information concerning the development of the United States postal system in Northern Maine is much sparser. The United States Postal Service has been a federal institution since 1789. As in British North America, however, the postal service more closely resembled modern private courier services than modern postal services. The mail was carried over individual routes by private contractors. By 1837, there were 121 postal routes in Maine. The mail traveled from Bangor to Mattawamkeag three times a week by coach. Another route took the mail from Mattawamkeag to Houlton three times a week, also by coach. Houlton was the northernmost United States post office at the time. In places not served by post offices, people could open private way offices and make their own arrangements to have mail carried to the nearest official post office. According to Dow's *Postal History and Postmaster of Maine*, there was such a way office at Fish River operated by S. Stevens at an unknown date. The federal government did not establish post offices in the disputed territory until after the resolution of the dispute. Stevens's post office may have opened during the Aroostook War. In 1843, post offices opened at Ashland, Monticello, Presque Isle, Fort Fairfield, and Fort Kent. The lack of convenient communications between the St. John and the rest of Maine may have hindered the development of postal communications. The unknown sender of an 1845 letter wrote:

Table 12-1: Northern Aroostook Post Offices

Name of Post Office	Date Opened	Name of Post Office	Date Opened
Houlton	1826	Central Madawaska	1875
Mattawamkeag	1830	Madawaska center	1875
Patten (Fish Mills)	1839	Upper Van Buren	1875
Aroostook (Ashland)	1843	Hamlin	1878
Fort Fairfield	1843	Upper Frenchville	1878
Fort Kent	1843	Eagle Lake	1883
Monticello	1843	Frenchville	1885
Presque Isle	1843	St. David	1885
Caribou (Lyndon)	1848	Wallagrass	1886
Madawaska	1851	Lower Grand Isle (Lille)	1890
Van Buren	1851	St. Agatha	1892
Mars Hill (Alva)	1854	Allagash	1894
Littleton	1857	Daigle (New Canada)	1899
Limestone	1858	Eagle Lake Mills	1903
Grand Isle	1859	Fort Kent Mills	1906
Dickeyville (Frenchville)	1869	Keegan (Van Buren)	1907
Upper Madawaska (Madawaska)	1869	Lille (Grand Isle)	1910
Lower Madawaska	1871	Saint. John	1910
St. Francis	1872	Seven Islands	1921

Fish River (Stevens Way office). Private office. No date.
Note: Post offices outside the Valley are in italics
Source: Dow (1943).

The road formerly cut out, from the Mouth of the Fish River, to the Aroostook is now impassable and the only means of communication with the United States is through her Majesty's Province 50 miles of which is by canoes—a company of U.S. troops under command of Cap. Melton, is stationed at the mouth of Fish River—55 miles from the Grand Falls, [unreadable] the river, and 110—from Houlton. Their only communication at present with the rest of the United States is a monthly express, through the Province of New Brunswick. The English P.O. in 28 miles distant, and it is very troublesome and expensive, to obtain letters or papers in that way—Their regulations impose such high postage, on pamphlets and American newspaper publications, as to amount to a prohibition.[1]

Madawaska and Van Buren acquired a post office in 1851 and Frenchville in 1869. (The other northern Aroostook County post offices are listed in Table 12-1.) In 1845, Congress drastically reduced the cost of postage to 5 cents for letters traveling up to 300 miles and 10c for letters traveling more than 300 miles (for letters up to half an ounce or 14 grams). In 1851, when postage stamps were introduced in the United States, letters traveling less than 3,000 miles cost 3 cents to mail if prepaid and 5 cents if postage was collected upon receipt.

C. News

Postmasters carried more than official dispatches and private letters; they also carried newspapers. In 1852, A. W. Raymond, the Grand Falls postmaster reported that he transported, on average, 64 letters and 178 newspapers every week. Some of this mail was merely passing through Grand Falls on its way to Canada. But E. Akerley of Grand River reported receiving an average of four letters and eighteen newspapers per week; J. M. Amiraux at Madawaska reported one letter and five newspapers per week; and P. Gagnon at Baker Brook reported one letter and twenty-three (!) newspapers. Newspaper subscribers were not always literate, either. During an investigation into electoral fraud at Madawaska in 1858, state officials found out, for instance, that the Van Buren post office received four copies of the *Aroostook Pioneer* and the Madawaska post office received four copies of the *Aroostook Pioneer* and one copy of the *Bangor Democrat* "the last named paper and one *Pioneer* [coming] to a man who cannot read." This is not as surprising as it may initially appear. Until literacy became widespread, the practice in western countries was for literate people to read the papers aloud in public places, such as coffee houses, taverns, inns, and general stores. One went to those places to *hear* the papers. There were plenty of reading locations at Madawaska. Bilingual individuals may also have translated papers written in English. The first Acadian paper, the *Moniteur Acadien,* started in 1867 and had some Madawaskayan subscribers. Papers could also be swapped across the river. Despite its imperfections, the postal system allowed Valley residents to know what was going on in the world around them.

D. The Telegraph

The telegraph reached the Valley in 1851. In 1847 Québec businessmen, including J. Tibbets, H. J. Noad, and J. Gilmour, created the British American Electric Telegraph to connect their city to Halifax. The line was initially going to pass through Campbellton and Dalhousie to keep it out of reach of possible American attacks. But since the shareholders had difficulties raising the necessary capital, the line was run through the Grand Portage and Edmundston to save money. The telegraph office, like the post office, was located in John Emmerson's store.

Public education for all children stands as one of the major social developments of the nineteenth century. New Brunswick and Maine authorities were equally convinced of the necessity to provide some form of public schooling to all children. However, officials and parents often disagreed over what exactly children should learn.

A. New Brunswick

1. First Schools in the Valley

Before the treaty, educational facilities in the Valley were very limited. Contemporary sources make occasional mentions of a local individual acting as a teacher or a priest attempting to teach a few pupils. The first one was the Reverend Lagarde, who outlined his plan in a letter to the bishop in 1819. The curriculum would include reading, writing, arithmetic, and, most importantly, religion. The school would be free "so that rich and poor may equally benefit, and the inhabitants may send those of their children who are able, except girls who won't be admitted."[2]

In 1831, land agents Deane and Kavanagh found only three schools in the entire Valley, located at Simon Hébert, William McRae, and David Cyr's residences. At Hébert's, Peter Amiraux, a recipient of provincial funding, gave French and English lessons for £20 per year. Deane and Kavanagh did not say how many students were enrolled in these schools and were not convinced that they served the community well.

2. The Civil Parish School System

Amiraux and the teacher at Cyr's received some government support and, therefore, had to run their school according to the provisions of the 1816 Parish School Act. The act provided for a provincial subsidy of no more than £10 per civil parish. Justices of the peace distributed the money and also appointed the school's trustees. The government appointed teachers

on the vaguest criteria. A new law to fund school districts was passed in 1833. The financing was complicated. According to historian Katherine F. C. MacNaughton:

> When a school had been kept to the satisfaction of the Trustees for not less than six months, the Trustees certified the facts to the Justices, these officers in turn made certificate to the Lt.-Governor, and the legislative grant—at the rate of £20 per school for one year was issued, provided that no parish received more than £160 a year, and no county a larger sum than would amount to an average of £120 for each parish in the county.[3]

The money limit was detrimental to Madawaska, which did not become a civil parish in its own right until 1833 and remained excessively large after that. The New Brunswick land agents who laid out settlers' lots under the treaty remarked on this fact:

> As the whole extent of the country from the Grand Falls to the St. Francis now forms but one Parish, it labours under the disadvantage of being deprived of a fair proportion of the public revenue, in consequence of the limited number of schools which are allowed by law to each Parish; thus the Parish of Madawaska, which extends seventy miles along the bank of the river St. John will only be entitled to receive the same amount for the support of its schools than a parish of not more than one fourth its extent.[4]

For this reason and other similar ones (parish expenditures for roads, for instance, were also capped), the land agents strongly recommended that the area be divided into several parishes. A Bill to that effect was passed by the Assembly but it was disallowed. New Brunswick's northern boundary had yet to be determined, and it could not organize a territory that may not belong to province. The successive boundary disputes, therefore, inhibited the establishment of publicly funded schools in the Valley.

3. School Reform Attempts

By the mid-1840s, the provincial elite had grown dissatisfied with the state of education in the province. Two reports in 1845 and 1846 identified a long series of problems: people's apathy; teachers' incompetence; unsatisfactory modes of payment for teachers (some were paid in store credit, other through the provision of room, board, and laundry); defective, or worse, American books; inadequate buildings; and imperfect supervision and control. The province passed a series of laws between the mid-1840s and mid-1850s to try to remedy the situation. Unfortunately, some of these laws actually made it harder for Madawaskayans to get a decent public education. The system that was gradually put in place was highly centralized. The Parish School Act of 1847 created a provincial board of education and established a normal and a model school in Fredericton (s normal school was a teachers' college; a model school was an elementary school attached to a normal school where student teachers practiced what they had learned). The course lasted ten weeks, and students received 10 shillings a week ($2) toward expenses. But the course was in English only. Only normal school graduates were supposed to get licensed, but two years later officials decided that those who had not attended it could still get third-class licenses. Licenses could also be issued to untrained teachers in remote areas. The population served by the schools was supposed to raise money and match the government grant. They were also allowed to contribute in kind, and boarding teachers with different families in the district instead of paying a salary remained common in poorer areas. This practice, however, did little to attract people into the profession. The province also encouraged the use of the Irish National Board of Education textbooks. Because they were carefully graded and non-sectar-

---

Sidebar 12-1: A Mid-Century End-of-School Fête

Arthur Hamilton Gordon, later 1st. Baron Stanmore, was New Brunswick lieutenant governor between 1861 and 1866. He was fond of traveling, fishing, and hunting and left an account of his travels in 1862 and 1863. Arriving at Madawaska at the end of the school year, he was asked to honor the end of year festivities with his presence. Gordon's biography can be found in the *Dictionary of Canadian Biography*.

On my way to Canada a few months later, I visited the parishes up the river, and was greatly pleased with all I saw at Edmundston. I was present at the vacation fete of the school of the settlement, and I do not know that, since I first landed in the Province, I have ever been more amused than by this festivity. The scholars were assembled in a large barn belonging to the Hon. F. Rice, M.L.C.,[1] which was decorated with true French taste, and there, they acted various dramatic scenes in French and English. Almost all the children appeared; the younger ones coming forward on the stage, and, after a bow to the audience, uttering some short English proverb, pronounced as though it were a word of one syllable, whilst the older boys and girls performed very creditable portions of the Bourgeois Gentilhomme, *and other pieces. At St. Basile, there is an excellent boarding-school for young ladies, conducted by the Sisters of one of the numerous religious orders which make education their special care. I mention these facts, because the few people in England who know anything at all of the Madawaska settlement probably imagine it to be a howling wilderness of pine forest and swamp, as indeed I remember hearing it termed in the House of Commons.*

Note 1: M.L.C : Member of the Legislative Council.
Source: Sir Arthur Hamilton Gordon (1864): 22.

Illus. 12-1: St. Basile Academy circa 1867. CDEM, PC3-30

ian, and understood children's psychology, those textbooks were considered the best in the English language at the time.

4. The Language Issue and the St. Basile Academy

Acadian districts faced an added problem: parish schools could only use textbooks approved by the provincial board, but the board approved almost no French texts. Elementary education in French was, thus, extremely limited. J. C. Pinguet, a Madawaska physician, member of the Victoria County Board of Education, and school inspector, reported in 1855 that while English-language schools had made very satisfactory progress, the same could not be said for French ones:

> In the French schools equal progress has not been made, owing to the want of proper elementary books, at the same time the exertions made by the French teachers in their schools has afforded me entire satisfaction.[5]

Pinguet recommended translating the official reading books. It did not help that before 1870 Madawaska teachers were almost always holders of third-class licenses granted by the county board.

This lack of training was alleviated for young women with the opening of the Madawaska or St. Basile Academy in 1858. Run by the Sisters of Charity of Saint John and subsidized by the province, it provided young women with an (English) secondary education and prepared them for the teaching profession. The provincial superintendent held the school in very high regard. In 1863, he reported that there were twenty-seven students in attendance. He added:

> Sixteen of these young ladies were engaged by Americans as teachers during the summer; these being preferred on account of their knowledge of both the French and English languages. After fulfilling their engagements, they re-enter the Academy. This Institution should, and in time,

Table 12-2: Percentage of Children Ages Six to Sixteen in School in New Brunswick Counties Between 1851 and 1861

County	1851	1861
Albert	62.4	52.8
Carleton	48.6	48.4
Charlotte	56.8	49.5
Gloucester	27.2	24.9
Kent	27.4	27.0
Kings	48.0	47.3
Northumberland	42.4	42.1
Queens	58.4	53.3
Restigouche	35.0	54.9
Saint John	68.1	78.8
Sunbury	39.0	45.4
Victoria	21.6	25.6
Westmorland	33.6	36.8
York	35.4	39.6
Province	39.6	44.7

Sources: PANB, Annual report of the Chief Superintendent of Schools, 1851 and 1861.

probably will supply one great want above the Grand Falls, namely, teachers who can both speak and teach the French and English languages.[6]

5. Educational Attainments

A closer look at the statistics provided by the Provincial Blue Books[7] demonstrate that educational levels in the area that later became Madawaska County were the lowest in New Brunswick. The region had the fewest schools and students. Table 12-2 shows that Victoria County ranked low in terms of educational achievements. Between 1850 and 1865, the county had an average of 17 parish schools and 465 students per year. Even Sunbury and Restigouche Counties, which, according to the 1841, 1851, and 1861 censuses, had much smaller populations than Victoria County, had more students and schools.

The province's emerging school system ill served its French-speaking population. This was not so much because the authorities saw the schools as a tool to keep the Acadians in their place but rather because they were indifferent to the specific needs of those districts. Their failure to provide normal-school training in French and their unwillingness to approve an adequate range of French textbooks could only marginalize the Acadians. Yet language does not seem to have been the root of the problem: authorities funded French-language schools like the others. And in Victoria County there were two French speakers on the county board of education—Pinguet and the Reverend Langevin—and at least one French-speaking inspector—Pinguet. More likely, the peripherally located Acadians were outside the central authorities' field of vision. The system was more Anglo-centric than anti-French.

B. Maine

1. Facing the "Alien" French

New Brunswick paid scant attention to its French-speaking population, but Maine did. As a matter of fact, state authorities developed an obsession with the Madawaska French, whom they viewed as almost an alien species. Language was, of course, the first and most obvious marker of this difference, and most felt that the new Americans had to understand the language of their country. Madawaskayan material culture was equally foreign. Few Americans were familiar with Madawaskayan house architecture. The shape of their carts, sleighs, and boats; outdoor bread ovens; Canadian stoves; the eating of pea soup instead of beans (New Englanders had switched from peas to beans in the eighteenth century); the cut of people's clothes; and their continued use of home-made fabric were all very strange. (See Appendix K, "The Way They Saw Us," for examples). Mainers' confrontation with Madawaska "exoticism" very often led to a deep sense of unease. The Acadians had no institutions or, at least, no institutions New Englanders were willing to recognize. How could one live without the institutional accoutrement of New England civil society? Where were town governments, registers of deeds, courts, and public schools? This institutional void suggested to Mainers that the St. John Valley French were lost in some time warp: they were either the remnant of some pre-civilization Golden Age or plain, backward peasants. New Englanders also misunderstood the Valley's land-holding customs and farming techniques. In Maine, farm lots were square or rectangular; some Mainers felt the Valley's long-lot farms with their narrow river fronts resulted from endless divisions of parental land by people lacking the initiative to carve out new farms away from the river. But we will see in chapter 16 that those assumptions were false. Valley people were also described as indifferent farmers, content to live off buckwheat. We will put this notion to rest in Chapter 14. Furthermore, Maine was on its way to becoming the first dry state in the Union, but the French saw nothing amiss with drinking alcoholic beverages. Nor could Yankees believe the size of the Valley families. Many a visitor left the area convinced that Valley women all had twenty children. They did not, as we saw in Chapter 7. By the middle of the nineteenth century, Anglo-Protestants no longer believed large families were something to be proud of. They believed that these families were, instead, outward signs of a lack of self-restraint: only the lower sorts of people made children for the fun of it. Besides speaking, eating, and dressing differently, Valley residents' values appeared antithetical to American ones.

2. Attempts at Americanization

Government officials visiting the Valley usually concluded that "Americanizing" the French was a very urgent matter. Not only did those new Mainers have to learn—and use—English, they also had to internalize the American values of self restraint and self discipline, and display a spirit of "improvement" similar to that of good Anglo-Protestants. If they could be persuaded to give up "Popery" in the process, all

the better. Mainers believed that to be integrated into American society, the French had to change their habits and adopt the numerous government agencies the Americans viewed as the bulwarks of freedom against despotism. Anglicization would therefore not be enough; it had to be accompanied by acculturation and assimilation, processes many, like the *Republican Journal,* felt would not happen quickly. "It will be a long time before they accustom themselves to the machinery of our institutions and a longer time before their distinct nationality is effaced or lost."[8] Initially, many officials believed English schools would easily take care of those problems.

3. The School System in Maine

The problem with this plan was that Maine's school system was much less centralized than the New Brunswick school system. Until the 1830s, education had been an entirely private matter. The first state measure to assist education dates back to 1828: Maine put aside twenty townships whose sale would be used to create a permanent school fund. In 1833, Maine also began to levy a tax on bank profits and directed the proceeds toward schools. Between 1846 and 1852, the Maine Board of Education surveyed the condition of education in Maine and found it wanting for about the same reasons as their colleagues in New Brunswick—namely a lack of qualified teachers, poor school attendance, inadequate textbooks, limited financial resources, and an insufficient number of graded schools. Maine passed a law in 1854 aimed at placing the state's common school education on a sound footing. School committees, elected by the townships, were responsible for raising money; erecting buildings; examining, certifying, and hiring teachers; establishing the curriculum; selecting textbooks; inspecting schools; and examining student progress two times per year. Although committees had the discretion to establish the curriculum, government officials laid out the spirit of education:

> ...all ...instructors of youth, in public or private institutions, shall use their best endeavors to

impress on the minds of the children and youths committed to their care and instruction, the principles of morality and justice, and a sacred regard for truth; love of country, humanity, and a universal benevolence; sobriety, industry, and frugality; chastity, moderation, and temperance; and all the other virtues which are the ornament of human society; and to lead those under their care, as their ages and capacities admit, into a particular understanding of the tendency of such virtues to preserve and perfect a republican constitution, and secure the blessings of liberty, and promote their future happiness; and the tendency of the opposite vices, to slavery, degradation, and ruin.[9]

The role of the state was more limited in Maine than New Brunswick. The state superintendent had to make sure school laws were obeyed. He collected statistics and generally acted as an advisor to the local committees. Teachers were not required to attend a normal school or secondary institution to apply for certification.

4. State-Run Schools in the Valley: 1842–53

State authorities did not believe the Valley French would spontaneously establish schools. They first had to be taught the value of education. Therefore, in 1844 the state legislature appropriated $1,000 for schools in the territory, which was formed as a single school district and placed under the authority of a governor-appointed agent. The agent was to act as the principal instructor and superintendent of the schools. Valley residents were expected to raise money for the schools through a subscription.[10] The first superintendent was the Irish Catholic James Madigan. Madigan faced a few major difficulties, such as finding enough qualified (bilingual) teachers, convincing Valley residents of the need to send children to school, and convincing Valley residents of the need to learn English. Most Valley people had little need for literacy, and those who felt reading and writing were useful skills wanted their children to learn to

Table 12-3: Summary of Madigan's 1845 Report

District	St. Francis	Ste. Luce	Sirois District	Daigle District	St. Bruno
Teacher	Miss E. Baker	Not identified	Not identified	Not identified	M. Stanley
Duration	3 months	4 months	5 months	5 months	4 months
Number of students	20[a]	33	31	37	33
Age range	Under 14	6 to 27	Under 14 [b]	5 to 22	6 to 27
Having previously attended school	All	7	Not specified	16	12
Subjects taken					
Alphabet			27	21[c]	
French alphabet		19			
Words		7			
Writing		5	7		
Beginners					21
Taking English	20	3	21	4	33

[a] All English speaking; [b] Plus four occasional adults; [c] The other students can read a little.
Source: Maine Public Documents. *Final report of the Superintendent…,* (1845).

The Land in Between

read and write French. During the first year of his tenure, Madigan established four schools enrolling a total of 117 students. Many of these students had never attended school before and were only beginning to learn the alphabet (see Table 12-3).

Some students, however, had attended school in New Brunswick, suggesting that parents sent their children to whatever school was convenient rather than to the one they should have attended. The following year, Madigan added two more schools, which raised the number of students to 140. They ranged from four to twenty-seven years of age. Interest in formal schooling was uneven. Enrollment numbers were low, and although various people gave some land for the building of schoolhouses, the Valley raised almost no money for their operation. Madigan, like several subsequent school agents, believed this was due to the Valley's poverty. But as we have seen, people in the Valley were no poorer than residents of other parts of New Brunswick or Maine. More likely people believed that if the state wanted schooling for all children, it should support it.

5. The State Shifts Responsibility for Schools to Local Valley Authorities: 1853–61

The state continued funding education in the hopes that the situation would change. In 1853, state policy changed, and Valley schools could no longer receive state funding unless they raised matching funds. School attendance remained anemic. An 1857 superintendent report estimated there were 1,516 young persons between four and twenty-one years in Hancock, Madawaska, and Letter G (Van Buren) plantations. Only 158 had registered for the summer term and only 140 for the winter term. This means that only one out of ten eligible youth had actually registered. Interestingly, most schools were private and charged tuition. This included all of the six schools in Hancock, eleven out of thirteen schools in Madawaska, and eight out of thirteen schools in Letter G. Some parents, therefore, were willing to part with their money to educate their children, but preferred placing them in tuition-based private schools

rather than free public ones. Valley residents' supposed lack of interest in schooling may actually have been a lack of interest in the type of schooling the state had decided they should receive. In 1859, the board of education investigated the state of schools in the Valley. The state superintendent concluded from his visit that many of the leading citizens were quite supportive of the education system. However, the few schools in the region were poorly managed and not all schools taught English to their students. The superintendent reported that that parents' main reason for sending their children to school was for them to learn to read French. Valley parents were not hostile to their children learning English, but they also wanted them to learn French.

6. The State Takes Over Again: 1861–70

Progress remained inadequate in the eyes of the state, and in 1861 officials placed the Valley under tighter control: teaching had to be mostly in English, and the state superintendent would select textbooks. The state superintendent would also report to the state twice a year on the situation in the former territory. He visited the Valley in 1862 to report that no money had been collected for school purposes, although the voters had approved the tax. Colonel David Page was then appointed as local school agent. He supervised twenty-six schools with about 530 pupils. The difficulty of securing bilingual teachers was somewhat alleviated with the opening of the St. Basile Academy. Nonetheless, the old problems continued. There were still not enough qualified teachers, adequate school buildings, funding, or textbooks.

In 1868, the state legislature repealed all previous school laws pertaining to the territory, voted a new appropriation, and prescribed the number and location of schools. There would be schools at Ste. Luce, Van Buren, Fort Kent, and the Madawaska/Grand Isle boundary.[11] Local money was still not forthcoming. The Maine School Report of 1869 recommended that a high school be opened to train teachers for the local schools. Moreover, the region still did not raise the funds required to establish and maintain its schools. That year, a land agent also visited the area; he found eight school districts in Van Buren, but only one was public. In District One (Violette Brook), the only school was a private one taught by Melle Modeste Cyr, who was regarded locally as "one of the best teachers in the territory, and former instructress of one of the public schools established by the Legislature in 1868."[12] She told the land agent that while boys over twelve did not attend school, girls did; she had female pupils as old as twenty-three. She taught English, but at a very elementary level. She had to give up teaching English composition because none of her pupils could write a proper sentence. The land agent concluded that "to Americanize this French colony of five thousand souls is indeed a difficult task, perhaps the work of a generation."[13]

7. The 1870 School Act and Its Aftermath

The school system in American Madawaska was not established on a permanent footing until the Act of 1870. Valley towns had to raise 25 cents per capita to support their schools. By 1870, there were forty-seven schools in operation, and money was finally being raised on a regular basis through taxes. Teachers were required to teach in English and use English textbooks, otherwise the schools could not receive state money. But in 1878, the state relented to allow the use of the English and French versions of the New Brunswick Royal Series textbooks. In 1875, there were 3,798 young persons between the ages of four and twenty-one in American Madawaska; 1,917 of them attended thirty-three different schools. (Eagle Lake and St. John plantations were still without public schools.) In 1871, provisions were made to open free high schools at Fort Kent and Frenchville. Only the Frenchville one opened, taking over a private academy set up in 1868 by Father Sweron. In 1875, the Free High School in Frenchville ran for thirty-two weeks over two terms and enrolled seventy-five students. Only twelve of those students were in the fourth reader or above; all seventy-five took math; sixty-eight took English grammar; twenty were studying modern languages (presumably French); and twenty were studying ancient languages (presumably Latin). The state provided $500 and the town $250 toward its budget; in the future, however, the state grant would equal the amount raised through taxes.

Conclusion

After 1842, both halves of the Valley gained public institutions designed to firmly integrate them into the political entities to which they belonged. These measures, however, largely failed. The postal system remained underdeveloped on the Maine side of the Valley, which either left local people reliant on the New Brunswick one or forced them to establish informal linkages across the river. Nonetheless, the post office made it possible for Valley people to get newspapers and gain knowledge of outside events. Those living on the Maine side probably did not limit themselves to American newspapers, especially after the *Moniteur Acadien* began publication in 1867.

The school systems also failed at integrating Madawaskayans into the United States or British American societies and on the southern bank of the river, the schools failed at Americanizing the next generation of children. The St. John Valley was divided at about the time Maine and New Brunswick authorities began to take public education seriously. The authorities also viewed elementary education as more than the teaching of basic academic skills. Besides teaching children reading, writing, and arithmetic (and needlework to girls), and imparting technical knowledge to more advanced students (measuring, surveying, and navigation, for instance), public schools pursued social and even political goals. Schools should instill the moral values required to be a useful, productive member of the community. In New Brunswick, schools were meant to counter the deplorable democratic tendencies spreading among the masses. They were expected to instill in their charges Christian values, respect for British institutions, and love of her gracious majesty, Queen Victoria. In Maine, schools were also expected to promote Christian values, as well as a love for American political institutions.

New Brunswick and Maine, however, followed different paths to reach their goals. New Brunswick, like the other British North American colonies, developed a centralized, top-down system of public education, largely inspired by the Irish system. The organization of the Maine public school system, on the other hand, promoted those democratic tendencies rejected by New Brunswick. The Maine system was very decentralized and allowed local school committees to certify teachers and determine content.

Centralization led to the neglect of the Acadian schools in New Brunswick. American Madawaska was not neglected; on the contrary, it was rather micro-managed. When left to its own devices, the American Madawaska population opened French schools using the catechism as a primer. Consequently, officials provided the region with a top-down system controlled by the state superintendent. This system did not serve the population any better than the New Brunswick one, and here language appears to have been the critical issue. Madawaskayans avoided the public schools and failed to raise taxes for their support. Instead, they sent their children to private schools, over which they had greater control and which probably taught more French. But parents had to bear the full tuition cost, which limited the number of students. On both sides of the river therefore, poorly organized, underfunded, and under-equipped schools provided little more than a smattering of education, resulting in a high rate of illiteracy.

ENDNOTES.
1. Maine Historical Society, unsigned letter, 1845, S-5108 109/37. Viewable on Maine memory network at www.MaineMemory.net
2. AAQ, Lettres des prêtres missionnaires..., February 2, 1819.
3. MacNaughton, "Development of Theory and Practice...," 71.

4. PANB, Journal of the House of Assembly, Letter from J. A. MacLauchlan and John Allen to the lieutenant governor, January 23, 1846, 599.
5. PANB, Journal of the House of Assembly, Report on Public schools, J. C Pinguet Report, 1856, 68.
6. PANB, Journal of the House of Assembly, Report on Public schools, 1863, 30,
7. The Blue Books were compilations of social and economic statistics that the provincial governments sent to the Colonial Office in London.
8. *Republican Journal,* Belfast, Maine, December 29, 1843.
9. Kingsbury, *The Maine Townsman,* 184.
10. *Resolves of Maine,* 1844 and 1845.
11. *Private and School Laws of Maine,* ch. 603, sections 1 and 2, 1868.
12. Chadbourne, *History of Education in Maine,* 261.
13. Ibid., 261.

FURTHER READINGS
Chadbourne, Ava Harriet. *A History of Education in Maine: A Study of a Section of American Educational History.* 1922.
MacNaughton, Katherine F. C. "The Development of the Theory and Practice of Education in New Brunswick, 1784–1900: A Study in Historical Background." Master's thesis, University of New Brunswick, 1947. (Available online from the University of New Brunswick Library web site: www.lib.unb.ca/)

SOURCES
Besides the two titles listed above, one can find some useful information about education in New Brunswick in Fitch (1930). For New Brunswick Acadians, see Landry and Lang (2001) and Couturier Leblanc, *et. al.* (1993). Education in Madawaska is discussed by Albert (1920), Michaud (1984), and G. Sirois (1977). Thériault (1998) and Vautour (1998) contain sections on the Saint-Basile convent. Statistical data can be found in the *Annual Report of the Chief Superintendents of Schools for New Brunswick* (at PANB), and in the Blue Books of Statistics for New Brunswick, volumes 4-48 (Library and Archives of Canada, Microfilm # B-1265 to B-1274). For Maine, see the *Reports of the Superintendent of Schools* (available at the Maine State Archives). Dow (1943) surveyed the history of Maine's postal services, and G. Sirois (1985) wrote an article about the postal services in Madawaska. The appendices of the Journal of the House of Assembly of New Brunswick contain reports about the province's postal services.

13

THE FOREST INDUSTRY AND THE INTERNATIONAL
ECONOMY OF THE UPPER ST. JOHN RIVER BASIN

W. H. Cunliffe and B. W. Mallett were fairly typical of a new breed of frontier entrepreneurs who appeared on the upper St. John after the settlement of the boundary dispute. Born in New Brunswick on February 2, 1820, Cunliffe moved to the upper St. John Valley in 1846. He clerked for American lumber operator Shepard Cary, who kept a store at Fort Kent. In 1857, he went into the lumber business on his own account. Soon, afterwards, Cunliffe bought the Cary property at Fort Kent, when his former employer went bankrupt. In 1865, he formed a partnership with Shepard Cary's brother, Holman, and Cary and Cunliffe became one of the most important lumber businesses on the upper St. John River. In 1873, Cary left, and Walter Stevens, a Fort Kent innkeeper, took his place. In 1866, Cunliffe partnered with Mallet, who had just moved back to Fort Kent, and began trading shingles. Mallett was an American from the Penobscot; he came to the upper St. John Valley in 1853 and moved from place to place but was always involved in the forest industry. Cunliffe and Mallet built a large store in New Brunswick across from Fort Kent. According to Aroostook County historian Edward Wiggin, "The firm of B. W. Mallett & Co. did a large business in trading, buying and shipping shaved cedar shingles which at that time was an immense industry upon the upper St. John…. The shingles were made both on the American and provincial sides of the St. John and the duty on provincial shingles formed the principal source of revenue at the Fort Kent custom house at that time." Stevens, Cunliffe, and B. W. Mallett &

Co. were all brought down in 1875 by the failure of a major merchant firm in Saint John: the American Jewett and Jewett. The men, however, recovered and started a new business shortly afterward.[1]

The experiences of Mallet, Cunliffe, and others highlight several important changes in the forest industry during the mid-nineteenth century. First was the fragility of the industry itself, which was overly sensitive to the vagaries of international demands. Second, Mallet, Cunliffe, and Cary produced lumber and other products as well as ton timber. In the mid-1800s, the forest industry shifted, from the production of ton timber for overseas markets to the production of lumber and other building material for the North American market. This led to the erection of large-scale lumber mills in the Valley; previously there had only been custom mills, (mills sawing lumber for local customers only). This new breed of operators engaged in multiple activities: Mallet clerked, milled, lumbered, farmed, and manufactured clapboard before going into storekeeping and shingle trading. Moreover, their activities ignored boundaries. Men from New Brunswick, Maine, and Lower Canada logged, made lumber, and traded in the upper St. John River basin, often financed by men from Boston, Saint John, Quebec City, and even Glasgow. The timber and lumber trade was truly international and had little use for boundaries. More than any other activity, it preserved the unity of the Madawaska territory, and firmly tied it to the port of Saint John at the mouth of the river.

After 1842, lumber operators could log in Maine on public land with a permit or purchase timberland. North of the border, Canada laid claim to the part of the former disputed territory that lay west of the Madawaska River. Operators who wanted to log in this area were not sure from whom to seek permission. New Brunswick decided not to issue permits until the boundary issue was resolved. The Canadian Crown Land Office issued permits to cut with the understanding that "they [the lumberers] remain liable to any duty New Brunswick may seem fit to levy on them." The Canadian Crown Land Office collected a quarter of the fees. New Brunswick was to collect the rest and put it in a fund "to be refunded to the parties entitled to it after settlement of the boundary."[2] This did not even guarantee immunity from New Brunswick officials, who could seize wood they deemed "illegally" cut. Those who got permits from Canada were either large firms that could afford the gamble, such as Bangor timber baron John Veazie; operators well established in the area, such as John Glazier; and a surprising number of local small operators, namely Enoch Baker, Abraham Dufour,

John Emmerson, William. B. Hammond, Joseph Michaud, and Jean-Baptiste Thibodeau. This was surprising given that the Canadian Crown Land Office was located in Kingston (now Ontario). Either those men were willing to make a very long trip to get permission to cut, or one of the larger operators got a permit for them. The settling of the interprovincial boundary solved the problem. After 1853, governments on both sides of the river clearly stated the legal procedures necessary to access timber.

The sliver of the former disputed territory that lay to the west of the upper St. John was quickly divided onto *concessions forestières,* or sections of public land where one could log under permit. Those *concessions* could be transferred and renewed at expiration. The bulk of the *concession* holders along the Maine and Lower Canada border were New Brunswick and Maine men. Glazier held *concessions* at the head of the Little and Big Black Rivers, as well as at Rivière Daaquam. Two roads linked Seven Islands with Saint-Roch des Aulnay and with L'Islet (Elgin Road) (see Map 9-3).

II.   COMPETITIONS

A. The Pike Act

After the settlement of the boundary dispute, New Brunswick also modified the system of fees and duties it levied on timber. It was obvious that licensing operators to cut a specified amount of timber made cheating too easy. Instead, the province began to levy stumpage fees over a specified acreage (the minimum was two acres). Since timber and lumber were almost entirely produced for export, the province simultaneously levied export duties on the wood as it left the ports. This did not sit well with operators on the American side of the St. John River. They could float the wood duty free on the river— but had to pay to get it out of the province and

return it to the United States. American operators claimed New Brunswick had deliberately changed its system to circumvent the Webster–Ashburton Treaty and tax them. They flooded Washington with petitions to obtain redress. Nothing happened until 1854, when the United States and British North America signed the Reciprocity Treaty (1854–66) establishing free trade in natural products between the two countries. Among other clauses, it exempted Aroostook lumber from provincial export duties.

Equally upsetting for American producers was the fact that timber cut on the American side of the Valley but milled in New Brunswick was subject to a 20 percent duty upon re-entry into the United States. Aroostook producers tried to get relief from

Illus. 13-1: The Grand Falls were a formidable obstacle to the log drives, as this picture from the 1880s clearly shows. PANB, George Taylor photograph, P5-185.

this duty as well, but the Penobscot Valley lumbermen opposed any measure to that effect for obvious reasons. Reciprocity again solved the problem, as it provided for the duty-free entry of British North American natural products into the United States and vice versa.

The repeal of Reciprocity in 1866 again raised the prospect of double duty on Aroostook forest products re-entering the United States. Lumbermen from southern Maine opposed letting those products enter duty-free; they claimed that provincial products would be passed as American ones to evade tariffs.

Aroostook County lumbermen, led by Shepard Cary, set up an association, organized numerous meetings, and petitioned Congress for exemption from the duty. They won. In 1866, Congressman Frederick A. Pike from Calais, Maine (another lumber-producing region along the boundary), got a bill passed allowing Americans who cut timber on the American side of the St. John River but milled it in New Brunswick to return their goods to the United States duty free. The "Pike Act" as it came to be known also covered agricultural products. It encouraged American interests to open mills in New Brunswick and provincial millers to take on American partners. The Pike Act lapsed in 1911. Lumbering, then, did not pit British American against American lumbermen but rather those exploiting the St. John River's resources against lumbermen from other regions.

B. The Telos Cut and Chamberlain Lake Dam

The rivalry between the St. John and the Penobscot basin producers did not play out only in the corridors of the United States Congress. It also led to more direct action on the ground. The headwaters of the south-flowing rivers (Saco, Androscoggin, West and East Penobscot, and Kennebec) and the sources of the north-flowing rivers (St. John, Allagash, and Fish) lie within a few miles of each other. The region was also rich in white pines. Bangor operators wished to bring this pine south to their mills, instead of letting their rivals drive it to Saint John. To do so they cut a channel, the "Telos Cut" between Telos and Webster Lakes (at the heads of the Allagash and Penobscot Rvers, respectively). They also dammed

the head of Telos Lake in 1841. Three additional dams—on Chamberlain Lake, at the foot of Eagle Lake, and on the Allagash—acted as locks and raised the water level. Timber cut on the headwaters of the St. John and Allagash could now be driven south through the cut. Most of the land in this area belonged to Pingree of Massachusetts, and between 1845 and 1846, extensive lumbering operations began on his land. Pingree owned the Chamberlain Dam, but not the Telos Cut. The latter belonged to Rufus Dwinel, who charged what lumbermen deemed "extortionate tolls." The dispute, which started in the woods, soon made it to the floor of the state legislature, leading to the creation of the Telos Canal Company. It was acquired in 1852, by the Great Northern Paper Company.

The Telos Cut, however, diverted more than timber: it also diverted water from the Allagash–St. John system toward the Penobscot. The St. John is not a very deep river, and lumbermen had to rely on the spring freshet to carry their logs. By summer, it was exceedingly difficult to raft timber above the Grand Falls. Allagash and St. John river operators bitterly resented what they viewed as an illegal diversion of water. John Glazier took matters into his own hands a couple of times: in 1847 and again in 1848, he and his men breached the Chamberlain Dam. In 1847, this led the river to rise three feet at the Grand Falls.[3] The Telos Cut and associated dams remained a bone of contention between the various timber operators until the construction of railway lines, which provided an alternative means of carrying timber out of the area.

III.   BIG MEN, SMALL MEN

The organization of the forest industry evolved in the second half of the century. In the earlier period, loggers worked together in small teams. They were either independent operators, or were outfitted by outside merchants. Some historians have argued that those small operators, who were usually local men,

were gradually marginalized or eliminated. This is not what happened in the Valley; although large-scale operators quickly dominated the industry after the 1842 treaty, they never monopolized it.

Operators were a varied lot. Some logged for only a few years, whereas others spent their whole

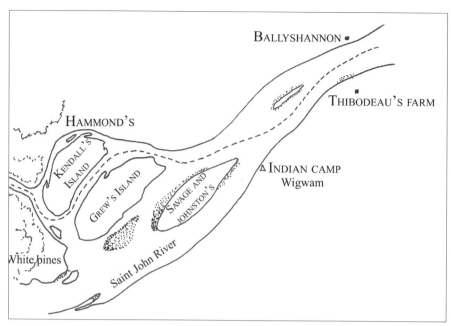

Map 13-1: David Thibodeau's homestead at St. Francis in the mid 1840s. David Thibodeau (1792-St. Francis 1847) was married to Celeste Cyr (1792-St. Francis 1864). He was father to Elie (see illustration 20-5), ("Olie") who was the target of Shepard Cary's ire.
Map by B. and S. Craig from LAC, G1116.F2 G72 1848. Maps of the boundary between the United States and the British possessions in North America as established by the Treaty of Washington, August 9th 1842, and surveyed and marked under the direction of the Joint Commission appointed under the 6th article of that treaty, vol. I map XV.

lives in the woods. Some came from southern Maine, and even as far as Massachusetts; others were from southern New Brunswick and Lower Canada. Some operators were complete outsiders, who worked through local agents and owned enormous tracts of timberland in Maine, such as Pingree. Others were state and provincial entrepreneurs who were directly involved in the day-to-day operations of their company, such as John and Stephen Glazier of New Brunswick or Shepard Cary of Maine. And then there were the smaller operators, who cut under license or on someone else's berth with—or without—his permission. Hired men stood at the bottom of the ladder. Acadian and French Canadian names are noticeably absent from the list of large-scale operators. The organization of the industry and its heavy reliance on credit explains this: only those with the proper contacts in Saint John and beyond could secure the credit necessary to set up large-scale operations. (For example, when local merchant and wholesaler John Emmerson died in 1867, John Glazier owed him £15,000.) Thus, Valley operators were limited by their own resources or the credit provided by area merchants.

Large operators tended to move upriver and onto the Allagash and Black River valleys. Small operators tended to be concentrated on timberland behind the St. John Valley settlement. Presumably, large operators were not interested in those tracts because they had long been culled their best timber. Small operators, however, lacked the resources needed to push inland in their search for timber. Quite a few of them were local farmers, anyway.

There were different ways to get involved in the

forest industry. In New Brunswick, logging on public land with a license was the norm. The license gave lumbermen permission to cut logs for the season in a specific area known as a timber berth. In the Valley, most licensees were outsiders. They logged for one to three years and then disappeared, never to be seen again. The industry's instability discouraged long-term involvement. In Maine, the government got rid of timberland at first opportunity. Documents about the activities of Maine timberland owners have now largely been lost. Nonetheless, we know that lumber barons like Pingree did not monopolize cutting. They allowed others to cut on their land, but we no longer know the details. John Glazier, for instance, was cutting on Pingree's land in the mid-1850s. Men who could not afford to pay stumpage fees either to the province or a proprietor could subcontract. For instance, in April 1846, Daniel and Milton Savage of St. Francis promised Shepard Cary that they would deliver to market 33 sticks of ton timber, or 80 tons of wood, cut on his limit. The Savages secured the agreement by posting an $800 bond. Subcontractors were known to sub-subcontract. In 1861, William Cook Hammond contracted with the Glaziers to deliver 8,500 board feet of spruce logs over the next four years. The Glaziers lent him $300 upon securing a mortgage on his wife's property. The mortgage was discharged in 1866. Hammond, though, did not do all the cutting himself and sub-subcontracted some of it to a J. Bourguoin in 1862. Bourguoin was to deliver $135 worth of spruce logs within twelve months. Hammond agreed to the contract after securing a mortgage on Bourguoin's farm. That mortgage was discharged in 1867.

And, of course, cutting on public or proprietors' land did not stop. In 1857, Cunliffe sent a letter to Cary informing him that:

> Olie (Elie) Thibodeau is a cutting timber on your land near the Fish river bridge. I don't think it is any use of trying civil means to prevent him from trespassing. The better way is to send the sheriff and take the damn scoundrel to jail.[4]

Old habits were hard to break.

IV. FRAGILITY

A. Roller Coaster Rides

The period under discussion begins and ends with two major crises in the forest industry; one in 1848–49 and another in 1875. The earlier one was a consequence of Britain adopting free trade. In 1842, Britain reduced the duties on timber from outside the Empire from $11 to $5 a load. Duties on colonial timber were reduced from $2 to 20 cents a load. After further reductions, foreign and colonial timbers were charged the same rate starting in 1860: 20 cents a load.[5] In the mid-1840s, colonial merchants rushed their products to Liverpool before additional reductions could take effect, and glutted the market. In 1848, the bottom fell out. Recovery was initially slow but accelerated in 1854 when the Crimean War broke out in Europe. It did not last very long. The American Civil War caused a recession in Britain, which depressed demand until 1863. Recovery lasted about ten years until the Panic of 1873, a severe economic depression in the United States.

The New Brunswick forest industry in the second half of the nineteenth century is still waiting for its historian, but we can get a sense of the industry's overall trends by looking at timber licenses issued during this time. After 1843, cutting fees were proportional to acreage. As output is probably roughly proportional to the number of square miles licensed, the numbers show that the industry collapsed in 1848 and ground to a halt in 1849 and 1850 (see Figure 13-1). The mid-1850s and late-1860s were good, the late-1850s and 1862, bad. The boundary dispute between New Brunswick and Canada provides us with more pre-

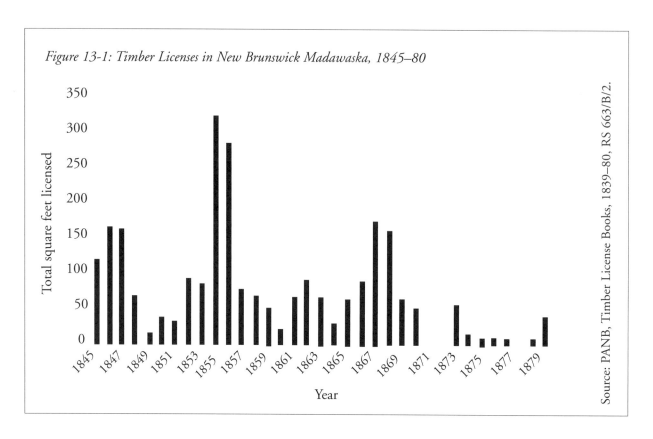

Figure 13-1: Timber Licenses in New Brunswick Madawaska, 1845–80

Source: PANB, Timber License Books, 1839–80, RS 663/B/2.

cise information about the impact of the 1848 crisis on logging activities in the New Brunswick side of the Valley (see Table 13-1). In 1849, the timber harvest was one-tenth of what it had been five years previously. One of the consequences of the collapse of the forest industry was a sharp drop in the price of fodder; oats, which sold for 2s 6d (50 cents) a bushel in 1846 was down to 1s 6d (30 cents) in 1848. On the whole, then, the industry moved in spurts: A few adequate years alternated with very bad ones. Lumbering on the British side of the upper St. John River basin, therefore, was a very unstable activity.

B. Panics

"Panic" was the word nineteenth-century North Americans used to describe an abrupt decline in business. Panics usually occurred when some large firm or bank ceased payments; this, in turn, made its creditors unable to meet their own obligations, and the creditors of the creditors found themselves in the same situation, and so on through the credit chain. People were very much aware of this domino effect and, when such a failure occurred, they rushed to present their bills and recall their loans, aggravating the cascading effect. Buoyant economies could absorb the failure of a few large concerns; sluggish ones could not. Consequently, panics usually inaugurated a recession. Those recessions were usually short lived (a year or two). The Panic of 1873 was different: business remained slow for the next twenty years.

Panics led to sharp contractions of credit. This was particularly bad for the forest industry because it was, by and large, a card castle built on extensive credit. Operators bought supplies in the fall. They did not have to pay for these supplies until they sold their wood in Saint John. Workers similarly were not entitled to their pay until the wood was sold (see Sidebar 13-1). In the meantime, they could get goods on credit at the camp store, and received an advance on their wages at the end of the logging season in

Table 13-1: Amount of Timber Brought to Market from the Territory in Dispute Between Canada and New Brunswick: 1845–49

Year	1844	1845	1846	1847	1848	1849
Number of licensees	20	7	17	18	4	4
Valley licensees	7	2	4	0	0	0
Tons of timber brought to market	28,873	10,088	26,838	32,960	5,990	2,881

Source: PANB, Journal of the House of Assembly, Canada Disputed Territory Fund, 1855: clviii-clx.

April. The merchants who bought the wood in Saint. John or Fredericton may similarly have made partial payment, the balance to be paid when the wood was sold on the outside market. Two years would often elapse between the men pushing into the woods with supplies and animals (in the fall), and the closing of the books for the "season." A problem anywhere in the chain could have disastrous consequences for anyone along it. A downturn in the demand in Liverpool could start a cascade of bankruptcies which ultimately left the shanty men in possession of worthless promissory notes and credit on stores that had failed.

An example of this domino effect is the fall of Jewett and Jewett and their partner, Jewett and Pitcher. George K. Jewett (of Bangor and Boston) and Edward D. Jewett (of Saint. John) had a lumbering and mercantile firm with offices in two cities. George managed the timberland in Bangor, Edward the mills in Saint John. Edward was also president of the European and North American Railway, and the failure of this line, in which both Jewetts held stock, played a role in their own difficulties. The Jewetts were partners with Jewett and Pitcher of Boston, who operated the largest lumberyard in New England. The Jewett and Pitcher scrip (merchant notes) circulated through Aroostook County like bank notes. The Panic of 1873 and a decline in demand for forest products put the firm in difficulties. George mortgaged some of his timberland with the Bangor

Savings Bank in 1873; Edward followed suit in 1874. In 1875, the Bangor Savings Bank foreclosed on the two men. In June 1875, Jewett and Pitcher announced they were suspending credit, leading to a rush on their scrip. Several Valley businesses collapsed as a consequence, including Mallet, Cunliffe, and Stevens. On April 16, 1874, The *Aroostook Times* reported:

> We hear of some lumber operators who have paid their men off wholly in this paper. The greater bulk is to be found in the upper part of the County, and must cause great pecuniary inconvenience and great distress.... The bills have been offered here (in Houlton) for 50 cents on a dollar, with no takers. What they will ultimately be worth no one knows. The protestation of the holders is loud and deep. That they never should have been allowed to pass as money in now fully realized.[6]

In July, Jewett and Pitcher announced they would make good on their scrip over a period of several years, but it was too late. People had lost trust in their "money" and the use of merchant notes in lieu of money ceased. Loggers could still receive scrip, but only their employers would willingly accept it at face value as payment for anything.

The Panic of 1873 and the fall of Jewett and Pitcher ushered some significant changes into the organization of the forest industry, especially concerning its use of credit. Operators had been in the

MEMORANDUM

I HEREBY obligate myself to labor for SHEPARD CARY and COLLINS WHITAKER, doing business in the name and under the firm of

"SHEPARD CARY & COMPANY"

at making Ton Timber or other Lumber, and at getting the same to market; during the season for Lumber operations next ensuing the date thereof, and until I shall be discharged by the said Shepard Cary and Company. I agree to labor as aforesaid at Black River, or at such other place or places as the said Cary & Co., their Agent or Agents, may from time to time designate, at the place or places where their said operations are to be carried on and matured.

I agree at all time to obey the orders and directions given me from time to time by the said Cary & Co., or by their Agent or Agents having the control and management of their operations in their absence; and to labor faithfully and to the satisfaction as far as may be in my power, of the said Cary & Co., and of their Agent or Agents under whose directions I may be placed from time to time.

I agree that in case I shall at any time, leave the employment of the said Cary & Co., during the period for which I have engaged to labor for them, against their wish or consent, or against the wish or consent of their Agent or Agents as aforesaid, to forfeit the full amount of wages due me, and to be liable to the said Cary & Co., in damage for any injury or loss by them sustained by reason of my so leaving their employment against their wish or consent or that of their said Agent or Agents.

I agree to receive the amount of wages due from the said Cary & Co. in the manner following, to wit: -- In such supplies of Clothing and other articles (always excepting money) as I may require while in their employment, and such balance as may be due me after deducting the amount of their account for supplies so furnished, in Current Bank Notes of either one of the Bank of the Province of New Brunswick, when the said Cary & Co. shall have sold the Timber or other Lumber at which I shall have been engaged in cutting and getting to market, while in their employment as aforesaid.

On settlement with the said Cary & Co., which shall be made at some time and place designated by them, at the time when I am discharged, I agree to receive from them, their Note or Due Bill, for the amount found due me payable as aforesaid, at their Store in Houlton, and until such settlement shall have been made, and such Due Bill shall have been taken by me, I shall have no right either by law or otherwise, to enforce from the said Cary & Co. any payment for the labor and services by me rendered them.

My time and wages to commence at the date hereof, the latter at the rate of   *twelve*
Dollars for every twenty-six days labor performed for the said Cary & Co., by me, in pursuance of this contract.
IN WITNESS WHEREOF, I have hereunto set my hand this *26th day of*
september A.D. One Thousand Eight Hundred and Forty *eight*

Signed in presence of
W. H. Cary Jr.

his
Charles X Terrio
Mark

Source: Shepard Cary papers, in the possession of Mr. Frank Peltier, of Houlton.

habit of settling accounts with their suppliers and workers only after the wood had been sold —a lag time that could last anywhere from eighteen months to two years. John Glazier's accounts with wholesaler John Emmerson, for instance, opened in the fall and were usually settled a year and half later. Lumbermen did not treat logging as an ongoing business, but as a succession of "seasons." Each cutting season was a separate venture, often with its own separate account. This reflected an archaic approach to accounting: operators imputed equipment and tool purchases to the season during which they occurred, even if they used those supplies for subsequent seasons. Lumbermen had no concept of amortization.

The way the men were paid was equally old-fashioned. Workers could get goods from their employer's store or in other stores on their employers' account during the season. In the spring, they received an advance on their wages, as well as a promissory note for the balance of their wages once the wood was sold. For instance, on June 26, 1847, Francis Berubé received a voucher from his employer, Cary, for $47.20 payable at the Fish River store "as soon as we sell the timber got by our parties the winter last on Black River."[7] Payments did not have to be in kind, however; workers could collect their wages in cash. The evils of the company stores did not take hold in the Valley. As the Cary-Thériault memorandum (see Sidebar 13-1) shows, men who did not finish their contract were not entitled to wages for the work done—and they could even be sued for damages. There was nothing unusual in these clauses, derived from English labor laws still in force in the United States during the first half of the nineteenth century. However, by the mid-1800s, the practice was beginning to look old-fashioned. The forest industry, in other words, was operating under very traditional, if not downright archaic, principles. The Panic of 1873 changed this. The business dealings of Robert Connors, lumberman and shingle manufacturer in New Brunswick, illustrate this change. Connors paid his suppliers as he received their invoices and his men as they were coming out of the woods in the spring. He could make these payments more easily than lumbermen twenty years previously because the Saint John mercantile firms to whom he sold the wood paid him upon receipt of the timber. The industry still relied on credit, but on a much shortened one.

V.   THE SHIFT TO LUMBER

Between the two depressions of 1848 and 1873, the forest industry underwent another change, from ton timber to lumber. In New Brunswick, the prized white pines were growing scarce. Britain was gradually turning to northeastern Europe for its supply of wood. Simultaneously, urbanization created a market for construction lumber, which can be manufactured both from pines too small for square timber and spruce. American builders began to get lumber from British North America. The Reciprocity Treaty facilitated this trade. The repeal of the agreement had little impact on the lumber trade because by 1866 American supply could no longer satisfy American demand for building material.

New Brunswick's Blue Books contain information about timber and lumber exports out of Saint John. Most of it was cut in the upper St. John Valley and its tributaries, the Tobique and the Aroostook. Export statistics confirm the shift from square timber to sawn lumber (see Figure 13-2). The 1850s marked the turning years. The switch to lumber was accompanied by the building of large lumber mills in Saint John and also at the production sites, such as the Valley. Those mills differed from the custom mills, which served local people: they were often larger and always in the hands of English-speaking people. The Madawaska French never managed to become large lumber manufacturers, for the same reason they never became large-scale operators.

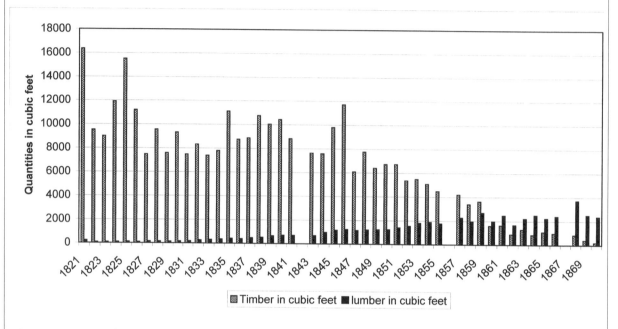

Figure 13-2: Quantities of Timber and Lumber Exported from the Port of Saint John, 1821–70

Sources: PANB, Schedule of taxes, fees, etc. RS536; Public Accounts of the Province of New Brunswick, RS845.

VI.   MILLING

A. The Baker's Mill

The mills catering to the export trade were almost all located in the western section of the Valley. First, there was John Baker's grist and sawmill on the Meruimticook, which became two separate mills after 1845. The mill, or shares of it, changed hands constantly: it was sold no less than twenty-eight times between 1847 and 1870. Buyers and sellers included an extremely varied group of people: Frederic Hatheway from Fredericton, Wiley and Burray from Madawaska, and Turner and Whitney from Maine; Jesse Wheelock, one of Baker's original confederates, and Hilaire Pelletier, a local French man,

both lumberman; Collins Whitaker; Cary's brother-in-law, and Edward Jewett, who paid $5,000 for the property; Prudent Gagnon, a local merchant and miller; and several members of the Baker family: John Senior; his wife Sophia; his sons Enoch and John Junior; Enoch's French Canadian wife, Madeleine Ouellette; and John's wife, Sarah. As a side note, most of the transactions involved one of those three women (and one would really like to know why the Baker women played such a prominent role in the mills' transaction history). In the 1871 census, Prudent Gagnon is listed as owning a gristmill under repair worth $1,100 on this site and Baker a sawmill worth $1,000 on the same site (see Appendix I-3).

B. The Fish River

On the American side of the river, the situation was similar. The 1850 census lists two sawmills on the Fish River about a mile above its junction with the St. John, in the newly named village of Fort Kent. They were worth quite a bit (an average of $10,000 each), and the total output was valued at $17,000. One of the mills had a long history, since it was the one started by the Peter and Wilmot firm in 1825 before it went bankrupt. Like the Baker mill, it changed hands often. In 1845, Niles, West, and Soper, an Old Town lumbering firm, bought the mill. Soper's share soon wound up in the hands of Bangor merchant James Jenkins. West and Niles moved to Fort Kent, removed the Savage mill, and built a new one containing an up-and-down saw and two clapboard and two shingle machines. Soon, they added a store, smithy, and boat house, as well as a house for each of them on the property; finally, they built a bridge across the river.

Silas Niles died in 1852, and Henry West entered into a partnership with Charles Jenkins. The 1854 freshet washed out the whole compound except the mill and cut a new channel through the river. The partners built a new mill to manufacture deals for the British market. The 1850 census lists West and Niles as owners of a mill valued at $8,000 that produced sawed lumber from logs. West and Niles employed forty-five men. They produced $8,000 worth of boards and clapboards but also $15,000 worth of ton timber. In 1866, they sold the mill to Asa Smith of Bangor. Shortly thereafter, George Seeley, a New Brunswick-born Fort Kent merchant bought it. It burned in 1868, and was never rebuilt.

The West and Niles mill was located on the east side of the Fish River. In 1847, Cyrus Bodfish from Gardiner (central Maine) and Colonel David Page from Waterville, north of Gardiner (Page may have come to the region with the Maine militia during the boundary dispute), purchased the part of the lot on the east side of the Fish River, half the dam, and some water privileges from West and Niles. They ran out of capital before their mill was completed, and Bodfish mortgaged the property to another Waterville man before finishing the work. Bodfish equipped the new mill with one saw, a clapboard machine and a shingle machine. In 1848, William Dickey, another Gardiner man, bought the property. The 1850 census listed the Bodfish and Dickey mill with a value of $12,000. It employed twenty men to produce $9,000 worth of boards and clapboards. Dickey later added a gristmill to the property but sold it in 1854. Levi Sears, who happened to be married to Silas Niles' widow, bought it. The Fort Kent industrial schedule of the 1860 census has not survived, but Sears is listed as a lumberman in the personal census; his real estate worth $8,000 and his personal estate $15,000. He lived with his wife, two stepchildren (Silas Junior was seven at the time), his daughter, a servant, and sixteen unmarried male laborers. In 1870, Sears was still in business, and now owned a five-sawmill with clapboard and shingle machines estimated at $2,000 and a gristmill with two runs of stones worth $1,000. The output consisted of two million shingles worth $16,000, 15,000 feet of clapboard worth $1,000, $10,800 worth of boards, and $11,500 worth of flour. He employed twelve men.

Like the Baker mill, the Fish River mills attracted the attention of outside investors as well as outside speculators. Americans were buying mills on the New Brunswick side and vice versa. The mills at the Fish River also played the role later historians ascribed to local mills: they attracted settlers, provided wage-earning opportunities for a considerable number of men, and became the nucleus of a small service center. In 1860, according to the census, Sears and West were neighbors to innkeepers Samuel Stevens and José Nadeau, dry goods merchant George Seeley, and variety store owner William Cunliffe. The four men were still in business in 1870 and had been joined by another merchant. By 1870, Fort Kent was also the township with the highest proportion of households not headed by a farmer. But although the mills encouraged settlement and development, they brought their owners uncertain rewards. Over the years, the value of the mills declined markedly. In the case of the Sears mill, it diminished to one-sixth of its value over twenty years despite the addition of extensive machinery.

C. The Hammond Mill

The last commercial mill was located at the other end of the settlement and, by 1870, had become the largest lumbering business in the Valley. William Cook Hammond, a native of Kingsclear near Fredericton, started the mill. He learned the lumbering business working for his uncles, Abraham and Charles Hammond. After his marriage, Hammond made a living by farming, logging, trading, and manufacturing lumber, at times in partnership with his brother-in-law. In 1848, there was a mill on his property in Van Buren. In 1870, Hammond had become a farmer in Hamlin Plantation. His son William Cook Hammond, Jr., on the other hand, was listed as a Van Buren merchant and board and shingle manufacturer, not as a miller. He was twenty-six, married, and perhaps a partner with his father in the W. C. Hammond and Cie, a company worth $12,000. The elder Hammond owned a mill equipped with two up-and-down saws, a hedger and a trimmer, and two clapboard, two shingle, two picket, and two lath machines. He employed ten workers. The mill's output was valued at $19,100 (half of it in clapboards). Within ten years, the business expanded, and Hammond acquired property in Montana under the name Hammond Lumber Co. The Hammond mill, unlike the Baker one, was only briefly owned by people outside the family. The Hammonds raised capital through family connections and through mortgages on their land. The Hammond enterprise was very much a family enterprise built over several generations, whereas the Fish River and Baker mills were disposable assets for most of their owners. The Baker and Fish River mills focused mostly or exclusively on timber and lumber manufacturing, whereas the Hammond diversified and produced items that were more than semi-

processed commodities, such as sash and moldings. Interestingly, the Hammond mills survived and prospered, whereas the mills closely linked with the lumber trade did not. Lumbering for export was no more a road to riches than making ton timber.

Conclusion

The diplomats behind the 1842 Treaty had not wanted to disturb the St. John River basin forest industry. They succeeded. The industry remained a truly international one, involving operators and men from different nationalities and providing British and American markets with wood products. The St. John River forest industry also emerged as a serious rival to the Penobscot Valley lumbermen, who sought to reduce this competition by demanding custom duties on re-entering lumber and diverting waters from the head of the Allagash toward the Penobscot. The extent of the lumbering activities in the region, however, should not mask the fact this was a highly volatile industry that moved in spurts and left all participants at the mercy of the next panic.

ENDNOTES
1. Wiggin, *History of Aroostook*, 176–77.
2. PANB, Journal of the House of Assembly, 1844, Appendix CXXIV, Northern Boundary, document 3.
3. See John Glazier's biography at http://www.biographi.ca/EN/
4. Shepard Cary papers, in the possession of Mr. Frank Peltier of Houlton.
5. Wynn, *Timber Colony,* 51. A "load" was equivalent to 50 cubic feet of wood.
6. *Aroostook Times,* April 16, 1874, quoted in Judd, *Aroostook,* 98.
7. Shepard Cary papers, in the possession of Mr. Frank Peltier of Houlton.

FURTHER READING
Dubay, Guy. "The land: in common and undivided, the lumber world of western Aroostook." In *The County: Land of Promise,* ed. A. Mcgrath. 1989: 145–52.
Dubay, Guy. *Chez Nous: the St. John Valley.* 1983: 35–54.
Judd, Richard W., et. al. *Maine: The Pine Tree State.* 1995: Chapter 13.

Judd, Richard W. *Aroostook: A Century of Logging in Northern Maine.* 1989.

Wood, Richard. *A History of Lumbering in Maine, 1820–1861.* 1961 (first ed. 1935).

Wynn, Graeme. *Timber Colony: A Historical Geography of Early Nineteenth-Century New Brunswick.* 1981.

SOURCES

The activities of the lumbermen on the New Brunswick side of the Valley can be traced in the Timber Licence Book, RS663B2/2n, 1839–1848; RS663B2/16, 1848-1860; RS663B2/2t, 1860-1870; RS663B2/2s, 1859–1872, at the Provincial Archives of New Brunswick. Contracts secured by a mortgage can be found in the land record books. The industrial schedules of the various censuses contain information about mills.

Useful biographical information can be found in the "Reminiscences of Thomas S. Glasier," written in 1914 and found in the Lilian M. Maxwell collection at the University of New Brunswick Archives; in the *Political Biographies* compiled by James C. Graves and Horace C. Graves, available at the Provincial Archives of New Brunswick, especially the biography of James Tibbits; information about the Hammonds can be found in the Family History Files, also at the Provincial Archives of New Brunswick. Besides the titles listed above, published sources include Wiggin (1922) and Dubay (1989); for information on the Telos Cut, see Rogers (1966) and Avery (1937).

14

AGRICULTURE AND THE FOREST INDUSTRY: SIAMESE TWINS?

We left the Madawaska settlers in the late 1830s in dire straits. They were facing the wheat midge, rust, and competition from western flour—and had yet to find a decent solution to any of these problems. After the Webster–Ashburton Treaty, the now-legal forest industry could provide an alternative market for farmers. The shanties required food for their workers, and more importantly, feed for their teams, providing farmers with one of their two primary markets. New farmers, as before, provided the other one, and a growing number of wage-earning families swelled the ranks of those who had to buy at least part of their food.

Contemporary observers noticed that lumber camps provided both a market and a source of employment for local people. The governor of Canada, Lord Elgin, for instance noted:

> The farmer who undertakes to cultivate unreclaimed land in new countries, generally finds that, not only does every step in advance, which he makes in the wilderness by removing him from the center of trade and civilization, enhance the cost of all he has to purchase; but that, moreover, it diminishes the value of what he has to sell. It is not so, however, with the farmer who follows in the wake of the lumber-man. He finds on the contrary, in the wants of the latter, steady demand for all that he produces, at a price not only equal to that procurable in the ordinary marts, but increased by the cost of transports from them to the scene of the lumbering operations.[1]

Contrary to Lord Elgin, most outsiders deplored farmers' involvement in lumbering and blamed it for perceived inadequacies in New Brunswick farming. They believed that if farmers attended to their farms instead of rushing off to the lumber camps in search of "easy" money, the province would not have to import food. (For whatever reasons, critics believed men went to the woods because they were too lazy to farm.) In their eyes, the long-term consequences of farmers working in the woods were even worse: they eventually abandoned their farms to move to the western United States, contributing to the depopulation of the province and even of British North America. James Robbs was one such critic:

> Under our present actual circumstances, a few days labour at a boom or mill-pond brings enough wherewithal to purchase a barrel of American flour; and the silver dollar *near the eye* of a settler, as it has been expressed to me, so conceal the view of the distant farm, that when the fall of one penny per foot of lumber in the markets of Liverpool throws him out of employment, he is surprised to find his fence down, his fields grown up with bushes and both himself and his snug little clearing generally, all gone to the bad.[2]

Historians initially shared this negative view of the relationship between the two sectors. Madawaska historian Georges Sirois, for instance, viewed the forest industry as an exploitive one:

> Generally speaking, lumbering was an important factor in early nineteenth century Madawaska economic development. This region depended

primarily on the Saint John market for the export of most of this natural resource. But Anglophones controlled the economic prosperity this activity brought. This situation consequently heightened the ambition of a small privileged group in the midst of an Acadian majority whose only reward was servitude.[3]

Recent historians have a more nuanced view of the relationship. They claim that in the early nineteenth century, when most teams were made of local men cutting close to home, lumbering allowed farmers to earn money with which to stock and equip a farm. In the later part of the century, farm households could use the supplementary income derived from lumbering to buy land for their sons and perpetuate a way of life based on relatively small-scale family farming. What then happened at Madawaska? Did the forest industry force Madawaska settlers into a detrimental form of dependence? Or did they benefit from its existence and, if so, under what conditions?

I. DESCRIPTIONS, 1850–70

A. Crop Shift

St. John Valley visitors began to notice a shift in crops between the the late 1830s and the early 1850s: buckwheat grew in importance and became a cash crop. Aroostook County historian Clarence Day, citing a mid-nineteenth-century state surveyor report, noted that it was a staple crop in the Aroostook and St. John Valley "used to fatten hogs and poultry, feed horses and oxen, and ground into flour."[4] Buckwheat had become to northern Maine farmers what corn was to their midwestern counterparts: an all-purpose commodity. This may explains why it was in such high demand. Aroostook historian Edward Wiggin went as far as to call it a "commodity currency," or a crop that local stores always accepted as payment.[5]

B. Impact of Lumber Camps

Visitors also identified lumber camps as a market and a source of employment for local people. In 1843, the Maine land agents stated:

> The only market now existing in Aroostook for ordinary agricultural production is that created by the lumbering operators. This is generally a good one to an extent sufficient to absorb the surplus which the settlers now tilling the soil have to dispose of; but it is by no means a uniform one, varying as it necessarily must, with the fluctuations of that interest (proverbially uncertain) which *creates it*.[6]

The lumber camps were still a market for farmers in 1857: a report by the Maine Board of Agriculture included that same statement, verbatim. British agronomist J. F. W. Johnston who visited the province in 1850 also noted that lumbering offered "a more ready market for farm producers. It kept prices up and gave employment to idle hands."[7] In the late 1860s, a local newspaper echoed the same sentiment:

> The farmers will share in the harvest [of lumber] by creating a demand and market for everything he can raise. As long as lumber is high, hay, oats, and all kind of farming produce will be high also. The winter will be as productive to him as the summers ... Raising most of his supplies, the farmer of Aroostook can convert the heavier and bulkier articles, such as hay, oats, buckwheat, potatoes, and all the coarser kinds of grain, which will not pay the cost of transportation to a distant market, into lumber which will float down the St. John to a market.[8]

Although contemporaries familiar with market conditions in Aroostook County recognized that farmers were at least partially dependent on lumber camps, they did not see the situation through rose-tinted glasses. Farmers were dependent on a market that was highly volatile, and since logging animals spent their winters in the woods, farmers could no longer use their manure as fertilizer.

Knowledgeable observers objected to Aroostook or Victoria farmers being described as incompetent by outsiders. The Maine Board of Agriculture was annoyed by the rumor that farmers did not spread manure on their fields. This erroneous notion was so widespread that the board felt the need to make it clear that Maine farmers *did not* empty their barns' contents in the nearest stream. This example shows that as a general rule, comments on farmers and farming by people outside the trade tended to be inaccurate.

C. The 1870s

French farmers attracted more than their fair share of contemptuous comments. Critics described Valley farmers as "indifferent," "improvident," and "more fond of the fiddle than the hoe." A report widely reprinted in the Maine press in the late 1850s described them as:

> ...generally ignorant and unambitious, each generation contenting themselves with simply existing. They subsist chiefly on pea soup and other vegetable foods which is raised on their patch of land.[9]

As we shall see below, this description was inaccurate. American tourists, government officials, and journalists frequently visited the Madawaska territory, but they were so convinced the French were living in a time warp that they invariably saw what they wanted: angel-like or backward peasants (depending whether they got their clues from Longfellow or Darwin), who were living the life—and eating the food—of their seventeenth-century French forbearers. New Brunswickers generally paid no attention to Madawaska, which tells us that there was nothing remarkable about the place, its people, or the way they conducted their business.

Reliable descriptions of St. John Valley farmers are scarce after 1850. Charles S. Lugrin, secretary of the Agricultural Board of New Brunswick, has provided one description of Victoria County (which also included several Catholic and Protestant-Irish civil parishes) farmers that is less supercilious. His report listed hay, oats, buckwheat, peas, and potatoes as staple crops in the county. Wheat production had increased a little of late but had not regained the importance it had enjoyed at the beginning of the century. Although local people blamed successive crop failures for this state of affairs, Lugrin believed, instead, that bad farming practices, which had exhausted the soil, were to blame. Buckwheat had replaced wheat, a development he deplored because he did not think this grain was as good a food as wheat. It did, however, ripen quickly. Peas also provided "a staple article of food, particularly among the French with whom pea soup is a deservedly favorite dish."[10] Oats were usually excellent, and "the whole county, but particularly the lower parishes [that is, the Irish ones], cannot be surpassed in their adaptation to the growth of potatoes." Intervale land and islands produced excellent hay, although the quality had begun to decline. Flax was grown mostly among the French "who are expert at weaving good, strong, and durable linen." Like many observers, Lugrin noted that Victoria County farmers practiced extensive agriculture; like most, he disapproved because he did not think this was the most profitable use of one's time.[11] Lugrin similarly deplored the farmers engaging in lumbering and shingle-making, "speculations" he felt could only lead to lifelong debts. He was, nonetheless, enough of a realist to understand logging as a form of supplemental income could not be eliminated entirely and advised farmers to limit themselves to small-scale ventures. He also recognized that while the lumber camps were the only cash markets available to local farmers, they could not absorb the entire farm production surplus. Thus, farmers had to make shingles or log to round up their income.

Lugrin's account of Victoria County agriculture is particularly useful for his descriptions of existing stock, the most detailed and thorough to date. He found faults with the animals, which he deemed ill-suited to the wants of the people. The horses lacked strength although they were descendents of the "hardy little French horses" imported from Canada at the beginning of the nineteenth century. The stock had, unfortunately, been weakened through indiscriminate cross-breeding. On the positive side, the horses had "nerve, energy, and speed." They were small, did not cost much to keep, but were strong enough to be useful on farms. They were not always the better draught animals to keep, though, and Lugrin believed the French kept too many of them. He believed poorer farmers would have been better off with a team of oxen, which could have done the same amount of work for half the cost. He described horned cattle as small, but good milk producers, and sheep as average in size and fleece. For pigs, he noted, "the common breed of pigs in the French parishes is very long in the leg, with an immense frame, and rather difficult to fatten." Cross-breeding easily improved the scrawny pig, however, and turned it into a very heavy porker.

Lugrin's extensive descriptions are helpful for several reasons. First, with the exception of crop mixes and markets, not much seemed to have changed between 1830 and 1870. The stock descriptions, especially, are very similar to those provided by Deane and Kavanagh, as well as Johnston. Second, Lugrin was visibly not impressed by Victoria County agriculture, whether French or Irish, in either its Catholic or Protestant varieties. Nonetheless, he found nothing that could not be easily remedied with a bit of manure here, a more judicious crop or stock selection there, and widespread cross-breeding of animals with better stock. Victoria County agriculture distinguished itself through neither its vices nor its virtues, but had great potential. Poor communication, not the farmers' lack of skills held it back. Like his neighbors in Aroostook County, Lugrin believed the arrival of the railroad would herald an era of prosperity for the region.

II. AND QUANTIFICATION, 1850–70

A. The Censuses: Misleading Sources

As in the previous period, existing quantitative sources corroborate the accounts left by observers who understood farming. Let us turn towards the agricultural schedules for the American and Canadian censuses. (We only have civil parish level aggregates for New Brunswick in 1851.) Tables 1 and 2 in Appendix H clearly show the crop shift noted by observers: wheat was replaced by buckwheat, and oats production was more important. Lumber operators did not impose this crop shift on farmers; if they had, the shift would have occurred much earlier. Farmers gave up on wheat only when it became unreliable and another market emerged for other crops. In this period, Madawaska farmers could still feed themselves, the increasing local non-farm population, and have some surpluses left to sell on extra-local markets.

But the data also indicate that farm production dropped precipitously after 1850. Is this evidence of the negative impact associated with farmers' dependence on the forest industry? Not really. The drop is, in part, an illusion caused by the nature of the source. Only farms worth $500 or more were included in the 1850 United States census. The 1860 and 1870 censuses included all farms worth at least $100 and the New Brunswick censuses of 1861 and 1871 included all farms regardless of their value. Intuitively, we know that a farm worth $50 should be less productive than one worth $500. Consequently, if we compare the production of all the farms listed in the various censuses, we should see a "decline" in the average production per farm, and also find that American farms "outperformed" New Brunswick ones. Not surprisingly, this is exactly what the tables indicate. But it would be a mistake to conclude that the real average production—which we would have been able to calculate if we had the information for all farms in all years—declined. The differences we observe are, in part, what historians call a "source artifact," or inaccuracies stemming from the nature of the source.

B. Evolution of Farm Productivity

This does not make the censuses useless—but we should only compare what is comparable: the 1860 and the 1870 figures for instance, or the ones for 1861 and 1871. We can also compare the figures for the operational farms in 1830 and in 1850 (about one-third of all holdings in each case). The performance of American farms improved between 1860 and 1870, whereas the performance of New Brunswick farms declined between 1861 and 1871. These contradictory trends are not as odd as they seem: New

Brunswick Madawaska was growing more rapidly than the American one between 1860 and 1870. There were 108 additional farms listed in the 1870 United States census (an increase of 17 percent) and 427 new farms on the New Brunswick side (an increase of 98 percent). More new farms mean fewer fully operational farms and, consequently, lower farm production averages.

C. Marketable Surpluses

Changes in average production per farm or per household can reflect genuine shifts in farm production, but also changes in the region's occupational structure, or even be a consequence of the ways in which the information had been gathered. Changes in the size of the marketable surpluses are a more reliable indicator of the evolution of agriculture. To work around the problem described above and make sure we do not compare apples and oranges, we will

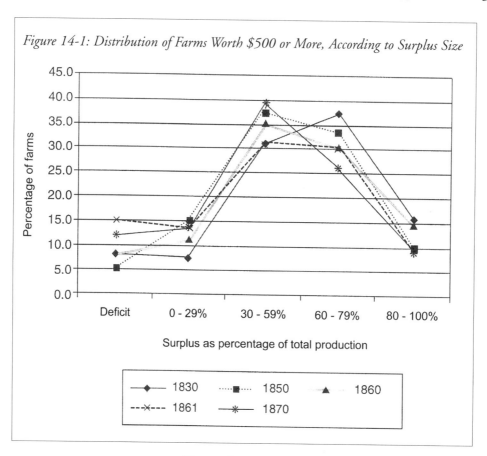

Figure 14-1: Distribution of Farms Worth $500 or More, According to Surplus Size

Table 14-1: Value of Farm Production and Farm Surpluses in Dollars

Year	1830	1850	1860	1861	1870	1871
Net value of farm production	420	545	333	374	337	249
Value of surpluses	316	338	172	213	152	67
Surpluses as a percentage of net production	66	62	52	57	45	27

Sources: see list of censuses p. 409.

Table 14-2: Value of Farm Production and Farm Surpluses in Dollars for Farms Valued at $500 or More

Year	1850	1860	1861	1870
Net value of farm production	545	506	442	518
Value of surpluses	338	324	264	311
Surpluses as a percentage of net production	62	64	60	61

Sources: see list of censuses p. 409.

first compare the farms worth $500 or more (unfortunately, we do not have farm values for 1871). Figure 14-1 shows the distribution of farms in terms of the size of their surplus. The surplus size on these farms hardly changed over the years. But when we compare the value of the surpluses of all American farms in 1860 and 1870, and of all the New Brunswick ones in 1861 and 1871, we see that they declined, especially in New Brunswick (see Tables 14-1 and 14-2). This confirms our initial hunch: the lower the value of a farm, the poorer the occupants.

As the population expanded and carved farms in rear lots (*les concessions*), farmers were forced to cultivate land less and less fit for agriculture. By 1871, new farmers who could not upgrade to better land along the St. John were likely to struggle all their lives. Madawaska had been a good place for families with limited means in the past: they could work for wages in the off-season while clearing the land for a farm. By the 1870s, this was no longer the case. Madawaska arable agriculture had reached its ecological limit.

Surplus size also varied from commodity to commodity. As early as 1860, not enough pigs were raised in the Valley to satisfy the needs of the entire population. Fodder production, on the other hand, increased, especially on the American side. Farmers with large overall surpluses were very often the ones who produced more hay than average because hay had become the Valley's primary commercial crop from 1860 to 1870. But the shanty market was shrinking, because the forest industry was declining.

Illus. 14-1: Although taken in the 1880s, this picture of the St. John Valley a few miles above Grand Falls depicts what was probably the landscape in most of the Valley by mid century. The long lot farms fronting the river are clearly visible on this photograph. PANB, Ketchum collection, Four miles above Grand Falls, P4 1-35

Declines in estimated farm surplus values indicate that farmers' incomes were slowly shrinking.

D. Mid-Century Changes

Soon after the middle of the century, Valley farmers ceased to cover some of their needs through production. Inability to raise certain crops, such as wheat, was one reason. Merchants selling food staples was another factor. They sold Upper Canadian superfine flour, biscuits, meal, wet and dry cured fish (from the Atlantic fisheries), and various grades of mess pork, rice, and molasses. These items were sold by the barrel or retailed by the pound. Between 1846 and 1868, Edmundston merchant John Emmerson ordered an average of 50 barrels of mess pork, 490 barrels of flour, and 56 barrels of herring and other "green fish," a year, as well as dry cod by the

hogshead or by the hundredweight.[12] This was to supply his store; he ordered additional goods for the lumbermen and to fulfill various individuals' special orders.

It is easy to understand why a Catholic population would start buying fish as soon as it became available: Catholics were not allowed to eat meat on Fridays. But fish purchases also reduced the need for other sources of protein; people who ate fish for lunch or dinner on Friday did not feel the need to compensate by eating more meat on Saturday. It is also easy to understand why Valley farmers bought wheat flour rather than gamble on raising an uncertain crop. But why did they buy mess pork instead of slaughtering their own pigs? Farm wives were usually responsible for slopping pigs. This was not a pleasant task. When these women became able to buy pork at the store, they did not quit raising pigs entirely but

The Land in Between

rather limited themselves to a couple of animals. Thus, the Valley could be self-sufficient in terms of food, but its inhabitants preferred buying staple food at the store to diversify their diets or reduce unpleasant chores.

This willingness to rely on the market for necessities is not what one would expect from impoverished farmers dependent on the goodwill of lumber barons for their income. Neither does this behavior fit the stereotypical image of the "self-sufficient" frontier farmer. Instead, it reflects the fact that farming families had access to various markets and were comfortable using them as sources of income and food.

III. COMPARISONS

Other historians have used the 1861 Canadian Census to estimate farm production and marketable surpluses in other regions. This allows us to see how Madawaska farmers compared to their neighbors. This comparison works to Madawaskayans' advantage. Madawaska farmers outperformed farmers in other Acadian districts in New Brunswick. They performed as well as their colleagues in Upper Canada and even as well as Nova Scotia's most prosperous farmers. Since historians consider that Upper Canada agriculture was the most commercial and the most-developed one in British North America in the mid-nineteenth century, Madawaskayans were very productive farmers.

There were differences among the regions: Nova Scotia exported beef to New England and thus had more cattle and hay. It grew less peas, a cultural trait: Anglo-Americans preferred beans. Historian Jean Roch Cyr found that Madawaska farms were larger, had more acres under cultivation, and devoted more space to other uses, such as buildings, meadows, and vegetable gardens, than the ones in other Acadian districts. The Valley devoted significantly more acres to the cultivation of buckwheat than the other Acadian districts; otherwise, acreages devoted to the main field crops (oats, hay, and potatoes) were similar across regions. The Valley also had more animals per farm than the other districts, with oxen as the one exception. Cyr concluded that the parishes of Dorchester in Westmorland County, St. Leonard, and St. Basile were the best-performing Acadian districts in New Brunswick. As for Upper Canadian farms, they did not out-produce Madawaska ones by much, despite enjoying a much longer growing season and having better access to urban markets. Upper Canada, like Madawaska, engaged in the same type of multiple crops and mixed agriculture, and relied heavily on family labor. And, despite the climate disadvantage, Madawaska's top-producing farmers had more surpluses to sell than their Upper Canadian counterparts. Valley farmers were, therefore, successful farmers by mid-nineteenth-century British North American standards.

IV. SIDE-ACTIVITIES

Farmers also benefited from the proximity of lumber camps in indirect ways. Some rented draft animals to lumber operators. This meant they did not have to feed or muck those animals during the winter. Other farmers transported supplies from the farms or stores to the camps. Storekeepers hired farmers to transport hay and oats to the shanties. John Emmerson also hired farmers to go and fetch merchandise at Rivière-du-Loup or Grand Falls, and then transport some of them to the shanties. Farmers supplied the labor, animals, and equipment, and, as they did most of the carrying in winter, they probably welcomed the opportunity to get out of the house and exercise the horses. They earned 25 shillings ($5) for taking four barrels of goods from Rivière-du-Loup to Edmundston (according to Emmerson's records, four barrels

Table 14.3: Per Capita Domestic Fabric Production, in Yards: 1851–91*

Years	Ontario	Quebec	Nova Scotia	New Brunswick	Victoria County**	Madawaska***
1851–52	1.79	2.84	4.08	3.21	2.96	2.47
1860–61	1.53	2.84	3.99	no data	no data	no data
1870–71	1.11	4.49	4.09	3.94	5.98	6.63
1880–-81	0.75	3.01	3.17	2.68	4.45	no data
1890–-91	0.25	1.86	1.69	1.48	2.59	no data

* The data on domestic textiles is only available for British North America and Canada, since American censuses did not include questions about farm cloth production. There is, however, no reason to believe that the American side of the Valley behaved differently in this respect than the Canadian one.
** The published census tables for 1881 and 1891 combine Victoria and Madawaska Counties. The manuscript schedules of the 1881 and 1891 census have been destroyed, and therefore one cannot recalculate the quantities.
*** In 1851, the area that later became Madawaska County produced 8,577 yards of fabric; in 1871, it produced 10,328 yards of linen and 37,697 yards of flannel.

Sources: See list of censuses p. 409.

was the normal carrying capacity of a sleigh). Traffic on the Témiscouata Road was particularly intense: on average, during the winter months, two supply-laden sleighs traveled from Rivière-du-Loup to Emmerson's every week. Since Emmerson was not the only storekeeper in the Valley, there must have been convoys of sleighs riding up and down the Témiscouata Road on a constant basis.

V.   MADAWASKA WEAVERS

Madawaska weavers are still remembered, in part, because Madawaska women continued making "homespun" (handwoven fabric) long after their New England counterparts gave up this activity. And indeed Madawaska was a high producer of "home-spun" (see Table 14-3). American visitors were often struck by the sight of these women spinning and weaving, which reinforced their belief that the Madawaska French were remnants of a self-suffi-cient, non-commercial world. Other less romantic types believed home weaving was a sign of poverty, that families that could not afford factory-made fabric had to make it themselves.

Both the romantics and critics were wrong. At Madawaska, it was not women from poor house-holds who wove but women who were better off (that is, the ones from farms with high surpluses). This is not paradoxical. Weaving required looms. The frame could be made by any farm boy who knew how to use his tools. But the heddle (the part of the loom that guides and lifts the warp threads) had to be purchased. Looms also took up quite a bit of space, and poor people had tiny houses. Poor women who wanted to weave had to borrow a neigh-bor's loom.

Women who wove did not do so to avoid

WOOLEN GOODS IN GREAT DEMAND

A.A. Miller & Co wish to purchase Homespun Cloth of all kinds in large quantities, also 2000 pairs of socks and Mitts, 1-2 ton Woolen Yarn, Over Socks, Home Knit Drawers, Shirts, Pants, &c., &c. in exchange for Dry Goods.
We are daily opening New Goods for the Fall and Winter Trade, and claim to have one of the Newest, Freshest, Cleanest and Best Assorted Stocks in Canada

A.A. MILLER & Co.
Opposite City Hall, Fredericton

Source: *New Brunswick Reporter* and *Fredericton Advertiser,* September 8, 1880.

LOOK SHARP

BUY YOUR COTTON WARPS AT

A.A. Miller & Co.,

AND MAKE UP

Homespun Cloth,
Socks, Mitts, &c.

early in the season, and you can be relieved of all such Domestic Goods at the Store of A.A. Miller & Co. opposite City Hall in exchange for DRY GOODS. We want about

4000 Yds. Of Cloth

Source: *New Brunswick Reporter* and *Fredericton Advertiser,* June 8, 1881.

expenses. According to the local storekeepers' books, the households buying lots of fabric were also the households making lots of homespun. Women who wove did so in part to clothe their families and in part for the market. Homespun was a scratchy but tough and warm material, suitable for the work clothes men wore in the woods or driving timber rafts down the river. It was also commonly used for men's work pants, even if the wearer did not go in the woods. Madawaska producers knew about this demand—and had taken advantage of it in the 1840s as shown by Isaac Stephenson's autobiography:

> At Hartland and Spring Hill [about mid-river] I saw as a child, the products of the forest go by in an endless stream of rafts, the towboats laden with supplies for the farms, the canoes of the Indians and white men, the pirogues of the Acadians carrying to market the woolen garments made from their own flocks of sheep and maple sugar obtained in the woods.[13]

There was still a heavy demand for homespun in New Brunswick later in the century (see Sidebar 14-1), and the material was expensive to purchase. John Emmerson sold it at $1.20 per yard. By comparison, he sold black silk for 80 cents a yard and cloaking (a heavy woolen material for coats) for 60 cents a yard. Female weavers could, therefore, make good money. Based on the cost of raw material and the time required to weave the fabric, a weaver could net from $2 to $2.50 per day. At the time, a female farm servant earned $2.50 a month, plus room and board, and a male farm laborer 50 cents a day. No wonder women gave up slopping pigs.

Two developments made it easier for women to weave, and may explain why the production of homespun increased after 1850. The first was the spread of carding mills, which spared women the labor needed to prepare fleece for spinning. The second was the availability of factory-spun cotton yarn. Weavers used cotton for warp and wool for weft. Cotton warp was available in the Valley by the mid-1840s when the Dufour brothers began selling it in their store; ten years later, John Emmerson was bringing enormous quantities of this material into the Valley. Between 1849 and 1858, he ordered an average of 1,000 pounds of cotton warp a year.

Conclusion

In this period, Madawaska households supported themselves through agriculture and participation in the forest industry. Contrary to what occurred in other regions where the two activities co-existed, they did not suffer from the combination. First, the land they occupied was suitable for farming, which was not true for all agro-forestry regions. Second, no lumber operator had a monopoly in the region as was the case in the Saguenay or along the Ottawa River. Farmers could play one operator against another. And, as they could live off their farms if they so chose, they could refuse to sell when prices or conditions were not to their liking. Shepard Cary found, to his dismay, that farmers around Fort Kent would not exchange fodder for credit at his store; they wanted cash. Since the population of the Valley was growing rapidly, farmers also had an alternate market for some of their surpluses. Their dependence on the shanty market was, therefore, not absolute. Farmers sold fodder to merchants, or directly to lumber opera-

tors—and in the latter case, they appear to have been paid in cash. They also sold food to new farmers and wage earners. Wage earners and new farmers made their money working in the shanties in winter. Established farmers did not work in the lumber camps, but could derive additional income by either renting out their animals or carrying supplies for merchants.

The farmer's double market is reflected in the commodities they produced between 1850 and 1870, including potatoes and buckwheat, oats, and hay. As in the early 1830s, farmers were not all the same. Some farmers produced much larger surpluses than others, and larger farmers were the ones most likely to be able to cover all their food needs from their land. But store ledgers during this time indicate that this was not their goal, since they also bought staple foods. Improved transportation along the Great Lakes/St. Lawrence waterway brought food to their door. And they could afford those goods because the various markets surrounding them provided them with the necessary means. The Valley had successfully responded to the emergence of the Great Lakes region as the continent's breadbasket and found alternative markets for its own production. Madawaska farmers were also as productive as those in better located regions, such as Upper Canada. And finally, women were not averse to producing for markets either, and when they did, they earned considerable profits.

ENDNOTES
1. Lord Elgin (governor of Canada from 1847 to 1854) in a letter to the Duke of Newcastle. Cited in Monroe, *New Brunswick,* 81
2. Robb, *Agricultural Progress,* 23.
3. " Pris dans son ensemble, la coupe du bois est certainement un facteur important dans le développement économique du Madawaska au début du XIXe siècle. Cette région dépendant surtout du marché de Saint Jean pour absorber la majorité des exportations de cette richesse naturelle. Mais la prospérité économique qu'elle apporte sera contrôlée par les anglophones. Cette conjoncture accélère donc les ambitions d'un petit groupe de favorisés au milieu d'une majorité acadienne dont la servitude sera l'unique récompense. " Sirois, "Les Acadiens et la naissance du commerce du bois...," 183–93

4. Day, *Aroostook: The First Sixty Years,* ch. XII.

5. Wiggin, *History of Aroostook,* 295.

6. "Abstract of land agent report." *Republican Journal* (Belfast, Maine), January 27, 1843.

7. Johnston, *Report on the Agricultural Capabilities...,* 51.

8. *Loyal Sunrise* (Presque Isle, Maine), October 12, 1866.

9. Elwell, *Aroostook, with some account of the excursions....* Ellwell is *not* a reliable source about the Valley.

10. PANB, Journal of the House of Assembly of New Brunswick, 1872, Appendix: "Description of Victoria County," by Charles Lugrin: XI.

11. The Maine Board of Agriculture seems to have been the only group supporting extensive farming. They actually advocated it as the most cost-effective method in a region where land is cheap, labor expensive, and markets limited. *Second Annual Report...,* 24.

12. A barrel weighed 196 pounds; a hundredweight (abbreviated cwt) could weigh between 100 and 112 pounds; the British hundredweight was equal to 112 pounds; a hogshead was a unit of volume, with the British hogshead worth 54 imperial gallons, or 65 U.S. gallons.

13. Stephenson, *Recollection of a Long Life,* 28.

FURTHER READINGS

Dubay, Guy. "The Garden of Maine." In *The County: Land of Promise,* ed. A. Mcgrath. 1989: 153–60.

Dubay, Guy. *Chez Nous: The St. John Valley.* 1983: 55–70.

SOURCES

This chapter is a summary of the chapters on agriculture in Craig's *Homespun Capitalists and Backwoods Consumers* (2009), without the technical information. The methodology is explained at length in Appendix I of this volume.

Those who are curious about the agro-forestry system may consult Hardy and Séguin (1984), Gaffield (1982), and Bouchard (1988 and 1996). Willis (1981) and Little (1991 and 1989) investigate the relationship between agriculture and the forest industry in two regions close to the upper St. John Valley.

Comparative material about Ontario, Nova Scotia, the lower St. John Valley, and New Brunswick can be found, respectively, in McInnis (1984), MacNeil (1990 and 1993), Acheson (1993), and Cyr (1988). Atack and Bateman (1984) have published similar studies on American agriculture, but a slight methodological difference makes comparisons between their work and the one of Canadian scholars difficult, especially for those unfamiliar with the technicalities involved.

Craig, Rygiel, and Turcotte (2001 and 2002) explain textile production at Madawaska in greater detail. See also Simard (1987).

15

HOW THE CONSUMER ECONOMY CAME TO MADAWASKA

In the previous chapters we saw that many Madawaska men and women engaged in commercial activities that often enabled them to make respectable profits. What did they do with their earnings? During the 1845–70 period, they used at least some of that money to go shopping. According to the 1870 and 1871 censuses, there were twenty-three merchants, storekeepers, and traders in the entire Valley, or one store for every hundred households. Opportunities to shop, therefore, were not lacking.

Going shopping in rural areas during the nineteenth century was an entirely different experience from shopping in modern times. There were no shopping malls and few specialized stores. Instead, one went to a general store that carried a very wide range of goods. Most purchases were made on credit, and were entered into the storekeepers' book; payments were similarly recorded when they were made. Those books provide historians with very useful information about the types of goods sold in a given area. Madawaska is blessed with an unusually large number of these documents.[1] They reveal that a surprising amount of money was in circulation at Madawaska by the mid-nineteenth century. They also show that a wide range of consumer goods from British North America, the United States, Europe, and the West and East Indies were available locally at affordable prices, and that people purchased those goods readily. The Madawaska economy was a cash economy to a larger extent than most other rural areas at the time; it was also a consumer economy and a consumer frontier.

I.   THE EMERGENCE OF A CASH ECONOMY

A. A Problem: Specie Shortage

It is surprising to find Madawaska customers paying in cash because this practice was uncommon during the nineteenth century. Historians have found that only 5 to 30 percent of customers in Upper Canada, New England, and New York State during the first half of the nineteenth century paid for purchases in cash. There were two reasons for this. The first one was a shortage of "specie," or metallic money. There were not enough coins in circulation to cover all the transaction needs of the American and British North American populations. Britain did not allow its colonies to mint coins and did not send them enough coins. The United States mint could not keep up with the needs of the American economy; as a result, it was legal to use Spanish silver dollars even for transactions with the government until the middle of the century. Bank notes as we understand them today did not exist. Banks issued notes, but those were private money and no one was obliged to accept them as payment. Merchants only accepted at face value notes from banks they knew; they either discounted (accepted for less than their face value) other notes or refused them altogether. British and American currencies both circulated in Madawaska during this time. During the 1840s, Mainer Shepard Cary paid his men in New Brunswick bank notes, which he obtained by selling timber in Saint John. And in 1846, the priest informed his bishop that "our paper is all from New Brunswick."[2] On the other hand, in 1858, storekeeper John Emmerson was swapping American dollars for British North American notes with Rivière-du-Loup merchant Georges Pelletier (who apparently needed American money).

B. And a Solution: Book Credit

Farmers may have been rich in goods they could trade, but they were also short on cash. Storekeepers then had to accept payments in kind. Moreover, since not all customers had something to trade when they needed to buy something at the store, many purchases were "put on the book," meaning done on credit. Farmers, for instance, had goods to sell at harvest and slaughtering time (late summer/early fall and around Christmastime, respectively). Every now and then, debits and credits were tallied, and the account "settled." Normally, the balance was very small and could be settled with the small amount of specie people had—or simply put back on the book.

Payments in kind were usually made in "country products," such as farm commodities, forest products, and, in some regions, mineral products such lime and potash (made from wood ash). The storekeepers then had to find a buyer for those goods in order to have money to pay their own suppliers. The shortage of specie meant that storekeepers experienced the same problem as their customers and struggled to pay their suppliers in Montreal, Saint John, or Boston. They too bought on credit and paid when they could. A merchant, therefore, acted as a sort of traffic controller, presiding over the movements of goods in and out of his community.

This reliance on credit made country merchants very vulnerable to economic downturns. The Dufour brothers learned this the hard way. By 1848, the bottom had fallen out of the market for forest products;

the price of fodder also plummeted, with oats dropping from 50 cents to 33 cents a bushel. As the Dufours' customers could not settle their accounts, the brothers could pay neither their suppliers nor their clerk. The various parties sued, and the Dufours, in turn, sued their customers. They were obliged to close the store in 1848. Their experience served as a warning to Emmerson, who went into the storekeeping business in the mid-1840s. Emmerson avoided credit like the plague, as we shall see below. So, apparently, did Charles Morneault, who operated a store across the river.

Valley residents also encountered the same kind of problems in their transactions with each other. For example, farmer Firmin may not have had the goods the blacksmith wanted when he needed his horse shod. So Firmin may have told the blacksmith he could go to the store and purchase goods on his (Firmin's) account. This was known as a third-party transaction. And if the blacksmith did not like or need anything at that store, he could pass his credit on Firmin's account to somebody whom he owed money. The storekeeper, thus, was a necessary player in the local circulation of goods and services.

C. The Valley's Cash Economy

Madawaska was different from other areas because cash quickly became a very significant form of payment (see Tables 15-1 and 15-2). In the mid-1840s, the Dufour brothers collected country products as payment (mostly fodder for the lumber camps); their customers also earned store credit transporting the said fodder to the lumber camps. Only ten percent (in value) of the payments were in cash.

At Emmerson's and Morneault's stores, on the other hand, cash was much more common. If customers could not pay in cash, they could get store credit by working for the storekeeper. Since Emmerson was doing a high volume of business, he always needed people to go and fetch goods at Grand Falls or Rivière-du-Loup. He clearly did not like trading in country products, which accounted for only a small

Table 15-1: Modes of Payment

Store	Year	Total payment in dollars	Cash as a percentage of all payments	Country products as a percentage of all payments	Third most popular type of payment as a percentage of all payments	Third type of payment
Dufour	1846	3,611	10.8	42.9	13.7	Transportation
Emmerson	1853	3,593	40.8	6.6	12.1	Labor
Emmerson	1863	3,764	24.6	17.1	16.6	Transportation
Morneault	1858	508	41.6	25.3	8.4	Wood products

Sources: See Endnote 1, p. 216.

Table 15-2: Frequency of Payments

Store	Year	Total number of people making payments	Percentage of people paying in cash	Percentage paying in country products	Percentage paying in a third kind of payments
Dufour	1846	208	28.4	40.7	34.1 [1]
Emmerson	1853	173	57.8	24.3	12.1
Emmerson	1863	162	42.0	38.7	27.6
Morneault	1858	68	60.3	54.4	7.4

Note 1. The totals exceed 100 percent because no one used only one form of payment.
Sources: See Endnote 1, p. 216.

part of his customers' payments. Morneault, for his part, accepted a fair amount of wood products as payment. One would think that over the years the use of cash would have become even more widespread. Yet, in 1863, cash payments had become less, not more, important. What happened?

The first thing that happened was the American Civil War. The American government began issuing greenbacks, but soon their value became suspect. By 1863, British North American officials had begun discounting American money, and Emmerson was accepting greenbacks at only three-quarters of their face value. American money still circulated at Madawaska but by 1863, neither residents nor storekeepers were willing to accept it. Second, a crisis in the forest industry not only curtailed farm profits by depressing fodder prices (the price of oats dropped from 50 cents to 25 cents a bushel), but also led to the bankruptcy of a New Brunswick bank. Emmerson had to begin accepting country products, thus

Illus. 15-1: John Emmerson's house, built in 1867, later served as Edmundston's city hall.
CDEM, PC-83

taking a risk. What if he could not find buyers willing to offer adequate prices? But Emmerson did more than buy his cutomers' goods. He went to see one of his suppliers in Quebec City and came back with $500 worth of silver coins, which he used to ease the shortage of trustworthy money. What is interesting about this is that Emmerson clearly felt that his customers' problems were also his problems, and that it was his responsibility to try to minimize it.

D. An Interventionist Storekeeper

John Emmerson handled considerable sums of money. Several times a year, he would collect his cash or quasi-cash—which included British and American coins, bank notes, lumberers' scrip, drafts on the treasury for public work, and lumbermen's letters of exchange—and send it all by mail to J. J. Hegan, his major supplier in Saint John. In return, Hegan sent him goods, notes from Montreal banks, and, after the start of the Civil War, British gold coins. In 1856, he sent $7,500 worth of cash; in 1858, $14,400; and in 1860, $28,600. Emmerson, who clearly pushed his customers to use cash, also paid his own supplier in cash as soon as he received their bills. He mailed to Québec the bank notes and gold coins received from Saint John. All those bags of money traveling from Saint John to Edmundston to Québec by post represent one of the more surprising aspects of Emmerson's activities.

Emmerson also did his best to push the Madawaska economy toward a cash economy where people settled their accounts promptly. Whereas most storekeepers made their customers settle their accounts once a year, Emmerson asked them to settle every three months. Other storekeepers followed suit. Cash payments dominated transactions at the Morneault store in the late 1850s, and Morneault had so few customers on his books (about seventy) that he could not have stayed in business without additional cash customers. The situation was the same at the Connors' store. In the mid-1870s, the only people who had book credit at the Connors' store were the ones who worked for him or were in business with him. The others, presumably, were cash customers. The days of payments in kind and long book credits were fast disappearing.

II.   TOWARD A CONSUMER ECONOMY

Emmerson and the Dufours brought large quantities of a wide variety of products in the region. They introduced their customers to the world of manufactured of goods. Their books tell us what kinds of objects were available in the region and the changes in consumption patterns that occurred between 1845 and 1870.

A. Wholesale Trade and Mail Order

Men like the Dufour brothers and Morneault purchased goods from wholesalers to sell back at Madawaska. On the other hand, Emmerson was acting as a middleman between wholesalers and retailers as early as 1858. He worked on commission. Most of the storekeepers he supplied were located at Fort Kent on the other side of the river. Emmerson either supplied his clients with goods from his own stock, or he ordered the goods on their behalf and had them delivered to them. The activities of one of his customers show how this worked. In March 1853, Joseph Nadeau, the innkeeper at Fort Kent, gave Emmerson £2 10s ($9). In July, Emmerson charged Nadeau's account 75 shillings ($14) for two barrels of flour (35s each plus an extra 5s for freight charges). Nadeau immediately mailed the payment.

Emmerson then billed Nadeau for freight charges on twenty-five barrels of flour, which Nadeau paid in person in September. The receiving book, however, shows Emmerson receiving six barrels of flour for Nadeau in July and twenty-five barrels of flour and two barrels of pork in August. Yet, Emmerson never billed Nadeau for the value of those barrels. (Twenty-five barrels of flour at 35s apiece would have been worth £43 15s or $175.) Nadeau probably paid for the goods when he placed his order or orders and paid for most of the freight in advance. Like Nadeau, various individuals placed orders for staple food, such as flour, pork, molasses, and fish, through Emmerson. They also ordered a great variety of other goods. For example, a blacksmith ordered a set of tools; three people ordered stoves; and Placide Thériault ordered a cabriolet.

Lumberers ordered shanty supplies. Emmerson's 1846 book lists eight of them (plus Glazier). They received 22 barrels of pork, 246 barrels of flour, 6 barrels of herring, 3 barrels of meal, and 1 barrel of molasses. Glazier, for his part, needed 20 barrels of pork, 84 barrels of flour, 6 barrels of herring, 7 barrels of molasses, 27 barrels of meal, and 8 barrels of beans. In addition, Glazier ordered tea, soap, axes, ropes, various tools, blankets, and "dry goods." In

1853, there were only two lumberers listed in the receiving book. (Emmerson supplied others, but kept their accounts in another book.) Peter Clare, who also ran an inn, ordered twenty-five barrels of flour, fourteen barrels of "sundries," and one barrel of sugar. Glazier, on the other hand, required an astronomical quantity of goods: 313 barrels of flour; 78 barrels of pork; various quantities of fish, molasses, tea, and tools; and casks, boxes, and chests whose contents were not identified.

B. Where Did Goods Come From?

Emmerson purchased large quantities of staple foods, such as flour, meal, fish, and mess pork, from Quebec City merchants. The flour originated from various mills in Upper Canada. (Retailers often identified the mill where the flour was produced.)

Apparently Emmerson did not pay customs duties on the goods' entry into New Brunswick. His competitor, John Costello, objected and tried, without success, to convince the New Brunswick government to take measures against this (see letter in Sidebar 15-1). Emmerson purchased most of his other goods from Saint John importers. For instance, he purchased all his textiles and notions from Hegan and Co., a merchant house that described itself in 1864 as "importers of British and foreign dry goods of every description." Some Saint John suppliers advertised lower prices for customers who paid in cash. Some of those importers also deliberately targeted country merchants; Hegan and Co. announced in their 1855 advertisement that "personal attention will be given to the selection of goods for all wholesale and retail orders received from the country." Wholesalers and the country merchants they serviced became key

---

Sidebar 15-1: Smuggling!

To the honourable attorney general, Fredericton
Little Falls, December 9th 1851

Honourable Sir,
When I saw you in Fredericton I complained to you with regards to partys treading between Here and Canada, and now I am prepared with facts. But not knowing how to State them unless that there is not scarcely a day But several partys passes my store door loaded with all sorts of merchandises from Canada vz liquors tea tobacco stoves & all other goods two numerous to mention. I find the principal part of what is a wanting in this part of the country is taken from their and I who has to purchase my stock in St John and take them as far as here I cannot compete with the River du Loup merchant to prevent this it is requisite to have a custom house officer here and such a course will benefit the government the St John merchants and the Treader who purchase them and keep the money in the country which is dreamed of day should the government think proper to make this appointment which I trust they will, they will find it to their advantage. I am sir your most obedient humble servant
    John Costello

Source: PANB, RS76 4a2a, Attorney General files, Boundaries, Madawaska, General Correspondence, 1818–51, Letter from John Costello to the Attorney General, 9 December 1851. Document kindly contributed by Gary Campbell; spelling as in the original letter.

---

players in the movement of goods from the manufacturing centers of Europe and the United States to remote rural communities.

Because Emmerson did a very large volume of business, he could afford to travel to Quebec City and Saint John and select goods himself. This also allowed him to spot useful innovations. In 1858, he purchased lamps, shades, and lamp oil from the New Brunswick Oil Works, a company that had just begun to advertise that year. The Oil Works, which also manufactured paraffin lamp oil, advertised "liberal discounts for wholesale dealers."[3] Emmerson got a 25 percent discount on his first order. The product was more popular than he had expected, and he reordered twice during the same year. Because he was prompt with his payments and always paid in cash, he often received discounts, which enabled him to sell the goods at competitive prices.

C. Consumer Choices

1. Food Items

So what did people actually buy? In descending order of popularity, they bought food—especially flour—fabric, clothing, footwear, hand tools, maintenance materials, and household equipment and supplies. It is in the details of the categories, rather than in the aggregate figures, that the true story of rural consumption emerges. Staple goods, namely flour, mess pork, fish, and meal, represented the bulk of food purchases. At Dufours' store, flour accounts for 10 percent of all purchases. Emmerson sold the same products, but the most popular product at his store was not flour but the cheaper, locally produced buckwheat meal. In fact, 16 percent of his customers bought the meal, which constituted 8 percent of the total value of all his sales. Only 10 percent of his customers purchased flour. Flour buyers, however, probably ordered a barrel or two from the store and paid cash. Poor people, who typically opted for the cheaper buckwheat meal over the more expensive flour,[4] were also more likely to make piecemeal purchases of a few pounds and put them on account.

Another 15 percent of Emmerson's customers bought biscuits, a product he appears to have carried from the day he opened his store (they are listed in his receiving book in 1845). Emmerson seems to have sold more fish to more people than the Dufours. That is, 10 percent of his customers purchased fish in 1863. Customers bought cod by the pound, herring by the dozen, salted fish by the half or whole barrel, and dry cod by the box. Similarly, 15 percent of his customers purchased pork, which was largely sold by the pound. Other customers, however, may have ordered barrels of mess pork in the same way they ordered barrels of flour and they may have paid cash; in that case, they would not appear in the books.

The Dufours sold very little white sugar, which is not surprising since the region was a major producer of maple sugar. Emmerson, on the other hand, sold sugar and molasses to 25 percent of his customers in 1853 and to 18 percent in 1863. He rented sugar kettles, (large pots used for boiling maple sap), and bought maple sugar from local people. He shipped some of this sugar to Georges Pelletier, the forwarder at Rivière-du-Loup who relayed his orders from Quebec City. Emmerson also sold some maple sugar back in the Valley; his 1867 inventory lists more than 2,000 pounds of maple sugar in November, which was well after the end of the sugaring season. But, as early as 1849, he was purchasing sugar loaves and molasses from his Québec suppliers, including Pelletier. Collectively, Madawaska residents were swapping local sugar for the West Indian variety, a strange phenomenon which will be explained below.

Baking techniques were evolving. The Dufours sold leavening agents (pearl ashes and saleratus) to 6 percent of their clients. Emmerson sold saleratus, baking soda, and baking powder to 10 percent of his clients. Drinking habits were also changing, but neither storekeeper sold alcohol. In 1863, almost 12 percent of of the Dufours' customers bought tea, but none bought coffee. Neither did Emmerson's customers buy any on credit, and yet, according to his inventory, he had coffee in stock. Tea was the bever-

Sidebar 15-2: Young Consumers

Store accounts were always in the head of household's name. Here, the Dufour brothers hired Marie Lagacé, François' daughter, as a servant for a month. Her wages were credited to her father's account. Marie, however, used her wages to buy things for herself. The purchases were also put on her father's account. The amounts in the left column are credits (payments towards the account) and the ones in the right column are debits (what the account holder owed the storekeeper). In 1845, the Dufours started a new page in a new book in Lagacé's name. He already had an account at the store, and they reported the balance from his page in a previous book (Folio I) at the beginning of this one (5 shillings and 9 pence). The values are in Halifax currency (One pound currency equal $4, and one shilling equal 20 cents; the / means shilling and the d, pence)

Owes François Lagacé		Credit	Debit
1844	Report from Folio I, p. 146		5/9
1845			
January 2,	1 barrel		7/6
	Goods delivered to his daughter Marie		1/6
February 5	Credit for 1 pr. slippers from Marie	2/3	
	¼ yd gingham		4d
July 26	Marie begins her time at 12/6 per month		
August 26	Credit for Marie's salary	12/6	
	1 pr. French shoes		8/
	1 yellow silk kerchief		5/
July 13, 1847	1 pr. suspenders		1/
	1 scythe to son		10/
August 7	By hay in the field	£1-5/	
	10½ pounds of bacon at 10d		
	Interest on 13/6 from May 1,		
	1845 to present		2/0 ½
Total debit			£3-17/4½
Total credit		14/9	

Source: Madawaska Public Library, Dufour Ledger, 1844–48. Translation by the authors.

age of choice, with 20 percent of Emmerson's customers purchasing a total of thirty-six pounds in 1863. The inventory taken after Emmerson's death in 1867 lists tea, tea pots (cheap tin ones and pricier earthenware ones), tea kettles, cups and saucers, and spoons known as "tea spoons." The growing fondness for tea may explain why people were swapping maple sugar for the imported variety. That is, maple sugar, like molasses, tastes fine with robust-flavored food, but tea tastes better with white sugar. And, if Madawaska residents had not sweetened their tea, they would have had no use for teaspoons.

Illus. 15-2: John Emmerson was sending large quantities of supplies to the lumber camps. Some of the supplies were boated in the fall. This picture shows the transporting of supplies on the Restigouche. Similar scenes could be seen along the St. John River and its tributaries. PANB, Central New Brunswick Woodsmen Museum Collection, P54-113.

2. Textiles

Fabric constituted one of the two main categories of purchases customers charged to their accounts; most of the recorded purchases were for cotton (both in terms of total value and in terms of frequency of purchases). Customers generally purchased factory-made material in such small pieces that the amount was insufficient to make a complete garment. The yardage purchased, such as Marie Lagace's quarter yard of gingham (see Sidebar 15-2), suggests customers used this fabric for caps and bonnets, aprons, and trimmings; small yardages of wool were probably used for cuffs and lapels, and the fronts of waistcoats. Silk purchases were extremely rare.

Emmerson was receiving an extensive variety of fabric from his Saint John supplier. In 1851, by no means a high-volume year, he received 2,287 yards of fabric, plus unspecified yardage of flannel. Most fabric was "grey" cotton (725 yards);[5] this was followed by a dozen different inexpensive cotton prints totalling 526 yards. He sold very little luxury fabric and did not carry much in his inventory, either. He did, however, carry a great variety of ribbons, lace, inserts, edging, and banding. Women who used to edge their clothing with bits of purchased fabric may have switched to material designed for the purpose, because it was easier to use and more varied. Emmerson also carried extremely large quantities of buttons, hooks, and eyes. Customers were purchasing slightly larger quantities of fabric in 1863, but the yardage was often still not enough to create a complete garment. For instance, of the twenty-eight customers who bought calico, half bought less than three yards—the minimum yardage needed to make a woman's blouse. Only five customers bought at least six yards, the amount needed to make a petticoat.

And although several people bought merino (a high quality woollen material), none bought enough for a dress—despite the material being relatively cheap (1s 8d to 2s 6d a yard). By contrast, another Edmundston storekeeper, John Costello, carried the fancy stuff Emmerson did not stock, such as silk linings, Scotch plaid, Delaine, Kerseys, Gros de Naples (a silk material), and imported linen (Brown Holland and Onasbruck). Emmerson may have sold relatively little fabric, especially high-end fabric, because other local stores were specializing in this line of products. He may have decided to focus on low-end cotton fabric because he was able to buy it at a discounted rate.

3. Tools and Hardware

Tools, hardware, and maintenance products were similar to the ones that had been available to North American settlers for centuries with some exceptions. Costello and Emmerson both carried the same assortment of hand tools, nails, tacks, spikes, and the curiously named "sparrow bills," a sort of fastener; they also stocked various colors of paint, oil for paint, turpentine, paint brushes, varnish, coal tar, and putty. They both carried all sorts of metal wares that could hinge, close, fasten, or lock containers and cupboards. Emmerson alone carried tarpaulin, oilcloth, and "patented" oilcloth, a product clearly advertised as a vast improvement over the usual variety. There were also two new items in Emmerson's 1863 account book and in his inventory: screws and screwdrivers. Screws were a product of the Industrial Revolution because threads were difficult to make by hand. They eventually replaced dowels. Monkey wrenches, available at Emmerson's but not at Costello's, were another new tool (using a threaded rod). They came from the United States; had they come from Britain, they would have been called spanners. While the male world of goods did not change much during the century, it did come to include timesaving innovations.

4. Household Items

The world of household goods tells a different story. The few Madawaska post mortem inventories[6] available suggest very Spartan homes. The common room contained a stove, table, seats, chests, a few pots and pans, and a limited amount of crockery and cutlery. It also contained women's tools, since the common room was the women's workshop, where they carded wool and scutched flax, spun, wove, sewed, mended, and knitted garments, and cooked food. The 1845 inventory of Jean-Baptiste Cyr, a saw-miller who drowned in 1843, leaving behind a wife and four children, includes two bedsteads with bedding, a bedstead settee, an iron stove, three tables (but no chairs or benches), and three chests. To cook and serve food, Cyr's wife, Marguerite, had a tea kettle, a frying pan, a soup kettle, an iron kettle, six spoons, forks and knives, six plates, six cups and saucers, a decanter, and an oval dish. The inventory also lists two smoothing irons, a candle mold, four tubs, kneading trough, spinning wheel, the mechanical parts for a loom (but apparently no loom frame), candlestick, mirror, and a $10 clock. With the exception of the beds, Cyr's inventory reads more like the description of a scullery than a home. It also suggests that Marguerite Cyr was a busy woman, who spun, wove (assuming her husband made a frame for her loom), baked bread, molded candles, and kept some people's clothes wrinkle free. She could also keep track of her time with the clock and steal glances at her appearance in the mirror. The 1860 inventory of Benjamin Madore, a wealthy farmer, lists a single and two double stoves, four beds with bedding, a dresser with crockery, two big and one small pot, two bake pans, two kettles, two tables, seventeen chairs, a chest, churn, frying pan, two firkins (a firkin was a tub used to preserve butter in a salt solution), a loom with reeds and pulleys, and two flax wheels. The inventory did not list a spinning wheel, despite the presence of forty pounds of wool. Madore's only luxuries were two mirrors. All his possessions were worth $146.40. He did have some new items, such as a dresser and more crockery than the administrator

Illus. 15-3: No picture of Simon and Abraham Dufour seems to have survived. This lady was their sister–in–law, Anastasie Thibodeau (1828–1912), wife of Cyrille Dufour. She is dressed in the style of the 1860s. Madawaska Historical Society.

to stock the Madore household in the 1860s. Both Emmerson and Costello offered a wide range of cookware, including griddles, frying pans, dippers (sauce pans), and tin bakers, as well as crockery, cutlery, and glassware. These items were available at different prices and were, thus, presumably of different qualities. Emmerson also sold blankets and counterpanes, as well as cotton batting or wadding, which could be used for quilts. (He was still selling these items in 1863 despite the high price of cotton.) Emmerson sold flatirons while Costello sold smoothing irons. Costello's inventory lists two types of carpet material valued at 80 cents and $1.50 a yard, as well as two types of carpet tacks to fasten material to the floor, and a piece of tablecloth fabric. Emmerson sold both carpet and carpet tacks in 1863. Neither of the two storekeepers' inventories nor Emmerson's books include curtains, drapes, or blinds; Costello, however, had ten window-blind curtain pulls, as well as latches for window sashes. One could buy wallpaper at both stores; Costello had eighty-eight rolls in stock, and Emmerson had "one lot" of room paper. Costello sold brass candlesticks and chandeliers (28 cents and 12 cents), and even two "plated" candlesticks for 50 cents apiece. Customers could purchase mirrors for anywhere from 12.5 cents to 50 cents. Emmerson did not carry brass items, but sold furniture, including two "show cases" for $20 and $30, and shelves. The inventory gives lot, not individual, prices for the shelves, and they were expensive, ranging from $45 to $75. Few of those goods appear in Emmerson's 1863 accounts, but since these items were durable or semi-durable, this is not surprising. Customers probably purchased flatirons only once in their lifetimes; nor did they purchase new carpeting every year. Some items sold at Emmerson's are not listed in his inventory probably because their turnover was high. These included candles (purchased by 9 percent of his customers), lamps and accessories (purchased by 7 percent of his clients), and oil (purchased by 23 percent of his customers and accounting for 9 percent of the debit).

cared to itemize. He also had enough stoves to heat at least three rooms, with two of those stoves of better type than the Cyrs'. The double stoves made oven baking possible, hence the baking dishes. And he had enough seats with backs for everyone in his family.

The Dufours sold few household items. What they sold was very basic, and resembled the items found in the Cyr household. Their most commonly sold item was candlewick. The Madore inventory suggests a less Spartan lifestyle. Emmerson's account books and inventory, as well as the Costello's inventory indicate that the stores sold the goods required

5. Patterns

The account books and inventories also indicate that a wide range of not very utilitarian but usually inexpensive items had become popular in the 1860s. They included whalebones, skeletons for bonnets (5 cents a piece), hoops for skirts, neckties or "cravats" instead of the traditional neckerchiefs, paper collars (8, 10, and 18 cents a dozen), paper cuffs, spectacles ($1.50), razors, shaving boxes, hairnets (a few cents each), hair oil, "fancy" or "toilet" soap, playing cards, flypaper, starch and bluestone (used to make a rinse for white fabric), cigars (Emmerson had 380 in stock when he died), umbrellas (30 cents to $1 depending on quality), parasols (75 cents), stove polish and stove blackening, and India rubber shoes ($1 to $1.50 a pair). The stores were starting to look more like dime stores than warehouses. Emmerson and his colleagues were acquainting their customers with new products. Surprisingly, even though Emmerson appears to have owned the largest store in the Valley, he did not carry nearly as many fancy goods as his neighbor Costello. Had the storekeepers begun to specialize, with Emmerson selling higher volumes of cheap goods and Costello selling lower volumes of expensive goods? Or were the fancy fabric and brass items in Costello's inventory the results of bad judgment or leftover goods he could not sell?

New consumption patterns emerged at Madawaska between 1846 and 1863, although these changes did not become significant until the late 1850s. The shift could merely reflect the opening of Emmerson's store. However, Emmerson's appearance cannot account for all the changes that occurred between 1853 and 1863. For instance, he was probably not responsible for tea's gain in popularity during this period or for all the cheap consumer items that were just beginning to show up in 1863. The "consumer revolution" at Madawaska took place between 1855 and 1860. This revolution occurred against the backdrop of a generally prosperous agriculture, during the peak years of the forest industry, and at a time when there was a relatively abundant supply of cash. People could and did earn money,

and they spent it at the store. They also spent their money quite differently from their parents and grandparents by buying different kinds of goods.

Rather than storekeepers shaping consumer preferences, customers shaped storekeepers' decisions. Stores supplied customers with indispensable manufactured objects, such as crockery, cutlery, pots and pans, tools, thread, needles, pins, paint, and glass panes. But even items like oil lamps and chamber pots, which are not, strictly speaking, necessities, became indispensable almost as soon as people tried them. Stores also provided customers with items that supplemented their own production. Households covered most of their food needs through their own work and exchange with neighbors, and they made their own clothes (even if they hired a seamstress to do the work using store-bought fabric). But storekeepers enabled them to buy items, such as carpeting, that made their houses more comfortable, their diets less monotonous, and the bread better tasting (white flour). Storekeepers also improved people's wardrobes with umbrellas, shawls, and shoes, and allowed them to follow fashion trends, such as wearing paper collars, should they be so inclined. Most customers preferred variety over ostentation and chose to buy, for instance, inexpensive rather than expensive fabric. Women preferred calico gowns over silk ones. A similar trend affected household items. The narrow range of inexpensive items broadened after 1846, but even as late as 1867, storekeepers were still not stocking costly crockery and cutlery. And yet, Emmerson's supplier advertised silver-plated items and other luxury goods in the *New Brunswick Almanac*. The new items crowding Emmerson's shelves were, instead, modestly priced.

Conclusion

Two parallel changes in consumer patterns occurred at Madawaska during the mid-nineteenth century. The first change was that barter and long book credits gave way to short book credits and increased use of cash. Modern purchasing practices were beginning to take hold. In times of crisis, however, merchants like John Emmerson were obliged to revert to old practices to help their customers out. Emmerson, however, tried to make credit unnecessary by ensuring there was always money in circulation locally. Merchants had begun to dislike credit and payments in kind.

The second change was the dawning of a consumer society at Madawaska. It translated into people being able to purchase cheap trifles, such as cotton stockings, horn combs, earthenware teapots, and perfumed soap. Those low-cost purchases put people in the habit of going to the store to acquire manufactured goods, which were often produced outside the region. Rural merchants were indeed conduits through which the products of industrial capitalism reached the countryside. The customers, however, were not passive. As noted, they could have preferred expensive display items. Or they could have purchased durable consumer items, such as home furnishings or tools. They did both of these to a point. But they also chose to become consumers, acquiring goods they used up quickly, such as hair oil and shoe polish, and accumulating inexpensive items.

Consumption, like production, made Madawaska a frontier. By the mid-1800s, a Valley resident could eat bread made from Upper Canadian flour (ground, perhaps, from American wheat) with Canadian mess pork or Newfoundland cod, drink East Indian tea sweetened with West Indian sugar in English earthenware, use American-made screws and nails manufactured in New Brunswick, wear shirts or aprons made of American cotton, don shoes mass-produced in New Brunswick or moccasins made by Natives, and wear homespun clothes to plow the fields or milk the cows. The Madawaska consumer, like the Madawaska producer, was blending local and regional goods with continental and transatlantic ones.

ENDNOTES

1. The Dufour brothers' store ledger (Madawaska Public Library) covers the 1845–48 period; the Morneault ledger (Madawaska Historical Society) covers the 1858–63 period; the Emmerson books (originals at the New Brunswick Museum, copies at the Acadian Archives and the PANB on microfilm reels F12229 to F 12333) covers the 1849–87 period (with some gaps); the Connor ledger (Clair Historical Society and PANB microfilm reel F1053) covers the 1875–1923 period; the Savage ledger (Madawaska Historical Society) covers the 1880s.

2. AAQ, lettres des prêtres missionnaires du Madawaska à l'évêque de Québec, February 19, 1846.

3. Oil lights were a recent invention. Abraham Gesner, who invented kerosene, gave the first demonstration of the product in 1846 and began marketing it in 1850. See Gesner's biography at http://www.biographi.ca/EN/. Ads for kerosene lamps can be found in New Brunswick's *Merchants' and Farmers' Almanac,* 1858, CIHM 36663.

4. Bought in bulk, buckwheat meal was worth 0.025 cents a pound and flour 0.037 cents a pound, assuming selling prices of $2.50 (12s 6d) per hundredweight of meal and $7 (35s) per barrel of flour.

5. "Grey" cotton is a corruption of the French word "grège" and refers to unbleached cotton. It is not really grey.

6. Post-mortem inventories were inventories of the goods owned by a person at time of his or her death. The two households inventories used in this chapter can be found at the Houlton Probate Court (Houlton, ME): J-Bte. Cyr, 26 December 1845, Benjamin Madore dit Laplante, 25 November 1860. Costello's and Emmerson's inventories are at the Provincial Archives of New Brunswick, RS73A , Victoria County Probate Court Records, Probate Record Books 1850-1926, microfilm reel F 7308; Estate Files 1850–1910 microfilm reel F 7296.

FURTHER READINGS

Dubay, Guy. *Chez Nous: The St. John Valley.* 1983: 55–70

SOURCES

For those interested in the history of consumption in general, Brewer and Porter (1993) provide a good starting point. For information on general stores, see McCalla (1990 and 1997) and Wainwright (1954). Madawaska stores are further discussed in Craig's *Homespun Capitalists* (Ch. 6 and 9), as well as in Craig (2003 and 2005). An English version of those two texts is available at the Acadian Archives under the title "Agents of modernization or struggling countrymen: rural merchants in Eastern Canada in the XIXth century." There are chapters on

American country stores in Bruegel (2002), C. Clark (1990), and Wermuth (2001). For material culture and the "World of Goods," see J. P. Hardy (2005) and Cook (2001). MacKinnon (2003) shows the direction and volume of traffic on back roads in eastern Québec and New Brunswick. I do not know of any equivalent work for Maine. Wholesalers' advertisements can be found in the *New Brunswick Almanac and Register* (1831–69), the *Merchants' and Farmers' Almanac* (1855–64), and *Barnes' New Brunswick Almanac* (1869–79). These almanacs are all available on CIHM microfiches.

16

HANDING DOWN THE FAMILY FARM, 1845–70

Instead of imitating the enterprise of the Yankee pioneer, by plunging into the forests and clearing new farms, each succeeding generation has divided the land patrimony of their fathers among the children, until nearly every farm has a river front of but a few rods.

—Reverend Dingley, in *The Maine Evangelist* (1858)[1]

The Reverend Dingley had a poor opinion of the Madawaska French, whom he described as "generally ignorant and unambitious." This led him to misinterpret his facts. When confronted with the Valley's long farm lots, so different from New England's square farms lots, he concluded they had to be the result of divisions among heirs who preferred slivers of cleared land over larger holdings carved from the forest. The maps of Frenchville in 1845 and 1877 (see Maps 16-1 and 16-2), show that Dingley was wrong. Valley residents seldom divided farm lots; nor were they averse to plunging into the forest. (And not all forest land was worth clearing, either.)

This leaves us with some interesting questions: If families were large, and farms were not divided among heirs, what happened when parents died? How was property transferred from one generation to the next? In Maine, New Brunswick, and Lower Canada, the law provided for division of the parents' estates among their children. However, as New Brunswick agronomist Charles Lugrin noted, elderly people often disposed of their property before their death to fund their retirement:

> They stick tenaciously to their old manners and customs.... One of these customs that bids fair to last for a few generations yet, is that of the father and mother, when they become old, giving their lands to their children, or to a stranger, in consideration that they support them during the remainder of their lives. This mode of becoming their own executors is very popular with the French farmers, and in their deeds they stipulate to a nicety how much sugar, tea and coffee, how many coats, shirts, and hats, they are to receive every year, not forgetting the tobacco and a few gallons of whiskey.[2]

This ensured that most farms were passed intact from one generation to the next.

I.   THE LAW

A. English Law

Variants of the English common law were in force in New Brunswick and New England during this period.[3] Under the common law, the husband was the owner of all real and personal property acquired by either spouse during their married years (real property was land and buildings, and personal property everything else). This ownership extended to all the personal property his wife owned on their wedding day. Women retained ownership only of the real estate they brought into marriage. If the wife died first, nothing happened, unless she had owned real estate, which then passed to her heirs. If the husband died first, all his property (and that included the personal estate his wife had brought into marriage) passed to his heirs, subject to the widow's dower rights: one-third ownership of her husband's personal estate plus the income from one-third of his real estate. A husband could modify these provisions through his will and leave more or less to his wife than the law required. The common law did not recognize prenuptial agreements, arguing that marriage made the husband and wife one, and that one cannot contract with oneself.[4] In the United States, children inherited equally regardless of birth order or sex since the American Revolution, unless their father stipulated otherwise in his will.

B. French Law

The common law probably seemed very peculiar, if not downright unfair, to the French. Canada and Acadia had used the Custom of Paris, which remained in force in Lower Canada until 1866 when it was replaced by a civil code. Under the Custom of Paris, communally owned property and equal inheritance were the rule. Everything the spouses owned at marriage, except real estate (referred to as the "*propres*" or patrimonial property), as well as everything acquired after marriage (except real estate inherited from parents), became common property (*La communauté*). When one of the spouses died, the survivor gained sole ownership of half the *communauté*, and the other half was divided among the heirs. In addition, widows were entitled to a dower, consisting of the income from half of their husband's real estate. Couples could opt out of the *communauté* or modify it through a prenuptial agreement (*contrat de mariage*). The British introduced testamentary freedom (the absolute right to dispose of one's property in a will irrespective of the law) to Lower Canada, but French Canadian parents very rarely took advantage of this new possibility to benefit one or more children at the expense of others.

Widows were treated very differently under English and French laws, French law treated spouses as equal economic partners entitled to an equal share of the property accumulated through their labor. (During marriage however, the husband could manage the *communauté* as he saw fit.) The common law (which referred to widows as "relicts") treated wives as noncontributing dependents, merely entitled to support after the death of their husband.

II.   AND THE PRACTICE—CONDITIONAL DEEDS

The differences between English and French family and property laws did not pose great problems for the French at Madawaska. They could write wills to distribute their estates as they saw fit, but few took advantage of this possibility. Maine passed a Married Woman's Property Act in 1844, and New Brunswick followed suit in 1855. Valley residents used these acts creatively, as we shall see below. More commonly, people disposed of their property before they died, a practice that had fallen into disuse throughout Anglo-America during the nineteenth century, with the exception of Upper Canada. It was this discrepancy that caught the attention of observers like Lugrin. Contrary to Dingley, Lugrin was very well informed (see Appendix J). The Custom of Paris made those arrangements, referred to as *donations entre vifs*,[5] straightforward and enforceable in court. One party gave another property in exchange for support or an annuity. If the second party did not fulfill his end of the contract, the first one could repossess the property. *Donations entre vifs* were usually recorded in great details. Those persnickety contracts could indicate mutual distrust. More likely, however, they provided a neutral third party, the *notaire* (a public lawyer who witnessed private contracts and ensured that they were written in the

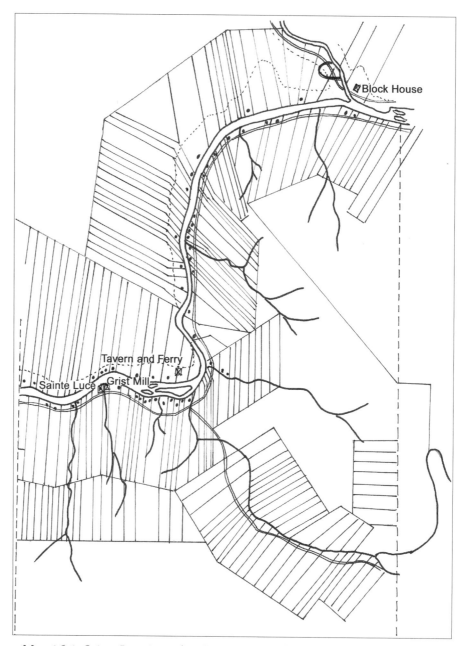

Map 16-1: Sainte Luce in 1845; Composite map based on the American surveyor's maps at the Maine State Archives and at the Acadian Archives, and British ones at the British National Archives (Kew). MPG 1/743/10-21; map by B. and S. Craig.

proper form) with an opportunity to prevent future misunderstandings. They also operated as a rite of passage into a new stage of life for both father and son, and were a pretext for a party. In his 1846 book *La Terre Paternelle, notaire*-novelist Patrice Lacombe

describes the drawn-out process of drafting a *donation*—a process he likely presided over many times in his legal capacity. Parents, the chosen son, other family members, neighbors, and friends all attended the proceedings. The father made sure no small detail

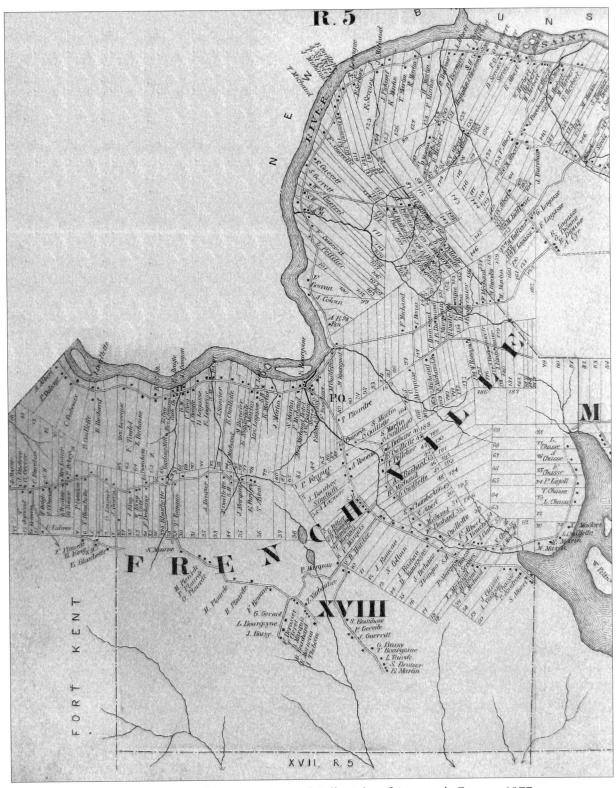

Map 16-2: Frenchville in 1877; Roe and Colby, Atlas of Aroostook County, *1877.*

was overlooked, while the son complained that his father's demands were growing burdensome. Here is our translation of Lacombe's portrayal of such a gathering:

Notaire (repeating the father's words): A fat pig, weighing at least 200 pounds. One...

Son (interjecting): But, Father, look, the payments are already so high. Let us say a lean pig. It will not cost you much to fatten it.

Father: No, no. We agreed on a fat pig. Let us stick with that.

(A long discussion ensues in which all those present take part. Finally, the notaire intervenes.)

Notaire: See, I am going to reconcile your differences. You, Chauvin Senior, are asking for a fat pig, while you, Chauvin Junior, find this demand excessive. Let us compromise on a fairly fat pig.

Audience: That's it! that's it!

Lacombe continues his depiction of this lengthy but convivial process and mentions that they almost always ended in festivities.

We will spare our readers the rest of the payments, clauses, and conditions of this contract, which were again debated at length and which stretched the procedure well into the afternoon. The discussions that took place before the *notaire* had been so frequent and lengthy that the sun was ready to set when Chauvin and his friends went back home. The elder Chauvin invited all attendants to spend the rest of the day and evening at his place. He also invited other neighbors and friends, as was the custom in such circumstances. All congratulated father and son on the transaction that had just taken place, and the day ended happily with a groaning table, where the culinary talents of Mrs. Chauvin and her daughter were prominently displayed.[6]

One should not be fooled by the mercenary appearances of these contracts. Community standards strongly shaped the clauses, and much of the proceedings had become ritualized.

The common law made no provision for condi-tional gifts; once individuals gave away property, they gave it away for good. Valley residents quickly found a way around this: they registered three contracts. One provided for the sale of a property by party A to party B, usually for $1; the second was an indenture in which party B agreed to support party A; and the third was a performance bond in which B pledged the property he had just bought for a dollar. Those transfers became known as "deeds of maintenance" or "conditional deeds."

Conditional deeds did not always go to sons, and rarely to the eldest. Rather, one's son-in-law could receive it, or it could even be given to strangers. Conditional deeds also provided for the support of children still living at home, including their marriage portion (boys usually received a horse and tools, while girls received a cow, a bed with bedding, spinning wheel, linen, and crockery). Until the 1860s, people supported parents and children with payments in kind. After 1860, support increasingly took the form of cash annuities or store credit, reflecting the commercialization and monetization of the economy. Marriage portions for unwed children similarly switched from material to cash payments.

Conditional deeds also increasingly fueled tensions. Children treated the land received from their parents as an asset that they could use as they saw fit. For instance, Benoni Parent acquired a large lot (315 acres) through a deed of maintenance in 1844. He sold it piecemeal; in 1851 and 1853, he sold sixty-three acres to William Corbin for $80; then he sold sixty-seven acres to his son Fabien for $60; two days later, Fabien sold it to Corbin for $100. His parents could not have been very pleased. More and more maintenance deeds were cancelled, replaced by another one with a second and sometimes even third recipient. In other cases, the grantee would sell the land (and the responsibility of the elderly) to a third party; the buyer then had to assume the support payments. Not surprisingly, clauses forbidding selling or mortgaging the land without the grantor's permission became more and more common. From the 1860s onward, conditional deeds were often converted into outright sales. A new option seems to have become available by the end of the nineteenth century: deeds to the Church. In 1862, fifty-year-old Urbain Martin and his wife gave a conditional deed for half a lot to their only daughter (who was married to Herménégilde Sirois). Twelve years later, in 1874, after the death of their daughter and son-in-law, the Martins conditionally deeded this lot to the St. Basile Convent, across the river in New Brunswick. In return, the convent was to provide the Martins with room, board, clothing, the use of a horse and cart once or twice a week, a first-class funeral, and twenty-five Low Masses for the repose of their souls. The deed also made provisions for their grandchildren Georges, twelve, and Marie-Ange, eleven. Georges was to be educated at the seminary or at the Jesuit College in Montreal, and Marie-Ange at the convent—"in all branches taught in their institution." (Georges eventually became a physician; see Sidebar 24-1.)

Conditional deeds suited parents just fine; they guaranteed them financial support until their death and spiritual support in this life and beyond (One hundred masses were not unheard of). They suited children less and less, not so much because of the deeds' cost but because they restricted their use of the property. Children could not mortgage it to raise capital, nor could they sell it to purchase a better one or to emigrate without their parents' permission.

Conditional deeds, in short, stood in the way of the commoditization of land. In the long run, though, parents lost their security and children won their commodity. Some elderly people ended up going through several support providers, who likely viewed the arrangement as an open-ended lease rather than a commitment until death.

Conditional deeds were common but not universal. Some people died before they retired. If there was no will, the property was distributed according to the law. Subdivision of the land remained, nonetheless, rare. Either one of the heirs bought the others' shares or the children sold the property to another party and split the proceeds. Widows with underage children usually stayed on the land, and the estate was not settled until the youngest came of age—at which point the widow could buy back her children's shares or exchange the property for support in old age. The process was complicated by the fact that, under common law, the farm did not belong to the widow but to her children. Children, however, seem to have thought the farm rightfully belonged to their mother, regardless of what the law said. One way around the problem was for children to sell their mother the land for a nominal price. For instance, in 1860, fifty-eight-year-old Louise Albert paid her children just $200 for the nine farm lots left by her husband. She subsequently sold the various parcels to her sons at market price.

III.   ESTABLISHING CHILDREN

In the nineteenth century, parents believed they had a moral obligation to "establish" their children—that is, to ensure they were economically independent. Conditional deeds provided for the establishment of one child on a farm. What happened to the others? Whether French, English, or immigrants of other nationalities, North American parents relied on a limited number of strategies to help their children. In recently settled areas, parents often acquired additional tracts of forest land, at little to no cost, for their sons. They then helped their sons clear the land

by lending them animals, tools, and helpers (typically younger sons); they also provided them with some provisions until the first crop. As noted by land agents Deane and Kavanagh, some early Madawaska settlers probably used this practice:

> When any of them have marked the front of a lot by spotting a few trees and cutting down some bushes, the claim, thus acquired, has been generally considered valid.... From our enquiries the violations of this custom are very rare.... Some have availed themselves of such rights for

the benefits of their children, while others have done it for the purpose of speculation.[7]

Firmin Thibodeau, for instance, had accumulated a lot of real estate by 1831 and was in the process of distributing it among his sons and daughters. He transferred his very large homestead at Green River to his younger son Vital, who had married a daughter of Firmin's second wife, in exchange for support during his old age. Not every father was this generous: Simon Hébert, another large landholder, sold his children his property at market value.

In older settlements, parents sometimes sold their farm for a high price and used the proceeds to move to a pioneer region. There, they could acquire enough uncultivated land for all their sons at a low price. This scenario was uncommon at Madawaska because, before 1870, people who married in the Valley did not migrate out. Another strategy, common in Connecticut and Upper Canada, consisted of leaving the farm to a son in exchange for parental support and compensatory payments for the other children. The other children could then use this capital to establish themselves. (This was known as the "single-heir-plus-burden" system.) There is no evidence that this strategy was employed at Madawaska,

where children only received support until they came of age. These children also usually had to work for their brother to receive their portion when they left home. Finally, one could set up one or several sons in a business or have them trained in a craft or the ministry. One could also train the daughters as school teachers. This appears to have been the strategy adopted by Celestin Pelletier, a blacksmith at St. Basile. Six of his children reached adulthood. His eldest son became a priest and was appointed pastor of Saint-François's Church in 1876. In 1861, Pelletier and his wife retired and went to live with him. A second son became a prosperous farmer but was not educated beyond the local primary school; a third son became "a less prosperous farmer with three years' education at Sainte-Anne de la Pocatière"; a fourth son became a merchant; and the fifth and youngest son was a student at Sainte-Anne who hoped to become a doctor in 1861 (see Sidebar 24-1). The only girl in the brood married a well-to-do farmer.[8] Pelletier, in other words, provided his children with education, land, and start-up capital. Consequently, they became farmers, tradespersons, and professionals.

IV. LATERAL TRANSMISSIONS: DEEDS TO WIVES

A few families resorted to transferring property not from parents to children but from husband to wife. Wills were uncommon in this region (there were only twenty-three written between 1845 and 1870).[9] Forty percent of men left some real property to their wives (and of that 40 percent, a quarter left *all* property to their wives); one out of five husbands left his wife a usufruct on all their land. ("Usufruct" literally means use of the fruit, in this case the right to the income from the property.) Personal estate was distributed exactly like real property—wives who got a share of the real estate got exactly the same share of the deceased's personal estate. The few men who left a will tended to benefit their wives over their children. In half the cases, the widow received uncondi-

tional ownership to a least half the family property. The will of Jean-Baptiste Daigle III is a good example. He left his wife, Emilienne Morin, two-thirds of the family farm, including the house, barn, furnishings, stock, and equipment; he divided the remainder of the property, namely one-third of the family farm and a larger lot requiring clearing, among the sons. The daughters were to receive $25 each when they came of age. The property and chattel left to Morin very likely amounted to more than half the value of the estate. In addition, she was given the usufruct of the entire estate to raise her nine children, who were between the ages of two and sixteen at the time.

Some men took advantage of the Married

The Land in Between

The two following wills are representative of the existing corpus.

GEORGE LONG'S WILL

I, George Long, of the parish of St. Francis, County of Victoria and Province of New Brunswick, farmer, knowing the uncertainty of life and being desirous of controlling the distribution of my property, do make publish and declare the following my last will and testament.

First, I give and bequeath to my beloved wife Adelaide Long a lot of land being and lying in the parish, county and province aforesaid, bounded south by the River St. John, upper side by land owned to Romain Long, lower side by land owned to Paul Long, containing two hundred acres more or less.

Secondly, a second lot, situated in the same parish, county and province bounded south side by the river St. John and up and down by land owned by Romain Long, measuring four acres in front. Both lots granted to me said George Long, with all houses, barns, edifices, buildings, farm improvements, profits, privileges, and appurtenances theron.

Thirdly, all my household goods, horses, cattle, sheep, cows, pigs, agricultural tools, in a word, all my personal estate to have and to hold all the above described premises to her, the said Adelaide Long, her heirs and assigned forever, she collecting and paying all my debts, funeral charges and expenses.

Lastly, I constitute and appoint my said wife Adelaide Long sole executor of this my last will and testament, the testimony whereof I have hereto set my hand and seal this twenty-fourth day of September in the year of our lord one thousand eight hundred and sixty four.

his
George X Long
mark

THEODORE VIOLETTE'S WILL

In the name of God, Amen, I, Theodore Violette junior, of the parish of Saint Leonard in the County of Victoria and province of New Brunswick, yeoman, and being very sick and weak in body and perfect in mind and memory, thanks be given unto God, calling into mind the mortality of my body and knowing that it is appointed for all men to die, do make and order this my last will and testament, that is to say, principally and first of all I give and recommend my soul unto the hand of the almighty God that gives it and my body I recommend to the earth to be buried in decent Christian burial at the discretion of my executor nothing doubting that at the general resurrection I shall regain the same again by the mighty power of God, and as touching such worldly estates wherewith it hath pleased God to bless me in this life, I give, devise and dispose of those same in the following manner and form.

First, I give and bequeath to Louisa, my dearly beloved wife whom I likewise constitute, make and ordain the sole executrix of this my last will and testament all and singular my lands, messuages and tenements by her freely to be possessed and enjoyed on the following condition, that is the said Louise shall have all our minor children taken care of until they become of age and remain under her control and protection attending to their employment faithfully and diligently during the said minority and also that the said Louisa shall transfer the said property without reserve to one of our children of her own selection for her support and maintenance during her natural life—I likewise bequeath to the said Louisa all my personal property of every description.

And I do hereby disallow, revoke and disowned all and every other former testament, will, legacies, bequests and executors by me in any ways before named, willed and bequeathed ratifying and conforming this and no other to be my last will and testament. In witness whereof, I shall hereunto set my hand and seal this eighth day of June in the year of our Lord one thousand eight hundred and sixty-three.

> *his*
> *Theodore X Violette*
> *mark*

Source: PANB, Victoria County Surrogate Court, 1863 and 1864.

Women's Property Act, which allowed married women to own property in their own name. Twenty-four men put all or part of their property in their wives' names. The process was tortuous, because the act specifically excluded property that a husband gave to his wife. To get around this, the husband had to sell his property to a third party for a nominal fee, such as a dollar; the third party would then sell the property back to the man's wife for a dollar.

The reasons behind these transactions varied greatly. Men who remarried younger wives would often take advantage of this act to ensure that she would have a way to support herself and her children when she inevitably became a widow. Children from the first marriage could not take the property away from her. Some men gave all their property to their wives, provided that the wives pay off their debts and support them. One gave half of his land to his wife to get rid of her (the deed was *very* explicit). Putting property in one's wife's name was also a good way of putting it out of the reach of creditors. Some individuals combined strategies. Like many in the forest industry, Benoni Pelletier, (born in 1803), experienced economic difficulties during the late 1840s; in 1848, he sold some of his land to his son Cyrille for $1,200 but bought it back from him in 1853. He then transferred some of that property to his wife

through a third party. In 1857, he retired and exchanged some of his wife's land with his son Jean Baptiste, who was in his mid-twenties, for a $160 annuity. His son later bought the land outright for $500. Pelletier sold the rest of his property to his wife for $20. He left a will confirming this division.

The Married Women's Property Act was, thus, a way of dealing with uncommon situations or a means of providing insurance. The common thread seems to have been to protect the economic position of the household, as well as improve a widow's economic position beyond the provisions of the law. Although not common, wills and transfers under the Married Women's Property Act uniformly improved a woman's economic position, often at the expense of both the heirs and the husband, who could otherwise wield control over his wife and property. When this population deliberately deviated from the ordinary prescriptions of the law, it did not curtail women's access to property but enlarged it.

Conclusion

Property transmission practices at Madawaska remind us of the need to look beyond the law to know what really happened. The Custom of Paris and the common law provided for an equal division of estates among the children, leading people to conclude that this led to the fragmentation of farm holdings. But fragmentation produced unviable economic units, and Madawaskayans made sure that such divisions happened as rarely as possible.

These transmission practices also remind us that the process of transferring property from one generation to the next was not a punctual event coinciding with a parent's death. They were instead processes that usually began a long time before the parents' death and took years to complete.

At Madawaska, as elsewhere in North America, this process was carefully planned. Families had to balance competing interests— the parents' need for a retirement income and the children's desire for independence. It also had to respect cultural notions of fairness (in this case, treating all children equally). Heads of households took special care to preserve the farm's ability to support a family. The process did not always work as planned, and conflicts sometimes arose. But, on the whole, Madawaskayans succeeded in their goals.

ENDNOTES

1. The Reverend Dingley in *The Maine Evangelist* (1858), quoted in Elwell's *Aroostook....*
2. PANB, Journal of the House of Assembly of New Brunswick, 1872, Appendix: "Description of Victoria County," by Charles Lugrin: XI.
3. "English" and not British because the common law originated in England, and never applied to Scotland, which kept its own body of laws after the union.
4. English prenuptial agreements, called "settlement," were only valid in a parallel body of law called Equity. Equity law did not exist in New England and existed only in theory in the Maritimes.
5. In French law, these contracts are also called *viagers or rentes viagères.*
6. Lacombe, *La terre paternelle,* 67–73 (translation by the authors).
7. Deane and Kavanagh, "Report," 454.
8. Andrew, *Development of Elites...,*107.
9. Wills can be found in the probate records, in the registries of the deeds, or both.

FURTHER READINGS

Craig, Béatrice. "Land Transmission Practices Among Northern Maine French Canadians in the Nineteenth Century." In *New England–New France, 1600–1850,* ed. P. Benes. 1992: 69–81.

SOURCES

Craig discusses property transmission practices at Madawaska in greater details in three publications (1991, 1992, and 2005). The topic of inheritance and property transmission was popular among historians in the 1980s, and there is abundant literature on the topic. For colonial New England, start with Waters (1976 and 1982) and Keyssar (1974); for Maine, see Taylor (1990). Ditz (1986), C. Clark (1990), and Bruegel (2002) take the story into the nineteenth century.

For French Canada, Bouchard (1985 and 1996) is a must-read. Maisonneuve (1985), Santerre (1990), Depatie (1990), and Gervais (1996) are also helpful. For the Maritimes see McNabb (1986), Wagg (1990), and Moody (1991),

Those interested in the place of women and property rights will be interested in Waciega (1987) and Wilson (1992).

Part Four

CAPITALISM'S BORDERED LANDS, FRENCH CATHOLIC BORDERLAND

The period extending from 1875 to World War I (1914 in Canada, 1917 in the United States) was a time of accelerated change. New means of transportation (railroads) and communication (telephone), new industries (potato and dairy farming, and paper pulp production), new activities (tourism), improved and expanded educational systems, the founding of French language newspapers, and new ideas (the "Acadian Renaissance") all combined to significantly and permanently alter life along the upper St. John.

Railroads triggered and accelerated many of these economic changes. At first, the railroads bound the entire former disputed territory even more firmly to the port of Saint John, but this changed at the turn of the twentieth century with the arrival of an all-American line in Aroostook County: the Bangor and Aroostook Railroad (B&A). The B&A line and growing American protectionism combined to divide the Valley into loosely connected economic entities—that is, into bordered lands.

Economic changes went beyond changing the nature of production and direction of trade. Control over economic resources inexorably slipped out of local people's hands, whatever their ethnicity. Until the early 1870s, there had been two transborder economies at Madawaska: a local/regional one and an international one. The local economy still had autonomy, and local people had been able, up to a point, to uncouple from the international economy when participation was disadvantageous. By 1900, this dissociation was no longer possible. For the first time, men with capital were able to directly or indirectly shape the entire regional economy. Local economies

became mere subdivisions of larger ones, and not everyone benefited from the changes.

But other changes were also afoot. Acadians, French Canadians, and Franco-Americans were acquiring better instruments to preserve their language and culture, and Valley residents were no exception. At the same time, renewed cultural awareness among the Maritime Acadians coalesced into an "Acadian Renaissance" that obliged Valley residents to question and define their own identity as a "people in between." Were they Acadians, French Canadians, British subjects, or American citizens?

In this section, we will discuss these various forces of change and their impact on the Valley. We will begin by talking about changes in transportation and communications and their economic and social impacts. Then we will discuss institutional transformations. We will finish with ideological and political changes, many of which stemmed from the above transformations.

Timeline Part Four, 1870–1918

	Maine	New Brunswick
1868	**Opening of the Frenchville High School**	
1871	Beginning of starch making in Aroostook County	
1871		Common School Act
1873	State of Maine starts subsidizing high schools	
1873		**Madawaska (N.B.) becomes a county**
1873		St. Basile Academy, opened 1858, closes its doors
1873		Sisters from Montreal's Hotel-Dieu take over the St. Basile convent
1873		First hospital in the Valley at St. Basile
1875		**New Brunswick Railway reaches Grand Falls**
1877		Elected municipal government established in New Brunswick
1878		New Brunswick Railway reaches Edmundston
1878	Opening of the Madawaska Training School	
1881		First Convention Nationale Acadienne at Memramcook
1882		Andrew Blair (Liberal) becomes premier
1886		Single and widowed propertied women get the right to vote in municipal elections
1887	First compulsory schooling law	
1887		Founding of *L'Evangeline*
1889	Chartering of the Van Buren College (St. Mary's)	
1889		Universal white male suffrage in provincial elections
1891	First cheese factory in Madawaska (Maine)	
1892	**XXIX Amendment to the state constitution—educational qualification of voters.**	
1893	Town school boards become the rule in Maine	
1894		Opening of the Superior school in Edmundston
1895	Incorporation of the Fort Kent Telephone Company	
1895	First bill to prevent the use of French on school grounds	
1896		Incorporation of the Madawaska Telephone Company
1896		Control of liquor licences reserved to a provincial board
1899		**Completion of the Temiscouata Railway**
1899	**Bangor and Aroostook Railroad reaches Van Buren**	
1899		First butter factory in Madawaska (N.B.)
1902	Bangor and Aroostook Railroad reaches Fort Kent	
1902	Founding of the Société Mutuelle de l'Assomption	
1902–06	Publication of the *Journal du Madawaska* in Van Buren	
1904	Completion of the Pont à José	
1904–09	The "Van Buren" War	
1904	Daughters of Wisdom (a French order) open their convent in St. Agatha.	
1907	Completion of the Maine and New Brunswick Electric Power Company	
1909	St. John River commission begins its work	
1910		Québec prohibits the export of logs cut on Crown land
1911	The Pike Act lapses	
1911		New Brunswick prohibits the export of logs cut on Crownland
1911		**Donald Fraser purchases the Murchie Mill in Edmundston**
1912		Mgr. Leblanc becomes the first Acadian bishop
1913		Founding of *Le Madawaska* in Edmundston
1914		Beginning of World War One—Canada enters the war
1914		Premier Flemming forced to resign by Dugal from Edmundston
1915	International Railway Bridge built between Van Buren and St. Leonard	
1915	St. John River commission publishes its results	
1916		Prohibition in New Brunswick
1917	The United States enters World War One.	
1917		Military Service Act in Canada
1918		Completion of the Fraser paper mill
1918	End of World War One	

17

THE ARRIVAL OF THE RAILROADS

New means of transportation and communication emerged in the Valley between 1875 and 1914. A Canadian railway line reached Grand Falls in 1875 and Edmundston in 1878, then connected to the Grand Trunk at Rivière-du-Loup in 1889. An American line reached Van Buren in 1899 and Fort Kent in 1902. The railroads at first tied Aroostook residents even more firmly to New Brunswick. However, the opening of the Bangor and Aroostook (B&A), severed the link between northern Aroostook and New Brunswick, reorienting most of its trade southward. Canadian and American lines, nonetheless, had no desire to turn their backs on each other and instead chose to facilitate cross-border traffic.

Despite calls for a railroad line as early as the 1830s, the first one to reach the Valley did not arrive until the 1870s. New Brunswick projects all fell under the larger plan of connecting New Brunswick to Lower Canada and promoting interprovincial traffic. Similarly, Maine projects intended to link the northern part of the state to the more populous south, facilitate the shipment of wood products, and open northern Maine to settlement (see Table 17-1). By the 1850s, many believed that neither Madawaska, Victoria, or Aroostook Counties could achieve their full potential unless they could reach their markets by rail. But as their population was too small to generate enough traffic to make the lines profitable, these schemes usually failed to attract potential investors, and the public ended up subsidizing most railroad lines. This was even true in Maine despite an 1847 constitutional amendment forbidding the use of state money for internal improvement projects.

I. EARLY PROJECTS

A. The St. Andrew and Québec Railway

The very first plan for a line reaching what became Aroostook County predates the 1842 Treaty. In 1829, a group of New Brunswickers proposed a plan for a line connecting St. Andrew to Quebec City, and in 1836, obtained a provincial charter for the St. Andrew and Québec Railway (see Sidebar 17-1). The proposed route, however, passed through the southern part of the disputed territory (see Map 17-1). Maine officials protested the survey, and Britain put the project on hold. Some people in British North America even asserted the Americans were claiming the territory as their own solely to prevent the building of this line, which could have turned St. Andrew into a rival of Boston for access to the continent's interior. When the southern part of the territory was awarded to the United States, the project was shelved, only to re-emerge in the late 1840s. In 1856, a line was built between St. Andrew

Table 17-1: Railroads in Nnorthern Maine and Western New Brunswick

Name	Subsequent Names	Year Chartered	Charter Sponsor	Promoters	Planned Route	Year(s) Built
St. Andrew and Quebec	New Brunswick and Canada (after 1856)	1836	New Brunswick	Canadian and New Brunswick businessmen	St. Andrews (N. B.), St. John Valley, Mars Hill, Allagash area, Quebec City	Not feasible due to boundary dispute
Halifax and Quebec		1840		Canadian and Maritime businessmen	Halifax, Shediac, Saint John, St. John River, Rivière-du-Loup	Not built
European and North American	Maine section: Maine Central (after 1882) Canadian section: New Brunswick Railroad (after 1883); Canadian Pacific (after 1890)	1850	Maine	John A. Poor	Halifax, Saint John, Bangor, Portland	Built Bangor to Saint John 1871; went bankrupt in 1875
European and North American		1850			Mattawamkeag to Houlton line	Not built
Grand Trunk Railway	Acquired by the Intercolonial Railway in 1879	1853	Dominion of Canada	Canadian businessmen	Detroit to Rivière-du-Loup	1860
New Brunswick and Canada	Canadian Pacific (after 1890)	1856			St. Andrew, Woodstock, St. John River, Rivière-du-Loup, Quebec City	1864 built line to Woodstock; bankrupt 1867.
Northern Maine Railroad		1859	Maine	To be built by public subscription		Not built
Northern Aroostook		1864	Maine		Patten, Ashland, St. John River	Not built; charter lapsed 1868
Houlton Branch Railway Company		1867		Local businessmen	Houlton to Debec junction onthe NB&C	1871
Intercolonial Railway			Dominion of Canada, with British public funding		Halifax, Shediac, Matapedia, Rivière du Loup	1876

Name	Subsequent Names	Year Chartered	Charter Sponsor	Promoters	Planned Route	Year(s) Built
Aroostook River Railroad				Central Aroostook businessmen	Caribou to Fort Fairfield and Aroostook junction on NB Railway; extended to Presque Isle 1881	1876
New Brunswick Land and Railway Company	New Brunswick Railway after 1881 Canadian Pacific after 1890	1870	Province of New Brunswick	Alexander Gibson	Fredericton to Edmundston	1878
Northern Aroostook		1871		W. Dickey, and W. C.Hammond	Bancroft to Fort Kent and Madawaska,	Not built
Temiscouata Railway		1885			Edmundston, Rivière-du Loup; extended to Connors, N.B., in 1891	1889
Restigouche and Victoria Colonization Railway	International Railway in 1906	1885			St. Leonard to Campbellton	1910
Bangor and Aroostook		1891	State of Maine	A. Burleigh and F. Cram; county funding	Old Town to Houlton, Caribou and Fort Fairfield (1895), Van Buren (1899)	1894
Fish River Railroad	Acquired by B&A in 1903	1902			Ashland to Fort Kent	1903
St. John River extension of the B&A		1909			Van Buren to Fort Kent and St. Francis	1909
National Transcontinental		1903		Dominion of Canada	Moncton to Winnipeg (Edmundston to St. Leonard and Moncton)	1912
Van Buren to St. Leonard International Railroad Bridge	Subsidiary of B&A	1913			Van Buren to St. Leonard	1915

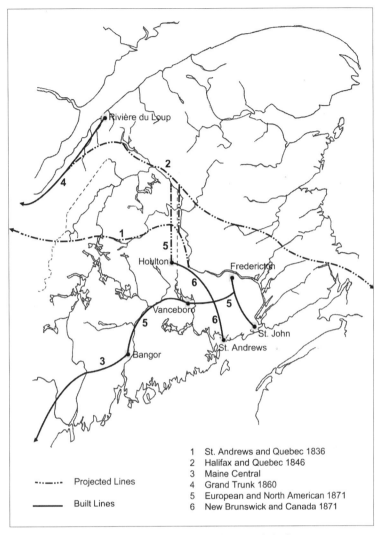

Map 17-1: Railways Projected or Built before 1870
Map by B. and S. Craig

Legend on map:

- - - - - Projected Lines

──────── Built Lines

1 St. Andrews and Quebec 1836
2 Halifax and Quebec 1846
3 Maine Central
4 Grand Trunk 1860
5 European and North American 1871
6 New Brunswick and Canada 1871

and Woodstock and renamed the New Brunswick and Canada. The company went bankrupt in 1867. Mainers, for their part, were toying with the idea of a line between Bangor and the upper St. John River. The only thing that came out of that plan was the Bangor and Old Town Railway Company. (Built in 1836, this line was the second railroad line built in the United States.) Another aborted project in the 1840s was the Halifax and Québec Railway, which would have connected Halifax, Shediac, Saint John, Rivière-du-Loup, and Quebec City. The plan fell through during the survey stage.

B. The European and North American Railroad (E&NA), and Morthern Maine Lines

The European and North American Railroad was the brainchild of Bangor lawyer John A. Poor. Poor had been instrumental in convincing Canadian promoters to choose Portland, rather than Boston, as the terminus of the Atlantic and St. Lawrence Railway, which connected Montreal to the Atlantic.[1] Before the Atlantic and St. Lawrence was completed in 1853, Poor had turned his attention to another scheme connecting Portland to Saint John and

Sidebar 17-1: St. Andrews and Québec Railroad

This prospectus, issued by the railroad's promoters, was meant to inform the public about the prospective line and, hopefully, attract additional investors. It reproduced several supporting documents, such as:

A. *Resolve of the House of Assembly of Lower Canada, December 18, 1835:*

Resolved: that a railroad operating between the port of St. Andrews in the Bay of Fundy, which is open at all seasons of the year, and the Port of Quebec,[1] would greatly diminish the disadvantages under which the province labours from the severity of its climate and the consequent periodic interruptions of the navigation of the river St. Lawrence.

Resolved: that the opening of such communication between the port before mentioned, would promote the settlement of the country, greatly facilitate the intercourse between this province and the United Kingdom—extend the interchange of commodities between the British possessions in America—increase the demand for British manufactures, and be the means of affording additional employment to British shipping.

B. Excerpt from *Resolve of the Legislative Council of Lower Canada, December 1835:*

The resources of 200 miles of rich forest country would at once be opened and rendered productive; and the timber and different kinds of lumber procured on the tract of the road would afford immediate employment and yields of itself a large income, besides giving rise to towns, villages and settlement along the whole line.

C. Expected Income and Expenses

From Québec:

Flour and provisions, wheat, barley, oats, breads, staves, ashes, passengers (80 shillings each)	£51,100

From the intermediate country:

100,000 tons deals, timber, boards, and planks at 7s6d/ton.	£37,500
Shingles, staves, saw logs, scantling, and other dimension lumber.	£7,500
Provisions, goods, passages, etc., for settlers and operatives.	£6,500
Imports into Québec:	£48,400
Estimated income	£151,000
	Or £134,667 sterling

In addition, the line would earn revenues carrying the mail.

Source: *Prospectus of the St. Andrews and Québec Railroad.* St. Andrews: Standard Office, 1836.

1. St. Andrew was the nearest open winter port to Quebec City on the British Atlantic shore. It was 200 miles away.

Halifax: the European and North American Railroad. Poor's initial plan included a branch line from Mattawamkeag to Houlton. The company was chartered in 1850. As usual, raising sufficient capital proved extremely difficult. By 1852, disagreement over both the best way to finance this line and the route it should follow paralyzed the project.

When it became obvious the E&NA was not going to build a line in Aroostook anytime soon, some Aroostook County promoters obtained a charter for the Northern Maine Railroad in 1859, with capital to be raised through public subscription. The American Civil War and the Panic of 1873 put the project on hold. During the war, promoters easily convinced Maine legislators that a railroad line was needed to defend the frontier with British North America. Consequently, in 1864, the Northern Aroostook Railroad was incorporated and granted large acreages of land in Aroostook County—under the condition that it build the line within four years. One proposed route, through Patten, Ashland, and Fort Kent, would have been useful for both transporting troops and shipping lumber. The project failed because of rivalry between lumber interests in Bangor and southern Aroostook (the latter led by Shepard Cary). When the Northern Aroostook charter lapsed, Poor convinced the state that the E&NA could build this line. In 1868, the state transferred the Northern Aroostook Railroad grant to the E&NA, adding 700,000 acres of land, mostly in Aroostook County, for good measure. In 1871, the main line of the E&NA was completed and connected Bangor to Saint John through Vanceboro.

The New Brunswick government, however, had had to take over the construction of the Canadian section of the line, as capital was as difficult to raise on that side of the border as on the American side.

When Maine issued the land grant to the E&NA, everybody assumed that the company had tacitly agreed to build a branch line to Aroostook County, because the grant's alleged purpose was to facilitate the defense of the northeast frontier. The route was surveyed, but the line was never built: the E&NA failed following the Panic of 1873. Subsequently, many concluded that the grant had been a theft of the public land. Those huge land grants soon became the source of a long conflict between railroad trustees and northern Aroostook settlers, a conflict that was not resolved until Maine purchased some of the land back from the owners (see Sidebar 17-2).

Some local people, however, had been skeptical of the E&NA promises from the start. In 1868, Fort Kent representative William Dickey petitioned the state legislature to charter a railroad line from Houlton to Madawaska; he had the support of Van Buren businessman William.C Hammond and others. As a result, a second Northern Aroostook Railroad—running from Bancroft (on the E&NA) to Van Buren through Houlton and to Fort Kent through Portage Lake—was incorporated in 1871. By that time, Dickey had lost his seat in the Maine legislature, and nothing came out of this project. Instead, the Houlton people built a short line linking their town to the New Brunswick and Canadian in 1871.

Sidebar 17-2: With Justice for All

This is the title of a play local historian Guy Dubay wrote as part of America's bicentennial Independence Day celebrations. It tells the story of a conflict that, for more than a generation, pitched Madawaska settlers against "great proprietors."

The root of the conflict lay in the grants of land Maine made to the European and North American Railroad (E&NA) in 1868. The first draft of the grant excluded lands reserved for settlement and for public use, but the actual deed made no such distinction. This inevitably created problems because people were already improving land set aside for settlement under the terms of an 1859 statute; some already qualified for a title.

By 1875, the E&NA was under receivership. Some bond holders (people who have loaned money to a corporation for a specified number of years) were getting concerned, especially since the E&NA had never even paid interests on its bonds. In 1876, two bond holders, Thomas N. Egery and Daniel B. Hinckley, co-owners of an iron foundry in Bangor, decided to place an attachment on the E&NA timberland in Aroostook to secure their bonds. But the settlers already occupying the land could potentially challenge the E&NA's ownership claim. Since they could not produce titles, Egery and Hinckley tried to evict them as squatters. Representative Peter Charles Keegan convinced the legislature to pass remedial legislation, but the governor vetoed it, and the matter went to court. Keegan convinced both judge and jury that the 1859 statute had precedence over the grant. This judgment only applied to settlers covered by the 1859 statute; others were left in a limbo.

In 1882, the E&NA trustees sold the existing tracks and rolling stock to the Maine Central Railroad but kept the timberland. They auctioned off some of it; most went to the Coe and Pingree interests, who already owned huge tracts of land in northern Maine. Some proprietors reached an agreement with the settlers, as Coe did in Frenchville. The E&NA trustees, however, refused to open the rest of the land for settlement and sold stumpage rights (the right to cut lumber) instead. They served the settlers eviction notices and took them to court. The first five suits (all in 1886) produced results that satisfied neither settlers nor proprietors. The jury decided the proprietors had to choose between evicting the settlers with proper compensation for the improvements they had made to the land or selling them the land for what it was worth before such improvements were made. The six pieces of land were valued at $305, the improvements at $4,400. The proprietors gave up the land.

There were other suits already pending in the courts, and local politicians (Keegan from Van Buren, Dickey from Fort Kent, and state senator Llewellyn Power) were pressing the legislature to act. The legislature appointed another commission, which concluded that the problem was of too great a magnitude for the courts to solve one case at a time. The proprietors by then were ready to sell anyway. The commissioners recommended the state purchase the land under contention, and then sell it back to the settlers, or, when appropriate, give it to them. The state legislature passed a resolve to that effect in 1889, and 659 deeds were issued in the following years:

Deeds Issued After March 8, 1889

T18R4	Madawaska	234
T18R5	Frenchville	179
T18R6	Fort Kent	174
T18R7	Fort Kent	72
Total		659

Sources: Maine State Archives, Maine Public Documents, Land Agent Reports: 1875, 1882, 1884, 1892; Commissioners' Report Regarding Settlers' Claims on Proprietors' Land in Aroostook County, Made Pursuant to Resolution Passed on February 27, 1873; Commissioners Report Investigating the Settlers Living Conditions in Madawaska, Appointed Following a Resolution on March 10, 1887; Burque (1900); Dubay (1976).

The Land in Between

A. The Intercolonial Railway

New Brunswick and Nova Scotia had long desired a rail connection to the rest of Canada. In 1864, they tried to convince the government of Canada (which at the time only included present-day Ontario and Québec) to join them in building an interprovincial line at public expense. Canada, however, pulled out at the last minute. In the late 1860s, the Maritime Provinces made the construction of this line a condition for their entry into Confederation. New Brunswickers wanted the Intercolonial Railway to pass through the St. John Valley, where most of the province's population resided. Britain, however, wanted a line that could be used for defense purposes. It therefore opposed the St. John Valley route, which it thought was too close to the border. The line was built through the Matapedia instead (see Map 17-2). It was finished in 1876.

B. The New Brunswick Railway

This was a serious blow to the people of the St. John Valley, who consequently resurrected schemes to build a line in the more populated western part of the province. Industrialist Alexander Gibson had

Map 17-2: Railways Projected or Built 1870–90
Map by B. and S. Craig

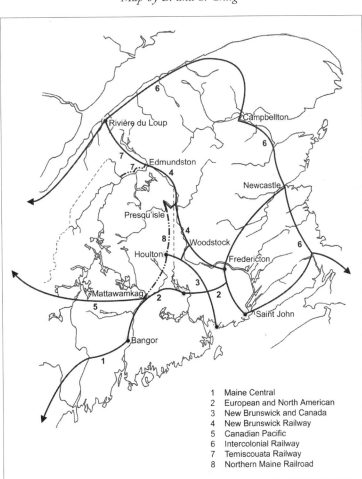

1 Maine Central
2 European and North American
3 New Brunswick and Canada
4 New Brunswick Railway
5 Canadian Pacific
6 Intercolonial Railway
7 Temiscouata Railway
8 Northern Maine Railroad

The Arrival of the Railroads

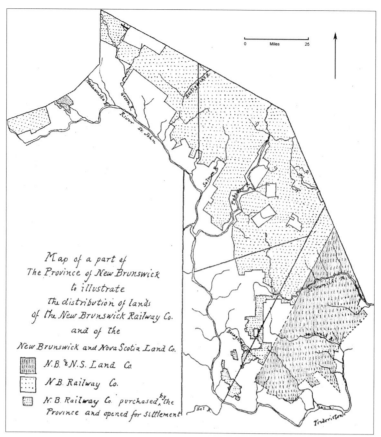

Map 17-3: LandGrants to New Brunswick Railway
W. F. Ganong, "A Monograph of the Origins of Settlement in the Province of
New Brunswick." Proceedings and Transactions of the Royal Society of
Canada, *1901, 105.*

commissioned a survey in 1866 for a line between Fredericton, where he had a mill, and the upper St. John Valley, where he owned timberland. He received a charter for the New Brunswick Land and Railway Company in 1870 (renamed the New Brunswick Railway Company in 1881). Although the line was supposed to extend to Rivière-du-Loup, it never went beyond Edmundston.

The New Brunswick Railway soon experienced financial difficulties that prevented the line's completion. To help the company, the provincial government granted it more than 380,000 acres of forestland in Victoria and Madawaska counties. Although most of this land was valuable only as tim-

berland, other sections were suitable for settlement, a point mentioned by Gibson, managing trustee for the New Brunswick Railway, in an 1880 report:

> I may state that I am informed by very reliable explorers, that on Green River, and some of the other tributaries of the Saint John above Grand River, as well as on that river and the head of the Restigouche, cedar is found in large size, and great abundance. I am also informed that there is considerable quantity of good settling land in the Railway Company's property between the Grand River and Saint Francis.[2]

The land grant, however, blocked all possibilities of expanding settlements in the region. In the early twentieth century, Madawaska residents put pressure on the provincial government to buy the land back. In 1902, New Brunswick purchased 50,000 acres of this land from the railway company and granted it to farmers in the region. It purchased additional acres in St. Leonard and Comeau Ridge in 1912 and opened them to settlement two years after. But the railway company remained the proprietor of more than 330,000 acres of land in Madawaska-Victoria.

The section of line from Fredericton to Newburgh, across the river from Woodstock, was completed in 1873, and the one from Newburgh to Grand Falls in 1875; the line reached Edmundston

Table 17-2: St. John Valley Products Exported through New Brunswick in 1879

Commodities	Quantity	Value ($)
Potatoes	30,000 bushels	9,000
Starch	1,300 tons from 5 factories	52,000
Long lumber	13 million feet	91,000
Sawn shingles	7 million	14,000
Sawed clapboard	325,000 feet	3,250
Lath	300,000 feet	300
Picket fences	200,000 feet	200
Shaved shingles	30 million	75,000

Source: Maine Public Documents, *Report of the Commission…to Locate Bridges…*, 1880.

Illus. 17-1: This view of Connors in the 1890s shows the Temiscouata railway station and water tower.
CDEM, PC2-1

Illus. 17-2: The Canadian National station in Saint Leonard. CDEM, PC3-152

in 1878. Central Aroostook residents did not waste time linking to this line. The Aroostook River Railroad (ARR), a narrow-gauge railway connecting Caribou to the New Brunswick Railway at Aroostook Junction, was completed in 1876, and this line was extended to Presque Isle in 1881. The ARR charter allowed the company to extend the line to Houlton and Fort Kent, but it did not make any effort to that effect. The New Brunswick Railway leased the New Brunswick and Canada (with which it connected) for 999 years in 1882, and the New Brunswick section of the E&NA in 1883. (By 1890, both lines were leased to the Canadian Pacific for 999 years.) In the Valley, one merely had to cross the river to bring products to the station; people immediately took advantage of this opportunity (see Table 17-2).

C. Other Canadian Lines

When the E&NA project got mired in disagreements among investors, Canadian promoters obtained a charter from their government for another transcontinental line (the Grand Trunk) in 1853. By 1860, the Grand Trunk connected Detroit with Rivière-du-Loup through Toronto, Montreal, and Quebec City. After 1878, the only thing needed to create a direct connection between Saint John, New Brunswick, and the rest of Canada was a short line over the old Grand Portage. Local interests also wanted this connection, which would enable them to ship wood products to the St. Lawrence more easily and would also help expand the region's forest industry. This connection was made when the Temiscouata Railway Company, chartered in 1885 to link Edmundston to Rivière-du-Loup, inaugurated its line on January 1, 1889. In 1891, the line was extended to Connors, opposite St. Francis, Maine. Promoters put forth some plans to extend this line westward, but it never got beyond the paper stage. Canada, for instance, incorporated a Québec and New Brunswick Railway, to be built from Connors Station to a place near Saint-Charles (Québec) in 1900, but nothing came of it. The

Temiscouata Railway never succeeded in rerouting logs to the St. Lawrence in significant quantities; rather, the line helped those traveling from Montreal to Halifax. One could shave off 155 miles by using this line rather than the Intercolonial.

Five years later, the province of Québec incorporated the St. Francis Railway to start at St. Francis and continue through Pohenegamook toward the St. Lawrence; this line was completed in 1914 as part of the National Transcontinental Railway (which became part of the Canadian National, or CN, in 1919). The line was built fairly close to the Maine-Québec border to promote settlement in sparsely populated back parishes. A last railway, the St. John Valley Railway Company, was incorporated in 1910, linking Gagetown, which lay south of Fredericton, to Grand Falls, where it could have connected to existing lines going to Québec. The project stalled, however, until Arthur Gould, president of the Aroostook River Railroad, intervened. He managed to receive the financial backing of the recently elected Conservative government in Ottawa. The line still went over budget, the province took it over in 1915, and built the line to Centreville. It opened to traffic in 1919, but as it duplicated other lines, it never made money and was sold to the Canadian National Railway in 1919.[3]

A first attempt at connecting the Valley with the Restigouche was made in 1885, when the Restigouche and Victoria Colonization Railway Company was incorporated. One of the goals of this line was to encourage settlement between the two rivers. Nothing came of this project until the late 1890s when construction finally began. The International Railway of New Brunswick took it over in 1906 and completed a line between St. Leonard and Campbellton in 1910. Many believed that this line would provide great economic opportunities: the Atlantic, Québec, and Western Railway intended to use the International's tracks to reach its terminal at Gaspé. Gaspé was a short three-and-a-half-day journey from Liverpool by steamer. Valley businessmen concluded that their region would inevitably become part of the normal route between England and North America.

Instead, the line lost money right from the beginning and the Canadian government bought it in 1914, later integrating it into the CN line. The Québec Central extended its line to Lac Frontière, on the Québec-Maine boundary, to serve the lumber industry during that same period. The section of the National Transcontinental Railway connecting Edmundston to Moncton via St. Leonard and Plaster Rock was completed in 1912. This turned St. Leonard into an important railway junction, and from this town, one could travel to Vancouver and points in between. This line, however, also facilitated migrations from the Valley to the Canadian Prairie Provinces, which were getting settled.

III.   THE BANGOR AND AROOSTOOK RAILWAY

The Canadian lines provided central and northern Aroostook with railway connections to the outside world. Some of those connections were, however, circuitous and cumbersome. Farmers in the Houlton or Caribou–Presque Isle regions who wanted to ship products to southern Maine had to put their goods aboard narrow-gauge railway cars going to Woodstock. At Woodstock, the goods were transferred to wider-gauge cars which traveled down to Fredericton Junction or McAdam Junction, where they were transferred to the E&NA, to pursue their journey to the United States. Besides delays and added costs, all the transfers could easily damage the merchandise (especially potatoes, which were susceptible to bruising). Merchants and farmers also accused the Canadians of charging exorbitant rates. This complicated system limited the region's access to international markets. Americans also chafed at their dependence on the Canadians. The *Aroostook Times* commented on this situation in 1890:

Illus. 17-3: The B&A railway station in Grand Isle in 1911. Madawaska Historical Society

Add to this the passenger traffic, and the inward bound freight and we have over a million and a half dollars paid by the people of Aroostook, yearly, to the Canadian Pacific Railway. This would go a long way toward building railroads into this country.[4]

In 1887, the Northern Maine Railroad Company was revived and was vigorously supported by A. W. Hall, editor of the Presque Isle *Aroostook Republican.* A route was surveyed, and the Maine Central Railroad (MCR) was supposed to build or at least lease the line once work was completed. The MCR, however, pulled out of the project. In 1890, the Canadian Pacific (CP), a Canadian transcontinental line, had leased the New Brunswick Railway and its feeders, including the New Brunswick and Canadian. It had also built the so called "Short Line" between the eastern townships of Québec and Mattawamkeag on the Maine Central line, enabling it to send traffic to (or withhold it from) the latter.

Rumors circulated that the Canadian Pacific had blackmailed the Maine Canadian Railway into dissociating itself from the Northern Maine Railroad because it did not want competition.

In 1890, Albert A. Burleigh, a resident of Houlton, businessman, and state and federal civil servant, shared with visiting journalist F. Wiggin a plan he thought would finally allow Aroostook to have a railroad. Wiggin communicated the plan to Hall, who not only endorsed it enthusiastically but also published the idea in the *Aroostook Republican.* Readers were very interested, but the memory of recently failed endeavors discouraged bankers and entrepreneurs. Burleigh then proposed that the county fund the project alone. The county, he said, could borrow the necessary funds, up to 5 percent of the value of its tax base. This became known as the "Burleigh Scheme." The railroad was to run from Van Buren to a point on the Maine Central line. Burleigh was very convincing; pledges poured in

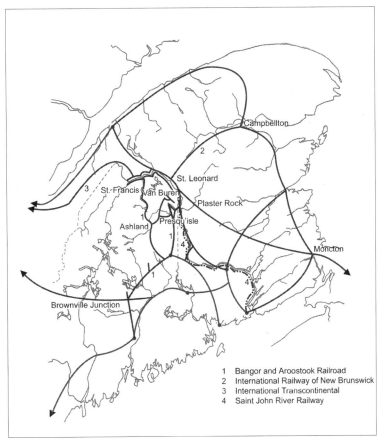

Map 17-4: Railways built after 1890
Map by B. and S. Craig

from Bangor and Houlton businessmen, and the Bangor and Aroostook Railroad Company (B&A) was formally created on February 13, 1891. John A. Nadeau of Fort Kent was one of its directors (see Sidebar 18-2). The newspapers remained involved, publishing interviews with informed individuals and promoting the project's benefits. Just five days after the company's creation, the required 5 percent of the railroad's capital stock had been raised. On April 21, the Aroostook voters approved the scheme in a county referendum (with 5,201 in favor of the plan and 505 opposed). The company's capital stock was set at $1,050,000 and the Maine legislature passed various laws to protect the company. For example, no competitor was allowed to build another railroad line within fifteen miles of the B&A for three years.

The Maine legislature also incorporated a construction company, the Aroostook Construction Company, headed by Burleigh, to build the line. Franklin W. Cram, former superintendent of the E&NA and former general manager of the New Brunswick Railway, became the B&A's general manager. (He took this offer over another by the CP.)

Construction began on July 1, 1893, at the Brownville station on the Maine Central line, the start of the B&A line. On January 1, 1894, the very first B&A train pulled in at Houlton. A year later the line reached Caribou and Fort Fairfield. The line to Van Buren took a little more time due to the company's financial difficulties. The situation got so bad that Burleigh had to pledge his personal credit before work could continue. He had good reasons to

The Arrival of the Railroads

do so; Van Buren residents, tired of waiting, secured a charter for a Van Buren and Caribou Railroad Company in 1899; the charter, however, would be void if the B&A completed the line before the end of the year. The B&A reached Van Buren in October 1899. And in 1903, the company acquired the recently built Fish River Railroad (from Sheridan to Fort Kent), which integrated Fort Kent into the network. In 1909, the B&A was granted a charter to build an extension from Van Buren to St. Francis. The St. John River extension was built in three parts: the Grand Isle Section from Keegan to Grand Isle opened in October 1909; the Fort Kent section from Fort Kent to Grand Isle opened in November 1910; and the St. Francis section from Fort Kent to St. Francis opened in December 1909. As a result, the entire Valley was now served by parallel American and Canadian lines. Unlike to other railway lines, the B&A made money; after paying $103,458 in dividends to stockholders, it ended the 1915 fiscal year with a net income of $132,032.

The B&A directors also realized that they could increase the company's traffic if they connected to the transcontinental railways across the river. Therefore, in 1913, they set up a subsidiary, the Van Buren Bridge Company, to build an international bridge near Van Buren. The company was authorized by both the United States and Canadian governments in 1913. In September 1914, various companies began work on the bridge. The Cyr Brothers Company of Waterville built the substructure of the bridge, while the Dominion Bridge Company, Ltd., of Montreal built the superstructure. Workers labored through subzero temperatures during the 1914–15 winter, and the project took only about seven months to reach completion. On May 1, 1915, the bridge was officially opened, linking Van Buren to the town of St. Leonard. All involved were surprised by the speed of the job. One of the engineers on site noted:

> Perhaps the most marked feature of the bridge project [was] the rapidity of its construction.... Beginning in the middle of last September

[1914] excavation and the laying of concrete were vigorously pursued throughout the winter months, although the temperature usually over around zero [Fahrenheit], and was at time much lower.[5]

With the B&A came American Express, a money-transferring business that had contributed $600,000 to the building of the main line. Soon, there were American Express offices in most B&A stations. Telegraph lines ran parallel to all railroad lines, since this was one of the legal conditions for operation.

Conclusion

The second half of the nineteenth century was the age of the railroads in Western Europe and North America—a phenomenon that touched northern Maine and western New Brunswick. Their residents believed the railroads would open new opportunities for their communities. They would provide, for example, a means of communication and transportation independent of water levels and weather conditions. In addition, the location of the Valley seemed to make it an inevitable part of a trans-Canadian line—and some went as far as to view the Valley as an inevitable part of a Europe-American connection. They quickly learned, however, that enthusiasm and dreams alone do not build railroads. Capital—and lots of it—is needed. Mainers and New Brunswickers believed railroads would bring immigrants to the region and contribute to economic development; but promoters believed the region was insufficiently populated and underdeveloped to make a line profitable. Consequently, railroad connections were slow in coming and rarely profitable.

While they existed, railroad lines to or through the Valley served their intended purposes: they moved people and goods, helped farmers link to new markets, allowed new industries to emerge, and redistributed people on the land. In particular, the transformations following the arrival of the B&A

were so dramatic that many Aroostook residents dated the real birth of their county to the first train pulling into Houlton station in 1894.

ENDNOTES

1. The purpose of this line was to allow Montreal merchants to ship goods to Europe even when the St. Lawrence was frozen.
2. Gibson, *The New Brunswick Railways,* 18.
3. One may wonder why the Canadian government bought unprofitable railway lines. Because it had promised interest payments on part of the stock of those lines, it had no choice; it would have to pay whether the lines were operating or not, or risk damaging its credit rating. The government, therefore, decided that if it was going to pay, it might as well own the lines. That way it could rationalize their operations. This was the beginning of Canadian National. The Canadian Pacific remained a private company.
4. White, *The Burleigh Scheme...,* 6.
5. Angier and Cleaver, *Bangor and Aroostook...,* 47.

FURTHER READINGS

Judd, Richard W. *Aroostook: A Century of Logging in Northern Maine.* 1989.

Judd, Richard W. *et. al. Maine: The Pine Tree State.* 1995: Ch. 14 (Judd includes a nice map of railroads in Maine).

Sirois, Georges. "Une vue rétrospective du développement des communications dans le haut de la vallée du Saint-Jean au XIXème siècle." *Revue de la Société historique du Madawaska* VI (Avril-Juin 1978): 2–13.

Michaud, Marie-Claude. "Le chemin de fer au Madawaska, 1878–1990." *Revue de la Société historique du Madawaska* XXXVI (Janvier–Juin 2008): 4–26.

White, John. W. "The Burleigh Scheme: An Idea that Became a Railroad." *New England Social Studies Bulletin* XV (March, 1958): 5–11.

SOURCES

For railroads in Maine, see Chase (1926) and Corliss (2000). For the Bangor and Aroostook Railroad, see White (1958), Angier and Cleaver (1986), and R. Sprague (1966). For Canadian railways, see Gibson (1880) and Stolz (1987) and visit http://www.the canadianencyclopedia.com. Information about rail workers can be found in Dubay (2002). Statistical data can be found in the annual reports of Maine's Bureau of Industrial and Labor Statistics. (Parts of Maine Public Documents; we used the 1880 to 1914 reports.)

18

COMMUNICATIONS AND ENERGY FOR THE MODERN AGE: BRIDGES, PHONES, AND ELECTRICITY

Railroads eventually divided the Valley; bridges, telephones, and electrical power plants had the opposite effect. Building bridges across the St. John turned out to be difficult. Publicly funded bridges required the cooperation of both the American and Canadian governments, but the former was not interested. Consequently, private interests built the first two international bridges but for very different reasons.

The first phones appeared shortly before the turn of the century, facilitating communications across the river. The various companies made sure their subscribers had access to lines outside the Valley and across the river. Electricity became available shortly before the outbreak of World War I. It was provided by a power plant on the Aroostook River, which gradually extended its grid north. By 1913, this plant even supplied Grand Falls. Attempts at harnessing the power of the Grand Falls before the war, however, failed.

I.   BRIDGING THE RIVER

In 1880, Fort Kent Representative William Dickey headed a commission appointed to locate and survey bridges across the St. John and St. Francis rivers, connecting the United States with Canada. The commissioners recommended building four bridges—one at Van Buren directly opposite the New Brunswick Railway depot, one west of the Madawaska River near the railway depot, one at Fort Kent, and one at St. Francis. To promote the plan, Dickey presented it as a means for American Madawaskayans to have easier access to the New Brunswick Railway. Northern Aroostook producers were already shipping significant quantities of goods through New Brunswick, and he believed bridges would double exports and increase local residents' profits (see Table 17-2). He hoped increased economic opportunities would also encourage people to stay in the area instead of migrating south or west.

Dickey had tried to get bridges built across the river before. In 1868, he had been instrumental in getting the state legislature pass a resolution requesting the United States and Canada to appropriate money for this purpose. The Canadian Parliament voted the money, but Congress did not. Dickey would have no greater success this time around. John Costigan got the Canadian Parliament to allocate the funds, but Congress sent the proposal to committee where it died. Dickey tried one last time during his last session in the state legislature in 1897. Two years previously, the Dominion of Canada had incorporated the Saint John River Bridge Company "to erect bridges for pedestrians, vehicles, and other traffic over the St. John River" at four designated locations. Dickey asked the state to subsidize any company willing to build a two-way bridge across the St. John River at Fort Kent, provided that both

Illus. 18-1: Until bridges were built, the only ways to cross the river were by canoes or boats (if one owned one) or by rope-ferry, like this one at St. Basile. Ferries are already mentioned on Wilkinson's 1840 map. CDEM, PC3-12

the Canadian and American governments match the funds. This bridge idea also failed.

The only bridges that crossed the river before World War I were the Bangor and Aroostook (B&A) Railroad bridge at Van Buren (see Chapter 17) and a suspension footbridge at Fort Kent, erected in 1903-04 by Joseph Long, an innkeeper at Clair (see Sidebar 18-1). The Fort Kent footbridge (Pont à José) was a private toll bridge, built after Costigan obtained permission from Ottawa and J. A. Laliberté (Fort Kent) from Augusta. It cost 5¢ to cross it, less than the 10¢ to cross the river by ferry. The bridge brought customers from dry Maine right to Lang's door (he served alcohol). No other international bridge was erected until 1922. In the meantime, people used ferries, which crossed the river pulling on a cable strung across it. A suspen-

sion footbridge was built at Grand Falls in 1858, but it collapsed two weeks later; it was rebuilt in 1860. This structure was located entirely in New Brunswick territory.

Illus. 18-2: The "Pont à José" was the first international bridge across the river. It was a private, toll pedestrian bridge. Madawaska Historical Society

Illus. 18-3: The first bridge across the river was the suspension bridge at Grand Falls, entirely in New Brunswick territory. PANB, Isaac Erb photograph, P11-200

The Land in Between

Sidebar 18-1: The "Pont à José"

Excerpts from Henri J. Souci's history of the *Pont à José,* published in *Le Madawaska,* December 10, 1936; translated by the authors.

The "Père José" (Joseph R. Long, husband of Alphonsine Bérubé) was a businessman with foresight. There were then at Clair three or four inns, each doing fantastic business because the sale of alcoholic beverages was forbidden in Maine. Père José had his own inn and thought that, if there was a bridge leading to his door, it would bring more customers to his bar and, hence, provide greater profits. With the toll he could, within a few years, recoup the cost of this bridge....

Drinks were then very cheap, and our brothers and friends in and around Fort Kent were coming to have a drink or buy a bottle in the inns in Clair. Père José's predictions were soon fulfilled, and he saw his clientele grow, and the income from the tolls proved that soon he would recoup his investment in this business....

Previously, one crossed the river in summer using a ferry held by cables. The ferry connected to a pulley gliding on a thick cable strung across the river. There were two of those ferries within three quarters of a mile of each other; later, there was a third one....

In 1918, the United States Department of Immigration required the installation of a gate to close the bridge at night—that is, between 10 p.m. and 7 a.m., to control the crossing of people of military age from one country to the other. This gate closed the bridge, but there were many in Clair and Fort Kent who knew or found a means of going around this obstacle. Because 10 o'clock Standard time, or 11 o'clock, Atlantic time, was not very late for many people, their drinking on the one side or their evening on the other was not always finished on time, and one had to become an acrobat to go over the gate and return home.

Source: Text reproduced in *Paroisse Saint-François d'Assise...* (n.d.): 150–52.

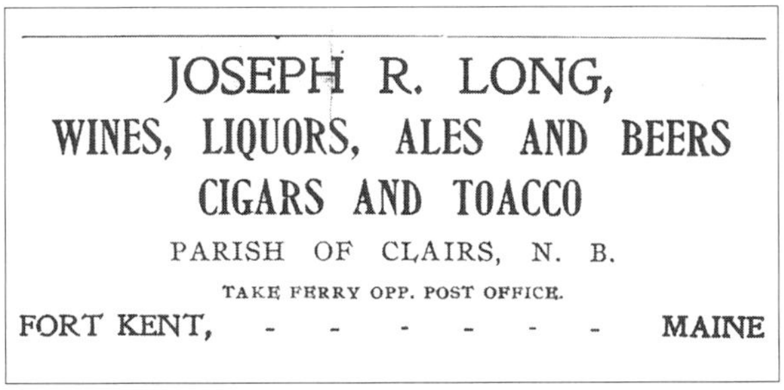
JOSEPH R. LONG,
WINES, LIQUORS, ALES AND BEERS
CIGARS AND TOACCO
PARISH OF CLAIRS, N. B.
TAKE FERRY OPP. POST OFFICE.
FORT KENT, - - - - - - - MAINE

Illus. 18-4: Joseph (José) Long's advertisement in the Aroostook County (Maine) Business and residential Directory, 1905-1906. *Newton, Mass.: Newton Journal Publishing Co., 1906. (Yes, there is a typo!)*

II. THE TELEPHONE

The first telephone company to operate in the Valley appears to have been the Fort Kent Telephone Company, incorporated in March 1895. The company was comprised of fourteen partners, including selectman and member of school committee Henry Nadeau, postmaster, and town clerk Frank Mallett, and local businessmen such as John A. Nadeau (see Sidebar 18-2). The capital was not to exceed $6,000.

A yearly subscription cost $18, but Page and Mallett's starch factory paid only $9. The company purchased its equipment in Montreal and hired a "telephone girl" (switchboard operator) at $100 a year. Initially, she was expected to work from 6:30 a.m. to 9:30 p.m. The following year, her hours were reduced to 7 a.m. to 8 p.m., with two half-hour breaks for lunch and supper. There were sixteen subscribers the first year. Fort Kent quickly became the hub of a network that included the Fort Kent

Telephone Company, St. Francis Telephone Company (1901), and Eagle Lake Telephone Company (1905). Another company, the Aroostook Telegraph and Telephone Company, served Van Buren. By 1910, the entire American side of the Valley had access to telephone services.

A year after the Fort Kent Telephone Company was incorporated, the Madawaska Phone Company was set up in Edmundston, with a capital of $5,000; the fourteen investors included four men from

---

Sidebar 18-2: Obituary of John A. Nadeau

Le Journal du Madawaska announces the death of John A. Nadeau, age fifty-five (born August, 3, 1850); translated by authors.

His father was the late Joseph Nadeau, one of Fort Kent's first residents, and his mother was Alice White. At about fifteen, he was sent to the collegiate institute in la Pocatière to begin his classical course of studies. After two years at la Pocatière, he attended St. Joseph College in Memramcook for five years. At twenty-two, he returned to Fort Kent.

He was involved in general trade and in the wood industry on a large scale. Through his ceaseless activities, his energy, and his superior qualities, he was able, in a relatively short time period, to achieve a comfortable standard of living and enable his family to live independently in one of the most elegant and most handsome houses in the beautiful village of Fort Kent.

In 1874, the late John A. Nadeau was elected to the state house to represent the electoral district of Fort Kent, an honorable position he fulfilled until 1877. He was a customs collector in Fort Kent for about fifteen years, and at his death, was still occupying this position. Until his death, he was president of the Fort Kent Bank, a position to which he had been unanimously elected as soon as this institution was incorporated....

With the death of the honorable John A. Nadeau, the entire region loses one of its distinguished children, an active, vigilant, and powerful defender. In particular, the village of Fort Kent loses a notable citizen, an agent of progress and development of this flourishing village. When one visits Fort Kent nowadays, one finds evidence of John A. Nadeau's activities everywhere: his industries, his railroad, his bank, and his normal school all display to our imagination the name of this regretted compatriot in sparkling gold letters.

He married Sarah McSweeny from Memramcook in 1889 and had two children, Arthur, twenty-three, a student at Washington University, and Thérésa, seventeen, a student at the Convent of Providence, Rhode Island. He leaves a brother, H. W. Nadeau, a merchant in Fort Kent, and two sisters, Mrs. John Sweeney and Mrs. Stephen Audibert.

Source: *Le Journal du Madawaska*, October 2, 1904.

The Land in Between

Table 18-1: Shareholders in Fort Kent and Madawaska Telephone Companies

Fort Kent Telephone Company (incorporated 1895)	Madawaska Telephone Company (incorporated 1896)	Residence
Nadeau, John A.	Nadeau, John A.	Fort Kent, ME
Nadeau, Henry W.	Nadeau, Henry W.	Fort Kent, ME
Mallet, Frank W.	Mallet, Frank W.	Fort Kent, ME
Niles, Silas	Niles, Silas	Fort Kent, ME
Pinkham, Asa M.	Pinkham, Asa M.	Fort Kent, ME
Cunliffe, G. V.	Cunliffe, G. V.	Fort Kent, ME
Bradbury, L. F.		Not specified
Bradbury, T .M.		Not specified
Mullin, John		Not specified
Bradbury, C. F.		Not specified
Bradbury, C. C.		Not specified
Page, J. H.		Fort Kent, ME
Mallett, B. W.		Fort Kent, ME
Dr. Sirois, F. G.	Dr. Sirois, F. G.	Fort Kent, ME
	Laliberté, Joseph A.	Fort Kent, ME
	Fenlason, A. G.	St. Francois, N.B.
	Long, Joseph	St. Francois, N.B.
	Michaud, Michael	Edmundston, N.B.
	Richards, J. Medley	Edmundston, N.B.
	Cochrane, Thomas J.	Edmundston, N.B.
	Guy, J. Adolphe	Edmundston, N.B.

Sidebar 18-3: Telephone Dos and Don'ts

—4. Face the transmitter, and do not talk sideways into it. Keep the mouth about two inches from the transmitter, and speak naturally, distinctly, and not too rapidly.

—6. Answer your calls promptly. This is necessary for good service. Do not blame the operator when kept waiting—it is because a party does not answer promptly.

—9. It is strictly against the rules of the telephone company for subscribers to play musical instruments of any kind over the lines for the entertainment of other subscribers.

—10. Do not use telephones during thunderstorms, since calls will not be answered by central at such times.

Source: St-Onge, "L'évolution du service téléphonique à Edmundston...," 8; translated by the authors.

Illus. 18-5: This street view of St. Francis (Maine) shows that growth and modernization were not limited to urban areas; note the telephone pole to the left of the store. St. Francis Historical Society

Edmundston, two from St. François (New Brunswick), and eight from Fort Kent, some of whom were already shareholders in the Fort Kent Telephone Company (see Table 18-1). The Madawaska Phone Company immediately linked with the Fort Kent network. In 1905, it extended its lines to the Québec border where it linked with the Kamouraska Phone Company. In 1904, the New Brunswick Telephone Company, (founded in 1889), extended its line from Grand Falls to Edmundston. At that time, the Madawaska Telephone Company had only thirty subscribers. In 1906, the New Brunswick Telephone Company bought the Mada-waska Phone Company for $4,000. The central remained in Edmundston. Services were often interrupted in winter when the lines broke under the weight of snow and ice. Users had to follow rules and regulations when using the phone, which nowadays would appear very quaint (see Sidebar 18-3). In 1907, the Madawaska Telephone Company had ninety-five subscribers in Edmundston. Although the majority of these clients were businesses, forty-four were private citizens. By 1910, it had 132 subscribers from all over the region including Edmundston, Saint-Jacques, Baker Brook, Frenchville (Maine), St. Hilaire, and St. Basile.

III.   ELECTRICAL POWER

Electricity was first used by large lumber mills built at the end of the nineteenth century. These mills operated their own generators, using the current to provide light for their activities. Mill directors' houses and plant boardinghouses were also wired. Those small generating plants were not intended to serve the general public. One would think that the Grand Falls would have provided Valley residents with an abundant and early source of electrical power. This was not the case. The first electrical power plant serving northern Aroostook County was located on the Aroostook River, and Grand Falls' first supplier was this plant.

A. The Maine and New Brunswick Electrical Power Company

On May 9, 1903, the New Brunswick legislature chartered the Maine and New Brunswick Electrical Power Company, Ltd., and granted it the water rights to Aroostook Falls. The original directors included three men from New Brunswick and two from Maine. The capital stock was set at $40,000, divided into 4,000 shares. The directors, however, soon realized that they lacked sufficient funds and sought the help of Arthur Gould, one of the largest mill owners in Aroostook County. Gould offered his assistance only if the directors would turn their charter over to him, which they did. Gould's first order of business was to secure a charter amendment allowing the company to increase its capital to $200,000. In 1905, the Maine State Legislature chartered Gould's company to operate in the state. The company was also allowed to acquire the Presque Isle Electric Light Company and the Fort Fairfield Electric Company. It also received permission to transmit electricity to Fort Fairfield, as well as sell electricity to both the Aroostook Valley Railroad and the town of Houlton.

In 1906, Gould started work on the Aroostook Falls dam in New Brunswick. The first years of construction were difficult. The company lacked capital and proper supervisory staff. One day, Gould arrived unexpectedly on the job site to find all of the workers sitting around waiting for the contractor to return from an errand. This lack of supervision and waste of manpower infuriated him. He fired the contractor and began supervising the workers himself. The project was completed in 1907. It included a 246-foot-long dam, and a 2,200-foot-long, 21-foot-wide, and 20-foot-deep canal. The total cost for the project was $275,000. In the following years, Gould expanded the grid. In 1909, he reported that the company supplied power to Houlton, Fort Fairfield, Mars Hill, Easton, Bridgewater, and Monticello in Maine, and Andover and Perth in New Brunswick. In 1912, he added Van Buren and

Fort Kent to the line. By 1913, he was also supplying power to Caribou and Grand Falls.

B. The Grand Falls Project

Sir William Cornelius Van Horne, one of the builders of the Canadian Pacific Railway (CP) was the first to consider building a power plant at Grand Falls. Van Horne had been instrumental in the CP acquisition of the New Brunswick Railway, a deal that included the company's huge timber reserves. In 1896, he developed a plan to build a pulp and paper mill near Grand Falls and an electric plant to power it, and he acquired development rights to the site from the province. At that time, however, it was uncertain how much access Canadian paper would have to the American market. Tariffs on paper exported to the United States were high, whereas pulpwood could enter duty free. The Canadian provinces wanted to both manufacture paper on their soil and restrict pulpwood exports. The issue was not resolved until 1911, when the United States, under intense pressure from the newspaper industry, dropped duties on imported newsprint. This protracted struggle delayed Van Horne's project. In 1903, New Brunswick began re-examining it. By then, new technology had been developed which made it possible to transmit electricity over greater distances, and New Brunswick politicians began to think the Grand Falls could supply more than just a paper mill. They envisioned a power plant supplying power to the entire St. John Valley.

This, however, raised some diplomatic problems. A power plant needs a steady supply of water, but New Brunswick only had access to 4 percent of the Grand Falls potential storage capacity. Another 23 percent of its capacity lay in Québec and 73 percent in Aroostook County. This meant that, at any given time, three-fourths of the water feeding the power station came from Maine. In 1909 and 1910, Maine and New Brunswick collaborated on preliminary studies of the water supply. This led historian C. Beach to conclude that:

For a brief period, it appeared that New Brunswick would succeed in re-establishing cooperative relations with Maine. Memories of earlier beneficial economic and social connections still survived, providing a basis for mutual appreciation of the development potential of Grand Falls in the border region.... Thus electrification presented an opportunity to create a new and unique transnational "artefact" based on the Grand Falls project; it would only occur if sufficient political will could be generated to overcome the narrower economic interests.[1]

Those "narrow interests" included downriver lumberers, who did not want obstacles to log drives on the river; Van Horne, who did not want to surrender his rights to the site; and the paper companies in Maine, who cared about getting their logs more than about diversified development. The American-owned International Paper Company— also the second largest holder of private timberland in New Brunswick after the CP—had fought to preserve tariffs against imported newsprint. When these tariffs were eliminated, it had to rethink its business strategy. Realizing that the Grand Falls was the largest untapped waterpower site in the Maritimes and hoping to keep that site out of competitor hands, the company struck a deal with Van Horne. Van Horne transferred his rights to International Paper, and became one of its directors. The province immediately chartered the new corporation that resulted from the agreement. However, instead of constructing a newsprint mill and power station, International Paper continued exporting pulpwood to its American factories, and no electricity was produced at Grand Falls before World War I.

Conclusion

Bridges, telegraphs, and telephone lines did not fire people's imagination in the same way that railroads did, but they played an important role in people's lives, and more importantly, in economic development. The telephone allowed businesspeople to communicate much faster with distant correspondents, and electricity extended the workday at the mill. But most ordinary residents had to wait until after the war to get electricity in their homes.

ENDNOTE
1. Beach, "Electrification and Underdevelopment in New Brunswick...," 69.

SOURCES
Not much has been written about those topics. For bridges, see Maine Public Documents, *Report of the Commission appointed... to locate and survey bridges across the St. John and St. Francis rivers...*, and *Paroisse Saint-Francois d'Assise (Clair) 1889–1989* for the *Pont à José*. For the telephone, see St. Onge (1990) and Grindle (1975). Beach (1993) and Stetson (1984) discuss electricity during this period.

19

THE GROWTH OF LUMBER MANUFACTURING AND THE EMERGENCE OF PULP AND PAPER

The railroads had a tremendous impact on the forest industry in the upper St. John River basin, by making large-scale production of long and short lumber economically feasible. The new mills, however, were expensive to run and, therefore largely financed by outside interests. They were almost all located on the American side of the Valley, in order to avoid paying customs duties on the finished products entering the United States. During World War I, another wood-based product made its debut in the Valley: paper pulp.

I. THE FOREST INDUSTRY BETWEEN THE PIKE ACT AND THE ARRIVAL OF THE RAILROADS

By 1876, the forest industry had recovered from the Panic of 1873. It remained transnational: whether cut in Maine or New Brunswick, wood was always shipped via the St. John River, to be turned into lumber in Saint John. Logging also expanded into the sliver of formerly disputed territory that had become part of the Côte-du-Sud, and wood cut there had to taken out via the St. John River. Lumber-operators continued to come from both sides of the border. The Maine Bureau of Industrial and Labor Statistics' 1883 annual report lists the Canadians Robert Connors and E. D. Jewett of Saint John among the fifteen loggers cutting on the American side of the St. John. The industry also continued to provide many jobs for local people, since logging still required a lot of man and animal power.

A. The Saint John Connection

After the middle of the century, the forest industry had shifted from pine ton timber for the British market to spruce long lumber for a largely American market. Saw logs cut in the upper St. John River basin enjoyed free navigation rights on the St. John River under the Webster–Ashburton Treaty. The reciprocity treaty with British North America (1854–66) and the Pike Act (1866–1911) allowed Aroostook wood milled in New Brunswick by Americans to re-enter the United States without paying customs duties. (Wood milled by New Brunswickers paid a 20 percent duty.) This led to the construction of several very large sawmills in Saint John, owned by Americans, or by Americans with New Brunswick partners. By 1872, the Americans were controlling the entire Saint John trade going to American ports. One of the largest such concerns was Stetson, Cutler Company founded in 1880. The partners, Stetson, Hayward, and Cutler, were from Bangor. Cutler worked from Bangor while Stetson supervised operations in Saint. John. The firm had warehouses in Boston and New York. Stetson, Cutler Company cut on the St. Francis, Big Black, Allagash, and upper St. John

Rivers. Thomas Phair of Presque Isle managed the ground operations. The Saint John mills, however, were only interested in the best logs (eleven inches in diameter or larger), and consequently, a lot of wood went to waste on the cutting sites.

B. The Uppermost St. John

In the 1870s, as in the 1850s, the men who exploited the forest resources in the part of the upper St. John basin that lay in Québec were usually from Maine or New Brunswick. William Murray, a Miramichi lumber merchant and shipbuilder, had permits for a staggering 1,446 km² (about 565 square miles). Morrow and Connors, and Cunliffe and Stevens had *concessions* for almost all the land that remained. The days of very large concession holders were nonetheless numbered, since by 1894 both sets of partners had abandoned their lots.

George H. Eaton took over a large number of permits and used the wood to feed his mill in Calais, Maine. In 1887, eighteen-year-old Flavien Chouinard, a native of Saint-Jean-Port-Joli, moved to Saint-Pamphile and began to trade in lumber and general merchandise. He also opened a sawmill, and worked as a sub-contractor for the St. John Lumber Company (see Part II below for information on this firm). Murray still had had permits for 777 km² (about 304 square miles) along the Maine boundary; he was the last of the larger concession holders. He floated all his wood down the St. John River.

C. Into the Woods and Out

Logging lasted anywhere from twenty to twenty-six weeks. The "swampers," who made tracks for workers to go into the woods were the first in the woods; they arrived at the camps in early fall. Next came the

Illus. 19-1: Lumber camp circa 1910. CDEM, PC1-6

The Land in Between

choppers, who cut down trees until about the beginning of February. They then hauled the wood to the rivers and streams. At the end of March, when the ice finally melted, they put the wood in the water under the care of log drivers and fastened it together in rafts. Drives typically involved teams of 10 to 300 drivers. This was extremely hard work, since the drivers had to direct the rafts with poles and pikes. Moreover, the St. John River was difficult to navigate, and water levels fluctuated up to a foot a day. There were also boulders, gravel, sandbars, and, of course, the Grand Falls to contend with. Drivers lost plenty of good timber when rafts went over the falls. As if this was not challenge enough, the drive also had to be concluded quickly. The St. John is shallow, and once the spring freshet ended, there was not always enough water left to carry the logs, which caught on the riverbanks or ran aground on sand bars. The operators then had to wait for the fall when water levels rose again, but by that time, the Saint John market would have slackened for the winter. For all their work, log drivers earned about $2 a day.

From the 1840s to 1904, most logs cut along the St. John and its tributaries were driven to the Fredericton boom where the logs were sorted and the rafts towed to Saint John to be milled or exported as ton timber. In 1886, the St. John River Log Driving Co., with exclusive rights to drive logs from Grand Falls to Fredericton, was created. The Madawaska Log Driving Company, which had been incorporated by Maine and New Brunswick, organized the drive between Allagash and Grand Falls. And, finally, the state of Maine incorporated the St. John Log Driving Company for the Baker and Southwest branches of the St. John to Allagash in 1911. Those companies were cooperative operations. The fees charged were proportionate to the number of logs brought in. "Prize logs," or logs without visible owner's marks, were sold at the end of the drive and the proceeds distributed among the different lumbering operations in proportion to the number of logs they had in the drive.

The composition of the labor force also gradually changed. In 1880, the Bangor *Whig* noted that Aroostook farmers "ceased to trouble themselves with lumbering operations and hence when winter gives way to spring, they are at home attending to their farming instead of being away on the river."[1] Lumbermen consequently, were less likely to be local men. By the beginning of the twentieth century, Acadians and French Canadians dominated the labor force. A 1904 study of three "typical" lumber camps in northern Maine by the Maine Bureau of Industrial and Labor Statistics noted that workers included twenty-six Mainers and ninety-one Canadians, most of whom were French-speaking.

Working conditions, however, improved. Food was better and more varied. A lumberman's diet used to consist of bread, beans, salt pork, and tea. By the late nineteenth century, fresh meats, vegetables, and fruits were added to their meals, which were now also prepared by professional cooks. New equipment, such as wagon sleds, also made the work easier and faster. New dams in strategic locations controlled the supply of water. Obstacles such as boulders, islands, and sandbars were also removed. Finally, the men's pay also improved. As a local veteran lumberman noted in 1899:

> Men who work in the woods are better fed and better paid now, than when I began the business.... Then the swampers got ten or twelve dollars a month, and the highest wages paid to any of the men was twenty dollars, while the head man's pay ranged from twenty-five to forty dollars. Now swampers receive from twelve to fifteen dollars a month, the choppers, teamsters, and sled tenders from twenty to twenty-six dollars, and the head man's pay ranges from thirty to sixty dollars.[2]

After the arrival of the railroads, fewer logs were driven to Fredericton. The railroads made it much easier to take short and long lumber out of the Valley; it also reduced transportation costs.[3] When the Bangor and Aroostook opened, the cost of transporting lumber to Boston dropped by 58 percent. The railroads also indirectly increased the forest industry's overall efficiency. Low-end products made from material previously considered refuse could now be sold profitably outside the region in the shape of telegraph poles, railroad ties, boxes, pallets, molding, flooring, and kindling wood, in addition to the shingle, clapboard, lath, and box shooks already in existence. Steam-operated mills also used the waste products to fuel boilers.

With two exceptions, the new mills were built on the American side of the river (see Tables 4 and 5 in Appendix I). The United States allowed unprocessed Canadian logs to enter the country duty free but charged duties on manufactured products. Some of the mills also preferred using Canadian rather than American logs because of lower stumpage fees in Canada. What emerged on the upper St. John at the turn of the century was, therefore, an American-based lumber manufacturing industry financed mostly by Americans but using wood cut almost exclusively by French Canadians along both sides of the river and processed by a local labor force residing on both sides of the river.

A. Van Buren and Its Vicinity

The largest lumber mills were located near Van Buren and owed their existence to the arrival of rail lines, first from Canada and then from southern Maine. They were highly capitalized steam-powered plants that produced their own electricity and were connected to the B&A via short feeder lines. They shipped wood products to markets in Massachusetts and New York.

1. The Van Buren Lumber Company.

To take advantage of the New Brunswick Railway, Stetson, Cutler Company founded the Van Buren Manufacturing Company in the late 1870s in conjunction with Edgar R. Burpee of Bangor. The mill produced mostly shingles, using wood from New Brunswick. The shingles were shipped to American markets through New Brunswick. In 1901, Burpee was dead and the remaining associates sold the mill to Allen E. Hammond (one of William C. Hammond's sons). Hammond owned a lumber mill at Violette Brook that he sold to the St. John Lumber Company in 1903 in order to build another mill next door. That same year, he also built a shingle mill at Grand Isle (known as the "Crawford Mill").

Hammond was also one of the directors of B&A, the line that had pulled into Van Buren two years previously. Hammond became one of the directors and general manager of the renamed Van Buren Lumber Company; the two other directors were E. J. Cochran of Montreal and S. A. J. Pluckett of Edmundston, who was also the company's president and treasurer. The company controlled 282 square miles of timberland on the Grand, Quisibus, and Green Rivers. In 1904, the Van Buren Lumber Company included a steam-operated mill above Van Buren Village, which linked to the B&A. The platform was so long that the mill could load nineteen railroad cars at a time. The main mill employed 150 men and could produce 100,000 feet of long lumber, 80,000 feet of lath, and 3,000 to 5,000 feet of clapboard daily. The company also operated a water-powered rotary sawmill on Violette Brook, which, in 1904, produced 10,000 feet of long lumber and 30,000 feet of shingles per day. The sawmill had to be rebuilt after fires in 1905 and 1916. Operations ceased after a third fire in 1918. This mill had employed twenty-five workers. Lastly, the company owned a shingle mill next to the railroad station. Hammond became its sole owner in 1913 and

Illus. 19-2: The St. John Lumber Company in Van Buren. Madawaska Historical Society

renamed it the "Hammond Lumber Company." It burned down in 1915 and was not rebuilt. The three mills combined employed 225 men; winter logging expeditions involved 1,000 men and 200 horses. The Van Buren Lumber Company also operated a store, the Van Buren Mercantile Company.

2. The St. John Lumber Company

The St. John Lumber Company was chartered in 1902. Its founder was Charles Milliken, an Augusta lumberman who turned his attention to Aroostook County when lumber supplies on the Kennebec declined. The Van Buren operations were his fifth in Aroostook County. The mills (a shingle mill and a sawmill), were situated two and a half miles above Van Buren on a 400-acre site, connected to the B&A. Managed by A. W. Brown (and therefore known as "Le Moulin à Brown," the plant began operating in 1904 and was, according to the Maine Bureau of Industrial and Labor Statistics, one of the

largest in New England. The shingle mill had a capacity of one million shingles a week and could produce 50 million shingles per year.[4] The mill could also produce 20 million feet of long lumber per year. During its first year of production, the plant employed 175 workers. The St. John Lumber Company purchased some timberland on the Little and Big Black Rivers. Most of the cutting was done under contract by William Cunliffe, Jr., and Joseph T. Michaud. The company's operations provided work for 1,500 men.

B. The Fish River Area

1. The Fort Kent Mill Company.

The founding of the larger Fort Kent concerns also coincided with the arrival of a railway line. During the 1891–92 winter season, four entrepreneurs from Limerick (C. C. Bradbury, T. M. Bradbury, C. F. Bradbury, L. F. Bradbury), and John Mullen founded the Fort Kent Mill Company and store (see Table 18-1). Over the years the company became, as a local promoter noted in 1908, "the leading industrial establishment in Fort Kent and vicinity."[5] The plant combined a water-operated sawmill equipped with a rotary saw, with a shingle-, grist-, and carding mill located along the B&A line and Fort Kent's main highway. The Maine Bureau of Industrial and Labor Statistics noted that the company could produce up to 25 million shingles, 1.5 million feet of long lumber, and 4 million feet of spruce and cedar timber per year. The gristmill was capable of processing 400 bushels of buckwheat daily. During the summer months, the company employed about 60 people in the mills and another 120 to 140 in the lumber camps. The company also operated a general merchandise store and doubled as a shipper. For example, in 1908, the company shipped large amounts of hay and grain, as well as more than 30,000 barrels of potatoes. The company sold a wide range of goods to local farmers, such as fertilizers,

seeds, carriages, sleighs, and farm and horse equipment. The partners were also shareholders in the Fort Kent Trust Company and provided loans to local farmers and entrepreneurs.

2. *Eagle Lake and Wallagrass*

The construction of the Fish River branch of the B&A led to the opening of several businesses processing wood products in Eagle Lake and Wallagrass. The most important was the Fish River Lumber Company (headquartered in Augusta, Maine), which ran steam-operated plants at Eagle Lake, Winterville, and Hill Plantations; this company employed 275 workers in its various plants, 600 to 700 workers in the woods, and 240 horses. The Eagle Lake plants were also heavily capitalized. By 1911, the Fish River Lumber Company had been joined by the Eagle Lake Mill Company and the Birch River Lumber Company, as well as the Standard Wood Company, a supplier of kindling wood. Further up the St. John River, Stadig &

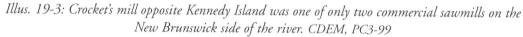

Illus. 19-3: Crocket's mill opposite Kennedy Island was one of only two commercial sawmills on the New Brunswick side of the river. CDEM, PC3-99

The Land in Between

Quincy opened a lumber and shingle mill at St. Francis in 1904. Oleg Stadig was already operating a sawmill at Connors with someone called McLean in 1902.

C. New Brunswick

Information about lumber mills on the New Brunswick side of the river is fragmented. There were two lumber manufacturers: Crockett's mill which operated a mill at Clair and the James Murchie & Son Company of Calais, Maine, which opened a sawmill at Edmundston in 1888. James Murchie & Son laid the groundwork for an industry that is still in operation today (see Section IV below). It employed a total of seventy-five workers. The mill also did custom work for local landowners. Although information about this mill is scarce, it is easy to see that its opening coincided with the construction of the Temiscouata Railway—which pro-

moters hoped would facilitate the transportation of logs to processing sites. Murchie sold the mill to a Canadian manufacturer in 1911, the year the Pike Act lapsed. Shortly after the completion of the Temiscouata Railway to Connors, Robert Connors built a steam-operated shingle mill at Connors (see Sidebar 19-1).

D. The Témiscouata and the Québec–Maine Border

Mills were few and far between in Madawaska County, but there were several large lumber mills around Témiscouata Lake and along the Transcontinental Railway line. This was the consequence of Québec's policies. Until 1910, Québec taxed logs cut on public land and exported; after 1910, it required the processing of these logs in the province. Logs cut on the Québec side of the upper St. John could be diverted away from the St. John

Illus. 19-4: The Murchie Mill was built in Edmundston by Calais (ME) entrepreneur James Murchie. This view is from 1886. Murchie sold the mill to Fraser in 1911, who demolished it to erect a pulp mill. CDEM, PC3-45

Illus. 19-5: The Connors Hotel. CDEM, PA1-62

Sidebar 19-1: Robert Connors

Robert Connors, born in Pictou, Nova Scotia, on December 18, 1829, moved to the upper St. Francis River as a boy. (A man by the same name appears fleetingly in merchant John Emmerson's record books in the 1850s; he was a trader in homespun pants and shirts.) Over the next two decades, Connors became an important lumber operator and merchant with connections in Saint John. He opened a general store at the place later named "Connors" in his honor. The store served as a railway depot at the end of the Temiscouata Railway

Illus. 19-6: Robert Connors. Chad Pelletier's Collection

line. In his *History of Aroostook,* Wiggin describes him as the largest lumber operator on the upper St. John. This was not an exaggeration. At the end of the 1876 logging season, Robert Connors sold $84,470 worth of pine and spruce (17 million feet spruce logs, 775,000 feet pine logs, and 467 tons of pine ton timber) to various lower St. John River merchants. Connors also built a nondenominational church in his community. He died in Hot Springs, Arkansas, on March 9, 1895. His heirs sold the store to Georges Bernier, who was still running the establishment at the beginning of the twentieth century.

When the Temiscouata Railway arrived at his doorstep, Connors took immediate advantage of the opportunity and built a shingle mill. Madawaska shingles, which enjoyed an excellent reputation in American markets, sold well despite being more expensive than others produced closer to the buyers. Connors bought a mill at Grand Falls in April 1892 from a Mrs. Brown for $1,500. He then moved all the machinery to Connors and added a boiler, rotary saw, and wood splitter. The mill, which cost $7,350 to build, was constructed over the summer and fall and began operations the following spring. Connors sold some shingles locally (a local church, for example, bought $63.45 worth of shingles). He shipped most of his shingles, however, across New England. W. S. Blanchard from Boston bought some of them for resale and charged a 5 percent commission. Connors' bookkeeping is confusing; however, it seems that in the first year, he sold about $8,000 worth of shingles, with expenses eating half his profits. The second year, he sold $14,000 worth of shingles. He could have, therefore, quickly paid off the mill.

Sources: PANB, Record Books of Robert Connors, Book B. Robert Connors Account, 1875–76; Book 2, Mill Construction Account, 1892–93; Shingle Accounts. Microfilm reel F. (Original at the Pioneer Historical Connors Museum, Connors, N.B.; Wiggin (1922).

River after the completion of the Transcontinental and the extension of the Québec Central to Lac Frontière. In addition, sawmills producing dimension lumber began springing up along the border. By 1915, half of the sawmills in Côte-du-Sud were located in the formerly disputed territory, namely at Lac Frontière, Saint-Pamphile, Sainte-Perpétue, and Lac de l'Est. Mill owners on the Québec side of the line also relied on the Maine forest for supplies: the mills at Sully and Lac Bleu processed logs cut along the uppermost St. John and Allagash Rivers. Villages gathered around the mills, and villagers even cleared some land, but farming was never more than a side activity: these were logging communities. The same pattern emerged around Témiscouata Lake, where there were several mills, including Donald Fraser's

Illus. 19-7: Alexis Morneault's sawmill at Grand Isle in 1906. Morneault manufactured shingles and other wood products. Note the barrels of water on the roof as fire protection. Madawaska Historical Society

The Growth of Lumber Manufacturing and the Emergence of Pulp and Paper

enormous mill at Cabano. Lumber manufactured in these mills could be shipped to Quebec City via the Temiscouata Railway. Settlers also cleared farms in the vicinity, but as in the Côte-du-Sud backcountry, agriculture remained marginal.

E. Custom Millers

In addition to these lumber manufacturers, there were still several custom sawmills catering to Valley residents' needs. Contrary to the large lumber mills, they were more or less evenly distributed on both sides of the river (eight on the New Brunswick side in 1902; nine on the American side in 1900). This division between commercial lumber mills for the outside market and custom mills for the local market was not new. Neither was the fact that custom millers were local people, while lumber manufacturers were outsiders. Hammond, a local man producing for outside markets was, again, an exception. A new trend, however, was the fact that lumber manufacturers remained outsiders; before 1870, they would have taken up residence in the Valley. Those were the men the nineteenth century called "capitalists"—that is, men with capital to invest. It mattered little to them where they invested their money and their connection to the place or places where they did business was much more tenuous than that of their forefathers.

III.   THE ROLE OF THE STATE

Government policies were responsible for the lack of lumber mills in Madawaska County—and their proliferation in Northern Aroostook and Temiscouata Counties. On the one hand, the United States taxed imported manufactured products but not raw material. Canadian logs thus entered duty free but not Canadian lumber. On the other hand, Québec adopted policies to force the manufacturing of lumber from its logs on its soil: that is, Québec taxed saw logs cut and exported from public land until 1910, after which it banned exportation altogether. New Brunswick passed a similar law in 1911. These laws, however, could not keep Madawaska logs in the county because the New Brunswick Railway—not the province—owned the timberland in the county. Québec policies regarding its public resources, American tariffs, and capitalist developments had turned the two banks of the river into two, if not three, bordered lands, even though cross-border personal and business links remained numerous.

IV.   PULP AND PAPER

By the 1880s, the pulp and paper industry was expanding rapidly throughout North America. The spectacular growth of the printed press, especially inexpensive or "penny" newspapers, was one of the reasons for this industry's rise. In the United States alone, 29 million copies of 2,000 different newspapers went to press every day. These penny newspapers were made possible by the invention of wood-based paper, which used material that hitherto had been wasted or had no commercial value (for example, smaller or gnarled trees). Lumbermen could thus comb through areas that had been stripped of their merchantable timber and find wood suitable for this use.

A. Maine

This new industry developed rapidly in Maine, thanks to an abundant water supply, rapid forest regeneration, and nearby markets. In 1899, there were fifty-eight paper mills in the state, but none in the Valley. By 1907, the counties with the most paper mills were Androscoggin, Kennebec, and Penobscot; there was only one mill in Aroostook (in Millinocket). Although some argued that the county could benefit from the industry, others feared that large paper mills would endanger the local lumber industry because of their large wood consumption. However, if St. John River wood was not turned into paper in the Valley, it would be turned into paper elsewhere. In 1914, the Great Northern Paper Company, the largest pulp and paper firm in Maine, contracted with Madawaskayan companies to provide it with wood. The Fish River Supply Company provided it with 1,500 to 2,000 cords of wood and the Fort Kent Mill Company with 3,000 to 3,500 cords.

In 1916, Great Northern bought land along the Fish and upper St. John Rivers. The company now owned some of the best timberland in the state, which it used it to supply its mills down south. That same year, a pulp mill, the Aroostook Pulp and Paper Company, opened at Van Buren; it failed and had to shut down two years later. It opened again in 1920 but failed within a few years. In Maine, the industry was, therefore, limited to the southern counties. Richard W. Judd noted that since the late nineteenth century, Aroostook journalists claimed that the region held "unparalleled advantages" for the pulp and paper industry, and they hoped that it would soon become the center of the industry in Maine. Unfortunately, "the dream was not to be realized...."[6]

B. New Brunswick

The story was different on the New Brunswick side of the border thanks to Donald Fraser. Thirty-year-old Donald Fraser arrived in New Brunswick in 1873 as part of a group of 600 Scottish immigrants who settled in Kincardine (Victoria County). As soon as he arrived, Fraser got involved in the forest industry. In 1874, he installed a sawpit on his farm, hired two men, and began producing around 500 feet of boards per day. In 1892, he founded the Donald Fraser & Sons Company, which invested in various wood-related enterprises.

In 1905, along with Alec Matheson and Andrew

Illus. 19-8: The Fraser Mill under construction in 1917. CDEM, PC2-56

Brebner, he formed Fraser & Matheson Lumber. A year later, the company purchased shares in the Tobique Manufacturing Company Limited, which had a sawmill at Plaster Rock. It seems that Fraser noticed rather quickly the economic potential of the region. In 1911, he formed Fraser Limited and purchased the James Murchie & Son Company sawmill in Edmundston. The other Fraser-owned companies continued to operate independently of each other in different parts of the province. Fraser died at the age of seventy-four in 1916. A year later, Fraser's son, Archibald, regrouped all the Fraser holdings under the name Fraser Companies Ltd.

In 1917, Fraser Companies closed the Murchie mill and built a pulp factory on the site. The factory cost a total of $4 million and could produce 120 tons of pulp per day. The choice of Edmundston for such a factory was a logical one, given its position at the confluence of the Madawaska and St. John Rivers and proximity to some of the province's best forests. Fraser Companies also acquired a hydroelectric plant (part of the James Murchie sawmill). Edmundston was also an important railway center on the Canadian National (formerly National Transcontinental), Canadian Pacific, and Temiscouata railway lines. Thus, it was easy to bring logs to Edmundston.

Hardy S. Fergusson & Company of New York City began construction of the factory in late 1917. Construction was very quick, since the factory was already producing pulp by June 1918. The plant was huge by regional standards:

> The plant, which will have the capacity of 120 tons a day, covers about six acres. It will consist of a storage room, machine room, screen room, blow pit room, digester house and plant boiler room, turbine room, wood room, machine shop, and hydraulic power plant. In the machine room there will be two drying machines. The digester house will contain four digesters each 17 feet in diameter and 56 feet high...in the boiler room there will be six 500-hp boilers; in the turbine room there will be two

1,000-kw electric generators directly connected to steam turbines; and in the hydraulic power plant there will be two 1,000-kw electric generators directly connected to vertical-shaft water wheels.[7]

No other industry can claim to have had as much of an impact on the region as the Fraser Company. As Nicole Lang noted, it played a key role in Edmundston's social and economic growth by providing hundreds of jobs. The management jobs were limited to Anglophones from outside the region—not very surprising, since Fraser Limited's offices had been located in Fredericton before moving to Edmundston. Most workers, however, were Francophones. They came from all over the region: some had worked at the Murchie mill; others had worked for another branch of the company at Baker Brook; while others had migrated to Edmundston in the hopes of finding a stable job. After World War I, the company hired returning veterans. In 1923, Fraser Limited opened a second factory in the town of Madawaska (Maine). The factory fabricated paper from the pulp manufactured in Edmundston. The pulp was sent across the river through a pipeline located under the International Bridge connecting both cities.

As large lumber mills opened along the upper St. John River and cutting intensified along the Allagash River and uppermost St. John River, conflicts erupted—first between the St. John and Penobscot River interests, then between Valley producers (both American and Canadian) and large mill operators in Saint John (mostly Americans), and finally among upper St. John Valley producers themselves. At stake was who controlled access to the logs and water.

THE VAN BUREN WAR AND THE ST. JOHN RIVER
INTERNATIONAL COMMISSION

A. Conflicts

1. St. John versus Penobscot Basin.

The point of contention here was the usual one: who had rights to the water flowing into the Allagash. In 1903, when Bangor lumber interests asked the state legislature to incorporate the East Branch Improvement Company to improve navigation on the East Branch of the Penobscot, Aroostook County and St. John River lumber interests were up in arms. The charter would have allowed the company to rebuild the dam on Churchill Lake, which, in turn, would have diverted waters away from the Allagash and into the Penobscot. Opponents argued that the project violated the Webster–Ashburton Treaty, which prohibited obstacles to free navigation on the St. John and its tributaries. The bill of incorporation was passed, but with an amendment forbidding the construction of a dam on Churchill Lake. And in 1905, Allagash lumbermen blew up the Chamberlain Dam, as they had in the 1840s—but this time they used dynamite.

2. Tidewater versus Headwater.

The alliance among producers up and down the St. John River lasted as long as they opposed Penobscot basin rivals. In 1903, American and Canadian lumbermen established the St. John River Dam Company, to build a sluice five miles upriver from Fort Kent, at Winding Ledge. The sluice would have created a sorting pond for logs; in addition, local people believed it would encourage the construction of additional mills, and perhaps even produce electricity along their stretch of river. But more lumber mills upriver was the last thing St. John mill owners wanted. They, too, claimed the project violated the Webster–Ashburton Treaty, and their delegation in Ottawa managed to scuttle the project (because half of the structure would have been in Canadian waters, Canada had to approve it).

3. Log Drivers versus Manufacturers.

Navigation along the river also needed improvement given the massive log drives required by the Van Buren mills. Relying on the traditional drive was impractical for the companies, and they began to sort the logs at Van Buren at their own boom and at their own expense. During the 1903–04 season, the Van Buren and St. John lumber companies used the string of islands above Van Buren to create a sorting pond above their mills. The Van Buren booms, however, trapped all logs floating downriver, and the log-driving associations complained that they brought the drives to an almost complete halt while workers from the two lumbers mills picked their own logs from the mass. They claimed the booms were an obstacle to free navigation and, therefore, illegal under the treaty. In 1909, Levi Pond of the Madawaska Log Driving Association, dynamited one of the two booms and tried to destroy the other by similar means. This incident came to be referred to as the "Van Buren War."

B. The International St. John River Commission

By then, it had become obvious that the free navigation guaranteed by the treaty would be unenforceable without improvements to the river to accommodate an increased volume of logs. These improvements included clearing channels, storing water for use during the dry season, and sorting booms—but under its current provisions, the treaty deemed all these improvements "obstacles." It was also obvious that the various groups involved in exploiting the forest resources of the upper St. John were using the treaty as a means of defeating their business rivals.

In 1906, the Canadian and American governments established the International St. John River Commission to investigate issues relating to log drives, water conservation, and waterpower. It was not able to meet until 1909 and produced its final report in 1915. Alexander P. Barnhill and John Keeffe of Saint John represented Canada; Peter C. Keegan of Van Buren and John Murchie of Calais represented the United States. The commission suggested two things: the creation of a Canadian-American corporation to resolve problems arising from the use of the St. John, and measures to increase water storage and improve channels. By then, however, the Pike Act had lapsed; the St. John milling industry was in decline; there was a world war going on; and the problems that had led to the creation of the commission had either lessened or were no longer very important. The commission's main legacy rests in the thousands of pages of detailed studies and testimony it produced and the Van Buren Bridge, whose construction it authorized.

Conclusion

The railroads led to a dramatic shift in the nature of the upper St. John forest industry. As long as the river remained the only way to transport products to markets, production consisted mostly of ton timber and saw logs. Other products had to be portaged around the Grand Falls, thereby escalating transportation costs. Trains, however, allowed for the fast and inexpensive shipment of any kind of wood products. Some entrepreneurs were prompt at taking advantage of this opportunity, and mills sprung up near railroad tracks. Those mills were usually large, heavily capitalized, and were beyond the means of the local people who continued to operate custom sawmills.

Government policies also shaped the manufacture of wood products in the Valley. Saw logs had floated down the St. John to be turned into lumber by large American-owned mills in Saint John because the Webster–Ashburton Treaty guaranteed free navigation for natural products on the river and legislation and treaties allowed free re-entry of Aroostook County wood products into the United

States. Kennebec and Penobscot lumbermen had always denounced these arrangements, saying they only benefited their competitors. Since they could not change the law, they began diverting St. John water away from them. Milling the wood in Aroostook County and shipping it directly south bypassed Saint John lumber merchants, allowing Penobscot and Kennebec interests to penetrate the upper St. John. All sides used the venerable Webster–Ashburton Treaty to try to thwart their competitors. The conflicts cut across national lines: Americans in Saint John were fighting Americans in both Bangor and the upper St. John, and Canadians were siding with the Americans in northern Aroostook.

The two camps may have ignored nationalities, but the boundary no longer ignored them. Congress passed increasingly high tariffs to block the importation of manufactured goods, but coupled those measures with low tariffs on raw material. This resulted in the construction of lumber mills only along the American side of the river. The situation was different for pulp and paper. The American market absorbed enormous amounts of paper, and the newspaper lobby in Washington was very powerful. When Québec (and Ontario) taxed and then prohibited the export of logs cut on Crown land, not only were the Americans unable to force them to change their policies, but Congress had to lower the duties on pulp and paper imported into the United States. New Brunswick benefited from Ontario and Québec's policies, and the New Brunswick side of the Valley acquired its own pulp mill. The transformation of the transportation and forest industries, coupled with different Canadian and American tariff policies, had succeeded where institutions had failed and made bordered lands of the two sides of the valley.

ENDNOTES

1. *Whig,* July 7, 1880, quoted in Judd's *Aroostook,* 99.

2. Maine Bureau of Industrial and Labor Statistics, *Thirteenth Annual Report (1899),* Augusta, ME: Kennebec Journal Printing, 1900, 71.

3. Short lumber consists of pieces shorter than 3 feet.

4. Maine Bureau of Industrial and Labor Statistics, *Eighteenth Annual Report (1904),* Augusta, ME: *Kennebec Journal* Printing, 1905.

5. Grindle, *"Glimpses of History,* [Mills at Fort Kent]," (1975).

6. Judd, *Aroostook,* 196.

7. *Paper Trade Journal,* September, 20 1917, quoted in Lang, "L'impact d'une industrie...," 24.

FURTHER READINGS

Dubay, Guy. *Chez Nous: The St. John Valley.* 1983: 35–54.

Grindle, Roger L. *Milestones from the St. John Valley.* 1977.

Acadian Culture in Maine, "Maine Acadians and the Land," Section 3, http://acim.umfk.maine.edu.

Judd, Richard W. *Aroostook: A Century of Logging in Northern Maine,* 1989.

Pelletier, Martine A. and Monica Dionne Ferretti. *Van Buren, Maine, History.* 1979.

Ouellette, Linda and Harold Underhill. "The Corriveau Mill: When carding cost six cents a pound." *Echoes: The Northern Maine Journal,* 58 (October–December 2002): 9–10.

SOURCES

Smith (1962) and Judd (1989) remain the obligatory starting point of any study of logging in northern Maine. Grindle (1977) contributes additional information about the Valley. Contemporary descriptions can be found in the 1899 *Thirteenth Annual Report* and especially in the 1904 *Eighteenth Annual Report* of the Maine Bureau of Industrial and Labor Statistics.

There is, unfortunately, hardly any printed material about the forest industry in New Brunswick Madawaska, besides "Évolution de l'industrie forestière en Marévie...." (1981). For the Témiscouata region, see Blanchard (1936), and for the Maine-Québec border, see Laberge, et. al. (1993). Information on the pulp and paper industry can be found in "Magnitude and Importance of Pulp and Paper Industry," published in the *Saint John Globe* (available at the New Brunswick Museum Archives & Research Library, F 201-2, Ganong Collection). Lang has done extensive work on the Fraser Company (1987). For information on the International St. John River Commission, see Stevens (1970).

20

THE NEW AGRICULTURE: POTATO CROPS AND DAIRY FARMS

It would seem logical that there would be more information about recent times than the past. In the case of Madawaska agriculture, the opposite is true: we have less data about agriculture after 1870 than before. The agricultural schedules of the Canadian censuses (information that we have used for the previous period) were destroyed in the 1960s without being microfilmed. Post-1880 schedules from American agricultural censuses have similarly disappeared. Now, historians must rely on aggregate tables published by the various census bureaus. In Canada, some, but not all, tables are at the parish/town level; in the other cases, however, the census unit is not Madawaska County, but Victoria-Madawaska combined. In the United States, the tables are compiled at county or even state levels. Madawaska data are lumped together with data from central Aroostook County and the Houlton region to produce the reported figures. This loss of data makes it difficult to determine whether the Madawaska region was similar or different from the

rest of Aroostook County or northwestern New Brunswick, and if the two sides of the river were similar or different from each other. The same problem emerges in the detailed documents produced by Maine state agencies, which provide information at the county level; when they do focus on a subregion, it is never on the Valley, which might as well not exist.

Late nineteenth- and early twentieth-century sources, therefore, do not provide us with a clear picture of Madawaska agriculture. Nor do they provide information about what individual farmers were doing. This is particularly unfortunate because both the Panic of 1873 and the emergence of railroads had a significant impact on northern Aroostook County farming. Did Madawaska farmers respond to access to new markets like their counterparts in central and southern Aroostook County or on the mid St. John River? The existing evidence suggests that by the turn of the century, American and New Brunswick Madawaska may have begun to diverge. Mainers probably turned to potato production for American markets, although not to the same extent as their colleagues in the southern part of Aroostook

Illus. 19-1: This unexpectedly candid picture was probably a "trial picture"- the photographer's back-room on wheels is even visible in the corner. It is very unusual to find photographs of people at everyday tasks, as here (women doing the laundry, a man doing mundane yard work). Ovilla Daigle's farm,
Courtesy St Francis Historical Society

County, whereas New Brunswickers appear to have continued to practice mixed farming for regional, national, and imperial markets. Moreover, potatoes were not always shipped as is; some of the crop was transformed into starch near the production sites before being shipped out. The potato boom was accompanied by the beginnings of a processing industry. Farmers on both sides of the river also began participating in the new dairy industry, but under different circumstances and with different outcomes.

I. THE "POTATO REVOLUTION"

A. Aroostook County

Historic accounts of Aroostook County have tended to depict 1894 as the "real" beginning of its history: before 1894, Aroostook County was stagnant, but after that year, it was finally able to achieve its enormous agricultural potential. The year 1894 is, of course, when the Bangor and Aroostook Railway began operations. The market the farmers seized was the one for potatoes and potato starch. The soil of eastern Aroostook County, Carleton and Victoria Counties in New Brunswick, and the Madawaska region was perfectly adapted for potato production—a fact the Maine Board of Agriculture had been advertising for many years. The number of farms did not increase much after the arrival of the B&A. What increased was the amount of land under cultivation and, the quantities of potatoes grown. This production had reached dizzying heights by 1910 (see Table 20-2 and Appendix H-3).

Aroostook County potatoes and potato seeds enjoyed a very good reputation; indeed, southern farmers used these seeds for their own crops. Aroostook potato seeds were sold in North and South Carolina, Georgia, Texas, Ohio, Michigan, and Minnesota. Potatoes were sold for consumption mostly in the New England and Great Lakes states. Potatoes became the main crop in Aroostook County, which eventually became the state's leading potato producer. At this time, average state potato production was around 225 bushels per acre. In Aroostook County, average production was 275

Table 20-1: Shipments Across the Two Branches of the New Brunswick Railway

	Bushels of Potatoes	Casks of Starch	Tons of Hay	Shingles
Houlton Branch				
1883	138,400	2,760	3,076	41,490,000
1886	179,718	3,260	2,958	55,949,000
Presque Isle Branch				
1883	62,250	5,052	329	28,000,000
1886	35,080	6,494	1,487	26,526,000

Source: Maine Bureau of Industrial and Labor Statistics, 1887: 38.

---

bushels per acre, and in the Aroostook Valley that figure reached 300 bushels per acre. According to the United States Department of Agriculture, Aroostook County was then producing 16 percent (or one-sixth) of the entire commercial potato crop of the United States. This turned Maine into one of the United States' major potato-producing regions. By 1900, the state produced 2 million bushels, and by 1918, annual production had grown to 18 million bushels. Maine state officials even worried that farmers were neglecting other crops. In 1904, the state Bureau of Industrial and Labor Statistics sounded the alarm:

> The county is one of the best agricultural sections of New England, and all the cereals, except for corn, can be raised in abundance.... While more grain is raised in Aroostook than in any other part of Maine, so profitable has been the raising of potatoes in late years that the raising of grain seems to be only of secondary consideration.[1]

This narrative, however, is not entirely accurate. The B&A did not bring commercial potato production to Aroostook County, and farmers continued growing other commercial crops. The census data show that oats and hay production continued to grow. It was only the other crops and animal products that declined. The lumber camps' demand for fodder did not decline, but increased, and farmers continued trying to satisfy that need. But the forest industry was an unpredictable market. The economic depression of the 1870s, which was triggered by failures in the timber and lumber industries, had forced farmers to look for alternative and more reliable markets. Many turned to potato production, which had been quite successful in other parts of the state. Until the arrival of railroads, the problem was how to ship these crops to market. Prior to the building of the B&A, the only way to ship goods was through New Brunswick, a route producers used often (see Table 20-1). Average potato production increased five-fold between the 1870s and 1880s due to the building of the New Brunswick Railway (see Table 20-2). Although the B&A considerably reduced freight charges, it merely accelerated a movement that was well under way.

Farmers' massive production, combined with the usually high price of potatoes ($3 per bushel on the average) should have brought prosperity to Aroostook County farmers. The Maine Bureau of Industrial and Labor Statistics noted in its 1904 report, "wealth came in bounteous measure to the Aroostook farmers as the outcome of the high prices prevailing during the year...."[2] Every county in the state, except Aroostook and two other counties, saw farm values decrease in the late 1800s. In Aroostook County, farm values increased by 48.1 percent during that period.[3]

Table 20-2: Aroostook County Agricultural Production: 1860–1910

	Number of Farms	Improved Acreage per Farm	Bushels of Potatoes	Bushels of Potatoes per Farm	Bushels of Oats per Farm	Tons of Hay per Farm
1860	1938	64	411,630	212	217	20.3
1870	3209	41	380,701	119	166	15.0
1880	5802	47	2,248,594	388	108	13.8
1890	6180	51	2,746,765	444	183	16.7
1900	6938	56	6,466,189	932	261	19.2
1910	7289	61	17,514,491	2,403	349	21.0

Illus. 20-2, above: A turn-of-the-century farm implement: a cradle.
Illus. 20-3, above right: A turn of the century farm implement: a locally made plough.
Illus 20-4, lower right: A turn-of-the-century farm implement: a locally made harrow.
All at the Tante Blanche Museum, Madawaska, Maine. Photographs by B. Craig

The potato was, however, a mixed blessing. By the end of the century, it was a speculative crop, and its prices fluctuated violently from year to year and even from month to month. The United States price index numbers for potatoes ranged from 43 in 1895 to 149 in 1881, but the price index did not reflect the size of the crop. Rather, it reflected what the buyers and sellers thought the demand was going to be. The potato market, in other words, was as unpredictable and unstable as the ton timber market had been, but this time, the ones bearing the brunt of the market's volatility were local farmers, not large-scale outside entrepreneurs. As the county's high yields could not be achieved without the extensive use of fertilizers, low prices could spell serious trouble for producers. According to the 1910 Census, 50 percent of Aroostook County farms were mortgaged, and the average mortgage amounted to 21.5 percent of the value of the land and buildings. The situation went from bad to worse. By 1924, 54 percent of Aroostook County farms were mortgaged (compared to 23 percent statewide), and the average mortgage represented 43 percent of the value of the land and buildings.[4] (The figures for 1910 exist only at county level; we do not know how many farms in the Valley were mortgaged.) This means the alleged prosperity from the potato industry may have been more apparent than real or, at least, unevenly distributed.

Sidebar 20-1: Pierre A. Cyr

Who was Pierre Cyr, the gentleman whose account book allows us to view the impact of the railroad on potato shipping (see Table 20-3)?

Pierre (*à Alexis à Paul à Paul*) was born in 1872 in Grand Isle, Maine. He died in Boston, where he was receiving medical treatment, in 1956. His great-grandparents, Paul Cyr and Charlotte Ayotte, were among the first French settlers in the St. John Valley. Their son, Paul, married Salomé, daughter of Firmin Thibodeau and François Thibodeau's sister (see Chapters 7, 8, and 21 for other family members). Thibodeau gave them a farm. By 1850, Paul was among the richest farmers in the Valley. He became a state representative (1852–59) like François Thibodeau. Paul sent his sons to Houlton Academy, then a secondary school. His son, Alexis (1836–87), finished his education at Worcester College, a Catholic institution in Massachusetts. He married Julie Anne Sirois. He, too, was a wealthy farmer, according to the 1870 Census. In 1880, he was postmaster at Grand Isle, and he was elected state representative in 1884, 1885, and 1886. Unlike his father and grandfather, Pierre received a French education: he attended St. Joseph College in Memramcook in the 1880s.

Pierre became a potato broker and shipper. His account book clearly illustrates the impact of the railroad on the potato trade. Before 1909, he was already shipping potatoes to Rhode Island and Massachusetts, but first he transported them across the river to St. Basile's station. After the building of the B&A, the potatoes were loaded at Parent and Lille sidings, and then traveled a long way, for instance, to Texas. Besides potatoes, Cyr also shipped considerable quantities of hay, which was in great demand in cities since all vehicles (except for a limited number of street cars) were still pulled by horse.

Most of Pierre's children either became, or married, professionals. Some followed the family tradition and got involved in politics. His son Patrick became a potato broker; another son, Amand, became a priest, as well as superintendent for all the Catholic schools in the Diocese of Portland; a third son, Edward, became a state senator. Two daughters entered religious orders and probably taught. Another daughter, Rose, married Lawrence Violette, author of *How the Acadians Came to Maine* and a school superintendent; a second daughter, Josephine, married Albert Cyr, also a school superintendent. One of their first cousins, Leo E. Cyr, son of Louis A. Cyr, went into the diplomatic service and became the United States ambassador to Rwanda under President Lyndon Johnson.

Source: Information courtesy of Guy Dubay.

Table 20-3: Pierre Cyr's Potato Shipments from Grand Isle (in bushels)

Season	Maine	Out of State	Not Specified	Total
1905–06	7,472	5,543	3,891	16,906
1906–07	5,409	…	1,548	6,958
1907–08	13,812	1,650	…	15,462
1908–09	10,626	…	…	10,626
1909–10	10,370	5,885	…	16,255
1910–11	13,429	18,376	5,272	37,076
1911–12	2,893	3,500	22,072	28,465
1912–13	14,823	9,503	25,084	49,409
Grand Total	78,833	44,457	64,197	187,486

Source: Pierre Cyr's Account Book (communicated by G. Dubay).

B. Potato Production in American Madawaska

Large-scale potato production seems to have taken longer to appear in the St. John Valley. The fragmentary sources available suggest that here, too, significant increases in production were linked to the opening of railroad lines connecting the Valley to external markets. In 1879, Northern Aroostook shipped 30,000 bushels of potatoes and 1,300 tons of starch (the equivalent of about 325,000 bushels of potatoes) through New Brunswick. Potato production in Fort Kent increased from 5,000 bushels prior to the railway's arrival to 100,000 bushels a year afterterwards. State officials believed that the Valley was as suitable for potato production as the rest of Aroostook County, and the state's Bureau of Industrial and Labor Statistics was convinced all the region needed to achieve its full potential was an American railroad line. For instance, it stated in its 1909 report, "The building of the new branch of railroad along this valley is opening up a large area of good potato land."[5] Pierre Cyr (see Sidebar 20-1)

from Grand Isle was already shipping potatoes and hay when the B&A's extension was built through Grand Isle. The volume of potatoes he shipped out certainly increased after that (see Table 20-3). Pierre Cyr's largest out-of-state purchasers lived in Boston, Massachusetts; Providence, Rhode Island; and Houston, Texas.

Bureau statistics indicate that as late as 1903, potato production in the upper St. John Valley may have been much lower than in neighboring regions. Potato storage capacity was certainly much lower than in the rest of Aroostook County. In 1903, there were eighteen potato houses in Caribou, with enough capacity for 199,000 bushels of potatoes. In Easton, there were eleven houses with enough capacity for 160,000 bushels. In the Valley (Fort Kent and Van Buren), however, there were only eight houses and only enough capacity for 79,500 bushels. (This meant that the Valley owned only 4.5 percent of the 201 potato houses in Aroostook County, and had 3.5 percent of the total capacity.) The 1903 Aroostook County crop shipments confirm this dis-

Illus. 20-5: A comfortable farming couple from St. Francis, Maine: Elie Thibodeau(1828–1908) and his wife Seconde Jalbert (1829–1910), circa 1875. He is the "Olie" who antagonized Shepard Cary in Chapter 11. Seconde is dressed in her best clothes for the picture, and her dress and hat reflect the fashion of the time. Elie is wearing a very crisp white shirt, clearly cut from factory-made fabric, a small bow tie, and thick homespun pants. His hairstyle and full beard are also typical of the period. By 1875, farm people in the plantations could afford to follow fashion and dress in factory-made material.
St. Francis Historical Society

crepancy between the Valley and the rest of Aroostook County. Houlton and Caribou were Aroostook County's most productive regions. That year, Caribou shipped 1,280 train cars of potatoes (704,000 bushels) and Houlton, 1,032 cars (567,600 bushels). By comparison, Van Buren shipped only 133 cars (73,150 bushels) and Fort Kent shipped only 72 cars (39,600 bushels).[6]

These figures suggest that, as in the rest of the county, large-scale potato producers depended on railroads to ship their produce out of the region. Moreover, it seems that the Canadian lines were less effective than the American ones in stimulating production. In the long run, potato production does not seem to have benefited farmers in American Madawaska more than farmers elsewhere in Aroostook County. In 1924, 52 percent of the farms on the American side of the Valley were mortgaged, to a slighter extent than in the rest of the county (40 percent of the value of land and buildings instead of 43 percent).

C. Starch Production

Starch was in great demand in the industrial centers of New England, as it was used to glaze cotton yarn to facilitate weaving (a process called "sizing") and to stiffen and give sheen to cotton fabric, especially cheap material. Starch, which can be made from grated potatoes, was a good way of turning an easily bruised, frost-sensitive, and bulky commodity into a more profitable and easy-to-transport product. As a result, starch factories followed the railway line as it was built across the boundary line. The first factory was built in New Limerick in 1871 and the second in Caribou in 1872. In 1904, there were sixty-six starch factories in Maine and sixty-four in Aroostook County; the majority were in the central and southern part of the county near Presque Isle and Houlton. Seven were in the St. John Valley at Fort Kent, Frenchville, Grand Isle, Hamlin, Madawaska, St. Agatha, and Van Buren. They represented 11 percent of Aroostook County's starch factories (see Appendix I-4).

Starch factories were often combined with shingle mills, since they used the same machinery at different times of the year. On average, starch factories operated forty days a year and employed about nine people. Business depended upon the price of potatoes. When potatoes prices were high, farmers took them directly to potato shippers; when prices were

Sidebar 20-2: Making Starch in St. Agatha

The St. Agatha Starch Company was founded in May 1904; it had eighty-six shareholders who agreed to haul all their starch potatoes to the company factory at the going rate (with the exception of those who lived too far to make this practical). Profits and losses were proportional to the number of shares one held. The three larger shareholders (who held fifty $10 shares apiece) were the parish priest, Father Gory; Michel Ouellette; and Israel Ouellette. Israel (1857–1920) was a lumberman and shingle-mill owner; Michel (1881–1948) was his son. According to a report issued by the Maine Bureau of Industrial and Labor Statistics, a mill worth $4,500 and employing ten men opened in St. Agatha in 1904. It was probably the St. Agatha Starch Company. The company was still in operation ten years later.

The largest shareholder, Israel Ouellette, was already listed as the owner of a starch factory and a shingle mill in St. Agatha in 1900. Abraham Bouchard built the first starch factory in St. Agatha, but he did not have enough money to complete it and borrowed half the required capital, or $3,000, from Thomas W. E. Egery and Daniel Hinckley, co-owners of Egery and Hinckley, an iron manufacturing company in Bangor. Egery and Hinckley were also creditors of the bankrupt E&NA and had sued settlers living on former railroad land. The factory, worth $6,000, opened in 1884; it employed twenty-five men, which was considerably more than the average nine to ten men usually employed by this type of business. By 1886, Bouchard was facing foreclosure and died a short time afterwards.

The property passed into the hands of Michel Michaud and his brother-in-law, Israel Ouellette. In 1898, they borrowed $2,000 from Bouchard's widow (now living in Pennsylvania), against a mortgage on the starch factory. By 1900, they had completed a new combination starch factory and shingle mill worth $6,000 and employing thirty men. The brothers-in-law then parted company. Michel Michaud continued running the starch factory. Israel appears in the records only as a shingle and lumber manufacturer, but obviously he had not given up making starch. The brothers-in-law were following two different strategies: Michel was a factory owner, who depended on farmers bringing him potatoes; Israel was a member of a cooperative venture. Although the St. Agatha Starch Company shareholders did not require the associates to bring a given amount of potatoes every year, nor did it fix beforehand the price they would pay for potatoes, they could be reasonably assured of a supply of potatoes (as all crops include a percentage of non merchantable tubers). Michaud assumed all the risk, but the others spread that risk around.

Sources: Maine Bureau of Industrial and Labor Statistics, *Reports* (1884 to 1914); *Maine Register* (1880, 1900, and 1910); *Centenaire de Ste. Agathe, Maine, 1899–1999* (1999).

low, they hauled them to the factory. This resulted in highly fluctuating starch prices (from 2.5 to 4 cents a pound).[7] Some starch factories, such as the St. Agatha Starch Factory, were farmers' cooperative (see Sidebar 20-2).

II.   THE CONTINUATION OF MIXED FARMING IN NEW BRUNSWICK

The New Brunswick Railway did not have the same impact on potato production along the New Brunswick side of the St. John Valley. The railway first reached Woodstock, in Carleton County, in 1867, subsequently moving upriver until it reached Edmundston in 1878. The arrival of the railway coincided with a significant increase (150 percent) in potato production in Carleton County. Carleton, however, never became the province's leading potato producer—that honor went to Kent and Gloucester. Instead, Carleton was the province's leading oats producer until World War I. In Victoria-Madawaska, potato, oats, and hay production actually decreased after 1871; the situation did not improve until the twentieth century (see Appendix H-4), nor were there any starch factories in Madawaska and Victoria before the war. Although New Brunswick potato production increased significantly in the second half of the nineteenth century, it was eventually outpaced by Maine. In 1901, for instance, New Brunswick produced 4 million bushels of potatoes compared to 6 million bushels in 1910 (one-sixth of it in Carleton County). Aroostook County produced 6.5 million bushels in 1901 and 17.5 million bushels in 1910.

Potato farmers in Madawaska County faced a disadvantage because other producers were closer to the markets than they were. Whereas Aroostook potatoes easily reached New England, Valley potatoes did not easily reach Quebec City, which was supplied mostly by farms in the lower St. Lawrence region, and potato production in this region had expanded significantly after the building of the Grand Trunk. As for starch, the biggest market was in New England—but because starch was a manufactured product, it was taxed when imported. New Brunswick starch simply could not compete with Maine starch.

New Brunswick farmers may also have shipped their goods to international markets. A 1901 report to the New Brunswick House of Assembly mentioned that hay remained one of the province's main crops, and that the prices were high because of demand from South Africa. Farmers also shipped potatoes overseas. A 1910 report quoted a local shipper stating that "he was paying $1.15 at Florenceville for shipments to Cuba, and he was buying on American territory at $1.00 a barrel." The report concluded that, "It was a new page in New Brunswick history that our own people can go over [to the US] and buy potatoes and ship them."[8]

British-American shippers obviously had different networks, and contacts in different places than American ones—but this did not translate into levels of production commensurate with those of Aroostook County. Agricultural reports frequently cited the various pests infesting potatoes and grain crops, which could also explain New Brunswick farmers' low performance—except one would expect those pests to cross the boundary. Less favorable location in regard to domestic markets, coupled with the higher volatility of world markets than domestic ones, provide likely alternative explanations. It would also be interesting to know if New Brunswick farmers mortgaged their property as much as their neighbors across the border. It is possible that the net worth of farmers on both sides of the boundary was not all that different.

Some New Brunswick Madawaska farmers also grew products for niche markets: some grew berries and shipped them to urban centers in Canada and the United States. *Le Journal du Madawaska* regularly informed readers about the prices fetched by berries. The quantities and the resultant gross income were significant.

By the early twentieth century, agronomists in both New Brunswick and Maine were concerned about the state of agriculture in their respective jurisdiction. Agronomists in Maine considered farmers' singular focus on potatoes worrisome. Similarly, agronomists in New Brunswick wanted farmers to diversify to boost the entire sector. Both viewed the expansion of the dairy industry as a good way to reach these goals. The dairy industry, however, did not fulfill this vision in either region. In New Brunswick, agronomists blamed the failure on the railroads, while in Maine, they blamed farmers who were reluctant to divert resources, especially land, away from their potato crop.

A. New Brunswick

In 1895, the New Brunswick minister of agriculture sent two agents around the province to give seminars to farmers on how to improve and expand the dairy industry. On June 25, one of the agents hosted a heavily attended meeting at St. Leonard. He noted that the area's cream and butter were of good quality, and participants discussed ways to increase production. This was the first of several such visits over the next few years. Initially, the efforts seemed to pay off. An association of dairy farmers, the St. Leonard's Dairy Association, was founded in October 1898 by Edouard Michaud and André Levesque of Grand Falls, Christophe Laforge of Poitras, and Béloni Violette of St. Leonard. The following year, Violette, a merchant; Joseph Martin, a Van Buren merchant; and J. St. Pierre, a Ste. Anne farmer, started the Ste. Anne Butter Factory. In 1901 Cyriaque Daigle, superintendent of Dairy District 3 (which included Madawaska), reported the building of three creameries in his district—one at Caron Brook "by Mr. L. Long, one at Albertine [St. Hilaire] by Vital Albert, and one at St. Leonards by...Martin & Violette & Co., all in the County of Madawaska."[9] However,

Daigle was not pleased with this development. Butter and cheese factories were dependent on farmers bringing milk to them, and most factories had a group of regular suppliers. Daigle feared the new factories would divert milk away from existing ones, and that, in the end, both the new and old factories would fail.

In 1901, there were ten cheese factories in Carleton County, one in Victoria, and three in Madawaska. There were also ten creameries, or butter-making factories, in Carleton County (nine of which belonged to W. C. Raymond), three in Victoria, and six in Madawaska. American farmers also patronized those plants. The newspaper *L'Évangéline* noted on August 2, 1900, that "the Americans from the neighboring republic are so satisfied with the productivity and performance of our creameries that they bring their milk to Madawaska to turn it into butter."[10]

The dairy products from the different factories were shipped to Quebec City, Montréal and Britain. In 1899, Madawaska county exported 36,343 pounds of cheese and 18,964 pounds of butter; in 1901, the figures rose to 70,000 pounds of cheese and 55,403 pounds of butter. Provincial agronomists believed exports of New Brunswick dairy products to Britain could be increased. British consumers were buying 400 million pounds of butter annually, but Canadian farmers at that time were only shipping 25 million pounds of butter to Britain. There was, therefore, room to grow, but the butter had to be shipped within a week of its production to remain fresh. Only under those conditions could Canadian butter compete on the British market with Danish butter. Unlike butter, the British market for cheese was close to saturation. Canada was already providing 75 percent of the cheese imported in Britain. The only thing New Brunswick producers could do was to increase their share of the exports, and to achieve this goal, their cheese needed to be identifiable as a New Brunswick product. Provincial authorities understood the concept of "branding" early on:

> Quality governs, or should govern, prices; but something must be done to place our cheese on the English market as a New Brunswick product, and with simply the word "Canadian" stamped upon the box, we can never hope to establish a high reputation for ourselves unless we can let the consumers know where or what country produced them.[11]

However, success appears to have been short-lived. By 1910, production levels were falling. In 1906, the two creameries in St. Leonard produced 37,235 pounds of butter. By 1908, they produced only 3,381 pounds. This downturn in production was not limited to St. Leonard. By 1913, ten of thirteen creameries had closed down. The remaining three were those in St. Basile, St. André, and St. Hilaire, which consolidated into one.

Cyriaque Daigle blamed the construction of the Pacific Grand Trunk (the International Railway) for the industry's demise. Although on the surface it would seem that the railway should have improved the industry by providing a means of transporting massive amounts of diary products to American and Canadian markets, it had the opposite effect. Daigle explains:

> ...the Grand Trunk Pacific furnished employment to many farmers with their horses, who worked on the road all summer, thereby neglecting much work on the farm.... This, of course, kept those farmers busy, and resulted in many herds of cows being neglected. High prices were obtained for hay and grain, and many were tempted to diminish their stock, and sell their oats and hay, instead of feeding it to the cows.... [12]

Farmers, in other words, made rational short-term choices, and worked for the most profitable— or more predictable—markets, as their fathers and grandfathers had always done. In this particular case, this was an unfortunate decision, because the con-

struction crews did not stay forever. Once they were gone, Valley farmers discovered that re-entering the dairy business was much harder than they had expected.

B. Aroostook

We have less information about dairy production on the American side of the border. The sources cover the industry at state, or at best, county level, and do not provide good information on dairy production in northern Aroostook County. Dairy farming does not seem to have been an important activity in Aroostook County as a whole. This was not due to a lack of encouragement from state officials. In 1878, the state commissioner of agriculture feared that the continuous production of hay and potatoes would soon destroy the soil. Diversification, he said, was needed. The county was well suited for dairy farming. The Maine Board of Agriculture noted it was capable of providing year-round fodder for its stock. An infusion of Jersey cows would allow existing cows to provide "the best butter and cheese in the world." Dairy production could also transform a high-volume, low-value commodity (hay) into the opposite. Wouldn't it be in the best interest of the farmers to sell less hay, oats, and potatoes and more beef, pork, butter, and cheese? Dairy products from other parts of the state enjoyed a great reputation and a huge market. Dairy producers shipped large amounts of these products to Massachusetts, Rhode Island, and southern states. In various New England cities, such as Boston and Providence, local merchants branded their stock with a sign: "Maine cream for sale here."[13] An Aroostook County factory, the Pine Tree Creamery Company of Sherman Mills, even received a gold medal at the Paris World Fair in 1900. The market, in other words, was ready for Aroostook County dairy products. Aroostook County farmers did not seize it, and the Bureau of Industrial and Labor Statistics blamed the popularity of potato-growing for this failure.[14]

Information about Maine Madawaska dairy

farming is extremely elusive. According to the Maine Bureau of Industrial and Labor Statistics, a cheese factory (built for $500 and employing three workers) opened at Madawaska in 1891, and a butter factory (build for $2,000 and employing two workers) opened at the same place in 1900. The Aroostook County Board of Underwriters (an insurance organization) listed a creamery run by L. B. Fournier in 1905, but made no mention of a cheese factory. Yet, in 1910, the Maine Board of Agriculture noted that there were only two creameries and one cheese factory in the county, located in Houlton and New Sweden. What happened to the Madawaska factory? The Maine Dairymen's Association annual report in 1910 also lists no dairy factories of any sort in the upper St. John Valley. This might explain why, as mentioned earlier, the New Brunswick side of the river received milk from the United States to turn into butter or cheese. Although sources from Maine seem to indicate that there were no dairy activities in the Madawaska region, we do know that some farmers were interested in this activity.

Conclusion

Inadequate sources prevent us from drawing definitive conclusions about Valley agriculture between 1870 and World War I. Nonetheless, some trends do seem clear. Until the early 1870s, New Brunswick and Maine Madawaska practiced the same kind of mixed, multi-crop agriculture. Statements made about one side of the Valley usually applied to the other, as well. By the early twentieth century, this was probably no longer true. Small-scale farms producing a wide range of crops and animals continued to dominate in New Brunswick Madawaska, whose producers sold to domestic and international markets. New Brunswick farmers, however, suffered a disadvantage on the Canadian market. The larger cities (Quebec, Montreal, and Toronto) were not only distant, but also surrounded by farmland; farmers in Québec, in particular, enjoyed a better climate and longer growing season than those in

New Brunswick. Agricultural products were exported to different parts of the Empire: cheese to Britain, hay to South Africa. Dairy producers may have processed milk from the Maine side of the Valley, as well.

Maine Madawaska appears to have followed in the footsteps of central and southern Aroostook County, and shifted to potato, hay, and oats cultivation to the near exclusion of everything else. This trend worried state agronomists, who realized that reliance on a limited number of crops would impoverish the soil. They were right, and farmers were forced to use more and more fertilizer. It also resulted in farmers becoming too dependent on volatile commodity markets. But since many of them had accumulated debts, they could no longer wait out disadvantageous market conditions.

The period also saw the emergence and development of new industries, such as potato starch in Maine (there were no such plants in Carleton, Victoria, or Madawaska counties) and butter and cheese factories in New Brunswick (there were several along the St. John River from Woodstock up but very few in Aroostook County). Although sharing the same physical environment, Aroostook County farmers and those who lived in the Carleton-Victoria-Madawaska region had gone their separate ways by the eve of World War I. The large-scale commercialization of agricultural production had turned the two sides of the Valley into agricultural bordered lands.

ENDNOTES
1. Maine Bureau of Industrial and Labor Statistics, *Eighteenth Annual Report,* Augusta, ME: Kennebec Journal Printing, 1904, 100.
2. Ibid., 19.
3. Maine Bureau of Industrial and Labor Statistics, *Sixteenth Annual Report,* Augusta, ME: Kennebec Journal Printing, 1902, 159–60.
4. State of Maine, Department of Agriculture, Bulletin, *Agricultural Census of Maine, by Towns, 1*925. (Maine State Library, A.27.10: Ag396/925 c. 2).
5. Maine Bureau of Industrial and Labor Statistics, *Twenty-Third Annual Report,* Waterville, ME: Sentinel

Publishing Company, 1909, 272.

6. Maine Bureau of Industrial and Labor Statistics, *Eighteenth Annual Report*, 77–78.

7. One bushel of potatoes (60 pounds) produced 8 pounds of starch; it took 250 bushels to produce a ton of starch.

8. PANB, New Brunswick Legislative Assembly, Agricultural Report for the Province of New Brunswick for 1910, published by order of the legislature, Fredericton: New Brunswick. 1910, 83, microfilm reel F209.

9. PANB, New Brunswick Legislative Assembly, Agricultural Report for Province of New Brunswick for 1901, report from the superintendent, Dairy District 3: 51, microfilm reel F200.

10. *L'Évangéline,* August 2, 1900, quoted in Michaud, *Brève Histoire du Madawaska,* 97 (translation by the authors).

11. PANB, New Brunswick Legislative Assembly, Agricultural Report for the Province of New Brunswick for 1901, 64

12. PANB, New Brunswick Legislative Assembly, Agricultural Report for the Province of New Brunswick for 1908, 74-5; and Lapointe, "Histoire de l'industrie laitière...," 29–30.

13. Maine Bureau of Industrial and Labor Statistics, *Fifteenth Annual Report,* Augusta, ME: *Kennebec Journal* Printing, 1901, 34.

14. Maine Bureau of Industrial and Labor Statistics, *Twenty-Third Annual Report,* Waterville, ME: Sentinel Publishing Company, 1909, 267.

FURTHER READINGS

Dubay, Guy. *Chez Nous: The St. John Valley.* 1983: 55–70.

Acadian Culture in Maine. "Maine Acadians and the Land." Section 3, http://acim.umfk.maine.edu.

SOURCES

Although there are books covering the agricultural history of Aroostook County, they either ignore Madawaska, or assume Valley farmers practiced subsistence agriculture. They also tend to write as if "true" agriculture did not develop until the arrival of the Bangor and Aroostook Railway (Judd's *Pine Tree State* is a case in point). Despite this drawback, Day (1963) remains the basic reference text for Aroostook County agriculture.

Public documents are the best place to start researching Aroostook and Madawaska agriculture; see, for instance, publications by the Maine Board of Agriculture, the Maine Dairymen's Association, and the Maine agricultural societies (at either the Maine State Library or at the Maine State Archives as part of the Maine Public Documents for the year; some individual reports can be found in various Maine libraries). For New Brunswick, see agriculture reports to the Legislative Assembly (at the Provincial Archives). The Maine Register and the Maine Bureau of Industrial and Labor Statistics annual reports contain data on starch, butter, and cheese factories (both available at the Maine State Archives). Data on agricultural production can be found in the aggregate tables produced by the United States and Canadian census bureaus. Lapointe's (1989) writings on the dairy industry in St. Leonard and G. Michaud's (1984) are also useful.

21

URBANIZATION

Railroads and the economic transformations they triggered contributed to the urbanization of the Valley. Urban areas are defined by their population (2,500 persons or more). They are also characterized by higher population densities, and, most importantly, by functional diversity. They are commercial, administrative, service, and educational centers. Their residents also have access to a wider range of services. Before the turn of the twentieth century, businesses and services had begun to cluster in Madawaska-Edmundston, Fort Kent, and Van Buren, but these three localities remained small. The largest town was still Frenchville which did not otherwise offer any services beyond those normally found in farm communities although it boasted the first high school in the Valley. After 1900, all this changed, and four true urban centers emerged: Fort Kent, Van Buren, St. Leonard, and Madawaska-Edmundston. St. Leonard and Van Buren's development were linked, and one could even refer to the two places as a single trans-border town.

I. GEOGRAPHY AND POPULATION

A. Geography

As Table 21-1 shows, the four urban centers were all located on railroad lines and soon became railroad junctions. The railroads, however, do not explain everything—if they were the sole cause of urbanization, urban centers would have appeared much earlier on the New Brunswick side of the Valley. The railroads, though, appear to have had a much greater impact in Maine than in New Brunswick. The population of Van Buren increased by 60 percent in the ten years following the arrival of the Bangor and Aroostook, and by another 60 percent in the ten years after that. While population increase was not as spectacular in Fort Kent (38 and 46 percent, respectively), it was still significant. Eagle Lake also went from 406 inhabitants in 1900 to 1,421 in 1910. This points to the real cause of urban development: large lumber mills. The communities experiencing the greatest growth were mill towns, and St. Leonard clearly benefited as much from the mills on the other side of the river as it did from its location on three different railway lines (the New Brunswick Railway/Canadian Pacific, National Transcontinental, and Restigouche lines). Edmundston, for its part, became a small city. It went from 1,821 residents in 1911 to 4,025 in 1921. Fraser had built his pulp mill in the intervening years.

The lumber mills employed a large number of workers, all requiring housing. The Fish River Lumber Company in Eagle Lake, which employed some 225 men, built 25 tenement houses and a boarding house for 125 people in the plantation; it

Table 21-1: Population Growth in Selected Localities

American Madawaska	1870	1880	1890	1900	1910	1920
Eagle Lake	143	233	313	406	1,421	1,772
Fort Kent	1,034	1,512	1,826	2,528	3,710	4,237
Frenchville-St. Agatha	1,851	2,288	2,560	2,712	2,947	3,285
Madawaska	1,041	1,391	1,451	1,698	1,831	1,933
Grand Isle	688	847	964	1,104	1,317	1,352
Van Buren	992	1,110	1,168	1,878	3,065	4,594

Canadian Madawaska	1871	1881	1891	1901	1911	1921
St. Francis-Clair-Lake Baker	1,752	1,600	2,040	2,577	3,050	3,146
Madawaska-Edmundston	1.816	966	1,683	1,882	2,809	4,911
Edmundston (alone)					1,821	4,035
St. Leonard-Ste. Anne-St. André	1.997	3,101	3,366	4,021	5,217	6,107

Sources: See list of censuses p. 409.

Sidebar 21-1: Eagle Lake in 1903

(This paragraph follows a description of Wallagrass.)

...a very large lumber mill, under the proprietorship of Mr. A. R. Cushing and Mr. P. P. Burleigh, is not the least of the industrial and commercial advantages of Eagle Lake. Mr. Cushing and Mr. Burleigh, who are very enterprising men and lovers of progress, have done much for the good of the town, which, by right, might be called theirs. They have built many pretty and comfortable houses for the use by their employees, which are either sold or rented to them at very reasonable terms. They also have, very near the pretty station of Eagle Lake, a large, fully supplied store where all customers are treated with courtesy and honesty. Many other very nice and large stores are being built on various streets of the town, where every branch of commerce and trade is represented. The town has also its own electric lights and its own first class hotels and boarding houses with conveniences of all kinds. Last but not least, a large Catholic church is being erected by the Reverend Father Marcoux (with lumber donated by Cushing and Burleigh).

Source: *Le Journal du Madawaska*, November 25, 1903; translated by the authors.

Those two photographs (opposite) illustrate the growth of Edmundston
Illus. 21-1, top: This 1865 picture is the first known photograph of the town. CDEM, PC2-15
Illus. 21-2, bottom: Edmundston in 1880. CDEM, PC2-40

Urbanization

Illus. 21-3: By 1912, St. Basile had turned into a pretty village. CDEM, PC3-207

built another 25 tenements at Winterville. The St. John and Van Buren lumber companies similarly had to build housing for workers in the village (the first built twelve houses, and the second thirty-nine tenements in Van Buren). In Van Buren, these tenements and boardinghouses were added to the existing housing stock of a well-established village. In Eagle Lake, they formed the town. With their twenty-five tenement houses and large boardinghouses, Eagle Lake and Winterville became industrial villages overnight (see Sidebar 21-1).

New houses led to the development of new schools and businesses. Stores, hotels, restaurants, barbershops, and grocery stores opened in the years following the construction of the mills. All these new people—including factory workers, merchants, and professionals—needed food, thus providing a growing market for farmers. The factories became the most important facet of the local economy. Unfortunately, this situation also had negative consequences, since the towns became dependent on the factories' success. Local stores also became reliant on the money they generated to remain in business. Riverside plants even affected towns across the river, since they employed workers from both sides.

B. Population Composition

The population of the new urbanized centers differed from that of neighboring farming communities in several respects. First, some of those people were not French Canadian or Acadian; many were not even British or Anglo-Americans, and must have seemed very exotic at the time. For instance, a handful of Jewish people settled in the Valley; the Klein family opened clothing stores in Van Buren and Fort Kent, and the Krasnic family opened a store in Baker Lake. The *Journal du Madawaska* refers to the "Syrian" community of Van Buren being visited by a missionary of their faith (a Maronite; the "Syrians" were from present-day Lebanon). According to the 1911 Canadian census, there were also twelve

Scandinavians, eighty-eight Italians, and thirty-four Bulgarians and Romanians living in the Valley. All except nine of the Scandinavians and half of the Italians lived in Edmundston. Thirty-two of the Italians lived in St. Leonard. Although the Valley was still 95 percent French, its towns now attracted small concentrations of people from other nationalities.

Second, a greater proportion of the population was made up of wage earners, salaried men, and professionals. For instance, in 1871, listings for the Van Buren Plantation in the *Maine Register* took up just fourteen lines. In addition to the various plantation officials, it listed five stores: Violet's, W. H. Hammond, W. H. Hammond, Jr., Chas. Hammond, and Richard Collins and Co. (full names are usually not given). There was one manufacturer (W. C. Hammond, Jr.) and one hotelkeeper (Haley). In 1910, Van Buren took up almost two pages of the *Maine Register,* not including its advertisements. Merchants sold everything from agricultural implements to watches and jewelry. One could purchase items ranging from clothing, fruit, and candies to furniture and sewing machines. Some merchants specialized in the wholesale trade of hay

and potatoes. The town had two dressmakers, three milliners, and seven barbers; one could go and have one's picture taken at J. M. Bouchard, Joseph J. Gagné, or Bruno Morin's. Entertainment was available for gentlemen at Théophile Violette and Paul Beaulieu's billiard halls. Visitors to the town could stay at the Hammond's hotel, and if they did not like the food served there, there were two restaurants in town. One could buy insurance policies from local brokers and real estate from two agents and even have one's earthly remains handled by an undertaker. A look at the *Register'*s entries for Fort Kent shows that the same variety of retailers and services were also available there. Armand Dugal epitomized the spread of new commodities: according to his publicity in *Le Journal du Madawaska,* he was a tinsmith, plumber, roofer, who also sold steam space- and water-heaters. What one could not find were places serving alcohol. Maine was a dry state. But New Brunswick had passed a local option law, and Madawaska County was wet. The bar was a key attraction of the hotels at St. Leonard and Clair, as we already saw in Chapter 18.

II.   TRADE AND RETAIL

A. Overview

Would-be Madawaska entrepreneurs with limited capital went into retail. Retailers on the American side advertised their recent returns from Boston and New York, where they reportedly had collected a stock of new merchandise for the season. The days of José Nadeau (see Chapter 15) getting his supplies from John Emmerson, who was getting his supplies from Canada (then a separate political entity), New Brunswick, and the United States, were apparently over. Those taking consumer goods across the river had to report their wares and pay high duties. Smuggling became commonplace as tariffs kept escalating. The account book of Georges Bernier (from Connors), on the other hand, suggests that

most, if not all, of his suppliers were Canadian. However, family lore claims that Georges Bernier was ordering goods on his American collegues' accounts, and smuggling them across the river after dark. Most trans-border trade probably escaped official scrutiny, and private individuals could still cross the border unhindered; pictures of ferries crossing the river do not show any customhouses at the landing. But customhouses were erected at both ends of the Van Buren International Bridge. The days when people could shop indifferently on this side or that side of the river were numbered.

Other changes affected trading patterns at the store. Payments at the time of purchase had become the rule. The 1870s, 1880s, and 1900s record books of Connors, Bernier, and Savage (from St. Francis) stores were usually general stores carrying a wide and heteroclite variety of goods, whereas villages also had specialized establishments. The newspaper editors began their list with the Van Buren Mercantile Company, a department store selling dry goods, groceries, provisions, shoes, and furniture. Next came Parent frères, two young and talented retailers with "friendly manners [and] reasonable prices." They carried general merchandises but specialized in farm implements and sewing machines. Fred Smith's store, really run by Mrs. Fred Smith, contained a "splendid assortment of hats"; H. A. Gagnon's stock was "well chosen, fashionable, tasteful, and could be purchased at reasonable prices." Gagnon was not choosy: he exchanged his goods for "farm products, wood, cattle, lamb, and when he cannot do better, he even accepts money." This could explain why he attracted many consumers. Joseph Gagné, on the road leading to the ferry, owned a second store that was run by his daughter and son at the new village of Chappel Eddy. Florent Sansfaçon's "Magasin Populaire," claimed it had everything on hand; sold to everyone; accepted money, grain, potatoes, and hay as payment; and "refused nothing" (*"Nous avons en main de tout, nous vendons à tous, nous ne refusons rien"*)

Illus. 21-4: Two very fashionably dressed ladies c. 1900. CDEM, PA1-52

B. The Nadeau Store in Baker Lake

Most retailers were men from local families, like the Nadeaux of Baker Brook. Denis Nadeau was born in Baker Brook in 1876. Prior to settling in the parish and opening his shop, he traveled to the American and Canadian west for profit and adventure. When he returned to Baker Brook in 1902, he began selling axes he made himself in a small makeshift shop. A few years later, he bought some land from Denis Hébert and William Cloutier and built a general store. His stock also expanded. Besides axes, he began selling items such as clothing, tools, and foods of all sorts. Like most of the region's retail stores, his was family-run. Nadeau was also constantly trying to improve his stock and provide the

show that the only people receiving credit at the store were either doing business with the storekeeper or working for him (the story of the Nadeau store below, however, demonstrates that cash exchanges were still not universal). Savage was even paying some of his workers half in money and half in store goods. But some storekeepers were still accepting payments in kind—they advertised the fact in the newspaper, suggesting that payment-in-kind was no longer the norm.

Storekeepers took advantage of the newspaper started in Van Buren in 1903, to advertise their wares. The advertisers were all from the American side of the river. In October 1903, the editors of *Le Journal du Madawaska* surveyed the retail scene in the Valley. The resulting article shows that the local latest fashions and products. In order to do so, he had to travel to places such as Montreal or Quebec City to purchase merchandise. While away on business, his wife, Laura Collin, managed the store. The store's clientele was mostly drawn from Baker Brook, but Nadeau also attracted customers from all over the region. Money was rare in that part of the Valley, and Nadeau often sold on credit. To help out his poorer customers, he accepted wood as payment: in 1904, a 4 by 8 cord of wood could be exchanged for $4 worth of goods.

Nadeau was a true entrepreneur. He started from nothing and created a store that lasted for decades after his death. Nadeau also engaged in other activities. For example, he taught English at Fort Kent. He traded in horses and enjoyed the reputation of being the man one had to see when buying or selling a good horse. Customers who did not have enough money could buy a horse on installments. It is this consumer-friendly service that made Nadeau one of the most successful entrepreneurs of the region and helped him survive the Great Depression. In 1950, when his son Uldéric took

over, customer relations remained one of the store owner's top priorities.

C. Kasner Brothers in Edmundston

Retailing was not exclusively in the hands of local French and English residents. Immigrants, such as the Kasner brothers, also started lasting enterprises. In 1910, Isack Kasner left his native Romania and settled in Edmundston; his brother, Osias (Nathan), followed a year later. Soon after his arrival, Isack began to lay the foundation for what would eventually become one of the best-known women's clothing stores in the region. Like Nadeau, Kasner started small. He visited villages by foot and went door to door peddling goods, such as combs, sewing thread, and socks that he carried in a bag over his shoulder. In 1911, he purchased a horse-drawn carriage and a sled for the winter. He improved his stock, adding clothes of all kind: formal, informal, work clothes, etc., which he acquired from wholesalers in Montreal and Quebec City.

That same year, Isack and Osias bought a parcel

Illus. 21-5: The Kasner Store celebrates its anniversary. CDEM, PC2-12

of land on the Canada Road where they built a store. In 1913, the brothers formalized their partnership, announcing it in the province's official paper, the *Royal Gazette*. It read:

> This is to certify that we, Isack Kasner of the town of Edmundston, in the county of Madawaska and Province of New Brunswick, Merchant, and Osias Kasner, of the same place, Merchant, have formed and entered into a general co-partnership for the purpose of carrying on the business of merchants in dry goods and furs, in wholesale and retail.[1]

The store specialized in furs and other clothing; like the Nadeau store, it outlived its founders and lasted until 1987 (the Kasner brothers also had a store in Montreal). The secret of the brothers' lasting success was their emphasis on quality and customer service. Nadeau, the local French Catholic boy, and the Kasners, Jewish immigrants from southern Europe, had used the same strategy: high-quality goods, excellent customer service, and responsiveness to the needs of the clientele to achieve the same results—a store that outlived them.

Illus. 21-6: Inside Dalfen's store at Grand Falls. CDEM, P54-113

The Land in Between

Illus. 21-7, left: Béloni Hébert's general store, built in the late 1880s. Downstairs was a general store and post office. Upstairs was the first Madawaska hotel. It was destroyed by fire in 1944.
Madawaska Historical Societ.

Illus. 21-8a and b, below: Advertisements from Aroostook County (Maine) Business and Residential Directory, 1905–1906.
Newton, MA: Newton Journal Publishing Co., 1906

Illus. 21-9 a and b: Advertisements from Le Journal du Madawaska, *1904.*

III. SOCIAL LIFE

Different forms of leisure also emerged, not only because of urbanization, but also because of higher levels of formal education and higher standards of living among the villages' middle class. Schools provided education and entertainment. The religious orders began cultivating students' musical talents, an endeavor that had the support of the community, and organized theatrical and musical evenings. In March 1904, the Van Buren Convent performed a rendition of *Marguerite Morus* (the plot centered on Margaret, daughter of Thomas Moore, Henry VIII's chancellor). The cast consisted in fifteen amateur actresses (there were no male parts in this play). Between the different acts, other young ladies displayed their musical talents. In May, the convent put on another play: *Tolbiac.* It told the story of French King Clovis' conversion to Christianity at the urging of his wife in the fifth century. Van Buren College also had an orchestra, which organized a gala in June 1904. Singers and musicians entertained family, friends, and neighbors. According to *Le Journal du Madawaska,* there was a small orchestra in Fort Kent, in which L. Martin, A. J. Thibodeau, Ed. Beaumont, I. Daigle, and F. Peters played.

This fondness for music was also reflected in the private and public dances held throughout the year. No decent wedding could occur without music and dancing (see Appendix K "Wedding at Wallagrass"). But dances could also be used as fundraisers. In June 1904, the *Court des Maccabées* of Madawaska (a fraternal insurance organization) organized a dance in Vital Beaulieu's public hall. The evening was to start at 7:30 p.m. and continue until 2:30 a.m. Drinking and smoking were prohibited, and the Maccabées charged admission. The following issue of *Le Journal du Madawaska* reported that the evening had been a success, and that there had not been any problems.

Public schools offered end-of-term fêtes for students and their parents. Students entertained adults with music and recitation; the adults also played cards (see appendix K, "School Fête"). Private entertaining also appears to have frequently included card playing. A typical evening (*soirée*) started with card playing, then food, and finally singing and instrument playing, usually by the younger members of the assembly. Sometime after midnight, the participants went home but not without first singing the ubiquitous *"Bonsoir mes amis, bonsoir"* ("Good night friends, good night"; see Appendix K, "Winter Soirées").

The railway also made traveling in and out of Madawaska possible. The trains stopped at every post and functioned like urban buses. People took advantage of them: passenger traffic accounted for about a quarter of the railroad's revenues before World War I. One could take the train to visit family and friends, shop, and play sports. School boys often took the train to play baseball. Van Buren College had a baseball team, which had played against Caribou in 1904 (a five-hour ride away). *Le Journal du Madawaska* kept informing its readers about the visits Valley residents were paying to rela-

tives who had left the region and about the visits relatives from afar were making to Madawaska. The railroads encouraged people to travel for pleasure. The Temiscouata Railway organized a daytrip to Rivière-du-Loup on July 24, 1904. The return ticket cost between $1.60 and $1.70. The trip was, however, not for people who liked to lie around in bed. Trains were slow. The excursionists, therefore, had to leave Clair at 5:40 a.m. to arrive at Rivière-du-Loup by 10 a.m.; the return train left at 7 p.m. and arrived back at Clair at 11:30 p.m. Both the B&A and Canadian lines organized excursions and pilgrimages of this sort. The B&A organized yearly pilgrimages to the famous shrine at Sainte-Anne de Beaupré near Quebec City with side trips to Quebec City and Montreal—a trip that cost $7. Excursionists were picked up in Van Buren and taken to Québec via Caribou and Old Town; presumably the train picked up other pilgrims along the way. The Canadian lines charged only $3.50 for the same trip, but limited the trip to Sainte-Anne. Railways also facilitated attendance at county events, such as the Northern Maine Agricultural Fair in Presque Isle, or political county conventions in Houlton, by reducing rates. There also was an international exhibition in St. Louis (Missouri) in 1904. The B&A offered a special rate from Van Buren: $54 for sixty days or $45 for fifteen days. (This amount included the price of the tickets on the various railroad lines between the Valley and St. Louis.)

Conclusion

The railroads, lumber mills, and increased commercialization of agriculture brought new employment and commercial opportunities to the Valley. Wage earners, businesspeople, and professionals clustered in localities served by one or more railroad lines, resulting in the emergence of small urban centers. The railroads gave people access to a wider range of consumer goods and greater travel opportunities, commodities the emerging Valley middle class could afford. By 1910, life in Fort Kent, Van Buren, and

Edmundston was visibly different from life in Grand Isle or Connors.

ENDNOTE

1. *The Royal Gazette,* Vol. 71 (July 16, 1913), quoted in Couturier, "L'entreprise Kasmer...," 215.

SOURCES

For migrations in and out of the Valley, see Vicero (1968), Allen (1974), and Brookes (1976). The storekeepers' stories are based on Lagacé (1989) and Couturier (1987). The depiction of social life during this time is based on the 1904 social columns of *Le Journal du Madawaska.*

22

TOURISM AND RECREATION IN THE ST. JOHN VALLEY, 1792–1914

The railroads allowed people to travel with greater speed and comfort, and in the previous chapter, we saw that Madawaska residents and former residents took advantage of the opportunity. The railroads also made it easier for outsiders to visit Madawaska, which led to the emergence of a modern tourist industry in the region. Traveling for pleasure was, of course, not a new concept, and Madawaska had long attracted its share of visitors. The railroads, however, attracted different kinds of people, and railroad companies and town merchants began to see these "vacation tourists" as sources of income. The Bangor and Aroostook even believed tourism could lure potential investors to Aroostook County.

I.   PRE-RAILROAD TRAVELERS

A. Early Nineteenth-Century Visitors

Throughout time, people have traveled to broaden their horizons, learn new things, and immerse themselves in other cultures. By the eighteenth century, travel was viewed as a necessary component of a young gentleman's education. Until the nineteenth century, however, travel was limited to the upper class, since traveling for pleasure was too expensive for the rest of the population. Those who could not travel in person could do so vicariously through others: travelogues were an established literary genre.

The St. John Valley had long been a well-traveled route. Whether going through the Valley for official or private business, travelers took note of the landscape—in particular the spectacular Great Falls. British officers were sketching it as early as 1782 (see Chapter 4). So did Québec surveyor-general Joseph Bouchette in 1816. During the early nineteenth century, those traveling for pleasure were mostly British officers on furlough, who used their leave time to see local and faraway attractions. Very early accounts of the upper St. John Valley tend to be matter of fact and descriptive—and were written for a British audience. These accounts include Patrick Campbell's *Travels in the Interior Inhabited Parts of North America in the Years 1791 and 1792* (Edinburgh, 1793); John Mann's *Travels in North America: Particularly in the Provinces of Upper & Lower Canada, and New Brunswick, and in the State of Maine, Massachusetts, and New York,* (Glasgow, 1824); George Head's detailed description of a winter journey from Fredericton to Quebec City in *Forest Scenes and Incidents in the Wilds of North America: Being a Diary of a Winter's Route from Halifax to the Canadas* (London, 1829); and Lieutenant E. T. Coke's *A Subaltern's Furlough: Descriptions of Scenes in Various Parts of the United States, Upper and Lower Canada, New Brunswick, and Nova Scotia During the Summer and Autumn of 1832* (London, 1832). Those authors either wrote descriptive, informative accounts detailing their

Illus. 22-1: Some sure footed sight-seers at the Grand Falls. PANB, George Taylor Photograph, P5-277

exact travels or more anecdotal and entertaining stories. The French character of the settlement was of minor interest for them.

B. Romanticism and the Cult of Nature

During the early nineteenth century, Romanticism led tourists to seek destinations besides the traditional cultural centers of Paris, Rome, Florence, and Athens. Romantics emphasized senses and emotions over reason and intellect. They regarded cities as corrupt and artificial. Truth and freedom were found in the mountains, lakes, rivers, and rolling country hills that Mother Nature had created. Romantic travelers thus journeyed to uninhabited lands and sought a mystical union with nature to open paths of self discovery. William Wordsworth (1770–1850), a

Romantic poet, wrote that nature was:

> The anchor of my purest thoughts, the nurse,
> The guide, the guardian of my heart, and soul
> Of all my moral being.[1]

In New England, the American Transcendentalists shared those views. These individuals believed that God resided in each person and in nature and that intuition was the highest source of knowledge. From the mid-1840s until his death, the most famous Transcendentalist, Henry David Thoreau, traveled through the Maine wilderness and published accounts of his journey, which were gathered after his death and published under the title *In the Maine Woods.* The following quote, part of a description of a hike up Katahdin, provides insight into Thoreau's mindset:

It is difficult to conceive of a region uninhabited by man. We habitually presume his presence and influence everywhere. And yet we have not seen pure Nature, unless we have seen her thus vast and drear and inhuman, though in the midst of cities. Nature was here something savage and awful though beautiful. I looked with awe at the ground I trod on, to see what the Powers had made there, the form and fashion and material of their work. This was that Earth of which we have heard, made out of Chaos and Old Night. Here was no man's garden, but the unhandselled globe. It was not lawn, nor pasture, nor mead, nor woodland, nor lea, nor arable, nor waste-land. It was the fresh and natural surface of the planet Earth, as it was made forever and ever.[2]

Thoreau traveled through the Maine woods several times, climbing Katahdin and paddling up the Penobscot and Allagash Rivers. Thoreau wrote *In the Maine Woods* with future sportsmen in mind (see his advice in Appendix L), and the book further popularized northern Maine among sportsmen and recreational travelers. Consequently, by the mid-nineteenth century, travelers' reasons for visiting the Valley and their subsequent narratives changed form. Many had read Thoreau, and they came to the area to commune with nature. Travelers during this period particularly sought wilderness areas and spectacular landscapes. The Great Falls of the St. John, therefore, became a popular destination among adventurous, pre-rail travelers—and hardiness was mandatory (see Appendix L). Northern Maine and New Brunswick also began to attract the attention of anglers and hunters, since such vast tracts of land teeming with game and fish were getting rarer in the Northeast, where many species had been brought to the brink of extinction.

Travels to the upper St. John remained major expeditions. Travelers took servants or companions with them, hired Native guides from Old Town if they came from the south, or Natives or French Canadians from Canada if they came from the north. Dogs usually joined the party, as well; in winter, they pulled sleds. Throughout the year, dogs kept wild animals interested in the travelers' provisions at bay. Traveling parties sometimes met others along the way, and decided to journey together for a while. Travelers often slept outside, eating whatever food they had brought with them—salt pork, sailor's bread or "hard tack," and black, sweetened tea or coffee. Food obtained through purchases from settlers, hunting, fishing, and wild-berry picking could improve their diets. During the winter, one traveled on snowshoes and, when the road permitted, on sleigh. During the summer, travelers did not have to worry about freezing to death during the night, but they did have to contend with insects, including mosquitoes, swarms of blackflies, and sand flies. By the mid-1800s, products had already been devised to protect travelers against insect bites, and veils had become a necessary travel accessory.

C. The Evangeline Myth

By the mid-nineteenth century, the image of the Valley as the land of the "Evangeline people" was also firmly fixed in many people's mind. Longfellow's 1849 poem about a young Acadian girl who spent her life searching North America for the fiancé she lost during the Deportation of 1755 was an instant success. In addition, educated New Englanders felt they knew about the "real" Acadians. Volume 4 of George Bancroft's *History of the United States,* published in 1852, contained an account of the Deportation that was very favorable to the Acadians; Bancroft's narrative had to have been made public prior to publication, perhaps in a literary magazine, because a Maine newspaper, the *Maine Republican,* had referred to Bancroft's account nine years previously (in 1843). Mainers learned about Acadians even earlier because of the boundary dispute. State officials and newspapers claimed the Valley's early settlers had moved onto territory they knew to be American to escape their persecutors (see Appendix M for examples).

The Acadians appealed to the educated public for the same reason the wilderness did: they were deemed untainted by the corrupting effects of civilization. It is no accident that the very first verse of Longfellow's poem refers to a "forest primeval," or to the forest as it existed before humans' arrival. Subsequently, visitors came to the Valley looking for the "lost tribe" of Acadia. These visitors immediately recast the Valley architecture, clothing, and foods that differed from those of surrounding regions as French traditions handed down unchanged from generation to generation since the seventeenth century—even if these traditions were only fifty years old. But the Acadians' lifestyle didn't bear much resemblance to their ancestors'; instead, it reflected adaptations to a very different physical environment. Nonetheless, the Valley was viewed as an Acadian historical park instead of a living agricultural community. But that wasn't the worst of it. Expecting fresh-faced maidens in crisp Norman caps and kirtle, visitors were appalled to find grubby and sweaty farmwives who spent their days milking the cows, tending the garden, and slopping the pigs; some then decided that the Valley French were nothing but backward French Canadian, popish peasants who were "content to remain stationary when everything around them progresses."[3]

II.   POST-RAILROAD TRAVELERS

After the mid-nineteenth century, steamboats and trains reduced travel costs and made trips shorter and more comfortable. Increases in the standard of living of the middle and working classes made it possible for people of modest means to take trips. Women also began to travel for pleasure. The governments of both Maine and New Brunswick used their new railway systems to attract tourists and sportspeople. The railways pursued the same goals. Their guidebooks and tourist pamphlets targeted nature lovers by highlighting the area's picturesque beauty, isolation, and possibility for adventure.

With thousands of square miles of untouched and uninhabited frontier, wild forests, and magnificent rivers, streams, and lakes, the St. John Valley was the ideal vacationing paradise for anyone seeking unity with nature. The railway companies and governments made note of the numerous activities that could fulfill the vacation needs of any traveler. Although enthusiastic adventurers were willing to vacation in the Valley, both governments were well aware of the fact that time mattered. If a location took too long to reach, travelers would most likely not visit the area, no matter how well the government promoted its beauty. In fact, all of the major tourist spots in both Maine and New Brunswick were within easy reach of a railway station. For example, New Brunswick guidebooks constantly stressed that miles and miles of railroad connected visitors to the area's hunting and camping grounds. Early on, visitors could reach the Madawaska region via the New Brunswick Railway; the region became even more accessible from New England after the opening of the B&A, which put it within twenty-four hours' travel time from Boston.

As a result, railroad-era visitors were less adventurous than those who came before them. Nonetheless, these new men and, increasingly, women, still sought a respite from the bustle and pollution of urban life through exercise in the open air. Hunting was also a competitive sport; the men shipped the animals by rail back to Boston or New York and had the heads mounted as trophies.

A. Canoe, Camping, and Fishing Adventures

The first activities eager travelers might have tried out during their vacation in the St. John Valley were canoeing and camping. These trips, which differed in length and difficulty, appealed to both the casual

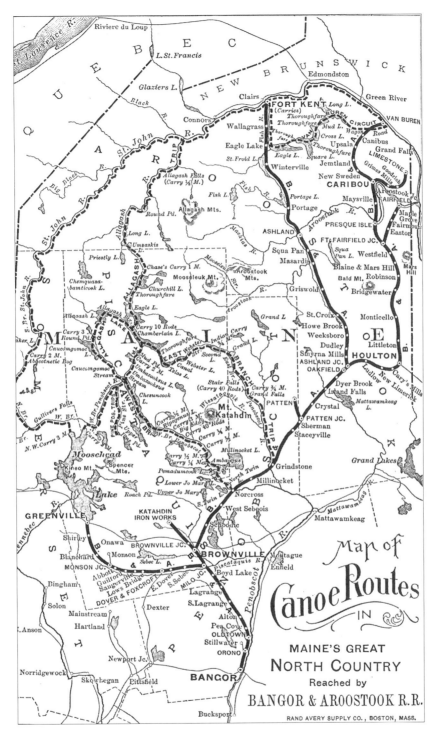

Map 22-1: Canoe routes in Maine
Clifford, Haunts of the Hunted, *1903, 92*

and serious adventurer. Some trips were advertised as suitable for families, and all visitors were promised that they would encounter places of beauty. Tourist literature suggested that, for the majority of trips, the assistance of a guide was advisable or required. These guides would ensure travelers' well-being and provide them with canoes and tents. In Maine, the state began regulating professional guides by 1904; the field was not restricted to men, and there were a few female guides. However, there were no registered guides in the Valley.

B&A promotional literature included not only a map of the canoe routes reached by the railroad, but also descriptions of the various circuits. The most famous canoe trip in the entire state was the one along the Allagash River. This 200-mile trip brought tourists to St. Francis. It was particularly attractive to romantic travelers since it took canoeists through various breathtaking sites. The first stop was Chesuncook Lake, an eighteen-mile-long and three-

mile-wide lake with a beautiful view of Katahdin. The next stop was Chamberlain Lake, the unique Allagash caves, and Allagash Falls. The Allagash trip could be extended to Fort Kent and beyond if the canoeists desired. The last part of the trip, from Fort Kent to Van Buren, took visitors through the heartland of the Madawaska region. At this juncture, visitors saw islands dotting the river, which added to region's charm. Once in Van Buren, travelers could return home on the B&A line.

The 111-mile Van Buren circuit took canoeists "through a country of wondrous beauty and into a fishing and hunting region that knows no superior." It was also "one of the prettiest and most comfortable canoe trips in all the B&A territory" and "an ideal outing for the man, woman, or family seeking a summer trip where ease and comfort can be combined with a reasonable amount of healthful outdoor exercise."[4] Canoeists typically arrived in Van Buren by early afternoon, where they were advised

Illus. 22-2: Canoeists camping at Edmundston
PANB, George Taylor Photograph, P5-603

The Land in Between

Illus. 22-3: Rafts could be used as pleasure boats. Fort Kent Historical Society

to immediately hire a guide. Then, it was suggested that they explore the town's points of interests: the college, convent school, and lumber mill. The next morning, guides took most visitors by road to Long Lake, the starting point of their canoe trip. Visitors could fish for trout and salmon in the lake if they were in no hurry. Cross Lake featured a good campground; those who preferred could also lodge at a nearby hotel. On the third day, the canoeists crossed Square Lake, where they could either camp or spend the night with local farmers at nearby Eagle Lake. People with time for only a short trip could catch the B&A there around noon and be back in Bangor by evening. Others could continue to Fort Kent. There, they could "tarry a day or two" to rest up and visit scenic and historic points of interests in the town. The Fort Kent to Van Buren portion of the trip could be completed in a day, thanks to a strong current. The return trip was easy, and before leaving Van Buren, voyagers could visit the Grand Falls, twelve miles away. *In the Pine Tree Jungles* mentioned that along this part of the river there was a French

settlement; it made a passing reference to the Acadian origin of the settlers but otherwise said little about its history. The outings the B&A promoted were not cultural adventures.

The New Brunswick Saint John Tourist Association proposed a canoe trip on the St. John River that covered 140 miles of wilderness. Canoeists started at Grand Falls and went downstream to Fredericton, their final destination. Grand Falls itself was easily reached, since it was a stop on the Canadian Pacific Railway. Eager travelers seeking to add more mileage to the trip could start from Lake Témiscouata. The trip brought travelers down the Madawaska River (a trout fishing area) to Edmundston. They then followed the St. John River back to the trip's starting point at Grand Falls. The Saint John Tourist Association promoted the beautiful scenery found along the river. The association knew that while most tourists wanted to rough it in the woods and sleep in tents, not all would. It therefore made sure that comfortable hotels were easy to reach at any point along the trip. Once in

Fredericton, the end of the trip, tourists were encouraged by the association's guidebook to take some time and visit the provincial capital's sites and surroundings.

At Grand Falls, guidebooks encouraged travelers to see what they considered as one of the greatest natural wonders of Canada. They described the waterfall, which was within walking distance of the village and boasted a fifty-eight-foot drop, as among the finest and largest in America—second only, perhaps, to Niagara Falls. A brochure titled *The Tourist's Guide to Saint John and the Province of New Brunswick* stressed the romantic qualities of the spectacle:

> It is a narrow and frightful chasm, lashed by the troubled water, and excavated by boiling eddies and whirlpools always in motion; at last the water plunges in an immense frothy sheet into a basin below, where it becomes tranquil, and the stream resumes its original features.[5]

Many travelers to the upper St. John Valley also took the Restigouche River canoe trip, which went through wild forests. Once again, travelers arrived at the starting point of the excursion by train—this time at St. Leonard on the Canadian Pacific. From there, the canoeists traveled twenty-five miles to the headwaters of the Restigouche. The trip itself was about ten days long and quite pleasant. It suited the casual adventurer, since the river was easy to manage, and there was a swift current all the way down, which meant easy paddling. The trip was also perfect for nature lovers, since the region was wild and remote.

The Squatook Lake trip was also described as a superior trip. From Van Buren, adventurers went on a 110-mile trip to the Fish and St. John Rivers, which guaranteed a healthy dose of outdoor exercise and fishing for some of the state's largest fish, such as twelve-pound trout and twenty-pound salmon. All in all, there were plenty of trip options and plenty of space for any nature lover seeking to vacation in Madawaska.

B. A Hunter's Paradise

The St. John Valley region was also renowned as a premier hunting ground. New Brunswick promoted the fact that it had more big game per square mile than any other province in Canada. This had not always been the case, though. During the mid-nineteenth century, a hunter would have had better luck hunting in Québec or Maine. However, while big game populations—especially moose, caribou, and red deer—had become much scarcer in those areas, they had actually increased in New Brunswick during the latter half of the nineteenth century. About seven million acres, approximately one third of the province of New Brunswick, had yet to be settled, allowing big game populations to flourish. As with canoe routes, hunting grounds were all within easy reach of the railway; indeed, some lines went directly into the heart of the best hunting territories. Government officials regulated hunting: the open season for moose, caribou, and deer extended from September 15 to November 30; killing moose calves was prohibited at all times; and non-resident hunters were required to buy a $50 license.

The St. John Valley was itself a popular hunting destination, especially for moose, deer, and caribou. According to a guidebook entitled *Big Game in New Brunswick,* almost all the hunting parties that visited the region in 1897 succeeded in capturing big game. The moose were of magnificent sizes: a Mr. Decatur, of Portsmouth, New Hampshire, had apparently killed a moose weighing about 900 pounds whose antlers measured 66 inches from tip to tip. A visitor from Philadelphia reportedly caught an even larger animal. Although these animals were already of significant sizes, the guidebook ensured its readers that they could catch much larger ones, and tried to attract hunters with the lure of a record-breaking hunt. The ground around the Green and Restigouche Rivers, the Third Falls, and the Little Forks, which were easily reached from either Edmundston or St. Leonard (both stops on the Canadian Pacific Railway), boasted many moose, as

Illus. 22-4: These hunters are waiting for the B&A, which will take them and their trophies (two moose) back home. Haunts of the Hunted, *86.*

well as, to a lesser extent, caribou and deer.

Northeastern Maine offered similar opportunities for the eager hunter. The Masardis region on the Aroostook River was a popular destination. The rail journey was quick, at least for the times, and comfortable. A hunter who left Boston in the evening on a sleeping car could reach Masardis the next day at noon, leaving him plenty of time to get into the field before nightfall. In the late 1800s, the Fish River extension of the B&A (which went from Ashland to Fort Kent) opened up fifty-two miles of deep virgin forest that was home to thousands of deer and moose. Ashland was less than twelve miles from Portage, which had a great reputation among hunters. In 1901, hunters caught some of the season's largest and most magnificent moose and deer

in this area. And as in New Brunswick, the number of big game had actually increased over the years. From there, hunters could take the train to Winterville or Eagle Lake, which also still offered great gaming opportunities. The last leg of the trip brought hunters to Fort Kent, where the B&A could take them home. Fort Kent was also the starting point for many other trips that took hunters to regions where moose and deer were abundant. Before leaving Fort Kent, travelers were encouraged to explore the town and visit the fort, after which the town was named. With its hundreds of gaming options, all within easy reach thanks to the Canadian Pacific and B&A, the St. John Valley was depicted as a true hunter's paradise.

Wealthy urban dwellers in the late nineteenth and early twentieth centuries were attracted to the St. John Valley's scenery, waterways, and hunting and fishing opportunities. The railroads put the region within relatively easy reach of Quebec City, Saint John, and Boston. Naturally, railroad companies wanted to encourage tourism because it increased passenger traffic. The bulk of the promotional literature produced by the railroads, government agencies, and various outdoor associations targeted outdoorsy people: canoeists, fishermen, and hunters. These organizations made only passing reference to the French character or history of the upper St. John Valley. Clarence Pullen's *In Fair Aroostook*, published by the B&A in 1902, was an exception. While this publication catered to outdoorsy sorts, it also introduced readers to the area's culture, particularly the recent Swedish immigrants living in New Sweden

---

Sidebar 22-1: Back to the Primeval Nature

At the end of the nineteenth and beginning of the twentieth century, many believed that urban life was artificial. People needed to get in touch with Nature to regain their "true" humanity. The Bangor and Aroostook Railroad publications were promoting this notion. The following paragraphs were allegedly penned by a "woman nature-lover", praising the beneficial influence of the Maine woods on over-civilized individuals.

Deep in the blood of every man worthy of the name, lies something of the primitive being as God first designed him. It may be a love of Nature, in its simple beauties as we find them in the woodland paths with the springs, and flowers, and birds, and beautiful foliage, or in the grander, more rugged outlines of mountains and lakes under a glorious sunset skies. Or it may be even more primitive—for is there a man who lives and breathes, who has never turned a listening ear to the "call of the wild" or felt it stir in his blood? Who has not felt a wild desire creep over him, to throw off the shackles of civilization and step out into the Garden of Eden—into true freedom and be for a time, his own master?...

The twentieth century with its airships, wonderful steel structure, and marvellous inventions and its civilization—and a journey of only twenty four hours and your social pets and the humble citizens; the millionaires and the bread-winners are again brothers just out of school.

The fetters are cast aside and man comes into his own. The log cabin becomes a palace, the open campfire—his mirror in which he sees his dream-life of freedom as it should be, wherin there is equality—brotherhood.

The simple, wholesome food from tin plates, the sparkling water from tin cups are dainties fit for a king, and indeed he feels himself a king among men—and yet he is living the life of the Indians. But the Superior minds knows and recognizes it to be a nearness to Nature and Nature's God. The society and civilization that the city life demands today are the iron bars that make your prison, through which you may only look upon the divine life of the free man.

Source: Hennessy (n.d.): 101–03.

and Westmanland and the Acadians living in the St. John Valley. But the publishers had an underlying, less visible motive for producing the booklet.

The B&A directors were aware that tourists from Boston and other cities to the south had money. They hoped that their vacation would open their eyes to the potential of the county and convince them to invest in its industries. Their involvement could in turn generate additional traffic—and profit—for the B&A. Consequently, the B&A aggressively promoted northern tourism, releasing four brochures between 1898 and 1906. But something more was needed. Outside investors had to be convinced that the county dwellers actually wanted economic development. Therefore, the common stereotype of Valley people as backward French Canadian peasants would not do. *In Fair Aroostook*

is thus a curious read, designed to encourage New Englanders to come and visit the land of Evangeline, while simultaneously working to convince business-people that Acadians were forward-looking people who embraced change. Pullen obviously knew about Longfellow and even quoted from *Evangeline*. But he also described well-tended and productive farms; large, modern houses along the river (with more primitive ones in new settlements); smart young professionals, such as Peter Keegan and Vincent Thériault, Esq.; and innumerable young female teachers, all invariably pretty, intelligent, and highly competent. *In Fair Aroostook* goes to great length to show that not only were the Valley's educational facilities (the Madawaska Training School and Van Buren College) without peer, but also its people were keen to have their children receive a solid edu-

---

Sidebar 22-2: The Future of Fort Kent

Following the completion of the railroad extension from Ashland, of which it will be the terminus, the town of Fort Kent will take rank among the foremost of the Aroostook towns. Its isolated position on the northern border of the State, with no railroad facilities except such as are afforded by the Temiscouata line across the St. John River, has so far retarded the development due to the natural advantages of the site. Even under such conditions, its growth has kept pace with the development of the country north of the Aroostook River and from the time of the Aroostook War, in 1839, it has been an important supply point for lumbermen and the trade center for a considerable population of Acadian farmers. The coming of the railroad will materially increase its availability as a distributing point, and as a place of customs entry from Canada, and will make profitable the extensive manufacture of lumber. Along this avenue of transportation a considerable part of the more than 110,000,000 feet of Aroostook lumber that yearly is driven down the St. John to be manufactured in New Brunswick will find its way through Maine to markets on American soil. Beyond the commercial prospects that are now at hand there is a promising future for Fort Kent in its eminent advantages as a health and pleasure resort....

Near the river, on the level plateau that includes the famous blockhouse is the handsome residence of Vincent M. Thériault, Esq., a wealthy land proprietor who is one of the leading lawyers in the Madawaska territory. He is of Acadian descent, and his wife was the beautiful Marguerite Elise Cyr of the family so prominent in all the annals of the Madawaska territory. From my visit to his place I brought pictures of his house and family which represent the most cultured phase of Acadian life.

Source: Pullen (1902): 44 and 61

---

cation. He claimed, "In no New England rural tract similar in extent and population are the common schools more numerous, the ratio of attendance greater, or the pupils apter to learn, than in Maine Acadia."[6]

His goal was to prove that while the Valley had a romantic past and exotic character, the younger generation was educated, smart, orderly, industrious, modern, and forward looking. In other words, Pullen wanted investors to realize Acadians were the kind of people who could make them earn dividends on their investments (see Sidebar 22-1). Pullen differs markedly from his contemporaries, who viewed the St. John Valley French as either Acadians frozen in time or backward French Canadian peasants left more and more behind by the modern world. It seems unlikely, however, that visitors to the Valley were really more interested in the Madawaska Training School than fishing and exploration.

Conclusion

During the late nineteenth century, rail lines allowed the St. John Valley to become a very popular vacation destination. Tour companies and the guide-books they produced stressed the abundance of recreational opportunities for tourists in all parts of the Valley. Tourist associations on both sides of the Valley concentrated all of their efforts on attracting nature lovers and adventure seekers. With their descriptions of remote rivers, wild forests, untouched frontiers, and beautiful landscapes, they promoted a very romantic picture of the region. This attracted those seeking an escape from city life and yearning for unity with nature. They also promoted more aggressive activities, such as hunting, to help those perhaps seeking domination over nature. And they hinted at potential investment opportunities for wealthy visitors.

ENDNOTES
1. From "Lines Composed a Few Miles Above Tintern Abbey," in *The Complete Poetical Works of William Woodsworth,* 194.
2. Thoreau, *The Maine Woods,* 1985 ed., 645.
3. Elwell, *Aroostook, with some account of the excursions...,* 25.
4. Clifford, *In the Pine Tree Jungles,* 113.
5. Mulhall, *Tourist's Guide...,* 58.
6. Pullen, *In Fair Aroostook,* 60.

FURTHER READINGS
Pullen, Clarence. *In Fair Aroostook.* 1902; reprinted by the Madawaska Historical Society in 1973.

SOURCES
For a very broad overview of tourism see Boyer (1996) and Holloway (1989). For the offshoots of tourism, see B. LeBlanc (2003).

Promotional brochures like the ones cited can be found in Aroostook County libraries. We used the following from the Aroostook Room at the University of Maine at Presque Isle: Churchward (1898), Clifford (1902 and 1903), and Hennessy (no date). We used the following equivalent information for New Brunswick: Fredericton Tourist Association (1909), Mulhall (1888), Reynolds (1898), and the Saint John Tourist Association (1905). Starting in the mid-1880s, the Maine Bureau of Industrial and Labor Statistics began publishing reports on Maine's hotels and boardinghouses and occasionally discussed the region's tourist industry. The Valley, as usual, tended to be overlooked.

23

PUBLIC EDUCATION, 1870–1914

During this forty-five year period, the educational system in the Valley greatly expanded, as it did in the rest of Maine and New Brunswick. New Brunswick secularized its common schools, a measure that the province's Catholics and Acadians bitterly opposed. Their opposition almost provoked a constitutional crisis in the new Dominion of Canada. In Maine, changes included the introduction of compulsory elementary schooling and the creation of the Madawaska Training School.

I.   NEW BRUNSWICK MADAWASKA

A. The New Brunswick School Crisis

In New Brunswick, many schools were initially denominational. The secularization of the public school system in 1871 led to serious political troubles and even to a "school strike," all to no avail since the schools remained secular.

By the 1860s, provincial authorities considered education in New Brunswick highly unsatisfactory. Schools were underfunded and operated only on an irregular basis; teachers were often unqualified, the curriculum was haphazard, and too many children grew up to be illiterate or semi-literate adults. The problem was even more pronounced in the Acadian districts. For instance, in 1860, the school inspector noted that while most Madawaska students could read, teachers taught them almost nothing else. Part of this problem stemmed from parents who were satisfied once the child could read; as a result, few students learned anything besides reading, writing, and spelling. In 1869, New Brunswick Premier George E. King decided to remedy this state of affairs by creating a tax-supported, tuition-free, non-denominational common school system throughout the province. The Common Schools Act passed in 1871 also required teachers to attend the normal school in Fredericton and become certified; textbooks had to belong to the province's approved list; and instruction had to be in English. It also prohibited religious education, the display of religious symbols in the schools, and the wearing of religious habits by teachers.

The Catholic Church immediately opposed the measure. In the nineteenth century, the Church opposed non-confessional schools which it considered "atheist." Acadians had an additional reason to be upset: the new common schools were going to be English schools. Opposition to the Common School Act was, therefore, stronger in Acadian districts than elsewhere in the province. Lévite Thériault, a member of the House of Assembly for Madawaska and a member of the provincial cabinet, had voted in favor of the act—only one of two Acadian legislators to do so. He never gave his reasons. In Madawaska, opposition to the Common School Act soon became opposition to Thériault.

Illus. 23-1: Levite Thériault
PANB, P37-139

The *Moniteur Acadien* depicted him as a traitor:

> We have learned from a reliable source that the ex-Honorable Lévite Thériault is suspicious since his electors have understood the consequences of his vote this last winter and his role in the iniquitous King Bill, which so outrageously insults Catholics. He has no friend left in the county and he can finish his days in the pleasant knowledge he has nothing left to do but run his mills.... The entire Madawaska County is a permanent meeting, as one hears from all quarters nothing but the expression of the deepest indignation at such an unfair law.... The refusal to be subjected to the overall provisions, as well as to the specific ones of this monstrous law, is unanimous.[1]

Thériault backtracked quickly, resigned from the government, and claimed Premier King had misrepresented the act to him. He also donated lumber to the sisters of the Hotel-Dieu de Montreal to rebuild the St. Basile Convent, thus ensuring that they stayed at Madawaska. He was easily re-elected in 1873 (475 to 210).

The act's opponents adopted two strategies to fight it. One was political. They argued that it went against the principles of Confederation. Because a school act passed in 1858 permitted religious instruction in the province, and because Canada's constitution secured all rights that minorities had enjoyed prior to Confederation, opponents claimed the act was unconstitutional. English and French Madawaskayans sent no less than seven petitions to the provincial Legislative Council and Assembly asking for the law to be amended or scrapped altogether. The provincial government did not change its mind. John Costigan (see Sidebar 26-1), then asked the federal government to disallow the act, which it had the right to do. The federal government refused to intervene: education was a provincial responsibility under the BNA Act (the Canadian constitution). In Québec, opposition to any restrictions on provincial autonomy in this matter was very strong. In addition, Prime Minister John A. Macdonald's Liberal-Conservatives had the support of the powerful Orange Order, a Protestant organization that violently opposed tax-supported Catholic schools. The federal Parliament merely adopted a motion regretting that New Brunswick had passed this legislation. The next step was to appeal to the Judiciary Committee of the Privy Council in London, the Supreme Court for the Empire. In 1873, the Privy Council upheld the Common School Act. In 1875, King's government was re-elected. One of the election slogans was "Vote for the Queen, against Popery." For many of the law's supporters, the act was as much a measure against Catholics as one to improve elementary education in the province.

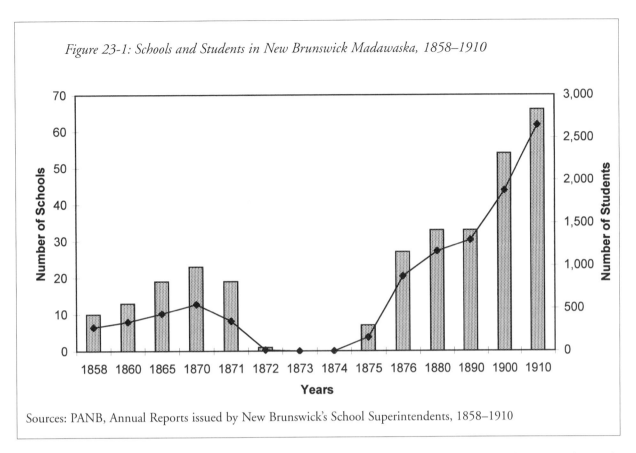

Figure 23-1: Schools and Students in New Brunswick Madawaska, 1858–1910

Sources: PANB, Annual Reports issued by New Brunswick's School Superintendents, 1858–1910

Opponents also used extra-legal tactics: they refused to pay taxes for the maintenance of common schools. The province even arrested and imprisoned the Reverend Joseph Michaud (originally from Madawaska) for this refusal. Parents also simply stopped sending their children to school, which led to several school closures. There were twenty-two schools in Madawaska County prior to the Common School Act. By 1874, there was only one school left in the entire county; it was not even attended by French students, but by Anglo-Protestant students living in the region (see Figure 23-1).

In 1875, the bishop of Saint John, Mgr. Sweeney, and the recently re-elected King reached a compromise: religious teaching would be allowed outside regular school hours; members of religious orders could teach wearing their habits; teachers who had not attended the province's normal school could get third-class licenses; and teachers could use

French in the Acadian schools' lowest grades, with students tested in both French and English at the end of each term. The compromise ended the opposition to common schools, but there were barely any schools left in Madawaska County, and the St. Basile Academy, which had once trained young women to become teachers, had closed its doors when it lost its provincial subsidy.

B. Education in New Brunswick Madawaska after 1875

The new superintendent, M. Balloch of Edmundston, rebuilt the educational system. By 1877, there were thirty-one schools, averaging thirty-three students, and the numbers kept growing. More and more teachers were women and by the twentieth century, male teachers had become a rarity. Female teachers did not stay very long in the profession: one-third of them taught for three years or less. More and more schools were graded, and in 1884, a superior school offering secondary level courses (for those in grades seven to nine) opened at Edmundston. This school remained rather small; in 1910, it had only thirteen students in grade nine. These students took Latin (twelve), algebra (thirteen), bookkeeping (four), and trigonometry (six), in addition to the subjects taught at the elementary level. The nearest grammar school (secondary school) was located in Grand Falls. It offered the usual high school subjects, including Latin. It did not, however, offer French until the late 1800s.

There were still serious problems with the state of education: the number of untrained and third-class teachers remained high until the eve of World War I. In addition, many parents did not send their children to school, or they took them out after their second or third year of schooling. The most common reasons for this were lack of money and the need for extra labor on the farm. Factors such as limited resources, the lack of French education except in the lower grades, and a non-compulsory education system collectively took their toll. French-speaking New Brunswickers had a higher-than-average illiteracy rate. In 1891, illiteracy rates across the Acadian counties included 27 percent in Kent and Restigouche, 36 percent in Gloucester, and 44 percent in Victoria-Madawaska. By 1911, some progress had been made. Illiteracy rates had dropped to 32 percent in Gloucester and 25 percent in Madawaska-Victoria (the provincial average was 14 percent). Those were also the counties with the highest proportion of French-speaking people. Men had a higher illiteracy rate than women (33 percent versus 23 percent in Madawaska-Victoria).

Higher levels of illiteracy among the Acadian population also stemmed from a different attitude toward education. Whereas English-speakers tended to view literacy as a basic life skill (especially Protestants who believed in Bible reading), the Acadians viewed literacy and numeracy as vocational skills. Consequently, they tended to keep one of their children (the most promising, academically) in school much longer than average and pull the others out very quickly. Education was a strategy to establish children; consequently, one often found families where one child was a school teacher, while his or her siblings were illiterate—a situation that baffled English-speaking authorities.

II.   AMERICAN MADAWASKA

A. Consolidation and Expansion

Legislation passed in 1870 (see Chapter 12) finally placed the Madawaska schools on sound footing, and the number of schools and students increased steadily. The Maine authorities, nonetheless, remained unsatisfied with the state of education in the state. Their concerns were the usual: irregular attendance, lack of parental interest, lack of discipline, incompetent teachers, and improper classification of pupils. They blamed the district system—which almost always meant a single, one-room school per district—for most of the problems. The 1870 legislation made it possible to abolish school districts and replace them with town school systems supervised by an elected school board along with an elected supervisor or a hired superintendent. By 1893, all the remaining district schools had been abolished, and town school boards had become the norm. In 1887, the state passed a law requiring all children between the ages of five and fifteen to attend school for at least sixteen weeks in the year, and in 1909, attendance became mandatory for fifteen- to seventeen-year-olds who could neither read nor write a legible sentence in English. This may be part of the reason why the proportion of young people eligible to attend school in the Valley (those between ages four and twenty-one) who actually did so increased, from about half the school-age population in 1870 to two-thirds by 1910.

Common schools with grade levels also expanded their curricula. In 1910, fourteen towns in

Illus. 23-2, above: A former one-room schoolhouse at the Tante Blanche Museum in St. David.
Photograph by B. Craig

Illus. 23-3, below: Grand Ruisseau School
Madawaska Historical Society

Illus. 23-4: Frenchville School building in 1900 (this was a one-room school).
Maine State Documents, Vol. 4, Report of the Superintendent of Schools for 1899, 25.

Aroostook County offered kindergarten through eighth-grade education; Island Falls and Stockholm offered kindergarten through ninth-grade education. Those more advanced schools were concentrated in central Aroostook; none were in the Valley. Only ten of the 117 Valley schools had grade levels, and none went further than grade six. Curiously, Eagle Lake had the highest number of graded schools of all the towns in the Valley (four).

B. The Use of French

The use of French in classrooms and even on school grounds remained a bone of contention. Nativism underwent a revival at the end of the nineteenth century. Nativists were hostile to immigrants preserving any aspect of their culture and were particularly hostile to immigrants communicating in their mother tongue. In 1895, they introduced a bill in the legislature mandating that schools still instructing in a language other than English lose their funding (see Sidebar 23-1). Major William Dickey, the representative from Fort Kent, denounced the measure. He had the support of Governor Llewellyn Power. Dickey said the bill violated the basic principles of fairness:

> On a stretch of 60 miles along the river St. John it is an impossible task to confer discipline and instruction but in English. Would it be equitable that for this reason thousands of children might lose the benefit of the schools? Would it be equitable to confiscate their rights to education, because being born of French parents and having learned in their prime infancy but the French tongue, one of the most beautiful languages in the world, they labor, as a matter of

Sidebar 23-1: Thou Shalt Not Speak French in School

State of Maine
Educational department

Augusta, May 1, 1896

To the teachers of Northern Aroostook

The examination which I made of your schools last summer and the more recent inspection which I have made of the books and accounts of your town make it necessary for me to call your attention to the following extracts from the Statute of Maine.

"No teacher shall be employed in any school receiving the benefit of the Madawaska Territory School Act, who is not able to speak and write the English language satisfactorily, and the English language shall be used in giving instruction and directing the discipline of the same." Also "the State Superintendent shall prescribe the studies to be taught in the common schools of this state."

By virtue of the power granted me by the above statutes, I prescribe that the studies enumerated in the School Laws of Maine shall be taught in your schools. To do this work as the law intends that it shall be done, will require the entire time of the school sessions, i.e. from 9 A.M. to 12 P.M. and from 1 to 4 P.M. It is clearly stated in the above extract that the instruction and discipline of the schools must be given in English. If this work is faithfully done, your children will, in a short time, be able to read, write, and speak the English language fluently. When I visit your schools next fall I shall be able to decide if you are complying with the requirements of the law cited above.

These statements do not debar you from giving instruction in another language, if your superintendent wishes you to do so. It does not prevent you from giving instruction in other subjects outside of school hours, if you are willing to do so. But I must insist that, during school hours, the work of the school shall be confined to teaching the subjects specified by the law.

I feel that this is a matter of great importance. Therefore, do not fail to have all the conversation of the school, both on the part of the teacher and pupils, carried on in English; and also have all the instruction, and all the explanations, directions, and commands given in this language.

A failure to do this will endanger the fund which your town draws from the State. This, together with the fact that the law requires that is stated above, furnishes sufficient reasons for your being very careful to live up to the letter and the spirit of the statute.

I trust that when I visit your schools next summer, I shall find the law complied with in all these particulars. I also would be glad to see some flower-beds in your school-yards, to see your rooms decorated with maps, pictures, and sketches made by the pupils or yourself; and I would likewise be pleased to see in the school rooms, flowers and such other simple and inexpensive decorations as you may be able to make or secure....

Very sincerely,
W. W. Stetson

Source: Maine State Archives, State of Maine, Office of the State Superintendent, 1896.

course, under the want that French may be, more or less, spoken to them for school discipline and instruction?[2]

Dickey advocated bilingual education in the lower grades and then all-English education in the higher grades, by which time a student should have become proficient in the language. The anti-French bill did not pass—at least not this time.

III.   POST ELEMENTARY EDUCATION

A. The High Schools

The state also turned its attention to post-elementary education. At mid century, academies which were chartered, endowed, fee-paying establishments provided this education. They offered college preparatory courses, although by the 1860s, the state paid for one academy per county to train common schools teachers. The academies nearest to the Valley were in Houlton (founded in 1847) and Patten (also founded in 1847). In the 1860s and 1870s, some towns began to open free high schools. There were twenty such high schools in the state by 1870. A high school also opened in Frenchville in the late 1860s, but initially it was private and subsidized by the parish priest, Father Sweron. To encourage more towns to open free high schools, the state began to subsidize them in 1873. They had to be open at least ten weeks a year and follow the state curriculum. If they met these conditions, the state reimbursed the town for half the teachers' salaries up to $500. In 1875, there were 165 free high schools in the state, including the one in Frenchville (see Sidebar 23-2). The law covering these free high schools was suspended for a year in 1879. These schools were accused of elitism because they had begun to teach college preparatory courses, deemed the responsibility of the academies: high schools existed primarily to educate future teachers. In 1880, it became illegal to use state money to support ancient and modern language education—except in schools where these languages were already taught. In 1887, lawmakers gave the superintendent the right to decide whether or not to teach second languages. In 1899, music moved into the same category as language education. However, since towns often contracted with academies to act as free high schools, the boundary between college preparatory schools and vocational high schools was often blurred.

B. The Madawaska Training School

Maine school officials had difficulties finding qualified teachers, and the state opened normal schools at Castine and Farmington in the 1860s. In the Valley, the problem was exacerbated because officials needed to find qualified bilingual teachers. Although instruction was in English, everyone recognized that teachers had to be able to communicate with their students. The authorities viewed schooling as doubly important in the Valley, since it would (they hoped) accelerate the Americanization of the population. In 1878, Dickey was instrumental in getting the state to support a special school to train teachers—the Madawaska Training School—for instruction in the Valley.

For the first ten years, the school alternated between Fort Kent and Van Buren. In 1887, it was permanently established at Fort Kent. The first principal of the school was the local-born Vital Cyr. Under both his direction and that of his successors, the school became an important asset for the region. The 1890 Maine Common School Report noted that "no school in the state is doing more important and valuable work than this, and none is growing more rapidly."[3] Attendance grew so much throughout the 1880s and 1890s that the school was forced

Sidebar 23-2: Upper St. John Valley High Schools, 1875–1910

	1875 Frenchville	1880 Frenchville	1885 Frenchville	1890 Frenchville	1895 Frenchville	1895 Madawaska	1910 St. Agatha
Operating costs in $	780		125	249	150	186	250
Funding from the town in $	250						
Funding from tuition in $	16						
Funding from the state treasury $	500	180	250	249	150	200	250
Number of terms	2		2	2			
Number of weeks	32		44	24	25	27	40
Registration	75	45	36	42	37	67	36
Attendance	70	35	24	34	25	41	32
Residents of township							36
Females							27
Males							9
In third reader or above	63	not taught		20	18	24	
In fourth reader or above	12	20	21	42	25	58	
English grammar	68	45	36	20	18	28	36
US history	not taught	20		42	25	67	36
Geography	35	0					
Ancient languages	20	0					
Modern languages	20	0		42	37	58	36
Sciences							11
Natural sciences	12			20			
Arithmetic	75	45	36	42	25	67	
Mathematics							36
Music							36
Drawing							36
Manual training							27
Bookkeeping	not taught	20	20	20	18	20	
Students who have taught or intend to teach within a year	24	24	12	22	13	8	

N.B.: Frenchville is not listed among the high schools after 1901, and Madawaska is not listed in 1905.
Sources: Maine Public Documents. *Reports of the State School Superintendent* (1875 to 1910).

Illus. 23-5: Madawaska training school
Acadian Archives/Archives acadiennes

to limit admission. In 1890, 59 students were admitted for the fall term and 68 for the winter term. In 1900, 112 new students were admitted and in 1910, 127.

The school's overarching goal was to teach potential teachers through drill work so they could, in turn, do the same with their students. During the first semester, students usually took reading, arithmetic, English grammar, and composition classes. During the second semester, they learned physical geography, civil government, art, and penmanship. They also devoted an hour a day to the theory and practice of teaching. The school boosted the regional schools' performance by providing them with many qualified teachers, but it also drew some criticism, since it was obviously aimed at assimilating and Americanizing its students. For example, prior to 1884, when French was finally added to the curriculum, training school students were only allowed to communicate in English. In addition, a training school diploma did not allow graduates to teach throughout the state; instead, they were restricted to the Valley. This problem was partly resolved when a normal school opened in Presque Isle in 1903, allowing some training school graduates to continue their studies and receive a diploma recognized throughout the state.

C. Colleges

There were no public colleges or universities in the Valley at the time. Some young people took advantage of English skills obtained in the local public school to attend Ricker Academy, a classical institute in Houlton. Florent Fournier, the first Madawaska-born physician, studied medicine at Bowdoin College. *Le Journal du Madawaska* mentioned a few young men who had studied, or were currently studying, out of state in 1904: Arthur Nadeau (son of John Nadeau), who had just been hired by a lawyer in Caribou, had studied law at Georgetown University; Ludger Pelletier was studying medicine at Laval University in Quebec City. Such opportunities were reserved for boys from families who could afford the tuition and boarding costs, as well as do without the labor of the adolescent in question. In the next chapter, we will discuss the private college and convent schools opened in the Valley by religious congregations.

Conclusion

Between 1870 and World War I, the school systems on both sides of the Valley were reorganized and literacy progressed as a result. On the New Brunswick side of the border, large numbers of third-class teachers, a faulty system that neither taught Acadian children English nor educated them fully in French, and different attitudes toward school led to a higher proportion of illiteracy in Acadian counties, Madawaska included, than elsewhere in the province. The American side, on the other hand, benefited from the opening of the Madawaska Training School and the introduction of compulsory education. The use of French in the schools, however, remained controversial, and attempts were made to prohibit it entirely. By 1910, there was one tax-supported high school on the American side of the Valley (in St. Agatha), a superior school in Edmundston, and a teachers' training school in Fort Kent. Although not accessible to all children, opportunities for education beyond the lower grades now existed in the Valley. They were supplemented by religious institutions (discussed in the next chapter).

ENDNOTES
1. Quoted in Desjardins, *Le Madawaska Raconté par le Moniteur Acadien,* 28. (Article dated February 23, 1872, translated by the authors.)
2. Burque, *Major Dickey,* 14.
3. Maine Public Documents, *Thirty-Seventh Annual Report of the State Superintendent of Common Schools,* Augusta, ME: Burleigh and Flint, 1891, 51.

FURTHER READING
Chadbourne, Ava H. *A History of Education in Maine: A Study of a Section of American Educational History,* 1922.
MacNaughton, Katherine F.C. "The Development of the Theory and Practice of Education in New Brunswick, 1784-1900: A Study in Historical Background." Master's thesis, University of New Brunswick, 1947. (Available online from the University of New Brunswick Library web site: www.lib.unb.ca/)

SOURCES
The biographies of Premier George Edwin King, Bishop John Sweeney, the Reverend Joseph Michaud, and MP John Costigan in the *Dictionary of Canadian Biography* (online at http://www.biographi.ca/EN/) provide context for the New Brunswick common school question. One can also consult Wilbur (1989). Toner (1967 and 1970) and Hatfield (1972 and 1975) both cover the 1873 controversy. Besides MacNaughton, one can find useful information about education in New Brunswick in general in Fitch (1930) and Hody (1964). Andrew (1997) explains the Acadian attitude toward education, and Couturier Leblanc, *et. al.* (1993) provides an overview of the subject. See also Lejeune (1989). Statistical data can be found in the Provincial Archives of New Brunswick (PANB) in the annual reports issued by New Brunswick's school superintendents.

Useful information and statistical data for Maine Madawaska can be found in the annual reports of the state superintendents of public schools. Those documents also contain reports about the Madawaska Training School. The history of this institution was the topic of Paradis' M.A. thesis (1964). Albert (1920), Michaud (1984), Desjardins (1992), Bélanger-Violette (1953), and Sirois (1977) also discuss education in American or New Brunswick Madawaska.

24

THE CHURCH AND PUBLIC WELFARE, 1870–1914

During this period, the role of the Catholic Church in both the lives of Maritime Acadians and New England French-speakers changed markedly, particularly in the areas of education, health, and welfare. First, as the Maritime Peninsula's Catholic population grew, the Church reorganized dioceses and created new parishes. More and more priests were of Acadian origin, and at the end of this period, an Acadian even became bishop—but not without a struggle against the Irish-dominated hierarchy. In the Maritimes and New England, parish priests and bishops also began to call on members of religious congregations to provide services—such as private schools, hospitals, nursing homes, and orphanages—to the Catholic (and even non-Catholic) population.

The Valley remained overwhelmingly Catholic throughout this period. Despite stock images to the contrary, the relationship between the laity and clergy were not always harmonious; the Valley, however, appears to have escaped the worst of the conflict, namely those that pitted French-speaking parishioners against Irish bishops.

I.   ACADIANIZING THE CHURCH IN THE MARITIMES

Prior to 1850, there were barely any Acadian priests in New Brunswick. This changed after the mid-1800s. The first Madawaska-born priest was Joseph Michaud, ordained in 1867. Fourteen years previously, however, in 1853, the Kamouraska-born, St. Basile-raised Joseph Pelletier had become a priest. Like many other Madawaska-born priests, he attended the college in Sainte-Anne-de-la-Pocatière. Between 1867 and 1930, more French-speaking priests came from Madawaska than any other county: twenty-seven from Madawaska County and five from the American side of the Valley. Additionally, twenty-six priests came from Westmorland County, twenty-five from Gloucester, and twenty-five from Kent.[1]

Despite this growth, the hierarchy remained in Irish or Scottish hands. In 1900, all five Maritime bishops were Scottish or Irish, despite the fact that there were more French Catholics than Irish Catholics. Bishop Sweeny (Saint John) and Bishop Rogers (Chatham) had reached retirement age. The Acadians believed that the time had come for one of their own to be nominated bishop. However, when the five Maritime bishops met to select the two names they would submit to the pope, they chose two Irishmen: Thomas Francis Barry and Timothy Casey. The Acadians were furious and even went as far as boycotting the installation ceremonies.

The Acadians were convinced that the Irish hierarchy was at best intent on monopolizing control of the Church in the Maritimes, or at worst downright hostile to the preservation of the French culture. Several incidents fed this conviction: the Irish bishops in the Maritimes had seen no point in starting French-language newspapers in the region, believing instead that English-language newspapers adequately served the public. The bishop of Chatham had withdrawn funding to the eight-year-old Saint-Louis-de-Kent classical college founded by Abbé Richard because he believed the school promoted French culture too vigorously. Sweeny, on the other hand, supported the supposedly bilingual St. Joseph College at Memramcook (in practice a mostly English school). The Acadians also claimed that the bishops encouraged Irish men to become priests, a courtesy they did not seem to extend to Acadian ones.

Tensions between Irish-dominated hierarchies and French-speaking laities were not unique to the Maritimes. Eastern Ontario French Canadians clashed with Mgr. Fallon, bishop of London (Ontario), over the use of French as the language of instruction in parish schools, and Maine's Francophone population clashed with the bishop of Portland over "national" (or "ethnic" in present-day terms) parishes. Language was always at the heart of the issue because the laity and clergy widely disagreed over the relationship between ethnicity and religion. The Irish believed that religion transcends ethnicity and culture: Catholics formed one community irrespective of language, citizenship, and national origins. Their singular duty was to protect and spread the faith. In North America, the Irish clergy believed that clinging to linguistic and cultural differences endangered this goal. They believed that Protestants would be less likely to approach a priest for information, and possibly conversion, if he belonged to a different cultural group or spoke a different language. Anti-French feelings were also quite strong in Canada outside of Québec, and the Irish considered the association of Catholicism with French an obstacle to acceptance by the Anglo-Protestant majority. In the United States, Americans viewed cultural and especially linguistic variation as a rejection of their culture. And even when sympathetic to the goal of cultural survival, English-speaking bishops believed this secular goal should have no

Illus. 24-1: The new St. Bruno Church, built in 1876, in 1895.
UMPI, Aroostook Room, Arts Work of Aroostook County, *Chicago, 1895.*

bearing on the running and administration of the Church.

Acadians and French Canadians held a different view. Language and religion constituted two key components of their identity. They believed that if their language was eliminated or even undermined, their religion would inevitably become endangered. Anglicization also would make them more vulnerable to Protestant conversion attempts. In short, they believed, *Qui perd sa langue perd sa foi* ("He who loses his language loses his faith").

Upset by the nomination of the two Irish bishops, the Maritime Acadians continued to agitate for an Acadian bishop in newspaper editorials and sent petitions and representatives to Rome to plead their case. The Irish, as can be expected, used the same tactics but to opposite ends. Rome, however, grew concerned over the growing rift between English- and French-speaking Catholics, and in 1912, the pope appointed Mgr. Edouard Leblanc as the new bishop of Saint John. New Brunswick Madawaska, however, remained under the authority of the Irish bishop of Chatham.

On the surface, Valley residents did not encounter problems with their bishops in either Chatham or Portland. But there are hints that their relationship with the bishop of Portland was less than ideal. When Father Gory invited the *Filles de la Sagesse* (Daughters of Wisdom) to open a convent in St. Agatha (Maine) in 1904, he advised them to build the convent on their own land instead of Church land in order "to be independent of the Bishop who is peculiar (*un original*)." Apparently, the bishop was prejudiced against the French sisters, but we know nothing about the reasons behind this prejudice.

II.   THE ROLE OF RELIGIOUS CONGREGATIONS

During the latter half of the nineteenth century, Catholic religious orders underwent a spectacular expansion; this was especially true for female orders in Québec. In 1854, Bishop Connelly of Fredericton brought the Sisters of Charity of the Immaculate Conception (later known as the Sisters of Charity of Saint John) to his diocese. His successor, Sweeny of Saint John (the seat of the diocese was transferred from one city to the other in 1860), called upon several male and female orders to help him develop a network of educational and charitable institutions. French-speaking orders saw their numbers increase after 1904 when the French government made it illegal for religious orders to teach and banned most religious congregations from the country. Sisters (and brothers) who did not wish to return to secular life joined or started congregations abroad, and many came to North America. Some of those exiled sisters resettled in St. Agatha in 1905. The presence of teaching orders even led to a curious phenomenon in American Madawaska: public schools staffed by members of religious congregation wearing the habit of their order.

A. The St. Basile Academy

The first religious foundation in the Valley opened in 1858. The St. Basile priest, Mgr. Langevin, had established a scholarship fund for boys at Sainte-Anne-de-la-Pocatière in 1855. In his will, he left a piece of property known as La Butte à Bellefleur in St. Basile to the bishop of Saint John, to open a convent school for girls. A year after his death in 1857, the Sisters of Charity of Saint John opened a school that received a small subsidy from the province; the St. Basile Academy prepared young women for the teaching profession. The academy closed in 1873, after losing its subsidy following the Common School Act. One of the graduates, Suzanne Cyr (daughter of Elie Cyr and Sophie Ayotte, 1850–1936), later joined the order under the name of Sister Marie-Anne and, much later, founded the *Congrégation des Religieuses de Notre-Dame du Sacré-Coeur,* an Acadian congregation.

The Religious Hospitallers of St. Joseph (*Religieuses hospitalières de Saint-Joseph*), a Montreal teaching and nursing congregation, immediately took over the vacated school building. The sisters quickly opened a sick room and dispensary and began teaching and taking boarders the following

Illus. 24-2: Hotel-Dieu (hospital) de Saint-Basile. CDEM, PC3-32

year. The St. Joseph Hospital (Hotel-Dieu Saint-Joseph) was the very first hospital to open in the Valley. The sisters also received help from Dr. Félix-Xavier Bernier, who offered his expertise free of charge. The community had a difficult beginning: the building was too small and not functional, and the first superior died after a few months, to be replaced by Sister Maillet. In 1876, the hierarchy seriously considered closing the convent. Sister Maillet, however, pleaded for another year, and Lévite Thériault donated the lumber needed to construct a new building. The expanded convent/school/hospital stayed. In 1884, the sisters began to take in orphans, and in 1885, they opened a small boy division (those aged five to twelve); in 1888, they began receiving provincial funding for the hospital. In 1884, they aligned their curriculum with the provincial one and started providing a preparatory course for the Fredericton Normal School. This made them eligible for government funding. Boys and girls were both eligible to take this preparatory course, but very few boys took

advantage of the opportunity. By 1910, both the school and hospital had begun to play an important role in the community, drawing students and patients from both sides of the river.

B. The "Public Parish Schools" of Maine

There was no opposition to sisters in Maine public schools, and parish priests quickly grasped the possibilities that came along with their presence. They wanted the children of their parish to receive a Catholic education. Meanwhile, school boards wanted to save money. To this end, they were hiring more and more female teachers. Sisters were even cheaper: they lived communally and donated their salaries to the community, which allowed them to subsidize other activities if needed. Father Beduneau, who was trying to bring the Daughters of Wisdom to St. Agatha in 1904, was very explicit:

> Give us three sisters who can teach in English, and they will immediately get $700 from the state; after a year, give us two additional sisters

Illus. 24-3: St. Agatha Convent
UMPI, Aroostook Room, Arts Work of Aroostook County, *Chicago, 1895.*

who can teach high school, and they will get $400; add a small wing to the hospital to take in the county's elderly, and each resident will bring in $60 a year; if you have a sister who understands pharmacy, she will make money hand over fist.[2]

A sister, in other words, was a financial resource.

And thus it happened that in September 1904, a group of sisters left France for St. Agatha, where they founded the first Daughters of Wisdom community in the United States. The sisters first opened a dispensary, then took the examinations needed to become certified teachers, and finally began teaching elementary and high school classes. They took in boarders (boys up to age twelve and girls up to their high school graduation). In France, the Daughters of Wisdom had catered to a mostly middle-class clientele. The community in St. Agatha similarly taught "accomplishments": piano, violin, singing, painting, and needlework. Every year, they organized an exhibition of their students' work and a public con-

cert. Interestingly, they also taught the boys how to sew. In 1906, the sisters opened a hospital with an operating room and nursing home. At the same time, they opened a convent school in Lower Grand Isle (Lille).

Other parishes already benefited from the services of religious congregations when the Daughters of Wisdom crossed the Atlantic. Father Sweron had invited the *Congrégation Notre-Dame du Saint-Rosaire* of Rimouski to open a boarding school and teach elementary classes in Frenchville in 1899. The Ste. Luce School became a tax-supported public school after Father Sweron was elected to the school board in 1900. Father Marcoux, who had been appointed to St. Joseph Parish in Wallagrass, immediately built a church, rectory, and convent; he invited the *Petites Franciscaines de Marie* of Baie-Saint-Paul in 1898. The sisters opened a boarding school, which accepted boys. By 1908, this convent was in financial difficulties. The new priest, Father Bourbeau had the sisters hired as public school

Illus. 24-4: St. Mary's College in 1895
UMPI, Aroostook Room, Arts Work of Aroostook County, *Chicago, 1895.*

teachers, but this did not solve their problems, and they left in 1913. Marcoux was, by then, a priest in Eagle Lake, where he had built a hospital staffed by members of a religious order; the school, however, had to wait until 1916. Father Decory called the Franciscaines to Fort Kent, where they opened a school in 1906 and began receiving public funding in 1907. They took female boarders after 1911 and male boarders after 1915.

C. Van Buren's St. Mary's College

Almost all the religious orders in the Valley were female ones, and these women did most of their teaching at the elementary level, except in St. Agatha and Van Buren. A few attempts had been made to attract a male teaching congregation to the Valley in the hopes that it would open a French secondary school for boys so that they would not have to travel to receive a post-elementary education. Usually, Valley boys went to Sainte-Anne-de-la-Pocatière;

when a bilingual Catholic college opened in Memramcook in the 1864, Madawaska boys began attending that school as well. Both of those institutions offered a seven-year collegiate, classical course leading to a baccalaureate degree, as well as a shorter commercial course.

Valley residents had contacted the Holy Cross Fathers in the 1860s, but they had declined the offer and gone on to run St. Joseph College in Memramcook. The Jesuits had been approached in the aftermath of the New Brunswick school crisis, but they also declined the offer. In 1884, St. Bruno Parish in Van Buren was handed over to the Marist brothers, a teaching order. The Marists opened St. Mary's College three years later; the state chartered the college in 1889 under the name Van Buren College and allowed it to grant baccalaureate degrees. St. Mary's, which included a high school and college division, was bilingual. The college was constructed in front of the church. It was at first a modest building with four 50-by-100-foot floors

The first physician to serve the Valley was Dr. Landry, the military surgeon at Fort Ingall (1839–40), who was allowed to take private patients in the community. Francis Rice tried in vain to convince him to open a practice in the Valley. J. C. Pinguet (1820–?), a French Canadian, was the first resident medical practitioner at Madawaska. Pinguet moved to Madawaska in 1841, and is listed in the 1851 New Brunswick census as a M.D. and surgeon. In a 1846 letter to the bishop of Québec, Mgr. Langevin, the parish priest, wrote that Pinguet preferred hunting, fishing, and good company to his patients and chosen profession. Indeed, Pinguet's activities were not limited to the medical field: he was also New Brunswick's first French-speaking school inspector (1850–55). Pinguet did not marry while at Madawaska, nor did he set up a household of his own. In 1851, he lived with merchant John Emmerson. In 1861, Pinguet boarded with Vital Hébert, the first French-speaking member of the House of Assembly from the Valley. We do not know what happened to him after this point.

Illus. 24-5: Florent Fournier, the first Madawaska-born physician. CDEM, PC1-21

Florent Fournier (1824–1900), the first Madawaska-born physician, was the sixth of Jean-Baptiste Fournier and Salomée Cyr's thirteen children. His maternal and paternal grandparents, Jean-Baptiste Fournier and Félicité Martin and Paul Cyr and Charlotte Ayotte, respectively, both arrived in the Valley before 1800. Langevin paid for his education at Sainte-Anne-de-la-Pocatière from 1839 to 1847; he then studied medicine at Bowdoin College in Brunswick, Maine (Bowdoin had a medical school during most of the nineteenth century). He set up a practice at the Petit Sault, and married his second cousin and neighbor, Elizabeth Tighe, in 1857. In 1858, he became a justice of the peace. Like all early Madawaska professionals, Fournier kept a farm, and according to the 1861 New Brunswick census, he also owned four town lots in Edmundston. In 1863, he ran for a seat in the assembly with the support of his cousin and uncle-in-law Francis Rice.[1] He failed in this endeavor. He served at St. Basile's hospital as early as 1877. When New Brunswick finally regulated the practice of medicine in 1882, he was grandfathered although his training did not meet the new requirements. He retired in 1895 and died at his daughter's house in Salem, Massachusetts, five years later.

The Québec-born François-Xavier Bernier (1840–91) played an important role in the development of the St. Basile hospital, since he provided it with free medical services from the day it opened its doors. Bernier studied at Sainte-Anne-de-la-Pocatière from 1854 to 1861 and received his degree from Lower Canada's College of Physicians and Surgeons in 1866. Bernier served as superintendent of the Madawaska School District from 1871 to 1874. In 1874, he ran against John Costigan for a federal seat and was soundly defeated. Subsequently he became a municipal councilor.

One of the first Madawaska young men to receive modern medical training was Félix Sirois (1864–1910), son of Herménégilde Sirois and Edith Martin, whom we met in Chapter 16. He was put in the care of the Religieuses Hospitalières de Montréal and studied classics at the Jesuit College at his grandparents' request, but then continued on to study medicine; he graduated with a degree in surgery in 1888. He married Catherine Martin at St. Basile in 1891 and practiced in both St. Basile and Fort Kent.

Note 1. Jean Baptiste Fournier's nieces Angélique and Marie Olive (daughters of Guillaume Fournier) married Michael Tighe, father of Elizabeth, and Francis Rice, respectively.

Sources: Andrew (1997): 130–33, 149, 159, and 163; AAQ, Lettres des prêtres missionnaires du Madawaska, letter dated February 14, 1846; St. Basile's hospital web site, http://www.umce.ca/hoteldieustbasile/en/.

Illus. 24-6: Louis Albert, from Rivière Verte (N.B.) studied medicine at the Montreal campus of Laval University and was licensed to practice medicine in Maine in 1904. Acadian Village-Van Buren, Maine. Photograph by B. Craig.

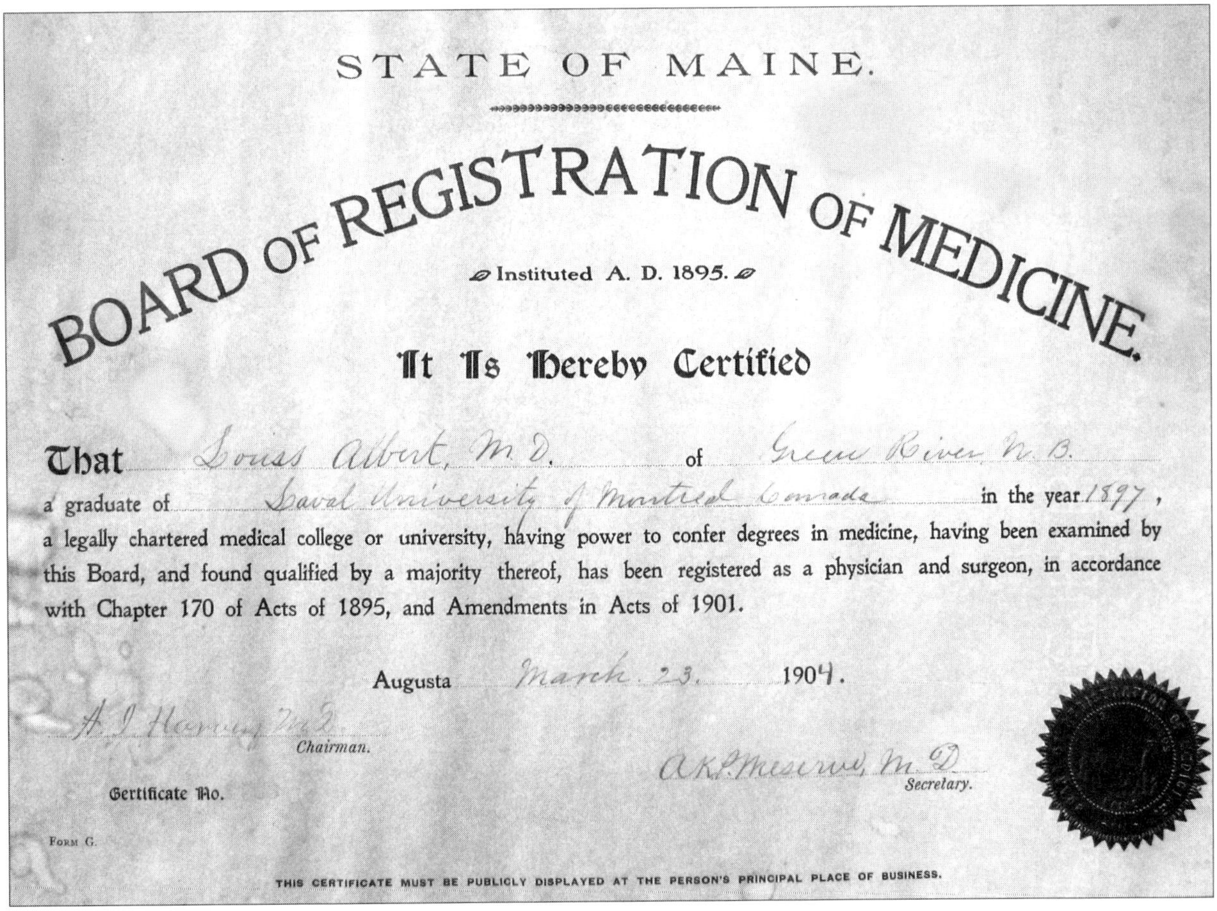

STATE OF MAINE.

BOARD OF REGISTRATION OF MEDICINE.

Instituted A. D. 1895.

It Is Hereby Certified

That *Louis Albert, M.D.* of *Green River, N.B.* a graduate of *Laval University of Montreal Canada* in the year *1897*, a legally chartered medical college or university, having power to confer degrees in medicine, having been examined by this Board, and found qualified by a majority thereof, has been registered as a physician and surgeon, in accordance with Chapter 170 of Acts of 1895, and Amendments in Acts of 1901.

Augusta *March 23.* 190*4.*

Chairman.

Secretary.

Certificate No.

Form G.

THIS CERTIFICATE MUST BE PUBLICLY DISPLAYED AT THE PERSON'S PRINCIPAL PLACE OF BUSINESS.

The Church and Public Welfare, 1870–1914

capable of accommodating seventy-five students—a capacity much lower than actual demand. The students came from all over Maine, New Brunswick, eastern Québec, and even farther away. St. Mary's did not accept girls, and the Van Buren priests invited the Good Shepherds Sisters of Québec to open a convent school in 1891. The sisters taught elementary classes under contract with the town, as well as a high school academic course, and they took female boarders. They sought permission to grant high school diplomas to graduates of the academic course, but they did not succeed until after World War I.

Conclusion

During the 1870 to 1914 period, the Catholic Church began providing its members and the communities under its jurisdiction with an increasing range of services. Members of religious congregations taught, even in public schools, and were the first to open post-elementary and collegiate institutions in the Valley. Sisters ran the three Valley hospitals, the orphanage, and the nursing home. Since those congregations were almost all French-speaking, they contributed to the maintenance of not only the French language, but also of a shared French Catholic culture that was not specifically "French Canadian," "Acadian," or "Franco-American."

ENDNOTES
1. Albert's *Histoire du Madawaska* contains a list of all the Madawaska priests ordained before 1910.
2. St. Agatha Historical Society, *Les Filles de la Sagesse*, St. Agatha, ME, 7–8

FURTHER READINGS
Brewer, Iris Field and Joseph Donald Cyr. "Cultivation of the Spirit in the Garden of Maine." *In The County: Land of Promise*, ed. A. Mcgrath, 1989: 75–94.
Dubay, Guy. *Chez Nous: The St John Valley*, 1983: 71–86.
Acadian Culture in Maine, http://acim.umfk.maine.edu, Section 2, "Roots of Maine Acadian Culture."
Archives des Religieuses Hospitalières de Saint-Basile, http://www.umce.ca/hoteldieustbasile/en/.

SOURCES
Spigelman (1975) and Thériault (1993) analyze the relationship between Acadians and the Irish Catholic hierarchy. Biographies of the Maritime Bishops in the *Dictionary of Canadian Biography* (online at http://www.biographi.ca/EN/) can supplement their research; Mgr. McEvay's and Mgr. Sweeny's biographies provide a quick and clear overview of the nature of the conflict. Goguen (1984) documents the Acadianization of the clergy.

The arrival of the various nursing and teaching sisters at Madawaska is described by Sœur Marie-Dorothée (1984), Georgette Desjardins (1992), Lefrançois (2001), the St. Basile's hospital web site, http://www.umce.ca/hoteldieustbasile/en/, and *Les Filles de la Sagesse, Ste-Agathe, Maine, 1904–2004.* Thériault (1998) and Vautour (1998) each have written chapters on the St. Basile establishments. The hybrid public-parochial schools of the Valley were the topic of Brassard's 1967 thesis.

Further information about the Church and religion at Madawaska can be found in Albert (1920), Bélanger-Violette (1953), and Dugal (1977). Readers interested in the relationship between French-speaking Catholics and Irish bishops in New England can consult Brault (1986), Guignard (1973), and Roby (2000).

25

THE ACADIAN RENAISSANCE AND MADAWASKA

During the latter half of the nineteenth century, members of the Maritime Acadian elite began to define the Acadians as a separate "nation" (nowadays, we would call it a cultural community, since they had no intention to press for an independent Acadian state).[1] They urged Acadians to engage in concerted actions to preserve their "nationality," defined in terms of language, religion, and traditions. This movement, since called the "Acadian Renaissance," was fraught with tensions: it pitted the Irish Catholic hierarchy in the Maritimes against the Acadian elite, the Acadians against French Canadians from Québec and even Maritime Acadians against their New England cousins. This renaissance was, moreover, an elite-led movement, and we really know very little about the impact it had on farmers, loggers, and fishermen.

The Acadian Renaissance placed Madawaska in an awkward position. Was Madawaska "Acadian"? The Acadian Renaissance posited that the Acadians belonged to a different nationality than Quebeckers—but Madawaskayans were of mixed Québec and Acadian origins. Moreover, they now included some Irish individuals, such as Francis Rice, and New Englanders, such as John Baker's grandson Jesse. How would they fit into the Acadian "nation"? And would residents on both sides of the river share the same nation? In short, was the Acadian Renaissance going to unite Maritime French-speakers or exclude Madawaskayans from the group? Was it going to drive another wedge between the Canadian and American sides of the Valley? Men like Thomas Albert answered these questions by defining Madawaskayans as members of both Acadia and French Canada, but also as part of a larger French-speaking and Catholic community that included Acadians, French Canadians, and Franco-Americans. Moreover, this larger community had a providential role to play in North America.

I. BEFORE THE ACADIAN RENAISSANCE

The first Acadian Convention in Memramcook in 1881 is traditionally viewed as the beginning of the Acadian Renaissance. This meeting (discussed below) resulted from several factors that had been gathering strength during the previous twenty years.

A. Social and Economic Factors

The first factor was demographic growth. In New Brunswick alone, the Acadian population represented 12 percent of the total population in 1870, and 25 percent in 1910. The second factor was the gradual emergence of an elite among the Acadian population, an emergence facilitated by the spread of education and the opening of French post-elementary schools (see Chapters 22 and 23). Consequently, in the early 1860s, a growing number of Acadians began to take political and economic leadership roles in the Maritime Provinces. Improved levels of education and a growing population helped Acadians get appointed to public service positions both inside and outside Acadian districts. For instance, in 1868, the Acadian Vautour, a former Sackville English Academy student, became postmaster in Richibouctou, in the mostly English county of Kent. His appointment triggered vocal opposition from a segment of the province's English population. The Acadian population, however, was scattered throughout the three provinces; even in New Brunswick, it did not constitute a single spatial block. Consequently, the various Acadian communities had little contact with each other until the first Acadian newspaper, the *Moniteur Acadien,* was founded in 1867. The *Moniteur* was politically conservative and battled against the New Brunswick Common School Act. The shared fight against this piece of legislation helped unite New Brunswick's Acadian communities—or at least their leaders.

B. *Evangeline* and the "Paradise Lost" Myth

Literature also fueled this growing collective identity. The publication of a French translation of Longfellow's poem *Evangeline* in 1865 was the starting point. The poem, originally published in New England in 1847, had been an instant success among Anglo-American readers. After it became available in French, St. Joseph College in Memramcook put it on its reading list, and the *Moniteur Acadien* published it in its first issue. Longfellow had not intended the poem to be a historical piece of work but a morality play praising the constancy of Woman: Evangeline was the archetypal faithful Woman. The Acadian elite read something different into it. The Deportation of the Acadians, a mere backdrop in Longfellow's story, became the dominant theme in the eyes of the Acadian elite, and came to symbolize the very essence of Acadian identity. The Deportation was what differentiated Acadians from other French-speaking Catholic North Americans. Evangeline became a historical

figure and the national heroine of the Acadians. In addition, the Acadian elite also accepted as fact Longfellow's depiction of pre-Deportation Acadia as a paradise lost, or a world unsullied by sin, uncorrupted by trade and materialism, and devoid of conflict.

Longfellow had borrowed this image of the lost Acadian paradise from Abbé Raynal's *Histoire des deux Indes,* published in France in 1770. Raynal was violently anti-colonial and anti-clerical—despite the fact that he was a priest. He systematically ignored all evidence that Acadians had engaged in trade or activities other than farming and disregarded the fact that warfare, not peace, had been the recurrent feature of Acadians' lives throughout the seventeenth and eighteenth centuries. Raynal also conveniently overlooked the fact that Acadia was a creation of the colonialism he denounced. In his account, imperial rivalries and priests acting as guerrilla leaders had disrupted the Acadian paradise. Under his pen, the Acadians became not only the people who suffered deportation in 1755, but the archetype for helpless, innocent victims.

One does not really know what ordinary Acadians—the ones who barely knew how to read and, even if they were literate, did not subscribe to the *Moniteur* or attend the college in Memramcook —saw in the poem; however, the theme of separated lovers is very common in folk tales, and this aspect of the story might have appealed to ordinary people.

C. Rameau de Saint-Père, Acadian's First French Historian

Raynal and Longfellow left their readers with the impression that Acadians had disappeared after 1755. It was another outsider, Rameau de Saint-Père, who reminded the world that there were still many Acadians left in the Maritime Provinces (see Sidebar 25-1). His first book, *La France aux Colonies,* published in France in 1859, drew attention to several French-speaking communities in North America—including one in Madawaska. He

François Edmée Rameau de Saint-Père was born in Gien, France, in 1820 and died in 1899. He possessed a modest fortune that allowed him to live off his means. Rameau was interested in the study of society and was a disciple of Frederick Le Play, one of the founders of the discipline of sociology. Le Play advocated rigorous, systematic observations of social systems (monographs) and a comparative approach. He created an association (*Société d'économie sociale*) that held yearly conferences and published its proceedings. Le Play was also a political reactionary who used his brand of sociology to promote his political views. The urban-industrial world repulsed him since, in his eyes, material progress led to social and moral degeneration. He also believed the philosophical principles underpinning the United States Declaration of Independence (1776) and the French Declaration of the Rights of Men and Citizens (1789) were completely wrong. To Le Play, individual rights doctrines could only lead to individualism and selfishness, which in turn led to social and moral disintegration. Needless to say, Le Play was no democrat; his ideal society was hierarchical, patriarchal, and agrarian, and the basic social unit was not the individual, but the family as represented by the father.

When Le Play's followers discovered Québec, they viewed it as an excellent example of the master's ideal. In 1888, Rameau, along with two French Canadians, co-founded the *Société Canadienne d'économie sociale*, contributing to the spread of Le Play's methods and theories in French Canada. Rameau, who was an imperialist, also sought to find out the key to the success of "dominant people." He came to the conclusion that their dominance did not rest in their military might, but in the nature of their social organization, their demographic vitality, and their mores.

In 1859, Rameau published a book in Paris whose title advocated a socio-political program: *La France aux Colonies—Etudes sur le développement de la race Française hors de l'Europe,* subtitled*: Les Français en Amérique—Acadiens et Canadiens (France in the Colonies—Studies on the Development of the French race outside Europe,* subtitled *The French in America—Acadians and Canadians.)* Rameau's correspondents in North America supplied him with much of the material and information for the book. Rameau's book became a revelation for Acadians—it showed not only that they had a history, but that, as a people, they had collectively survived the Deportation of 1755. For the first time, they could read this history in French. Madawaska received its fair share of attention, but Rameau's information was often inaccurate. Rameau, who had access to the French colonial archives, concluded that the French government was to blame for losing Acadia. It was also indirectly responsible for the Deportation, which might not have happened if the French had made a real effort to defend their colonies. Like both the late-eighteenth-century French historian Abbé Raynal and the American poet Henry Wadsworth Longfellow, Rameau depicted pre-Deportation Acadians as contented peasants and passive bystanders in historical events, rather than as agents in their own right. Nonetheless, Rameau's devoted less than half of his book to Acadian history before 1755.

Rameau was conscious of the fact that the few available historical accounts of pre-deportation Acadia, including his own, provided too few details. The following year, he embarked on a tour of Québec and the Maritimes where he collected material for his next work and met new people. Back in France, he strove to assist the Acadians as best he could: he made donations to St. Joseph College in Memramcook and supported *Le Moniteur Acadien.* He also convinced French Emperor Napoleon III to subsidize the founding of the Saint-Paul de Kent Parish. In 1877, he published *Une colonie féodale en Amérique, L'Acadie,* a book which covered the pre-Deportation period; in 1889, he republished *Une colonie féodale* as part of a two-volume book that brought the reader to the present.

The Acadians of the time viewed Rameau not only as a historian of their people, but as one of their intellectual leaders. He is still considered one of the founders of French-language Acadian historiography. As an understanding of history played a critical role in how Acadians constructed their collective identity, Rameau's works played a key role in the Acadian Renaissance.

Sources: S. Rameau (1948), Bruchési (1948), P. and L. Trépanier (1978), P. Trépanier (1979, 1980, and 1987), and Clarke (1993). Rameau de Saint-Père's papers are available at the Centre d'études acadienne, Université de Moncton. *La France aux Colonies* is accessible online on *Gallica:* http://gallica.bnf.fr/. *Une colonie féodale en Amérique c*an be viewed online at http://www.canadiana.org.

argued that the Acadians were distinct from French Canadians.

> These two colonies [Acadia and the St. Lawrence Valley] were separated by a wide space through which it was very difficult to travel; they communicated but little with each other, and only by sea. The people who settled them were of different origins; the two colonies developed differently; they led completely separate existence, and gave birth to two races at present still very distinct from each other, the *Acadians* and the *Canadians*.[2]

The Acadians, continued Rameau, could not take the future of their "race" for granted and had to make a concerted effort to preserve and strengthen it. He made a list of specific recommendations. First, new territory needed to be opened to settlement and agriculture, especially to the north and northwest of New Brunswick. This would stem out-migration, create a solid Acadian territorial bloc, and protect the "true" Acadian culture, which Rameau believed was rooted in agrarianism. Acadians also had to stop fishing and logging, because those activities ran contrary to their nationality. Second, education had to be expanded, especially post-elementary education, since it was the one that produced leaders. Third, the Acadians had to publish a newspaper to link the dispersed Acadian communities and help reinforce their unique culture and traditions. Fourth, they should found a national society similar to the French Canadian *Société Saint-Jean-Baptiste*; and fifth, they should establish a national day dedicated to a patron saint. Rameau's agenda was fulfilled a generation later by the *Conventions Nationales Acadiennes*.

II.   THE NATIONAL CONVENTIONS

In 1880, Quebeckers organized a convention in Quebec City to discuss issues affecting French Canadians. They invited Acadians to participate but only as members of the "French Canadian" nation. As far as Quebeckers were concerned, all French-speaking Canadians were French Canadians. As early as 1868, the Québec newspaper *Le Pays,* in a review of Rameau de Saint-Père's work on the Acadians, had questioned the very existence of an Acadian nationality. It countered that Acadians had no common culture, no consciousness of themselves as a people, and no common goals as a community. Therefore, an Acadian identity separate from the French Canadian one did not exist. The Acadians were merely French Canadians who happened to live in the Maritime Provinces, nothing more.

The Acadian delegates, however, came back from this gathering unconvinced that they were part of French Canada and persuaded others in their communities to hold a similar event—for Acadians. This led to the first Acadian National Convention at Memramcook on July 20 and 21, 1881. The theme of the convention was cultural renaissance. Its purpose was to raise Acadian consciousness by increasing their own awareness of their existence as a distinct people, identifying the problems facing them, and investigating possible solutions. This emerging cultural consciousness immediately became rooted in a specific interpretation of history fed by *Evangeline*: the Acadians were a victimized people, and this victimization lay at the root of their current problems. In his opening speech, future senator Pascal Poirier declared:

> We are the descendants of a small people, formerly vanquished, dispersed, despoiled in an atrocious and shameful manner; as a vanquished race, we have been accustomed to distrust our abilities and resources, to walk with lowered brow, and to think of ourselves as incapable of matching the talents and merits of neighbors better favored by Fortune. We want, through this convention, to sustain our numbers and evaluate our resources. We live in a free, privileged country, where all can aspire to the highest positions and reach the highest rung of the social and political ladder.[3]

The text is revealing on two counts. First, it shows that *Evangeline,* in historian Naomi Griffith's words, had become for the Acadians "the most powerful tool at their disposal to construct an Acadian identity."[4] The Deportation was also a way for Acadians to present themselves as distinct from Quebeckers. The Conquest of Québec (by the British in 1759) was the touchstone of French Canadian identity; the Deportation of 1755 became the one of the Acadians. Second, the text reveals a seldom mentioned dimension of Acadian nationalism that further distanced them from Quebeckers: the Acadian elite was pro-British. Poirier hinted the

Dominion of Canada was a "land of opportunity."

Convention-goers discussed the various measures needed to consolidate this emerging sense of Acadian "nationhood" or cultural identity. A central issue was the choice of a national holiday. There were two options: Saint-Jean-Baptiste (the French Canadian national holiday) or *l'Assomption* (a Catholic holiday celebrating the rising of the Virgin Mary's body to Heaven after her death). Opponent of Saint-Jean-Baptiste argued that the Acadians were distinct from their French Canadian cousins and therefore needed a distinct holiday. The Reverend J. Doucet argued:

> We want to choose a *national* holiday, don't we? Well, let us choose one that is specific to our nationality, one that our people will share with no other. Preserving our nationality is the important point. This is what we must keep in mind while taking our decision. Is our nationality distinct from the one of the Canadians? Are the Acadians a distinct people, however small this people may be? If the answer is yes, and who could deny it? Let us choose a holiday that is our own.[5]

Poirier similarly noted:

> The Acadian national holiday mustn't, if we want to be faithful to the past, be the one of the Scots, the Irish, nor even the one of the French Canadians. Each of those nationalities has its national day, its family holiday. Why couldn't the Acadians have their own as well?[6]

The delegates chose *l'Assomption* (twelve votes to four). The next convention chose the flag and a national hymn (*Ave Marie Stella*). Quebeckers continued to refuse to accept that the Acadians were members of a different nation, arguing "we all belong to the same race and to the same religion." By 1905, the Acadians ceased to invite Quebeckers to their conventions. In the meantime, a permanent structure had emerged from the convention's organizing committee: the *Société Nationale de l'Assomption*. The society's seven vice presidents each represented a different Acadian district, and most of the society's council members were politicians.

At each convention, promoting agriculture stood at the forefront of the delegates' agendas. The Acadian elite believed that old Acadia had been a self-contained peasant society. To stay true to their roots and preserve their traditions, the coming generation thus had to remain on the land. French Canadians were saying the same thing at the time: their elite also claimed that agriculture was the key to survival as a distinct community. Because urban life, trade, and industry facilitated Anglicization, they had to be avoided. Much later, in the 1960s,

Québec and Acadian scholars and activists virulently denounced this attitude, accusing the clerical elite of having tried to keep Acadians and French Canadians on the farm in order to control them and preserve their own power. The 1881 convention-goers also agreed that the educational system needed improving. The delegates believed education was an important tool for progress; without it, the Acadians could never achieve their material, political, and social goals. Finally, Acadian newspapers were to educate the population on the pressing issues of the day and promote and defend Acadian culture.

III.   IMPACT OF THE ACADIAN RENAISSANCE

A. The Press

Several Acadian newspapers such as *l'Étoile du Nord, Le Réveil, l'Avenir,* and *l'Evangéline* were founded to be the voice and defenders of the Acadian minority in the wake of the first national conventions. Valentin Landry started *l'Evangéline* in 1887 and promised that the newspaper would do all it could to assist in the Acadian awakening. He stated that the daily "would always do its part to promote the important cause of education among the Acadians."[7] *l'Evangéline* promoted the two most important values of the Acadian Renaissance: the central role of agriculture and the importance of education. The newspaper also defended the Acadian minority from attacks by Irish and Anglo-Protestant New Brunswickers.

B. Challenges
1. The Catholic Hierarchy
Quebeckers were not the only ones to think the conventions were encouraging the French-speaking Maritimers to stray from the flock. The Maritimes' Irish Catholic hierarchy felt much the same way. A second Acadian convention was held in Miscouche in 1884, and a third convention was held in Pointe-de-l'f glise (Church Point, Nova Scotia) in 1890. There was then a hiatus until 1900 (Arichat, Nova

Scotia). The Irish Catholic hierarchy attempted to discourage these meetings because the delegates continued to discuss the matter of an Acadian bishop (see Chapter 23). Bishops forbade some priests from attending the 1890 convention; in 1900, the hierarchy strongly advised the delegates to avoid discussing ecclesiastical matters without their bishops' permission.

2. American Acadians
Expatriated Acadians also challenged the *Société Nationale.* By 1900, there were several important Acadian communities around Boston, where Acadian carpenters were in great demand (the rationale being that "he who can build a boat can build a sturdy, tight house"). Most of those Acadians came from Westmorland and Kent in New Brunswick, Cape Breton, Baie-Sainte-Marie in Nova Scotia, and Prince Edward Island. In 1900, the question of the Acadians in the United States had been one of the topics discussed by the Arichat convention, which had even set up a commission for the purpose. In 1902, the New England Acadians held a *Congrès Acadien* in Waltham, which led to the founding of the *Société mutuelle de l'Assomption,* a mutual benefit society, the following year. The insurance services provided by the *Société* were really just a means to an end: organizing Acadians in local

associations called *succursalles* (chapters). The *Société mutuelle* also offered scholarships to Acadian students. In 1907, the *Société mutuelle de l'Assomption* was incorporated in New Brunswick, and soon thereafter, its headquarters moved to Moncton.

3. The Challenges of Modernity

The *Société mutuelle* was typical of other associations created outside the framework of the conventions. The conventions encouraged Acadians to keep to themselves and have as little contact as possible with the Anglo-American, urban-industrial society expanding around them. In addressing problems of the day, they always proposed the same solutions: clear the forest, create new settlements, establish family farms, live off the land as much as possible, and resist the sirens of commerce and urban life.

Everyday Acadians, however, led different lives than their elite cousins and were not inclined to follow this advice. Some Acadians, like the Madawaskayans, engaged in commercial agriculture and worked in the woods and lumber mills; similarly, Westmorland Acadians were commercial farmers and, increasingly, railroad workers. In northeastern New Brunswick, Acadian fishermen were banding together to escape the control of the fish merchants. And those who could not find work at home or hoped for a higher standard of living were taking the road to Boston or New England mill towns. Mutual benefit societies, teachers' associations, and even the Acadian trade unions in Moncton (although more limited in scope) better fitted the needs of twentieth-century Acadians than the agrarianism promoted by the conventions. At the 1908 convention in St. Basile, an attempt at merging the *Société mutuelle* with the *Société Nationale* led to an acrimonious dispute between the *Moniteur Acadien* and *l'Evangeline* because the old and new elites had different visions of the Acadians' future. Older elites advocated traditional solutions (separateness and agrarianism) for Acadian problems, whereas newer elites were far more willing to embrace change and modernity. Consequently, the new elite seemed more in touch with ordinary Acadians than the old clerical elite.

IV.   MADAWASKA AND THE ACADIAN RENAISSANCE

There was a final problem with the institutions coming out of the Acadian Renaissance that directly concerns us: the Acadian conventions furthered the gap between the people of Madawaska and other New Brunswick Acadians.

A. Madawaska Keeps Its Distance

Four New Brunswick Madawaskayans had been invited to the 1881 convention– but none from Maine, which angered their cousins across the St. John. The Madawaska representatives were usually at odds with the majority. Father Joseph Pelletier and Lévite Theriault, members of the national holiday commission, voted in favor of Saint-Jean-Baptiste. Nor were there any representatives from Madawaska at the 1884 and 1890 conventions. Georges Sirois noted that by that time, "Madawaska people seem to want to keep to themselves and 'politely' dissociate themselves from patriotic matters."[8] The Acadian national holiday, *l'Assomption*, was not even celebrated in the region; on the other hand, *Le Journal du Madawaska* mentions the local celebration of Saint-Jean-Baptiste, the Québec national day, in 1904. Madawaskayans attended the conventions in 1900 and 1905 as observers; in 1905, there were only twenty of them in attendance. To redress the situation, the convention's organizers decided to hold the next meeting (1908) in St. Basile. This time Madawaska participation was massive—but remained superficial. People attended because in was in their backyard. As for the *Société mutuelle,* it had more than 5,000 members in 1910, but apparently no chapter in the St. John Valley.

Madawaskayans were not sure if they belonged to these organizations. They were very much aware that their family trees included both French Canadians and Acadians. Claire Sirois noted that this mixture and the region's geographic position played an important part in shaping different "national" aspirations for the people of Madawaska. She noted that the institutions that shaped Madawaskayans' cultural identity were different from those that shaped other Acadian populations. Acadians could receive a secondary education at three Maritime institutions: St. Joseph College in Memramcook, Sainte-Anne College in Pointe-de-l'Église, and Sacré-Coeur College in Caraquet. Madawaskayans who sought such an education usually went to Sainte-Anne-de-la-Pocatière in Québec. French Canadians' influence on the region's primary and secondary education was also important. After the 1871 Common School Act, it became difficult for Acadians to study in their own language. Although teachers were allowed to teach in French after 1874, most textbooks remained in English. In Madawaska, however, the schools were able to get French books from Québec. Madawaska priests also usually came from Québec, as did the sisters who staffed the local schools and hospitals. The Madawaska economy was also different from the economies of other Acadian districts in the Maritimes. The rivers and later the railroads firmly tied the Madawaska region to Saint John (New Brunswick), the lower St. Lawrence Valley, and finally, Bangor, and points farther south on the rail line. At school, at church, and for the few boys in secondary schools, Madawaskayans were exposed to French Canadian or even American, not Acadian, culture.

There were Acadian communities in New England (the nearest in Rumford, Maine), but Madawaskayans had little in common with those people. Their own geographic origins, occupations, and ways of life were completely different from those of other New England Acadians. Madawaskayans who left the Valley for *les États* normally did not go to Boston, but to the textile towns of southern Maine or elsewhere in New England—or to the American and Canadian West where they became farmers. When the Boston branch of the *Société de l'Assomption* was founded in 1903, it included eighty-six members: thirty-eight originally from Kent and Westmorland, seventeen from Cape Breton, six from the Magdalene Islands, and a lone individual from Madawaska.

B. Defining a Madawaskayan identity

But if Madawaskayans were neither Maritime Acadians nor New England Acadians, what were they? Were Madawaskayans going to be defined as two different people based on the side of the Valley they lived on? Who then was a Madawaskayan? We do not know what the rank-and-file Madawaskayan thought—or even if they were concerned with the issue. This lack of concern did not hold true for Dr. Thomas Pelletier and Abbé Thomas Albert.

1. *Dr. Pelletier and* Le Journal du Madawaska
The New Brunswick-born, Québec-educated Dr. Thomas Pelletier,[9] founder and editor of the short-lived *Journal du Madawaska* (published in Van Buren from 1902 to 1906), acknowledged both the dual origin of the Madawaska French and the fact that the residents of both sides of the river formed one people. However, he had more affinity with French Canadians than Acadians. He shared the French Canadians' anti-British stance. In the pages of his paper, he systematically described the mother country as a wicked and selfish stepmother. Pelletier longed for the day when the United States annexed Canada, because Britain certainly would never grant her independence.[10] He also promoted celebrating Saint-Jean-Baptiste and referred to his readers as Franco-Americans. Likewise, the 1915 *Dictionnaire des Franco-Américains* included several Madawaskayans, but none residing in New Brunswick

(although some were Canadian born). But of course, Pelletier's New Brunswick readers could not be Franco-*Americans*. Pelletier not only broke the link between Madawaskayans and Acadians, but also drove a wedge between those residing on different sides of the upper St. John.

2. *Thomas Albert and* Histoire du Madawaska

Madawaska-born, Québec-educated Thomas Albert had no desire to create divisions. In his *Histoire du Madawaska,* he argued that the people of the Valley were both Acadian and French Canadian. He began by restating Rameau de Saint-Père's thesis: North America's French settlers divided between the Canadians on the banks of the St. Lawrence and the Acadians along the Bay of Fundy. Each subsequently developed a distinct character and culture. Like most of his contemporaries, Albert believed in folk psychology (members of the same "nation" or "race" display the same psychological traits, which they then pass on to their descendents along with physical traits, such as hair and eye color). However, the two cultures reunited in Madawaska which became a mini melting-pot:

> But at Madawaska, where both elements have met again and mixed in almost equal proportions for more than a century, the original differences have been weakened by constant interactions, through intermarriage, from sharing the same way of life and the same needs, to meld into a complex personality drawing from both sources, and which constitutes the true Madawaskayan type, simultaneously Breton and Normand, stubborn and cunning, honest and merry, active and intelligent, generous and enterprising, hospitable but secretive, clannish without being exclusive....[11]

There was, however, little room in Albert's melting pot for other founding people: the Native Americans vanished into the forest as if on cue, the role of the Irish and occasional Scot shrunk, and the New Englanders emerged as troublesome outsiders. To be a true Madawaskayan, one had to be not only French-speaking and Catholic, but also of French and Catholic ancestry. As Adrien Bérubé noted, Albert stressed ancestry over shared geography or experiences, and nostalgia for a lost agrarian golden age over the need to develop the region's economic base. It is not an accident that Albert's Madawaskayans are mostly farmers who occasionally dabble in logging or the professions, and never engage in trade. Nor is it an accident that there are no businesses or factories in his Madawaska. In his eyes, modernity and the Madawaskayan identity were incompatible. His Madawaskayans fit the same portrait of the ideal French Canadian or Acadian as both groups' clerical elite—and he expounded the same values as those set forth at the Acadian conventions.

Moreover, Albert stressed the commonalities between Acadians, French Canadians, and Franco-Americans: all were French-speaking, Catholic North Americans, invested with the same God-given mission to re-conquer the continent by producing large families, settling their sons on farms, shunning Anglo-Saxon "materialism," and preserving the faith, language, customs, and traditions of their forefathers. This perspective allowed him to fit the mixed Acadian-French Canadian Madawaskayans into the seamless fabric of French North America—and deftly sidestep the question of Madawaska's "Acadianess." By the time he published his book, however, this form of agrarian traditionalism was getting old-fashioned, and some members of the clergy were even beginning to reject it, noting that agrarianism inevitably condemned French Canadians and Acadians to economic and social marginalization: there could be no cultural survival without modernity.

Conclusion

Regional changes, such as demographic growth, improved education and communications, and economic development, made the late-nineteenth-century Acadian Renaissance possible. Its ideology was, however, largely borrowed. It drew on ideas common throughout the late-nineteenth-century Western world, such as biologically determined concepts of nations and race, as well as ideas put forth by conservative French Canadians: religion and language protected each other; French Canadians were farmers by their very nature; French Canadians had a God-ordained mission to populate North America. Their elite further defined the Acadians as a separate people whose history had unfolded independently from that of the St. Lawrence Valley and culminating with the Deportation of 1755. They even borrowed the image of pre-Deportation Acadia as a self-contained community of pious, peaceful peasants from foreign authors, namely a French opponent of colonialism, a New England Romantic poet, and a French social scientist with a highly conservative agenda. This image of Old Acadia was completely at odds with reality, a fallacy that later historians have since uncovered. The image of a lost paradise swept away by imperial forces during the seventeenth and eighteenth centuries proved to be a myth. Nonetheless, the elite held fast to this mythical past to define Acadian identity—a past that became superimposed onto the folk memories it modified. We do not know how the farmers, loggers, and fishermen who made up the bulk of the Acadian population initially remembered their past, but as they learned to read and attended schools or catechism, the elite's view of the past slowly bled into their own.

This emergence of an Acadian identity at odds with the French Canadian one placed Madawaskayans in an awkward position. It forced Madawaska's elite to come up with their own cultural identity, one that reflected not only their dual origins but also their dual citizenships (British and American). Pelletier, who emigrated to the United States, rejected Madawaska's British heritage, called American Madawaskayans "Franco-Americans," and hoped the United States would annex Canada. The British Albert viewed Madawaska as a frontier where two "races" had melded into one. As in modern times, Madawaskayans were a people in between, and Albert's definition appears to have resonated better with its intended audience than Pelletier's definition, as this one left New Brunswick Madawaskayans in a no-man's-land. Both men's perceptions, however, reflected the awareness that on the eve of World War I, Madawaska was increasingly becoming two bordered lands.

ENDNOTES

1. At times, the Acadians also referred to themselves as a "race." Both the words "nation" and "race" enjoyed broader meaning in the nineteenth century than they do now. "Nation" could include any self-conscious cultural community, usually with a shared language; "race" referred to distinct ethnic groups. In this context, there was an English race, a Scottish race, a Welsh race, etc.

2. Rameau de Saint-Père, *La France aux Colonies,* 10–11; Rameau obviously was unaware of the historical significance of the St. John-Témiscouata route!

3. Quoted in Robidoux, *Conventions Nationales des Acadiens,* 29–30, translated by the authors.

4. Griffith, "Longfellow's *Evangeline...*," 37.

5. Quoted in Robidoux, 46-47, translated by the authors.

6. Quoted in Robidoux, 55, translated by the authors.

7. Boucher, *L'Évangéline de Valentin Landry,* 22.

8. G. Sirois, "La participations des Madawaskayens aux Conventions Nationales," 124.

9. Thomas Henri Pelletier (1845–1921) was the son of Célestin, the blacksmith in Chapter 16. He attended the college in Sainte-Anne-de-la-Pocatière from 1857 to 1862. After completing his medical studies, he opened a practice at Grand Falls in 1868. He married Frenchville teacher Malvina Chenard in 1869 and moved to Van Buren in 1871. He lived in Lewiston, Maine, for a while as well. Pelletier started *Le Journal du Madawaska* in 1902 and handed it over to his son-in-law Lévite Thibodeau (see Chapter 26) in 1905. The newspaper folded soon thereafter.

10. Canada gained its independence by the Statute of Westminster in 1931.

11. Albert, *Histoire du Madawaska,* 11, translated by the authors.

FURTHER READING

Landry, Nicolas and Nicole Lang. *Histoire de l'Acadie,* 2001: Ch. 4 and 5.

Thériault, Léon. "L'Acadie de 1763 à 1990, synthèse historique." In *L'Acadie des Maritimes, études théma-*

tiques des débuts à nos jours, Jean Daigle, (dir.), 1993: 45–92.

SOURCES

The origins of the Acadian Renaissance are discussed in Thériault (1993) above, Mailhot (1993), and Wilbur (1989). Andrews (1997) provides useful background. One can find biographies of P. Poirier, F-X Lafrance, François Richard, and P-A Landry in the *Dictionary of Canadian Biographies* (online). Robichaud (1981) analyzes the ideology of convention participants. Massicotte (2005) discusses how convention-goers chose a flag, and Basque (2006) covers the history of the *Société Nationale*. To study colonization and the promotion of agriculture, see R. Leblanc (1988). In 1907, Robidoux published the texts of the speeches given at the first three conventions.

On the role of history and myth in defining Acadian identity see Griffiths (1982), Viau (2006), Richard (2006), and Johnston (2004 in English, and 2005 in French translation). For information on Rameau de Saint-Père, see Clarke (1993).

Harvey (2000), Thériault (2000), and Boucher (2000) analyze the relationship between Acadians and French Canadians. Information about Acadians in New England is scarce; see Brun (2001), Chevalier (1972), and Quintal (1984). G. Sirois (1974) has researched Madawaskayans' participation in the conventions. C. Sirois (1973 and 1975) and G. Michaud (1991 and 1994) have investigated Madawaskayan identity. Bérubé (1980) has looked at the role Albert played in its development.

26

POLITICAL AND INSTITUTIONAL LIFE, 1875 TO WORLD WAR I

Politics continued dividing Madawaskayans after 1870. Not only were New Brunswick and Maine Madawaskayans part of two different political systems, but they also faced different issues at the state/provincial and national levels. Their ability to exercise political influence was not the same, either. In New Brunswick, the French-speaking population went from 15 percent of the province's total population in 1870 to 24 percent in 1914; pragmatic politicians quickly recognized their growing strength. In Maine, native French speakers represented less than 10 percent of the state population in 1900. The Acadians were the second group to settle in New Brunswick after the Natives and remained the majority group in most of the counties they inhabited. (To simplify the narrative, we refer to all French-speaking New Brunswickers as Acadians in this chapter.) With the exception of Madawaskayans, Maine's French-speaking population was comprised of mostly latecomers. In 1860, Maine counted only 7,490 Franco-Americans, as they were later called; there were 77,000 in 1900. The Franco-Americans came mostly from Québec, attracted by factory jobs in southern Maine. Consequently, they moved into areas that had been long settled by New Englanders. Their status as immigrants, coupled

with their small numbers, created a different dynamic in Maine than in New Brunswick. Even the most anti-French or anti-Catholic New Brunswickers recognized that the Acadians, though a minority, were there to stay, and their strategy was to try to contain the Acadians and limit their political influence. Mainers, on the other hand, tended to view Franco-Americans as a foreign element requiring assimilation.

Moreover, many Madawaskayans were not immigrants, since they had settled in the Valley before part of it became American. Nonetheless, many Mainers treated them as if they were newcomers and expected them to adopt the language, culture, and values of Anglo America. This resulted in New Brunswick's Valley residents wielding greater political influence than Maine Valley residents. This difference in political clout and influence is also reflected in our knowledge of these groups' political activities. Acadian participation in New Brunswick politics has attracted more attention than Franco-American participation in Maine politics; this is especially true of Madawaskayans, since we know almost nothing about Valley politics on the American side of the border.

A. Local Government

1. Madawaska Becomes a County

The four parishes of St. Francis, Madawaska, St. Basile, and St. Leonard were erected into a single county—Madawaska—in 1873. Edmundston became the shiretown. Madawaskayans were not the driving force behind this change. *Le Moniteur Acadien* denounced it as ridiculous. The new county numbered just under 12,000 inhabitants and could barely support the costs that came along with county status. *Le Moniteur* was convinced that James Tibbits, one of Victoria's two legislative assembly members, had convinced his colleagues to divide Victoria county because he feared he would not be re-elected: Madawaskayans were lukewarm toward him. The provincial House of Assembly went along because Tibbits was a stalwart government supporter. After the split, Victoria and Madawaska were each entitled to one assembly member.

The division of Victoria into two counties, one almost entirely French and another overwhelmingly English, fits, however, into a wider context. During this period, the anti-French and anti-Catholic Saint John *Daily Telegraph* advocated dividing multi-ethnic counties where Acadians formed either the majority or a large enough minority to have electoral weight. In 1869, Urbain Johnson (Acadian despite his last name) defeated Robert Hutchinson in Kent County for an assembly seat. This was the first time Kent had sent an Acadian to the House of Assembly. In the mind of the *Telegraph,* this scandalous outcome resulted not from "an intelligent decision," but from "calls to religious and national [i.e., ethnic] prejudices entirely unworthy of the county and its people." One thus had to find a way to "guarantee the Protestant population of Kent against similar results in the next or subsequent elections." And the only way to do so was to divide the county along ethnic lines. The paper advocated a similar measure in Victoria where the same danger lurked:

The French paper published in Shediac,[1] M. Renaud, M.P. for Kent,[2] the St. John *Freeman,*[3] and other nefarious agencies—some coming from the province of Québec—work energetically to suppress the legitimate influence the English population of Kent and Victoria should exercise in the Legislature. We shall soon find out if the current House of Assembly will continue to bow to such diktats.[4]

Since Kent County had not been divided, the government and assembly had obviously established Madawaska County not out of a need to please ultra-Anglo-Protestant elements in the province but out of political expediency.

2. New Brunswick Democratizes Its Local Government

Municipalities governed by elected men who held the power of taxation and appropriation had been introduced into the United Province of Canada in 1841. New Brunswickers were generally hostile to the idea because these municipal governments could levy taxes. In New Brunswick, the House of Assembly financed local improvements and public buildings (byroads, bridges, wharves, courthouses, county jails, etc.), usually at the initiative of the local politicians whose popularity among electors depended largely on their ability to secure provincial money for local projects. Because it would have deprived them of a means of getting re-elected, most politicians opposed municipal government. Their constitutents, who did not want to pay taxes if they could avoid it, shared this dislike,

In 1851, the House of Assembly passed legislation authorizing the incorporation of counties into municipalities. Voters attempted to incorporate Carleton, Victoria, Charlotte, and Northumberland Counties, a measure that succeeded in Carleton alone. Other counties obtained the necessary two-thirds majority, but the assembly rejected their petitions on the grounds "that the majority was obtained by intimidation at the hands of rowdies brought into the county by interested parties."[5] The 1877 General Act, on the other hand, made the incorporation of counties mandatory. The civil parishes became the basic electoral units, and each parish was entitled to two county councilors. (There was no local government at the parish level; the county was the lowest level of government.) Until 1886, the same people had the right to vote in municipal and provincial elections: since 1877, one needed to own $600 worth of real estate to vote. In 1886, the municipal franchise (right to vote) was extended to single and widowed women who met the property qualifications. After 1889, a leasehold worth $600 also qualified individuals to vote, and after 1912, one could qualify by owning $1,200 worth of assessed personal property in place of real estate. As the government did away with property qualifications for provincial elections in 1889, the municipal franchise was more restrictive for men than the provincial one, but less restrictive for women, who could not vote in provincial elections until 1919. Urbanized areas could be detached from the county to which they belonged and be separately incorporated. Until 1896, the assembly incorporated towns through special acts. Fredericton and Moncton were the only towns incorporated before the First World War.

3. Prohibition: From Local to Provincial Control
There were Prohibitionists in both New Brunswick and Maine, but they were never as powerful in the province, in part, because the Irish Catholic and Acadian populations, who opposed outright Prohibition, were proportionally more important. Nonetheless, liquor legislation became more restrictive during the latter half of the nineteenth century, and control over the sale of liquor gradually escaped local authorities. The House of Assembly repealed the Prohibition Laws of 1851 and 1855 almost immediately after it had passed them; the Prohibition Law of 1870 allowed rate payers (that is, those who paid local property taxes) to forbid liquor licensing in their community by winning a two-

thirds majority vote—reduced to simple majority in 1871. After 1878, local authorities could also introduce Prohibition measures under the Canada Temperance Act. By 1880, ten counties were dry, but the five northern counties (including Madawaska and Victoria) and Saint John County were wet. In 1896, control over liquor regulations was taken away from the municipal authorities and placed in the hands of a provincial liquor board. The issuing of liquor licenses became a form of political patronage, as well as a way of exercising electoral pressure (that is, candidates could make it known that if they were not elected or re-elected, the county's liquor licenses could be in jeopardy).

B. Provincial Politics

Provincial politics slowly democratized during this period, which also saw the emergence of parties and party-based politics, as well as increased Acadian political participation.

1. Constitutional Changes
The Election Act of 1889 introduced universal male suffrage for provincial elections. However, lunatics, prisoners, paupers, and Natives were specifically excluded from the franchise. Officials also modified electoral procedures, and after 1879, polls had to be opened at the same time throughout the province rather than at the discretion of county officials.

2. Slow Emergence of Partisan Politics
a. The Continuation of "Compact Politics"
In 1866 and 1867, provincial politicians had been forced to declare their views on the matter of Confederation. The school crisis (see chapter 23) similarly compelled them to identify themselves as either proponents or opponents of the Common School Act: candidates lined up under either the "Non-Sectarian Free School Party" or the "Separate School Party" banner. Only one member of the assembly out of forty-one remained neutral on the issue during the next election. Once this was settled,

New Brunswickers reverted to compact politics as usual, and the premier felt free to include in his government both people who had run for election as "friends of the government" and independent and opposition candidates. The one thing government members had in common was their support for Confederation. Therefore, if they declared a political affiliation, they usually called themselves "Liberal-Conservatives," the name of the coalition that had achieved Confederation and remained in power in Ottawa until the 1890s. Candidates who ran as independent continued to declare their willingness to join the government if asked. There were still no electoral platforms common to all candidates supporting or opposing the government. As Woodward noted, "The lack of fixed party lines served the

---

Sidebar 26-1: Our Man in Ottawa: John Costigan

We first met John Costigan in 1861, when he won a seat in the New Brunswick House of Assembly on a platform that opposed Confederation (Chapter 11). In 1868, he was elected to the federal Parliament; he first made his mark by trying to get the Canadian House of Commons to intervene in the New Brunswick school question (see Chapter 23), in spite of the prime minister's determination to do nothing about it. This gained Costigan the support of the New Brunswick bishops—and the lasting distrust of Prime Minister Macdonald who pointedly did not appoint him to any cabinet positions until 1882 (when he was nominated minister of inland revenue). His main role in that position, in Macdonald's view, was to gain the Irish-Catholic vote. Costigan held this portfolio under both Macdonald and his successor, John Joseph Caldwell Abbot. He then became secretary of state and finally minister of marine and fisheries under three successive and short-lived Conservative prime ministers (Macdonald died in

Illus. 26-1: John Costigan. CDEM, PA1-1

1891). Costigan's relationship with the Conservatives steadily deteriorated. Macdonald, of course, resented him for trying to force his hand on the New Brunswick school question, especially since the Orange Order was one of the pillars of the Liberal-Conservative Party. Costigan believed Macdonald did not allow him as many patronage positions as he was entitled to, and he even tried to resign over the matter; Macdonald refused to accept his resignation, and Costigan did not press the issue. Costigan, nonetheless, secured an appointment as House of Commons mail clerk for Prudent Mercure. After Macdonald's death, the Orange Order's influence over the party grew stronger, until Costigan announced in 1899 that he was quitting the Conservative Party and would sit as an Independent. He argued that the party was no longer the inclusive, nation-building one that existed in Macdonald's time. In 1907, the Liberal prime minister Sir Wilfrid Laurier appointed him to the Canadian Senate. During his last year in the cabinet, he joined others trying to extend the right to vote to women. He died in 1916.

Source: "John Costigan," *Dictionary of Canadian Biography* (http://www.biographi.ca/).

ambition of the elected, since they were free to join and leave associations according to the dictates of their self interests."[6] Many politicians merely wanted to control local patronage—such as appointing people to government jobs, securing public work contracts, and controlling liquor licenses—and therefore waited until after the election results came out to declare their affiliation.

Despite their initial hostility to Confederation, Acadians often supported Liberal-Conservative candidates after 1867. Their only newspaper for a long time, *Le Moniteur Acadien,* was also Liberal-Conservative. But there were no clear patterns at the voting booth. Gloucester, Kent, and Madawaska Counties—or the three counties with the greatest proportion of Acadians in their populations—all voted differently. Gloucester was "Liberal" (meaning its members opposed the government) at the provincial and federal levels. Kent was a swing county, voting Liberal-Conservative at the provincial level in 1874, Liberal from 1874 to 1882, and Liberal-Conservative again after that. At the federal level, Kent County voters elected two Liberals, followed by an Independent, and finally three Conservatives from 1878 to 1900. In Victoria County, and after 1873 in Victoria-Madawaska electoral district, the federal Member of Parliament (MP) was the Liberal-Conservative John Costigan (see Sidebar 26-1). In Madawaska, Liberal-Conservative Lévite Thériault won every provincial election save one between 1870 and 1894, after which he became county registrar. The one election he lost—in 1882, by one vote—resulted in part from the continuing hostility of *Le Moniteur Acadien,* which had not yet forgiven him his support for the Common School Act of 1871. *Le Moniteur* pointed out that Thériault was not a genuine resident of the county, noting that although he sat on the municipal council as representative for St. Basile, he resided in Rivière-du-Loup, home of his second wife. He even sat on that town's municipal council. But Thériault remained popular among his electors because he was successful at attracting government money to his electoral

district. His initial endorsement of the Common School Act (see Chapter 23) did not harm him in the long run; he was even re-elected by acclamation in 1878 and 1890. However, Thériault represented an old political culture that, by 1882, had begun to profoundly change.

b. The Emergence of the Provincial Liberal Party
Changes in the province's political culture appeared under the leadership of Premier Andrew G. Blair. Blair was first elected to the Assembly in 1878. Although he supported the federal Liberal-Conservatives along with the existing provincial government, Blair was soon at the heart of a group of opposition members in the provincial legislature. They advocated constitutional reforms, such as broadening the franchise, abolishing the appointed Legislative Council, and employing cost-saving measures in the government's daily operations. During the 1882 election, provincial Liberal newspapers endorsed Blair and his supporters. During that election, Blair introduced a new practice: he campaigned at both the local and provincial levels. That is, in addition to campaigning in his own electoral district, he issued an electoral manifesto as a reference for candidates sharing his views.

The electoral results were inconclusive, but the Liberal-Conservative premier had alienated too many Independents, and his government fell after a vote of no-confidence. Blair then became premier and replaced the Liberal-Conservative "compact," the coalition that had brought New Brunswick into Confederation, with another one that lasted for the next sixteen years. Blair is considered the founder of the modern New Brunswick Liberal Party because he was the first to both act as a party leader and campaign province-wide. He also introduced party platforms and the practice of nominating candidates through party conventions.

Blair's successive governments, nonetheless, continued to include non-Liberals. In that sense, he was still an old-style premier. Blair believed in cultural pluralism and, recognizing the numerical strength of the Catholics and Acadians, he began nominating some of them to official positions. New Brunswick's multi-member constituencies facilitated this process, as it was desirable to balance tickets according to the county's ethnic mix. Blair refused to heed calls for a Prohibition law (like the one in Maine) from the various temperance societies and from the ultra-monarchist, ultra-Protestant Orange Order. He also refused to reopen the compromise reached by George King and Mgr. Sweeny in 1874 (see Chapter 23), despite complaints by Protestants in Acadian Bathurst who contended that the local school commission was using tax money to support two Catholic schools. This led Herman Pitt, the Orange Order editor of the *Reporter and Fredericton Advertiser,* to dub him the "Champion of Rum and Rome." Pitt feared that Blair's policies would destroy the Protestant character of New Brunswick.

During his second term, Blair extended the provincial franchise to all males ages twenty-one or above (1889) and abolished the Legislative Council (1891). Seats in the House of Assembly were redistributed in 1895 to the benefit of the predominantly Acadian counties (Madawaska, Gloucester, Kent, Victoria, and Carleton each got an extra seat). The Blair government was re-elected by a landslide. Victoria switched from Liberal-Conservative to Liberal. Acadian Gloucester and Kent elected one member from each party, as well as an Independent candidate, a pattern that they repeated in 1899 and 1903. Gloucester elected Peter John Veniot, co-founder of the Liberal *Courier des Provinces Maritimes.* He later served as the first Acadian premier between the two world wars.[7] Madawaska elected a Liberal-Conservative slate: the merchants Alphonse Bertrand and Mathias Nadeau, and farmer Cyprien Martin. At the next two elections (1899 and 1903), however, Madawaska voted Liberal (Fred Laforet and Narcisse Gagnon in 1899 and Gagnon and J. Thomas Clair in 1903). In 1896, the Liberals, headed by French Canadian Wilfrid Laurier, won the federal elections. Laurier appointed Blair, minister of railroads and canals.

c. The New Conservatives

In the meantime, the Conservatives had finally regrouped under the able leadership of John D. Hazen, who introduced another change: the positive party platform. Instead of denouncing the government's shortcomings in almost libelous terms, Hazen explained what he—and the Conservatives—would actually do if they were elected. In 1908, he placed the fight against government corruption at the heart of his platform. His party won, ending sixteen years of Liberal domination. The Acadian counties were again divided, returning a Conservative slate in Kent, a Liberal slate in Gloucester, and two Independents (Charles L. Cyr and Jesse Baker, grandson of John Baker) in Madawaska. The Independents supported the Hazen government once elected—adhering to the "old way" of doing politics. Cyr became party whip (the whip is responsible for rounding up members of his party when a vote is taken). Baker discovered that he disliked politics and did not seek a second term in 1912. During his time in office, he voted against a bill that would have given women the right to vote at provincial elections in 1909, and in 1910, he supported subsidies for the St. John Valley Railway Company (also known as the Saint John and Québec Railway Company).

In 1911, the Laurier government was defeated over the reciprocity issue, (the resumption of limited free trade with the United States). In Madawaska, electors voted for the Liberal candidate, incumbent Pius Michaud. The Conservative Robert Borden became prime minister, and Hazen was appointed minister of marine and fisheries. His successor as premier was James K. Flemming of Woodstock. In May 1912, Flemming inaugurated the construction of the St. John Valley Railway, which he described as a symbol for the new era of prosperity and advancement in the province. The line was his baby: under his supervision, the House of Assembly guaranteed $4 million of the railway's bonds.

Two days after this ceremony, Flemming dissolved the assembly and called the elections. His platform's key elements included support for the St. John Valley Railway, promises to help the pulp and paper industry, to implement a farm settlement scheme to stem the exodus of young men to the United States, and the tightening of liquor regulations. The Liberal opposition accused him of grossly increasing the provincial debt, wasting government money on road building and agriculture development on Crown land, and doing nothing to prevent emigration from the province. Liberal candidates also argued that the government had no intention of ever extending the St. John Valley Railway to the upper St. John. Nonetheless, Flemming's government was re-elected by a landslide (forty-four seats out of forty-six). The only two Liberals in the assembly were from Madawaska: the mayor of Edmundston, Louis Auguste Dugal, and Joseph A. Pelletier. Dugal soon became instrumental in Flemming's forced resignation.

d. Kickbacks

In 1914, Dugal introduced motions in the assembly that accused Flemming of receiving kickbacks from the contractors building the St. John Valley Railway and from lumberers in exchange for timber license renewals. Dugal was acting as the mouthpiece for a group of three Liberals, including Veniot who provided the two first-term opposition members with the evidence they needed. Neither Pelletier nor Dugal had good command of the English language, and Dugal received permission to present his motions in French. This marked the first time a member addressed the House of Assembly in French. The assembly appointed a provincial royal commission to investigate the kickback charges; the commission concluded that a government insider had asked for Conservative Party contributions from timber license applicants and that Flemming himself had asked for contributions from railway contractors. Widespread condemnation throughout the province and by Conservative provincial and federal politicians forced Flemming to step down as premier and resign from the assembly in 1914. In

Illus 26-2: Louis Alexandre Dugal, mayor of Edmundston and member of the Legislative Assembly of New Brunswick. PANB, P37-147

1915, the St. John Valley Railroad defaulted on its obligations, and the province took over its stock. Its American promoter, Arthur Gould (see Chapter 17), admitted to the commission investigating the matter that he had paid Flemming $100,000 before the 1912 election. The commission concluded that this had been an attempt at "placing the most trusted public man in the Province under his control," and at protecting Gould's interests should he have to default on his obligations to the company's stockholders. The scandal damaged Gould's later political career. When he was elected a Maine senator in 1926, his opponents challenged his right to serve his term on the grounds that he had bribed the premier of New Brunswick.

3. Conservatives and Acadians Part Company

When Veniot became Liberal Party organizer in 1912, his goal was to turn the Acadians into a Liberal voting bloc; he succeeded. In the period between the world wars, the terms "Acadian," "from the North," and "Liberal" became synonymous. Yet, as late as 1900, the Acadian counties were either Liberal-Conservative or swing constituencies. The Conservatives' behavior played as much a role in the Acadians becoming Liberals as did Veniot's skills, and the switch had its roots in the period preceding World War I.

Acadians' growing political consciousness and subsequent determination to play a role in provincial politics angered some segments of the Anglo-Protestant population. Some evangelical Protestants, many of whom lived side by side with Catholics, as well as Orange Order members, were determined to minimize Catholic and Acadian influence to the greatest possible extent. The drive to divide Kent and Victoria counties so that, in the words of the *Telegraph,* the "legitimate Protestant influence over the Legislature" could be preserved represented an early example of this attitude. The same story repeated itself at the national level, where the goal was to confine French Catholic influence to Québec. This led provincial Conservative governments to abolish French language education rights in Manitoba in 1896, and in Ontario (Bill 17) in 1912. (When Manitoba entered Confederation in 1869, its population was almost equally divided between English and French speakers, but over the years, immigration had tipped the balance in favor of English. The opposite trend occurred in Eastern Ontario, where the French-speaking population had grown steadily since 1870.) The federal and provincial Conservatives were increasingly tainted by their association with ultra-Protestant or anti-French elements. Costigan left the federal Conservative party in 1898, claiming it no longer was the inclusive, nation-building party of John A. Macdonald. Acadians were, therefore, becoming weary of Conservatives, and three events, (two provincial and one federal) during the war permanently alienated them from the Conservatives.

First, Conservative Premier James A. Murray introduced a Prohibition bill in the assembly in 1916. Acadians viewed this as unwarranted meddling in local affairs, as well as an Anglo-Protestant attempt at imposing their values on others. The Prohibition law was widely violated, even in the south, and the St. Leonard-Van Buren area became the hub of massive liquor-smuggling operations. Second, Murray proposed a resettlement scheme under which veterans would receive free land. Unfortunately, the counties specifically targeted as appropriate places to settle these "men from the British Isles" were the northern, or Acadian, counties. The Acadians interpreted this scheme as an attempt to Anglicize them by flooding their counties with Anglo-Protestants.

Third, at the federal level, the 1917 conscription crisis was equally damaging to the relationship between Acadians and the Conservative Party. In 1917, the federal Parliament passed the Military Service Act (MSA) at the initiative of the Conservative-dominated, wartime, Union government. The MSA allowed the government to draft soldiers to replace those getting killed in massive numbers across Europe. Farmers across the country opposed conscription, irrespective of ethnicity; so did most French Canadians and Acadians, who did not see why they should get killed to fight the king of England's European war. As a result, war and conscription supporters hurled insults at Acadians. Those criticisms were particularly strong in Conservative newspaper columns.[8]

In truth, not all Acadians opposed conscription, but support was confined to members of the elite, such as Kent Conservative member of the House of Assembly F. J. Robidoux, most members of the clergy, and the editors of *Le Moniteur Acadien.* Dugal's son enlisted and came back in 1916 minus the leg he lost on the battlefield. At the 1917 federal elections, Acadians voted in favor of Wilfrid Laurier's Liberals because they opposed conscription. The pro-conscription Unionists won eleven of the fifteen New Brunswick seats, but the Liberals carried all the ridings (electoral districts) with large Acadian populations. In Kent, Robidoux lost his seat by a margin of 3,563 to 1,323 votes. In Gloucester, Liberal Onésiphore Turgeon won by acclamation after Unionist candidate Édouard DeGrâce, dropped out of the race. Finally, in the new riding of Madawaska-Restigouche, voters elected Liberal candidate Pius Michaud by a large majority (3,059 to 1,111).

Therefore, after 1917, many Acadians had come to view the Conservative Party as the party of Anglicization, conscription, and anti-Catholic hostility, and deserted it for good.

II. MAINE: REPUBLICAN ASCENDANCY, NATIVISM, PROHIBITION

A. Republican Ascendancy, Nativism, Prohibition

Our knowledge of Maine Madawaskayans' political activities is much more limited. Three issues, nonetheless, deserve attention. First was the issue of citizenship: who among Madawaska residents had the right to participate in the political process? This was not as clear as one would think and led to charges of electoral fraud in 1878. Second, anti-French and anti-Catholic hostility was not a purely Canadian phenomenon; it also occurred in Maine, leading to an amendment to the state constitution in 1892. Third, and perhaps surprisingly, the Valley slowly turned Republican.

1. Contested 1878 Elections: Who Is a Citizen?

In 1878, the state legislature again had to investigate allegations of electoral fraud in northern Aroostook County (St. John Valley and Fort Fairfield). Some men on the list of electors had not been entitled to vote at the time they cast their ballot. The legislature appointed commissioners to go to the county and interview the men in question to ascertain their electoral qualifications. The commissioners struck eighty-three names from the voters' lists. In Fort Kent, most deleted names were English. In St. Francis and Frenchville, some of the voters in question missed the interview. And, in several instances, the commissioners could not determine whether an individual had the right to vote or not. The commissioners further confused the issue with a circuitous explanation that tried to show that, while assessors and electors might not have fully understood the voting process, they had not made deliberate attempts at fraud:

> It is undoubtedly true that in this part of Aroostook County, in determining the rights of men claiming to be citizens, questions of laws and fact of some nicety arise under the treaty and upon general principles. Questions of birth, parentage and residence, and of the character of the residence, whether temporary or permanent, on one side of the boundary line or the other, and it is believed by all the members of the Commission that the illegal voting in the Towns and Plantations to which their investigation extended is not upon a very large scale, and that to the extent to which it occurs, it results in most instances rather from the character and number of the questions of law and fact arising to be determined than from a design to act fraudulently on the part of the voters or the officers of towns.[9]

The incident is revealing, because it shows that as late as 1878, both area residents and state officials struggled to ascertain the citizenship of Valley residents and, consequently, the rights of an individual to vote in one specific township over another. Since only three months' residence was required to qualify as an elector, it seems that the population was largely transient.

2. The 1892 Constitutional Amendment: Who Should Be Allowed to Vote?

In June 1904, Thomas H. Pelletier, editor of *Le Journal du Madawaska*, denounced American "members of secret societies," who had been behind an act that "annihilated" their electoral franchise and deprived half their present population of the right to vote, and which, within a few years "would eliminate the vote of ⁹/₁₀ of their total population." The act he was referring to was an amendment to the state constitution (Amendment XXIX—Educational Qualifications of Voters) stipulating that:

> No person shall have the right to vote or be eligible to office under the constitution of this state, who shall not be able to read the Constitution in the English language and write his name; provided however, that the provisions of this amendment shall not apply to any person prevented by a physical disability from complying with its requisition, nor to any person who now has the right to vote, not to any person who shall be sixty years of age and upward at the time this amendment will take effect.[10]

Members of the sixty-fourth legislature voted to put the amendment to the popular vote by a two-thirds majority. The referendum took place in September 1892 at the same time as county elections. Almost 60 percent of the voters (25,775 in favor to 18,061 against) approved the amendment, which took effect in January 1893.

Pelletier presented his readers with an apocalyptic vision of the future. His argument is peculiar, however, in that it only holds true if Acadians and Franco-Americans were all illiterate in English and planned to remain so indefinitely. But, since school attendance had been compulsory in Maine since 1887 (see Chapter 23), it seems likely that this new generation of Madawaskayans would have met the amendment's proposed educational qualifications. Even if one assumes that most naturalized immigrants from Québec could read no English, it seems doubtful that this amendment could disenfranchise

nine-tenths of the French population in Maine.

Pelletier was prone to exaggeration, but he was probably right in asserting that the amendment targeted the state's Franco-American population. Its adoption paralleled other measures designed to Anglicize the French (see Chapter 23, Sidebar 23-2). In any case, it did not unite the Anglo-American population. As one can expect, Madawaskayans voted strongly against the amendment—but places like Portland and Augusta were not as strongly in favor as might be expected. And even those who supported the amendment may not have done so because they were anti-French, but merely because they believed American citizens should be functional in English, regardless of the language they used in private or taught their children. There were Nativists in Maine, but not all Mainers were Nativists. (For the origins of Nativism, see Chapter 11.)

3. Did the Valley Become Republican?

Madawaska was Democrat when the state was Democrat (see Chapter 11) but remained Democrat when the state became Republican in the late 1850s. Ethnic minorities and Catholics tended to favor the Democratic Party—and the behavior of the Madawaskayans was therefore not unexpected. However, by the end of the nineteenth century, the Valley was increasingly supporting Republican gubernatorial candidates. Did this make it an emerging Republican stronghold? Because turnout for presidential elections remained low, the results of those elections cannot be treated as indicative of political preference. And because voters elected state representatives and senators based as much on personality as on party affiliation, researchers cannot treat local elections as accurate indicators of political preference. However,, Madawaska voters began to regularly send Republicans to the state legislature at about the time they began to favor Republicans for governor (see Figure 26-1). On the eve of World War I, Madawaska was no longer a predictable Democratic stronghold.

Local elections were another story. *Franco-*

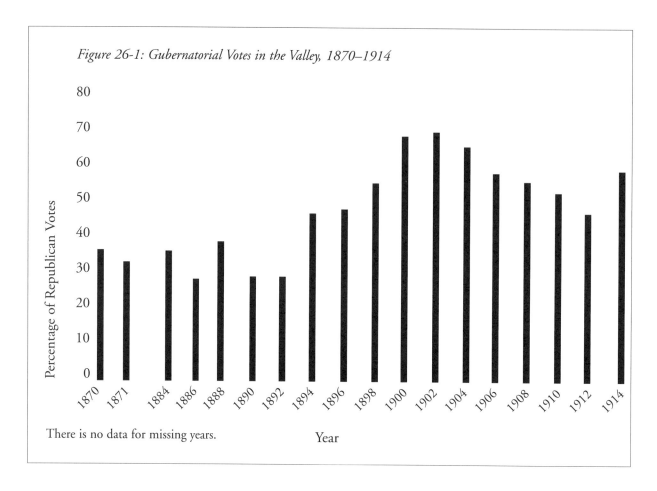

Figure 26-1: Gubernatorial Votes in the Valley, 1870–1914

Percentage of Republican Votes

Year

There is no data for missing years.

Americans of the State of Maine, offers an overview of the careers of many successful Franco-Americans, including Valley citizens. The volume identifies only four Republicans among the latter: Lévite Thibodeau, Joseph Dumas, Willie F. Paradis, and Émile Lebrun. Their support ranged from a simple declaration of affiliation to running for office. Thibodeau was the only one of the four to run for a seat in the Maine legislature. He was defeated. Many of the men who appear in this volume took part in local politics or ran for a seat in the state legislature, and those who were Democrat appear to have been more successful. Voters elected Irénée Cyr (Fort Kent) to the Maine legislature in 1911 and 1913, where he served on various committees. They also elected storekeeper Henry Gagnon (Van Buren) twice, and he served on the state roads, state land, and Indian affairs committees. Van Buren lawyer

Jean B. Pelletier served in the Maine legislature in 1911, and many believed he was very influential among Franco-Americans. Insurance agent and automobile dealer Paul D. Thibodeau was Van Buren town treasurer and served in the legislature in 1915.

If we are to believe Thomas H. Pelletier, Aroostook County Republicans were not a particularly welcoming group. The Democrats always proposed Valley candidates, including French Catholic candidates, for county elections. The Republicans did not. The absence of any Franco candidate on the 1904 Republican ticket elicited violent denunciations of the "hypocritical Houlton gang and their Orange associates that the Maritimes have vomited onto our soil over the past few years."[11] *Le Journal du Madawaska* believed that too many people in Aroostook County automatically assumed that

Lévite V. Thibodeau was born on April 14, 1868, in St. Leonards, New Brunswick. After graduating from Ricker Classical Institute in Houlton, Maine, he studied law in Caribou, eventually becoming one of the most prominent lawyers of Aroostook County. He was the second French-speaking St. John Valley resident to be admitted to the state bar. In January 1898, he married Alma Pelletier, daughter of Dr. Thomas Pelletier of Van Buren, and they settled in the village. Thibodeau joined the Republican Party and tried without success to get on the ticket as the candidate for county commissioner. He ran for the Maine legislature in 1914, but was defeated by Fortunat O. Michaud, a Democrat. He then served as town treasurer for a year and town solicitor for five. Thibodeau engaged in "boosterism"—or the relentless promotion of his town using any and all possible means. He was a promoter and stockholder for the Van Buren Trust Company and the First National Bank of Van Buren, as well as a shareholder in the Van Buren Light and Power Company and the Van Buren Water District. He co-founded *Le Journal du Madawaska* with his father-in-law and operated a real estate agency that sold land in the northwestern United States. Like most prominent men of his time, he belonged to several fraternal organizations and mutual benefit societies, including the Union Saint-Jean-Baptiste, the Independent Order of Foresters, the Catholic Order of Foresters, the Benevolent and Protective Order of Elks of Houlton, and the Modern Woodsmen of America. Lawton and Burgess in the *Franco-Americans of the State of Maine* describe him as a man "held in high esteem personally" and "essentially public spirited and patriotic, hence he takes a deep interest in the advancement and future prosperity of Van Buren and the great surrounding farming country."

Source: Lawton and Burgess (1915): 189.
Illus. 26-3 and 4: Photo of Lévite Thibodeau from E. C. Bowler, An Album of the Attorneys of Maine, 1902. Publicity for his real eestate agency from Le Journal du Madawaska, *1904.*

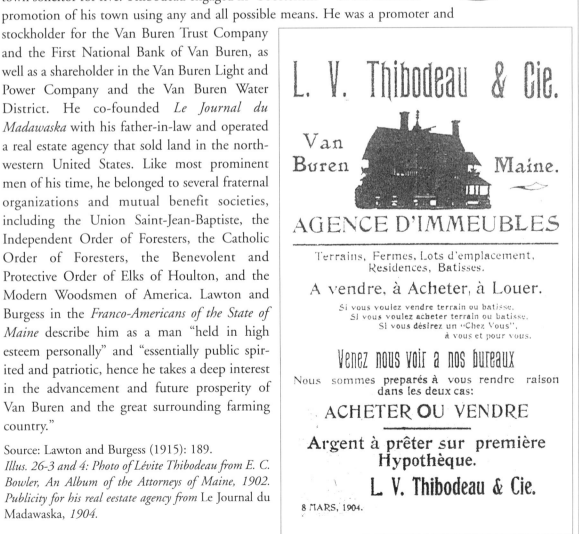

L. V. Thibodeau & Cie.

Van Buren   Maine.

AGENCE D'IMMEUBLES

Terrains, Fermes, Lots d'emplacement, Residences, Batisses.

A vendre, à Acheter, à Louer.

Si vous voulez vendre terrain ou batisse,
Si vous voulez acheter terrain ou batisse,
Si vous désirez un "Chez Vous",
à vous et pour vous.

Venez nous voir a nos bureaux

Nous sommes preparés à vous rendre raison
dans les deux cas:

ACHETER OU VENDRE

Argent à prêter sur première Hypothèque.

L. V. Thibodeau & Cie.

8 MARS, 1904.

Sidebar 26-3: The "Duke of Fort Kent"

The "Duke" was William Dickey, Fort Kent state representative from 1868 to 1870 and 1878 to 1899 (the year he died). Dickey earned his nickname because he had "done more than any other man to promote her [Aroostook County] interests out of the State treasury."[1] In the nineteenth century, a politician's value was still based on his ability to deliver the goods—and Dickey delivered.

Dickey would never have taken up residence in Fort Kent had it not been for several fortuitous events. Born in Damariscotta, Maine, in 1810, he lost his father, a ship captain, in 1819 when his vessel was lost at sea. His mother moved the family to Strong, in Franklin County, where they started a farm.

After completing his education at Farmington Academy, he returned to Strong to clerk in a store, and opened his own store in 1831. In 1832, he was elected captain of the local militia and was promoted to major two years later. He also worked as a postmaster and deputy sheriff before being elected to the state legislature in 1841. There, he adamantly

Illus. 26-5: William Dickey
Fort Kent Historical Society

opposed the Webster–Ashburton Treaty for giving away Maine land to the British. In 1842, he married Lydia Bodfish of Gardiner, moved to her hometown, and began working in the lumber and milling business.

In 1849, Dickey, who was suffering from an incapacitating lung condition, moved to Fort Kent, renowned for its healthy air, with a stock of goods to open a store. He purchased half of the Fish River mill privilege, rebuilt the saw mill, built a gristmill, and cleared a farm. Five years later, his health restored, he divested himself of his business interests in Fort Kent and moved to Haverhill, Massachusetts, where he opened a door and sash factory. Unfortunately, the factory burned to the ground two years later, and in 1857, Dickey was back on his farm in Fort Kent. In 1858, he was appointed deputy collector of customs (a federal patronage job), a position he kept for three years.

Dickey became the unbeatable Fort Kent state representative in 1878. He was by then sixty-eight years old, a well-established businessman, and an experienced politician. Dickey bragged that he always got what he wanted—and as long as the state legislature had the ability to deliver on what he wanted, he was right. Dickey secured appropriations for local roads, bridges, and schoolhouses. A former superintendent, he is also credited with founding the Madawaska Training School. He secured a reduction in local school taxes without any loss of state appropriation. When the bill banning instruction in a language other than English was introduced in the state legislature, he scuttled it, arguing that it was pointless to instruct children in a language they did not understand. Dickey also played an active role in resolving conflicts between timberland owners and settlers (see Chapter 17). He spearheaded efforts to rebuild downtown Fort Kent after the disastrous flood of 1888 and secured funding for repairs on the blockhouse. Dickey, however, never fulfilled his dream of seeing bridges across the St. John. The state legislature appropriated funds, as did the Canadian federal Parliament (thanks to Costigan), but Washington always turned down such requests. Dickey was indeed the patron of northern Aroostook County, and he used his powers and abilities to develop the local infrastructure, promote education, and protect the interests of local people.

Note 1: Burque, *Major Dickey,* 8.
Source: Burque (1900).

Franco-Americans were morons unworthy of political consideration. T. H. Pelletier's outrage might have derived from personal factors: his son-in-law Lévite Thibodeau had sought nomination as county commissioner candidate and lost.

If Valley voters were showing a greater inclination to vote Republican at the end of the nineteenth century, were New Brunswick and American Madawaskayans evolving in opposite directions? In other words, is it not true that Democrats are "liberal" and Republicans are "conservative"? Not really, since those are late-twentieth-century equations with little relevance to the past. For instance, Prohibitionists were reformers, a fact that should have made them "liberal," but in Maine, they were mostly Republicans. In New Brunswick, Prohibitionists were at first mostly Liberal before becoming largely Conservative. In short, past party ideologies cannot be ascertained through their twentieth-century equivalents.

What caused Madawaskayans to switch from Democratic before and during the American Civil War to Republican at the turn of the twentieth century is not known. Were they attracted by the policies or values of one party, or repelled by the other, or both? Were county Republican leaders really New Brunswick Orange Order members who had immigrated to Maine? How did Nativism really affect Madawaskayans' political participation? At the

moment, we do not know because researchers have not investigated these questions.

Conclusion

Over the course of the fifty years preceding World War I, Acadians in New Brunswick and Franco-Americans in Maine became political forces in their own right. Madawaskayans were no different and not only participated in elections but sought, and sometimes gained, public office. The growing number of Acadians in New Brunswick made them an important constituency, and they began to secure patronage jobs. In Maine, on the other hand, French Madawaskayans could rarely win non-local elections. Residents elected Frenchmen from the Valley to the state legislature (local electoral districts) but not to county offices, and no French Madawaskayans won a seat in the state senate before 1907 (Patrick Thériault). Significant segments of the state and province's Anglo-Protestant majorities adamantly opposed French-speakers or Catholics gaining political power, but we do not know how this affected Madawaska on either side of the border. We know why the New Brunswick Acadians turned their backs on the Conservatives in the early years of the twentieth century, but not why American Madawaskayans slowly moved away from the Democrats during the same period.

ENDNOTES

1. *Le Moniteur Acadien.*

2. Auguste Renaud, a French immigrant, won the Ottawa election in 1867, with 64 percent of the vote, defeating both an Anglophone Liberal and an Anglophone Conservative. Renaud was a Liberal. He was defeated by an Anglophone Liberal in 1872 and 1874.

3. An Irish Catholic daily newspaper.

4. Quoted in *Le Moniteur Acadien,* April 3, 1873.

5. MacNutt, *New Brunswick, A History: 1784–1867,* 346.

6. Woodward, *The History of New Brunswick Provincial Election,* 2

7. Peter John Veniot, (born Jean-Pierre Vigneault, 1863–1936) was first elected to the New Brunswick Assembly in 1894; he left politics in 1900 to take an appointment as customs collector. In 1912, he was hired to reorganize the Liberal Party and re-elected in 1917. Veniot set out to turn the Acadians into a voting bloc, an effort that paid off after the war. Veniot also became the first New Brunswick Acadian premier in 1923 but lost the elections in 1925. He was elected to the federal Parliament in 1926 and joined the government the same year.

8. *Le Madawaska* (Edmundston), March 15, 1917.

9. Maine Public Documents, *Report of the Commission Appointed to Investigate Alleged Election Frauds...,* 7.

10. The text of 1892 amendment can be found in *Revised Statutes of the State of Maine, 1903, Published by Authority of the State Legislature,* Augusta, ME: Kennebec Journal Printing, 1904.

11. *Le Journal du Madawaska,* Van Buren, August 17, 1904.

FURTHER READINGS

Judd *et. al.*, *Maine: The Pine Tree State;* Buckner and Reid, *Atlantic Canada Since Confederation;* and Mac Nutt, *New Brunswick: A History* all provide a good overview of political life in Maine and New Brunswick during the period under consideration

Landry and Lang's *Histoire de l'Acadie* and Doucet's *La Politique et les Acadiens* can help contextualize Madawaskayans' political activities.

SOURCES

New Brunswick electoral results can be found in G. Boucher (1973), Garland (1979), and Woodward (1976); Dubay (1994) compiled Aroostook County electoral results. Results for all Maine elections from 1870 onward are available on microfilm at the Maine State Archives (Secretary of State, Election returns, official vote tabulation, 1870–1916.) For the 1892 constitutional amendment, see Dirnfeld (2008).

The Reverend Burque, a priest in Fort Kent, published a biography of Major Dickey the year following his death; other political biographies can be found in Lawton and Burgess (1915). For biographies of Canadian politicians (Lévite Thériault, John Costigan, Leonard Tilley, James Kidd Flemming, Andrew George Blair, and Pierre Amand Landry), see either the *Dictionary of Canadian Biography* (http://www.biographi.ca/EN/) or Graves's typewritten account, "Political Biographies," at the Provincial Archives of New Brunswick. G. Sirois (1980) tells the story of John Baker's grandson. Whalen (1964) explains local government in New Brunswick. For an equivalent explanation in Maine, see Kingsbury (1878) and Stetson (1898).

Newspapers also covered political life during this time. One can consult Desjardins' *Le Madawaska Raconté par Le Moniteur Acadien, 1867–1926,* which contains transcripts of all articles relating to Madawaska. The Acadian Archives have microfilm copies of *Le Journal du Madawaska,* 1904–05 (the only issues that have survived). For the conscription crisis in Canada, see Theobald (2004).

CONCLUSION

The upper St. John Valley emerged from the Ice Age to become the axis around which the region revolved. First, the entire area tilted north, allowing rivers and lakes to drain into the future St. Lawrence estuary; then it tilted south, and the waters began to flow toward the Bay of Fundy, as they do today. The region's geological past foreshadowed its human history as a "land in between"—a frontier or borderland until the beginning of the twentieth century. When the first humans reached it, the upper St. John Valley became a link between two regions; subsequently, it became a link between two colonies and two economies.

In the millennia before the first contact with Europeans, the upper St. John Valley functioned as both a bridge and a crossroads. It allowed animals, humans, ideas, technology, raw material, and objects to travel back and forth between the St. Lawrence and the Gulf of Maine/Bay of Fundy. It was also a place where cultures could blend. Native artifacts found in the area, besides providing evidence of long-distance trade, show unmistaken clues to such blending. The upper St. John Valley was a true frontier, an intermediary region where people interacted without outside interference.

This did not change during the first century of European presence in the northeast. The Europeans, who were few in number, fished and traded. The Natives incorporated European goods into their lives. Those who controlled the St. John River or the coast attempted to control the traffic of those goods. Those people became middlemen between the Europeans and tribes living farther southwest. The Maritime Peninsula had become a commercial frontier between Natives and newcomers, and the St. John River–Témiscouata and St. John–St. Francis routes played a pivotal role in this development.

France and England, however, soon tried to turn the northeast into bordered lands. The French established colonies on the Bay of Fundy (then called *Baie Française*) and the St. Lawrence, while the English established colonies along Massachusetts Bay. Although the colonies' nuclei were clearly identifiable, their boundaries existed only on paper and were constantly challenged. Furthermore, Natives challenged the very existence of colonies—of North American territories under the exclusive authority of an overseas monarch—arguing that this was their land. At the heart of the contested territory lay the St. John River and its tributaries. This communication route was part of a military borderland extending first to the Kennebec River and then to the Penobscot River. New Englanders constantly challenged the control members of the Native-French alliance exerted over the route. In times of peace among the Europeans, the St. John Valley acted as a commercial frontier, or part of a fur-trading network involving French, Natives, and Bostonians. It was also a borderland between hostile Anglo-Americans and Natives trying to retain sovereignty over their land. Moreover, Natives used it as a haven from aggressors.

When Britain briefly gained control over the entire Atlantic Seaboard, the St. John River temporarily lost some of its usefulness for official communications. But the end of the military conflict led to the intensification of economic activities, namely those involving the exploitation of natural resources. Those activities, orchestrated by Québec and New England merchants, involved Natives, Canadians, Acadians, and newly established New Englanders. The St. John Valley again emerged as a frontier—albeit an economic one—but this did not last long. The Revolutionary War turned it back into a contested borderland with a divided population. During this time, it served as a vital communication route for the British military.

Up to that point, the upper St. John River and Témiscouata had been critical components of the Maritime Peninsula communication network, but their banks were not permanently occupied. Even if we take the Natives' way of life into account and define "permanent occupation" as the converging of a relatively stable group of people at predictable times of the year in a given place, there were no permanent settlements on the upper St John River. Native travelers, hunters, and occasionally refugees from the south, however, constantly used this region, which therefore was essential to their survival, and even the French deemed it part of Maliseet territory. The Europeans used the St. John–Témiscouata waterways as a travel and trade route.

This changed during the Revolutionary War. A sizeable Native village appeared at the junction between the Madawaska and St. John Rivers in the late 1770s. This village probably included people pushed north first by coastal warfare and then by Loyalist intrusion onto their hunting grounds. It lasted less than a generation: a large village at the limit of the region's carrying capacity, it had to compete with Québec Hurons and north-shore Montagnais for resources. Canadian fur traders engaged in intensive trapping and moose hunting in the area, accelerating the depletion of natural resources. The arrival of a significant number of Euro-American families after 1785 aggravated the

situation. This hunting frontier became incapable of supporting this enlarged population, and the Natives migrated to the Tobique or Ile Verte, where competition was less severe.

The Acadian-Canadian settlement on the upper St. John occurred when the provincial governments' needs merged with those of the people. The provincial governments pursued two goals: ensuring the security of government couriers along the St. John–Témiscouata route as soon as possible and reaffirming British jurisdiction over the area against possible American claims. Settling the Valley and the Témiscouata route with British subjects was part of the attempt to turn the St. John River into a bordered land. As far as New Brunswick was concerned, settling the upper St. John meant asserting the province's jurisdiction over that part of British North America. Lieutenant-governor Carleton viewed the upper St. John as an interprovincial bordered land. The Acadians along the lower St. John River left because their economic base was undermined by the Loyalists' arrival, their sons' futures were uncertain, and they were a tiny Catholic minority surrounded by Protestants. Those who were familiar with the upper St. John or already had connections to the St. Lawrence communities moved there, to be joined soon thereafter by other relatives from the St. Lawrence. As far as they were concerned, the Valley was still a frontier.

Diplomats drawing red lines on maps (and usually on inaccurate maps to boot) were one thing. Translating those lines into meaningful divisions on sparsely populated, underdeveloped ground that lay a considerable distance from the seats of power was another matter altogether. Local people ignored the boundaries. They also ignored the formalities of acquiring land or gaining the legal right to exploit natural resources. They traded with northern and southern merchants with blithe disregard for customs regulations. Whatever British and American authorities chose to believe, late-eighteenth and early nineteenth-century Madawaska was a frontier—until some purses began to suffer. Timber was a valuable resource, and neither Maine nor New Brunswick wanted its proceeds to line the other's pocket. Some at that time even believed that a plan to run a rail line through the Madawaska territory linking Quebec City to St. Andrew played a role in the boundary dispute: such a railway could have hurt Boston's economic interests. State political rivalries exacerbated the situation. The time had come to turn the upper St. John River Valley into bordered lands. Red lines were again drawn on maps: Maine got a slice of the pie, New Brunswick another, and Québec got two slivers. Each government built customhouses, post offices, and roads, as well as issued land grants, held elections, and appropriated school funds. Despite this flurry of activity, life went on as usual for the people of the Valley.

London, Washington, Quebec City, Fredericton, and Augusta may have entertained the illusion that they had established real borders, but geography defeated them. The region's resources were farm and wood products. The only means of communications between the Valley and the rest of the world were the St. John River and the portages to the St. Lawrence. Timber could be taken out of the former disputed territory only through the St. John, regardless of whether it had been cut in Maine, New Brunswick, or Lower Canada. American producers usually succeeded in getting legislation passed allowing them to process their lumber in New Brunswick and then ship the finished product back to the United States without duties.

The St. Lawrence portages, especially the Grand Portage to Rivière-du-Loup, linked the upper St. John Valley to the St. Lawrence. These routes channelled immigration from Lower Canada to Madawaska and made trade possible. Farmers exported grain out of the region, and imported staples, such as barreled flour, meat, and fish, as well as household goods, such as Canadian stoves from Lower Canada. Money flowed in both directions. For example, merchant John Emmerson paid for his purchases in Quebec City with money he earned

from supplying local lumber operators who nonetheless paid him in Saint John. People moved across the river freely, sending their children to whichever school seemed best and patronizing stores on both sides of the river. The mail crisscrossed the border using the most convenient route. As late as 1857, the Maine Board of Agriculture noted that:

> As traffic ever seeks the most profitable channel as naturally as water seeks its level, we cannot wonder, however much we may regret, that it has nearly all passed into the Province; nor can we wonder more to find that the social intercourse and sympathies of the people have followed the same direction, and that, except in the matter of jurisdiction, this vast and fertile region is (almost if not quite) as really annexed to new Brunswick, as if so stipulated in the Treaty of 1842. The boundary line never here a practically serious obstacle to interchange of commodities has, since the Reciprocity Treaty came in operation, been little more than a nominal one.[1]

This situation would last as long as the only practical means of communication were in British territory: the rivers, and eventually, the railroads. The building of the Bangor and Aroostook Railroad represented a turning point in the region's history. Aroostook County farmers and loggers could finally ship their agricultural and forest products quickly and directly to other parts of the United States over an all-American route. Aroostook County became a potato-growing, starch-producing district, while Madawaska-Victoria continued to produce fodder and tried to diversify through dairy production. Government policies restricting the export of raw materials (Québec) or taxing the import of manufactured goods (the United States) intensified the impact of the Bangor and Aroostook on lumber production. The lumber industry consequently split along geographic lines. Lumber mills using Maine and New Brunswick logs were established in Maine, while others using Maine and Québec logs appeared in the Québec part of the former disputed territory.

New Brunswick Madawaska became a mere supplier of raw material and labor.

Madawaska was still a borderland, but the borders were becoming increasingly intrusive. Cultural factors did not necessarily minimize the changes. Madawaskayans shared a language and a religion with French Canadians, Acadians, and Franco-Americans. Madawaskayan children attended schools in greater and greater numbers. Although public schools were supposed to be secular on both sides of the river, and teaching was supposed to be in English, Canadian or French sisters often taught children French on both sides of the river. While the school systems could be bent to preserve language and religion, could they provide Madawaskayans with a shared cultural identity?

Quebeckers claimed Catholic French-speakers were "French Canadians," including even those who had migrated to New England. Acadians, however, drew a sharp distinction between themselves, descendents of deportees, and French Canadians.

Madawaskayans fell somewhere in between: while they were descendents of French Canadians and Acadians, their Acadian ancestors had not been deported. Thomas Albert defined them as a bridge people, but his biological-cultural definition ignored citizenship, which was becoming an increasingly pressing issue south of the border. On the eve of World War I, the old Madawaska territory was still part cultural and economic frontier and part borderland. But the forces that would turn its different parts into so many bordered lands over the next fifty years were already in place. Indeed, the "land in between" was on the brink of becoming the "land divided." How this happened will be the topic of the second volume of this narrative.

ENDNOTE
1. Maine Public Documents, *Second Annual Report of the Maine Board of Agriculture,* 1857, 32.

Epilogue

UNTOLD STORIES

Readers should not be fooled by the size of this volume; these are not the final words on the history of Madawaska. Time constraints prevented us from exhausting all sources of information. There remains a lot that is not known but perhaps could have been unearthed with several more years of research. Besides unearthing new facts, additional research might have provided us with new perspectives on old issues. And, of course, documents shedding new, if not contradictory, light on the aspects of Madawaska history explored in these pages may still surface. In the paragraphs that follow, we want to identify some areas that need additional research. This list is not exhaustive, and we hope that readers will come up with their own questions (and answers).

What are the gaps in our knowledge?

Natives: The Maliseets are this story's poor parents. We were surprised to find how little research has been conducted on them, especially compared to the Mi'kmaq, Passamaquoddy, and Penobscots. American scholars ignore the Maliseets because most live in New Brunswick, and Canadian scholars are much more interested in the Mi'kmaq. The Indian Affairs series at the Provincial Archives of New Brunswick is a good place to start researching this group.

Religion: Our coverage of religion and religious life needs fleshing out. Researchers can do this by using records available at Archevêché de Québec, the Diocese of Chatham, the Diocese of Portland, and even the Diocese of Boston. While we know when parishes were founded and who the priests were, we have little information about parish life. In particular, it is obvious that having a profound attachment to faith and yet being conflict with the priest or bishop was not as uncommon as one might assume: the parishioners of Fathers Langevin, Dionne, and McGuirk, to name a few, denounced them to the bishop, and the relationships between Acadians, French Canadians, and Franco-Americans and their Irish bishops were often acrimonious. Why, or how, did Madawaska escape the latter problem? In addition, we know that priests got involved in politics. We suspect that power struggles between priests and Valley leaders were behind the denunciations mentioned above. The relationship between the priests and governors of Maine and New Brunswick also deserves a second look. Dionne's correspondences in French with former Governor Hubbard asking him to intervene on Madawaskayans' behalf is a little surprising. How frequent was that type of relationship? Historically, how long did this type of relationship last?

Military: Readers will also notice that we have left military issues aside. Finding lists of veterans is not difficult—the militaries in both the United States and Canada keep detailed records. But we did not have the luxury to go to Washington, D.C. Madawaskayan participation in the Civil War, the Spanish-American War, the Boer War (if they lived in New Brunswick), and World War I deserves further investigation. During World War I, the presence of many Americans on Canadian soil and vice versa even led Britain and the United States to sign a treaty allowing American citizens and British subjects to serve in the other country's military without jeopardizing their citizenship. Did American Madawaskayans serve in the British armed forces—and vice versa?

Economy: As Chapter 20 amply shows, we do not know much about post-1870 Madawaska agriculture, especially on the American side. In all likelihood, interesting changes took place after 1880. Between 1878 and the building of the B&A, for example, farmers shipped potatoes through New Brunswick. Customs records may contain information about these exports. Otherwise, as routine official sources are unlikely to shed much light on this matter, researchers should try to find private documents similar to the Cyr account book, such as farmers' account books and shippers' business records.

We know even less about small businesses. Various documents provide us with lists of storekeepers, merchants, and craftsmen, but we know almost nothing about them. Here especially, our hope is that some private records will surface. The emergence of similar documents for bigger businesses (like the lumber mills) would also considerably enhance our knowledge of the industry.

Newspaper advertisements demonstrate that retail trade was well developed in the Valley at the turn of the twentieth century. How did consumption patterns change at the end of the nineteenth and beginning of the twentieth centuries?

Advertisements in the local paper suggest that merchants on the American side of the border received their stock from Boston or other American centers; on the New Brunswick side of the border, merchants tended to advertise wares acquired in Quebec City or Montreal. American and British clothing styles were slightly different. Did American Madawaskayans dress "American" and New Brunswick Madawaskayans dress "British"? Or did Valley residents shop on both sides of the border and create their own fashion blend? And how did metropolitan fashions affect the countryside? Photographs, which are numerous for this period, could provide some answers.

Infrastructure: The development of a modern financial and communication infrastructure (banks, postal services, telegraphs, and telephones) has merely been sketched in this volume and deserves further investigation. It would be worth looking at United States Post Office records to see if they provide information regarding the volume and direction of traffic, and the nature of the material carried, such as letters, newspapers, and other materials.

Associational Life: The biographies of Madawaskayans contained in *Franco-Americans of the State of Maine and Their Achievements* suggest that many of the leading men of the Valley belonged to fraternal organizations. This aspect of Madawaska social and civic life has never been investigated. For that matter, the role of fraternal organizations in small towns and rural communities at the turn of the twentieth century is waiting for its historian. The participation of Madawaskayans in Acadian associations (in New England and the Maritimes), French Canadian associations (like the Saint-Jean-Baptiste), and in Franco-American associations also requires further exploration.

Politics: As the various chapters on politics make it plain, we know almost nothing about political life in American Madawaska. Even worse, we really know little about political life in nineteenth-century Maine. Maine political history, by and large, covers political activities in Augusta. For instance, we did not find material telling us who supported what party and why. Did residents along the coast vote differently from those in the interior? Did town dwellers vote differently from rural inhabitants? Did merchants vote differently from craftspeople? Did Anglo-Protestants vote differently from Catholics? And did the Irish vote differently from Franco-Americans? We do know that Irish Catholics flocked to the Democratic Party, but how much did tensions between Franco-Americans and the Irish influence the former's political affiliation? What motivated Madawaska's slow shift toward the Republicans at the end of the nineteenth century? These are very basic questions for which we have found no answer in the writings of historians.

One could also ask whether Maine and New Brunswick politics were really so different from each other. "Compact politics" gave way to partisan politics earlier in Maine than New Brunswick, but how important were parties in local elections? Maine's absorption of a territory where compact politics was still strong, when the state's political life was becoming unmistakably partisan, could provide researchers with a good start to investigate this transition. When, how, and why did people switch their allegiance from a person to a party? What did parties have to do to attract people who hitherto had supported individuals? By using Madawaska as a laboratory to investigate this process, one is much less likely to fall into the trap of seeing it as "uniquely American" or as "typical of colonial societies."

International Issues: We have dealt summarily with international issues, such as the use of the St. John River for transportation, construction of international bridges, and taxation of goods produced in Aroostook but exported through New Brunswick. The debates in Washington leading to the Pike Act and the government's refusal to allocate funding for international bridges should be looked into. This, in turn, would shed light on the rivalry between timber and lumber producers in the St. John and the Penobscot valleys. One also suspects that similar rivalries must have affected the building (or non-building) of railroads in Maine. It would also be interesting to find out how New Brunswick and Canada reacted to those debates in Washington. Did they try to lobby for a particular outcome? What position did they support and why? Who was behind the lobbying efforts? Along the same lines, it would be interesting to research why New Brunswick took so long to enact legislation restricting the export of saw logs cut on Crown land—something Ontario and Québec had done earlier. Who favored such legislation and who did not? What was the position of Valley producers in this debate?

We did not look at customs records (in the Canadian and American national archives). We can take for granted that a lot of cross-river purchases escaped official scrutiny. Large volumes of goods, on the other hand, probably could not. While customs records may underestimate the amount of merchandise that crossed the river, they can tell us about the type of merchandise and help us detect trends and shifts in the direction of trade.

Identity: Madawaska is also a good locale to investigate questions of identity. First, of course, is the matter of the identity of the Valley residents. In Maine, they call themselves Acadians; in New Brunswick, they avoid the term. When did American Madawaskayans began to see themselves as Acadians, and why? Why this disregard for their French Canadian ancestors, not to mention the Irish, Scots, "Yankees," and Natives? And why were New Brunswick Madawaskayans so cool toward the Acadian Renaissance? We have sketched a few answers to those questions, but they should be treated more as working hypotheses than definitive conclusions.

The lasting power of the story of the *petit dérangement* (Fredericton Acadians forcibly evicted by Loyalists or even New Brunswick government officials) is also a phenomenon worth investigating. W. O. Raymond debunked this story before World War I, but his conclusions have been largely ignored. The Acadian Renaissance linked Acadian identity to the Deportation of 1755, but the Madawaskayans' ancestors had not been deported. Was the insistence of a *petit dérangement* an attempt at fitting into the existing definition of an Acadian?

Language: By the late nineteenth century, language had become a key component of national identity. This had not always been the case. In the eighteenth century, the elite did not expect their social inferiors to speak their language, and language issues were considered unimportant. For instance, the 1763 Treaty of Paris attempted to protect French Canadians' religious rights, but never mentioned language. While the American Constitution also ignored the issue, many Americans in the middle colonies spoke Dutch, German, or Swedish at the time. Members of the elite were learning the language(s) of their social inferiors instead of the other way around. (After all, the elite had leisure time, whereas their social inferiors were busy doing other things, such as working to pay their rents!) In the 1840s, traveler William Baird met young members of the New Brunswick social and political elite who were spending their summer with Madawaska families to learn their language. When, how, and why did language acquire such significance on both sides of the American-Canadian border?

"Them" and "Us": How did Mainers and Anglo New Brunswickers view Madawaskayans? One of us looked at this issue before 1870 (see B. Craig's chapter in *New England and the Maritime Provinces,* as well as "Cultural Face-Off" in the *River Review*). But what happened after 1870? How did English-speakers view Acadian/Franco-American/Madawaskayans? Who were most likely to hold anti-French sentiments? Or, who was most likely to defend them and why? Dr. Thomas Pelletier denounced the nefarious influence of the Orange Order, which was crossing over into southern Aroostook County, in the pages of the *Journal du Madawaska*. Did members of the Orange Order really infiltrate Maine and attack the French? Local newspapers published at that time could shed light on this issue. Discrimination against Catholics and French-speakers on both sides of the border also needs further investigation. And finally, how did Madawaskayans become "Americans"—that is, when and how did being citizens of the United States become part of their identity?

As mentioned, this list of questions is not exhaustive. In the introduction to this volume, we expressed the hope that our efforts would stimulate further research. The questions raised here are merely intended as starting points. And now, readers, it is up to you.

WHAT IS CANADA?

What a stupid question, our readers may say! Everybody knows what Canada is. It is that country that sits north of the United States on the map and sends Alberta Howlers down every winter.

That is true, but only since 1867. Since the emergence of "Canada" as we know it forms the backdrop to our story, and since the process intruded on the lives of the people of the St. John Valley, we must clarify what "Canada" (and a "Canadian") has been before we start.

Until June 30, 1867, Canada was a British colony comprising what is now southern Québec and southern Ontario (called Canada East and Canada West, respectively). The single colony of "the Canadas" was the result of the union of two separate colonies, Lower and Upper Canada, in 1840. Lower Canada was 90 percent French, and the British government hoped that merging it with the fast-growing and 90 percent English Upper Canada would result in its assimilation. It did not work, and the United Province of Canada proved ungovernable as a result.

Upper and Lower Canada had been created in 1791 by an act of the British Parliament that divided what is now referred as "the Old Province of Québec," a territory stretching from Gaspé to the Great Lakes and until 1783 including the Ohio Territory as well. The "Old Province of Québec" had been a French colony (known as "Canada") since the beginning of the seventeenth century. In 1763, France lost the Seven Years War (which lasted seven years in Europe, but nine in North America) and had to give its colonial empire, which also included part of India, to Britain. France kept two sugar islands, fishing rights around Newfoundland, and some trading posts in India and the west coast of Africa.

In 1791, the French and long-settled part of the province became Lower Canada, and the rest became Upper Canada (*lower*, because it was on the lower part of the St. Lawrence River; the lower part of a river is the one nearest its mouth, even if it is more to the north on the map). There were about 165,000 people in Lower Canada at the time. Upper Canada was sparsely populated, and its 10,000-odd white settlers were all very recent arrivals. They were Loyalists, people who had left the United States because they wanted to remain loyal to the king or who had been driven out by their patriot neighbors. They came from New England or upstate New York. They disliked Québec's language, religion, forms of landholdings, and legal system. They wanted an elected assembly, but Catholics were not allowed to vote, and the British authorities balked at the prospect of a small number of Protestants ruling over a much larger Catholic population. The British authorities directed the Loyalists to the west, along the St. Lawrence River and the north shore of Lake Ontario. And finally, they formed this territory into a separate province.

The two provinces, like all British colonies in North America, were independent of each other; they could, for instance, levy custom duties on each other's products. Interestingly enough, the term "Canadian" was used only to refer to the French inhabitants of Lower Canada. The others, like all English-speaking inhabitants of the British colonies, were simply "British" or more precisely "British Americans."

Between the first Treaty of Paris in 1763 and the second one in 1783, which recognized the independence of the United States, British North America encompassed the territories east of the Mississippi and north of Florida, as well as undefined land west of the Great Lakes. There were altogether sixteen colonies in 1769. Besides the thirteen that became independent, there was the Old Province of Québec, Nova Scotia, and Prince Edward Island. In addition, Britain held Newfoundland, which did not yet have colonial status, and claimed territories unsettled by whites to the west of the Great Lakes.

But, asks the observant reader, where was New Brunswick? And Maine, for that matter? Both were parts of other colonies. Maine was the "district of Maine" and belonged to the Commonwealth of Massachusetts. New Brunswick was known as "continental Nova Scotia" as opposed to "peninsular Nova Scotia," which is the same as the province we know today. In the same way as the arrival of the Loyalists triggered the partition of the Old Province of Québec, the arrival of Loyalists in Nova Scotia triggered the partition of this province. On January 1, 1783, there were about 18,000 people in Nova Scotia, including some 1,800 in the area that is New Brunswick today. A year later, there were almost 50,000 in peninsular Nova

Scotia and 14,000 in continental Nova Scotia. The 12,000 who landed at the mouth of the St. John River found a sparsely populated valley, where white people barely numbered 1,000. There were no roads worthy of the name, no local government, and only two justices of the peace. Nothing could be done without going to Halifax, and Halifax could only be reached by boat, a journey of several days. This was not workable. The Loyalists who were directed towards the St. John River were disbanded regiments of colonial volunteers, so they were organized, had leaders (their former officers), and had some connections in London. London agreed to their demand for separation within six months.

Collectively, all those provinces—Prince Edward Island, Nova Scotia, New Brunswick, Upper and Lower Canada, as well as Newfoundland and the western territories—continued to be known as British North America. The different colonies were separate political entities, independent of each other, each governed by a London-appointed governor. The one in Québec, who normally was the commander-in-chief of the British troops in North America, was the governor general.

Our Canada, then called the Dominion of Canada, was born July 1, 1867 (Canada's national day) of the union in a federal state of four provinces: Nova Scotia, New Brunswick, and the now-divorced Canada East and West, re-baptized Québec and Ontario. British Columbia joined in 1871, Prince Edward Island in 1873. The western territories were transferred to the Dominion in 1869, and three provinces created from their southern sections: Manitoba in 1870, and Alberta and Saskatchewan in 1905. Newfoundland joined last, in 1949. As for "Canadian," one has to wait until 1947 for the term to be legally defined. This is when Canadian citizenship was instituted; before 1947, people born in Canada were plain, old "British."

Appendix B

A NOTE ON MONEY AND CURRENCY

The readers will note that in this volume we often give prices in pounds and shillings, followed by the dollar equivalent. This occurs when the pound is the currency used by the documents we are using (land records or store ledger, for instance). We have chosen not to convert all pound values in dollars because we did not want the readers to inadvertently (and inaccurately) get the impression the dollar had been the currency of all of Anglo-North America since the Revolution. It was not; the pound was the currency used in the St. John Valley until the 1850s, when Canada adopted the dollar (and even afterwards, many people continued using the pound with which they had grown up).

The pound was not a decimal currency. There were 20 shillings (abbreviated as /) in a pound, and 12 pence (abbreviated as d for denarium) in a shilling. Ten shillings is then half a pound; five shillings, a quarter of a pound; and 2/6 (two shillings 6 pence), one eighth of a pound. People were also in the habit of expressing relatively small pound values in shillings. One pound for instance could be expressed as 20/. A barrel of flour was worth 55/, 60/, or 65/ depending on the year. In 1821, the Province of New Brunswick fixed the rate of exchange at 5/ for a U.S. dollar (or $4.00 for a pound). This is the rate merchants Abraham and Simon Dufour and John Emmerson were using at mid-century, and the one we are using.

The pound in question, however, was not the same as the pound sterling (Stg £) used in Britain, but the "Halifax currency" (Halifax cy) with a different value. The provincial governments fixed the value of foreign coins in currency. Here are the values adopted by the government of New Brunswick:

	1786	1821	1844	1852
Sovereign (gold coin worth Stg £1)	Not rated	1:2:3	1:4:0	1:4:4
Crown (gold coin, one quarter of a Stg £)	5/6	5/6	6/	6/1
Shilling (silver coin)	1/1	1/1	1/ 2.5	1/ 2.5
Eagle (American gold coin,)		2:10:0	2:10:0	2:10:0
Spanish milled dollar (silver)	5/	5/4	5/	
American dollar (silver)	Did not exist	5/	5/	

(1:2:3 reads 1 pound, 2 shillings, 3 pence)

The reader will note that the provincial government was manipulating the value of the gold sovereign. This was to encourage holders to keep the coins in the province and not use them to buy imported British goods. In February 1846, Joseph Lizotte showed up at the Dufour store in St. Basile and put on the counter "one gold coin," for which he was credited 1:4:6 currency. The coin in question was a British sovereign, and since they did not appear often, it must have attracted plenty of attention. The Dufours also paid a 6d premium on it. The provincial government was not the only one who wanted sovereigns.

Before the American Revolution, the situation was even more complicated. Besides the Halifax currency, there was also a Massachusetts currency and a New York one. Their values, fixed by the British government, were all different. At the official rates, 100 pounds sterling should have bought 133.33 pounds Massachusetts currency; in Halifax, one should have received 111.11 pounds, and in New York, 177.77. Imagine being a Boston merchant trading with Halifax, New York, Boston and London and having to deal with four different kinds of pounds.

Those "pound currencies" were funny beasts, because there were no coins in currency. The currencies were "money of account"; that is, they were used for keeping the books. The Massachusetts and New York currencies disappeared when the United States adopted the dollar as their currency. In 1857, the government of the province of Canada decided to change its money of account and use the dollar instead. Its value was fixed at par with the American one. In 1860, the New Brunswick government followed suit, and in 1867, the dollar became the currency of the newly formed Dominion of Canada.

Everyday transactions, even though they were expressed in currency, used real coins. But Britain never allowed the minting of coins in her colonies, resulting in a shortage of specie (the term used to refer to metal coins). People therefore made do with whatever they could put their hand on. In the eighteenth century, the preferred coins were the Spanish silver ones, especially the Spanish "piece of eight" or milled dollar. The piece of eight could be cut in eight pieces to provide smaller units (this is why a "quarter" is worth "two bits"). But Portuguese and French colonial coins were also used, and of course, British currency was used as well. In 1776, the Continental Congress recommended that the Spanish piece of eight be adopted as the monetary unit of the independent colonies, as it was widely used, and its value had always been stable. The dollar was chosen as the currency of the United States in 1785, its value fixed at the value of the Spanish milled dollar. But there were still no U.S. dollar coins. The mint act of 1792 provided for the coinage of silver dollars, and the first U.S. silver dollars were produced in 1794. The U.S. Mint did not produce enough coins to satisfy demand until 1857, however, and until then, it remained legal to use the Spanish dollar. British North Americans had to wait for the constitution of the Dominion of Canada to be able to issue their own currency. They initially got their coins from Britain; the Canadian Mint was established only in 1908.

To give an example, the New Brunswick Blue Book for 1851 (the Blue Book was an annual statistical report sent to London) listed as circulating in the province:

Gold: British guineas and sovereigns (a guinea was worth 21/); Portuguese milled doubloons; Spanish milled doubloons; French Louis d'or; Napoleon 20 f pieces; American eagle

Silver: British coinage; Spanish milled dollar; Old French crowns; French ten franc pieces; Spanish pistareens; American dollars

Copper: British mint pence and half pence; and a provincial copper coinage recently imported from England

Paper currency: Notes from the Bank of New Brunswick; the Commercial Bank; the Bank of North America; the Central Bank of New Brunswick (central only because of its location—it was not a central bank in our sense of the word); the St. Stephen Bank; and the Charlotte County Bank. There were about £200,000 worth of notes in circulation. The Blue Book could not tell how much coinage was in circulation.

Besides coins, Americans could use bank notes. Contrary to present-day bills, bank notes were really private money issued by the banks; in 1800 there was $1 million worth of bank notes, issued by twenty-nine different banks, in circulation in the United States. As banking was poorly regulated in the United States, people did not much trust bank notes. There were no banks—and thus no bank notes—in British North America until 1822. British banks (including the ones in North America) were very tightly regulated, and their money was more trustworthy. The British military made its payments in the colonies in "Army Bills," which were like bank notes, only issued by the military. Army bills could be exchanged at will for gold or silver coins. As they were backed by the government of Britain, people accepted them willingly.

How much was a dollar or a pound from then worth in today's money? Past values translate very badly into today's money, and with the exception of economic historians establishing long-term trends, historians do not even try. Economic historians have devised five different ways of translating old prices into new ones—each producing extremely different results. One can find rates of exchanges between dollars and Sterling, as well as 2003 values of older prices in the "How much is that" page of the eh-net web site (http://eh.net/hmit/). A quick look at the site will show why we have refrained from translating values into contemporary money: in most instances the result is meaningless. We believe the best way to contextualize prices is to compare them with what people earned. Unfortunately we do not have Valley wages before 1845. Farm laborers' wages remained relatively stable from the 1840s until late in the century: 2/6 or US$ 0.50 a day during the year; and 5/ or US$ 1.00 a day at haying and harvest time. Female servants made 2/6 a month with room and board.

Wages went up at the beginning of the twentieth century. In Madawaska County, the same farm laborers earned CAN$ 5.6 a week (six days) with room and board in 1901.

Summary: One pound	=	20/ (shillings)
One shilling	=	12d (pence)
One pound	=	240d
One pound cy	=	US$ 4.00
One shilling cy	=	US$ 0.20
One US$	=	5/ (shillings cy)

Appendix C

THE ST. JOHN RIVER AND GRAND PORTAGE IN THE SEVENTEENTH AND EIGHTEENTH CENTURIES

Thomas Albert, quoting J. A. Maurault's *Histoire des Abénakis,* claims Jesuit missionary father Gabriel Druillette was the first European to have left an account of a journey to Madawaska in 1652. However, the source Maurault used (*Les relations des Jésuites*) never mentions Madawaska, and Druillette's description of the river suggests instead that he and his party traveled on one of the south branches of the St. John River above Seven Islands.[1] Druillette nonetheless is the first European to have left a description of the uppermost St. John. The first descriptions of the upper St. John Valley and Madawaska by European travelers were penned half a century later. The following are passages written by Europeans who traveled through this region in the seventeenth and eighteenth centuries.

1. The Account of Mgr. de Saint-Vallier de la Croix, Bishop of Québec, 1688

In 1688, Mgr. de Saint-Vallier traveled from Canada to Acadia through the St. John route. He and his party used the St. Francis rather than the Madawaska River.

We navigated on the four rivers: Du Loup, Des Branches, St. François, and St. John; one does not tarry long on the first two, but spends more time on the two others. The St. Francis is a rapid more than a river; it is fed by several streams falling down from the two chains of mountains lining it to the right and to the left; it can be navigated only from the tenth or twelfth of May until the end of June; at that time, it is so swift that one could easily cover twenty to twenty-four leagues per day, if it were not for the trees that cut it in three or four spots and occupy some 15 feet of its width in each place; the passage would be free if they were cut down, which could be done at little cost, for one does not believe it would cost more than two hundred pistoles to clear the channel from those encumbrances which slow travelers down considerably.

The St. John River displays more breadth and beauty that that one; it is said to be some 400 leagues long, and there are 160 leagues from the place where we entered it to its mouth; its course is always even, and the land one can see on its banks seems good; several very pleasant islands can be found along the way, and numerous rivers full of fish flowing into it from the north and the south keep its channel open. We were of the impression one could open some flourishing colonies between Meductic and Jemseg, especially at a place we named Sainte Marie, where the river widens and is dotted by a great number of islands which would probably be very fertile if they were improved. This would be a good location for a Native Mission; the land does not yet have a master as neither the King nor the Governor have granted it to anyone.

As early as the second day we were on this river, we encountered for the first time the hut of some Christian Natives from the Sillery Mission, who, to go hunting, had transported themselves to the mouth of a river they call Madauaska [*sic*] and which we renamed St. François de Sales River. Traveling up this river, the Natives reach another river which falls swiftly into the St. Lawrence near Le Bic.

One can hardly convey the joy those poor Christians expressed at seeing us, nor the one we felt at meeting them; they presented us with part of their provisions, at a time when ours were in short supply; and the same day, we found a greater number of Natives in three cabins, who entertained us in the same manner, and who asked insistently that we send them a missionary to instruct them; a few of them had come from Percé Island and I was surprised to find a few who spoke a bit of French and had been to France.

The next day, May seventeenth, we arrived to the place called St. John the Baptist's Great Falls; the St. John River drops from the top of the rock as a tremendous fall into an abyss and produces a spray that hides it from sight, and a sound which warns the travelers at a distance to disembark from their canoes. This is where a man coming out of Acadia, where he had been sent by Mr. the Intendant [the province of Québec's civil administrator] gave me one of his letters and I took advantage of the opportunity to give him news about my journey for His Lordship the

Governor, who may be worried about us.

On the eighteenth, we went to sleep at Meductic, the first fort of Acadia, where I greatly comforted about a hundred Natives, as I told them, when I went to visit them, that I had come for the express purpose of establishing a mission for their benefit in their country. It would be desired that the French who have established residence on this route be of sufficiently good mores to attract those poor people to Christianity by their example, but one must hope that with time, the reform of the ones will lead to the conversion of the others

Source: Saint-Vallier, *Estat présent de l'Église*, 78-84. Translation by the authors.

2. The Account of John Gyles, New England Captive

John Gyles was captured by the Maliseets in 1689, when he was nine years old. One winter, a group of Maliseets took him with them to go hunting.

We moved still further up the country after the moose so that by the spring we had got to the north-ward of the Lady Mountains [near the St. Lawrence]. When the spring came and the rivers broke up, we moved back to the head of the St. John River, and then made canoes of moose hides, sewing three or four together and pitching the seams with balsam mixed with charcoal. Then, we went down the river to a place called Madawescook. There, an old man lived and kept a sort of trading house, where we tarried several days. Then we went further down the river till we came to the greatest falls in these parts, called Checanekepaeg, where we carried a little way over the land, and putting off our canoes we went down stream still. And as we passed down by the mouth of any large branches, we saw Indians; but when any dance was proposed, I was bought off. [Dances involved tormenting captives; Gyle's masters paid the dancers to leave him alone.] At length we arrived at the place were we left our birch bark canoes in the fall, and putting our baggage into them, went down to the Fort [Meductic].

Source: Gyles, *Nine Years a Captive*, 14.

3. Cadillac's Account of the St. John River, 1692

Antoine de la Mothe Cadillac, who later founded Detroit, appears to have traveled up the St. John as far as Témiscouata Lake in the summer of 1692.

This fall [the Reversing Falls at Saint John, New Brunswick] is no sooner passed than the river broadens all at once to a half league. It is also very deep, and a vessel of 50 to 60 tons can ascend for 30 leagues. But it is needful to take care not to pass this abyss except at slack water, for then one surely be lost.

It must be agreed that this is the most beautiful, most navigable, and richest river of l'Acadie; the most beautiful for the variety of trees found there, such as nut trees, wild cherry trees, hazel trees, cherry trees, elms, oaks, maples, and vines, which bear pretty good grapes. In brief, there is no kind of trees which is not found here.

There is a pinery around a lake near gemsèq [Jemseg] at 15 leagues from the sea, where can be found the material for making very fine masts, which could be passed through a little river that falls into this one [the St. John]. Near the lake is a mine of lead. I have seen the Indians melting it, and there-from making bullets for their hunting.

It is the most navigable on account of its width and depth, which results from the number of lakes and rivers that empty therein.

It is the richest because it has the best soil, and because the fishery for salmon there is incomparable, and can be made for eighty leagues of its length. Bass, trout, gasperau [gasparot], eels, sturgeons, and a hundred other kinds of fish abound there. It is the richest also because it furnishes beaver and other furs. I have ascended this river more than a hundred and fifty leagues without reaching its source, which I believe is in the vicinity of Montreal.

One thing that is regrettable, which is that in the most beautiful parts, where the country and ground is flat, it is found to be overflowed every spring at the melting of the snow, and this inundation is long continued because the water cannot empty off, on account of the two rocks whereof I have spoken [the Reversing Falls at the mouth of the St. John], which narrow the entrance of this river, where marble occurs.

Thirty leagues up the river is a fort of the mike-makes, [Mi'kmaq] at a place called naxouak [Nashwaak], and at 30 leagues farther, at a place called medoctèk [Meductic], is one of the marisis [Maliseets]. This nation is passably warlike. They are well built and excellent hunters. They apply themselves to raising Indian corn, beans, kidney beans, and pumpkins.

At 44 leagues higher is another fort which is the usual retreat of the Canibas or Abenakis when they

The Land in Between

fear something in their own country. It is on the shore of a little river which discharges into this one [St. John], and which comes from a lake called madagoüasca [Temiscouata Lake, which was referred to as Madawaska Lake], which is 12 leagues long and one in width. It is very deep and abounds in trout and pike. It is a fine country for moose hunting. This river and lake turn up to the north and it is the route that is taken to reach the river of kebeg [the Québec River was another name for the St. Lawrence] opposite tadoussac. I leave it here for it would lead me too far.

Source: Ganong. "The Cadillac Memoir on Acadia." (Original French translated by Ganong.)

4. Captain Pote's Account, 1744

Captain Pote was captured by the Native-Canadian expedition against Annapolis Royal in 1744. His captors took him back to Québec. Pote kept a logbook of his travels, complete with latitude and longitude measurements.

Friday June 12th, left Medocatik for Canedy. Paddled against strong current. Little to eat. Camped NNWGL.

Saturday June 13th, paddled about nine leagues north; scant provisions, no catch.

Sunday June 14th. Went past the Tobique River. Caught plenty of salmon. Passed by the Aroostook. [The Natives told him it led to the Penobscot.]

Monday June 15th. Arrived at the Grand Falls.
At this place, it appears to me like the head of the river and the water entirely still like a pond, and the land exceedingly high, the Indians told me we should carry over this high land, about ³/₄ of a mile, and find the river as large, and the current set as strong, as any part of the river, and they told me the River runs under this high land although there was no manner or signs to be perceives of it.

Tuesday June 16th. Packed the baggage and carried the conew [canoe] over the high mountain and into the river of Saint Johns. Came about 8 leagues CD and camped.

Wednesday June 17th. Paddled about five leagues and took another small river, that led into a large lake. This night we camped by the side of the small river. We computed we came 14 leagues. [The small river is the Madawaska River.]

Thursday June 18th. In the morning we arrived to a "large pond" about ten leagues in length, when we arrived to the other side of the pond our people the Indians, went to a place where they had hid provisions, in their journey to Annapolis the winter past, they often told me, that when they arrived to the lake, we should have a sufficient supply of provisions to carry us comfortably to Canady [Canada]. But when they came to the place where they had hid their provisions they found that some Indians had been there before them and taken the greater part. This was heavy news, both to the Indians and us prisoners, we carried our connews [sic] and baggage about a league, and came to another small pond [Eagle Lake or Lac des Aigles] which we crossed and encamped about 12 leagues NBW.

Friday June 19th. Camped on Three Pistole River.
Saturday June 20th. Stayed there.
Sunday June 21st. Arrived on St. Lawrence.

Source: Pote, *The Journal of Captain William Pote*, 65–70 (selected entries).

Note 1: Albert, *Histoire du Madawaska*, 32–33; Maurault, *Histoire des Abénakis*, 147; *Relations des Jésuites, 1647–1655*, tome 4, 22–24.

MURDER ON THE UPPER ST. JOHN

In July 1784, Charles, son of Nichau Noïte, "hunter and laborer" at Madawaska, and member of the Penobscot Nation, killed William Archibald Mc Neill from Quebec City and his guide Joseph Dufour of Kamouraska. (Dufour's sons David and Joseph moved to Madawaska in 1799.) Mc Neill was on his way to Halifax. On the way, he and his guide stopped at James Kelly's trading post above the Maliseet village at Madawaska. The next day, they stopped at a cabin some six miles below the village. Noïte and his companion, a Maliseet called François Arguibo, met the travelers at their cabin and spent the afternoon drinking with them. In the evening, they left to go moose hunting. Noïte, however, soon decided to come back to kill the two men to take revenge on the English who had killed seven of his relatives, although they were not at war. He found more alcohol in the travelers' canoe and drank it before entering the cabin, where he started a fire and axed the two men, who never woke up. Arguibo, who had refused to join in the deed, was watching from outside. The following day, the two men went back to the village, where Noïte bragged about the deed and claimed he would kill more Englishmen if he had a chance.

Upon hearing this, the Madawaska Natives assembled and decided to hand him over to the authorities in Quebec City. Noïte went along, declaring he was not afraid: he had been drunk, and would not have committed the murders if he had been sober (the Natives had long held that a man was not responsible for his actions while drunk). Madawaska Grand Chiefs Francois Xavier and Grand Pierre, eight other Maliseets, and an unspecified number of Hurons from Lorette, accompanied by James Kelly, took Noïte and Arguibo to Quebec City. The two men were jailed awaiting the trial, which was to take place in November.

The events in Quebec City show Anglo-Native diplomacy at work. The chiefs explained their action. Peace had prevailed on the Témiscouata Route for the past twenty-six years, but Noïte had sullied it with a "bloody branch." When told Noïte deserved the death penalty, they replied that had he belonged to their nation, they would have killed him themselves. The Natives had made their peace with the British after the fall of France; Noïte had disturbed this peace. When they made their peace, the Natives had recognized King George's sovereignty. They were therefore subject to English law. However, if the murder had been committed on their territory by one of them, they would have dealt with the matter themselves. They called on the British courts only because Noïte was from another nation.

The British authorities were very much aware of the fact the Natives were more than individual subjects of the king; they were also members of allied nations, whose friendship may prove critical again if further conflicts erupted on the frontier. They consequently had to take into account what the Natives believed were fair procedures. The Maliseet chiefs requested that two messengers be sent to the Penobscot Nation so that they could send observers to the trial. They were concerned that if this was not done, the Penobscot would blame them for Noïte's death and take revenge upon them. They also pleaded very insistently that the governor do something to put an end to liquor traffic, which was the cause of too many problems.

Charles Nichau Noïte was tried on November 2, 1784, and sentenced to death by hanging. The Natives asked that he be executed by firing squad, since they considered hanging to be degrading. Noïte was executed on November 11, 1784. He was fifteen.

The Verdict of Charles Nichau Noïte's Trial
(The verdict was in English)

At his Majesty's court of King's Bench begun and holden at the city of Quebec on Tuesday the second day of November in the year of our Lord one thousand seven hundred and eighty four. Before the Honourable Adam Mabane and Thomas Dunn esq. Commissioners appointed to execute the office of Chief Justice of the province of Quebec.

The Jurors for our Lord the King, upon their oath present that Charles Nichau Noïte, late of the village of Madoaska in the District of Quebec, in the province of Quebec, huntsman and labourer, not having the fear of God before his eyes, but being moved and seduced by the instigation of the devil, on the twentieth day of July one thousand and seven hundred and eighty four, in the twenty fourth year of the reign of our sovereign Lord George the third, King of Great Britain and the territories and dominions thereunto belonging; with force and arms, near unto the said village of Madoeska in the district aforesaid, and Province aforesaid, in and upon one Archibald Mc Neill, in the peace of God, and of our said Lord the King, then and there being feloniously, willfully, and of his malice aforethought, did make and assault, and that the said Charles Nichau Noïte, with a certain ax, of the value of one shilling, which he the said Charles Nichau Noïte, in and upon the head of him the said Archibald Mc Neill, then and there, feloneously [sic], willfully and of his malice aforethought, did strike, penetrate and wound, giving to the said Archibald Mc Neill, then and there, with the ax aforesaid, in and upon the head of him the said aforesaid Archibald Mc Neill, several mortal wounds, of the breadth of three inches, and of the depth of two inches each, of which said mortal wounds the said Archibald Mac Neill then and there instantly died.

And so the jurors aforesaid, upon their oath aforesaid do say, that the said Charles Nichau Noïte in manner and form aforesaid, feloneously, willfully, and of his malice aforethought, did kill and murder the said Archibald Mc Neill against the peace of our said Lord the King, his Crown and Dignity; and against the laws and statutes, in such case made and provided.

David Lynd. Act. C. Crown.

Sources: Archives du Québec à Québec, Cours de justice du régime anglais, TL 999 (old QBC 28/17); LAC, Haldimand papers, MG21 addition to ms. 21810, 363–67, microfilm reel H-1745. Delage et Gilbert, "La justice coloniale et les Amérindiens au Québec 1760-1820."

POPULATION, 1790–1920

Table E-1: Aggregate St. John Valley Non-Native Population, 1790–1920

Year	Population	Increase	Annual Increase (%)
1790	174		
1799	418	244	15.6
1808	456	38	1.0
1820	1,171	715	15.7
1830	2,476	1,305	11.1
1833	2.518	42	0.6
1834	2,272	-246	-9.8
1840	3.460	1,188	8.7
1850	6,180	2,720	7.9
1860	10,600	3,820	6.2
1870	14,900	4,200	4.0
1880	18,500	3,600	2.4
1890	21,500	3,000	1.6
1900	26,000	4,500	2.1
1910	35,000	9,000	3.5
1920	41,200	7,000	2.0

Note: The figures for 1850–1920 are estimates (U.S. Census figures were added to Canadian figures; the two censuses were taken one year apart).
Sources: See list of censuses p. 408–09.

Table E-2: Madawaska County Population by Civil Parish, 1851–1921

Civil Parish	1851	1861	1871	1881	1891	1901	1911	1921
Saint-François	732	578	1,752	1,600	2,040	2,577	1,200	1,269
Saint-Hilaire				893	992	1,150	1,566	1,702
Madawaska	858	1,247	1,816	966	1,683	1,882	988	876
Saint-Jacques				766	874	1,073	1,272	1,625
Saint-Basile	1,037	1,345	1,669	1,350	1,557	1,608	2,287	1,543
Sainte-Anne				911	973	1,283	1,638	2,050
Saint-Léonard	637	1,384	1,997	2,190	2,393	2,738	2,026	2,034
Lac Baker							953	985
Saint-André							1,553	2,023
Clair							897	892
Rivière Verte							1,011	
Native reserve							229	
Edmundston							1,821	4,035

Civil Parish	1851	1861	1871	1881	1891	1901	1911	1921 (continued)
Total population	3,264	4,554	7,234	8,676	10,512	12,311	16,430	20,045
Total increase		1,290	2,680	1,442	1,836	1,799	4,119	3,615
Annual increase (%)		4.0	5.9	2.0	2.1	1.7	3.3	2.2

Sources: See Table E-1.

Table E-3: American Madawaska Population by Town, 1850–1920

Town[1]		1850	1860	1870	1880	1890	1900	1910	1920
T18 R10	Glazier Lake			51	44	49	78	9	35
[2]	Allagash Pl.		149	156	202	200	190	245	359
Letter L R2	Cyr Pl.		218	376	558	420	502	531	479
T16 R7	Eagle Lake		104	143	233	313	406	1,421	1,772
T18 R6/R7	Fort Kent		879	1,034	1,512	1,826	2,528	3,710	4,237
T18 R5	Frenchville[3]		1,031	1,851	2,288	2,560	1,316	1,414	1,586
Grand Isle			623	688	847	984	1,104	1,217	1,352
Letter G R1	Hamlin		507	558	612	484	574	657	602
	Hancock[4]	592							
	Madawaska (US)[5]	1,276	585	1,041	1,391	1,451	1,698	1,831	1,933
T17 R6	New Canada		182	83	177	301	419	590	573
	St. Agatha[6]						1,396	1,533	1,699
T17 R9	St. Francis		241	253	299	451	568	918	1,241
T17 R8	St. John		99	127	166	226	271	571	549
	Van Buren[7]	1,050	616	992	1,110	1,168	1,878	3,065	4,594
T17 R7	Wallagrass		242	297	431	595	784	1,004	1,144
Total population		2,916	6,068	7,650	9,870	11,008	13,712	18,226	21,582
Total increase			3,150	1,582	2,220	1,158	2,684	5,004	3,439
Annual increase (%)			10.8	2.6	2.9	1,2	2.4	3.6	1.8

Notes:
1. Until they were incorporated (mostly in the late 1860s), townships were known by their letter/number.
2. T16 R10/R11 and T17 R10/R11.
3. Called Dickeyville in 1870.
4. Included Fort Kent, Saint John, St. Francis, New Canada, and Wallagrass
5. Included Madawaska, Frenchville, St. Agatha, and part of Fort Kent in 1850.
6. Part of Frenchville until 1899.
7. Included Grand Isle, Van Buren, Hamlin, and Cyr in 1850.

Sources: See Table E-1.

FAMILIES MENTIONED IN THE ST. BASILE PARISH REGISTER BEFORE 1801

Entry #	Head First Name	Last Name	Wife First Name	Last Name	Date of Marriage	Place of Marriage	Residence in 1780
1	Albert	Alexandre	Sirois	Marie-Madeleine	1778	Kamouraska	Canada
2	Albert	François	Boucher	Josette	1736	Kamouraska	Canada
3	Albert	François	Paradis	Marie-Anne	1774	Kamouraska	Canada
4	Albert	Firmin	Martin	Théotiste	About 1800	Unknown	Probably Canada
5	Auclair	Joseph	Garant	Marie-Geneviève	1791	Madawaska	Probably Canada
6	Ayotte	Alexandre	Saucier	Charlotte	1761	Ste Anne de la Pocatière (QC)	St. John R.
7	Ayotte	Charles	Paradis	Catherine	1795	Kamouraska	Probably St. John R.
8	Ayotte	Joseph	Martin	Marie Perpétue	About 1800	Unknown	Probably St. John R.
9	Ayotte	Zacharie	Cyr	Madeleine	1792	Madawaska	Probably St. John R.
10	Beaulieu	Antoine	Talbot-Gervais	Marie Florence	Unknown	Unknown	Probably Canada
11	Beaulieu	Mathurin	Dumont-Guérette	Marie	1767	Kamouraska	Probably Canada
12	Chouinard	Jean-Marie	Pinet	Marie-Anne	1793	Kamouraska	Canada
13	Cormier	François	Fournier	Charlotte	About 1793	Madawaska	St. John R.
14	Cormier	J-Bte	Landry	Madeleine	1762	Kamouraska	St. John R.
15	Cormier	Pierre	Soucy	Marie-Rose	1799	Madawaska	St. John R.
16	Costin	Thomas	Chamard	Marie-Anne		Quebec City	Canada
17	Cyr	Alexandre	Thériault	Victoire	About 1800	Madawaska	St. John R.
18	Cyr	Antoine	Violette	Geneviève	1792	Madawaska	St. John R.
19	Cyr	Firmin	Ayotte	Josette	1791	Madawaska	St. John R.
20	Cyr	Firmin	Roy	Ursule	1791	Kamouraska	St. John R.
21	Cyr	François	Guilbaut	Marie-Anne	1770	St. John R.	St. John R.
22	Cyr	Hilarion	Tardif	Marie-Charlotte	1795	Kamouraska	St. John R.
23	Cyr	Jacques	Bélanger	Ursule	1779	St Jean Port Joli (QC)	St. John R.
24	Cyr	J-Bte	Dumont-Guérette	Judith	1767	Kamouraska	St. John R.
25	Cyr	J-Bte	Violette	Marguerite	1793	Madawaska	St. John R.
26	Cyr	Joseph	Daigle	Marie-Madeleine	1785	Madawaska	St. John R.
27	Cyr	Joseph	Thibodeau	Marguerite-Blanche	1758	Beaubassin	St. John R.
28	Cyr	Michel	Thibodeau	Madeleine	1786	Unknown	St. John R.
29	Cyr	Olivier	Lebrun	Anastasie	1779	Unknown	St. John R.

Entry #	Parents of	Children of	Siblings of	Origin of family - male/female (Acadia or Canada)	Residence after 1790	Grant, if any
1		2	3	C/C	Madawaska	
2	1, 3			C/C	Madawaska	
3	4, 59	2	1	C/C	Madawaska	Mazzerolle SB #34
4		3, 52	59	C/A	Madawaska	
5				C/C	Canada	Mazzerolle SB #31
6	7, 8, 9			C/C	Madawaska	Mazzerolle SB #17
7		6	8, 9, 58, 19, 30, 31	C/C	Madawaska	
8		6, 52	6, 9, 19, 30, 31	C/A	Madawaska	Mazzerolle SB #8
9		6, 21	6, 8, 19, 30, 31	C/A	Madawaska	Mazzerolle SB #7
10			sister of 35?	C/U	Canada	
11	42			C/C	Madawaska	Mazzerolle SB #6
12		65		C/C	Kamouraska in 1828	
13	82	14, 44	15, 66, 74, 79, 80, 82; 41, 42, 43	A/C	Madawaska	Soucy Grant-Grand Isle
14	13, 15, 66, 74, 79, 80, 82			A/A	Madawaska	Soucy Grant-Grand Isle
15		14, 67	13, 66, 74, 79, 80, 82	A/C	Madawaska	Soucy Grant-Grand Isle
16				British/C	Ste Anne des P-B, then Canada	Mazzerolle NB #31; exchanged with Michel Mercure 1796
17		21, 70	6, 58, 72, 69	A/A	Madawaska	Mazzerolle NB #5
18		84	19, 21, 23, 24, 27, 29,	A/A	Madawaska	Mazzerolle SB #16
19		6	18, 21, 23, 24, 27, 29, 30, 31; 7, 8, 9, 58	A/C	Madawaska, then Lacadie in Quebec	Mazzerolle SB #24
20		27	22, 26, 32, 34, 60	A/C	Madawaska	Soucy grant-Grand River.
21	9, 17, 58, 72		18, 19, 23, 24, 27, 29, 30, 31, 33	A/A A/A	Madawaska	Mazzerolle SB #25
22		27	20, 26, 32, 34, 60	A/C	Madawaska	Soucy grant-Grand River
23	84		18, 19, 21, 24, 27, 29, 30, 31	A/C	Madawaska; On Chaleur Bay in 1790-91	Mazzerolle SB #26
24	25, 28, 49		18, 19, 21, 23, 27, 29, 30, 31	A/C	Madawaska	Mazzerolle SB #4
25		24, 84	28, 49	A/A	Madawaska	Mazzerolle SB #23
26		27, 33 32, 34, 47	20, 32, 34, 60,	A/A	Madawaska	Mazzerolle NB #28 & Soucy grant-Grand River
27	20, 22, 26, 32, 34, 60	76	18, 19, 21, 23, 24, 29, 30, 31	A/A	Madawaska	Soucy grant-Grand River
28		24, 78	25, 49, 28, 72, 79, 80, 81	A/A	Madawaska	Mazzerolle SB #22; mill site sold to Louis Mercure, and by Mercure to Duperré in 1789; rest of lot sold to Duperré in 1796
29			18, 19, 21, 23, 24, 27, 30, 31	A/U	Madawaska	Mazzerolle NB #29 & 30; sells part of 29 to Antoine Gagné in 1799

Entry #	Head First Name	Last Name	Wife First Name	Last Name	Date of Marriage	Place of Marriage	Residence in 1780
30	Cyr	Paul	Ayotte	Charlotte	1780	St. John R.	St. John R.
31	Cyr	Pierre	Ayotte	Madeleine	1780	St. John R.	St. John R.
32	Daigle	J-Bte	Cyr	Anne-Marie	1794	Madawaska	St. John R.
33	Daigle	Joseph	Guilbaut	Marguerite	1762	St. Thomas de Montmagny (QC)	St. John R.
34	Daigle	Joseph	Cyr	Marie-Théotiste	1790	Madawaska	St. John R.
35	Desnoyers	J-Bte	Talbot-Gervais	Marie-Constance	Unknown	Unknown	St. John R. or Kennebecassis
36	Dubé	Augustin	Dionne	Ursule			Canada
37	Dubé	Germain	Bourguoin	Marie-Geneviève	1797		?
38	Dufour	David	Potier	Charlotte	1799	Madawaska	Canada
39	Dufour	Joseph	Thériault	Marie-Rose	1799	Madawaska	Canada
40	Duperré	Pierre					Canada
41	Fournier	Charles	Dumont-Guérette	Marie-Catherine	1797	Madawaska	Probably Canada
42	Fournier	Guillaume	Beaulieu	Marie-Madeleine	1795	Madawaska	Probably Canada
43	Fournier	J-Bte	Martin	Félicité	Before 1784	Unknown	Probably Canada
44	Fournier	Jean Marie	Dionne	Angélique	1757	Rimouski	St. John R.
45	Gagné	Antoine	Grand-maison	Marie	1786	Kamouraska	Canada
46	Guimond	Joseph	Dionne	Josette	Unknown	Unknown	Probably Canada
47	Hébert	Simon	Daigle	Marie-Josephte	About 1783	Madawaska	St. John R.
48	Levasseur	J-Bte	Landry	Madeleine	1775	Kamouraska	Canada
49	Lizotte	Pierre	Cyr	Marguerite	1794	Madawaska	Canada
50	Martin	François	Dumont-Guerette	Euphrosine	1777	Kamouraska	St. John R.
51	Martin	Jean Marie	Levasseur	Marie-Anne			St. John R.
52	Martin	Simon	Bourguoin	Marie-Geneviève	1777	Kamouraska	St. John R.
53	Mazzerolle	Joseph	Tardif	Françoise	1794	Madawaska	St. John R.
54	Mazzerolle	Joseph	Thibodeau	Rosalie	1764	Boston	St. John R.
55	Mercier	Jean Juste	Thériault	Théotiste	1795	Madawaska	Canada
56	Mercure	Louis	Thibodeau	Madeleine	Unknown	Unknown	St. John R.

Entry #	Parents of	Children of	Siblings of	Origin of family - male/female (Acadia or Canada)	Residence after 1790	Grant, if any
30		6	18, 19, 21, 23, 24, 27, 29, 31, 7, 8, 9, 58	A/C	Madawaska	Mazzerolle NB #7
31		6	18, 19, 21, 23, 24, 27, 29, 30, 7, 8, 9, 58	A/C	Ste Anne des P-B 1787-1790; then back to Madawaska	Mazzerolle NB #8
32		33, 27	22, 26, 34, 47	A/A	Madawaska	Mazzerolle NB #26 & 27
33	26	33, 27	21	A/A	Madawaska	Mazzerolle SB #29
34		33, 27	22, 26, 32, 47	A/A	Madawaska	Mazzerolle SB #27 & NB 25
35			sister of 10?	A/U	Kennebecassis; Rivière Ouelle in; 1790; Madawaska 1792–97; gone afterwards	Mazzerolle NB #22 (1791); sold to Pierre Cyr in 1793
36			37, 68	C/C	Canada	Mazzerolle SB #37
37			36, 68	C/C	Ste Anne des P-B 1808–18; Back at Madawaska 1822	
38		62	39	C/A	Madawaska	
39		69	38	C/A	Madawaska	
40			49	C	Madawaska	Mazzerolle SB #38; sold 1792 to Joseph Saucier, merchant in Lower Canada
41		44	13, 42, 43,	C/C	Both died Ste Anne des Pays Bas, 1816-18	
42		44, 11	13, 41, 43	C/C	Madawaska	
43		44	13, 41, 42	C/A	Madawaska	Mazzerolle SB # 28
44	13, 41, 42, 43			C/C	Madawaska	
45				C/part A	Madawaska	Mazzerolle NB #A
46				C/C	Probably Canada	Mazzerolle NB #4
47		33	26, 32.34	A/A	Madawaska	Mazzerolle SB #35
48	69, 81		14, 51	C/A	Madawaska	Mazzerolle NB #6 & Soucy GD Isle
49		24	25, 28, 40, 49	C/A	Madawaska	Mazzerolle SB #36
50			51, 52	A/C	Madawaska	
51			48, 50, 52	A/C	Madawaska	Mazzerolle SB # 15; sells half on side of lot 14 to Pierre Lizotte in 1800
52	4, 8		50,51	A/C		Purchased lot 34 Mazzerolle grant NB from L. Mercure
53		54, 68		A/C	Ste Anne des P-B after marriage	Mazzerolle SB #32; sold to Simon Hébert in 1807
54	53, 63			A/A	Died Ste Anne des Pays Bas 1815 and 1819	Mazzerolle SB #1
55		70	69	C/A	Left after 1798	In a dispute over possession of part NB lot 21 with P. Cyr
56			57	A/A	At Rivière de Chute in 1809	Mazzerolle SB # 37

Entry #	Head First Name	Head Last Name	Wife First Name	Wife Last Name	Date of Marriage	Place of Marriage	Residence in 1780
57	Mercure	Michel	Potvin	Angélique	1777		St. John R.
58	Michaud	Joseph	Cyr	Marie-Rose	1796	Madawaska	Canada
59	Nadeau	Jean	Albert	Marie-Anne	1788	Kamouraska	Canada
60	Ouellette	Louis	Cyr	Marie-Geneviève	1792	Madawaska	Canada
61	Pelletier	Nicolas	Sirois	Geneviève	1786	Kamouraska	Canada
62	Potier	Paul	Thibodeau	Judith	1765	Ste Anne de la Pocatière (QC)	St. John R.
63	Robichaud	Joseph	Mazzerolle	Brigitte	1798	Madawaska	? Kennebecassis 1787
64	Sansfacon	Louis	Thibodeau	Madeleine	1765	Unknown	St. John R.
65	Sirois	Joseph	Chouinard	Francoise	Uunknown	Unknown	Probably Canada
66	Soucy	Germain	Cormier	Marie-Rose	1791	Madawaska	Canada
67	Soucy	Joseph	Thibodeau	Marie-Louise	1778	Kamouraska	Canada
68	Tardif	Jean	Dubé	Marie-Anne	1777	Kamouraska	Canada
69	Thériault	Joseph	Levasseur	Euphrosine	1799	Madawaska	Kennebecassis
70	Thériault	Joseph	Thibodeau	Madeleine	1768	St. John R.	Kennebecassis
71	Thibodeau	Etienne	Paradis	Judith	1795	Kamouraska	Probably St. John R.
72	Thibodeau	Firmin	Cyr	Marie	1795	Madawaska	Probably St. John R.
73	Thibodeau	J-Bte	Savoie	Marie-Anne	1780	Shepody (NB)	St. John R.
74	Thibodeau	J-Bte	Cormier	Marie	Before 1792	Unknown	Probably St. John R.
75	Thibodeau	J-Bte	Babin	Marie-Anne Françoise	1755	Rivière aux Canards (Acadie)	Probably St. John R.
76	Thibodeau	J-Bte	Leblanc	Marie	1727	Grand Pré	Probably St. John R.
77	Thibodeau	Joseph	Coté	Marie-Josephte	1795	Ile Verte	Probably St. John R.
78	Thibodeau	Olivier	Potier	Madeleine	1765	Ste Anne de la Pocatière (Qc)	St. John R., then Kennebecassis
79	Thibodeau	Olivier Jr.	Cormier	Marie-Josephte	1792	Madawaska	Probably Kennebecassis
80	Thibodeau	Paul	Cormier	Marie-Madeleine	1799	Madawaska	Probably Kennebecassis
81	Thibodeau	Grégoire	Levasseur	Madeleine	1794	Madawaska	Probably Kennebecassis
82	Thibodeau	Toussaint	Cormier	Marie-Théotiste	1799	Madawaska	Probably Kennebecassis
83	Violette	Augustin	Cyr	Elizabeth	About 1800	Madawaska	Kennebecassis
84	Violette	François	Thibodeau	Marie-Luce	1770	St. John R.	Kennebecassis
85	Bernard (Native)		Noël				Madawaska

Entry #	Parents of	Children of	Siblings of	Origin of family - male/female (Acadia or Canada)	Residence after 1790	Grant, if any
57			56	A/C	Madawaska	Mazzerolle SB #35
58		21	9, 72	C/A	Madawaska	Mazzerolle SB #14; sells part to Pierre Lizotte 1796
59		3	4	C/C	Madawaska	Mazerolle NB #19 (1791)
60		27	20, 22, 26, 32, 34	C/A	Madawaska	Mazzerolle SB #11 (1792)
61				C/C	Madawaska	Purchased lot 4, 7 and 8 Mazzerolle grant NB in 1808
62	38	76	70, 75, 78, 84	A/A	Madawaska	Mazzerolle SB #34
63		54	53	A/A	Tracadie	
64				C/A	Madawaska	Mazzerolle SB #5
65			12	C/C	"Rivière Bomouctou" then Ste Anne des Pays Bas	South side in front of Green River, next to #1, in 1793
66		14	13, 15, 67, 74, 79, 80, 82	C/A	Madawaska	Soucy Grant-Green River SB
67	15	75	66, 67, 71, 73, 77	C/A	Canada	Mazzerolle SB #8 & Soucy Grant
68	53		36, 37	C/C	Madawaska	Mazzerolle NB #36; sold to Simon Hébert 1799
69	39	70, 48	55	A/C	Madawaska	Soucy grant-Green R.
70	17, 39, 55, 69	76	62, 75, 78, 84	A/A	Madawaska	Soucy grant-Green R.
71		75	67, 73, 77	A/C	Madawaska	Mazzerolle NB #1
72		21, 78	28, 79, 80, 81, 82	A/A	Madawaska	Soucy grant-Green R.
73		75	67, 71, 73, 77	A/A	Madawaska	Soucy grant-Green R.
74			14	A/A	Madawaska	Mazzerolle SB 17 (1792)
75	67,71,73,77	76	62, 70, 78, 84	A/A	Madawaska	Soucy grant-Green R.
76	62, 70, 75, 78, 84			A/A	Madawaska	Mazzerolle SB #3
77		75	67, 71, 73	A/C	Madawaska	Mazzerolle NB #2
78	28, 72, 79, 80, 81, 82	76	62, 70, 75, 84	A/A	Madawaska	Soucy grant-Green R.
79		78, 14	13,15, 28, 72, 80, 81, 82	A/A	Madawaska	Soucy grant-Green R.
80		78, 14	13,15, 28,72,79,81	A/A	Madawaska	Soucy Grant-Grand Isle
81		78, 48	28, 72, 79, 80, 82	A/ part A	Madawaska	Soucy Grant-Grand Isle
82		78, 14	28, 72, 79, 80, 81	A/A	Madawaska	Soucy Grant-Grand Isle
83		84, 23		A/A	Madawaska	Soucy grant-Grand River
84	83	76	62, 70, 75, 78	A/A	Madawaska	Soucy grant-Grand River
85					Madawaska	Mazzerolle NB #24

Abbreviations:

A/A: husband and wife were Acadians; A/C: husband was Acadian and wife French Canadian; C/A: husband was French Canadian and wife Acadian.

Mazzerolle SB: Lot in Mazzerolle grant, south bank of the river.

Mazzerolle NB: Lot in Mazzerolle grant, north bank of the river.

Notes:

4. Applied for a grant on the north side of river opposite Frenchville in 1806.

5. Present in 1791.

6. His sister is a mother to 36, 37, 68.

8. Remarried Charlotte Tardif, widow of Hilarion Cyr (22) in 1836.

13. Miller.

18. Granddaughter of 76.

19. Left for Lacadie in the Richelieu Valley after the War of 1812.

20. Remarried to Euphrosine Cyr's daughter 24 in 1795.

25. Remarried to Catherine Dufour.

26. No children. Marie Madeleine was the only woman to get a grant of land at Madawaska.

27. "Tante Blanche."

29. Remarried Madeleine Thibodeau, widow of Joseph Thériault (69).

33. Remarried Charlotte Lefebvre in 1775 at St. Thomas Montmagny.

36. Nephew of 6.

37. Nephew of 6. Marie-Geneviève widow of 52; niece of 48 and 51. He remarried Marguerite Roy ou Denis, native of New York.

45. Granddaughter of 76.

48. Madeleine half-sister of Madeleine (14); J-Bte uncle of M-G. Bourguoin (37 and 52).

50. Sister of 24?

51. M-A aunt to M-G Bourguoin (37 and 52).

52. She is a niece of 48 and 51 and remarries Germain Dubé in 1797 (37).

54. 1790 grant named after him; died in Ste Anne des Pays Bas in 1815; only settler to have been deported (Boston). His wife is not a member of the Thibodeau family below.

56. Relationship to Thibodeau below unknown.

58. Remarried Marguerite Gagné, daughter of 45.

59. Remarried Joseph Sirois-Duplessis.

62. Miller.

64. She is probably a daughter of 76; remarried Marie-Anne Savoie , sister of 73, in 1791.

66. She remarried François Violette in 1803 (84).

67. He is a son of Rose Dumont Guérette, sister of 24; he died in St Nicolas (Qc) in 1812.

68. She is a niece of 6.

73. She is the sister of Louis Sanfaçon's second wife (64).

74. He seems to be a nephew of 76.

84. Remarried Rose Cormier, widow of Germain Soucy (66), and Genevieve Tardif, daughter (68).

SETTLERS LSTED IN 1840 MACLAUCHLAN REPORT AND REPORTING FORTY YEARS OF RESIDENCE OR MORE

First name	Last name	Country/ place of origin	Years in residence	Year of establish-ment	Bank of the St. John River	Location	# in previous table
Anselme	Albert	Canada	40	1800	SB	(1)	
Firmin	Albert	Canada	40	1800	NB	(2)	4
David	Dufour	Canada	40	1800	SB	(1)	38
Michel	Martin	Canada	40	1800	NB	(1)	
Michel	Mercure	New Brunswick	40	1800	NB	(1)	Son of 57
J-Baptiste	Souci	Madawaska	40	1800	SB	(1)	
Paul	Thibodeau	New Brunswick	45	1795	SB	(1)	80
Grégoire	Thibodeau	New Brunswick	45	1795	SB	(1)	81
Joseph	Martin Sen	New Brunswick	48	1792	NB	(1)	
Hilarion	Thériault	New Brunswick	50	1790	NB	(1)	
Firmin	Thibodeau	New Brunswick	50	1790	NB	(1)	72
J-Baptiste	Thibodeau	New Brunswick	50	1790	NB	(1)	74
Oliver	Thibodeau	New Brunswick	50	1790	SB	(1)	79
Vincent	Albert	Canada	52	1788	SB	(2)	
Simon	Hebert Sr.	Canada	54	1786	SB	(1)	Son of 47
Michel	Cyr	New Brunswick	55	1785	NB	(1)	28
Joseph	Thibodeau	Canada	55	1785	NB	(1)	77
Bénoni	Thériault	New Brunswick	57	1783	NB	(1)	Son of 70
J-Baptiste	Cyr	Canada	58	1782	SB	(1)	25

1. Between the Grand Falls and the Madawaska River.
2. Between the Madawaska and Fish Rivers.
Note that none of the individuals who claimed to have been at Madawaska before 1787 received a licence of occupation in that year.

TOWNSHIPS, PLANTATIONS, TOWNS, AND COUNTIES

Whereas New Brunswick's local government had been modeled on the English county system, Maine local government was a variant of the New England town system. The basic administrative unit was the township; in Northern Maine, townships were normally 360-square-mile blocks of land. Unincorporated township residents did not have to levy taxes for any purpose. Townships could be incorporated solely for school purposes upon application by three voters. This allowed the residents to levy taxes to support schools. In 1840, a law allowed electors in unincorporated places to vote in adjacent towns or organized plantations. The same year, a law known as the "Wildcat Law" provided for the organization, for electoral purpose only, of any unincorporated place upon the request of three electors. Hancock Plantation was thus incorporated in October 1840; it encompassed 1,300 square miles. Soon after the Webster–Ashburton Treaty, Van Buren and Madawaska Plantations were similarly organized for election purposes.

As soon as the population of a township reached 200, the residents could apply for incorporation as a plantation. Plantations had to support their own poor citizens and were responsible for maintaining the roads and bridges within their limits. Fort Kent, Frenchville, Madawaska, and Grand Isle became plantations in 1869; Van Buren in 1881; and St. Agatha in 1899.

The transformation of a plantation into a town was contingent on population and valuation—its tax base had to be sufficient to support the services for which it was responsible. Town officers were elected annually at the town meeting and included the selectmen, town clerk, town treasurer, constables, three or more assessors, three or more overseers of the poor, and a school superintendent.

Once large enough, towns could get a charter from the state legislature to become cities. Cities were governed by a mayor and a board of aldermen and were divided into wards. City governments were responsible for street maintenance and lighting, water supplies, municipal police, fire fighting, etc.

The county was also an incorporated body, with a three-branch government: the legislative branch was represented by three county commissioners elected for six-year terms; the sheriff (elected for two years) was the executive; and the county court was the judiciary. The other county officers were the probate judge, register of probate, clerk of the court, and register of the deeds (elected for a four-year term), and the county treasurer and attorney (two-year term). The county was responsible for the building and upkeep of the county courthouse and county jail.

Sources: Stetson, W. W. *History of Civil Government of Maine;* Kingsbury, *The Maine Townsman;* Dubay, *Light on the Past.*

AGRICULTURAL PRODUCTION

Table H-1: Production per Farm, 1799–1871

Year	Number of farms	Wheat	Buckwheat	Other bread grains	Oats	Peas	Potatoes	Hay
1799	56	53	1	2	11	8	70	...
1830s	159	111	3	11	74	39	356	...
1833	159	37	3	6	29	13	229	16
1835	156	41	7	16	36	14	216	...
1840*	41	38	22	40	55	28	268	...
1841*	54	35	...	34	90	24	232	...
1842*	61	46	7	44	81	19	227	...
1850	167	8	142	26	134	24	171	21
1860	667	6	93	23	89	15	133	13
1861	435	9	71	22	88	16	110	13
1870	775	2	125	6	95	11	109	10
1871	862	6	73	6	73	10	121	7

Units: Grains, peas, and potatoes in bushels; hay in toms.

* Ste. Luce parish only

Sources: See list of censuses p. 409.

Table H-2: Production per Household, 1799–1871

	1799	1807	1830s	1831	1832	1833	1835	1840	1841	1842*	1850	1851	1860	1861	1870	1871
# House-holds	72	100	403	475	113	403	[403]	149	175	250	466	550	880	621	1,042	1,166
Wheat	42	44	45	29	29	15	16	15	11	11	3	4	2	5	2	5
Buck-wheat	1	...	1	...	...	1	3	10	...	2	51	59	34	34	94	55
Oats	9	11	30	6	10	11	13	24	28	20	46	61	41	42	73	55
Other grains	1	...	4	...	...	3	6	20	10	10	11	11	17	15	4	4
Peas	66	8	16	9	10	5	6	11	7	5	9	13	6	8	8	7
Potatoes	56	78	143	41	88	90	101	121	72	55	61	106	46	47	82	85
Hay	...	...	...	...	...	9	...	...	...	...	8	...	5	6	8	5

Units: Grains, peas, and potatoes in bushels; hay in tons

Note: 1832, 1840–42, Ste. Luce only; 1850, 1860, and 1870, American side only; 1851, 1861, and 1871, New Brunswick side only.

Sources: See list of censuses p. 409.

Table H-3: Agricultural Production, Aroostook County, 1860–1910

County Production

	# Farms	Improved acreage	Unimprove acreage[a]	Cash value of farm[b]	Value of products[b]	Potatoes[c]	Oats[c]	Wheat[c]	Buckwheat[c]	Cheese[d]	Hay[e]	Wool[d]
1860	1,938	124,117	326,699	2,217,136		411,630	419,783	34,763	230,442	22,011	39,267	61,312
1870	3,209	133,024	295,426	3,010,130		380,701	532,151	46,846	360,450	21,011	48,052	86,173
1880	5,802	270,442	453,308	5,151,151	1,826,348	2,248,594	628,435	138,236	296,793		80,316	190,636
1890	6,180	316,253	406,763	7,518,870	2,643,230	2,746,765	1,128,909	41,722	388,037	29,898	102,935	164,733
1900	6,938	389,232	403,973	14,683,421	4,553,169	6,466,189	1,807,435	99,090	385,370	30,019	133,338	218,310
1910	7,289	443,007	421,353	44,220,004		17,514,491	2,524,893	76,126	231,026	6,280	153,242	25,031

Production per Farm

	Improved acreage	Unimprove acreage[a]	Cash value of farm[b]	Value of products[b]	Potatoes[c]	Oats[c]	Wheat[c]	Buckwheat[c]	Cheese[d]	Hay[e]	Wool[d]
1860	64.0	168.6	1,144.0	0.0	212.4	216.6	12.8	118.9	11.5	20.3	31.6
1870	41.5	92.1	938.0	0.0	118.6	165.8	14.6	112.3	6.5	15.0	26.9
1880	46.6	78.1	887.8	314.8	387.6	108.3	23.8	51.2	0.0	13.8	32.9
1890	51.2	65.8	1,216.6	427.7	444.5	182.7	6.8	62.8	4.8	16.7	26.7
1900	56.1	58.2	2,116.4	656.3	932.0	260.5	14.3	55.5	4.3	19.2	31.5
1910	60.8	57.8	6,066.7	0.0	2,402.9	348.9	10.4	31.7	.9	21.0	3.4

a In acres
b In dollars
c In bushels
d In pounds
e In tons

Sources: See list of censuses p. 409.

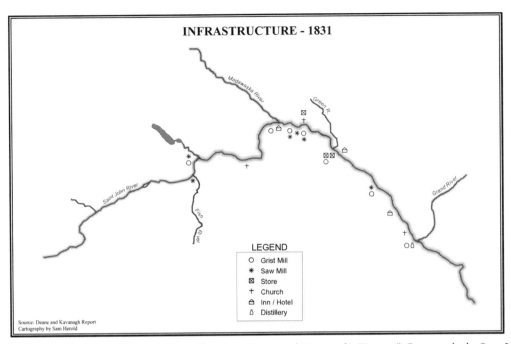

Upper St. John Valley infrastructure in 1831, based on Deane and Kavanagh's "Report." Cartography by Sam Herold.

Table I-1: Businesses Listed in Deane and Kavanagh's Report, 1831

Type of business	Owner	Side of river	Location	Comments
Sawmill	Daniel Savage	South bank	Fish River	Started 1826 or 1827
Saw- and gristmill	John Baker	North bank	Mouth of Meruimti-cook	Started around 1818 by Nathan Baker
Disused gristmill	David Dufour	South bank	Almost opposite mouth Madawaska River	Paul Potier's old mill
Saw- and gristmill	Simon Hébert	South bank	On Anselme Albert's lot	
Sawmill	Joseph Mercure	South bank	On a back lot across the river from St. Basile	
Saw- and gristmill	Louis Bellefleur	South bank	Across the river from St. Basile	Formerly Fraser and Robinson's and before, Duperré's
Store	François Thibodeau	South bank	Almost opposite mouth of Green river	
Store and gristmill	J-Bte Soucy	South bank	Almost opposite mouth of Green river	
Saw- and gristmill	Firmin Thibodeau	South bank	Opposite Grand Isle	Formerly François Cormier's
Distillery	William McRae and John Keaton	South bank	Below St. Bruno church	
gristmill	François Violette	South bank	Below St. Bruno church	His father had one on the same lot
Store	Antoine Bellefleur	North bank	Next to St. Basile church	

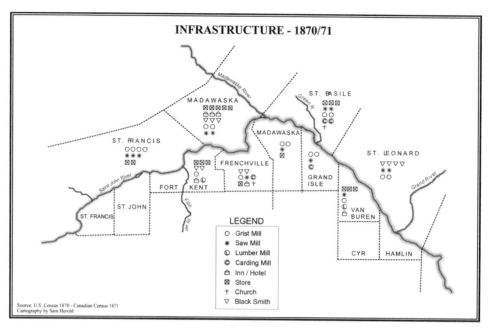

Upper St. John Valley infrastructure in 1870-71, based on the Canadian and U.S. censuses. Cartography by Sam Herold.

Table I-2: Mills Listed in the 1870 US Census

Location	Owner	Type	Equipment	Capital invested ($)	Value of raw material ($)	Value of output ($)
Fort Kent	Levy Sears	Clapboard and shingle mill	5 single saws	2,000	No data	16,000
Fort Kent	Levy Sears	Flour mill	2 runs of stones	1,500	No data	1,100
Fort Kent	Lindor Daigle	Flour mill	1 run of stones	1,000	No data	1,000
Dickeyville	Cyrille Daigle	Sawmill		300	500	900
Dickeyville	Edwin Gray	Carding mill	1 machine	300	1,800	2,200
Dickeyville	Régis Daigle	Gristmill	1 run of stones	1,200	7,000	8,000
Madawaska	Louis Leveque and son	Gristmill	1 run of stones	500	1,250	1,250
Madawaska	Sylvain Daigle	Gristmill	1 run of stones	500	5,000	5,000
Grand Isle	Joseph Corriveau	Gristmill	1 run of stones	1,200	2,500	2,500
Grand Isle	Joseph Corriveau	Carding mill		450	450	
Grand Isle	Michel Martin	Sawmill	1 circular saw	500	1,200	2,000
Van Buren	Israel Michaud	Sawmill	Single saw	500	500	762
Van Buren	Israel Michaud and son	Flour and gristmill	2 runs of stones	2,000	10,000	12,000
Van Buren	W. C. Hammond	Lumber mill	1 up-and-down saw 1 edge trimmer 2 clapboard machines 2 shingle machines 2 lath-and-picket machines	12,000	17,000	4,500 (boards and planks) 8,000 (clapboards) 6,000 (shingles) 600 (lath and pickets)

Source: United States, Bureau of the Census, 9th Census of the United States, State of Maine, County of Aroostook, Industrial Schedule.

The Land in Between

Table I-3: Mills Listed in the 1871 Canadian Census

Location	Owner	Type	Capital invested ($)	Value raw material ($)	Value of output ($)
St. Francis	Paul Silva	Buckwheat mill	100	400	560
St. Francis	Magloire Albert	Sawmill	400	600	1,000
St. Francis	Hilaire Nadeau	Sawmill	1,000	750	1,000
St. Francis	Hilaire Nadeau	Gristmill	1,000	1,000	1,250
St. Francis	Prudent Gagnon	Gristmill	1,100	300	500
St. Francis	Enoch Baker	Sawmill	1,000	500	950
St. Francis	Charles Ouellette	Gristmill	1,000	2,000	2.400
St. Francis	Ferdinand Ouellette	Sawmill	400	800	1,600
Madawaska	Pierre Plourde	Gristmill	1,000	500	400
Madawaska	Pierre Plourde	Sawmill	700	225	800
Madawaska	Eloi Otis	Gristmill	2,500	1,120	1,660
Madawaska	Régis Daigle	Sawmill	500	1,200	1,660
St. Basile	Lévite Thériault	Grist- and carding mill	2,000	800 (wool)	1,000 (wool)
St. Basile	Lévite Thériault	Sawmill		750	1,350
St. Basile	Denis Thériault	Sawmill	600	500	1,260
St. Basile	Denis Thériault	Gristmill	1,000	350	3,930
St. Basile	Denis Thériault	Carding mill	700	800	1,600
St. Leonard I	P. O. Byram	Gristmill	600	6,000	6,560
St. Leonard I	P. O. Byram	Gristmill	300	2,000	2,580
St. Leonard II	W. and E. J. Bijeau	Sawmill	1,000	350	1,000
St. Leonard II	Isaac Bijeau	Gristmill, buckwheat and other grains	500	4,800	4,800
St. Leonard II	Isaac Bijeau	Bakery			600

Sources: Canadian census, 1871 Province of New Brunswick, County of Victoria, Industrial schedules (schedule 6), Madawaska , St. Basile, St. Leonard, and St. Francis.

Table I-4: St. John Valley Businesses, American Madawaska, 1900

Location	Activity	Name	Sources
Connor Pl.	Sawmill, steam powered	Peter Powers	3
Connor Pl.	Sawmill, water powered	P. J. Pomeroy	3
Connor Pl.	Starch factory	Jacob Hedman	3
Cyr Pl.	Starch factory	Peter Ouellette	1
Eagle Lake	Saw- and grist mill	D. B. Laferriere	3
Eagle Lake	Sawmill	C. Baker	1, 3
Fort Kent	Brick work	Nadeau and Mallet	1
Fort Kent	Gristmill	A. Corriveau	1
Fort Kent	Gristmill	S. Daigle	1
Fort Kent	Lumber, grist, and carding mill	Fort Kent Mill Co.	1, 3
Fort Kent	Starch factory	Page and Mallett	3
Fort Kent	Tannery	M. Gagnon	1

Fort Kent	Woodwork shop, steam powered	Joseph O. Michaud	3
Frenchville	Cloth dressing	E. Guy	1
Frenchville	Gristmill	Régis Daigle	1
Frenchville	Gristmill	Grégoire Gagnon	1
Frenchville	Saw mill	Israel Ouellette	1
Frenchville	Starch factory	Israel Ouellette[1]	1, 3
Frenchville	Starch factory	M. A. Gagnon	1, 3
Frenchville	Tannery	M. A. Gagnon	3
Grand Isle	Grist- and shingle mill, steam powered	Remi Plourde	1, 3
Grand Isle	Ggris mill	A. Plourde	1
Grand Isle	Gristmill, water powered	W. A. Cyr	3
Grand Isle	Gristmill, water powered	Thomas Roy	1, 3
Grand Isle	Long and short lumber, steam powered	Alexis Morneault	1, 3
Grand Isle	Lumber mill, water powered	A. Parent	1, 3
Hamlin pl.	Saw mill	Isidore Martin	1
Madawaska	Butter factory		2
Madawaska	Gristmill	Philippe Morin	3
Madawaska	Gristmill	Vital Cyr	1, 3
Madawaska	Saw- and gristmill, water powered	Vital Levesque	1, 3
Madawaska	Starch factory	Daigle and Smith	3
New Canada	Lumber mill	Vital Daigle; Chas Rousseau	3
St. Agatha	Sawmill	Octave Cyr	1
St. Agatha	Shingle mill	Israel Ouellette	1, 2
St. Agatha	Starch factory	Michel Michaud	1, 2
St. Francis	Gristmill	Xavier Cyr	1
St. Francis	Shingle and lumber mill	Jones and Stadig	1
St. John	Gristmill	J. Wheelock	1
St. John	Lumber mill	D. Sinclair	1
St. John	Shingle mill		1, 2
Van Buren	Grist- and carding mill	Fred Violette	1
Van Buren	Lumber mill	Van Buren Shingle Co.	1, 3
Van Buren	Lumber mill	Hammond and Martin	1, 3
Van Buren	Machine shop		1, 2
Van Buren	Potato store house	Peter C. Keegan	3
Van Buren	Sawmill, water powered	Joseph Martin and son	3
Van Buren	Starch factory	Hammond and Martin	1, 3
Wallagrass	Lumber and gristmill	A. Michaud and Co.	1, 2
Wallagrass	Shingle mill	R. Nelson and Co.	1

Note 1: Listed under Edith Ouellette's name in the *Board of Underwriters Tariff Rates.*
Sources: Businesses listed in the *Maine Register* for 1900 (1); the 1902 *Report of the Maine Bureau of Industrial and Labor Statistics* (2); and the 1900 *Aroostook County Board of Underwriters Tariff Rates.*(3). Note that the different sources enumerate different businesses. No single source, therefore, gives a complete listing of all businesses in the Valley at any given time.

Table I-5: Manufacturing Establishments, New Brunswick Madawaska, 1900

Location	Business	Owner
Baker Brook	Sawmill	Joseph Ouellette
Connors	Sawmill	McLean and Stadig
Clair	Sawmill	Georges Corriveau
Edmundston	Sawmill	Emile Gagné
Edmundston	Lumber mill	James Murchie & Son of Calais
Edmundston	General store and shingle mill	Van Buren Lumber Co.
Edmundston	Saw- and gristmill	Joseph Verette Jr.
Green River	Saw- and gristmill	Jean Roy
Kennedy Island (near Clair)	Lumber mill	Crockett mill
Ste. Anne	General store and shingle mill	Van Buren Lumber Co.
St. Basile	Gristmill	Octave Corriveau
St. Hilaire	Sawmill	Albert and Cyr
St. Hilaire	Butter factory	Daigle, Daigle & Michaud
St. Jacques	Sawmill	H. L. Maddock and Co.
St. Jacques	Sawmill	Lévite Michaud
St. Leonard	Sawmill	I. H. Bijeau
St. Leonard	Lumber mill	D. H. Keswick
St. Leonard	Gristmill	Paul Plourde

Source: "Evolution de l'industrie forestière en Marévie."

DEEDS OF MAINTENANCE

I. The oldest deed of maintenance we found was between "Oliver Cyr and Mary" and "Beloni Theriault and Mary, his sister in law." It is dated September 22, 1803.

Benoni and Mary were to deliver to Oliver and Madeleine (Mary) on every year on the 1st of December, 6 years from now:

24 bushels of wheat	1¹/₂ lb of tea
2 bushels of peas	15 lb brown sugar
150 lb of pork	1 lb chocolate
50 lb of beef or mutton	1 gal of rum
6 lb of hog's lard	1 gal wine
¹/₂ lb of pepper	15 lb leaf tobacco
5 lb of candle	and their clothing
1 bushel of salt	

In return, they were to get the south side of lot 79 (in Mazzerolle grant), 30 rods wide, between J. B. Fournier and Joseph Daigle to the north, 100 acres. This includes a log house, a frame barn, and a good stable.

They also got a half lot on the north side between J. B. Fournier and Francis Martin, 100 acres.

Source: PANB, York County Registry office, 1785–1815, entry 999, Microfilm. F5618.

II. Almost as old is the deed between "Josephte Potter dit Marigau" and "David Dufour and Charlotte and Joseph Dufour and wife Nancy," dated August 5, 1806.

The names had been altered by the English-speaking registrar. The deed was between Judith Potier, widow of Paul Potier (Miller); her son-in-law David Dufour; and his brother Joseph, married to Marie Rose Thériault.

The Dufour were to deliver to Judith Potier:

12 bushels of wheat ground into flour	³/₄ lb tea
3 bushels of pease	¹/₂ bushel salt
100 lb pork	¹/₄ lb pepper
12 lb beef or mutton	3 lb rough wool
4 lb tallow or hog's lard	1 gal rum
15 lb maple sugar	

and clothing (included muslin caps, calico nightcap, and cotton kerchiefs). Judith was also to have the use of her garden and of a milk cow.

The Dufours got lots 31 and 34 in the Mazzerolle grant, and a lot one mile above the Madawaska River, 60 rods wide, 200 acres. They also got 2 horses, 1 yoke of oxen, 3 cows, 21 sheep, and 4 pigs. Three days later the brothers divided the property between themselves.

Source: PANB, York County Registry office, 1785-1815, entry 1005, Microfilm. F5618.

III. Deed dated June 30, 1824, and registered March 19, 1832, between "John" Thibodeau and "Nannie," and Léon Bellefleur.

Jean Baptiste and Nannie will receive:
Yearly:

Best room in house they now occupy	50 lb pepper
20 bushels wheat into flour	4 lb soushong tea
4 bushels peas	2 gal. espirit [*sic*]
200 lb pork	1 bushel salt

| 1/4 beef, or mutton in proportion | 10 bus. potatoes |
| 20 lb hog's lard | 20 lb candles |

Clothing: 2 pairs trousers, one jacket, 3 shirts, and 3 shifts for each yearly; 3 pairs *moggasins*, 2 pairs women's shoes, 1 pair men's shoes every four years; 1 beaver hat, every 4 years, 1 ditto common yearly, one silk handkerchief every 3 years, 1 ditto cotton, 4 pairs socks worsted yearly, 2 pairs women stockings, 20 lb Canadian tobacco, 1 petticoat of homespun cloth every year, 4 yds calico, 2 cotton handkerchief yearly, 2 pairs mittens each yearly, 4 lb of snuff, one paper of pins, 1/2 yd muslin, thread and needles, one pocket knife, likewise a horse and *cariol* to be kept in good order and a good milk cow likewise to be well fed, and shall provide for their washing and lodging and everything also necessary for their comfort and accommodation in sickness and health.

After their death: 5 services and 20 masses of requiem each

Leon to get lot 3 in grant to Jos. Mazzerolle, north bank, 63 rods, 203 acres.

Source: PANB, York County Registry office, 1829-1834, entry 5241, Microfilm. F5622.

IV. Deed dated June 12, 1846, between Vital Martin, yeoman, son of Joseph Martin, Sr., farmer at Madawaska, and Geneviève. Vital agreed to provide them with the following articles for their natural life:

1. The use of their house, with kitchen and cellar privileges; the use of a kitchen garden.

2. On December first yearly (and half to survivor):

24 bushels of wheat or 4 barrels wheaten flour	1 gallon of rum and 2 gallons best port wine
2 bushels of peas	60 lb of sugar
200 lb pork	12 lb good souchong tea
1/4 of a beef	1 lb chocolate
8 lb of suet	1 lb pepper
1 bushel of salt	12 lb tobacco

3. Wood as needed; one milk cow; the use of a horse and cariole, with harness and buffalo skin; one sheep and six hens to be changed as often as needed; after their death, 2 services and 40 low masses each.

4. For him:

Yearly: 1 suit homespun;

Every other year: 2 silk neckerchiefs; 2 cotton handkerchiefs, 2 pairs of socks, 3 pairs of shoe packs, 2 pairs of stockings, one pair of shoes, 1 beaver hat, one fur cap; 1 woollen nightcap and one cloth one, one coat.

5. For her:

Yearly: 1 suit of homespun; 4 shifts, 2 silk handkerchiefs, 1 pair of shoes, 3 pairs of shoe packs, 2 pairs of stockings, 2 pairs of socks, 1 yard of muslin, 1 yard of calico, 1/2 lb of pins, 1 shawl, 1 calico dress.

Every other year: 1 great cloak and one silk bonnet

6. To his sisters Ositée and Vitaline during their maidenhood: food, drink, and apparel, washing and lodging and attendance in sickness.

Also: Yearly: One suit of homespun, 4 shifts, 2 silk handkerchiefs, 1 pair of shoes, 3 pairs of shoe packs, 2 pairs of stockings, 2 pairs of socks, 1 yard muslin, one yard calico, 1/2 lb pins, 1 shawl, and one calico dress. A cloth cloak and a silk bonnet every 3 years.

When his sisters married, he was to pay all wedding expenses and provide then with one feather bed, 5 sheep, 1 cow, 1 spinning wheel, 1 hog, 1/2 dozen knives and forks, 1/2 dozen cups and saucers, and enough sheets and blankets for one bed.

In exchange Vital was to receive the lower half of #35 bounded by the upper half of #35 (the Bishop's land) and by # 34 in possession of the widow of Simon Martin, 38 rods front, 130 acres and the upper part of # 31, bounded by the rest of lot 31 and by lot 32 granted to Alexis Cir, 30 rods, 100 acres, less a kitchen garden in the first tract, as well as one yoke of oxen, 45 sheep, 5 cows, 2 horses, and 8 hogs.

Source: PANB, Carleton County Registry Office, entry 3292.

V. Deed dated January 5, 1865, between Vital Cyr and Susan, farmer, from Madawaska Parish, and Elie Cyr and Susan of St. Leonard.

Vital and Susan to get $400 yearly or maintenance for their natural life, as well as maintenance of Alexis Cyr until he comes of age or as long as he may live with them. When he comes of age, Vital is to give him a guaranteed deed to the lower half of the lower tract within the described indenture.

Source: PANB, Victoria County Registry office, entry E1618.

Appendix K

SOCIAL LIFE IN THE VALLEY (1904)

The articles are in French. Translation by the authors.

School Fête

Thursday, January 29, [1904], Mr. Théodule Daigle and Miss Lizzie Daigle threw a magnificent party for their pupils at St. David's Upper School. The meeting began around six o'clock and since the room was large and suitable for it, the evening started with a performance of the Grand March and Circle by the pupils. This first dance was vigorously applauded by all present. The evening consisted of a dance in one of the rooms and card playing (whist, euchre, etc.) in the other one. Around nine o'clock, a dialogue entitled "Welcome" [in English in the text] was delivered by Florine St. Amand, Marie Hébert, Olive Fournier, Joséphine Dufour, Agnès Cyr, Olive Hébert, and Eugénie Lebrun. English and French recitations by Loisse Dufour, Caroline Dufour, Caroline Lebrun, and Eugénie Lebrun followed. Several beautiful songs were performed by the pupils, accompanied by the teacher, Mr. T. Albert, on the violin. About 85 people took part in this select meeting, 50 pupils and 35 citizens. The evening ended with a "native dance" performed by four little girls who were very much admired and applauded. At ten-thirty, the audience left singing "Bonsoir mes amis, bonsoir" [Good night, friends, good night].

Source: *Le journal du Madawaska,* February 3, 1904.

Visitor from Afar

A pleasant family evening was organized on February 7 by Mr. and Mrs. Charles Dufour to honor Mr. Damase Cyr, Mrs. Dufour's brother. Mr. Cyr has lived in Pincher Creek, in the Canadian Northwest Territories, for several years and is at the moment visiting his native land. There were about 30 guests, and the evening was very pleasantly spent making music, singing, and playing whist. Mr. Théodule Albert and Miss Nathalie Albert sang several very pretty pieces with musical accompaniment by Mr. Dufour and George Hébert. Generous amounts of refreshments, sweets, and cakes, which received plenty of attention, were displayed on the tables.

None of this was enough for Mr. and Mrs. Dufour. Toward the end of the evening, all had to sit down for a sumptuous meal, a marvellous midnight feast. After the meal, the young Misses Dufour and William Lebrun sang sentimental little ditties that visibly moved the hero of the day. Mr. Damas Cyr gave away several ringing coins, items children always greatly appreciate. At a relatively tardy hour, everyone withdrew, pleased with the evening and wholeheartedly thanking Mr. and Mrs. Dufour.

Source: *Le journal du Madawaska,* February 10, 1904.

Wallagrass Wedding

On January 11, 1904, Mr. Fred C. Violette of Van Buren led Miss Zéline Labbé to the altar at Wallagrass (Maine). Holy Mass was celebrated in honor of the young couple by the Rev. Marcoux, parish priest. The best man was Ludger Levasseur, escorting Miss Mattie Clark. After celebration of the wedding, the young couple went to the bride's father's, Mr. Frank Labbé, for lunch. Numerous friends and relatives followed the newlywed to Mr. Labbé's. A magnificent meal was served. In the evening, a pretty little dance was organized for the benefit of all the guests.

The next day, one had to go and pay a visit to the bride's grandmother, Mrs. Martin of Fort Kent. There, the supper was followed by a nice evening of music and singing, then one went to visit the groom's uncle, Mr. Henry Lafrance. Here again, a delicious supper was followed by a pleasant evening gathering of relatives and friends. On Thursday evening, the 14th, the newlyweds were entertained by a dance at the Fort Kent Hall.

Source: *Le journal du Madawaska,* January 1, 1904.

Winter Evenings

Last Thursday, there was a big card game and oyster supper at Mr. Alex Dionne's (Van Buren). Around ten o'clock, after numerous card games, the guest were ushered into the dining room filled by the enticing aroma of a rich oyster soup. Fifteen couples had been invited; fifteen couples answered the call. After doing ample justice to the delicious stew [in English in the text] and to the mouth-watering cakes, the friends withdrew, delighted by their evening, singing "Good night, friends, good night," and heartily thanking Mr. and Mrs. Dionne for their generous reception. Mrs. Madore helped Mrs. Dionne prepare the feast, and the latter is happy to express her gratitude for her gracious assistance.

Source: *Le journal du Madawaska,* January, 22 1904.

Fort Kent Social News

Sunday evening, Mr. and Mrs. Isidore Bourgoin threw a nice euchre evening for the benefit of their friends in the village. Mr. and Mrs. J. A. Nadeau, John Sweeney, Henri Nadeau, Vin. Thériault, Félix Morneault, Dr. Archambault, Philippe Morneault, Stephen Audibert, and Levite Martin were invited. At eleven o'clock, a sumptuous supper was served by the Misses Maggie Sweeney, Allie Audibert, and Catherine Morin. After supper, Miss Catherine Morin performed a very pretty solo accompanied at the piano by Dr. Archambault. Euchre's first prizes were won by Mrs. Philippe Morneault and Dr. Archambault. The evening ended at one o'clock with the song "Good night, friend, good night," and the guests parted after warmly congratulating Mr. and Mrs. Bourguoin.

Source: *Le journal du Madawaska,* 1904.

Appendix L

TRAVELING BEFORE THE RAILROAD— OR, WHAT FUN WE HAD ON THE ROAD

A Fright

In 1792, Patrick Campbell was traveling with a servant and a friend, George McGregor, by canoe. Because the canoe was too small for the three of them, one of the men would always walk along the shore. On the day after they left Preskeel, at the mouth of the Prestile Stream, Campbell was walking along the shore in the evening, while the two other men were in the canoe.

> Towards evening I turned a point of land, and got considerably a-head of the canoe, which at this time was on the opposite side [of the river]. I sat down to rest and to write my journal, and intended to wait until the canoe came up. Having rested here for double the time I judged the canoe would have taken, I became very uneasy, lest it was overset, and both the men drowned; but still I continued where I was, in hopes that I might have mistaken the distance and

the difficulty of getting up the frequent and almost perpetual rapids; until at length I concluded, without a possibility of doubt, that some misfortune had befallen them, and that it could be no other than that they were for ever lost. I knew my servant could not swim, nor did I believe George could.

> I now found myself in a very disagreeable situation indeed, without clothes to cover me at night, provisions or ammunition but one shot in my gun, hungry, and much fatigued, having traveled a good deal, and eaten nothing in the morning but one slice of cold frosty meat, and three days journey from any human being or thing that could sustain life. In my desponding condition, I returned to make the best of my way to Preskeel, and was in great doubt if ever I could reach it, considering the frosty nights, ruggedness of the woods, and every other impediment that was to fall my way. I had not returned half a mile,

when, to my no small joy, I espied the canoe coming along on the opposite side of the river. What had detained them was, that the pole of the canoe broke just as I was getting out of sight. They had to land, cut another pole, put up a fire, toast and peel it, before it was fit for use. This induced me to resolve not to travel more by land without my gun, powder and shot, steel, sponge and flint; for striking a fire, and a piece of bread in my pocket; and I determined to cause my servant have the same when he walked; so that if the canoe should be lost, we would at least have some means of supporting ourselves, be the next Indian or white settlement at what distance it would.

Source: Patrick Campbell, *Travels in the Interior Inhabited Parts of North America*, 92–93.

Animal Stories c. 1828

George Head had just spent the night at David Dufour's inn.

> *January 15*—A party of persons had collected for the purpose of proceeding with our guides towards Québec; and so we all started together.... The picture of our caravan was now totally changed. A dozen persons of various descriptions had joined our party, some at the end and some at the beginning of their respective journeys. They pelted each other with snowballs, and sang and whistled, smoking and hallowing.... The guides had procured dogs to draw the toboggans, and several of these great creatures, from the coast of Labrador and Newfoundland, were loose and followed in our train. The noise of the party frightened a Caraboo [*sic*] deer from his lair, and urged him, unfortunately for himself, to cross over the ice of the river just in front of us. Immediately, there was a general hullabaloo, and men and dogs all at once gave the chase. I quite forgot I was lame, and made a tolerable run too, and to my surprise found that the dogs had come up with their game, which had entangled himself by the horns on the branches of a fallen tree. There they pinned him, till one of the Canadians despatched him with his axe; and we had one of his haunches the same night cut into steaks for supper, which, although tough, were well flavoured....
>
> *January 16*—At last we arrived at the house of Mr. Long, situated at the extremity of Lake Tamasquatha.... We found a new set of travelers, who had established themselves in the house; and these being reinforced by our numbers, a confusion of tongues

prevailed in our room which set at defiance all description. We had thirty-six persons in it, besides six or eight large dogs belonging to the tobogins [sic]. We were obliged to lay on the ground like so many pigs. My next neighbour was a major in the army, whom I never saw before and have never met since; he seemed more fatigued than I was, and did nothing but groan all night. The dogs disturbed us; for they ran about and trod upon us; they growled; and twice before morning, there was a battle royal among them, with the whole room up in arms to part them by throttling and biting the ends of their tails. What with the noise, and the shouting, and the swearing in bad French, we were in a perfect uproar. For this, the natural remedy, of course, would have been to turn the dogs out; but the masters would not allow it, as they were of too much use by far on a journey. The gabble of tongues, the smell of tobacco smoke, and the disturbance altogether, was really dreadful; and there was, besides, a truckle bed in the room, on which two women reposed—the mistress of the house and her sister.

Source: George Head, *Forest Scenes and Incidents,* 136–38 and 141–42.

Fast Food and Discomfort Inn, 1824 Style

John Mann, who knew not a word of French, traveled by foot from Quebec City to Temiscouata Lake, where he hitched a ride with three Natives (a man, his wife, and their teenage son) in a canoe. They took him down the lake and the Madawaska River. At the beginning of this story, they are eight miles from Little Falls (Edmundston) and have no provisions left.

> ...we set off, and in a little, we discovered a small cottage, bordering on the river. I called there, and bought a few potatoes to my companions, which they boiled with great haste, and having a few herrings, they partook of the mess with great cheerfulness. I got some bread and milk to myself, which formed one of the most palatable meals I ever took. After this repast, we proceeded and arrived late at the next Settlement. As we approached the first house on the river side, we heard the murmur, as of a water fall, right before us. The two Indians both stood up in the canoe, setting their paddles against the rocks and stones to keep the canoe at leisure, as the current was quite rapid.... The noise of the falls rendered me a little uneasy, being close to them, and could not get ashore until we went farther down the face of the

rock.... My anxiety, however, was in a little relieved by the prospect of a landing place just at the edge of the falls. Here we hauled our canoe ashore, carried it up to the house, which was not far off, and stepped in, not knowing whether welcome or not. The people were remarkably civil, and as they had accommodation for travelers, they entertained us very kindly. Need I mention how comfortable I felt myself before a good fire, with a plentiful supply of agreeable provisions? After supper, the landlady made me a bed before the fire. The sunap and his squaw were accommodated on one side of it, and the boy on the other. The landlord and landlady retired to a kind of a bed in one of the farthest corners of the house; and the two sons lay on the floor in the other corner, with the skin of a buffalo below them, and another above them. The daughter slept also on the floor, at the foot of the parents' bed, with a couple of old thread-bare blankets rolled about her.

Source: John Mann, *Travels in North America,* 39–41.

Traveler Beware

E. T. Coke was a British officer; his 1832 sightseeing tour started in Philadelphia and Washington, D.C., and thence to New York, New England, Niagara Falls, York (Toronto), Montreal, and Quebec City. In this excerpt, he and a Mr. Reid from Georgia are making their way to New Brunswick.

Upon enquiring at Kamouraska, we met with a Yankee pedlar who was returning with his cart to the States, and would travel 55 miles upon the same route as ourselves. He volunteered to carry our trunks for four pounds, with a proviso that we should walk by his side; alleging at the same time that it was impossible to perform the journey under three days.... Fortunately, we had no occasion to close this disinterested offer, a by-stander offering to furnish two carts for the same sum.... The chagrin of our Yankee friend at losing so good a bargain was very evident, notwithstanding all the assurances that his only desire was to see us safe to the end of the journey, and prevent our being imposed on. He took his leave of us, saying that the man who offered to accompany us neither knew what he said nor what he was undertaking; and finally, that we should not travel the 55 miles agreed upon under four days, and that the flies in the woods would bite our ears off, if we did not tie them on with a strong handkerchief. We also experienced much difficulty in replenishing our commis-

sariat department, and could obtain only a loaf of bread and a cold shoulder of mutton—a short supply for seven days, which we calculated our journey would last. But our severest loss was not discovered until were on the point of starting; the pilot [of the boat which had carried them from Quebec City to Kamouraska] had appropriated our whole stock of brandy, consisting of two bottles, to his own use.

Source: E. T. Coke, *A Subaltern's Furlough,* 102–03.

Camping in the Maine Woods

Poet Henry David Thoreau's essay *The Maine Woods* (1864) was full of advice to those who wanted to explore the state's wilderness areas.

Equipment:

The following will be a good outfit for one who wishes to make an excursion of twelve days into the Maine woods in July, with a companion, and one Indian for the same purposes that I did.

Wear,—a check shirt, stout old shoes, thick socks, a neck ribbon, thick waistcoat, thick pants, old Kossuth hat, a linen sack.

Carry,—in an India-rubber knapsack, with a large flap, two shirts (check), one pair thick socks, one pair drawers, one flannel shirt, two pocket-handkerchiefs, a light India-rubber coat or a thick woollen one, two bosoms and collars to go and come with, one napkin, pins, needles, thread, one blanket, best grey, seven feet long.

Tent,—six by seven feet, and four feet high in middle, will do; veil and gloves and insect-wash, or, better, mosquito-bars to cover all at night; best pocket-map, and perhaps description of the route; compass; plant-book and red blotting-paper; paper and stamps, botany, small pocket spy-glass for birds, pocket microscope, tape-measure, insect-boxes.

Axe, full size if possible, jackknife, fish-lines, two only apiece, with a few hooks and corks ready, and with pork for bait in a packet, rigged; matches (some also in a small vial in the waist-coat pocket); soap, two pieces; large knife and iron spoon (for all); three or four old newspapers, much twine, and several rags for dishcloths; twenty feet of strong cord, four-quart tin pail for kettle, two tin dippers, three tin plates, a fry-pan.

Provisions,—Soft hardbread, twenty-eight pounds; pork, sixteen pounds; sugar, twelve pounds; one pound black tea or three pounds coffee, one box or a pint of salt, one quart Indian meal, to fry fish in; six lemons, good to correct the pork and warm water; perhaps two or three pounds of rice, for variety. You will probably get some berries, fish, &c., beside.

A gun is not worth the carriage, unless you go as hunters. The pork should be in an open keg, sawed to fit; the sugar, tea or coffee, meal, salt, &c., should be put in separate water-tight India-rubber bags, tied with a leather string; and all the provisions, and part of the rest of the baggage, put into two large India-rubber bags, which have been proved to be water-tight and durable. Expense of preceding outfit is twenty-four dollars.

An Indian may be hired for about one dollar and fifty cents per day, and perhaps fifty cents a week for his canoe (this depends on the demand). The canoe should be a strong and tight one. This expense will be nineteen dollars.

Such an excursion need not cost more than twenty-five dollars apiece, starting at the foot of Moosehead, if you already possess or can borrow a reasonable part of the outfit. If you take an Indian and canoe at Old Town, it will cost seven or eight dollars more to transport them to the lake.

Setting Up Camp:
I will describe, once for all, the routine of camping at this season. We generally told the Indian that we would stop at the first suitable place, so that he might be on the lookout for it. Having observed a clear, hard, and flat beach to land on, free from mud, and from stones which would injure the canoe, one would run up the bank to see if there were open and level space enough for the camp between the trees, or if it could be easily cleared, preferring at the same time a cool place, on account of insects. Sometimes we paddled a mile or more before finding one to our minds, for where the shore was suitable, the bank would often be too steep, or else too low and grassy, and therefore mosquitoey. We then took out the baggage and drew up the canoe, sometimes turning it over on shore for safety. The Indian cut a path to the spot we had selected, which was usually within two or three rods of the water, and we carried up our baggage. One, perhaps, takes canoe-birch bark, always at hand, and dead dry wood or bark, and kindles a fire five or six feet in front of where we intend to lie. It matters not, commonly, on which side this is, because there is little or no wind in so dense a wood at that season; and then he gets a kettle of water from the river, and takes out the pork, bread, coffee, &c., from their several packages.

Another, meanwhile, having the axe, cuts down the nearest dead rock-maple or other dry hard wood, collecting several large logs to last through the night, also a green stake, with a notch or fork to it, which is slanted over the fire, perhaps resting on a rock or forked stake, to hang the kettle on, and two forked stakes and a pole for the tent.

The third man pitches the tent, cuts a dozen or more pins with his knife, usually of moose-wood, the common underwood, to fasten it down with, and then collects an armful or two of fir-twigs, called in Rasle's Dictionary, Sediak, arbor-vitae, spruce, or hemlock, whichever is at hand, and makes the bed, beginning at either end, and laying the twigs wrong-side up, in regular rows, covering the stub-ends of the last row; first, however, filling the hollows, if there are any, with coarser material. Wrangel says that his guides in Siberia first strewed a quantity of dry brush-wood on the ground, and then cedar twigs on that.

Commonly, by the time the bed is made, or within fifteen or twenty minutes, the water boils, the pork is fried, and supper is ready. We eat this sitting on the ground, or a stump, if there is any, around a large piece of birch-bark for a table, each holding a dipper in one hand and a piece of ship-bread or fried pork in the other, frequently making a pass with his hand, or thrusting his head into the smoke, to avoid the mosquitoes.

Next, pipes are lit by those who smoke, and veils are donned by those who have them, and we hastily examine and dry our plants, anoint our faces and hands, and go to bed, — and the mosquitoes.

Though you have nothing to do but see the country, there's rarely any time to spare, hardly enough to examine a plant, before the night or drowsiness is upon you.

Source: Thoreau, *The Maine Woods,* 639–40 and 738–39.

THE WAY THEY SAW US:
OUTSIDERS' VIEWS OF THE MADAWASKA SETTLEMENT

The Madawaska Settlement in 1790

This account of a 1790 trip to the St. John River by Park Holland, surveyor of the Bingham Purchase, is the earliest we have located.

> We go 300 rods on the 138th mile and strike the St. John's River running westerly. This was a joyful time for us, as we were now entirely out of provisions, and had been out of bread for several days. We move down river, expecting to find some inhabitants, soon come to a hay stack, which raises our hopes of once more seeing a human creature. It rains, and we must camp and go supperless. Next morning we go on two miles and find a French family on the opposite side of the river, who came after us in a canoe and inform us it is 11 miles to the village. The Frenchman had on the fire, when we entered his house, a pot of hulled wheat, to which he made us welcome, telling us to eat all we wished, which was no trifle, as he found, and it proved a good substitute for bread, which we had not seen for more than a week. This old man had followed hunting all his days. Early in life he had hunted with the St. François Indian, some where in the vicinity of Lake Memphremagog, had married a squaw of that tribe, and moved on to the St. John's River, where we found him, sometimes before the French settled at Madawaska. He had two sons grown to manhood, one as white as anybody, the other pure Indian. In the afternoon, Mr. Lequires took us in his boat, to go to the village, but the wind began to blow, accompanied by rain, hail and snow, and after going two or three miles, we halted for the night, where there was a small grist-mill, a temporary thing, built of logs, and covered with bark, which answered the purpose of dwelling house and mill. Here we supped and lodged, and procured 150 lbs of flour which was manufactured in the course of the night. We proceeded next morning to the village to get our flour manufactured into bread.
>
> Oct. 1st. At the village of Madawaska, which is very pleasantly situated on intervale land, on the St. John's River, high enough to be out of reach of the freshets, which here rise sometimes to a great height. The Madawaska River empties into the St. John's, not far from the village, which was settled by the French at the close of the Revolution. The British gave their American soldiers land upon the St. John's, where these people had settled, 60 or 70 families in number, and who, in their anger, moved up river, determined to have no communications with them. They appear happy and contented, though they begin to suffer for the want of edge tools, etc. They have never used any salt since they came here. They have a church and priest, cattle, horses, sheep and hogs, raise wheat, oats, barley and peas, and flax, and tobacco, which, though of a poor quality, answers for smoking, make their own cloth, etc. Their houses are built of logs, and those we entered were neat and in order. They make their meat into soup, to which they add onions and garlic, which grow wild upon the bank of the river. They are very kind and hospitable. We scarcely entered a house, that they did not ask us to take soup with them. We met among them a Mr. Everett formerly from New Hampshire, who was a hunter, and who had been here three or four years. He was of great service to us as interpreter, and gave us a small yellow dog, which, with our provisions, the second day after our arrival, we took on our journey up river, passed the night with the Frenchman at the mill who gave us a half peck of hulled wheat to use instead of rice in broth and pushed on our unknown and dreary way.

Source: Park Holland, "Life and Diary" (unpublished manuscript, 1790), transcript at Bangor Public Library (Bangor, Maine).

Crop Failures

Conditions on the upper St. John occasionally attracted the attention of people outside the region. The Shediac newspaper informed its readers the crops had failed at Madawaska in 1829.

> The present unfortunate condition of the Madawaska settlement excites our sincerest sympathy. We hope the causes of the evil will in the future be prevented, and that the exertions which are making for

the immediate relief of the distressed inhabitants will be successful. Meantime the following statement (from a correspondent of the *Colonist*) cannot fail to be read with much concern:

The public generally are not acquainted, that unparalleled distress now exists in the French settlement of Madawaska, occasioned by the failure of the two last years, of the wheat crop. The circumstances of being wedded to ancient notion, is strongly perceptible in the habits of all the settlers of Canadian origin. Wheat has been the standard of food with these people from time immemorial, and they have never attempted to raise oats or any other kind of grain for subsistence, excepting small quantities of pease and barley, for their own indispensable soups. The consequence of this unyielding system of cropping is deplorably felt after a succession of bad seasons for the wheat; and it is now experienced in a lamentable degree, among the settlers in that district who have lately come from Lower Canada. A petition from that settlement was presented to his honour the President[1] a short time ago, stating that unless relief were soon afforded, many families must perish. With that humane consideration which so eminently distinguishes the personage who now directs the government, and with the same prompt and bland attention which is extended to all who have business to transact with him, arrangements were instantly made for the rendering of such assistance as the exigencies of the case might seem imperiously to require, under the superintendence and disposition of the Commissioner of Crown land, who was proceeding to the neighbourhood in the execution of his duty, and volunteered his services on so charitable an errand. That gentleman accordingly proceeded to the spot, and a scene of unspeakable misery was presented to his view, in the humble habitations of upward of seventy families. A meeting of the principle persons in the settlement took place in the presence of Mr. Baillie and four gentlemen were appointed a committee to visit the sufferers, and to report their numbers and particular situations. Two hundred bushels of Indian Corn were then purchased at Woodstock, and immediately placed at the disposal of the committee, for the purpose of present relief.

Many families have for some time existed on the flour made from blighted wheat, kneaded into bread with the inner bark of the white birch. Berries and roots, procured from the forest, have been the sole dependence of others; and the prospect of procuring even such a miserable fare was obscured by rapidly increasing weakness. In one house which Mr. Baillie visited, there were sixteen children, five of whom were unable to walk from the united causes of untended infancy and pinching debility.

Source: *Gleaner and Northumberland Schediasma,* July 28, 1829.

When French Canadians Were Desirable Immigrants

After various land agents reported on the Madawaska settlement, newspapers started commenting on the region, its potential and its inhabitants. This is part of an article on the construction of the Aroostook Road, which had been completed from the heads of the Penobscot and Aroostook rivers. It was continued to Madawaska (a distance of 60 miles) the following year.

It will be seen, that this avenue opens to the tide of emigration, a vast and partially explored region capable of sustaining a dense population. There can be no better barrier along our frontier than a numerous and hardy population, ready to repeal invasions and capable of co-operating with regular troops. The British well understands this, and have within a few years totally changed their policy in regard to Crown land. Settlers in the upper parishes of New Brunswick, are now totally exempt from taxation; and the government pays to every man a bounty of twenty cents for each bushel of wheat, and 15 cents for every bushel of barley and 12 cents a bushel, for all the corn he may raise. Our government ought to encourage emigration to our sides of the lines. A gift of their lands and other favors to the French settlers at Madawaska would unquestionably induce many Canadian French to emigrate into that vicinity.

Source: The *Republican Journal,* September 22, 1831. (Reprinted from the *Bangor Republican.*) The *Republican Journal,* from Belfast, Maine, was Democrat, despite its name.

And Acadians Were Embraced by Maine

This description predates Longfellow's *Evangeline* by eighteen years, but displays the same feelings towards the Acadians as the poem.

About the close of the American Revolution, they [the Madawaska French] were discovered by their old enemy, the English, and their lands were granted by the British Crown to a band of American refugees. The poor Arcadians [*sic*], driven, once more from their homes and reduced to beggary, plunged again into the wilderness, a hundred and seventy miles from Fredericton, and occupied their present position, which they, knowing the terms of our treaty with Great Britain and being familiar with the geography of the country, considered as without the bounds of English jurisdiction. Here, after the lapse of half a century, they feel anew the rod of the oppressor. They are a frugal, industrious, pious, and amiable people, among whom vice, immorality, crime, and contention are unknown. They are governed by the simple principles of natural justice, settling their affairs without the aid of the civil code of courts or of lawyers. How unfortunate that they are disturbed by the footsteps of modern civilization.

Source: The *Republican Journal,* December 1, 1831.

A New Brunswick View

In 1838, Peter Fisher, the first historian of New Brunswick, published an anonymous description of the province which contains an extensive description of the Madawaska territory.

Commencing at the Canada line the first settlement of any extent is the Madawaska. There are however a few settlers scattered along the banks of the river above this place, as far up as the river Saint Francis which falls into the St. John about thirty miles above this settlement. From the Saint Francis downward to the Meruimticook there are a number of beautiful islands scattered along the St. John, and the banks of the river as well as the adjoining country are well stored with pines of the loftiest growth; a stream called Fish River falls into the St. John from the westward, about five miles above the Meruimticook. A road was formerly surveyed by the American government, from the Metawamkeag, a branch of the Penobscot, to the river St. John, which strikes the left bank of the Fish river, a distance of one hundred and twenty miles, but this road has not yet been opened.

At the Meruimticook, which is about 12 miles above the Madawaska River, there is a considerable settlement of American squatters, who have some buildings and mills at this place. It was on a point formed by the junction of the stream at this place with the St. John, that the noted John Baker on the 4th of July 1827, raised the American standard, and took formal possession of the territory for the state of Maine. There are some fine islands along this part of the river, and strips of good intervale, which are settled by the French. At the junction of the Madawaska

River, with the St. John River, the main settlement commences and extends down to near the Great Falls. The Meruimticook River has the Tamisquatta Lake near its head, from which there is a portage of thirty six miles to the Rivière du Loup in Canada. There are few settlers on this lake and along on the portage, it being part of the great road of communication over land from Halifax to Québec.

The main settlement of the French commences near the mouth of the Madawaska River, and extends down the St. John within a few miles of the Great Falls, a distance of nearly 40 miles, the whole distance being well settled on both sides of the river. The face of the country being pretty level, the soil is generally light clay of loam, easily tilled and very productive, some low districts containing large spots of alluvial soil, with fine islands in their neighbourhood. This settlement is well watered; several small rivers fall into the St. John at different points of the settlement; one of which is called Green River, from the colour of its waters, which at the place they mingle with the St. John are of a beautiful pea-green and very clear. Another stream called Grand River about 15 miles above the Grand Falls, rises from the northward, near the head of the Restigouche; a short portage connects the communication between the two rivers. This is the usual route in this part of the country from the river St. John to the bay of Chaleur.

Madawaska is an old flourishing settlement. The inhabitants are mostly all French, many of whom have been settled here over fifty years, and have always considered themselves as British subjects, being warmly attached to that Government. Madawaska is the name originally given to the whole district occupied by the French. It has lately been divided into three sections: the upper section being called Saint Emilie, the middle Saint Basil, and the lower Saint Bruno: the whole however still retaining the general name of Madawaska.

The inhabitants confine themselves principally to agriculture. Their soil is well adapted to the growth of wheat, of which they raise great quantities. It is also productive in oats, peas, barley, etc. and is also well adapted to grazing. The French have no great taste for building and improving, being generally content with the necessaries. Their dwellings consists chiefly of log huts, some of which are very large, being comprised of two buildings joined together. Within a few years some of them have begun to imitate the English in constructing frame houses, which is making a great improvement in the face of the country. They are a peaceable, contented people, and in possession of all the substantial comforts of life. Being all of the Romish [Roman Catholic] church, they have three chapels for divine service in the settlement: the oldest and principal chapel, which may be called the mother Church, is situated in the upper part of the middle district, and is a substantial spacious building with a bell, etc.... Here the Divine Service is duly and regularly performed according to the rites of the Catholic religion by a missionary from Canada, who resides near the chapel; and, in addition to his spiritual duties, also contributes much of his influence and exertions to the quiet and good order of the settlement. Indeed so successful have been the exertions of those missionaries in keeping the settler in peace and harmony, that till within a few years, there were no magistrates in the whole district. Of late years, however, a number of different traders and other strangers having settled in different parts of the settlement, [and so] a few magistrates have been appointed.

The French in their manners are very lively and hospitable. Most of their clothing is made by their women, and consists of coarse cloth, kersey and linen. They procure salt and other European goods from Canada and Fredericton. The French women are usually very stout and short, and slovenly housekeepers. The population of Madawaska is upwards of 3 000 souls.

Source: (Peter Fisher,) *Notitia of New Brunswick*, 96–97.

Emerging Stereotypes

After 1842, American descriptions of the Madawaska settlements became less positive. The difference in attitude is noticeable when one compares this *Republican Journal* article with the ones published ten years previously. In this piece, the poor Acadians are beginning to turn into primitive peasants. The *Journal* relied on information obtained from the Commissioners appointed to adjust and determine the land titles of the inhabitants; the author of the article had not traveled to Madawaska.

Between the Fish River and the St. Francis, about one third of the lots are occupied by a mixture of English, Scotch, Irish, Americans, and Frenchmen. Above the St. Francis there is but one settlement, and that consisting of only three or four families at the mouth of the Allagash. Below Fish River and to the East line of the state, all the lots are believed to be improved, and with the exception of perhaps 20,

they all have houses built upon them. The inhabitants here are all of French extraction. The settlements are confined entirely to the river lots, the back lots not as yet being thought of any value. When the lots are subdivided, it is always lengthwise, so as to preserve a river front to each part. In one instance, the commissioners found a family had subdivided in this way, into five parts, a lot in which the whole had a front of only 25 rods. The average front of the lot is about 60 rods, and they extend back from a mile to a mile and a half.

It results from these statements, that the whole distance upon the St. John from the Fish River to the east line of the state, is continuously and compactly settled. The number of families must be about 250, and it is quite certain the population exceeds considerably the amount returned in the census of 1840. The families are large. One with less than ten or twelve children is thought to be small. The commissioners saw two women, sisters, one of whom had born sixteen and the other seventeen children. Such instances are common.

The religion of the people is Roman Catholic. There are two chapels with officiating priests: one 8 miles below the mouth of the Fish River, and the other twelve miles of the St. John from the east line of the state. The only medical assistance obtained is from a physician who resides on the British side of the river. There is no public instruction, although there are two school masters employed by certain families. Very few of the people speak anything but the French language, and very few can either read or write.

The people live chiefly by agriculture. A few of them engage in lumbering. They hunt but little. They however employ themselves considerably in fishing, particularly in the Fish River Lake. Their husbandry is rude; their implements poor; and their breeds of cattle, sheep, and hogs of the worst description. Their chief crops are wheat, barley, oats, potatoes, and grass. Their grain crops generally come to maturity. They do not attempt to raise Indian corn. Their wood is of a tolerable quality, the growth being in some cases hard wood, but generally mixed. They have but few meadow intervals and those generally small. Their houses are most frequently built of hewn timber: sometimes of logs, and sometimes they are shingled or clapboarded. They are warm and comfortable. There are a few gristmills, of an inferior description. They buy and sell but little, producing nearly everything they consume, and hardly anything more. Their trade, such as it is, is with Fredericton and Québec, principally with the latter place.

Amid all the apparent hardship of their condition, they exhibit a vivacity, cheerfulness and buoyancy: characteristics of the nation from which they sprung. Their winters are devoted almost entirely to amusements, of which the most favorite are horse racing and dancing. A house is thought little of, which does not have any room large enough to accommodate a dancing party. Possessing in abundance all the necessaries, and according to their standard, all the comforts of life, and enjoying good health, they are content with the present and careless of the future. They ordinarily attain old age.

Knowing nothing of our government and laws, they are quite indifferent to the recent changes in their political conditions. If not treated as well as under the late New Brunswick rulers, they have only, as they say, to pass to the other side of the St. John. It will be a long time before they accustom themselves to the machinery of our institutions and a longer time before their distinct nationality is effaced or lost.

Such is a brief picture of the conditions of this remnant of those unfortunate Acadians whose cruel expulsion from their ancient homes in Nova Scotia has been immortalized by the pathetic eloquence of Bancroft. May they receive from us that kindness and protection, which are due to their own simple virtues, and to the misfortunes of their ancestors.

Source: The *Republican Journal,* "The Settlement on the St. John," December 29, 1843.

A French-Canadian View of the Settlement

The Canadians believed that the part of the former disputed territory west of the Madawaska River was going to be incorporated into their province; consequently, they sent their own land agents to investigate and describe the region. Although contemporary, M. Bureau's image of the area was different from the one of the *Republican Journal.*

The Madawaska River, into which flow the waters of Lake Témiscouata, is a pretty river, two to three rods wide and navigable by horse boats (*chalands*) and canoes only at this time of year, but could be used by larger vessels with the help of three or four locks. The view is particularly pleasant at the place where settlement on this river begins because the first farms are well cleared and make it possible to see well constructed buildings. The river offers beautiful points

on which lots of hay is made. The mountains are at a reasonable distance from the river, and although high, they are sought by the farmers who find them easy to clear and very productive. The inhabitants of this place are usually comfortable and live well. Houses are generally built on the shore or near the road that travels to the west of the river and reaches the Petit Sault before crossing the St. John River. Although the eastern section is well settled, a road has yet to be opened in this part, and when people have to travel, they must cross the river or take their trip by canoe....

Several mills can be found on the Iroquois River, such as grist, saw, carding, and fulling mills. The inhabitants are almost all French-Canadians, except for a few Irish whose names can be found in my diary. There are two villages taking shape at the Petit Sault, one to the east and one to the west of the river. At the moment, the one to the east is more important; there is there a military establishment, a block house, and other dependencies erected on a high rock and which command a wide view of the St. John River. The Petit Sault is a pretty place, where considerable business is conducted. The islands on the river have all been cleared and great quantities of hay are made there. There are good points of land on the river and farmers know how to take advantage of them. There are 179 settled lots between the Madawaska and St. Francis River, in addition to others not yet taken; those lots are all occupied by Canadians and Acadians. They were surveyed by the New Brunswick surveyors.

Bureau continued describing the river above the Petit Sault. He noted the existence of a gristmill and sawmill on an unidentified river, and a chapel under construction nine miles east of the St. Francis River. The "Rivière à la Tortue," fifteen miles above the Petit Sault, was fed by important lakes, and lots of ton timber and saw logs were cut on it. Finally, he noted that a grist and sawmill belonging to Mr. John Baker, who had there "a beautiful establishment" could be found near the mouth of the Meruimticook.

Source: LAC, Report of J-Bte Bureau, to D. B.Papineau, commis des terres de la couronne, following instructions received 7/2/1846, 12 Avril 1847. *Papers Relatives to the Settlement of the Disputed Boundaries between the Provinces of Canada and New Brunswick, Presented to Both Houses of Parliament by Command of her Majesty* (London: William Clover and Sons, 1851), 18. (Report in French; translation by the authors.)

A Not-So-Sympathetic British View of Acadian History

Not everybody believed the Acadians had been passive victims of the Seven Year War. This gentleman clearly remembered the "French and Indian War."

> Between the Grand and Little Falls are the Acadian settlements, established here in 1783, the settlers amount to upwards of 3,000; they live in small wooden houses scattered along the banks of the St John's. I observed also a small cluster on the left bank of the river. The Acadians are the descendents of those early French settlers, who, in conjunction with the Indians, were continually burning and laying waste the English settlements on the lower St. John's and who, when the English got the mastery, were removed to a safer distance. Those about the Madawaska being more shut out from the world than their French Canadian brethrens on the St. Lawrence seem to be less intelligent and industrious. When the North eastern boundary was finally settled by the Ashburton treaty, half of the Madawaska settlers, or those on the right banks of the St. John's, necessarily became American citizens. It will be a curious subject to enquire a few years hence, what has been the effect of this transfer.

Source: Alexander, *L'Acadie, or Seven Years' Exploration in British North America*, vol. II, 67.

A Definitively Unsympathetic and Greatly Inaccurate Depiction of the Settlement

Edward Elwell's *Aroostook* includes an account of a trip taken by Maine journalists in 1858, at the instigation of state officials, in order to make Aroostook County better known and to encourage settlement. Additional comments written at the time of publication (1878) are included at the end of this text. Elwell was poorly informed and prompt to repeat old stereotypes about immigrants, Catholics, and Canadians. His characterization does not stand confrontation with facts.

> About twenty miles north of Fort Fairfield are the famous Madawaska settlements, where the descendants of the ancient Acadians preserve in all their primitive simplicity, the manners and customs of their French ancestors. Like their kindred of Canada, they cling to the river bank, each farm having its river front and extending in a long narrow line to the forest. They are light hearted, improvident, unenterprising people, more fond of the fiddle than the hoe, and content to remain stationary while all around is pro-

gressing. Knowing nothing of our political institutions, they readily sell their votes to politicians, and he who bids highest carries the day.

Elwell next quotes an article in the *Maine Evangelist* that describes the Madawaska settlers as the "Evangeline People," before continuing:

> On the banks of the St. John they settled with all the habits and tastes which their fathers brought from France. Those habit—the habits of the peasantry of France—they still retain, having made scarcely an advance step in civilization, since the days of Louis XIV.

> The French settlers upon the Western and Southern Banks of the St. John were declared citizens of the US by the treaty of 1842, and by the same instrument the title to the land on which they were settled was confirmed to them. Although they have increased from a population of about five hundred to as many thousands, yet they have not gone back from the river. Instead of imitating the enterprise of the Yankee pioneer, by plunging into the forests and clearing new farms, each succeeding generation has divided the land patrimony of their fathers among the children, until nearly every farm has a river front of but a few rods. They are generally ignorant and unambitious, each generation contenting themselves with simply existing. They subsist chiefly on pea soup and other vegetable foods which is raised on their patch of land. A gentleman who visited them a few years since, informed us that he stopped at a small cabin in which there was but one room, where the happy head of the family could call around him twenty-three children. He counted fifteen houses near each other, averaging twelve children to each house. They make large quantities of maple sugar, but in general content themselves with the simple fare of their fathers. The state has made several attempts to educate and civilize them, and in some instance with good results. They are, however, a peculiar people, distinct in taste, habits, and aspirations from the Anglo-Saxon race.

Twenty years later (September 1878). Elwell refers to a Mr. Jones, who has found one great advantage in the cheap labor of the Acadian French.

> The road just beyond him is settled by them away to Violet Brook, a distance of twenty two miles. They live in small, untidy looking houses, two to a lot and two families in every house. And children- they have no end of them. A stranger riding one day exclaimed: In the name of goodness, are these all school houses? We counted one, two, three, four, five, six, seven,

eight little girls all playing in front of one house. Their fecundity and lack of thrift keeps them poor, though some have tolerable farms. They hire out for low wages. Every morning in planting, haying, or harvest time, numbers of them drive past Mr. Jones's door and ask for work. He sends them into the fields, gives them 75 cents a day, and pays in buckwheat.

Source: Elwell, *Aroostook.*

And a Sympathetic, But Highly Romanticized One

The narrator and his friend Penman[1] were on a recreational trip in Aroostook County. The story is written in the third person.

The Madawaska

We seem to have been suddenly transported by some wand of enchantment into another country, the smoothness of the fields, the absence of woods, the evidences of long-tilled lands, contrast so strangely with the tangled forests and new clearings only a few miles back. But pause! This fertile and enchanting valley was settled almost a century ago! Here was heard the sound of the loom, the ring of the axe, and the busy hum of labor, when all around was a wilderness.... We are now about to tread the almost classic ground of Acadia—land of a hundred romances. Before us are the golden portals of the Madawaska!...

Could the breath of life be breathed into those who suffered and died, and they in the flesh be transported hither, their faces would kindle with surprise that time had wrought so few changes during their long absence—so perfectly have their descendants retained the peculiarities of former days - their style of dress, mode of cooking, the forms of their houses, the antique-looking wind-mills for threshing grain, the clumsy wains, and rude cabriolets.... The road runs parallel with the river, perhaps half a mile distant, but the houses are for the most part riparian, with projecting roofs, and porticoes overlooking the smooth lawns that slope to the margin, and outdoor seats, where now, as in the olden time, gossiping looms are heard " mingling the noise of their shuttles with the whir of the wheels." Here the family sits at evening and receive the calls of their neighbors who come in boats; for the river is the thoroughfare most used by the Acadians in their daily intercourse with each other. The interval between it and the road is a continuous line of pastures and cultivated fields....

The neatly white-washed house to whose door they drove promised substantial comforts for tired and hungry travelers; and confident of a hearty welcome, they mounted the steps and knocked. Presently the door was opened by an impassive little Frenchman with a melancholy face and dark-blue homespun trowsers, who received them with a quiet recognition, and, with a step as cat-like as an undertaker at a funeral, ushered them into the presence of a pensive-looking Madame in plaited hair and blue woolen petticoat, and a group of reserved and thoughtful children in blue....

The house itself was built of squared logs, a single story high, and divided into two apartments, perhaps twenty feet square. From his wooden-bottomed seat, then, Penman thoughtfully contemplated the huge Canadian stove, six feet high, that stood in the partition wall, so as to warm both rooms alike, and calculated the number of cords of wood that would be required to feed the monster during a six months winter, and its cost at New York market prices. Then he looked at the loom and the spinning-wheel, and thought of Longfellow's *Evangeline.*

Source: Hallock, "Aroostook and the Madawaska," 695–96.

Note 1: President of the Executive Council, who replaced the lieutenant-governor in his absence.

Appendix N

THE AUDIBERT LETTERS

Letters sent to Joseph Audibert by his parents-in-law, Chrisostome "Thomas" Martin and Marie- Luce Cyr, while he was residing in Portland. (Original texts in French; translation by the authors.)

Ste. Luce, Madawaska, July 25, 1852

Dear children,

I received your affectionate letter dated from the 11th current, which caused us, as you can expect, the greatest pleasure in learning that you were all in perfect health. I told myself the Lord deign answer our prayers. I bless him and would bless him even more if he deigned make our wishes come true and bring you back among us.

Dear children, I do not doubt that you are missing us, but do not doubt either that we are grieving to be separated from you. Your mother especially is extremely lonesome but nonetheless one must trust the Providence concerning the time of your return. If I was not afraid to cause you trouble I would ask you for a remedy to quiet our lonesomeness. But I have the happiness of prosterity at heart and leave the whole thing to the Divine Providence.

If you decided to follow your wife's advice and come back here, write to me, and I will do my best to get a double cart to go and meet you at Mr. Jackson's.

Marguerite[1] must let me know in the next letter whether I should send her wool through Mr. Jackson if he comes, or whether I should turn it into homespun or flannel. I have some shoes made for the children; I would like to know whether I will have the happiness to give them to them in person or whether I should send them.

I have a lot of news to convey to you. I will start with the crops, which look good. It hailed here on the 17th and lots of windows were broken, but thanks be to God, caused little damage to the grain. Hilarion Daigle has married his boy on the 20th of the current month to one of the girls of Lairiche Cyr.[2] Eloi Pelletier marries his Théodore on the 27th of this month with the daughter of Francois Daigle.[3] We are all invited, and so are you.

I intend to do a bit of timbering. If the land agent is near you, can you find out whether I could get a permit and how I should go about getting permission. You will tell me all that in your next letter.

Modeste[4] had a big girl who is worth two, and she lets you know that if you have forgotten her, she has not forgotten you, and she gave her little girl the name of Marguerite.

Suzanne[5] lost her little one on the 10th last, and she is determined to double up in the future, and Modeste wants to get three times as many as you.

It pains me to inform you that Desir[6] is determined to leave for the Illinois country with his brother-in-law if he can sell his land. This is another source of grief.

Statutory labour has started on the roads all the way to St. François; from the Fish River Chapel, they have done for $750 worth of work. I will start cutting your hay at the beginning of next month.

School begins at my place Monday the 26th of the current month, and the teacher is Mr. Jacques Hamel and he sends you his regards, as well as his wife, and they pray you present their greetings to Marguerite and Sara[7] and kiss the children for them.

Nothing more. Running out of space.

Your mother, your brothers and sisters, and the entire family and all your friends join us to kiss you.

Hug for me, my dear Joseph L. and Betsy M.[8] Farewell.

Ste Luce, Madawaska, August 7, 1852

Dear children,

I recently received two of your letters, one dated from the 18th and the other from the 25th of July last, and it caused all of us the greatest pleasure to hear that you were all in perfect health. As for us we are enjoying a perfect health, thanks be to God, and let it please the Lord that this one will find you in perfect health as it leaves us.

You are telling me through your letter that Marguerite and Sara are very lonesome, and if they continue to be lonesome you will be obliged to come. Your return among us is our greatest desire. As for the deed and other papers that the two of us had, I still have them. You would have with me the same advantages that you enjoyed when you left if you come back, and I would even do all that is in my power to make room for you; you would have a horse at your disposal until little Joseph's colt is able to serve you.

You are probably desirous to hear the news from this place, and this is what I am going to tell you. I will inform you that Firmin Crock's little girl drowned at the age of four about two weeks ago. Here is a really bad piece of news, of course, but among the bad ones that can sadden you there are others that could rejoice you, like learning that your father went to a wedding last week at Joseph Daigle's with me, and he put into his head to dance with Dominique Daigle, Goodman Caron,[9] Goodman Mimiche and Goodman Le Naigre and her majesty the queen [Reine, which in French means queen], the wife of Christophe Marquis and Goodwife Caron. I cannot tell you what kind of dance it was, but all I can say is that it resembled the puppet dance a lot. Your father and the queen were dancing very well and played the role of Punch very well. Goodman Mimiche and Goodwife Caron played the ones of partner Peter and his wife; Goodman Le Naigre, the one of the devil; and Dominique Daigle, the one of Pulchinella, and you would have though that any moment they were going to fall into pieces, but they came out of there in one piece as they got into, and I can assure you that they had more luck than the floorboards because splinters were flying all over the place.

Ferdinand and Modeste are in good health and greet you and let you know they are still suffering from fièvre bourbonnaises,[10] and they are intending to go there, and they have vowed to go though [unreadable] and they ask for your advice on the subject.

Your father has started haying this week, and he must come back tonight from upriver and he had repeatedly told me to inform you how much you [unreadable] above mentioned, and there is nothing he wishes more in the world than your return and your prosperity. Oh, he misses all of you so much, as well as his dear Joseph and the little girl.

Eléonore[11] is attending school and learning Latin and reading and soon she will learn to write, and then she says that she will be in a position to offer her lips to whomever wants to kiss them, but not for nothing, because she says that goods as rare as she should not be given away.

Nothing has changed with Mrs. Michaud and she joins us in greeting you as well as Romain and his family.[12]

Nothing more to add.
I remain for life your affectionate mother
Marie-Luce Martin

Your father has arrived on time to add a word. He is upbraiding you and says that if your wife and Sara are lonesome, it is because you do not show them the sights, and at the same time it seems the place is not as good because here the crow still has its wings, and it has lost them in your place.

Sir,
With Mrs. Martin's permission, I humbly take the liberty to drop you a line to greet you, and my wife and my family join me to offer their salutations as well as to your wife and to Sara.
I have the Honor of being
Sir,
Your humble servant
Jacques Hamel

Dear children, I was happy to learn that you had some relatives in Quebec City. I would like to know the name and the occupation of your sisters' husbands. Perhaps M. Hamel knows them and how you have learned those peculiarities.
In the meantime,
I remain for life your affectionate father
Thomas Martin

Letters from his sisters and brother-in-law:

Quebec City, December 24, 1852
Dear brother,
This is the third time that we write to you without your receiving our letters. According to the story in your last, we at least have the pleasure of getting news about you, and we hope that the [unreadable] third of ours as we have taken all possible precaution to this effect, we hope that if you receive it you will not wait too long to answer it. We all enjoy a perfect health, thanked be the Lord, and wish that this letter reaches you and finds you, as well as your wife and your little family, in equally good health. Our husbands join us to assure you of our most tender friendship.
We are for life your three sisters,
Charlotte
Marie   Audibert dit Lajeunesse
Elizabeth

Quebec City, October 29, 1854
Dear brother and sister,
We take our pen in hand with pleasure to let you know about us. We are doing very well, thanks be to God, and hope that this letter will reach you and find you in good health.
We have not been in a hurry to write to you since we have been back to Quebec City, for the reason that we

often had the opportunity to send you some news about us and to receive some from you through people from your area that we had the pleasure to see in Quebec.

We must tell you that we have been very lonesome since we have been back in Quebec, and our spirits are among you and we wish we could have stayed a few more days.

We are nonetheless satisfied with our nice trip to your place, having seen there your fine situation and the means you have to raise your family comfortably, having finally seen personally that you both deserve the respect and friendship of all those who know you in your place.

We pride ourselves on being able to say in truth that you are both endowed with the required qualities to prosper and attract on you and your family happiness and contentment.

So we are comforted and full of joy every time that we think of you. As God has meant for us to live so far apart from each other, we satisfy ourselves to write as often as we can so that nothing strange ever happens in our families without our knowing it or letting it know. As for the rest, we will each other have to trust the Divine Providence.

We do not have anything new to add. We will close by asking you to present our most tender respects to Mr. and Mrs. Martin, the respectable old people, and assure them that we remain for life their devoted and obedient friends. Similarly, present our greetings to Mr. Registe and his lady and to Miss Sara Martin as well to Mr. Nadeau and his lady and to all our Madawaska friends whom we met at your place.

Our husbands are joining us to send you our greatest respect and friendship for life from your three sisters.

Charlotte
Marie   Audibert dit Lajeunesse
Elizabeth

20 October 1854

Sir,

Please inform Mr. Martin Sr. that flour is currently selling for 9 dollars a quart. One is under the impression that the price is going to go down in a few days; also please let me know whether Mr. Nadeau is satisfied with the goods I sent him on your order. I would like to know whether the stuff [in English in the letter; it is a kind of fabric] was wide enough for what Mr. Nadeau intended to do with it.

The lathe Mr. Blouin [another brother-in-law] had told you about is ready; we are waiting for the first good opportunity to send it to Rivière du Loup, and as soon as the lathe will be on board to be brought down to Rivière du Loup, I will let you know, and I will send it to Mr. George Pelletier, merchant.

I remain your affectionate servant,
Charles Beaupré

Notes:
1. Marguerite Cyr, daughter of Thomas and Joseph Audibert's wife.
2. Régis, born in 1831, married Anastasie Cyr, born 1831 as well, daughter of Hilaire Cyr and Judith Lizotte on July 13, 1852.
3. Théodore, son of Eloi and Anastasie Nadeau, born 1829, married Marguerite Daigle, daughter of Joseph and Suzanne Martin, on July 27, 1852.
4. Modeste Martin, born 1825, married Ferdinand Albert February 9, 1847 (à Joseph and Séveriste Lagassé). Little Marguerite, born July 11, 1852, was her fourth child. Ferdinand and Modeste are last mentioned in the parish register in November 1857; they are not in the 1860 or 1861 census.
5. Suzanne Nadeau, daughter of David and Théotiste Daigle, married Désiré Martin on August 12, 1851. The little one was Josephat, born on June 16, 1852, who died on July 11, 1852. Suzanne had another child, a daughter, ten months later on April 24, 1853.
6. Désiré Martin, born on September 11, 1827; he and Suzanne are last mentioned in the parish register in October 1858. Thomas Martin, Jr., (born 1818) and married to Marie-Cédille Albert, similarly disappear after the birth of his son Régis on June 26, 1857. He is not in the 1860–61 censuses.
7. Sara (Marie-Sara) Martin, was born September 13, 1829; she married Isidore Daigle, son of François and Barbe Cyr, on November 6, 1855.
8. Joseph L. and Betsy M. were Joseph Audibert and Marguerite Cyr's children.
9. Probably François Hubert Caron, married to Théotiste Dubé, who lived in St. Francis, dying in 1854 at age sixty-eight.
10. Bourbonnais, in Illinois, could still boast an identifiable population of French Canadian origins between the two World Wars. Langellier, *Tickling the Past...*, 33-37. The Bourbonnais French were farmers, like K. Langellier's grandparents.
11. Eléonore Martin, was born on January 22, 1832; she married Michel Daigle on January 25, 1853.
12. Romain Michaud, a.k.a Bénoni, son of Joseph and Marie-Anne Albert, married Flavie Martin, daughter of Thomas and Marie-Luce, on October 19, 1840. Flavie died on September 28, 1852, of unknown causes. Marie-Anne Albert died in 1858, at eighty-seven.

ECCLESIASTICAL PATRONAGE

In New Brunswick

Letter from Mgr. Langevin to Harvey, lieutenant governor of New Brunswick, November 7, 1838. (The letter was written in French and has been translated by the authors.)

Sir John Caldwell had just brought Mgr Langevin, the local priest, a letter from the lieutenant governor. Langevin's reply begins with a discussion of the Madawaska settlers' logging activities:

The inhabitants have always been under the impression they could cut the lumber needed for the construction and repairs of their houses and outbuildings on their land, and even beyond. The government has never seemed hostile to the practice, without which it would have been impossible to settle the district

Sir John Caldwell wanted to prohibit the floating of saw logs down rivers, at the same time as he would have been given permission to buy logs from the settlers for his mill. Langevin, did not want the lieutenant governor to allow this:

As for the saw logs [in English in the letter] your Excellency refers to in his letter, I would say, like most of my parishioners, that if the inhabitants are restricted to sell locally the saw logs they cut without being able to take them to town, that it will be of no benefit to them, but to the advantage of Sir John Caldwell, who is the only one at Madawaska in a position to buy them and will pay the price he chooses; and I can assure you that only the poorest who are forced by hunger will contract to cut saw logs for Sir John, as some have already done, and that this will complete their ruin.

As for me, I declare very frankly to your Excellency that if the Madawaska inhabitants cannot have the privilege of floating their saw logs and their ton timber to town to get the best profit possible from them, and thereby secure necessities for their families, I repeat that I cannot take care of this affair any more, because I would earn the hostility of the right-thinking people of my parish, who would think I am conspiring with Sir John Caldwell to prevent them from taking their wood further than the Grand Falls.

I will also beg your Excellency to allow me to remind him that at the evening I had the honor of spending with him, we discussed wood, but only ton timber; saw logs never entered the conversation.

Your Excellency told me then that he would take it upon himself to give the poor people from this place permission to cut a small specified amount of ton timber, permission granted to each head of household who had deserved the privilege by abstaining to cut wood for sale in 1837, on account of your Excellency's prohibition.

We then discussed the quantity, which could be 80 to 100 ton each, that would constitute a small raft that a father and his son or his hired man could take to town to bring back objects they absolutely need for their houses such as window panes, nails, etc... because it is only with wood that people from here can earn a bit of money to get those things.

Source: PANB, MG9 A2 Vol., 7

In Maine

The Canadian Henri Dionne was parish priest at Ste. Luce from 1841 to 1860. Like Mrg. Langevin, he acted as a representative of his community and sought to secure appropriations and favor for his parishioners by appealing to well-placed men. (The letters were written in French and have been translated by the authors.)

Ste. Luce of Madawaska, February 4, 1853
Dear and Honored Sir,[1]
I include in this letter a recommendation for our president;[2] this is but a poor way of expressing my gratitude to you. If I can do more, I am always ready to do so at any time.

I was greatly honored and pleased to be the recipient of your favor; but I am sill profoundly sad you are no longer our governor. I would be very happy and would congratulate you warmly if you could obtain the Liverpool post.[3] If I can still ask you for a few favors for us, can you secure an appropriation for an academy? I think that two to three thousand dollars would not be too much to build and support this house. Secondly, a sum of 200 dollars to open a road from the church to the back lots, and this for the convenience of about fifty families currently without a road.

A sum of about six hundred dollars for other roads in the lots between the Old Portage and the first lake, another road from Mr. Durepos' to go to the back lots, and finally a road at Augustin Cyr's or in the vicinity of his place.

All those requests were in the hands of Mr. Jos. Nadeau,[4] but as he is at present at home, and as his child's illness may keep him there for a while, it would be appropriate to have those requests introduced in the House by Mr. Tabor and Mr. Cary. One should not forget to tell Mr. Tabor and Mr. Cary that Mr. Nadeau is a truly honest man, and that all his requests for payments for the Fish River Bridge are fair, honest, and reasonable. Therefore, a sum of at least three hundred dollars would only be justice done to Mr. Nadeau. It is too much for Mr. Nadeau to pay this amount alone. The government is richer than he is.

If Mr. Tabor and Mr. Cary take your advice, as I think they will, they will help Mr. Nadeau as much as they can, and will introduce his request in the House, although he [Mr. Jos. Nadeau] is not there.

I insist particularly on this last request; I find it fair and reasonable. I myself gave 825 dollars to Mr. Nadeau for the work on the bridge, because I saw that he was putting too much of his own money in it.

I beg you, dear sir, to accept my most sincere thanks for all the favors you have bestowed on us, and to believe that, with the highest regards, I am

You most humble and devoted servant and sincere friend

Henri Dionne, missionary priest

Ste. Luce, Madawaska
October 4, 1853

To the most honorable John Hubbard,

I have the honor to reply to your letter, which was received, with the greatest pleasure, only Sunday last. The delay occurred at the Fort Kent Post Office, I think. But even if I had received it earlier, I could not have done anything more for the elections. One must now *remain* silent, or consent to be insulted, abused, and mistreated by those who call themselves Whigs, and who are, in these parts, nothing more than *first rate rascals* without any *manners*. One must not forget to include *among them* Colonel Page, this

officer from the Fort Kent Custom Office. He said that I had written phony letters against his friend Patee,[5] that I was a liar, and that he would drive me out of this place. You can imagine my reply and my fears of the threat of such an insolent character. I do not think there are greater bold-faced impudent liars and calumniators on the face of the earth than this miserable David Page and a few others of his party.

As for Madawaska, I need not tell you that the money obtained by the Whigs and their [unreadable] governor has left our roads in the same shape as we put them last year, thanks to your generous efforts. Therefore, if we have been able to travel on fairly good roads on the American side since last year, we can say we owe this to your generosity and your great and beautiful friendship for us. My good friends and I will be grateful and will never cease to thank you when the opportunity arises. Our schools are in the status quo. We are supporting one near my church for a year thanks to a subscription by eight or ten and an $80 grant from the government for the last session—or rather, we will get the money after we have supported it for a full year. I was told I was its agent, and I act as such, spending my money in the hope of receiving the money voted by the House at the end of the session, at least. You know I got nothing for my academy. There has been no other school in the entire Madawaska district for at least a year, and I do not know why.

Presently, allow me to ask you something. The inhabitants cannot cut saw logs or ton timber without paying a two- to three-dollar tax per ton to speculators like Mr. Cuillis, or to the government, and this on land they have occupied some for eight years, others ten years, and some even fifteen years, and they tell me that they do not have the papers [deeds or grants] from the government, but General Weber and other commissioners who drew the granted lots surveyed and marked their lots some eight years ago. Can we prevent the taking of timber from these lots, if we want to cut it ourselves (that is for those who do not own those lots), and are we obliged to pay the two or three dollars required, and is it possible to get the contracts [deeds] for those lots?

Why do foreigners get better deals than the poor inhabitants?

Some say that Mr. Samson and Mr. Morril[6] made reserves of these lots and that the wood belongs to the inhabitants. Is it true? I do not dare to write to Mr. Morril any more, because he forwarded one of my letters to that effect to Mr. Small last spring, and this letter compromised me with Mr. Weber. This was careless of him. Forgive me all these requests; treat them for what they are worth.

I have the honor to be, dear sir, with the greatest respect, your most humble and obedient servant.

H. Dionne, priest

Sources: Acadian Archives, Letters from Father Dionne to J. Hubbard.

Notes:

1. John Hubbard, a physician from Hallowell and a Democrat, was governor of Maine from 1850 to 1852 and gubernatorial candidate in 1853.
2. The president of the United States.
3. Probably a position as US Consul in Liverpool.
4. State house representative for Fort Kent.
5. Whig from Madawaska who was elected representative in 1854.
6. Lot Morril, a Free Soiler and Prohibitionist, was governor between 1853 and 1855.

BIBLIOGRAPHY

We have limited this bibliography to printed material, with the exception of censuses and census-like material (easily available on microfilms). For readers' convenience, we have also grouped all Maine Public Documents (usually annual reports of various public officers and institutions) together under this heading, instead of listing them by author or title. These documents are bound by year at the Maine State Archives. Miscellaneous individual reports are also located in various libraries throughout the state. Archival documents have been cited in footnotes only when quoted, and are not listed here for the sake of brevity.

CENSUSES AND CENSUS-LIKE MATERIAL

POPULATION

Disputed Territory
1790: *Censuses of Canada, 1665-1871/ Recensements du Canada, 1665-1871. Statistics of Canada/statistiques du Canada.* Vol. IV. Ottawa: L.B.Taylor, 1876: 64-80.
1820: LAC, Mercure Papers, 4th Census of the United States, 1820, photographic reproduction. Microfilm reels C-3109 and 3110; US National Archives, M33, microfilm reel 37.
1830: US Bureau of the Census, 5th Census of the United States, State of Maine, Washington and Penobscot Counties. US National Archives, M19, microfilm reel 47 and 51.
1833: PANB, Papers of the Legislative Assembly Relating to the Settlement of Madawaska, 1834; Report of the Commissioner of Affairs at Madawaska, 1834.
1834: PANB, Journal of the Legislative Assembly of New Brunswick, Appendix, Census of the Province.
1840: US Bureau of the Census, 6th Census of the United States, State of Maine, Aroostook County. US National Archives, M 704, microfilm reel 136.

New Brunswick
Manuscript Schedules:
Microfilms are available on interlibrary loan from the Library and Archives of Canada only.
1851: LAC, Provincial Census of New Brunswick, 1851, County of Victoria, Parishes of St. Francis, Madawaska, St. Basile, and St. Leonard. Microfilm reel C 996. PANB microfilm reel F 1591. Accessible on the LAC web site: http://www.collectionscanada.gc.ca/archivianet/1851/001005-130.01-e.html
1861: LAC, Provincial Census of New Brunswick, 1861, County of Victoria, Parishes of St. Francis, Madawaska, St. Basile, and St. Leonard. Microfilm reels M558 & M559. PANB, microfilm reels F1598 and 1599. Dominion Census of Canada, New Brunswick, Parishes of St. Francis, Madawaska, St. Basile, and St. Leonard, schedules 1 and 2. Microfilm reels C10385 and C10386. PANB, microfilm reel F1584.

Published Tables:
1881: *Census of Canada, 1880-81/ Recensement du Canada, 1880-81.* Four volumes. Ottawa: Printed by Mclean, Roger and Co., 1882-1885.
1891: *Census of Canada, 1890-91/Recensement du Canada, 1890-91.* Four volumes. Ottawa: Printed by S. E. Dawson, 1893–1897.
1901: *Fourth Census of Canada, 1901.* Four volumes. Ottawa: Printed by S. E. Dawson, 1902-1906.
1911: *Fifth Census of Canada, 1911.* Five volumes. Ottawa: Printed by S. E. Dawson, 1912-1915.

United States
Manuscript Schedules:
1850: US Bureau of the Census, 7th Census of the United States, State of Maine, Aroostook County, Hancock, Madawaska, and Van Buren Plantations. US National Archives, M432, microfilm reel 248.
1860: US Bureau of the Census, 8th Census of the United States, State of Maine, Aroostook County, St. Francis, St. John, Glazier Lake (T17R10), Eagle Lake, Wallagrass (T17R7), Fort Kent, Allagash (T16R10), Frenchville, New Canada, T14R11, T12R16, Madawaska, Grand Isle, Van Buren, Letter GR1, Letter LR2, Letter FR1. US National Archives, M653, microfilm reel 434.
1870: US Bureau of the Census, 9th Census of the United States, State of Maine, Aroostook County, St. Francis, St. John, Eagle Lake, Unincorporated territory above St. Francis, Wallagrass (T17R7), Fort Kent, Allagash (T16R10), Dickeyville, New Canada, Madawaska, Grand Isle, Van Buren, Connor, Hamlin, Cyr, T18R10, T17R6. US National Archives, M593, microfilm reel 538.

Published Tables:
1880: United States Census Office. *10th Census,1880, Compendium of the Tenth Census (June 1, 1880).* Washington: Govt. Printing Office, 1885.
1890: United States Census Office. *11th Census, 1890, Abstract of the Eleventh Census.* Washington: Govt. Printing Office, 1896.
1900: United States Census Office.*12th Census, 1900, Abstract of the Twelfth Census.* Washington: Govt. Printing Office, 1904.
1910: United States Bureau of the Census. *Thirteenth Census of the United States taken in the year 1910, Abstract of the Census.* Washington: Govt. Printing office, 1912.

AGRICULTURAL PRODUCTION

Disputed Territory
1799 and 1807: AAQ, Lettres des prêtres missionnaires du Madawaska à l'évêque de Québec, 3 mars 1799; 22 juillet 1799; 15 août 1807.
1830s: PANB, Papers of the Legislative Assembly Relating to the Settlement of Madawaska; Report of the Commissioner of Affairs at Madawaska, 1834.
1832: AAQ, Lettres des prêtres missionnaires, 16 Juillet 1832 (Ste. Luce parish only).
1835: Archives de la Côte-du-Sud et du Collège de Sainte-Anne, Fonds Collège de Sainte-Anne, Fond Abbé Henri Dionne, Cahiers des dimes de l'Abbé Dionne, F100/34/V.
1840–41: AAQ, Lettres des prêtres missionnaires, 16 septembre 1840; 10 juillet 1841.
1842: Fond Abbé Henri Dionne, Cahier de dimes de Sainte Luce, 1842–43, F100/34/XIII.

New Brunswick
1851: PANB, Journal of the Legislative Assembly of New Brunswick, 1852, Appendix 1, Population returns and other statistics, Victoria County: 228–30 (the agricultural schedule was not preserved).
1861: See agricultural schedules of the censuses listed in the population section.
1871: See schedules 4, 5, and 6 of the censuses listed in the population section.
1881–1911: See the agricultural production tables of the censuses listed in the population section.

United States
1850, 1860, and 1870: Maine State Archives, US Census, State of Maine, Agricultural Schedules, microfilmed by the Maine State Archives.
1880–1910: See published tables listed in the population section.

Annual Report of the Land Agent of the State of Maine for the Year ending November 30, 1885. Augusta, ME: Sprague and Son, 1886.

Annual Report of the Secretary of the Maine Board of Agriculture. Augusta, ME: Various printers, 1858 to 1910.

Annual Report of the Superintendent of Common Schools. Augusta, ME: Various printers, 1857 to 1910.

Annual Reports of the Bureau of Industrial and Labor Statistics for the State of Maine. Augusta, ME: Various printers, 1880 to 1914.

Final Report of the Superintendent and Instructor of Schools in Madawaska Settlement for the Year 1844. Senate Report # 9, Twenty-fourth Legislature, 1845.

Maine Department of Agriculture. *Maine Agricultural Statistics: Resources and Opportunities.* Augusta, ME: Kennebec Journal Printing, 1910.

Maine Seed Improvement Association. *Report of the Fifth Annual Meeting of the Maine Dairymen's Association 1902.* Augusta, ME: Kennebec Journal Printing, 1903.

Maine Seed Improvement Association. *Report of the Thirteenth Annual Meeting of the Maine Dairymen's Association 1910.* Augusta, ME: Kennebec Journal Printing, 1911.

Report of the Commission Appointed by the Governor and Council of Maine to Locate and Survey Bridges Across the St. John and St. Francis Rivers, Connecting the United States with the Dominion of Canada. Augusta, ME: Sprague and Son, 1880.

Report of the Commission Appointed to Investigate Alleged Election Frauds in Certain Towns and Plantations in Aroostook County. Augusta, ME: E. F Pillsbury and Co, Printers, 1879.

Report of the Commissioners Appointed under the Resolve of February 21, 1843 to Locate Grants and Determine the Extent of Possessory Claims Under the Late Treaty with Great Britain. n.p, n.d.

Report of the Commissioners on Claims of Settlers on Proprietors' Land in the County of Aroostook in Pursuance of Resolve of February 27, 1873. Augusta, ME, 1874.

Report of the Joint Committee appointed to investigate frauds in the late elections among the French Population in the County of Aroostook. Senate Report #8, Thirty-eighth Legislature, 1858.

Second Annual Report of the Secretary of the Maine Board of Agriculture, 1857. Augusta, ME: Stevens and Sayward, 1858.

Maine State Yearbooks

Maine State Year Book and Annual Register for the Year 1871. Portland, ME: Hoyt, Fogg, and Breed, 1871.

Maine State Year Book and Annual Register for the Year 1873–74. Portland, ME: Hoyt and Fogg, 1873.

Maine State Year Book and Legislative Manual for the Year 1880–81. Portland, ME: Hoyt, Fogg, and Donham, 1880.

Maine Register or State Year Book and Legislative Manual from April 1890 to April 1891. Portland, ME: G. M. Donham, 1890.

Maine Register or State Year Book and Legislative Manual, no 31-June 1900. Portland, ME: G. M. Donham, 1900.

Other

Revised Statutes of the State of Maine, passed Sept.1, 1903 and taking effect Jan. 1, 1904, by authority of the State legislature. Augusta, ME: Kennebec Journal Printing, 1904,

State Chamber of Commerce and Agricultural League. *History of the Land Grant to the European and North American Railway Company of 1868.* Portland, ME: State Chamber of Commerce and Agricultural League Headquarters, 1923.

State of Maine, Department of Agriculture, Bulletin, *Agricultural Census of Maine, by Towns,* 1925. (Maine State Library, A.27.10: Ag396/925 c. 2).

PRINTED SOURCES

CIHM stands for Canadian Institute for Historical Microreproduction, which has microfiched all pre-1900 Canadian publications and publications relating to Canada. The number is the microfiche number. Most Canadian university libraries own the collection. Canadian theses are available on microform from the Library and Archives of Canada.

Acheson, T.W. "New Brunswick Agriculture at the End of the Colonial Era: a Reassessment." In *Farm, Factory, and Fortune: New Studies in the Economic History of the Maritime Provinces,* ed. Kris Inwood, 37–60. Fredericton, N.B.: Acadiensis Press, 1993.

Albert, Abbé Thomas. *Histoire du Madawaska.* Québec: Imprimerie franciscaine missionnaire, 1920.

Albert, Thomas. *Histoire du Madawaska: Entre l'Acadie, le Québec et l'Amérique.* Lasalle, Qc: Éditions Hurtubise, 1982.

Allen, James P. "Franco-Americans in Maine: A Geographical Perspective." *Acadiensis* 4 (1974): 32–66.

_____. "Migration Fields of French Canadian Immigrants to Southern Maine." *Geographical Review* 62 (1972): 366–83.

Andrew, Sheila M. *The Development of Elites in Acadian New Brunswick, 1861–1881.* Montreal and Kingston: McGill-Queen's University Press: 1997.

Angier, Jerry and Herb Cleaver. *Bangor and Aroostook: The Maine Railroad.* Littleton, MA: Flying Yankee, 1986.

Arno, John. *Soil Survey, Aroostook County, Maine, Northeastern Part.* United States Department of Agriculture, Soil Conservation Services, in cooperation with the University of Maine Agricultural Experiment Station, 1964.

Aroostook County Board of Underwriters. *Articles of Association, By-Laws, Rules, Forms, and Tariff of Rates for Aroostook County, Maine.* Boston: Frank Wood, printer, 1900.

Arsenault, Bona. *Histoire et généalogie des Acadiens.* Montreal: Lémeac, 1978.

Atack, Jeremy and Fred Bateman. "Marketable Farm Surpluses: North Eastern and Midwestern United States, 1859 and 1860." *Social Science History* 8 (1984): 371–94.

Avery, Myron H. "The Telos Cut." *Appalachia* (June 1937): 380–95.

Baillie, Thomas. *An Account of the Province of New Brunswick, Including a Description of the Settlement, Institutions, Soil and Climate of that Important Province, with Advice to Emigrants.* London: Printed for J. G. & F. Rivington, 1832. CIHM 21383.

Baird, William Thomas. *Seventy Years of New Brunswick Life: Autobiographical Sketches.* Saint John, N.B.: G. E. Day, 1890. CIHM 02502.

Baron, William R. and David C. Smith. *Growing Season Parameter Reconstruction for New England Using Killing Frost Records, 1697–1947.* University of Maine, Maine Agricultural and Forest Experiment Station, Bulletin 846, Nov. 1996.

Basque, Maurice. *La société Nationale de l'Acadie. Au cœur de la réussite d'un peuple.* Moncton: Éditions de la Francophonie, 2006.

Bastarache, Michel and Andréa Boudreau-Ouellet. "Droits linguistiques et culturels des Acadiens et des Acadiennes de 1713 à nos jours." In *L'Acadie des Maritimes, études thématiques des débuts à nos jours,* ed. Jean Daigle, 385–430. Moncton, N.B.: Chaire d'études acadiennes, 1993.

Beach, Christopher S. "Electrification and Underdevelopment in New Brunswick: The Grand Falls Project, 1896–1930." *Acadiensis* XXIII (Autumn 1993): 60–85.

Bear Nicholas, Andrea and Harald Prins. "The Spirit of the Land, the Native People of Aroostook." In *The County: Land of Promise, a Pictorial History of Aroostook County, Maine,* ed. Anna Fields Mcgrath, 19–38. Norfolk, Va.: The Donning Company, 1989.

Beck. Jane C. "The Giant Beaver: A Prehistoric Memory?" *Ethnohistory* 19 (Spring 1972): 109–22.

Bélanger Violette, Marcella. "Le fait français au Madawaska Américain." Ph.D. thesis. Université Saint-Louis, Edmundston, N.B., 1953.

Belliveau, John Edward. "Sir Albert Smith, the Acadians and New Brunswick Politics, 1852-1883." Société Historique Acadienne, *Cahiers* 8 (1977): 65–79.

Bentley, D.M.R. "Charles G. D. Robert's Use of 'Indian Legend' in Four Poems of the Eighteen Eighties and Nineties." *Canadian Poetry* 51 (2005): 18–38.

Bernard, Antoine. *Histoire de la survivance acadienne.* Montreal: Clercs de Saint-viateurs, 1935.

Bérubé, Adrien. "Thomas Albert et la République du Madawaska." Société historique du Madawaska *Le Brayon* VIII (mars 1980): 10–13.

Bérubé, Benoît. "Le Journal du Madawaska et la crise de la conscription de 1917." *Revue de la Société historique du Madawaska* XVI (janvier-juin 1988): 4–34.

Bits and Pieces of Allagash History. Madawaska Maine: Allagash Historical Society, 1976.

Blais, Christian. "Pérégrinations et conquête du sol (1755–1836). L'implantation acadienne sur la rive nord de la Baie-des-Chaleurs." *Acadiensis* XXXV (Autumn 2005): 3–23.

Blanchard, Raoul. *L'Est du Canada français*. Montreal: Beauchemin, 1935.

Bonnichsen, Robson *et. al.* "The environmental setting for human colonization of northern New England and adjacent Canada in late Pleistocene time." In *Late Pleistocene History of Northeastern New England and Adjacent Quebec*. Geological Society of America, Special Paper 197 (1986): 151–59.

_____. "Paleoindian Sites in the Munsungun lake region, Northern Maine." *Archeology—Current Research* 1 (1984): 3–4.

Borns, H. W. "Changing Models of Deglaciation in Northern New England and Adjacent Canada." In *Late Pleistocene History of Northeastern New England and Adjacent Quebec*. Geological Society of America, Special Paper 197 (1986): 135–38.

Bouchard, Gérard. "Co-intégration et reproduction de la société rurale: Pour un modèle Saguenayen de la marginalité." *Recherches sociographiques* XXIX (1988): 283–310.

_____. "Family Structures and Geographic Mobility at Laterrière, 1851–1935." *Journal of Family History* 2 (Dec. 1977): 350–69.

_____. *Quelques arpents d'Amérique, Population, économie, famille au Saguenay, 1838–1971*. Québec: Boréal Express, 1996.

_____. "Représentants du Madawaska à l'assemblée législative du Nouveau Brunswick 1786-1965." Société Historique Acadienne, *Cahiers* 5 (octobre-décembre, 1973): 26–30.

Bouchard, Gérard et Régis Thibeault. "L'économie agraire et la reproduction sociale dans les campagnes saguenayennes (1852-1871)." *Histoire sociale—Social History* 36 (Nov. 1985): 237–58.

Boucher, Neil J. "L'Eglise, l'État et l'élite du Québec en Acadie néo-écossaise, 1880-1960: réconforter les minorités par un Québec fort." In *Les relations entre le Québec et l'Acadie de la tradition à la modernité*, ed. Fernand Harvey and Gérard Beaulieu, 73–96. Québec, IQRC—Éditions d'Acadie, 2000.

_____. "L'Évangéline de Valentin Landry, 1887–1910: Vivre et mourir pour le bien-être de la nation." In *L'Évangéline, 1887-1982: Entre l'élite et le people*, ed. Gérard Beaulieu, 73-96. Moncton, N.B.: Éditions d'Acadie, 1997.

Bouchette, Joseph. *A Topographical Description of the Province of Lower Canada with Remarks upon Upper Canada, and on the Relative Connexion of Both Provinces with the United States of America*. London: Printed for the author and published by W. Faden, 1815. CIHM 44373.

_____. *The British Dominions in North America, or, A Topographical and Statistical Description of the Provinces of Lower and Upper Canada, New Brunswick, Nova Scotia, the Islands of Newfoundland, Prince Edward, and Cape Breton: including Considerations on Land-Granting and Emigration: to which are Annexed, Statistical Tables and Tables of Distances, etc.* London: H. Colburn and R. Bentley, 1831. CIHM 42806-42808.

Bourque Campbell, Joan. "The Seigneurs of Acadie: History and Genealogy." Société Historique Acadienne, *Cahiers* 25 (octobre-décembre 1994): 285–313; *Cahiers* 26 (janvier-mars 1995): 23-27; *Cahiers* 26 (avril-juin 1995): 99-105; *Cahiers* 26 (octobre-décembre 1995): 173–75.

Bourque, Bruce J. "Ethnicity on the Maritime Peninsula, 1600–1759." *Ethnohistory*, 36 (1989): 257–84.

_____. *Twelve Thousand Years: American Indians in Maine*. Lincoln, NE: University of Nebraska Press, 2001.

Bourque, Bruce J. and Ruth Holmes Whitehead. "Tarrentines and the Introduction of European Trade Goods in the Gulf of Maine." *Ethnohistory* 34 (1985): 327–41.

Boyer, Marc. *L'invention du tourisme*. Paris: Découvertes Gallimard, 1996.

Brassard, Francis. "The Origins of Certain Public Schools in the St. John Valley of Aroostook, Maine." M.A. thesis, University of Ottawa. 1967.

Brault, Gerard J. *The French Canadian Heritage in New England*. Montreal-Kingston, McGill-Queen's University Press, 1986.

Brewer, Iris Field and Joseph Donald Cyr. "Cultivation of the spirit in the Garden of Maine." In *The County: Land of Promise, a Pictorial History of Aroostook County, Maine,* ed. Anna Fields Mcgrath, 75–94. Norfolk, VA: The Donning Company, 1989.

Brewer, John and Roy Porter, eds. *Consumption and the World of Goods*. London: Routledge, 1993.

Brookes, Alan. "Out-Migration from the Maritime Provinces, 1860–1900: Some Preliminary Considerations." *Acadiensis* V (1976): 26-56.

_____. "The Exodus: Migration from the Maritime Provinces to Boston during the Second Half of the Nineteenth

Century." Ph.D. thesis, University of New Brunswick 1979.

Bruchési. Jean. "Rameau de Saint-Père et les Français d'Amérique." *Les cahiers des Dix* 13 (1948): 225–48.

Bruegel, Martin. *Farm, Shop, Landing: The Rise of a Market Society in the Hudson Valley, 1780–1860.* Durham, NC: Duke University Press, 2002.

Brun, Régis Sigefrois. "Histoire socio-démographique du sud-est du Nouveau Brunswick, migrations acadiennes et seigneuries anglaises, 1760–1810." Société Historique Acadienne, *Cahiers* III (janvier-mars 1969): 58–88.

_____. "Le réveil du patriotisme acadien-américain, 1895–1905: la fondation de la société de l'Assomption. " Société Historique Acadienne, *Cahiers* 32 (2001): 40–68.

Brymer, Douglas, *Report on Canadian Archives for 1891.* Ottawa: S. E. Dawson, 1892.

Buckner Phillip A. and John G. Reid. *The Atlantic Region to Confederation: A History.* Toronto: University of Toronto Press, 1994.

Burke, Adrian L. "Témiscouata: Traditional Maliseet Territory and Connections between the St. Lawrence Valley and the St. John River Valley." *Papers of the Algonquian Conference* 32 (2001): 61–73.

_____. *Lithic Procurement and the Ceramic Period Occupation of the Interior of the Maritime Peninsula.* Ph.D. thesis, State University of New York, Albany, 2000.

_____. "Le site CjEd-5, Lieu d'habitation coutumier et lieu de rituel dans le Bas-Saint-Laurent. " *Recherches amérindiennes au Québec* XXXVI (2006): 23–35.

Burque, Rev. F. X. *Major Dickey. Sketch of his Life.* Bangor: Commercial Print, 1900.

Burrage, Henry F. *Maine in the North Eastern Boundary Controversy.* Portland, ME: Marks, 1919.

Campbell, Patrick. *Travels in the Interior Inhabited Parts of North America in the Years 1791 and 1792.* Edinburgh, 1793. Reprint, Toronto: The Champlain Society, 1937.

Campbell, W. E. [Gary]. *The Road to Canada, The Grand Communication Route from Saint John to Quebec.* New Brunswick Military Heritage Series, vol. 5. Fredericton: Goose Lane Editions and the New Brunswick Military Heritage Project, 2005.

Carroll, Francis M. *A Good and Wise Measure: The Search for the Canadian-American Boundary, 1783–1842.* Toronto: University of Toronto Press, 2001.

Chadbourne, Ava Harriet. *A History of Education in Maine: A Study of a Section of American Educational History.* Bangor: Furbush-Roberts Printing Co., 1960. (First published, 1928)

Chalifoux, Éric., A. L. Burke et C. Chapdelaine, eds. *La préhistoire du Témiscouata, occupation amérindiennes dans la haute vallée de la Wolastokuk. Paléo-Québec* 26 (1998).

Chalifoux, Éric and Adrian Burke. "L'occupation préhistorique du Témiscouata (est du Québec), un lieu de portage entre deux grandes voies de circulation." *Paléo-Québec* 23 (1995): 237–70.

Chapdelaine, Claude. "Des chasseurs de la fin de l'âge glaciaire dans la région du lac Mégantic: Découverte des premières pointes à cannelure au Québec." *Recherches amérindiennes au Québec* 34 (2004)**:** 3–20.

_____. "Réflexion sur l'ancienneté du peuplement initial du Québec à partir de nouveaux indices matériels du paléo-indien récent de la région de Rimouski, Québec." *Géographie physique et quaternaire* 50 (1996): 271–86.

_____. "Les Iroquoiens de l'est de la vallée du Saint-Laurent." *Paléo-Québec* 23 (1995): 161–83.

_____. "Les origines de la culture Plano, Il y a 8000 ans à Rimouski. " In *Il y a 8000 ans à Rimouski. Paléoécologie et archéologie d'un site de la culture Plano. Paléo-Québec* 22 (1994): 267–74.

_____. "Sur les traces des premiers Québécois." *Recherches amérindiennes au Québec* XV (1985): 3–6.

Chase, Edward E. *Maine Railroads.* Portland, ME: The Southworth Press, 1926.

Chevalier, Florence-Marie, Sister. "The role of French national societies in the socio-cultural evolution of the Franco-Americans of New England from 1860 to the present an analytical macro-sociological case study in ethnic integration based on current social system models." Ph.D. thesis, Catholic University of America, 1972.

Chipman, Ward. *Remarks upon the Disputed Points of Boundary: Under the Fifth Article of the Treaty of Gent.* Saint John, N.B., 1838. CIHM 21635.

Churchward, James. *A Big Game and Fishing Guide to North-Eastern Maine.* Bangor, ME: Bangor & Aroostook Railroad, 1898.

Clark, Christopher. *The Roots of Rural Capitalism; Western Massachusetts, 1780–1860.* Ithaca: Cornell University Press, 1990.

Clark, Ernest. *The Siege of Fort Cumberland, 1776. An Episode in the American Revolution.* Montreal-Kingston: McGill-

Queen's University Press, 1995.

Clarke, P. D. "Rameau de Saint-Père, Moïse de l'Acadie." *Journal of Canadian Studies* 28 (1993): 69–95.

Clifford, Fred H. *Haunts of the Hunted.* Bangor, ME: Bangor & Aroostook Railroad, 1903.

_____. *In Pine-Tree Jungles: A Handbook for Sportsmen and Campers in the Great Maine Woods.* Bangor, ME: Bangor & Aroostook Railroad, 1902.

Collins, S. W. *LumberingThen and Now.* [Caribou: ME]: The Company, [1954].

Complete Poetical Works of William Woodsworth, The. Philadelphia: Porter and Coates, 1851.

Connell, Allison. "Governed by Nature: Bioregions in the St. John River Watershed." *Echoes, Northern Maine Journal.* 51 (Jan.-March 2001): 32-34 and 47.

Connors-Carlson, Shirlee. "A Pocketful of Irish Settlement in the Woods." In *The County: Land of Promise: A Pictorial History of Aroostook County, Maine,* ed. Anna Fields Mcgrath, 59-62. Norfolk, VA: The Donning Company, 1989.

Cook, Jane. *Coalescence of Styles, the Ethnic Heritage of St John River Valley Regional Furniture, 1763–1851.* Montreal-Kingston: McGill-Queens University Press, 2001.

Corliss, Carleton J. "Railway Development in Maine." In *Along the Rails: A Survey of Maine's Historic Railroad Building,* ed. Kirk F. Mohney. Portland, ME: Maine Preservation, 2000.

Couturier Leblanc, Gilberte, Alcide Godin and Aldéo Renaud. "L'enseignement en français dans les Maritimes, 1604–1992." In *L'Acadie des Maritimes, études thématiques des débuts à nos jours,* ed. Jean Daigle, 543–86. Moncton, N.B.: Chaire d'études acadiennes, 1993.

Couturier, Luc. "L'entreprise Kasner's: 1910 à 1987. D'une activité de colportage à la création d'un magasin spécialisé dans la chaîne régionale des magasins Michaud." *Revue de la Société historique du Madawaska* XV (juillet-septembre 1987): 21–33.

Cozzens, Frederic S. *Acadia or a Month with the Blue Noses.* New York, 1859.

Craig, Béatrice. "Agriculture and the Lumberman's Frontier: The Madawaska Settlement, 1800-1870." *Journal of Forest History* 12 (July 1988): 125–37; reprinted under the title "Occupational Pluralism in British North America" in *Interpreting Canada's Past,* vol. 1, (*Pre-Confederation*), ed. J. M. Bumsted, 366–94. Toronto: University of Toronto Press, 1993.

_____. "Agriculture et marché au Madawaska, 1799-1850." *The River Review/La revue rivière* 1 (1995): 13–38.

_____. "Agriculture in a pioneer region: The Upper St. John Valley in the First Half of the Nineteenth Century." In *Farm, Factory, and Fortune, New Studies in the Economic History of the Maritime Provinces,* ed. Kris Inwood, 17–36. Fredericton, N.B.: Acadiensis Press, 1993.

_____. "Before Borderlands: Yankees, British, and the St. John Valley French." In *New England and the Maritime Provinces: Connections and Comparisons,* ed. Stephen J. Hornsby and John G. Reid, 74-93. Montreal and Kingston: McGill-Queen's University Press, 2005.

_____. "Early French Migrations to Northern Maine, 1785-1850." *Maine Historical Society Quarterly* 25 (Spring 1986): 230–47.

_____. "Économie, société et migrations: le cas de la vallée du Saint-Jean au 19e siècle." in *L'émigrant Acadien vers les États-unis, 1842–1950,* ed. Claire Quintal, 120–32. Québec: Conseil de la vie française en Amérique, 1984.

_____. "Entrepôt de l'Empire: Le magasin général rural au milieu du XIXe siècle." In *Familles, rapports à la terre et aux marchés, logiques économiques, France et Suisse, Canada et Québec, 18e-20e siècles,* ed. Gérard Béaur, Christian Dessureault and Joseph Goy, 33–46. Rennes: Presses Universitaires de Rennes, 2005.

_____. "Farm transmission and the commercialization of agriculture in northern Maine in the second half of the nineteenth century." *The History of the Family—An International Quarterly* 10 (2005): 327-344.

_____. *Homespun Capitalists and Backwoods Consumers: The Rise of a Market Culture in Eastern Canada.* Toronto: University of Toronto Press, 2009.

_____. "Kinship and Migration to the Upper St. John Valley, 1785–1842." *Quebec Studies* 1 (Spring 1983): 151–64.

_____. "La femme face à la transmission des patrimoines au XIXe siècle: Droit, coutume et pratiques." in *Transmettre, hériter, succéder. La reproduction familiale en milieu rural, France-Québec, XVIII-XX siècles,* ed. R. Bonnain, G. Bouchard and J. Goy, 231–42. Lyons/Paris/Villeurbane: Presses Universitaires de Lyons/L'école des hautes études en sciences sociales/Programme pluriannuel en sciences humaines Rhône-Alpes, 1992.

_____. "La transmission des patrimoines fonciers dans le Haut Saint-Jean au XIXe siècle." *Revue d'histoire de l'Amérique française* 45 (décembre, 1991): 207–28.

_____. "Land Transmission Practices Among Northern Maine French Canadians in the Nineteenth Century." in *New England—New France, 1600–1850*, ed. Peter Benes, 69–81. Boston: Boston University Press, 1992.

_____. "Le développement agricole dans la haute vallée du Saint-Jean en 1860." *Revue de la Société historique du Canada* 3 (1993): 13–26.

_____. "Marchés et transmission des patrimoines fonciers au XIXe siècle." In *Nécessités économiques et pratiques juridiques. Problèmes de la transmission des exploitations agricoles (XVIIIe-XIXe siècles),* ed. G. Bouchard, J. Goy, and A. L. Head-König. *Mélanges de l'Ecole Française de Rome. Italie et Méditerranée* 1998 110 (1): 405–08.

_____. "Migrant Integration in a Frontier Society: The Madawaska Settlement, 1800–1850." *Histoire sociale—Social History* 38 (Nov. 1986): 277–98.

_____. "Solder les comptes: les sources de crédits dans les magasins généraux ruraux de l'est canadien au milieu du XIXe siècle." *Journal of the Canadian Historical Association* 13 (2003): 23–48.

_____. "Y-eut-il une 'révolution industrieuse' en Amérique du nord?" in *Famille, terre et marchés, logiques économiques et stratégies dans les milieux ruraux (XVIIe-XXe),* ed. Christian Dessureault, John A. Dickinson and Joseph Goy, 33–48. Montreal: Septentrion, 2003.

Craig, Béatrice et Judith Rygiel. "Femmes, marchés et production textile au Nouveau Brunswick au XIXe siècle." *Histoire et mesure* XV, 1 (2000): 83–112.

Craig, Béatrice, Judith Rygiel, and Elizabeth Turcotte. "Survival or Adaptation? Domestic Rural Textile Production in Eastern Canada in the Later Part of the Nineteenth Century." *Agricultural History Review* 49 (2001): 140–71.

Craig, Béatrice, Judith Rygiel, and Elizabeth Turcotte. "The Homespun Paradox: Market-Oriented Production of Cloth in Eastern Canada in the Nineteenth Century." *Agricultural History* 76 (Winter 2002): 28-57.

Cross, William and Ian Stewart. "Ethnicity and Accommodation in the New Brunswick Party System" *Journal of Canadian Studies* 36 (Winter 2002): 32–58.

Cyr, Georges. "Le programme 'Chance égale pour tous' et la réforme du système de gouvernement municipal du Nouveau Brunswick." *Revue de la Société historique du Madawaska* XVIII (janvier-mars 1990): 2–35.

_____. "Le programme 'Chance égale pour tous' et la réforme du système de gouvernement municipal au Nouveau Brunswick." M.A. thesis, political science, University of Ottawa, 1990.

Cyr, Jean-Roch. "Aspects de l'agriculture chez les francophones du Nouveau-Brunswick au XIXe siècle: le recensement de 1861." *Revue d'histoire de la culture matérielle / Material History Review* 27 (Spring 1988): 51–60.

Daigle, Jean, ed. *Les Acadiens des Maritimes. Études thématiques.* Moncton, N.B.: Éditions d'Acadie, 1990.

_____, ed. *L'Acadie des Maritimes, Études thématiques des débuts à nos jours.* Moncton, N.B.: Chaire d'études acadiennes, 1993.

_____. "L'Acadie de 1604 à 1763, synthèse historique." In *L'Acadie des Maritimes, études thématiques des débuts à nos jours,* ed. Jean Daigle, 1–44. Moncton, N.B: Chaire d'études acadiennes, 1993.

Davis, R. B. and G. L. Jacobson, Jr. "Late Glacial; and Early Holocene Landscapes in Northern New England and Adjacent Areas of Canada." *Quaternary Research* 23 (1985): 341–68.

Day, Clarence. *Aroostook: The First Sixty Years.* Presque Isle, ME: University of Maine at Presque Isle, 1981. (First published as a serial in the *Fort Fairfield Review,* 1951–57).

Deal, Michael and Susan Blair. *Prehistoric Archaeology of the Maritime Provinces— Report on Archaeology.* Fredericton: Council for the Maritime Provinces, 1991.

Deane, John G. and Kavanagh, E. "Report of John G. Deane and Edward Kavanagh to Samuel E. Smith, Governor of the State of Maine." In *State of the Madawaska and Aroostook settlements in 1831,* ed. W. O. Raymond. New Brunswick Historical Society *Collection*, III, 1907.

Deane, John G. and Kavanagh, E. "Wilderness Journey, A Nineteenth Century Journal." *Maine History Newsletter* 16 (April 1980): 3–4 and 15; *Maine History Newsletter* (July 1980): 5–7 and 15–16; *Maine History Newsletter* (October 1980): 8–11 and 16.

Delâge, Denys and Etienne Gilbert. "La justice coloniale britannique et les Amérindiens au Québec, 1760–1820. II – En territoire colonial." *Recherches amérindiennes au Québec* XXXII (2002): 107–17.

Depatie, Sylvie. "La transmission du patrimoine dans les terroirs en expansion: un exemple canadien au XVIIIe siècle." *Revue d'histoire de l'Amérique française* 44 (1990): 171–98.

Desjardins, Georgette. *Saint-Basile, berceau du Madawaska, 1792–1992.* Montreal: Méridien, 1992.

Desjardins, Gérard. *Le Madawaska raconté par Le Moniteur acadien, 1867–1926.* Dieppe, N.B.: G. Desjardins, 1999.

Dickason, Olive Patricia. "Amerindians Between French and English in Nova Scotia, 1713–1763." *American Indian Culture and Research Journal* 10 (1986): 31–56.

Dickinson, John. " Les chemins migratoires et l'établissement des Acadiens à Saint-Denis au XVIIIe siècle." Société Historique Acadienne, *Cahiers* 29 (janvier-mars 1998): 57–69.

_____. "Les réfugiés acadiens au Canada, 1755–1775." *Études canadiennes/ Canadian Studies* 37 (Dec. 1994): 50–61.

Dionne, Raoul. *La colonisation acadienne au Nouveau-Brunswick, 1760–1860: données sur les concessions de terres.* Moncton, N.-B.: Chaire d'études acadiennes, 1989.

Dirnfeld, Rebecca. "Controlling the 'Chinese of the Eastern States?' Electoral Reform and the Franco-American Vote in Maine in 1893." M.A. thesis, University of Ottawa, 2008.

Ditz, Toby. *Property and Kinship, Inheritance in Early Connecticut, 1750–1820.* Princeton: Princeton University Press, 1986.

Doucet, Philippe, "La Politique et les Acadiens." In *L'Acadie des Maritimes, études thématiques des débuts à nos jours,* ed. Jean Daigle, 299–340. Moncton, N.B.: Chaire d'études acadiennes, 1993.

Dow, Sterling T. *Maine Postal History and Post Marks.* Portland, ME: Severn-Wylie-Jewett Co., 1943.

Doyle, R. A., *et. al.* "Late Paleo-Indian Remains from Maine and their Correlations in Northeastern Prehistory." *Archeology of Eastern North America* 13 (1985): 1–35.

Dubay, Guy, comp. *"In the Family": Bangor and Aroostook Railroad Workers of the St. John Valley.* Fort Kent, ME: Fort Kent Historical Society, 2002.

_____, comp. *Aroostook County Delegation 1840–1994.* Madawaska, ME: G. Dubay, 1994.

_____. *"With Justice for All": A Three Act Play.* [Madawaska, ME: n.p.], 1976.

_____. "The Land: in common and undivided, the lumber world of western Aroostook." In *The County: Land of Promise, a Pictorial History of Aroostook County, Maine,* ed. Anna Fields Mcgrath, 145–52. Norfolk, VA: The Donning Company, 1989.

_____. "The Garden of Maine." In *The County: Land of Promise, a Pictorial History of Aroostook County, Maine,* ed. Anna Fields Mcgrath, 153–60. Norfolk, VA: The Donning Company, 1989.

_____. *Chez Nous: The St. John Valley.* Augusta, ME: Maine State Museum, 1983.

_____. *Light on the Past: Documentation on Our Acadian Heritage.* [Madawaska, ME: Town of Madawaska]: Caribou, ME: Rainbow Printing, 1995.

_____. *The Story of Germain Dubé of Hamlin: and some of his descendants as told by them.* [Madawaska, ME: St. John Valley Publishing Co.], c. 1989.

Dugal, Mgr. "Notice historique sur l'Hôtel-Dieu de Saint-Basile de Madawaska, N.B. (de 1873 à 1910)." *Revue de la Société historique du Madawaska* XXV (octobre-décembre 1997): 3–22.

_____. "Notes historiques sur la paroisse de Sainte-Luce, Madawaska. " Société historique du Madawaska, *Le Brayon* V (mai-août 1977): 5–10.

Dumais, Pierre. "The La Martre et Mitis Late Paleo-Indian sites; a Reflection on the Peopling of Southeastern Quebec." *Archeology of Eastern North America* 28 (2000): 81–112.

Dumais, Pierre et Gilles Rousseau. "De limon et de sable, Une occupation paléo-indienne du début de l'Holocène à Squatec (CIEe-9), au Témiscouata." *Recherches amérindiennes au Québec* XXXII (2002): 55–75.

Elections in New Brunswick 1784–1984— Les élections au Nouveau-Brunswick 1784–1984. Fredericton: New Brunswick Legislative Library, 1984.

Elwell, Edward H. *Aroostook, with some account of the excursions tither of the editors of Maine in the years 1858 and 1878.* Portland, ME: Transcript Printing Co, 1878.

Facey-Crowther, David. "Militiamen and Volunteers: The New Brunswick Militia 1787-1871." *Acadiensis* 20 (1990): 148–73.

_____. *The New Brunswick Militia, 1787–1867.* Fredericton, N.B.: New Ireland Press, 1990.

_____. *The New Brunswick Militia. Commissioned Officer's List, 1787–1867.* Fredericton, N.B.: Capital Free Press, 1984.

Fisher, Peter. *History of New Brunswick. As Originally Published in 1825, with a Few Explanatory Notes by W. O. Raymond.* Saint John, N.B.: New Brunswick Historical Society, 1921. Originally published as *Sketches of New Brunswick.* Saint John, N.B.: Chubb & Sears, 1825. CIHM 37396.

_____. *Notitia of New Brunswick for 1836 and Extending into 1837, Comprising Historical, Geographical, Statistical and*

Commercial Notices of the Province, by an Inhabitant. Saint John, N.B.: Printed for the author by H. Chubb, 1838. CIHM 10424.

Fitch, J. H. *A Century of Educational Progress in New Brunswick, 1800–1900.* Toronto, n.p., 1930. CIHM 06047.

Flagg, Gale L. "Pearls along the River: Scattered among the common flora along the St. John River are dozens of Maine's rarest plants." *Echoes, Northern Maine Journal,* 27 (Jan.-March 1995): 34–35, 38.

Folster, David. " 'I am a St. John River Person:' Creating a mystique." *Echoes, Northern Maine Journal,* 35 (Jan.-March 1997): 2, 48–52.

Fortin, Jean-Charles, Antonio Lechasseur *et. al. Histoire du Bas-Saint-Laurent.* Québec: IQRC, 1993.

Fredericton Tourist Association. *The Celestial City, Fredericton, New Brunswick and the St. John River for the Tourist and Sportsman.* Fredericton, N.B., 1909.

Frenette Yves, *et al. Histoire de la Gaspésie.* Québec: IQRC, 1981.

Gaffield, Chad. "Boom and Bust, the Demography and Economy of the Lower Ottawa Valley in the Nineteenth Century." *Communications historiques/ Historical Papers* (1982): 172–95.

Ganong, William F. "A Monograph of the Origins of Settlement in the Province of New Brunswick." Royal Society of Canada, *Proceedings and Transactions,* 2d. ser. 10 (1904): 3–186.

_____. "A Monograph of Historic Sites in the Province of New Brunswick." Royal Society of Canada, *Proceedings and Transactions,* 2d. ser. 5 (1899): 268–70. CIHM 12510.

_____. "A Monograph of the Evolution of the Boundaries of the Province of New Brunswick." Royal Society of Canada, *Proceeding and Transactions,* 2d. ser. 7 (1901): 137–49. CIHM 74004.

_____. "A Monograph of the Place-Nomenclature of the Province of New Brunswick." Royal Society of Canada, *Proceeding and Transactions,* 2d. ser. 3 (1896–97). CIHM 12511.

_____. "Additions and Corrections to Monographs in the Place Nomenclature, Cartography, Historic Sites, Boundaries, and Settlement—Origins of the Province of New Brunswick." Royal Society of Canada, *Proceedings and Transactions,* 2d. ser. 12 (1906): 146–47.

_____. (ed.) "The Cadillac Memoir on Acadia of 1692." New Brunswick Historical Society *Collections* 13 (1930): 90–93.

Garland, Robert E. *Promises, Promises: An Almanac of New Brunswick Elections, 1870 to 1980.* Saint John, N.B.: University of New Brunswick at Saint John, 1979.

Garner, John. "The Enfranchisement of Roman Catholics in the Maritime Provinces." *Canadian Historical Review* (Sept. 1953): 208–09.

Gervais, Diane. "Succession et cycle familial dans le comté de Verchères, 1870–1950." *Revue d'histoire de l'Amérique française* 50 (1996): 69–94.

Gesner, Abraham. *New Brunswick: with Notes for Emigrants: Comprehending the Early History, an Account of the Indians, Settlement, Topography, Statistics, Commerce, Timber, Manufactures, Agriculture, Fisheries, Geology, Natural History, Social and Political State, Immigrants, and Contemplated Railways of that Province.* London: Simmonds & Ward, 1847. CIHM 35386

Ghere. David L. "The Maine experience during the French and Indian War." *Papers of the Algonkian Conference* (1993): 188–98.

Gibson, Alexander. *The New Brunswick Railways and its Land Grants.* Fredericton, 1880. CIHM 06026.

Goguen, Jean Bernard. "Le clergé acadien du Nouveau-Bunswick, 1850–1930." *Société Historique Acadienne, Cahiers* 15 (March 1984): 4–20.

Gordon, Arthur Hamilton. *Wilderness Journey in New Brunswick in 1862–63.* Saint John, N.B.: J&A. MacMillan, 1864. CIHM 23135.

Grave, Donald E. *The 1812 Journal of Lieut. John Le Couteur, 104th Foot: "Merry Hearts make Light Days."* Ottawa: Carleton University Press, 1993.

Green, Jere W. "Aroostook becomes a County." In *The County: Land of Promise, a Pictorial History of Aroostook County, Maine,* ed. Anna Field Mcgrath, 63-73. Norfolk, VA: The Donning Company, 1989.

Griffiths, Naomi, E. S. "Longfellow's *Evangeline:* The Birth and Acceptance of a Legend." *Acadiensis* 11 (1982): 28–41.

_____. "Petition of the Acadian Exiles, 1755–1785, A Neglected Source." *Histoire sociale-Social History* XI (May 1978): 215–23.

_____. *From Migrant to Acadian: a North-American Border People, 1604–1755.* Montreal-Kingston: McGill-Queen's

University Press, 2005.

Grindle, Roger L. *Milestones from the Saint John Valley.* ESEA Title VII, Project Brave Bulletin, 1977.

_____. "Fort Kent Historical Association: Glimpse of History: Mills at Fort Kent." (1975).

_____. "Fort Kent Historical Association: Glimpse of History: The Fort Kent Telephone Company I. III. IV." (1975).

Guignard, Michael J. "Maine's Corporation Sole Controversy." *Maine Historical Society Newsletter* 12 (1973): 111–26.

Gyles, John. *Nine Years a Captive, or John Gyles' Experience among the Malecite Indians, from 1689 to 1698 with an Introduction and Historical Notes by James Hannay.* Saint John, N.B.: Daily Telegraph Steam Job Press, 1875. CIHM 24033.

Hale, Richard W. "The Forgotten Maine Boundary Commission." *Proceedings of the Massachusetts Historical Society* 71 (1957): 147–55.

Hallock, Charles. "Aroostook and the Madawaska." *Harper's Monthly Magazine* XXVII (1866): 688–98.

Hannay, James ed. "The Maugerville Settlement, 1763–1824." New Brunswick Historical Society *Collection* 1-3 (1893–94): 63–88.

_____. "The maiden's sacrifice: an Indian legend of the Saint John River and Grand Falls which tells how a Malecite Indian maiden in order to save her people led a large party of Mohawk warriors over the cataract to their doom." [Saint John, N.B.: n.p., 1910?] Originally published in the *Saint John Telegraph* in 1873. CIHM 74160.

_____. *History of New Brunswick.* Saint John, N.B.: A. J. Bowes, 1909.

Hardy, Jean Pierre. *La vie quotidienne dans la vallée du Saint-Laurent, 1790—1835.* Montreal: Septentrion, 2001.

Hardy, René and Norman Séguin. *Forêt et société en Mauricie, 1830–1930, la formation de la région de Trois-Rivières.* Montreal: Boréal, 1984.

Harvey, Fernand. "Les historiens canadiens-français et l'Acadie, 1859–1960." In *Les relations entre le Québec et l'Acadie de la tradition à la modernité,* ed. Fernand Harvey and Gérard Beaulieu, 19-48. Québec: IQRC—Éditions d'Acadie, 2000.

Hatch, Louis Clinton. *Maine: A History.* New York, American Historical Society, 1919.

Hatfield, Michael F. "*La guerre scolaire:* The Conflicts over the New Brunswick Common Schools Act, 1871–1876." M.A. thesis, Queen's University, 1972.

_____. "H. H. Pitts and Race and Religion in New Brunswick Politics." *Acadiensis* 4 (1975): 46–65.

Head, George Esq. *Forest Scenes and Incidents in the Wilds of North America, being a Diary of a Winter's route from Halifax to the Canadas.* London,1829. CIHM 35433.

Hebert, Richard A. *Modern Maine.* New York: Lewis Historical Publishing Company Inc. 1951.

Hennessy, Wilfrid A. *In the Maine Woods.* Bangor, ME: Charles Glass and Co., n. d.

Hicks, Charles C. "The Bangor and Aroostook Railroad and the Development of Northern Maine." M.A. thesis, University of Maine, 1940.

Hobbs-Pruitt, Bettye. "Self-Sufficiency and the Agricultural Economy of Eighteenth-Century Massachusetts." *William and Mary Quarterly* 3d. ser., XLI, (July 1984): 333–64.

Hody, M. H. "The Development of the Bilingual Schools in New Brunswick." D.Ed. thesis, University of Toronto, 1964.

Holland, Park. "Life and Diary," unpublished manuscript. 1790. Transcript at Bangor Historical Society, Bangor, ME.

Holloway, Christopher. *The Business of Tourism.* London: Pitman, 1989.

Hudon, Paul-Henri. "Jean-Baptiste Grandmaison (1716–1793), un ancêtre fort actif." Société de généalogie de Québec, *L'ancêtre* 25 (octobre-novembre 1998): 19–27.

Hudon, Paul-Henri. "Jean-Baptiste Dupéré, marchand de Rivière-Ouelle." Société de généalogie de Québec, *L'ancêtre* 22 (mars 1996): 243–54.

_____. "Jean-Baptiste Bonenfant, marchand de Rivière-Ouelle." Société de généalogie de Québec, *L'ancêtre* 21 (mai 1995): 323–34.

_____. "Les négociants de Kamouraska, le Madawaska et les anglophones." Société de généalogie de Québec, *L'ancêtre* 25 (décembre-janvier 1998-99): 77–92.

Hughes, T. and H. W. Borns *et. al.* "Models of Glacial Reconstruction and Deglaciation applied to Maritime Canada and New England." In *Late Pleistocene History of Northeastern New England and Adjacent Quebec.* Geological Society of America, Special Paper 197 (1986), 139–50.

Inwood, Kris. ed. *Farm, Factory, and Fortune: New Studies in the Economic History of the Maritime Provinces.*

Fredericton: Acadiensis Press, 1993.

Jack. Edward, "Maliseet Legends." *The Journal of American Folklore,* 8 (Jul.- Sept. 1895): 193–208.

Johnson, Laurence. "Louis Thomas Saint-Aubin et sa famille. Deux siècles et demi de diplomatie et de revendications Malécites." *Paléo-Québec* 27 (1998): 187–98.

Johnson, Laurence and Charles A. Martijn. "Les Malécites et la traite des fourrures." *Recherches amérindiennes au Québec* XXIV (1994): 25–44.

Johnston A. J. B. "La séduction de l'archétype face au défi de l'histoire de l'Acadie." Société Historique Acadienne, *Cahiers* 36 (mars 2005): 12–46.

_____. "The Call of the Archetype and the Challenge of Acadian History." *French Colonial History* 5 (2004): 63–92.

Johnston, James Finlay Weir. *Notes on North America: Agricultural, Economical and Social.* Edinburgh and London: W. Blackwood, 1851. CIHM 35749 and 35750.

_____. *Report on the Agricultural Capabilities of the Province of New Brunswick.* Fredericton: J. Simpson, 1850. CIHM 43053.

Jones, Howard. *To the Webster Ashburton Treaty: A study in Anglo-American Relations, 1783–1843.* Chapel Hill, NC: University of North Carolina Press, 1977.

Journal du Madawaska, 1904.

Judd, Richard W. *Aroostook: A Century of Logging in Northern Maine.* Orono, Maine: University of Maine Press, 1989.

Judd, Richard W., Edwin A. Churchill and Joel W. Eastman. *Maine: The Pine Tree State from Prehistory to the Present.* Orono, ME: University of Maine Press, 1995.

Kendall, Thomas Augustus. *Travels through the Northern Parts of the United States in the Years 1807 and 1808.* Vol. III. New York: J. Riley, 1809.

Keyssar, Alexander. "Widowhood in Eighteenth-Century Mass.: A Problem in the History of the Family." *Perspectives in American History* 8 (1974): 83–119.

Kingsbury, Benjamin, Jr. *The Maine Townsman or Laws for the Regulation of Towns.* Portland: Bailey and Noyes, 1872.

Kite, James Stevens. "Late Quaternary Glacial, Lacrustine and Alluvial Geology of the Upper St. John River Basin, Northern Maine and Adjacent Canada." Ph.D. thesis, Department of Geography and Geology, University of Wisconsin, 1983.

Kite, J. Steven and Robert Stickenrath, "Postglacial evolution of drainage in the middle and upper St. John Basin." In Maine Geological Survey, *Studies in Maine Geology* 6 (1989):135–41, edited by Robert G. Marvinney and Robert D. Tucker.

_____. "Postglacial History of the Upper St John Drainage Basin." In *Contribution to the Quaternary Geology of Northern Maine and Adjacent Canada,* ed. Steven J. Kite, Thomas V. Lowell, and Woodrow B. Thompson. Maine Geological Survey, *Bulletin* 37 (1988): 117–29.

Laberge, Alain, *et. al. Histoire de la Côte-du-Sud.* Québec: IQRC, 1993.

Lacombe, Patrice. *La terre paternelle.* Montreal: Hurtubise, 1972.

Lagacé, Lucille. "Le magasin UlRéric Nadeau de Baker-Brook." *Revue de la Société historique du Madawaska* XVII (juil-let-septembre 1989): 4–10.

Laing, David. "Out of Chaos." In *The County: Land of Promise, a Pictorial History of Aroostook County, Maine,* ed. Anna Fields Mcgrath, 9-17. Norfolk, VA: The Donning Company, 1989.

Landry, Nicolas et Nicole Lang. *Histoire de l'Acadie.* Québec: Septentrion, 2001.

Lang, Nicole. "L'impact d'une industrie: Les effets sociaux de l'arrivée de la Compagnie *Fraser Limited* à Edmundston, N.B., 1900–1950." *Revue de la Société historique du Madawaska.* XV (janvier-mars 1987): 2–71.

Langellier, Kristin M. "Tickling the Past: Straining to Catch the Sound of my Own Voice." *Echoes, the Northern Maine Journal* 45 (July-September 1999): 33–37.

Langlois, Mgr. Henri. *Dictionnaire généalogique du Madawaska. Répertoire des mariages du diocèse d'Edmunston, N.B. et du comté d'Aroostook, recherches et compilations par Henri Langlois.* 8 volumes. St. Basile, N.B.: privately published, 1971.

Langmaid, K. K., J. G. Losier ,and J. K. McMillan. *Soils of Madawaska County, New Brunswick. New Brunswick Soil Survey Report No.8.* Ottawa: Government of Canada, Department of Agriculture, Research Branch, 1980.

Lapointe, Jacques F. "Histoire de l'industrie laitière à Saint-Léonard." *Revue de la Société historique du Madawaska* XVII (avril-juin 1989): 28–30.

Lavoie, Claudia, Soeur. "Le pensionnat de l'Hôtel-Dieu de Saint-Basile." *Revue de la Société historique du Madawaska* XXV (octobre-décembre 1997): 23–27.

Lawton, R.J. and J.H.Burgess, eds. *Franco-Americans of the State of Maine and their achievements.* Lewiston, ME: Royal Press, 1915.

Leavitt, Robert M. *Maliseet and Micmac: First Nations of the Maritimes.* Fredericton, N.B: New Ireland Press, 1995.

LeBlanc, Barbara. *Postcards from Acadie: Grand-Pré, Evangeline, and The Acadian Identity.* Kentville, N.S.: Gaspereau Press, 2003.

Leblanc, Robert. "L'émigration, colonisation et rapatriement: the Acadian perspective." Société Historique Acadienne, *Cahiers* 19 (juillet-septembre 1988): 71–104.

Lefrançois, Émilie. "La contribution des religieuses hospitalières de Saint-Joseph dans le domaine de la santé au Madawaska, 1873 à 2001." *Revue de la Société historique du Madawaska* 29 (octobre-décembre 2001): 4–35.

Lejeune, J-Théodule. "Document: Progrès en éducation française au Nouveau-Brunswick." Société Historique Acadienne, *Cahiers* 20 (juillet-septembre 1989): 132–39.

Little, Jack I. "Public Policy and Private Interest in the Lumber Industry of the Eastern Townships: The case of C.S. Clark and Company, 1854–1881." *Histoire sociale—Social History* 37 (May 1986): 9–38.

_____. *Crofters and Habitants: Settler Society, Economy, and Culture in a Quebec Township, 1848–1881.* Montreal-Kingston: McGill-Queen's University Press, 1991.

_____. *Nationalism, Capitalism and Colonization in Nineteenth-Century Québec, The Upper St Francis District.* Montreal-Kingston: McGill-Queen's University Press, 1989.

Lowell, Thomas V. "Late Wisconsin Ice-flow Reversal and Deglaciation, Northwestern Maine." In *Late Pleistocene History of Northeastern New England and Adjacent Quebec,* Geological Society of America, Special Paper 197 (1986): 71-83.

Lowenthal, David. "The Maine Press and the Aroostook War." *Canadian Historical Review* 32 (Dec. 1951): 315-36.

Lugrin, Charles. *Facts Concerning the Fertile Belt of the New Brunswick Land and Lumber Company (Limited) New Brunswick (Canada).* Saint John, N.B.: J. & A. McMillan, 1884. CIHM 09213.

MacGregor, John, Esq. *British America.* 2 vol. Edinburgh: William Blackwood and London: T. Cadell, 1832. CIHM 36844.

_____. *Historical and Descriptive Sketches of the Maritimes Colonies of British America.* London: Longman, 1828. CIHM 38031.

MacKinnon, Robert. "Roads, Cart Tracks, and Bridle Paths: Land Transportation and the Domestic Economy of Mid-Nineteenth Century Eastern British North America." *Canadian Historical Review* 84 (June 2003): 177–216.

MacNaughton, Katherine F. C. "The Development of the Theory and Practice of Education in New Brunswick, 1784-1900: A Study in Historical Background." M.A. thesis, University of New Brunswick, 1947. (Available on the University of New Brunswick Library website: www.lib.unb.ca/)

MacNutt, W. S. *New Brunswick: A History, 1784–1867.* Toronto: University of Toronto Press, 1963.

Mailhot, Raymond. "Prise de conscience collective acadienne au Nouveau-Brunswick (1860–91) et comportement de la majorité anglophone." Ph.D. thesis, Université de Montréal, 1973.

Maisonneuve, Daniel. "Solidarité familiale et exode rural: le cas de Saint Damase, 1852–1861." *Cahier québécois de démographie* 14 (octobre 1985): 231–40.

Mann, John. *Travels in North America, Particularly in the Provinces of Upper and Lower Canada and New Brunswick and in the States of Maine, Massachusetts and New York.* Fredericton, N.B.: Saint Anne's Point Press, 1978. First published in Glasgow, 1824.

Marie-Dorothée, Soeur. *Une pierre de la mosaïque acadienne.* Montreal: Léméac, 1984.

Marie-Victorin, Frère. "Le portage du Témiscouata, Notes critiques pour servir à l'histoire dune vieille route coloniale." Société Royale du Canada, *Proceedings and Transactions,* section I (1918): 55–93.

Martijn, Charles A. "The Iroquoian Presence in the Estuary and Gulf of the Saint Lawrence River Valley: A Re-evaluation." *Man in the Northeast* 40 (1990): 45–63.

Martin, Paul Louis. Book review of Janet Cook, *Coalescence of Styles, the Ethnic Heritage of the St. John River Valley.* In *Revue d'Histoire de l'Amérique française* 55 (Printemps 2002): 610.

Massé, Jean-Claude. "La guerre des fourrures au Madawaska-Témiscouata." Société de généalogie de Québec, *L'ancêtre* 26 (novembre-décembre 1999): 89–97.

Massicotte, Julien. "La Sainte Vierge et le Drapeau." *Égalité* 52 (2005): 69-79.

Maurault, Joseph-Pierre Anselme, Abbé. *Histoire des Abénakis depuis 1605 jusqu'à nos jours.* Sorel, Qc.: Atelier de la Gazette de Sorel, 1866. CIHM 29555.

McCalla, Douglas. "Retailing in the Countryside: Upper Canadian General Stores in the Mid-Nineteenth Century." *Business and Economic History* 26 (Winter 1997): 393–403.

_____. "Rural Credit and Rural Development in Upper Canada, 1790-1850." In *Merchant Credit and Labour Strategies in Historical Perspective,* ed. Rosemary Ommer, 265–72. Fredericton: Acadiensis Press, 1990.

McDonald, Sheila. "The War after the War: Fort Kent Blockhouse, 1839–1842." Maine Historical Society *Quarterly* 29 (Winter-Spring 1990): 142–68.

Mcgrath, Anna Fields, ed. *The County: Land of Promise, a Pictorial History of Aroostook County, Maine.* Norfolk, VA: The Donning Company, 1989.

McInnis, Marvin. "Marketable Surpluses in Ontario Farming, 1860." *Social Science History* 8 (1984): 395–424.

McNabb, Debra A. "Land and Settlement in Horton Township, N.S. 1760–1830." M.A. thesis. University of British Columbia, 1986.

McNeil, Alan. "Early American Communities on the Fundy: A Case Study of Annapolis and Amherst Townships, 1767–1824." *Agricultural History* 62 (1989): 101–19.

_____. "Society and Economy in Rural Nova Scotia, 1761–1861." Ph.D. thesis, Queen's University, 1990.

_____. "The Acadian Legacy and Agricultural Development in Nova Scotia, 1760–1861." In *Farm, Factory, and Fortune: New Studies in the Economic History of the Maritime Provinces,* ed. Kris Inwood, 1–16. Fredericton: Acadiensis Press, 1993.

Melvin. Charlotte Lenentine. *Madawaska, a Chapter in Maine–New Brunswick Relations.* Madawaska, ME: St. John Valley Publishing Co, 1975.

Mercier, Ernest. *Influence du traité Webster-Ashburton sur la colonisation dans le centre et le haut du comté de Montmagny.* La Pocatière, Société historique de la Côte-du-Sud, 1981.

Mercure, Prudent L. *Papiers de Prudent L. Mercure: Histoire du Madawaska.* Roger Paradis comp. Madawaska, ME: Madawaska Historical Society, 1998.

Michaud, Guy R. *Brève histoire du Madawaska; débuts à 1900.* Edmundston: Les éditions GRM, 1984.

_____. *Au Madawaska: Identité des gens. Le fort du Petit-Sault et le monument.* Edmundston, N.B., 1994.

_____. *L'identité des gens du comté de Madawaska.* Edmundston, N.B: Les Éditions GRM, 1991.

Monroe, Alexander, Esq. *New Brunswick; with a Brief Outline of Nova Scotia and Prince Edward Island. Their History, Civil Divisions, Geography, and Production.* Halifax, N.S.: Printed by Richard Nugent, 1855. Reprint, Belleville, Ontario: Mika Studio, 1972. CIHM 33945.

Moody, Barry. "Land, Kinship and Inheritance in Granville Township, 1760–1800." In *Making Adjustments: Changes and Continuity in Planter Nova Scotia, 1759–1800,* ed. Margaret Conrad, 165-79. Fredericton. N.B.: Acadiensis Press, 1991.

Muir, J. Lloyd. "The New Brunswick Militia, 1787–1867." *Dalhousie Review* 44 (1964): 333–38.

Mulhall, James M. *Tourists' Guide to Saint John and the Province of New Brunswick.* Saint John: Canadian Railway Co., 1888. CIHM 27278.

Murphy, Terrence. "The Emergence of Maritimes Catholicism, 1781–1830." *Acadiensis* 13 (1984): 29–49.

New Brunswick and Nova Scotia Land Company. *Practical Information Respecting New Brunswick, Including Details Relatives to its Soil, Climate, Production and Agriculture.* London: P. Richardson, 1843. CIHM 21463.

Newman, William A. "Pleistocene Geology of Northeastern Maine." In *Late Pleistocene History of Northeastern New England and Adjacent Quebec.* Geological Society of America, Special Paper 197 (1986): 59–70.

Nicholas, George P., J. S. Kites, and Robson Bonnischen. *Archeological survey and testing of the late Pleistocene-early Holocene landform in the Dickey-Lincoln school reservoir area, Northern Maine.* University of Maine at Orono: Institute for Quaternary Studies, final report, April 1981.

_____. "The Archeology of the Upper St. John River: Overview and Interpretation." In *Contribution to the Quaternary Geology of Northern Maine and Adjacent Canada,* ed. Steven J. Kite, Thomas V. Lowell, and Woodrow B. Thompson. Maine Geological Survey, Bulletin 37 (1988): 133–45.

"Notice historique sur l'Hôtel-Dieu de Saint-Basile de Madawaska, N.B. (de 1873 à 1910)." *Revue de la Société historique du Madawaska* XXV (octobre-décembre 1997): 3–22.

Ouellette, Linda and Harold Underhill. "The Corriveau Mill: When carding cost six cents a pound." *Echoes, the Northern Maine Journal* 58 (Oct-Dec. 2002): 9–10.

Paradis, Roger. "A History of the Madawaska Training School, 1878–1963." M.A. thesis, University of Maine, 1964.

_____. "John Baker and the Republic of Madawaska; An Episode in the Northeastern Controversy." *Dalhousie Review* 52 (1972): 78–95.

_____. "La bourse Langevin, une page de l'histoire des Acadiens au Madawaska." Société Historique Acadienne, *Cahiers* 7 (1976): 118–30.

_____. "Louis Mercure, fondateur du Madawaska." Société Historique Acadienne_*Cahiers* 28 (1989): 49–56.

Parent, Michel *et al.* "Paléogéographie du Québec méridional entre 12500 et 8000 ans BP. " *Recherches amérindienne au Québec* XV (1985): 17–37.

Paroisse St Francois d'Assise (Clair) 1889–1989, n.p., n.d.

Pawling, Micah A. *Wabanaki Homeland and the New State of Maine: The 1820 Journal and Plans of Survey of Joseph Treat.* Amherst: University of Massachusetts Press, 2007.

Pelletier, Martine A. and Monica Dionne Ferretti. *Van Buren, Maine, History.* Madawaska, ME: St. John Valley Publishing Co., 1979.

Perley, Moses Henry. *A Handbook of Information for Emigrants to New Brunswick.* Saint John, New Brunswick: H. Chubb, 1854. CIHM 22479.

_____. *Reports on Indian Settlements.* [n.p.]: J. Simpson, 1842. CIHM 61724.

Plessis, Mgr. "Le journal des visites pastorales de Mgr. Joseph Octave Plessis, Evêque de Québec en Acadie 1811–1812–1813." Société Historique Acadiennes, *Cahiers* (mars-septembre 1980): 124–29.

Plourde, Michel. "Le Sylvicole supérieur à l'embouchure du Saguenay est-il iroquoien?" *Recherches amérindiennes au Québec* 29 (1999): 27–39.

Pote, William. *The Journal of Captain William Pote, Jr., During His Captivity in the French-Indian War. From May, 1745, to August, 1747.* Edited by J. F. Hurst. New York: Dodd and Mead, 1896. CIHM 12097.

Prins Harald E. L. "Cornfield at Meductic: Ethnic and Territorial Reconfigurations in Colonial Acadia." *Man in the Northeast* 44 (1992): 55-72.

_____. "Micmacs and Maliseets in the St. Lawrence Valley." *Actes du dix-septième congrès des Algonquinistes.* Ottawa: Carleton University Press, 1986: 263–78.

Prospectus of the St Andrews and Quebec Railroad. St. Andrews: Standard Office, 1836. CIHM 37183.

Prospectus of the St Andrews and Quebec Railroad. [Saint John, N.B.: H. Chubb], 1846. CIHM 37182.

Pullen, Clarence. *In Fair Aroostook: Where Acadia and Scandinavia's Subtle Touch turned a Wilderness into a Land of Plenty.* Bangor, ME: Bangor and Aroostook Railroad Company, 1902.

Quintal, Claire. *L' émigrant Acadien vers les États-unis, 1842–1950.* Québec: Conseil de la vie française en Amérique, 1984.

Rameau. S. "Souvenirs d'Edmée Rameau de Saint-Père." *Vie française* 2 (1948): 400–04.

Rampton, V. N. "Quaternary Geology of Madawaska County, Western New Brunswick: a Brief Overview." In *Contribution to the Quaternary Geology of Northern Maine and Adjacent Canada,* ed. Steven J. Kite, Thomas V. Lowell, and Woodrow B. Thompson. Maine Geological Survey, Bulletin 37 (1988): 99-106.

Rand, Rev. Silas Tertius. *Legends of the Micmacs.* New York and London: Longman, Green and Co., 1894.

Ray, Roger B. "Maine Indians' Concept of Land Tenure." Maine Historical Society *Quarterly* 13 (1973): 28–51.

Raymond, William Odber. "Earliest route of Travel Between Canada and Acadia. Olden-time Celebrities who Used It." Royal Society of Canada *Proceedings and Transactions,* section II (1921): 33–46.

_____. "Introduction" to "State of the Madawaska and Aroostook Settlement in 1831. Report of John G. Deane and Edward Kavanagh to Samuel E. Smith, Governor of the State of Maine, and Other Documents." New Brunswick Historical Society *Collections* III (1907): 344–86.

_____. "The First Governor of New Brunswick and the Acadians of the River Saint John." Royal Society of Canada *Proceedings and Transactions,* section II (1914): 415–52. CIHM 86607.

_____, ed. "Letters Written at Saint John by James Simonds, A.D. 1764–1785." New Brunswick Historical Society *Collections* I (1894–98): 160–86.

_____, ed. "Papers Relating to the Townships of the River St. John in the Province of Nova Scotia." New Brunswick Historical Society *Collections* 6 (1905): 287–357.

_____, ed. "Selections from the Papers and Correspondence of James White, Esq., A.D. 1762–1783." New Brunswick Historical Society *Collections* I (1894–98): 306–40.

_____, ed. "The James White Papers, Continued, A.D. 1781–88." New Brunswick Historical society *Collections* II (1894–98): 30–72.

_____, ed., *Winslow Papers, AD 1776–1826.* [Saint John, N.B.: Sun Print. Co], 1901. Reprinted Boston: Gregg Press, 1972. CIHM 74571.

_____. *The River St. John.* 1910. Reprint, Sackville, N.B.: Tribune Press, 1943. CIHM 74579.

Relations des Jésuites (Les). 6 volumes. Montreal: Éditions du jour, 1972.

Reid, John G. *Acadia, Maine, and New Scotland. Marginal Colonies in the Seventeenth Century.* Toronto: Toronto University Press, 1981.

Reynolds, W. K. *Big Game in New Brunswick: A Sportsman's Guide to the Principal Hunting Grounds of the Province.* Saint John, 1898.

Richard, Chantal. "Le récit de la Déportation comme mythe de création dans l'idéologie des Conventions nationales acadiennes (1881–1937)." *Acadiensis* XXXVI (Autumn 2006): 69–81.

Richard, Pierre J. H. "Couvert végétal et paléo-environnements du Québec entre 12000 et 8000 ans." *Recherches amérindienne au Québec* XV (1985): 39–56.

Robb, James. *Agricultural Progress: an Outline of the Course of Improvement in Agriculture, Considered as a Business, an Art and a Science, with Special Reference to New Brunswick.* Fredericton, N.B.: J. Simpson, 1856. CIHM 22568.

Robichaud, Deborah. "Les Conventions nationales (1890-1913). La société Nationale l'Assomption et son discours." Société Historique Acadienne, *Cahiers* XII (1981): 36–58.

Robidoux, Ferdinand J. *Conventions Nationales des Acadiens: Recueil des Travaux et Délibérations des Six Premières Conventions.* Shediac, N.B.: Imprimerie du Moniteur Acadien, 1907.

Robinson, Brian S., James B. Petersen and Ann K. Robinson. *Early Holocene Occupation in Northern New England.* Augusta. ME: Maine Historic Preservation Commission, Occasional Publications in Maine Archeology, Number 9, 1992.

Roby, Yves. *Les Franco-Américains de la Nouvelle-Angleterre, Rêves et réalités.* Québec: Septentrion, 2000.

Roe, Frederick B. and Colby N. George. *Atlas of Aroostook County, Maine.* Philadelphia: Roe & Colby, 1877.

Rogers, Lore A. "The Telos Cut." *Northern Logger* (May 1966).

Rouillard, Eugène. *La colonisation dans les comtés de Dorchester, Bellechasse, Montmagny, L'Islet, Kamouraska.* Québec, [n.p.], 1901.

Saint-Vallier, Jean-Baptiste de la Croix de Chevrière de. *Estat présent de l'Église et de la colonie française dans la Nouvelle France, par Mgr. l'Évêque de Québec.* [London]: S. R. Publishers, 1965 (First ed. 1688). CIHM 22588 (reproduction of 1856 edition).

Sanger, David. "Archaeological Survey in the Dickey-Lincoln School Lakes Area, Northern Maine." Maine Archaeological Society *Bulletin* 18 (1978): 10–23.

Santerre, Renaud. "Donations de fermes et sécurité des agriculteurs âgés, 1850–1990." In *Famille, économie et société rurales en contexte d'urbanisation, XVIIe-XXe siècles,* ed. Gérard Bouchard and Joseph Goy, 35-48. Paris: EHESS, 1990.

Scott, Geraldine Tidd. *Ties of Common Blood: A History of Maine's Northeast Boundary Dispute with Great Britain, 1783–1842.* Bowie, MD: Heritage Books, 1992.

_____. "Fortifications on Maine's Northeast Boundary, 1828–1845." Maine Historical Society *Quarterly* 29 (Winter-Spring 1990): 118–40.

See, Scott W. *Riots in New Brunswick: Orange Nativism and Social Violence in the 1840s.* Toronto: University of Toronto Press, 1993.

_____. "Variations on a Borderland theme: Nativism and Collective Violence in Northeastern North America." In *New England and the Maritime Provinces, Connections and Comparisons,* ed. Stephen J. Hornsby and John G. Reid, 125–43. Montreal-Kingston: McGill-Queen's University Press, 2005.

Simard, Cyril. "Le lin au Madawaska au 19e siècle: Les 'Brayons' n'étaient pas les seuls à filer ce 'mauvais coton.'" Revue de la Société historique du Madawaska 15 (octobre-décembre 1987): 9–254.

Sirois, Claire. "Le Madawaska, trait d'union entre l'Acadie et la province qui se souvient." Société historique du Madawaska, *Le Brayon* II (octobre 1974): 8–10; *Le Brayon* III (décembre 1974): 9–15; *Le Brayon* III (février 1975):

13–17; *Le Brayon* III (octobre 1975): 15–20.

_____. "Le Madawaska, trait d'union entre l'Acadie et la province qui se souvient; Étude du milieu madawaskayen et de l'idéologie du journal régional de la période 1935-1945." M.A. thesis, University of Ottawa, 1973.

Sirois, Georges. "90 ans d'histoire postale à Edmundston, 1837-1927." *Revue de la Société historique du Madawaska* XIII (janvier-mars 1985): 4–31.

_____. "Jesse Baker: militaire et politicien." Société historique du Madawaska, *Le Brayon* VIII (septembre-décembre 1980): 3–15.

_____. "L'évolution de l'enseignement public au Madawaska durant le XIXième siècle." Société historique du Madawaska, *Le Brayon* V (janvier-mars 1977): 4–29.

_____. "La participations des Madawaskayens aux Conventions Nationales (1880-1908)." Société Historique Acadienne, *Cahiers* V (avril-juin 1974): 120–25.

_____. "Les Acadiens du Nord Ouest du Nouveau Brunswick et la Confédération." Société Historique Acadienne, *Cahiers* IV (1973): 8–20.

_____. "Les Acadiens et la naissance du commerce du bois, 1820–1840. " Société Historique Acadienne, *Cahiers* 7 (décembre 1976): 183–93.

_____. "Un aventurisme spirituel. La mission baptiste de Saint-François (1855–1867)." *Revue de la Société historique du Madawaska* XXIV (avril-juin 1996): 3–37.

_____. "Une vue rétrospective du développement des communications dans le haut de la vallée du Saint-Jean au XIXième siècle." Société historique du Madawaska, *Le Brayon* VI (avril-juin 1978): 2–13.

Smith, David C. "Maine and its Public Domaine: Land Disposal in the Northeastern Frontier." In *The Frontier in American Economic Development, Essays in Honour of Paul Wallace Gates,* ed. David M. Ellis, 113–40. Ithaca: Cornell University Press, 1969.

_____. *A History of Lumbering in Maine, 1861–1960.* Orono, Me: University of Maine Press, 1972.

Snow, Dean R. and Kim L. Lamphear. "European Contact and Indian Depopulation in the Northeast: The Timing of the First Epidemics." *Ethnohistory* 35 (1988): 15–33.

Sorg, Marcella Harnish. "La formation d'une communauté à Old Town, Maine, 1835–1930: endogamie et origines natales parmi les Acadiens." In *L'émigrant Acadien vers les États-unis, 1842–1950,* ed. Claire Quintal, 133–47. Québec: Conseil de la vie française en Amérique, 1984.

Sorg, Marcella H. and Béatrice C. Craig. "Patterns of Infant Mortality in the Upper St. John Valley French Population: 1791–1838." *Human Biology* 55 (Feb. 1983): 103–13.

Spigelman, Martin S. "Les Acadiens et les Canadiens en temps de guerre : le jeu des alliances." Société Historique Acadienne, *Cahiers* 8 (mars 1977): 5–23.

_____. "Race et religion: les Acadiens et la hiérarchie catholique irlandaise du Nouveau-Brunswick." *Revue d'histoire de l'Amérique française* 29 (1975): 69–85.

Sprague, J. F. "Documentary History of the North Eastern Boundary Controversy." *Collection of the Piscataquis County Historical Society,* Vol. 1. Dover, Observer Press, 1910.

Sprague, Richard. *The Bangor and Aroostook, 1881–1966.* Bangor, ME: B&A, 1966.

Saint-Pierre, Jacques. "Les chemins de colonisation." http://www.encyclobec.ca.

St. Agatha Historical Society. *Centenaire de Ste-Agathe, Maine, 1899–1999.* St. Agatha, ME, 1999.

_____. *Les filles de la Sagesse, Ste-Agathe, Maine, 1904–2004.* St. Agatha, ME, [2004].

Stanwood, Owen. "Unlikely Imperialist: The Baron of Saint-Castin and the Transformation of the Northeastern Borderlands." *French Colonial History* 5 (2004): 43–62.

Stephenson, Isaac. *Recollection of a Long Life.* Chicago, 1915.

Stetson, Hazel C. *From Logs to Electricity: A History of the Maine Public Service Company.* N.A.: Maine Public Service Co., 1984.

Stetson, W. W. *History of Civil Government of Maine.* New York: American Book Company, 1898.

Stevens, Thalia Olive. "The International Commission Pertaining to the St. John River (1909–1916)." M.A. thesis, University of Maine, 1970.

Stevenson, Michael D. and Graeme S. Mount, "The Roman Catholic Diocesan Boundary and American Madawaska, 1842-1870." Maine Historical Society *Quarterly* 32 (1992): 174–89.

Stolz, D. E. *A Statutory History of Trains in Canada 1836–1986.* Kingston: Queen's University, 1987.

St-Onge, Patricia. "L'évolution du service téléphonique à Edmundston, de 1896 à nos jours." *Revue de la Société historique du Madawaska* XVIII (janvier-mars 1990): 4–35.

Sweetser, M. F. *The Maritime Provinces: A Handbook for Travellers.* Boston: James R. Osgood, 1875. CIHM 44873.

Taylor, Alan. *Liberty Men and Great Proprietors: The Revolutionary Settlement on the Maine Frontier, 1760–1820.* Chapel Hill: University of North Carolina Press, 1990.

Tehatarongnatase Paul, Jocelyn, "Le territoire de chasse des Hurons de Lorette. " *Recherches amérindiennes au Québec* XXX (2000): 5–19.

Theobald, Andrew. "Une Loi Extraordinaire: New Brunswick Acadians and the Conscription Crisis of the First World War." *Acadiensis* XXXIV (Fall 2004): 80–95.

Thériault, Léon, "L'Acadie de 1763 à 1990, synthèse historique." In *L'Acadie des Maritimes, études thématiques des débuts à nos jours,* ed. Jean Daigle, 45-92. Moncton, N.B.: Chaire d'études acadiennes, 1993.

_____. "L'acadianisation des structures ecclésiastiques aux Maritimes, 1758–1953." In *L'Acadie des Maritimes, études thématiques des débuts à nos jours,* ed. Jean Daigle, 431–66. Moncton, N.B.: Chaire d'études acadiennes, 1993.

_____. " Les religieuses hospitalières de Saint-Joseph en Acadie." Société Historique Acadienne, *Cahiers* 29 (juillet-septembre 1998): 143–63.

_____. "L'Acadie du Nouveau Brunswick et le Québec (1880–1960), Froideur ou méfiance. " In *Les relations entre le Québec et l'Acadie de la tradition à la modernité,* ed. Fernand Harvey and Gérard Beaulieu, 49–72. Québec: IQRC—Editions d'Acadie, 2000.

Thoreau, Henry David. *Walden and Other Writings.* New York: Modern Library, 1965.

Thwaites, Reuben Gold, ed. *The Jesuit Relations and Allied Documents: Travels and Explorations of the Jesuit Missionaries in New France, 1610–1791.* 73 volumes. Cleveland. OH: Burrow Brothers, 1896–1901. Reprint, New York: Pageant Book, 1959. CIHM 07535 to 07607.

Toner, Peter Michael, "The New Brunswick Schools Question." *Study Sessions: Canadian Catholic Historical Association* 37 (1970): 85–96.

_____. "The New Brunswick Separate School Issue, 1864–1876." M.A. thesis, University of New Brunswick, 1967.

Tourist Association of Saint John. *Canoeing, Camping, Fishing in New Brunswick.* Saint John, 1905.

Tremblay, Ronald, ed. "L'Éveilleur et l'ambassadeur, essais archéologiques et ethno-historiques en hommage à Charles A. Martijn." *Paléo-Québec* 27 (1998).

Tremblay, Sandra. "Les territoires des Malécites." *L'Estuaire* XXI (janvier 1998): 21–28.

Trépanier, Pierre. "Les influences leplaysiennes au Canada français, 1855–1888." *Revue d'études canadiennes/ Journal of Canadian Studies* 22 (1987): 66–83.

_____. "Rameau de Saint-Père et l'histoire de la colonisation française en Amérique." *Acadiensis* 9 (1980): 40–55.

_____. "Rameau de Saint-Père et le métier d'historien." *Revue d'histoire de l'Amérique française* 33 (1979): 331–55.

Trépanier, Pierre and Lise. "A la recherche d'un homme et d'une société: Rameau de Saint-Père et l'Acadie." *Bulletin du Centre de Recherche en Civilisation Canadienne Française* 16 (1978): 15–17.

Tyrrell, Merle E. "The Year with No Summer: Snow and Ice in June." *Echoes, Northern Maine Journal,* 36 (April-June 1997): 2, 18–20.

U.S. Congress. Senate. *Message from the president of the United States with documents relating to alleged aggressions on the rights of citizens of the United States by the authorities of New Brunswick on the territory in dispute between the United States and Great Britain, March 4, 1828.* Washington: Duff Green, Printer, 1828.

U.S. Department of Agriculture. Soil Conservation Service in Cooperation with the University of Maine Agricultural Experiment Station. *Soil Survey; Aroostook County, Maine, North-eastern Part 25,* 1958.

_____. *Soil survey, Aroostook County, Maine, Northeastern Part 27* 1959.

Vautour, Sœur Thérèse. "Historique des religieuses de Notre-Dame-du-Sacré-Cœur." Société Historique Acadienne, *Cahiers* 29 (décembre 1998): 207–21.

Viau, Robert. "L'épée et la plume: la persistance du thème de la Déportation acadienne en littérature." *Acadiensis* XXXVI (Autumn 2006): 51–68.

Vicero, Ralph.D. "Immigration of French Canadians to New England 1840–1900: A Geographical Analyses." Ph.D. dissertation, University of Wisconsin, 1968.

Waciega, Lisa Wilson. "A 'Man of Business,' the Widow of Means in Southeastern Pennsylvania, 1750–1850." *William and Mary Quarterly* 3d. ser. XLIV (1987): 39–60.

Wagg, Phyllis. "The Bias of Probate: Using Deeds to Transfer Estates in Nineteenth-Century Nova Scotia." *Nova Scotia Historical Review* 10 (1990): 74–87.

Wagner, Michael D. "A Few Days Later in Coming": Major General Winfield Scott's Role in the Aroostook War." Maine Historical Society *Quarterly* 34 (Winter-Spring 1995): 162–77.

Wainwright, Kennedy. "A Comparative Study in Nova Scotian Rural Economy, 1788–1872, Based on Recently Discovered Books of Account of Old Firms in Kings County." Nova Scotia Historical Society *Collections* 30 (1954): 78–119.

Ward, Edmund. *An Account of the St. John and Its Tributary Rivers and Lakes.* Fredericton, N.B.: Sentinel Office, 1841. CIHM 49831.

Waters, John J. "Family, Inheritance and Migration in Colonial New England: The Evidence from Guildford, Connecticut." *William and Mary Quarterly,* 3d. ser., XXXXIX (Jan. 1982): 64–86.

_____. "Patrimony, Succession and Social Stability: Guilford, Connecticut in the Eighteenth Century." *Perspectives in American History* 10 (1976): 131–60.

_____. "The Traditional World of the New England Peasants: A View from Seventeenth Century Barnstable." *New England Historical and Genealogical Register* 30 (Jan. 1976): 3–21.

Wermuth. Thomas. *Rip Van Winkle's Neighbors. The Transformation of Rural Society in the Hudson River Valley, 1720–1850.* Albany: State University of New York Press, 2001.

Whalen, Hugh. *The Development of Local Government in New Brunswick.* Fredericton, N.B: Department of Municipal Affairs, 1964.

White, John. W. "The Burleigh Scheme: An Idea that Became a Railroad." *New England Social Studies Bulletin* XV (March, 1958): 5–11.

Wilbur, Richard *The Rise of French New Brunswick.* Halifax: Formac publishing company, 1989.

Wiggin, Edward. *History of Aroostook.* Presque Isle, ME: Star Herald Press, 1922.

Willis, John. "Fraserville and its Temiscouata Hinterland, 1874–1914, Colonization and Urbanization in a Peripheral Region of the Province of Quebec." M.A. thesis. Université du Québec à Trois Rivières, 1981.

Wilmot, Thomas Ashby. *Complete History of Aroostook County, and Its Early and Late Settlers.* (n.p., 1978) (Originally published as a series of articles in the *Mars Hill View,* published in Blaine, ME, from Dec. 23, 1909 to Jan. 12, 1911).

Wilson, Lisa. *Life after Death, Widows in Pennsylvania, 1750–1850.* Philadelphia: Temple University Press, 1992.

Wood, Richard. *A History of Lumbering in Maine, 1820–1861.* Orono, Maine: University of Maine Press, 1961. (First edition: 1935).

Woodward, Calvin A. *The history of New Brunswick provincial election campaigns and platforms, 1866-1974: with primary source documents on microfiche,* [Toronto]: Micromedia, c. 1976.

Wynn, Graeme. "New Brunswick Parish Boundaries in the pre-1861 Census Years." *Acadiensis,* VI (Spring 1977): 95–105.

Wynn, Graeme. *Timber Colony: A Historical Geography of Early Nineteenth-Century New Brunswick.* Toronto: University of Toronto Press, 1981.

INDEX

fur trade: at Madawaska, 57, 60-61, 75, 102; in
        Maritime Peninsula, 28, 31-32, 38-40, 48-49

G

Gagnon, Prudent, 162, 188

Gardner, John, 140

Garland, Robert (hist.), 151

Gaspé, 22, 47, 241

Gaspereau, fort, 45

genealogy, 372-8

George III, 47

Germain, Father, 44

Gibson, Alexander, 237-08

glacial lakes 3-4; Glacial Lake Ennemond, 4; Glacial
        Lake Guerette, 4; Glacial Lake Madawaska, 4;
        Glacial Lake Shields Branch, 4, 18

Glazier, Beamsley, 48, 51

Glazier, John, 120, 122, 134, 152, 179, 181-82, 187,
        208-09

Glooscap, 21

Gloucester County, 342, 343

Goldthwait Sea, 6

Gordon, Arthur Hamilton, Lord Stanmore, 170

Gory, Father, 320

Gould, Arthur, 241, 253, 344

governor and Council (definition), 103

grain bonuses, 79-80, 396

Grand Falls (place name), 119, 153, 166, 199, 205, 230,
        239, 241, 253, 301-02, 310, 367

Grand Falls (waterfall), 9, 34, 35, 45, 54, 86, 101, 295,
        297

Grand Falls: drift dam, 4; footbridge, 247; grammar
        school, 310; power plant, 254

Grand Isle, 258, 274, 276, 275, 322

grand juries, 103-04

Grand Portage, 45, 58, 61, 63, 75-77, 117, 168, 199,
        240; settlers along it, 63

Grand River, 397

Grand Sault, 9. *See also* Grand Falls.

Grand Trunk Railroad, 240

Grande Rivière, 83, 122

Grandmaison, J-Bte, 45-46

Great Falls of the River Saint John's, 9. *See also* Grand
        Falls.

Great Northern Paper Co., 261, 265, 266

Greenbacks, 206

Griffith, Naomi (hist.), 331

gristmills, 80, 116, 141, 188-89, 383-86

Grotius, Hugo (jurist), 36

guidebooks, 298

Gyles, John, 25-26, 38, 366

H

Haldimand, Sir Frederick, 51, 61

Halifax currency (definition), 363

Halifax: founding (1749), 45; journey from St. John
        River to Halifax in 1780, 64

Hamel, Jacques, 98

Hamlin Plantation, 190

Hammond (family), 105, 179, 183, 190, 235, 258-59,
        264, 287

Hammond Lumber Co., 259

Hammond, Sir Andrew Snape, 68

Hancock Plantation, 158, 160, 39. *See also* Fort Kent.

Hannay, James (hist.), 50

Hannay, James (poet), 34

Hartland, 201

Harvey, Sir John (NB lieut.-gov.), 122-23, 405

hay, 197

Hazen, John (NB premier), 343

Hazen, William, 49-50, 69

Head, George, 392

Hébert (family, at Madawaska), 75, 76, 80, 88, 105,
        152, 169, 224

Hegan J. J., 209

Henderson, John,140

Higginbottom, David, 60

Histoire des Deux Indes, 328

Histoire du Madawaska, xix, 335

history: as opposed to the past, xx; frameworks in, xxii ;
        methods, xix, xx; revisionism in, xx, xxii

Hobbs-Pruitt, Betty (hist.), 74

Hochelaga, 27

Hodgson, John T., 166

hogshead (weight of), 203

Holland, Park (American surveyor), 89, 395

Holland, Samuel (Québec surveyor), 101

Holocene Era, 6

homespun (domestic textile), 93, 199

hospitals, 321, 322-23, 324-25

Houlton, 167, 235, 240, 243, 253, 271, 276, 317

houses, 86, 90, 398, 401

Hubbard, Governor John, 159, 405-07

hundredweight (weight of), 203

Hunnewell, Barnabas, 129

hunting, 302-03

hydroelectricity, 253-54, 266

I

Ile Royale (Cape Breton Island), 43

Ile Saint-Jean (Prince Edward Island), 43

Ile Verte, 31, 61

immigration to the Valley, 142-43

In Fair Aroostook, 304-05

incorporation of Madawaska towns, 380

ABOUT THE SPONSORING ORGANIZATIONS

The Maine Acadian Heritage Council is very proud to publish *The Land in Between* in cooperation with the National Park Service, for this publication would not have been possible without their generous funding. We wish to also thank the following: Deb Wade, chief interpreter at the Acadian National Park, for her efforts in making this publication possible; Béatrice Craig for generously allowing us to publish her work in this manner; Lisa Ornstein, Guy Dubay, Maxime Dagenais, and Louise Martin for their contributions and research.

The Maine Acadian Heritage Council is a regional organization dedicated to preserving and promoting Acadian culture, language, and history throughout northern Maine's St. John Valley and beyond. It was incorporated in 1997 by the Maine Acadian Cultural Preservation Commission as a consortium comprised of the St. John Valley's municipalities, historical, and cultural organizations, and chambers of commerce to preserve and promote the French Acadian culture of northern Maine.

Since 1998 the Maine Acadian Heritage Council has been fortunate to receive financial support from the National Park Service (NPS) on an annual basis. The funds we receive have allowed the people of the St. John Valley to continue their work in preserving and promoting the Maine Acadian culture and its historic treasures. Along with the funds for our administrative expenses, we receive additional funding for the following tasks, which have been agreed upon with the NPS: distributing funds to the local historical societies for preservation initiatives, support for trained guides at the local historical societies' museums, as well as support for speakers and performers at local festivals; awareness efforts that inform residents of the St. John Valley, and those culturally connected to the Valley, about news of organizations interpreting and preserving Maine Acadian culture; and education development, which also allows us to develop a series of workshops for teachers and teaching materials on various aspects of Acadian culture for teachers to implement projects directed toward making students and teachers aware of Acadian culture.

Through the management of two sites—Saint Croix Island International Historic Site and Acadia National Park—and the support of the Maine Acadian Heritage Council, the National Park Service also protects and promotes French history and culture in Maine.

Saint Croix Island International Historic Site, located along the St. Croix River near Calais, Maine, is preserved as a monument to the beginning of the United States and Canada. St. Croix Island is the 1604 site of the first French attempt to colonize the territory they called Acadie, and the location of one of the earliest European settlements in North America. Members of a French expedition led by Pierre Dugua, Sieur de Mons, settled the island in 1604. Seventy-nine members of the expedition, including Samuel Champlain, passed the severe winter of 1604–05 on the island. Despite the assistance of the Passamaquoddy, who traded game for bread, thirty-five settlers died of scurvy, malnutrition, and exposure and were buried in a small cemetery on the island. In summer 1605 the survivors left the island and founded the settlement of Port Royal, Nova Scotia. From St. Croix Island—and the hard lessons learned—grew Acadia, New France, and an enduring French presence on this continent.

Today, visitors to the mainland site can explore a self-guiding trail with interpretive panels and cast bronze figures that convey messages about the French settlers and Passamaquoddy people who once used the site. Visits to the island itself are not encouraged due to its fragile nature. www.nps.gov/sacr

Acadia National Park is a land of varied environments—granite mountains, clear lakes, evergreen forests, and ocean shoreline—with a rich human history. Most of the park is located on Mount Desert Island (l'isle des Monts-deserts), named by Samuel Champlain when Pierre Dugua dispatched him from St. Croix Island to explore the coast in 1604. The French presence on the island began in 1613, when French Jesuits established the first French mission in America. The mission was destroyed shortly thereafter by an English ship, leaving ownership in a state of uncertainty between the French to the north and the English to the south. For the next 150 years Mount Desert Island was used primarily as a landmark for seamen. In 1688 Frenchman Antoine Laumet received a grant for 100,000 acres along the Maine coast, including Mount Desert Island. He hoped to establish a feudal estate in the New World but soon abandoned his effort. In 1760, English settlers arrived.

People have been drawn to Maine's rugged coast throughout history. Awed by its beauty and diversity, early twentieth-century visionaries donated the land that became Acadia National Park. The park is home to many plants and animals, and the tallest mountain on the U.S. Atlantic coast. Today visitors come to Acadia to hike granite peaks, bike historic carriage roads, or relax and enjoy the scenery. www.nps.gov/acad

ABOUT THE AUTHORS AND COLLABORATORS

Béatrice Craig holds a Ph.D. in Canadian-AmericanHistory from the University of Maine. She is a full professor of History at the University of Ottawa (Canada), and the author of *Homespun Capitalists and Backwoods Consumers,* University of Toronto Press, 2009, as well as numerous articles on the history of the upper St John Valley.

Maxime Dagenais is a doctoral candidate in nineteenth-century Canadian History at the University of Ottawa. He obtained his B.A. in History from Concordia University in 2003 and his M.A. from the University of Ottawa in 2006. His thesis "When on Active Service: Discipline and Illegal Absences in the 5th Canadian Infantry Brigade" deals with French-Canadian military history.

Lisa Ornstein holds a Master's degree in Ethnomusicology from Université Laval. She was the director of the Acadian Archives at the University of Maine at Fort Kent from 1990 to 2007, and recipient of the 2007 Clio prize in Atlantic History from the Canadian Historical Association for her work promoting St. John Valley history and culture.

Guy Dubay holds a Master's degree in Education from the University of Maine. A retired teacher and former school principal, he is now an independent scholar, author of several regional history books (among others, *Chez Nous: The St. John Valley,* 1983, and Light on the Past: Documentation on Our Acadian Heritage, 1995). He contributes regularly to the *St. John Valley Times* and lives in Madawaska.

This volume has also benefited from the assistance of:

Louise M. Martin is a St. John Valley native and has been the office manager of the Maine Acadian Heritage Council since 2001. Louise returned to the Valley after working in Boston, Massachusetts, for ten years as an executive assistant. In early 2007, Louise published *Heritage Sites of the St. John Valley,* a passport and guide featuring ten historic sites. Her monthly newspaper columns for the Maine Acadian Heritage Council have been featured in the *St. John Valley Times* since 2004.

Sam Herold (B.A. Geography, University of Ottawa) and **Séverine Craig** (B.A. History, Concordia University) produced the maps. Séverine also conducted some of the archival research required for this volume.

The following readers have provided valuable advice and input:

Michel Bock is assistant professor of History at the University of Ottawa and holder of the research chair in Histoire et francophonie. His book *Quand la nation débordait les frontières* (2005) won the Prix littéraire du Gouverneur général du Canada, catégorie "Études et essais," the Prix Michel-Brunet de l'Institut d'histoire de l'Amérique française, the Prix littéraire Champlain du Conseil de la vie française en Amérique (catégorie "ouvrages d'érudition") and a Médaille de l'assemblée nationale du Québec.

Adrian Burke has a Ph.D. from SUNY Albany and is associate professor of Archaeology in the Anthropology Department of the Université de Montréal. His specialty is prehistoric archaeology of the northeastern North America. His current research focuses on recent prehistory of the upper St. John River basin.

W. E. Campbell (Gary), a Ph.D. candidate at the University of New Brunswick, is the author of *The Road to Canada, The Grand Communication Route from Saint John to Quebec.* New Brunswick Military Heritage Series, vol. 5. Fredericton: Goose Lane Editions and the New Brunswick Military Heritage Project, 2005.

V. P. Gagnon (Chip) is associate professor in the Department of Politics at Ithaca College, New York. He obtained his Ph.D. in Political Aciences from Columbia University and is the author of *The Myth of Ethnic War: Serbia and Croatia in the 1990s,* Cornell University Press, 2004, winner of the 2005 American Political Science Association's Prize for the Best Book on European Politics and Society. Chip also created and maintains a web site on the upper St. John River Valley. http://www.upperstjohn.com/

Stéphane Lang is a native of Clair (N.B.), and received his Ph.D. from the University of Ottawa. He is currently an archivist at the National Archives of Canada, and was a postdoctoral fellow at the Chaire de recherche sur la francophonie et les politiques publiques of the University of Ottawa. He wrote his doctoral thesis on "La communauté franco-ontarienne et l`enseignement secondaire (1910–1968)" and his M.A. thesis on "Les enseignants acadiens et la 'Révolution tranquille' au Nouveau-Brunswick, 1960–1970: vers de nouveaux rapports avec les enseignants anglophones et l'État."

Cleo Ouellette, a retired teacher of high school French and English, is a member of the Maine Acadian Heritage Council Educational Resource Development Committee and is a secretary of Le Club Français du Haut St. Jean (among her many offices and interests). Her theme paper, "A New Look at French in the St. John Valley" (1993), which she wrote for her Master of Education degree, is now on the Internet as a resource for Franco-American studies. She lives in Frenchville and is president of the Frenchville Historical Society.

Lise Pelletier is a Fort Kent native and holds a Bachelor of Arts degree in English and French from l'Université de Moncton, and a M.A. in French from the University of Maine. She is currently finishing a Ph.D. in French Literature at the University of Maine. A former director of Le Club Français at Madawaska, she succeeded Lisa Ornstein at the helm of the Acadian Archives in 2007.

Charles Kenneth Theriault, Jr. (Ken) has a B.A. in History from the University of Maine at Fort Kent, where he received the 1991 Presidential Award for Academic Excellence. He did graduate work in Historical Sociology at Clark University before becoming a librarian. After working at the Worcester Public Library in Worcester, Massachusetts, he came back to the Valley and is now the library director of the Madawaska Public Library. Ken is also the vice president of the Maine Acadian Heritage Council and sits on the board of directors of the Madawaska Historical Society.